To put the matter in language not easy for moderns, . . . Christianity [is at its] center concerned with grace — if that word is given its literal meaning. Grace simply means that the great things of our existing are given us, not made by us and finally not to be understood as arbitrary accidents. Our making takes place within an ultimate givenness. However difficult it is for all of us to affirm that life is a gift, it is an assertion primal to Christianity. Through the vicissitudes of life — the tragedies, the outrages, the passions, the disciplines and madnesses of everyday existence — to be a Christian is the attempt to learn the substance of that assertion.

                        George Grant, "Two Theological Languages,"
                        Addendum (1988), in *Collected Works of George Grant*,
                        vol. 2, 1951-1959, edited by Arthur Davis
                        (University of Toronto Press, 2002), p. 60

Ordering Love

*Liberal Societies and the
Memory of God*

David L. Schindler

William B. Eerdmans Publishing Company
Grand Rapids, Michigan / Cambridge, U.K.

© 2011 David L. Schindler
All rights reserved

Published 2011 by
Wm. B. Eerdmans Publishing Co.
2140 Oak Industrial Drive N.E., Grand Rapids, Michigan 49505 /
P.O. Box 163, Cambridge CB3 9PU U.K.

Library of Congress Cataloging-in-Publication Data

Schindler, David L., 1943-
 Ordering love: liberal societies and the memory of God / David L. Schindler.
    p.   cm.
 ISBN 978-0-8028-6430-7 (pbk.: alk. paper)
 1. Love — Religious aspects — Christianity. 2. Love. 3. Civilization,
Modern — 21st century. 4. Life. 5. Conduct of life.   I. Title.

BV4639.S3425   2011
241′.4 — dc22

                                                          2011016000

www.eerdmans.com

For Stella, David, and Bryan
  and
    For Cornelia Capol

Contents

Preface ix

Introduction: Ordering Love 1

PART I: LIBERAL SOCIETIES AND THE MEMORY OF GOD

"Keeping the World Awake to God": Benedict XVI in America 19

Cultural Implications of Religions in Public Life:
Recuperating the Deeper Questions 26

The Dramatic Nature of Life: Liberal Societies
and the Foundations of Human Dignity 34

Truth, Freedom, and Relativism in Western Democracies:
Pope Benedict XVI's Contributions to *Without Roots* 53

Civil Community Inside the Liberal State:
Truth, Freedom, and Human Dignity 65

Charity, Justice, and the Church's Activity in the World:
A Reflection on *Deus Caritas Est* 133

Does the Free Market Produce Free Persons? 154

Market Liberalism and an Economic Culture
of Gift and Gratitude 166

The Significance of World and Culture for Moral Theology:
Veritatis Splendor and the Nature of the Body 219

The Embodied Person as Gift and the Cultural Task in America 242

PART II: THINKING AND ACTING IN A TECHNOLOGICAL AGE

George Grant and Modernity's Technological Ontology 277

Liturgy and the Integrity of Cosmic Order:
The Theology of Alexander Schmemann 288

Living and Thinking Reality in Its Integrity:
Originary Experience, God, and the Task of Education 310

Religion and Secularity in a Culture of Abstraction:
On the Integrity of Space, Time, Matter, and Motion 328

Modernity and the Nature of a Distinction:
Balthasar's Ontology of Generosity 350

The Given as Gift: Creation and Disciplinary
Abstraction in Science 383

The Anthropological Vision of *Caritas in Veritate*
in Light of Economic and Cultural Life in the United States 430

Index 450

Preface

The argument of this book is that reality, most basically considered, is an order of love. Reality at root is a matter of love and love is a matter of order, a bearer of a "word" or "logic" (*logos*) that presupposes an ordering intelligence. I take this claim to be entailed by the Christian understanding of creation *ex nihilo*.

The main critical judgment of the book, in this light, is that modern culture marginalizes love. The logical tendency of modernity, in its dominant liberal form,[1] is to look on love as at best a matter of piety or good will, and not as the very stuff that makes our lives and the things of the world *real*, the *basic order* of our lives and of all things. Indeed, modernity's marginalization of love is bound up indissolubly with its technological understanding of order. Modernity's technological logic, or ordering intelligence, can be said to consist in "theoretical manipulability" (Hans Jonas), or in the conflation of knowing and making (George Grant), or again in the assumption that something is true or good not in itself (*qua ens*) but only insofar as it is made so by man (*quia factum* or *faciendum*) (Joseph Ratzinger).

By technology or "technological," I thus do not refer in the first instance to what is customarily understood as the practical application of

---

1. Of course, as is often rightly argued, liberalism can be distinguished into several forms, most notably into European or Continental liberalism on the one hand, and Anglo-American liberalism, on the other. The critique of this book has mainly the latter in mind. Nevertheless, it is important to see that the pluralism within liberalism is best conceived in analogical as distinct from nominalistic terms. The differences within liberalism, in other words, even when they are important, bear in their deepest implications an ontological unity. But all of this will be sorted out in the following chapters.

knowledge. Nor do I refer to the devices resulting from such application, as indicated in a phrase like "new technologies for information storage." I refer rather to a particular ordering of being and consciousness.

Insofar as order and intelligence are technological, then, love cannot be judged *real* in any *reasonable* sense, and thus cannot be judged as essential for building an authentic human culture. The notion that love is "unrealistic" lies at the heart of the problems that increasingly threaten Western, and indeed global, civilization. Each chapter of this study takes up this concern in a distinct way, attempting to show, in the context of politics, economics, science, and cultural and professional life generally, that it is love, or more precisely God-centered love, that gives things their deepest and most proper order and meaning, always and everywhere.[2]

This claim will appear to many, *a priori*, to be counterintuitive and overly bold. Distinctions therefore must be undertaken to forestall misunderstanding, and arguments offered to demonstrate how and why the claim is worthy of consideration. These tasks are the burden of the book as a whole.

The chapters comprising *Ordering Love* were written on different occasions and thus with distinct audiences and purposes in mind. Most of them have already appeared in print, but, even where this is the case, they have been edited, sometimes substantially, for the present study. The chapters do not appear in the order in which they were written, though I have recorded below the date and occasion of their earliest versions, and added further information at the beginning of those chapters where such information seemed important for understanding the context of the original argument. Since each chapter thus has its own unity in light of the occasion for which it was conceived, it is inevitable that there be some repetition in the key terms of the book's argument. The distinctness of context on each occasion nevertheless serves to draw forth and develop new aspects and layers of meaning in those terms.

"'Keeping the World Awake to God': Benedict XVI in America" was a talk given at Columbia University in New York and at the Pope John Paul II Cultural Center in Washington, D.C., in anticipation of the visit of Pope Benedict to America in April 2008.

2. Cf. the argument developed by Benedict XVI in his most recent encyclical, *Caritas in Veritate*. Unfortunately, this encyclical appeared too late for Benedict's discussion to be incorporated in any substantive way into the present work. I have nonetheless added several pertinent footnote references to the encyclical, and included a chapter that treats the anthropological vision undergirding its social teaching.

"Cultural Implications of Religions in Public Life: Recuperating the Deeper Questions" was given as part of a panel on ecumenism composed of various religious leaders at the Pope John Paul II Cultural Center in Washington, D.C., in April 2009.

"The Dramatic Nature of Life: Liberal Societies and the Foundations of Human Dignity" was presented at a conference in May 2006 commemorating the twenty-fifth anniversary of the founding of the Pontifical John Paul II Institute for Studies on Marriage and Family at the Lateran University in Rome.

"Truth, Freedom, and Relativism in Western Democracies: Pope Benedict XVI's Contributions to *Without Roots*" was a talk given on the occasion of the publication of *Without Roots: The West, Relativism, Christianity, Islam* (Basic Books), co-authored by Joseph Ratzinger and Marcello Pera, at Columbia University in New York in February 2006.

"Civil Community Inside the Liberal State: Truth, Freedom, and Human Dignity" is a substantially different version of a paper originally presented at the College Theology Society at the University of Dayton, Ohio, in May 2007.

"Charity, Justice, and the Church's Activity in the World: A Reflection on *Deus Caritas Est*" was written for *The Way of Love: Reflections on Pope Benedict XVI's Encylical* Deus Caritas Est (Ignatius Press), a book presented to Benedict XVI in May 2006 on the occasion of the twenty-fifth anniversary of the founding of the Pontifical John Paul II Institute for Studies on Marriage and Family at the Lateran University in Rome.

"Does the Free Market Produce Free Persons?" was a paper written in conjunction with a debate on the nature of the free market, sponsored by ISI and The Tocqueville Forum, at Georgetown University in Washington, D.C., in April 2009.

"Market Liberalism and an Economic Culture of Gift and Gratitude" was written as a critical summary article for a collection of essays co-edited with Doug Bandow and published as *Wealth, Poverty and Human Destiny* (ISI Books) in 2002.

"The Significance of World and Culture for Moral Theology: *Veritatis Splendor* and the Nature of the Body" was originally presented at an international theological congress commemorating the tenth anniversary of *Veritatis Splendor,* held at the Lateran University in Rome in November 2004.

"The Embodied Person as Gift and the Cultural Task in America" has a dual origin, first in a conference on the question of homosexuality in Rome in September 2008, second at a conference on the body and the anthropology of love at the Pontifical John Paul II Institute for Studies on Marriage and Family in Washington, D.C., in November 2008.

"George Grant and Modernity's Technological Ontology" was written over different intervals of time, beginning in 2003, as the introduction to what was originally conceived as a book on technology.

"Liturgy and the Integrity of Cosmic Order: The Theology of Alexander Schmemann" was presented in an earlier form in Rome in May 2000 at one of the annual seminars with Cardinal Joseph Ratzinger, on the Marian Dimension of the Church.

"Living and Thinking Reality in Its Integrity: Originary Experience, God, and the Task of Education" was written for a conference on the nature of experience at the Pontifical John Paul II Institute for Studies on Marriage and Family in Washington, D.C., in December 2009.

"Religion and Secularity in a Culture of Abstraction: On the Integrity of Space, Time, Matter, and Motion" was written in its earliest form for a conference in New York sponsored by the Center for Catholic and Evangelical Theology in September 2000, and later published in *Pro Ecclesia* in Winter 2002.

"Modernity and the Nature of a Distinction: Balthasar's Ontology of Generosity" was originally written for *How Balthasar Changed My Mind: 15 Scholars Reflect on the Meaning of Balthasar for Their Own Work* (Crossroad Publishing Company) in 2008.

"The Given as Gift: Creation and Disciplinary Abstraction in Science" was originally written for the international symposium "Science, Reason, and Truth," co-sponsored by the John Templeton Foundation and Euresis, at the Repubblica di San Marino in August 2007.

"The Anthropological Vision of *Caritas in Veritate* in Light of Economic and Cultural Life in the United States" was written for different forums following the appearance of the Pope's encyclical. The version appearing in this book was originally written for the Vatican II International Symposium of University Professors in Rome in June 2010.

Given the distinct character of the chapters that is due to the great variety of their original purposes and audience, it may be helpful to draw attention to certain chapters which are particularly important for the argument of the book as a whole. "Civil Community Inside the Liberal State" is the most comprehensive and sustained argument regarding the political order, as is "Market Liberalism and an Economic Culture of Gift and Gratitude" regarding the economic order. "Living and Thinking Reality in Its Integrity" and "The Anthropological Vision of *Caritas in Veritate* in Light of Economic and Cultural Life in the United States" are the two most recently completed articles. The former is helpful in highlighting the fundamental context of experience in which the question of technology must be asked, and also treats more explicitly the question of what is called a "state of life," which is important for understanding the overall burden of the book, particularly as it bears on technology. The final chapter of the book provides a recent summary overview that picks up the threads of the argument throughout the book as a whole.

* * *

It is impossible to recall all those who have contributed to the chapters making up this study. Sometimes help has come in seemingly offhanded remarks by a friend or colleague that were filed away in memory, only to lead over time to important new directions of thought. Conversations with many persons have in any case been decisive for me in thinking through the matters taken up here. First and foremost have been the conversations with my son David (who has been nothing short of unstinting in his efforts to bring light to bear on the shadows of my arguments). I wish to thank all the members of the Arkwood group that met in New Hampshire to discuss cultural and ontological matters for several summers in the late 90s and early years of this century. I am grateful more than I can say to my colleagues on the faculty and staff at the John Paul II Institute, especially to my dear assistant Susan Shaughnessy, who passed suddenly from us in November 2008; and also to the students of the Institute for their goodwill and genuine inquiry after truth; and to Carl Anderson, Supreme Knight of the Knights of Columbus, for his friendship and for his visionary leadership and thoughtful support of the Institute. I am grateful for many years of interesting and helpful conversations with Stratford Caldecott, Larry Chapp, Clinton Froscher, Rodney Howsare, Glenn Olsen, William Portier, and Katherine Tillman.

Several people have assisted me in the final revising of arguments and editing of text. They have, by their attentive and astute reading, spared the book many lapses of cogency and clarity in style and in substance. I thank here especially Lesley Rice, whose meticulous work over several years invariably improved the arguments developed in the book; Caitlin Shaughnessy Dwyer, who managed her ever-thoughtful review of the book while guiding her son, Jack, through the early months of his life; and Michael Camacho and Carla Galdo, who offered many substantive comments and painstaking corrections toward the end of the editing process. I also want to thank Emily Rielley, Managing Editor of *Communio*, who edited many of the chapters of the book that first appeared as articles in *Communio*. Wherever you happen to discover a short and clear sentence in this book, it is likely due to the influence of Emily, whose fearless and always intelligent editing has significantly affected my approach to writing.

Finally, I want to thank in a special way William B. Eerdmans Jr., president of Eerdmans Publishing Company, for his generosity and friendship now for over twenty years. His company celebrates its hundredth anniversary in 2011, with only two persons having directed the company: William Sr. and William Jr. — a remarkable achievement in American publishing! It is a genuine pleasure for me to continue to work with the cordial and efficient members of the Eerdmans staff, especially, on the present occasion, with Linda Bieze and Jennifer Hoffman.

*   *   *

This book is dedicated to my children, Stella, David, and Bryan, who have borne up my life in more ways than they can ever imagine. And to Cornelia Capol, in gratitude for all that she has taught so many of us through her obedient, intelligent, and hidden life of service.

Washington, D.C.
25 May 2011

Introduction: Ordering Love

Love is the basic act and order of things. Such is the judgment that gives the essays in this book their unity. The judgment is a comprehensive one, to be sure, and begs for explanation and justification. Love is that which first brings each thing into existence, and that in and through and for which each thing continues in existence. I take the radicality of this claim to be demanded by the Christian understanding of creation, and also by a rightful understanding of the "ontological difference," or what is termed in Thomistic metaphysics the "real distinction" between *esse* (*act* of being) and *ens (what* being *is)*. This distinction shows us that created being is the *subject* of its own act of existence only as *given to itself*. Thus God creates and sustains being out of love; and being itself, all of being, as disclosed in the distinction between *esse* and *ens,* is most truly conceived as at root a *logos* or "logic" of love. The chapters of this book unfold the meaning of this judgment in a variety of contexts, though without claim of synthetic or systematic completeness. In this introduction, however, it will be helpful to clarify briefly what is, and is not, entailed by the radicality of the judgment, by qualifying its meaning relative to several objections that appear initially to tell most strongly against it. The objections are six.

The first objection is that love is a *personal* reality. Love in the sense proposed in this book consists in a mutual giving and receiving that is fruitful. But acts of giving and receiving presuppose consciousness and freedom, and thus spirit. Since only persons are conscious and free in the full and proper sense, there would seem to be no warrant for speaking of non-personal realities, such as the biological and physical entities of the cosmos, as in themselves matters of love. On the contrary, these latter participate in love only insofar as they become *instruments* of human-personal love. It would therefore seem necessary that my overarching thesis be restricted at best to human beings: love is the basic act or order of human persons.

Connected with this objection is a second one: love is an *act* of personal *freedom* and the *will*, but it is not properly a matter of *intelligence*, hence *order*, in the strict sense.[1] Love is a matter, not of *ordering* things, but of the *exercising* of *goodwill*. Thus, while we might say that love is the basic act of human persons, in the sense that it signals the basic meaning of human *freedom*, it cannot be said properly to constitute the *logic* of persons, or *a fortiori*, of the cosmos.

A third objection further sharpens this second one: love has nothing proper to do with what constitutes the basic identity of a person, or a thing. Love does not, strictly speaking, reach to the *substance*, hence substantial order, of persons or things, but has to do rather with how persons relate to each other. Love affects persons in terms of how each *acts relative* to others, not in terms of *what* each is in its own constitutive reality. Love, in a word, is a *process* of *relating* among persons, not integral to the *structure* of reality. It therefore follows once again that we cannot speak of love as properly involving the *basic or substantial meaning* of the entities of the cosmos, personal or nonpersonal.

There is, fourth, an objection that arises in light of Christian faith and the nature-grace distinction: viz., that it is the *nature* of human beings, considered apart from Christian revelation and the grace of Christ, to turn in on themselves.[2] In the parlance of modernity, human beings in their na-

---

1. See "The Significance of World and Culture for Moral Theology: *Veritatis Splendor* and the Nature of the Body," pp. 219-41 in this volume.

2. "For Albert the Great, indeed, it was a self-evident truth that nature is totally self-referential; taking over a term from Augustine, he writes, 'Natura semper re curva in se ipsa' [Albertus Magnus, *Summa Theologica* II.tract.IV.14.2]. The love that is saved by grace can as a consequence only be understood as a departure from nature, i.e., ecstatically" (Robert Spaemann, "Natur," in *Philosophische Essays* [Stuttgart: Reclam, 1993], pp. 19-40; English translation forthcoming in a volume of Spaemann's essays [ISI Books]).

Needless to say, this turning in of each thing on itself is taken for granted in modernity especially. It is reflected in the dominant account of subhuman beings, for example, in terms of the survival mechanism as interpreted in various forms of Darwinian theory. The problem with such a theory is not so much the drive for self-survival as the failure to understand self-survival as itself a (self-transcendent) *good* among other *goods*. The turning in of each thing on itself is also presupposed in any mechanistic account of non-living nature. Questions regarding the mechanistic account of nature are treated in "The Given as Gift: Creation and Disciplinary Abstraction in Science," pp. 383-429 in this volume.

ture as human, and without the addition of grace, act most basically out of their own self-interest. Community thus consists in self-interested acting become mutual. In a word, the deepest *natural* inclination of each human being is toward a *self*-centered happiness, except insofar as the self is promoted through the grace of Christ out of this self-centeredness toward other-centered love. A love that would include other-centered reference, on this account, cannot therefore be rightly said to indicate a meaning that is intrinsic to all things in their original constitution, but one that comes to things only via the addition of grace. Other-centered love indicates not the natural but only the *supernatural or Christian* meaning of things.

A fifth objection is that the thesis fails for the simple reason that it flies in the face of massive evidence to the contrary. What seems manifestly to prevail in the world as we know it is not love but evil and sin and brokenness. Realism seems most commonly to disclose man's inhumanity to man, as manifest in history's endless wars and violence. And indeed the central fact of existence in the subhuman world of nature appears to consist in the struggle of each entity to defend itself against the predatory behavior of others. That love is the basic act and order of things thus seems much more an ethical wish, or *moral value* or *duty*, on the part of humans than something already integral to the *fact* of created reality as such, either personal or non-personal.

A sixth objection is that love might well represent the basic act or order of things, but that such language is legitimate or "realistic" only in the "private" and not the "public" realm. Thus the separation of church and state, and indeed the secularity and "realism" of the political order, would seem to demand that human beings employ two languages: a "metaphysical" and "faith-ful" language of love among one's own family or church, on the one hand, and a "political" and "peace-ful" language of juridical rights and factional or self-interested preferences, on the other. Similarly, the economic order in its legitimate secularity would seem to require its own proper language of self-interest, best conceived in terms of an "enlightened" mutuality of self-interests. Finally, the secular academy employs as its predominant methodological language that of mechanism in the physical sciences complemented by self-interested survival mechanism in the life sciences. The language of love seems therefore, in the end, much more an expression of private piety than of anything like the basic order of things. Certainly it is not a language appropriate or "realistic" for the public-institutional order as expressed in the state, the economy, and the academy.

Now all of the above objections do, or at any rate should, hold some compelling power for us, since in fact they all bear important, albeit partial, truths. Indeed, the thesis I have proposed regarding love requires affirmation of each of these truths, though only as qualified in light of that thesis itself, rightly understood. It will suffice here to highlight the principles invoked in the case of each objection, indicating how these principles together articulate the meaning of the thesis.

In response to the first objection, this book's comprehensive claim about love is conceived analogically, in keeping with a venerable tradition of Catholic theology and philosophy. By this I mean first of all that the book's horizon is set more basically by being rather than merely by *human being*. The horizon is set by being in its most radical and comprehensive sense, and thus in terms of its origin and including relation to God as creator. The love, or gift-giving, to which the book's thesis refers is thus not the love that begins with human agency, and hence is not in the first instance human-centered love. It is on the contrary the love rooted first in God as creator, and is most basically God-centered. But further, it is the love in which all the beings of the cosmos participate, by virtue of their being creatures of God — the love that is therefore centered in the cosmos itself, but only from inside the cosmos's own centeredness in God. In a word, creation and the distinction between *esse* and *ens*, rightly understood, demand a love that begins and ends with God as creator and in which the created universe itself participates in its entire depth and breadth.

The point of terming this love analogical, then, is that each being truly participates in this creational love of God, even as each does so in a way proportionate to its distinct way or kind of being. All beings share in the unity characteristic of their being created *gifts*, by and in God's loving generosity, even as each shares in this unity differently, in terms of the ever-greater difference *(maior dissimilitudo)* proper to each kind of being, from non-living to living to human.

The human person is central in mediating the love between God and the rest of the creatures of the cosmos (see, for example, the work of Maximus the Confessor), and this claim lies at the heart of all that is proposed in the present collection. The human person recapitulates via his freedom and intelligence the love that all of creation shares in analogically. The pertinent point here, however, is that the human person is a creature and, as such, he mediates this love only as one who has himself first received his own reality as a gift from God, and indeed in a significant sense from all other creatures inside the common relation of all creatures to God.³

The problem with respect to the first objection, therefore, is that, living within the horizon of modernity, we have become accustomed to its distorted anthropocentrism. This problem, however, does not lie in the fact that we have focused on man, but that we have done so while forgetting being and God; such forgetfulness both presupposes and helps to bring about the forgetfulness of our own creatureliness and that of all other cosmic entities. The presupposition of the book's thesis in this light is that we need to recover a genuinely being-centered and God-centered way of thinking, precisely as the necessary condition for recovering an authentically human-person-centered vision of reality.

Thus, in a word, love is the basic act and order of all things because all things are created by God. The most basic *fact* or *truth* of all things is at once their analogically conceived *goodness* or *value* as *gift*, a giftedness that is intrinsic to each thing by virtue of its being generated by the generosity of God. The goodness of things in the cosmos is not rooted most basically in human freedom or intelligence, and thus in human spirit, nor is it first granted by human freedom and intelligence. On the contrary, it is rooted in the creative freedom and intelligence of the creator, in which *all things of the cosmos truly participate, and which they just so far "image," each in its own analogical, creaturely way.*

The response to the second objection follows from this fact of creation. Creation, mediated to the world through the "real distinction" between *esse* and *ens*, establishes a logic of gift at the heart of the creature. There can be no act of human freedom or consciousness that does not bear a memory of this logic or idea. Cardinal Ratzinger/Benedict XVI has emphasized the meaning of conscience as an *anamnesis* of God, a memory that he says is "identical to the ground of our existence."⁴ This memory carries an ever-present, albeit implicit, recollection of our origin from another. As Thomas Aquinas, following Augustine, says in a similar vein, every cognitive being knows and loves God in whatever it knows and loves.⁵ More needs to be developed regarding the sense in which this implicit awareness of God and of a transcendent origin implies a notion of creation

---

3. On the filial meaning of the creature, see, *inter alia*, "The Embodied Person as Gift and the Cultural Task in America," pp. 242-74 in this volume.

4. Joseph Ratzinger, *On Conscience: Two Essays by Joseph Ratzinger* (Philadelphia/San Francisco: The National Catholic Bioethics Center/Ignatius Press, 2007), p. 32.

5. St. Thomas Aquinas, *De Veritate*, q. 22, a. 2, ad 1.

and love as indicated in response to the first objection. But it suffices in response to the second objection to realize that this awareness is a *primitive* awareness. Which is to say, with Benedict XVI, that it is *given with our being*. To be conscious is to be implicitly aware of God as transcendent origin and thus of *ourselves as always already related* to God.[6]

The point, in sum, is that this *anamnesis* carries an implicit *order*, and just so far *logos* or *idea*, of the relation between ourselves and God, or a transcendent origin. This is the logic of the "real distinction" as mentioned earlier. The primitive act of human freedom, or indeed primitive human experience, is never empty of this order or idea, but is on the contrary always mediated from its core by an implicit memory of this order. It follows that, while love *is* properly an act of human freedom or will, it is and can be such only as also anteriorly participant in the deepest logic of being itself.

Regarding the third objection, the love characteristic of being could not bear the feature of generosity if it did not genuinely transcend itself and thus terminate in something genuinely *other*.[7] The logic of creation, expressed metaphysically in the logic of the distinction between *esse* and *essentia*, implies a constitutive *relation* on the part of the creature consisting in reception from and movement toward (*esse ab, esse ad*) God. This relation does not undermine but on the contrary demands the substantial identity of the creature. Indeed, this distinct identity of the creature is the *term of otherness* demanded by a genuinely creative, hence generous, love. In the language of Thomism, the act of creation brings about, even as it then-simultaneously presupposes, the substantial identity or "in-itselfness" (*esse in*) of the creature.[8]

The crucial point, then, in sum, is that, to secure the substantial identity of persons or things, we do not need to oppose or even simply juxtapose the substantial character of identity and the relationality of love. On the contrary, each in its own way is an inner condition of the other, and each thus enters into the original meaning of the other. For this reason, we

---

6. See "The Embodied Person as Gift and the Cultural Task in America."

7. Of course, in terms of God himself, this otherness is found *within* the Creator as a Trinity of divine persons. In other words, God's generosity does not *require* creation, although creation is innerly consistent with the infinite generosity already characteristic of God's own *Tri*-unity.

8. Cf. Kenneth L. Schmitz's "Created Receptivity and the Philosophy of the Concrete," in *The Texture of Being*, ed. Paul O'Herron (Washington, D.C.: Catholic University of America, 2007), pp. 106-31.

can indeed speak of love as the basic meaning of things, of each thing at once in itself and in its receiving from and moving toward all others.[9]

Thus, relative to the fourth objection, we can see from the ontology of the act of creation as expressed in the "ontological difference" that being always already bears within it a natural structure of generosity, in an analogical, creaturely way. As indicated, this natural structure of generosity is disclosed in the mutual receiving and giving between a one and an other, a mutual relating that presupposes the "in-itselfness" of the one even as the one promotes the "in-itselfness" of the other. This relation, which thus promotes the integrity of the other as other, implies a being and acting toward the other for its own sake. And this being and acting reveals the root meaning of the other as intrinsically, hence "transcendentally," true and good and indeed beautiful.[10]

What is crucial to see here, then, relative to the fourth objection, is that this generosity is characteristic of being already in its natural logic *as being*, and is indeed signified and expressed in the transcendental convertibility of being and truth and goodness. This does not at all imply attenuation of the newness, or indeed infinite difference, of the generosity of God revealed in Jesus Christ. Nor does it imply a "pure nature" actually existing in abstraction from or independent of the grace of Christ. What it implies, simply, is that the generosity of the one God is revealed already in and through his creation. This natural revelation of the generosity of God in creation is from the beginning open to the new *self*-revelation of his generosity in Jesus Christ, a divine or supernatural revelation that has been effective in history from its origin.[11]

---

9. Michael Waldstein, in his article "'Constitutive Relations': A Response to David L. Schindler," in *Communio: International Catholic Review* 37, no. 3 (Fall 2010): 496-517, raises important questions regarding the meaning I assign the term "constitutive relations," in light of what he argues is a rightly Thomistic-Aristotelian reading of the metaphysical principles of *esse*, substance, accident, and relation. Though the present book contains aspects of a reply to his questions, the article arrived when the book was already substantially complete, and will therefore be responded to more thoroughly and systematically elsewhere.

10. Of course only spiritual, e.g. human, beings in the cosmos can be related to for their own sake in the full and proper sense, because only spiritual beings have the capacity for the reflexive interior reception of the other, properly speaking. All beings, however, retain some *analogical capacity* for relation to another, because they all bear an interiority proportionate to their kind or level of being. No being of the cosmos can be exhaustively conceived simply as an instrument of what is outside it, because no being is simply outside of — simply without interior relation to — God and other creatures. Cf. Kenneth L. Schmitz's *The Gift: Creation* (Milwaukee: Marquette University Press, 1982).

11. Steven Long's *Natura Pura* (New York: Fordham University Press, 2010) raises

It is in this sense, then, that we can say that generous love begins already within the nature of being itself, and is not simply an addition to, or a reversal of, what some would take to be a more properly inward-turning nature or self-seeking love, an addition that would indeed then be elicited only arbitrarily and simply from outside. Indeed, it is in this sense that the call to generous love can be said naturally, and hence reasonably, to include all cosmic entities, in an analogical way and through the mediation of man. But once again, this generous love characteristic of being qua being is open to, and in the one concrete order of history always already affected by, the Eucharistic love of Jesus Christ.[12]

We come to the fifth objection. It is a fact of experience that the world offers massive evidence of sin and brokenness, and this seems radically to call into question the universality of human and non-human being's constitutional generosity as claimed in the foregoing. However, we do not need to deny this massive evil in order to sustain the claim of a natural participation in and tendency toward generosity that is structured into the original constitution of being. Indeed, the generosity of God's act of creation presupposes just the relative autonomy on the part of the creature that makes possible the creature's turning away from that generosity and its refusal to participate in it in the first place. Central to the overarching argument of this book is that this natural tendency continues to be operative despite, or indeed even within, this turning away or refusal.

What is indispensable for my argument, in other words, is that an echo or memory of the natural tendency toward what is good in itself and toward God continues to abide inside this refusal; what is "ideal" always remains *real*, in and through the *anamnesis* of God and our creatureliness that is given with our very being. The act of creation rightly understood thus implies that no being, however broken, can ever at its core be indifferent to or wholly forgetful of the call to generosity. What creation implies, in a word, is that, even in the face of massive sin and brokenness, there re-

---

questions regarding my position on this point, but this book, like Waldstein's article, arrived too late to be taken into account and will consequently be responded to elsewhere.

12. Cf. John Paul II, *Dominum et Vivificantem* (1986), n. 50: "The Incarnation of God the Son signifies the taking up into unity with God not only of human nature, but in this human nature, in a sense, of everything that is 'flesh': the whole of humanity, the entire visible and material world. The Incarnation, then, also has a cosmic significance, a cosmic dimension. The 'first-born of all creation,' becoming incarnate in the individual humanity of Christ, unites himself in some way with the entire reality of man, which is also 'flesh' — and in this reality with all 'flesh,' with the whole of creation."

mains in the depths of the human heart a recognition, even if not fully conscious, of the need *to sacrifice* and *to suffer* the good and God into one's own life in history.

The position outlined here holds in an analogical sense in the subhuman cosmos. As is clear in Genesis, things were made to be taken up into the service of man, in and through the familial-marital fruitfulness of Adam and Eve. As Karol Wojtyla put it, subhuman beings are apt for being taken up into the mutual gift-giving among human beings.[13] All things are thus meant to serve and show forth the love that is properly expressed in freedom only by human persons. Things are just so far intended as instruments of human love.

It is crucial to understand, however, that the instrumental character of things follows ontologically from what is always already their inherently given truth and goodness and beauty, because it is the nature of the good to share itself *(bonum est diffusivum sui)*. The instrumentality of nature, in other words, can never be taken legitimately to mean that things in their natural givenness are merely "brute facts," awaiting the simply utilitarian meaning that is to be assigned them, now arbitrarily, by human beings.[14] The necessary and legitimate *instrumentality* of nature, in a word, must be seen from within, and as a *sign and expression of,* what is the intrinsic or transcendental truth and goodness and beauty of things qua *created* and thus *given:* as a sign and expression, indeed, of things' basic liturgical and covenantal meaning in relation to God.[15]

To be sure, the original harmony and integration of things in their

---

13. "[C]ulture . . . forms a kind of organic whole with nature. It reveals the roots of our union with nature, but also of our superior encounter with the Creator in the eternal plan, a plan in which we participate by means of reason and wisdom. . . . There exists in nature, or the world, an anticipation of . . . human activity and . . . a radiation of humanity through praxis. There is also in nature, or the world, a kind of readiness to put itself at our disposal: to serve human needs, to welcome within it the superior scale of human ends, to enter in some way into the human dimension and participate in human existence in the world." Karol Wojtyla, "The Problem of the Constitution of Culture Through Human Praxis," in *Person and Community* (New York: Peter Lang, 1993), pp. 263-75, at 269-70.

14. See Joseph Ratzinger's related comments regarding the truth as given *(verum est ens)* as distinct from truth as made *(verum quia factum,* or *faciendum)* in connection with the Italian philosopher Giambattista Vico (1668-1744) in *Introduction to Christianity* (San Francisco: Ignatius Press–Communio Books, 1990), pp. 31ff.

15. See "Liturgy and the Integrity of Cosmic Order: The Theology of Alexander Schmemann," pp. 288-309 in this volume. See also Joseph Ratzinger, *The Spirit of the Liturgy* (San Francisco: Ignatius Press, 2000); and Psalms 104 and 148.

goodness and their service of human love was lost through the sin of man. Nevertheless, as already suggested above, the natural order of things perdures within what is now widespread fragmentation and violence. Nature retains its transcendental truth and goodness and beauty and its basic order toward praise and worship of God, albeit now with deep distortion. But we should take note of the fact that this distortion within subhuman nature itself is introduced by human sin, for this provides a significant lesson: the things of nature are bound into an ontological-cosmological community with man, such that realization of their own integrity as transcendentally good and as made for the service of man and for the praise of God depends in an utterly profound way on the integrity of man's own love and worship of God.

The sixth objection is that the language of love has its place in the "private" sphere, for example, of family and church, but that such language is neither adequate nor appropriate for the "public" sphere as expressed in secular academic, economic, or political institutions. The argument of this book presupposes that there is indeed a warrant for a distinction, by way of analogy, between the language proper to family and church on the one hand, and to public institutions, on the other. But this distinction between languages is legitimate only insofar as it preserves what is always a deeper anterior unity within them, and within the things to which they refer.[16] The pertinent point, in other words, is that there can be no language regarding the things and persons of this world that is neutral or indifferent with respect to their created-gifted nature and destiny. There is no language of simple strategic or methodological "purity," no language that is barren of implications, with respect to the meaning of nature as created in love and called to love, or with respect to nature's originally given openness to and "restlessness" for the divine love revealed in the Eucharist of Jesus Christ.[17] This holds true whether the strategic or methodological purity be claimed in the name of the economy, or the academy, or the state.

Relative to these three public institutions, then, the point is neither simply to *replace* nor simply to *add to* the legitimately autonomous lan-

---

16. See "Civil Community Inside the Liberal State: Truth, Freedom, and Human Dignity" and "Market Liberalism and an Economic Culture of Gift and Gratitude," pp. 65-132 and 166-218 in this volume. More generally, in relation to distinction within anterior unity, see "Modernity and the Nature of a Distinction: Balthasar's Ontology of Generosity" and "The Given as Gift," pp. 350-82 and 383-429.

17. It is important to see that this "restlessness," as generous, is always formed anteriorly in "patience."

guage proper to each domain. It is rather to insert within each a dynamic for transformation rooted in memory. Transformation, rightly understood, involves securing in their integrity the truth and goodness of things as articulated in the various public or institutionally specialized languages, all the while re-forming that truth and goodness from within a deeper and broader framework of integration. The newness is not only by way of a new context, but enters into the original content of truth itself; otherwise we slip back into so-called "integration" by way of "addition." In a word, the burden of transformation is that the truth and goodness of things as conceived in "public" and specialized languages is preserved, *even as* the meaning of this truth and goodness is now recuperated from the inside out and re-appears with a greater depth and breadth.[18]

Thus with respect to the dominant liberal economic order, the burden of my thesis is that self-interest is most truly realized *as* self-interest only inside the human act's always already given dynamic for other-centered love. It is not a question of eliminating self-love, which indeed is entailed in *being a self* in the first place, but of recuperating self-love from inside the always anterior movement toward love for others and for God above all things, a movement that cannot but be always "remembered" in the depths of one's being, even if only implicitly. In a word, other-centered love, rightly understood, is not a simply voluntary act understood as a private addition to the dominant public logic of economic life. On the contrary, it is naturally exigent in the heart of every human self, hence in every self-interest. Only by recognizing that this is so can the freedom intended by the liberal market itself be truly liberated.[19]

---

18. Cf. Benedict XVI's encyclical *Caritas in Veritate*, n. 30: "Faced with the phenomena that lie before us, charity in truth requires first of all that we know and understand, acknowledging and respecting the specific competence of every level of knowledge. Charity is not an added extra, like an appendix to work already concluded in each of the various disciplines: it engages them in dialogue from the very beginning. . . . Going beyond, however, never means prescinding from the conclusions of reason, nor contradicting its results. Intelligence and love are not in separate compartments: *love is rich in intelligence and intelligence is full of love*" (emphasis original).

19. See "Market Liberalism and an Economic Order of Gift and Gratitude," pp. 166-218 in this volume, for further argument of this point in an economic context. For elaboration of the anthropological foundations for this argument, see "The Significance of World and Culture for Moral Theology" and "The Embodied Person as Gift and the Cultural Task in America." On the mutual inherence of "self-interest" and other-centered love, see Benedict XVI's *Deus Caritas Est* (2005); for the social-economic implications of this mutual inherence, see his *Caritas in Veritate* (2009).

Similarly with respect to the academy: the presupposition of my thesis is that the logic of love can account without reduction for the legitimate mechanical properties of things, even as this will properly entail a new reading of these mechanical properties (recall here the parallel discussion regarding substantial identity in response to the third objection). The relevant point, of course, is that this account must be given in terms of a more adequate interpretation of *nature and reason themselves*.[20] The burden of my argument, in a word, is to criticize post-Enlightenment science, not for too much emphasis on reason, but for a too narrow and reduced idea of reason; and in this light to broaden and deepen our idea of reason.

Finally, regarding the distinctions between state and church and state and society, there are three main presuppositions demanded by a rightly conceived reading of the universal call to love as expressed in my thesis. The first is that there is no positive law that does not carry the implication of metaphysical — which in turn bear on theological — claims of truth. This means that there is no purely procedural state, nor are there any purely juridically conceived rights. On the contrary, juridical procedures always invoke a metaphysical claim of truth of some kind. It follows that no state in its *legal-constitutional order* can successfully avoid the question of truth.

As is well known, the modern liberal-juridical conception of the state, in contrast to the ancient and classical view, affirms that the "political" must take primacy over the "metaphysical," or again that, in accord with the Hobbesian dictum, it is authority and not truth that makes law (*auctoritas, non veritas, facit legem*). The thesis of my book requires demonstration of the fact that the putative priority of the political over the metaphysical itself expresses a metaphysical claim, even as the would-be priority of "authority," or merely positive law, over "truth" itself expresses a metaphysical "truth." Once this is shown, the question becomes that of *which* truth best secures the main purpose of civil society. This purpose, consistent with the implications of the thesis of this book, is to secure the common good, above all by safeguarding the inherent dignity of all human beings, especially the weakest and most vulnerable.

But here it is important to take note of the famous dictum that the state governs by truths of which it is not the source. Rightly understood, this means *both* that the state in its governance relies as a matter of inner neces-

---

20. See Part II of this book. See also Pope Benedict XVI's "Address to the Representatives of Science at the University of Regensburg," 12 September 2006.

sity on some truth, *and* that the state is never the original or final source or arbiter of truth. What my thesis requires in this context, therefore, is twofold.

First of all, the truth that government would best appropriate, on grounds of nature and reason and in terms of the purpose just stated, is the truth of freedom as an essential inner feature of love, or better, the truth of freedom as an order of love, a love anchored in the memory of God and others and their inherent goodness. The point, in other words, is to secure freedom as a genuine achievement of the liberal-juridical state, while avoiding the reduction of freedom to a would-be purely juridical freedom that has never been, nor as a matter of principle can ever be, actualized in history.

But again, secondly, this truth does not have its most basic source in the state. On the contrary, it has its origin in God, and in the citizens themselves as creatures bearing a nature, and a natural law and love, that participates in God's eternal law and love. The truth therefore resides in the *state* only as always mediated through the human beings who make up civil *society*, and indeed via the nature or natural logic of their being.

The upshot of the foregoing is that the truth about freedom in its root meaning as natural love is legitimately infused into the state only through citizens' appealing to their nature via the exercise of their reason, both of which are matters intrinsically of a love that moves toward others and toward God above all things. Citizens must properly make their proposals in ways consistent with this love, which is to say, in ways centered in authentic dialogue rather than in strategic manipulation and external management. They must understand that love, rightly understood, has its own way of dialoguing, which presupposes truth and is indeed intended to end in truth. This latter notion of dialogue stands in clear contrast to the merely procedural dialogue of the juridical state, which tends of its inner logic to trail off into interminable, fruitless chatter.

Many of the issues evoked here will be discussed further in the chapters to follow, above all in the chapter "Civil Community Inside the Liberal State: Truth, Freedom, and Human Dignity." My present concern has been only to indicate that the book's thesis makes a twofold claim: that the truth about freedom as love is an intrinsic matter of responsibility for the state, even as the exercise of this responsibility can never legitimately take any form that implies that the state is the source or final arbiter of the truth of things. The state, again, must always govern on the basis of a truth of which it is as such never the original source. With this crucial qualification, we can say that the argument of this book presupposes that the purpose of the state is to secure justice as a common *good*. It is to secure the equal freedom of all human beings in their inherent dignity, a dignity that can be truly recognized and sustained only from within the natural love of each human being for others in their transcendentally given truth and goodness, and for God above all things.

Thus the overarching thesis of this book holds true: all things are to be formed in love in accord with the *logos* of the original gift, including the state in a *lay* sense. The call to a love that is at once natural and ever-restless for the supernatural love disclosed in the Eucharist of Jesus Christ embraces everything, the order of public institutions not excepted.

* * *

I conclude this introduction with a comment about the methodology of this book. The book's intention, simply, is to reflect ontologically on basic realities of experience, vis-à-vis the contemporary cultural situation and in light of Christian faith. My way of proceeding presupposes that the things reflected upon have a nature, and indeed that the people reading this book also share a nature. It also presupposes that the realities reflected upon, as well as myself as the agent of reflection, are all affected by the divine love revealed in Jesus Christ and mediated through the "ontological difference," in ways that in principle can never be fully articulated. The book presupposes, finally, that there can be no metaphysical account of things which does not open of its inner dynamic into a natural theology (as Aristotle recognized long ago), and which does not thereby always already bear implications with respect to any divinely revealed theology.

The book's anchor in nature and thus in reason is key: the presupposition is that the arguments developed with respect to current cultural problems are accessible in principle to any reader. At the same time, it must be clearly acknowledged that even the arguments claimed thus to be rooted in nature, and hence to be reasonable and universal, bear within them the influence of Christian faith. The arguments bear this influence, however, in ways that I take to deepen and not distort the meaning of nature and reason, rightly understood in their concrete historical reality.[21]

Indeed, I should say in this connection that I take the demand that a metaphysical argument be free of the influence of faith, or the claim to be able cleanly to abstract what in such an argument is a matter purely of na-

---

21. See the Pastoral Constitution on the Church in the Modern World, *Gaudium et Spes*, n. 22: "Since human nature as he assumed it was not annulled, by that very fact it was raised up to a divine dignity in our respect too."

ture or purely of reason, to be in the end Cartesian rather than, say, authentically Thomist. Such a demand at any rate is not consistent with the view of Christian philosophy affirmed in John Paul II's encyclical *Fides et Ratio*, which contains many helpful reflections pertinent to the methodology indicated here.[22] Of course, whether the Christian ambience of my arguments does in fact deepen rather than distort the meaning of nature and reason can be ascertained only by entering intrinsically into the arguments themselves. The merit of the arguments can be assessed only in terms of what seems to one, in the light of the whole of one's experience — informed as this experience will also necessarily be by one's own stance toward the whole of reality and its origin, with the "faith" that this implies — to be the integrity of nature and reason; and if necessary only by providing the counter-arguments that one takes to be more adequate.

Gabriel Marcel states that "in the long run all that is not done through Love and for Love must invariably end by being done against Love. The human being who denies his nature as a created being ends up by claiming for himself attributes which are a sort of caricature of those that belong to the Uncreated."[23] This statement captures the burden of my argument: any act or order not formed in the logic of love — which is forgetful, that is, of being and its Source — must invariably end up, by implication, subverting the nature and destiny of things.

Love consists in this, "not that we loved God but that he loved us and sent his Son . . ." (1 John 4:10). The love characteristic of the being of the cosmos, in which the cosmos participates by virtue of its creation, is not a love that is first *produced by* the cosmos, but one that is always first *given to* the cosmos. As such it is a love that must first be received, through the power that is most basically that of the giver become effective *in* the gift, a power in which the creature is therefore always, properly, a filial participant. The burden of my proposal is that the mostly implicit ontology of modern Western culture is one essentially of technology, in the sense developed in the various chapters of this book. Such an ontology abstracts from the logic of love proper to created being, and in so doing assumes a version of power that can only become in the end a caricature of the power of God, a power not of love but of a technical manipulation tending ultimately toward tyranny.

---

22. See John Paul II's encyclial letter *Fides et Ratio*, especially n. 75f. on Christian philosophy. See also Hans Urs von Balthasar's statement regarding nature and grace in the Introduction to his *Theo-logic*, vol. I: *Truth of the World* (San Francisco: Ignatius Press, 2000), pp. 11-13.

23. Gabriel Marcel, *Man Against Humanity* (London: Harvill Press, 1952), pp. 55-56.

PART I

LIBERAL SOCIETIES AND THE MEMORY OF GOD

"Keeping the World Awake to God": Benedict XVI in America

For Pope Benedict XVI the main issue of our time, as it has been for all the saints and doctors of the Church down through the ages, is the memory of God and his centrality in our lives. Thus he asserts that the problems of the West can be traced finally to a forgetfulness of God. It is this question of God, of his presence or absence, that lies at the heart of the faith-reason problematic on which I have been asked especially to comment. My question is this: How does Benedict understand the task, as he puts it, of "keeping the world awake to God,"[1] and what does his understanding imply for America?

(1) Regarding God in America, the principal phenomena are two. On the one hand, as public opinion polls attest, God does not seem to be absent: the great majority of Americans continue to believe in God and indeed to give him an important place in their lives. And there is no need to doubt the sincerity of what people have recorded in these polls. In America the thesis that modernity brings with it secularism, or the death of God, therefore seems to be contradicted.

At the same time, equally pervasive in America is the view that the reality of God is not properly a matter of reason. However important it

---

1. Cf. Pope Benedict XVI, Chrism Mass Homily, Holy Thursday, 2008.

This chapter reproduces a panel presentation given for the Crossroads Cultural Center, "'Only Something Infinite Will Suffice': A Discussion on the Teachings of Pope Benedict XVI and Their Relevance for American Culture," held at Columbia University in New York and at the Pope John Paul II Cultural Center in Washington, D.C., 9 and 11 April 2008. The New York event included panelists Msgr. Lorenzo Albacete, Fr. Richard John Neuhaus, and Carl Anderson. The Washington event included Msgr. Albacete and John Allen, Jr.

may be as a matter of inspiration, relation to God cannot be integrated into the logic of reason as exercised in the public life of the academy, politics, economics, or indeed morality. In short, the God who appears to be pervasively present in America remains absent to reason in what the culture considers reason's legitimate meaning. The God of believers appears to non-believers to be an arbitrary God who is a threat to the integrity of public argument.

(2) For Benedict, a God who is truly God must make a difference to everything all the time. Affirming the truth of Romans 1:20 that, since the creation of the world, God can be seen in the things he has made — and not only by believers — Benedict stresses that the question of God is inescapable.[2] This indeed was one of the main (and often overlooked) points of his 2006 Regensburg lecture, whose burden was twofold: to insist, vis-à-vis the problems posed by some forms of Islam, that God is inherently reasonable; but to insist, at the same time, in relation to the West, that reason realizes its integrity only when it comes to terms with its constitutive or structural openness to God.

The whole of the theology of Joseph Ratzinger/Benedict XVI as it bears on culture and cosmos may be said to be centered on this basic fact that "I do not come from myself; rather, I come from another."[3] What reason most basically is, therefore, is a dialogue with God: whatever the content of our conscious acts, we always speak at least implicitly about the reality of God and of our relation to him. No act of creaturely consciousness remains neutral or can remain silent with respect to the Creator.

It follows that the religious dimension of our existence can never be rightly understood as a merely voluntary, extra-rational, or private addition to the life of reason. What Benedict's work shows, in a word, is that the marriage of modernity and religion in America is a marriage between modernity and a religion already formed mostly in the reductive terms of a peculiarly modern — post-Puritan, post-Enlightenment — understanding of God, creation, and reason.

(3) Now it is important for Benedict, if he is not to fall into the kind of reductive religion of which he is critical, that he give reasons for this argument that are persuasive at least in principle to those who do not share

---

2. Cf. *To Look on Christ: Exercises in Faith, Hope, and Love* (New York: Crossroad, 1991).

3. From a Saarland radio broadcast cited in *Co-Workers of the Truth: Meditations for Every Day of the Year*, ed. Sr. Irene Grassl, trans. Sr. Mary Frances McCarthy, S.N.D, and Rev. Lothar Krauth (San Francisco: Ignatius Press, 1992), pp. 97-98.

his faith. To be sure, Benedict makes his proposal as a Catholic and hence as a theologian. Speaking from within his faith, he nevertheless offers a renewed interpretation of the conscience and the natural law that are common to all human beings, and in so doing makes also a *philosophical* claim that makes *reasonable* demands on all human beings.

Regarding conscience: Benedict suggests that, to the traditional meaning of conscience as *synderesis* (moral awareness), we add, at an even more basic level, conscience as *anamnesis* (primitive recollection of God). Notably, Benedict makes this proposal also in terms of Socrates, who did not have the benefit of Christian revelation. Socrates witnessed by his life and argument that I become truly self-aware only by recalling in some primitive if unarticulated way the "more," stemming from the presence of a transcendent source, that is always implied in my self-awareness and is somehow more interior to me than I am to myself.[4] This is so, Benedict says, because "the *anamnesis* of the Creator . . . is identical to the ground of our existence."[5]

Regarding natural law: Benedict has appealed often in his pontificate to natural law, but it is a version of natural law that has recuperated its finality and center in God.[6] He affirms and develops Aquinas's understanding of the natural moral precept to seek to know the truth about God and to live in community with others. Note also that Benedict emphasizes the nature of law as a matter of desire and thus love, in contrast to the modern tendency, following Kant, to conceive law more basically as duty. As stated in his first encyclical, *Deus Caritas Est* (2005), what the human being *desires (eros)* is most basically to love God above all things and others for their own sake *(agape)*. The point is thus that this desire to generously love God and others arises naturally. It is not merely a function of grace, although the desire is fully realized only in grace.[7]

The task of Christians, then, is to awaken this desire and give witness

---

4. Cf. Augustine, *Confessions* 3.6.11: "tu eras interior intimo meo et superior summo meo." See also Aquinas, *ST* I, q. 8, a. 1: "God is in all things, and innermostly."

5. Joseph Ratzinger, *On Conscience: Two Essays by Joseph Ratzinger* (Philadelphia/San Francisco: The National Catholic Bioethics Center/Ignatius Press, 2007), p. 32.

6. It is his appeal at once to *natural* law and to a natural law *intrinsically ordered toward God* that grounds Benedict's conception of a dialogue open simultaneously to the West and to major world religious traditions such as Islam.

7. Thus Benedict develops more fully the Thomistic dictum, in which Thomas expressly follows Augustine (see Aquinas, *De Veritate*, q. 22, a. 2), that every cognitive being knows and loves God implicitly in whatever he knows and loves.

to it: to show that the restlessness driving every act of human consciousness in its depths is, even in America, a restlessness for God and for love. This is what is meant by the "pursuit of happiness," rightly conceived.

(4) What Benedict's views on God, creation, and reason imply for the various areas of life in America can only be hinted at here. (a) Suffice it to say, first, with respect to the academy: the search for truth, concerning being as love and finally concerning God, needs to take its place at the heart of the modern university, in a way that respects while reconfiguring the rightful autonomy of the disciplines. Renewing this search implies the deepening of reason to include interiority and contemplativeness — or more concretely, humility and obedience — as integral to the methods of research proper to the academy. Experience must find its proper place as more basic than experiment as a source of knowledge in the sciences, both social and natural.[8] And so on.

Benedict's understanding of reason does not reject the heritage of the Enlightenment. For him, the problem with the Enlightenment is not that it overemphasized reason, but that it unduly narrowed reason to a matter of technical control. Benedict means to recover reason in its full scope and depth. Insofar as post-Enlightenment reason has been concerned with infinity, it is the "bad infinity" of endlessly fragmented objects, as distinct from the good infinity that opens to integration in a universe of beings under God. What post-Enlightenment reason has done, in a word, is to cut human knowledge off from the natural desire for the truth about God as the *Logos* of love.

A final point in connection with education: in his January, 2008 letter to the diocese of Rome regarding the education of young people, Benedict recalls the importance, given that education must be rooted in the search for truth, of ensuring that young people are taught openness to suffering. The search for truth involves the self-sacrifice integral to love. He says that the danger in shielding young people from difficulties and the experience of suffering in their search for truth is that they will grow up to become brittle and ungenerous adults.

(b) Regarding freedom and rights: freedom for Benedict is most basically an act of love in search of God, which includes even as it transforms America's dominant view of freedom as an originally indifferent act of choice or exercise of options. "Rights" for Benedict flow from the natural

---

8. Cf. *Die Krise der Katechese und ihre Überwindung. Rede in Frankreich* (Einsiedeln: Johannes Verlag, 1983), pp. 13-14, cited in *Co-Workers of the Truth*, pp. 227-28.

desire and thus responsibility to love God and others, and this includes even as it transforms America's dominant view of rights as simply "immunities from coercion" by others.

(c) Finally, regarding religion and the political order. Benedict unequivocally affirms the West's separation between Church and state.[9] However, he rejects the idea of a purely juridical state. The fact that the state is not the source of truth about man and God does not mean that the state can ever be neutral or indifferent to that truth.[10] Indeed, the pervasively juridically conceived state in America has been an integral part of the public ethos that permits and encourages ongoing debate, but only so long as the debate does not terminate in any substantive truth that would be binding on all citizens. For Benedict, the purely juridical state implies a reductive view of human conscience and a formalistic notion of natural law. In fact, the juridical state, with its proceduralist public ethos, leads logically to nothing less than what Benedict has termed a "dictatorship of relativism."[11]

In sum, Benedict's theology does not reject the distinctive goods realized in America's institutions. On the contrary, he accepts these goods in their most basic and natural intentions. This does not mean, however, that he accepts America's achievements in their dominant present form, to which he would then wish merely to *add* a Christian difference — a difference that would inevitably be received as a merely private difference, in the end not making much of a difference at all. Rather, Benedict's theology endorses America's achievements, but with a dynamic for transformation that begins from inside our cultural and institutional logic. This dynamic changes the dominant notions of reason and freedom all the while taking

---

9. Benedict sees the difference between America's version of this separation and that which is more common in the post–French Revolution continental version. America's version, in short, had the purpose of protecting and even fostering religion in society. The problem, as is implied in my statements that follow, is that America already from the beginning interprets this separation too much in terms of an endorsement of the juridical state, with the problems ensuing from this as I have noted them — problems of which Benedict is aware in his general treatment of religion-state issues.

10. Cf. his statement on 1 January 2008, for the World Day of Peace: "the *juridic norm*, which regulates relationships between individuals, disciplines external conduct, and establishes penalties for offenders, has as its criterion the *moral norm* grounded in nature itself. Human reason is capable of discerning this moral norm, at least in its fundamental requirements, and thus ascending to the creative reason of God which is at the origin of all things."

11. Joseph Ratzinger, Homily, Mass "Pro Eligendo Romano Pontifice," 18 April 2005. For further discussion, see "Civil Community Inside the Liberal State: Truth, Freedom, and Human Dignity," pp. 65-132 in this volume.

over, now in an enlarged sense pointing toward their final Gospel meaning, all that America wishes to protect regarding human autonomy and dignity, by means of its dominant notions of reason and freedom.

(5) Lastly, a brief word about the nature and "realism" of the transformation indicated here. The main principles are three. First, Benedict's argument, in the spirit of Augustine, presupposes that all human beings have some primitive experience of restlessness for love and for God, however much this experience gets diverted in our culture into a pursuit of happiness conceived largely as the consumption of commodities. Benedict's theology thus presupposes that lives and indeed arguments that testify to this movement toward love and toward God will find resonance within the minds and hearts of others in the broader culture.

Second, Benedict insists over and over again that this task of cultural transformation is in the first instance not a matter of working up plans for new structures. As he puts it, "what the Church needs to respond to the needs of man in every age is holiness and not management."[12] What is needed is that Christians *reform themselves* patiently and from the inside, a reformation which, as inclusive of the whole human being and thus also of the body, will include a patient but genuine reformation of structures.

Third, Benedict stresses that cultural transformation will never be realized without suffering. This point cannot be overemphasized. There seems to be a widespread assumption today, often unspoken, that if Jesus had only had the benefit of liberal institutions and access to the Internet, he could have secured the power and influence necessary to avoid an ignominious death on the Cross. Needless to say, such is not the view of Benedict.

Benedict insists on the contrary that the "the Cross is revelation.... It reveals who God is and who man is."[13] What this means is that suffering the Cross is not necessary only for one who lives his or her Christianity faithfully; suffering the Cross already has its presentiment in the person who lives the fullness of his humanity justly. Which is to say, in the concrete order of history, it is "reasonable," and not only a function of one's faith, to expect to suffer crucifixion. Ratzinger/Benedict refers again to the case of Socrates:

---

12. Joseph Ratzinger, *The Ratzinger Report* (San Francisco: Ignatius Press, 1985), pp. 52-53.

13. Joseph Ratzinger, *Introduction to Christianity* (San Francisco: Ignatius Press, 1990), pp. 222-23.

> In the *Republic* [Plato] asks what is likely to be the position of a completely just man in this world. He comes to the conclusion that a man's righteousness is only complete and guaranteed when he takes on the appearance of unrighteousness, for only then is it clear that he does not follow the opinion of men but pursues justice only for its own sake. So according to Plato the truly just man must be misunderstood and persecuted in this world; indeed, Plato goes so far as to write: "They will say that our just man will be scourged, racked, fettered . . . , and at last, after all manner of suffering, will be crucified. . . ." This passage, written four hundred years before Christ, is always bound to move a Christian deeply. Serious philosophical thinking here surmises that the completely just man in this world must be the crucified just man; something is sensed of that revelation of man which comes to pass on the Cross.[14]

This expectation of the Cross, which finds its warrant in Christian faith but is also somehow already prefigured in reason, cannot be forgotten, even for a moment, in the Christian's engagement with the culture.

(6) To return in conclusion, then, to our opening question: What is distinctive about Benedict's theology, and what does it mean for us? Simply, Benedict proposes a new sense of the integrity of nature and reason, now understood in light of the statement of *Gaudium et Spes* (1965) that Jesus Christ, in his revelation of the Father's love, reveals the mystery of man to himself (n. 22). Relative to America, *Gaudium et Spes* as interpreted by Benedict entails a new sense of the reasonableness of God- and love-centeredness — in short, of the call to holiness — and consequently a new sense also of the reasonableness of the demand for openness to God and to love precisely at the heart of America's *public* culture.

---

14. Ratzinger, *Introduction to Christianity*, p. 293. The citation from Plato is from *The Republic*, Book II, 361e-362a.

Cultural Implications of Religions in Public Life: Recuperating the Deeper Questions

I begin by citing from the striking statement Pope Benedict XVI made last year at this Center on the occasion of his Meeting with Representatives of Other Religions:

> [R]eligious freedom [and] interreligious dialogue . . . aim at something more than a consensus regarding ways to implement practical strategies for advancing peace. The broader purpose of dialogue is to discover the truth. What is the origin and destiny of mankind? What are good and evil? What awaits us at the end of our earthly existence? Only by addressing these deeper questions can we build a solid basis for the peace and security of the human family, for "wherever and whenever men and women are enlightened by the splendor of truth, they naturally set out on the path of peace" *(Message for the 2006 World Day of Peace).*
>
> We are living in an age when these questions are too often marginalized. Yet they can never be erased from the human heart. . . .
>
> Spiritual leaders have a special duty . . . to place the deeper questions at the forefront of human consciousness, to reawaken mankind

---

A form of this chapter was given at a panel discussion titled "The Purpose of Dialogue Is to Discover the Truth." The discussion was sponsored by Crossroads Cultural Center and took place at the Pope John Paul II Cultural Center in Washington, D.C., 21 April 2009. The other panelists were Archbishop Pietro Sambi, Apostolic Nuncio of the Holy See; David Farber of the American Jewish Committee and the Jewish Federation of Greater Washington; Imam Yahya Hendi, Muslim chaplain at Georgetown University and member of the Islamic Jurisprudence Council of North America; and Marcello Pera, former president of the Italian senate.

to the mystery of human existence, and to make space in a frenetic world for reflection and prayer. . . .

While always uniting our hearts and minds in the call for peace, we must also listen attentively to the voice of truth. In this way, our dialogue will not stop at identifying a common set of values, but go on to probe their ultimate foundation.[1]

In a preface to Professor Marcello Pera's new book, *Why We Should Call Ourselves Christians,* Benedict notes the clarity of the professor's argument that, while an interreligious dialogue in the strict sense is not possible without setting one's faith aside, "intercultural dialogue on the cultural consequences of the basic religious decision has become all the more urgent." In what follows I will focus not on the sense in which interreligious dialogue may or may not be possible, but on what Benedict terms intercultural dialogue. That is, taking the cue given by Pope Benedict, I will focus on what he suggests is a basic task common to religious leaders: "to place the deeper questions at the forefront of human consciousness." What is entailed by this task, and how might common engagement with this task lead on to dialogue regarding the ultimate foundations of this task? Needless to say, what follows is offered in my own name and not that of Benedict, though, as will be clear, the line of reflection is influenced deeply by my reading of Benedict's theology.

(1) I'd like to begin by drawing on some events dramatically described in a recently translated book by the late Archbishop Kazimierz Majdanski of Poland. The book, *You Shall Be My Witnesses: Lessons Beyond Dachau,* recounts the experience of himself and other Polish seminarians and priests during their time in the early 1940s in the Sachsenhausen and Dachau concentration camps. Archbishop Majdanski notes some of the rules and principles governing behavior in the camp. One of them is well known: "*Arbeit macht frei:* Work sets one free." Another, which is less well known, states: "*Im Lager nur Laufschritt:* Only running (brisk walking) is permitted in camp." The burden of both, of course, is to further "productivity." Only through incessant movement can time and space, and thus work, be thoroughly instrumentalized. Stillness or rest in such a context becomes subversive. Two experiences noted by Majdanski bring out what is implied by this. He says, for example, that "the snowy Alps were visible

---

1. Benedict XVI, "Address to Representatives of Other Religions," at the Pope John Paul II Cultural Center, 17 April 2008.

in the distance from the camp, but no one was able to muster it within himself to give any thought to how beautiful they really are; this can only be done by one who is able to look at the world with the eyes of a man, not a slave." Majdanski also speaks of the talks he and his fellow clergy organized clandestinely, each talk given to the others based on one's own background of study. The Archbishop says that the talk he remembers most explained "how the arch of Titus can be considered the synthesis of the art of Ancient Rome."

The Archbishop's point is that one can see reality truly only with the eyes of a free man — with free eyes. And we should ponder the "useless" meaning (and beauty) of the topic chosen for discussion by the community of priests, which the Archbishop experienced as the most memorable during his time in the camps! Majdanski witnesses to us, in extreme circumstances, what is implied in keeping the mystery of things, and the deeper questions, alive.

What I want to say in light of these examples, simply, is that true freedom can be realized only through an essential link with "useless" meaning: beauty and goodness. Sustaining this link involves two presuppositions. First, there is a stillness lying at the heart of time and movement; and second, reality is *given to* us before it is *constructed by* us.

Regarding the first: the stillness to which I refer does not signify inactivity but something like what T. S. Eliot means when he says that the still point is at the heart of the dance;[2] or what Benedict means when he says that "life itself . . . becomes a movement towards [God]."[3] In other words, time *in each of its moments* reveals eternity, because time bears a relation to the Creator who *abides,* and invites *abiding,* in the sense of the Gospel of John (15:4).

Regarding the second: the meaning of reality, of truth and goodness, is inherent in things as naturally given. In more technical terms, we would say that a thing is *verum et bonum* first *qua ens* (true and good qua being) and not simply *quia factum*.[4] To be sure, things in their naturally given reality are open to and invite human thought and making, but only as re-

---

2. T. S. Eliot, "Burnt Norton," in *The Four Quartets* (New York: Harcourt, Brace, and Co., 1943).

3. Benedict XVI, "Address to Representatives from the World of Culture," at the Collège des Bernardins, Paris, 12 September 2008.

4. That is, true and good because and insofar as it is made to be so by human beings: cf. the Italian philosopher Giambattista Vico (1668-1744).

sponsive to their *originally given* order. Most basically, reality is a gift that is always *first to be received*, again because of its relation to the Creator.

It is in living the intersection of time and eternity and the givenness — or better, the giftedness — of reality in these senses alone that we are enabled to look at the world with the eyes of free men and women, and thus to see reality as it is: to see the beauty of things and especially the dignity of the human person for what they are, and to rethink and remake reality in accord with this beauty and this dignity.

Genuine freedom and seeing, in a word, human action, are realized only when liberated by and formed in wonder.

(2) To be sure, the examples I have noted above are tied to extreme circumstances. But we should recall here that, as Benedict noted last year in his address to the UN General Assembly, the United Nations[5] and the Universal Declaration of Human Rights[6] came into being not least because of "the profound upheavals that humanity experienced [during the events surrounding World War II] when reference to the meaning of transcendence and natural reason was abandoned, and in consequence, freedom and human dignity were grossly violated."[7] Benedict's point is that loss of a sense of the transcendent origin of things in a Creator — which is to say, in the terms I have adopted, loss of the eternal meaning of things in time, and of the truth and goodness of things in their natural givenness — drains of their objective foundations all the values intended by the United Nations: its founding concern for peace and justice and humanitarian cooperation and rights. The Pope emphasizes this point, of course, because he believes that loss of this sense continues to threaten human civilization. The lesson, in a word, is still, and always, to be learned.

What I mean to suggest, in this light, is that global culture today has its own liberal-technological version of a world viewed merely instrumentally: its own version of a public order that effectively permits *"nur Laufschritt"*: only endlessly dispersing movement and instrumentalized activity that are, *eo ipso*, closed to eternity, empty of the stillness or *abiding* necessary for living time in its genuinely creaturely sense.

As Ratzinger says, "Technological civilization is not in fact religiously and morally neutral, even if it believes it is. It changes the way people inter-

---

5. The United Nations was founded in 1945.
6. The Declaration was issued in 1948.
7. Benedict XVI, "Address to the Members of the General Assembly of the United Nations Organization," New York City, 18 April 2008.

pret the world, from the very bottom up. [It] is like an earthquake that shakes the spiritual landscape to its foundations."[8] But the response, he says, is not "a flight into the irrational, but . . . opening up reason to its true height and breadth."[9] Which is to say, opening it up to eternity.

In sum, human action, in Pope Benedict's view, is a matter most basically of *ora et labora:* of both prayer and work, that is, both together, but in that order. As the first monks affirmed in their founding contribution to European culture, life rightly understood has its roots in a community formed around *quaerere Deum,* the search for God. This search involves *eruditio,* the formation and education of man in "useless" truth and goodness and beauty, even as this *eruditio* then forms from within all "useful" movement and work.

Benedict reminds us: "What gave Europe's culture its foundation — the search for God and the readiness to listen to him — remains today the basis of any genuine culture."[10]

(3) I have not mentioned the strictly political dimension of the matters raised here. It is often said today, rightly, that the state is not the source of truth and indeed is not properly responsible for the ultimate truth of anything. However, as the Pope makes clear in his United Nations address, this does not mean that the state can govern without *intrinsic reliance on some truths.* Despite the claims of many proponents of liberal democracy in Europe and America, the state cannot take a purely juridical-procedural form. Indeed, what I am suggesting in this connection is that the (would-be) purely juridical state in fact embeds an instrumentalist view of truth. It is not the truth as such but "truth" qua *self-interested expression* of factions alone that is legally-publicly protected by the state, and this is as much the case in America as in Europe, though of course in different ways.[11] The result is that the values intended by de-

---

8. Joseph Cardinal Ratzinger, *Truth and Tolerance: Christian Belief and World Religions,* trans. Henry Taylor (San Francisco: Ignatius Press, 2004), pp. 76-77.

9. Ratzinger, *Truth and Tolerance,* p. 78.

10. Benedict XVI, "Address to Representatives from the World of Culture."

11. The implication of what I have suggested here is not that religions qua institutions should enter directly into the task of state governance, but only that they have the cultural task of encouraging their members, in their capacity also as citizens, to assist the state in favoring *de jure* those institutions in society which most properly do have responsibility for protecting the transcendent truth and goodness of creation *qua given* (by the Creator): namely, the institutions of religion and of family, and indeed of the local communities necessary for genuine subsidiarity.

mocracy are undermined by what Benedict terms a "narrow utilitarian perspective"[12] leading to relativism.[13]

(4) In conclusion, then: what I mean to propose is that the greatest cultural divide of our age is between those who live human action from inside the intersection of time and eternity and those who do not; between those who affirm the truth and goodness of the world as first given, thus as gift, and those who do not. The gravest cultural threat to humanity today, in other words (and I take this to be the view also of Benedict XVI), lies in humanity's loss of the capacity to wonder, which capacity alone in the end enables us to *see:* to see humanity and all of reality in their truth as naturally given rather than as primarily instruments, and hence as not true in a finally binding sense at all. Here, then, is the root of the relativism that Ratzinger says "is the most profound difficulty of our age."[14]

It is at just this cultural juncture, it seems to me, that a dialogue among the representatives of the world's great religious traditions might most fruitfully begin. Jointly they can work to keep alive the link between meaning and transcendent mystery that is due to time's openness to eternity, and in so doing keep alive the deeper questions embedded in man's nature. Permit me to cite two exemplary texts in this connection. First, the Jewish thinker Abraham Heschel says that "Spiritual life begins to decay when we fail to sense the grandeur of what is eternal in time";[15] that "Judaism is a *religion of time* aiming at the *sanctification of time*" (8); and that the "moment we become oblivious to ultimate questions, religion becomes irrelevant, and its crisis sets in."[16] Second, the Islamic scholar Seyyed Nasr says:

> Man . . . penetrates into the inner meaning of nature only on the condition of being able to delve into the inner depths of his own being and to cease to lie merely on the periphery of his being. Men who live only on the surface of their being can study nature as something to be manipulated and dominated. But only he who has turned toward the in-

---

12. Benedict XVI, "Address to the Members of the General Assembly of the United Nations Organization."

13. See "Civil Community Inside the Liberal State: Truth, Freedom, and Human Dignity," pp. 65-132 in this volume.

14. Ratzinger, *Truth and Tolerance*, p. 72.

15. Abraham Heschel, *The Sabbath* (HarperCollins Canada, 1951), p. 6.

16. Abraham Heschel, *God in Search of Man* (New York: Farrar, Straus & Giroux, 1955), p. 3.

> ward dimension of his being can see nature as a symbol, as a transparent reality and come to know and understand it in a real sense.[17]
>
> [In the end, only] he who is at peace with God is also at peace with His creation, both with nature and with man.[18]

We can surely find in these statements a community of perception sufficient for dialogue in the face of the modern cultural crisis.

To be sure, there are differences in the meaning of these statements that are tied already to differences in the ultimate religious foundations. Nevertheless, as Ratzinger puts it, here we "cannot avoid reference to the metaphysical dimension. A meeting of cultures is possible because man, in all the variety of his history and of his social structures and customs, is a single being, one and the same."[19] Thus both the cultural and religious differences can and should be engaged as honestly and truthfully as possible, but always while keeping focused on what is the crucial concern uniting us: to protect against the dissolution of the *humanum*, of the order of creation itself with the human person at its pinnacle. Here, it seems to me, is a way of beginning a genuine dialogue among representatives of the world's great religions: through gestures of friendship. It is only in friendship — as Benedict says, in "countless small acts of love, understanding, and compassion"[20] — that we develop the courage to speak openly to each other, living in time the mystery of giftedness that englobes all of us.

I summarize with two statements by Ratzinger:

> Christianity has more in common with the ancient cultures of mankind than with the relativistic and rationalistic world that has cut loose from the fundamental insights of mankind and is thus leading man into a vacuum, devoid of meaning, which risks being fatal for him unless the answer to it comes to him in time. For the knowledge that man must turn toward God, and toward what is eternal, is found right across all the cultures; the knowledge about sin, repentance, and forgiveness; the knowledge concerning communion with God and eternal life; and finally the knowledge of the basic rules of morality, as they are found in the form of the Ten Commandments. It is not relativism that

---

17. Seyyed Nasr, *Man and Nature: The Spiritual Crisis of Modern Man* (ABC International Group, Inc., 1997), pp. 96-97.
18. Nasr, *Man and Nature*, p. 136.
19. Ratzinger, *Truth and Tolerance*, p. 64.
20. Benedict XVI, "Address to Representatives of Other Religions."

is confirmed; rather, it is the unity of the human condition and its common experience of contact with a truth that is greater than we are.[21]

Confronted with these deeper questions concerning the origin and destiny of mankind, Christianity proposes Jesus of Nazareth. He, we believe, is the eternal *Logos* who became flesh in order to reconcile man to God and reveal the underlying reason of all things. It is he whom we bring to the forum of interreligious dialogue.[22]

---

21. Ratzinger, *Truth and Tolerance*, p. 79.
22. Benedict XVI, "Address to Representatives of Other Religions."

The Dramatic Nature of Life: Liberal Societies and the Foundations of Human Dignity

Human life and action realize their integrity only insofar as they are dramatic, and they are truly dramatic in the end only insofar as they engage to the full their creaturely nature before God. This, I believe, is the burden of the thought of John Paul II. *Evangelium Vitae* (1995) speaks of a struggle in our time between good and evil, between a "culture of life" and a "culture of death" (n. 28). Such a struggle would surely seem to suggest a drama. Though there is much movement and much noise and sometimes great violence in democratic societies today, there is virtually no drama, and it is just the absence of drama that highlights the nature of our societies' drift toward a culture of death.

I.

First, some brief and basic etymological notes. "Drama," from the Greek, means literally "deed" or "act." But the term refers more commonly to a life or theatrical performance involving tension and conflict that stirs the imagination and evokes the passions. These two meanings cannot be cleanly separated: we are not disposed really to count as a human action one that is bereft of passion or lacking in dynamic quality and depth.

The term "life," rightly understood, indicates more than bare physical existence. As we know from Aristotle, it signifies an ordered power that comes from within, a power bearing interiority and hence depth. The term "interior" comes from the Latin, *interior,* which means inner, and can also mean from the depth of something. This interior power enables the richness and intensity characteristic of what we spontaneously judge to be alive, in contrast to the dull repetition of a machine-like entity, whose movement remains superficial (*super-facies:* on the surface) and merely a function of external forces.¹ *Human* life, whose interiority takes a spiritual form, manifests the fullest richness and intensity of life among the beings of the world.

The term "passion" comes from the Latin, *patior,* "to suffer, undergo, experience, permit," and in turn from the Greek, πάσχω, "to receive an impression from without, to suffer evil, and to suffer as opposed to doing."

It is passion and interior power, then, that enable human life and action to be truly dramatic. But what is it, concretely, that gives passion and interior power their substantive content?

Answering this question requires attention to the creaturely nature of man. To be a creature is, *eo ipso,* to bear a relation to God that presupposes a "space" inside what is deepest and most original in the creature, one that reaches from within the roots of the creature outward. Human action is a matter of *passion* because at its root it remains an *undergoing* of this relation to God that is originally-anteriorly *given.* Human life is a matter of interior power for the same reason: it is above all an enactment of a relation that comes *from within,* a relation that, in the words of St. Augustine, is more deeply interior to us than we are to ourselves and reaches toward the highest heights, infinitely beyond us.² Passion and interiority, in short, disclose the deepest depths of what characterizes our creaturely openness to the infinite. They indicate the human receptive capacity for relation to God.

In the summary words of the *Compendium of the Social Doctrine of the Church* of John Paul II's pontificate, "*the essence and existence of man are constitutively related to God.* . . . This relationship is not something that comes afterwards and is not added from the outside. The whole of man's

---

1. Of course, no being in the cosmos is altogether lacking in interior power. On the contrary, every being participates analogically in a kind of metaphysical interiority, by virtue of creation. Cf., *inter alia,* the work of Kenneth L. Schmitz, *The Gift: Creation* (Milwaukee: Marquette University Press, 1982).

2. God is "more inward than my inmost self [*intimior intimo meo*] and higher than my topmost height" (Augustine, *Confessions,* 3:6). In the words of Aquinas, God is in all things *(intime),* and innermostly *(magis intimum)* (*ST* I, q. 8, a. 1). Further, Aquinas says that all cognitive beings know God implicitly [*implicite*] in whatever they know, and naturally tend implicitly to God in every end they seek or desire, thus affirming Augustine's statement that "Whatever can love, loves God" [*Deum diligit quidquid diligere potest*] (*De Veritate,* q. 22, a. 2).

life is a quest and a search for God. . . . [M]an of his inmost nature is a capacity for God *(homo est Dei capax)*."³

Further, John Paul II says that "creating the human race in his own image . . . , God inscribed in . . . man and woman the vocation, and thus the capacity and responsibility, of love and communion. Love is therefore the fundamental and innate vocation of every human being."⁴ Life and freedom are inextricably linked in this vocation to love (*EV*, n. 95), such that, "[f]ar from being achieved in . . . the absence of relationships, freedom only truly exists where reciprocal bonds . . . link people to one another" (*CSDC*, n. 199; cited from the Congregation for the Doctrine of the Faith, Instruction *Libertatis conscientia*, n. 26).⁵

All that I have to say regarding the nature of human life as drama follows from this understanding of the creature as *capax Dei et alterius*, and from the fact that this creaturely capacity "can be ignored or even forgotten or dismissed, but . . . never . . . eliminated" (*CSDC*, n. 109) and in relation to which therefore no act of intelligence or freedom can even for a moment remain neutral. My intention is to comment on what this means and why it takes us to the heart of the problem of the opposition between a culture of life and a culture of death in democratic societies as announced by *EV*.

We begin with a brief look at this encyclical's account of the drift in democratic societies toward a culture of death, focusing on the root causes of this drift.

---

3. *Compendium of the Social Doctrine of the Church (CSDC)*, n. 109. On the nature of spirit as the capacity for relation, cf. Josef Pieper, "The Philosophical Act," in *Leisure the Basis of Culture* (New York: Mentor, 1963).

4. John Paul II, *Go in Peace: An Enduring Gift of Love* (Chicago: Loyola Press, 2003), p. 211.

5. Thus the compendium affirms the constitutive social nature of human beings (*CSDC*, n. 37). In light of what we have proposed in section 1, cf. Cardinal Ratzinger's comments regarding the nature of creaturely autonomy, human freedom as shared freedom, the human being as openness to the infinite, that is, to God, and regarding the fact that it is martyrdom (see *EV*, n. 90) that shows us, "at one and the same time, the path to understanding Christ and to understanding what it means to be human beings," thereby revealing what is finally entailed in what we have termed the dramatic nature of life (Joseph Cardinal Ratzinger, "The Renewal of Moral Theology: Perspectives of Vatican II and *Veritatis Splendor*," *Communio: International Catholic Review* 32, no. 2 [Summer 2005]: 357-68; here, 366-68).

II.

The first chapter of the encyclical is devoted to an analysis of the lights and shadows of the current cultural situation as it bears on human life. There are many initiatives that serve as signs of hope. Democracy today, however, insofar as its peculiar quest for tolerance in the public order drives it to relativism, threatens to turn its intended defense of rights on its head, paradoxically becoming a kind of totalitarian freedom of the strong over the weak (n. 19-20).[6]

EV identifies two problematic tendencies at the source of the inversion of rights indicated here. First, there is a self-centered concept of freedom (n. 13)[7] that is characterized in various ways: for instance, a false concept of subjectivity that "recognizes as a subject of rights only the person who enjoys full or at least incipient autonomy and who emerges from a state of total dependence on others" (n. 19); also, a tendency to equate "dignity with capacity for verbal and explicit, or at least perceptible, communication" (n. 19), with a consequent loss of "place in the world for anyone who, like the unborn and the dying . . . , can only communicate through the silent language of a profound sharing of affection" (n. 19); in a word, a failure to understand that "freedom possesses an inherently relational dimension *(quae essentialem necessitudinis rationem secum fert)*" and an "essential link with the truth *(constitutivum veritatis vinculum)*" (n. 19).[8]

Along with this defective concept of freedom, the problem that threatens us even more profoundly is "the eclipse of the sense of God and of man" (n. 21). As the Second Vatican Council states, "when God is forgotten, the creature itself grows unintelligible" (*Gaudium et Spes*, 1965, n. 36). The result of this forgetfulness is that man "no longer grasps the transcendent character of his 'existence as man.' He no longer considers life as a splendid gift of God. . . . Life itself becomes a mere thing, which man claims as his exclusive property, completely subject to his control and

---

6. See "Civil Community Inside the Liberal State: Truth, Freedom, and Human Dignity," pp. 65-132 in this volume.

7. Self-centered, that is, in an ontological and not always psychological or moral sense.

8. As the Vatican summary of *EV* puts it: "[D]emocracy's peculiar inversion of rights stems from a notion of freedom which is seen as disconnected from any reference to truth and objective good, and which asserts itself . . . without the constitutive link of relationship with others" (The Vatican Summary of *Evangelium Vitae*, 1 [*Origins* 24, no. 42, 6 April 1995, p. 728]).

manipulation" (n. 22). Man "is concerned only with doing *(faciundi)* and using all kinds of technology *(ad omnes artes se conferens);* he busies himself with programming, controlling, and dominating birth and death. Birth and death, instead of being primary experiences demanding to be 'lived' *(agantur),* become things to be merely 'possessed' or 'rejected'" (n. 22). "Nature itself, far from being *mater* (mother), is now reduced to being 'matter,' and is subjected to every kind of manipulation," in accord with "a certain technical and scientific way of thinking" (n. 22).

More generally, "the values of being are replaced by those of having" (n. 23). Suffering is rejected as useless (n. 23). "The body is . . . no longer perceived as a properly personal reality, a sign and place of relations with others, with God and with the world. It is simply . . . a complex of organs, functions and energies to be used according to the sole criteria of pleasure and efficiency" (n. 23). Thus "the criterion of personal dignity . . . is replaced by the criterion of efficiency, functionality and usefulness: others are considered not for what they 'are,' but for what they 'have, do and produce.' This is the supremacy of the strong over the weak" (n. 23).

EV sums up as follows the response needed in the face of these characteristic tendencies of a culture of death:

> It is therefore essential that man should acknowledge his inherent condition as a creature *(originalem perspiciat suae condicionis evidentiam qua creaturae)* to whom God has granted being and life as a gift and a duty *(donum et munus).* Only by admitting his innate dependence *(innatam dependentiam in propria existentia)* can man live and use his freedom to the full and at the same time respect the life and freedom of every other person.[9] Here especially one sees that "at the heart of every culture lies the attitude man takes to the greatest mystery: the mystery of God" [*CA*, n. 24]. Where God is denied and people live "as though he did not exist" . . . , the dignity of the human person and the inviolability of human life also end up being rejected or compromised. (*EV*, n. 96)

Now, an important qualifier would seem necessary with respect to *EV*'s claim here of a link between the patterns characteristic of the culture of death and the absence of freedom's relation to God, and to others in

---

9. The freedom proper to creatures is "a freedom given as a gift, one to be received like a seed to be cultivated responsibly" (*CSDC*, n. 138; cited from *Veritatis Splendor* [1993], n. 86).

God. In the United States, for example, and hence in at least one liberal society, polling evidence continues to indicate extremely high belief in God (as much as 92 percent);[10] and the disposition of American society to help those in need likewise seems high. And yet abundant, and growing, signs of the culture of death as depicted in *EV* coincide with Americans' characteristically sincere belief in God and voluntary generosity toward others.[11]

Recalling our opening comments, we can anticipate that the nature of the qualifier needed to clarify the argument of *EV* lies in the nature of drama, with its presupposition of passion and interiority. The absence of God that correlates with the culture of death, in other words, is in the first instance a matter not of moral intention but of ontological depth. The problem lies in the professed neutrality of liberalism's concepts of reason and freedom, that is, in the ontological indifference expressed in liberalism's failure to take account of the *constitutive* nature of man's relation to God and to others and hence of the implications of creaturely *origin* and *destiny* in and for reason and freedom in each of man's acts.

What I am proposing in the name of *EV*, in a word, is that the real magnitude of the problem confronting us in the growing culture of death in liberal societies comes into view only when and insofar as we see that the absence of God is a phenomenon taking place precisely *within* what can otherwise be granted as a sincere belief in God and concern for social justice on the part of even the majority in some of these societies (at least in America).

My questions thus are two: What are the key conditions that must be realized to show reason and freedom in their rightful ontological depth? And in what way does liberalism typically tend to ignore or deny these conditions?

III.

First, we must recognize that our being originates as a gift: it has always *first* been *given* to us by God, and indeed by others in God. It follows that human life and action, in their innermost nature and destiny, are, and are meant to become, *responses* to this gift of love that consists in God's always

---

10. Pew Forum on Religion and Public Life, U.S. Religious Landscape Survey: "Religious Affiliation: Diverse and Dynamic" (Washington, DC: Pew Research Center, 2008).

11. See "Religion and Secularity in a Culture of Abstraction," pp. 328-49 in this volume.

loving us first, and indeed, in Jesus Christ, in loving us unto a suffering death (cf. *CSDC,* n. 39). All that needs to be said about the dramatic nature of life derives from this original-constitutive meaning of human life and action as *responsive* to a relation initiated, first and sustained by, God in Jesus Christ.

Second, this relation to God that is first given by God is meant *to last forever,* and calls the creature *to love God forever in return.* Thus Joseph Ratzinger has said that "the world is created in order to provide a setting for the Covenant by which God binds himself to man." The world "is created, so to say, in accordance with the inner structure of the Covenant . . . , and the Torah . . . [already] sets out both the Covenant and the marriage."[12] Thus we can say that creaturely freedom realizes its proper subjectivity only as always already objectively bound to God, and to other creatures in God. This objective binding is a binding in love, after the manner of spousal love,[13] and its "obligatory" nature thus comes in the form of a gift eliciting response, a call that moves through attraction, and hence passion. Creaturely freedom in its deepest reality is thus neither indifferent nor arbitrary subjectivity, nor is its objective binding to another a simple imposition from without. This duality, or dual unity, of subjective freedom and objective binding to another takes its meaning from the love by which the Creator God always first loves us, and this love is meant, in mutual if radically asymmetrical ways on the Creator's side and the creature's side, to bind forever.

In a word, creaturely freedom is ordered in its inmost structure toward a Covenant initiated by God and calling forth a creaturely response taking the form of what may be termed a vow.[14]

The nature of drama, then, lies in the fruitful tension implicit in the constitutive coincidence of this subjectivity that remains inherently free and this subjectivity's objective binding to another, ultimately to God. The free subject, and that to which the free subject is constitutively bound (God), each bear — in radically different *(maior dissimilitudo)* ways — an

---

12. Joseph Ratzinger, *God and the World* (San Francisco: Ignatius Press, 2002), p. 113.
13. Cf. *Deus Caritas Est* (2005), n. 3, 11, and 13.
14. See the following articles by David S. Crawford: "Christian Community and the States of Life: A Reflection on the Anthropological Significance of Virginity and Marriage," *Communio: International Catholic Review* 29, no. 2 (Summer 2002): 337-65; "Consecration and Human Action: The Moral Life as Response," *Communio: International Catholic Review* 31, no. 3 (Fall 2004): 379-403; and "Love, Action, and Vows as 'Inner Form' of the Moral Life," *Communio: International Catholic Review* 32, no. 2 (Summer 2005): 295-312.

infinite depth bearing an intention of remaining bound together, in freedom, forever. What we properly term drama, in a word, has its ontological origin in the abiding depth and fruitful tension presupposed in the simultaneous unity-within-duality of subject (self) and object (other) in the free act.

But all of this is fully realized only in the New Covenant begun in Jesus Christ. God's steadfast gift of love takes an infinitely new form in and through the gift of his own being in Jesus Christ. This gift takes the form further of a sacramental-Petrine Church, and thus of an infallibly effective presence of God in history. The new initiative by God in Jesus Christ is met with a new creaturely response in Mary, the nature and depth of which is disclosed in Mary's spousal *fiat*, which in turn becomes her *Magnificat* and makes her the *Theotokos*, the Mother who bears God into the world.

Here, then, we learn the full meaning of God's covenantal initiative with respect to creation: that it involves God's entering history himself and staying there all the way through to his suffering forsakenness on the Cross. And we learn the full meaning of the creaturely vow in response to this new covenantal initiative: that it involves a *fiat*, a permitting passion so deep that it enables giving birth to God and thus as it were giving God himself in response to God. And we learn the full meaning of this exchange between God and the creature in Jesus Christ and Mary in and through the sacramental Petrine-Marian Church that keeps the exchange infallibly — effectively and passionately — alive for the duration of history.

My summary point is thus that the true passion and interior power of the creature can be seen and realized only in terms of this new Covenant and vow embodied in Jesus Christ and Mary and the sacramental-Marian Church. It is here alone that we learn the radical meaning of the drama characteristic of human life and action: of the fact that, as creatures, *we are freely-responsively (spousally) ordered to the whole God with the whole self, in a way that includes all of creation, forever.*

It is drama in this sense that alone, finally, shows us the truth of the link between freedom and reciprocal or constitutive binding with God and others that *EV* insists upon as the presupposition for sustaining the *unconditional dignity* of the human person. To be sure, it is only those who live within the Covenant, within the sacramental-Marian Church, who, *eo ipso*, can understand this link in its full implications, and I will return to this point later. It is crucial to see here, however, with *EV*, that the supernatural vocation to share the life of God, and the Gospel of Life rooted in this vocation, have "a profound and persuasive echo in the heart of every person, believer and non-believer alike" (*EV,* n. 2).¹⁵ As the encyclical says, "[b]ecause he is made by God . . . , man is naturally drawn to God. When he heeds the deepest yearnings of the heart, every man must make his own the words of truth expressed by St. Augustine: 'You have made us for yourself, O Lord, and our hearts are restless until they rest in you'" (*EV,* n. 35).¹⁶

---

15. "Even in the midst of difficulties and uncertainties, every person . . . can, by the light of reason and the hidden action of grace, come to recognize in the natural law written in the heart (cf. Rom. 2:14-15) the sacred value of human life from its very beginning until its end . . ." (*EV,* n. 2).

16. The point made here is well summarized in the statement by Cardinal Ratzinger/Pope Benedict XVI, following his citation of Romans 2:14-15:

> We find an impressive formulation of the same idea in the great monastic rule of St. Basil: "The love of God is not based on some discipline imposed on us from outside, but as a capacity and indeed a necessity it is a constitutive element of our rational being.' Basil uses an expression that was to become important in medieval mysticism when he speaks of 'the spark of divine love that is innate in us" [*Regulae fusius tractatae, Resp.* 2:1]. In the spirit of Johannine theology, Basil knows that love consists in keeping the commandments. This is why the spark of love that we possess as creatures of God means the following: "We have received in advance the capacity and the willingness to carry out all the divine commandments. . . . They are not something imposed from outside ourselves." Augustine presents the simple core of this truth when he writes, "We would not be able to formulate the judgment that one thing is better than another unless a basic understanding of the good were imprinted upon us" [*De Trinitate,* 8.3:4].
>
> Accordingly, the first level, which we might call the *ontological level,* of the phenomenon "conscience" means that a kind of *primal remembrance of the good and the true* (which are identical) is bestowed on us. There is an inherent existential tendency of man, who is created in the image of God, to tend toward that which is in keeping with God. Thanks to its origin, man's being is in harmony with some things but not with others. This anamnesis of our origin, resulting from the fact that our being is constitutively in keeping with God, is . . . an inner sense, a capacity for recognition, in such a way that the one addressed recognizes in himself an echo of what is said to him. If he does not hide from his own self, he comes to the insight: *this* is the goal toward which my whole being tends, *this* is where I want to go.
>
> This *anamnesis of the Creator,* which *is identical with* the *foundations of our existence,* is the reason that *mission* is both *possible* and *justified.* The Gospel may and indeed must be proclaimed to the pagans, because this is what they are waiting for, even if they do not know this themselves (see Is. 42:4). Mission is justified when those it addresses encounter the word of the Gospel and recognize that *this* is what they were waiting for. This is what Paul means when he says that the Gentiles "are a law unto themselves" — not in the sense of the modern liberalistic idea of autonomy, where nothing can be posited higher than the subject, but in the much deeper sense that nothing belongs to me *less* than my own self, and that my ego is the place where I must transcend myself most profoundly, the place where I am touched by my ulti-

My proposal in the name of *EV*, then, is that liberal societies, by virtue of their neutral concepts of freedom and reason, ignore this restlessness with all the heights and depths of passion and interior power and hence drama implied therein. In a word, there is in liberalism, even on its best reading, no significant sense of, let alone provision for, what is most characteristically human: the self as constitutively-structurally *capax Dei et alterius*. How so?

IV.

First of all, the problem we have identified here regarding the nature of human life and action manifests itself where liberalism takes its most characteristic form and indeed is at its strongest and not at its worst, and hence not merely in extreme expressions such as abortion and embryonic stem cell research, and the like. The basic problem, in other words, lies in the assumptions that create liberal democratic societies' peculiar vulnerability toward these moral evils in the first place. We need to look first, therefore, at these societies' characteristic and most significant achievements, which, arguably, lie in human rights and in technology. We can rightly understand the sense in which these are truly positive achievements of the human spirit — and it bears emphasis that indeed they *are* such — only insofar as we understand the sense in which these achievements, *in their characteristic liberal form*, also simultaneously signify an *ontological absence* of God.

(1) In liberalism, the self is understood to be originally *unbounded* by, hence *indifferent* to others. The self first constructs or creates its relations to others, which are not already, constitutively, *given with* his being. Relation to others thus devolves into a matter first and most properly of a freedom conceived as a simple act of choice, the exercise of an *option* on the part of the self, even if liberalism at its best urges the importance of exercising that option. Consistent with such an understanding, the self's claim on others is conceived as ontologically prior to others' claim on the self. Rights, in other words, are conceived primarily as claims of protection against others, claims of immunity in relation to any possible undue influence by others, which influence cannot but be viewed, *eo ipso*, as arbitrarily introduced from outside, hence as in principle intrusive and liable to coerciveness.

---

mate origin and goal. (Joseph Cardinal Ratzinger/Pope Benedict XVI, *Values in a Time of Upheaval* [New York/San Francisco: Crossroad /Ignatius Press, 2006], pp. 91-93; cf. also Ratzinger, "The Renewal of Moral Theology," p. 367).

To be sure, some liberal defenses of rights, for example, that of the American Thomas Jefferson, link their notion of rights with a Creator, insisting, accurately, that such rights are endowed in us inalienably by our Creator. The pertinent question, however, is whether even these liberal notions of rights that recognize God as their source take account of the fact that the creature's basic act as a creature occurs *from within* God's original and abiding offer of love that always already "binds" the creature and others in love. The creature's act at the most profound level is always *responsive* in nature, and that act cannot but begin, in its root meaning and however unconsciously, as an act of obedient love and loving obedience. It follows, in the words of *EV*, that "being and life [are] a gift and a duty (*donum et munus*)" (n. 96). Rights flow from the "demands" implied in this gift and duty, and are "rightly" conceived only from within these demands.[17] I know of no liberal notion of rights that properly recognizes the order indicated here.

All of this entails no attenuation whatsoever of the importance of rights. The point is simply that it is the constitutive call to other-centered service that requires the right of the self to all those conditions of its being that are necessary for the fulfillment of this call to service. This does not mean that the self is not a bearer of rights already in its own substantial identity. It means, rather, that the self in its substantial identity is originally constituted as and toward response to God and others. The burden of our argument is thus not to deny rights but only to indicate the sense in which rights in their dominant liberal interpretation serve both as a sign and as a cause of the *ontological absence* in the self of God and others.

The freedom proper to the creature of course leaves the self the power to reject its anterior ontological subordination to God and others. What is crucial, however, is to see that this freedom is not, and cannot be, even for a moment, indifferent to the gift from God and others eliciting response, because the anterior relation to God remains the very condition of freedom's

---

17. Note, for example, how the notion of right is understood in the following statements: "Thus, work is primarily a right because it is a duty arising from humanity's social relations. It expresses humanity's vocation to service and solidarity" (John Paul II, *Go in Peace*, p. 193); "The Second Vatican Council reaffirms the traditional Catholic doctrine which holds that men and women, as spiritual creatures, can know the truth and therefore have the duty and the right to seek it" (referring to *Dignitatis Humanae* [1965], n. 3) (Benedict XVI, *Angelus*, St. Peter's Square, 4 December 2005, honoring the fortieth anniversary of *Dignitatis Humanae*). Note that it is the capacity for and duty to seek the truth about God, and not immunity from coercion, that most basically undergirds the nature of the right to religious freedom, even as this capacity and duty as a matter of principle require such immunity.

exercise, even when ignored or denied. Indeed, liberalism's implicit claim of an original indifference in the self's exercise of freedom already implies a wrongful priority of *self*-assertion, a re-centering of the power of choice in a self now conceived, *eo ipso*, apart from the attractive initiative of God that always-anteriorly liberates the self's freedom into being.[18]

The importance of what some may judge an arcane qualifier here can be seen in recalling the original creation and "original sin" of Adam and Eve. What transforms Adam's act of freedom from an image of God, of God's creativity, into a sin against God is just its original indifference to the creaturely order initiated by God. In enacting such indifference, Adam fractures the original community given not only with God but with Eve and with all other creatures. By virtue of his failure to take account of the constitutive claim of the other *in* the original act of his self, which is to say, by virtue of his precipitous, precisely non-obedient, assertion of his rights before creation, Adam institutes the original absence of God resulting in the first culture of death.[19]

In a word, Adam's sin did not consist in wanting to be like God — rightly understood, that is the calling of every human being. Adam's sin, rather, consisted in his wanting to be like God on his own terms, in abstraction from the filial obedience characteristic of the logic of his being as a creature.

We must face the irony implied in the above argument in all of its depth and breadth: liberalism's defense of individual rights presupposes an original-ontological indifference of the self toward the other that implies an inner dynamic for undermining the universal protection *intended* by this defense. However, contrary to liberalism's own best moral intentions, such indifference implies a logic of the priority of the "strong" and "independent" over the "weak" and "dependent": that is, of those who can assert their rights over those who cannot. It fails to recognize the ontological dependence of *all selves* upon God and indeed others that alone enables the

---

18. See D. C. Schindler, "Freedom Beyond Our Choosing: Augustine on the Will and Its Objects," *Communio: International Catholic Review* 29, no. 4 (Winter 2002): 618-53.

19. Cf. the statement of Cardinal Ratzinger in his *A New Song for the Lord: Faith in Christ and Liturgy Today* (New York: Crossroad, 1996): "In the account of the Fall one sees what it looks like when one accepts Satan's offer of power. *Power appears as the opposite of obedience and freedom as the opposite of responsibility* . . ." (p. 44, emphasis added). Again: "[T]he power of being is not one's own power; it is the power of the creator" (p. 45). And cf. the statement regarding the power of Jesus that Ratzinger cites from Guardini: "Jesus' entire existence is a translation of power into humility . . . into obedience to the will of the Father. Obedience is not secondary for Jesus, but forms the core of his being . . ." (p. 42).

true strength and justifies the unconditional dignity of all selves, even — especially — the weak and the dependent.

The upshot, then, is that, as Western democracies succeed in making their liberally conceived rights pervasive in their cultures, these democracies will tend *of their inner logic* to back ever more completely into totalitarianisms of the strong over the weak.

(2) We turn, then, to liberalism's sense of intelligent order as primarily technological.[20]

Once again our focus is not so much on morally evil practices of (bio)technology like cloning and in vitro fertilization, as on the deeper assumptions of liberalism that create the ontological vulnerability toward these practices in the first place, and are thus present already in the *achievements* of technology.

Consider, for example, the patterns of order implied in liberal society's achievements in the media of communication such as cell phones, the Internet, daily newspapers, television, and the like. These media invite communication that tends toward extroversion (turning outward) and superficiality (remaining on the surface); experience as the acquisition and manipulation of digitally accessible bits of information, or again as the encounter with fragmented parts, the instantaneous addition of which yields but fragmented wholes; experience without a receptive sensorium; extensivity without intensification; dispersal into the bad infinity of endlessly successive surface presences, as distinct from gathering into the good infinity of depths and heights; and so on.

The above media of communication, in short, by their inner logic promote inattentiveness, an incapacity for the patient attentiveness and memory necessary for the self in its integrity to relate to the other in its integrity.[21]

---

20. As discussed in the chapter on George Grant, technology is the ontology of modernity.

21. Plato perceived the order that is borne in technological aids to communication, and the ambiguity of that order. In *Truth and Tolerance,* Joseph Ratzinger quotes the *Phaedrus,* in which the Egyptian king Thutmose of Thebes expresses his reservations about the new art of writing, which "has been invented as an aid to the memory as well as for wisdom":

> This will bring forgetfulness into men's souls . . . through the neglect of remembering, in that by trusting in writing they will draw remembrance from without . . . and not from within, from their own selves. You have not, therefore, invented a means of remembering but of recording, and you pass on to your pupils only the appearance of wisdom, not the thing itself. For they are people who hear much without learning anything and will therefore think themselves very knowledgeable, since in general

It is scarcely accidental that liberal society's characteristic act is an act of consumption and its characteristic exchange an exchange of commerce.

The conventional objection to the foregoing, of course, is that, whatever the supposed logic of the instruments mentioned, it is how we choose to use them that counts in the end. Given present limits, I can only point out that my argument is that, *insofar* as our culture's experience of reality is mediated by such instruments, its modes of thinking and acting will be rendered increasingly incapable of a genuine immanent-transcendent relation to God and others.[22] I would say in fact that one can almost define liberalism as a massive Attention Deficit Hyperactivity Disorder (ADHD).

I referred at the outset to a kind of movement and noise indicative not of the presence but the absence of genuine drama. The lack of appreciation in a liberal society for the patience and silence required for any truly dramatic human movement and speech inevitably expresses itself, in the face of pain and the demand for self-sacrifice, in the marginalization unto elimination of those who cannot move and cannot speak, on the basis of

---

they are ignorant, and they are people who are difficult to deal with, in that they are apparently wise but not truly so. (Plato, *Phaedrus* 274d-275b)

Ratzinger goes on:

Anyone who thinks of the way television programs from all over the world overwhelm people with information and thus make them apparently knowledgeable; anyone who thinks about the further possibilities of computers and the Internet, which make available, for instance, to anyone searching, all the texts of some Church Father containing some particular word, yet without the person's having worked his way into his thinking, will not consider these warnings to be exaggerated. Plato is not rejecting writing as such, just as we do not reject the new information media but rather give thanks and make use of them; but he sets up a warning sign, the seriousness of which is demonstrated every day by the consequences of the "linguistic turning point" and by many developments of which we are all currently aware. H. Schade points out the essence of what Plato has to say to us today in this text: "What Plato was warning us about was the domination of a philological method and the accompanying loss of reality."

When writing, when what has been written, becomes a barrier to the content, then it has itself become an anti-art that does not make man more wise but sentences him to a sick appearance of wisdom. (Ratzinger, *Truth and Tolerance: Christian Belief and World Religions*" [San Francisco: Ignatius Press: 2004], pp. 187-89)

22. We can also invite attention here to the vast absorption of time, resources, and energy in the production of such instruments in the first place, and to what such absorption implies about the intellectual habits and ontological (theological, anthropological, spiritual) priorities of a culture.

the rights and interests of those who can. We need to understand the extent to which the security of one's rights in a liberal culture is roughly coextensive with the capacity to move around and make noise.[23]

(3) But, further, the burden of my earlier argument in the name of *EV* is that the creaturely relation to God and others that is needed to respond adequately to liberalism's rights and technological order can be conceived and carried through *finally* only insofar as that relation is sustained by the New Covenant initiated in Jesus Christ, in and through his sacramental Petrine-Marian Church. The implication of my argument, in other words, is that the absence of God indicated in liberal societies' notions of freedom and rights and technologically rationalized order cannot but, in some significant sense, both presuppose and promote the effective absence of a sacramental-Marian Church.

This effective absence takes at least two forms. First, in American liberal society there was of course no sacramental-Marian Church that shaped the dominant patterns of its thought and action and institutions from the beginning. Max Weber was right to see that the crucial difference of Calvinism, in the Puritan form that prevailed in America, from Catholicism, lay in Puritanism's elimination of sacrament, especially the sacrament of Confession, even if Weber himself did not develop the full implications of this difference.[24] Which is to say, there was in Puritanism no recognition of an infallible effective (Petrine) presence of God in history, nor was there any permanently abiding Marian response from the side of the creature that first enabled that infallible effective presence.[25] The Puritan therefore could never be assured of his salvation, of a redeeming relation to God become effective in him.[26] He could never be certain that such a relation was truly *given.* To be sure, this does not mean for the Puritan that this relation was simply to be constructed by him. It does imply, however, that he had to look

---

23. Cf., e.g., the statement cited earlier from *EV*, n. 19, which notes the tendency today to equate dignity with capacity for verbal and explicit, or at least perceptible, communication (p. 37).

24. Max Weber, *The Protestant Ethic and the Spirit of Capitalism* (London: Routledge, 1992).

25. See Hans Urs von Balthasar, "Who Is the Church?" in *Explorations in Theology,* vol. II: *Spouse of the Word* (San Francisco: Ignatius Press, 1991), pp. 143-91.

26. Of course, this does not mean that Catholics are certain of salvation, only that they are certain, in faith, of God's infallible effective presence in history: in the sacraments, they are certain in the sense of really making contact with God's saving presence in history, and that they "merely" have to make themselves available to this presence, so to speak *(ex opere operato).*

to himself as an individual, to his individual behavior, to find signs of God's redeeming action in him. The result is a logic whereby *sola fide* (which seems to denote the ultimate receptivity) undergoes an inversion into an emphasis on man's rationalized worldly *activity, rationalized* in order that one's life will be a *sign* of the effective presence of God's redemptive act.

To be sure, the Puritans scarcely denied the Covenant! The point is simply that, with the removal of Petrine sacrament and Marian responsiveness, and hence with the loss of the Church as the perduring extension of God's entry into history in Christ, covenantal freedom tends to become on man's part simply contractual in nature, even as that contractual freedom reinforces individualistically conceived rights and Cartesianized-technological rationalization of worldly order. It is important to ponder the link between this absence of a sacramental-Marian Church in America and the ontological indifference of American liberalism's contractual freedom (ontologically self-centered rights)[27] and neutral intelligence (technological order).[28]

Secondly, then, insofar as a sacramental-Marian Church does exist in a liberal society, the risk is that it will seek to evangelize the culture in terms taken over from the dominant liberalism. The risk, in other words, is that this Church will conceive its task primarily in terms of taking over rights in the terms given by the dominant culture, and then seeing to it that these rights are applied in the hard cases where they are increasingly not applied today: to human beings at the very beginning or the very end of their lives. Of course it is important that members of the Church do this. The difficulty, if what we have argued is accurate, is that such an approach to evangelization tends to leave ambiguous the notion of rights that has rendered weak human beings vulnerable in the first place.

The further risk in this connection is that even members of the sacramental-Marian Church themselves will undertake evangelization efforts in a way that relies disproportionately on the very media that presuppose and promote the dominant liberal-technological patterns of movement and sound. Consider the production of paper, the calling of meetings, the assembling of committees of experts, the multiplication of

---

27. As distinct from psychologically self-centered: recall what was said earlier about the evidence of widespread sincere belief in God and voluntary generosity of Americans.

28. What is key here, then, is the absence of a sufficiently deep and integrated sense in Puritanism of what is *abidingly-objectively given* by God in the orders, respectively, of creation and redemption (and of how the loss of what is objectively given in one order affects the idea of what is objectively given in the other order as well); but this is for further development elsewhere.

ministries and inflation of ministerial titles, all of which are aided and abetted by the faxes and cell phones and computers and email services and news reports that generate still higher piles of paper, more frequent meetings, and more extensive chatterings by committee. The risk, in short, is that, in the Church's evangelizing efforts, she will have eliminated the old authoritarian clericalism only to replace this with a mellow democratic clericalism appropriate for the age of Starbucks managers — clericalism in the form of secular management skills.[29]

To be sure, and once again: it is indispensable that we defend rights, and we surely cannot function today without the use of electronic media and the like. The simple but basic point is that we need to transform these from the inside out from their dominant liberal-technological understanding. How are we to do this?

V.

Simply by being who we are in our creaturely origin and destiny and as members of the sacramental and Marian Church.

In light of the foregoing, we can highlight two important aspects of what this entails.

First, we need to recuperate the *Dies Domini*, the day of the Lord. We need to recuperate this, that is, in its comprehensive meaning as expressed in the Eucharist and in Mary's *fiat*, and not only on one day of the week but in the time that is inside every day. We must, as often insisted by Cardinal Ratzinger, recover the meaning of our being as created for worship.[30]

---

29. The key to avoiding clericalism is suggested in the following statement by Cardinal Ratzinger: "The *true meaning of the teaching authority of the pope* is that he is the *advocate of Christian memory*" (*Values in a Time of Upheaval,* p. 95; cf. his footnote 13 for an amplification of what is meant by memory here). Clericalism thus might be said, in light of this and in the context of the present argument, to indicate management techniques that are insufficiently integrated by and into Christian memory. And here it is helpful to recall Ratzinger's abiding presupposition that Mary's *fiat* is the anterior condition for Petrine memory. See in this connection the *Catechism of the Catholic Church,* n. 773, which refers to John Paul II's apostolic letter *Mulieris Dignitatem,* n. 27. See also *Mulieris Dignitatem* (1988), n. 55, which cites a brief elaboration of the Marian and apostolic-Petrine profiles of the Church from Hans Urs von Balthasar's *Neue Klarstellungen,* published in English as *New Elucidations* (San Francisco: Ignatius Press, 1986).

30. "Worship, understood in the correct sense, means that I am truly myself only when I form relationships. . . . Worship means [reaching beyond finite goals] into being in-

We must recover the still point lying at the heart of every authentic human action and of all authentic human speech, the stillness which, Ratzinger reminds us, is not inactivity but a matter of sinking the roots of our being in the fruitful stillness of God.[31]

In the words of St. Ambrose cited in *EV*, when God rested from every work, "he rested in the depths of man, . . . in man's mind and in his thought" (*EV*, n. 35). It is our resting in God who in turn rests in us that must be unfolded into an entire way of life and culture.

Second, and as an integral expression of our recovery of the *Dies Domini*, we need to embody the true meaning of freedom in its constitutive order as the truth of a love destined for expression in a vow. Such a vow takes historical-ecclesial form in two states of life: consecrated virginity and sacramental marriage. Both of these states express a permanent spousal relation to God, involve the whole self and, each in its own way, include relation to the whole world. These two states of life, though of course they have always been of fundamental importance for the Church and the world, take on a special significance in light of Pope John Paul II's distinctive mission to culture, and indeed of Vatican II's profound opening to the world and renewed sense of the laity's ecclesial-secular vocation.

(a) Regarding the virginal state of life: in light of the above, there is particular need for that form of consecrated virginity that goes to the heart

---

wardly at one with him who wished me to exist as a partner in a relationship with him and who has given me freedom precisely in this" (Ratzinger, *God and the World*, [San Francisco: Ignatius Press, 2002] pp. 111-12). See also "Liturgy and the Integrity of Cosmic Order: The Theology of Alexander Schmemann," pp. 288-309 in this volume.

31. Joseph Cardinal Ratzinger, *Co-Workers in the Truth* (San Francisco: Ignatius Press, 1992), p. 338. Cf. in this connection the comprehensive statement of *EV*:

> We need first of all to foster in ourselves and in others a contemplative outlook. Such an outlook arises from faith in the God of life who has created every individual as a wonder (cf. Ps 139:14). It is the outlook of those who see life in its deeper meaning, who grasp its utter gratuitousness, its beauty and its invitation to freedom and responsibility. It is the outlook of those who do not presume to take possession of reality, but instead accept it as a gift, discovering in all things the reflection of the Creator and seeing in every person his living image (cf. Gn 1:27; Ps 8:5). This outlook does not give in to discouragement when confronted by those who are sick, suffering, outcast or at death's door. Instead, in all these situations it feels challenged to find meaning, and precisely in these circumstances it is open to perceiving in the fact of every person a call to encounter, dialogue and solidarity.
>
> It is time for all of us to adopt this outlook and with deep religious awe to rediscover the ability to revere and honor every person. (n. 83)

of the world and remains there (cf. the secular form of consecrated life: secular institutes), so that the meaning of man as *capax Dei*, as meant for worship, can be lived truly from inside every thought and every action, assisting every creaturely being and every aspect of every creaturely being to realize its deepest truth, at once in its own legitimate autonomy and in relation to God.

(b) Regarding the marital state of life: as the domestic Church and as the original home of human community, the family plays a constitutive role in the revelation of the meaning of freedom as an order of permanently-naturally binding love that is fruitful. Fatherhood, motherhood, and childhood each make an indispensable contribution to the meaning of life as fruitful gift-giving and receiving. It is in the family that we learn the meaning of the unconditional, and not merely contractual, worth of the small and the weak and the vulnerable. We learn that the true, the good, and the beautiful originate in being and not in having or producing, that they are in the first instance neither acts of consumption nor commercial transactions. We learn the proper meaning of time and space and motion, and of *technē*, as matters first of the patient and organic unfolding of life and love.

Conclusion

The cultural problem in liberal societies, including Anglo-American liberal society, and notwithstanding the sincerity of this society's religious intentionality, is what it is in every time and place of history: the absence of God. The problems with respect to a growing culture of death in such societies are moral and political only as more basically theological-ontological and spiritual. This is why John Paul II made his own André Malraux's statement that "the twenty-first century will be the century of religion or it won't be at all."[32] The heart of my argument has been that action can finally be dramatic only by entering life in its depths, all the way down into the encounter with the divine Source of being, down to the echo of the Marian *fiat* and *Magnificat* welling up from within the core of creaturely-human being,[33] an encounter that then must be unfolded into an entire way of life.[34] Passion, interiority, and God live and die together, and it is the absence of these together — and the absence of drama in this sense — that most basically accounts for democratic societies' drift toward a culture of death.

32. *Crossing the Threshold of Hope* (New York: Alfred A. Knopf, 1994), pp. 228-29.
33. Cf. Maurice Zundel, in *Magnificat*, 27 March 2006, p. 375.
34. Cf. in this connection Ratzinger's comments on martyrdom as cited in note 5 above.

Truth, Freedom, and Relativism in Western Democracies: Pope Benedict XVI's Contributions to *Without Roots*

This presentation consists of three unequal parts: first, a very brief (and necessarily presumptuous!) summary of what seems to me the theological center of Pope Benedict XVI; second, an outline of some main points of his two contributions to *Without Roots*;[1] and, third, a formulation of an important issue for reflection, particularly with respect to North America, that emerges from the Pope's contributions.

I.

First of all, we belong to the truth before the truth belongs to us. Although both of these statements are true, a reversal in their order changes the meaning and integrity both of the truth and of ourselves.

Second, this truth to which we belong is ultimately a matter of love. What is ultimately true and supremely real — God — is love. Hence Benedict's first encyclical, *Deus Caritas Est* (2005). God is a Trinitarian circle of divine love.

Third, this divine truth as love has a human face and a human heart

---

1. Joseph Ratzinger (Pope Benedict XVI) and Marcello Pera, *Without Roots: The West, Relativism, Christianity, Islam* (New York: Basic Books, 2006).

A version of this chapter was presented at a panel discussion with co-author Marcello Pera, former President of the Italian Senate, and George Weigel, titled "Freedom Without Roots: The Predicament of Western Liberalism and the Teaching of Pope Benedict XVI." The panel was sponsored by Crossroads Cultural Center and Basic Books and took place at Columbia University on 6 February 2006.

in Jesus Christ. In Christ, God assumes flesh and blood, hence the whole of human being, and this assumption takes a Eucharistic form: the total gift of self as the way of communion.

In sum: to belong to the truth is to belong to a love that, especially as seen in the light of the Incarnation, is simultaneously God-centered and human-centered.

II.

How are we to understand Benedict's contributions to *Without Roots* in this context? What are the key elements in his assessment of the spiritual, political, and cultural situation in the West and especially Europe today, as set forth in these contributions?

Marcello Pera in his Preface says that "[t]he only thing worse than living without roots is struggling to get by without a future" (xiv). Of course the two are related, because absence of memory is itself already a forgetfulness of destiny. Without a living memory of who we are, there can be no hope in the face of what we are to become.

The question, then, is: Who are we? The "we" here of course refers primarily to Europe but thereby also to the West, and hence includes America.

Passing over the rich historical reflections of Benedict, I will mention only the key moral elements that he sees as central to European identity. "Is there," Benedict asks, "a European identity that has a future and to which we can be wholeheartedly committed?" (74). Though he does not wish to enter into discussion of the new European Constitution and the controversy over whether the contribution of Christianity should be made explicit in this document, he indicates the three basic elements that he says should not be omitted.

First, there is "the unconditionality with which human rights and human dignity should be presented as values that take precedence over the jurisdiction of any state" (74). "The value of human dignity . . . refers to the Creator: only He can establish values that are grounded in the essence of humankind and that are inviolable" (75). "The existence of values that cannot be modified by anyone is the true guarantee of our freedom and of human greatness; in this fact, the Christian faith sees the mystery of the Creator and the condition of man, who was made in God's image" (75). Although today almost no one would deny the primacy of human dignity outright, says Benedict, "in the concrete sphere of the supposed progress of medicine, there are very real threats to these values," for example, cloning, storage of fetuses for research or organ harvesting, the whole field of genetic manipulation, and the like (75f.).

"A second element that characterizes European identity is marriage and the family. Monogamous marriage — both as a fundamental structure for the relationship between men and women and as the nucleus for the formation of the state community — was forged already in the Biblical faith" (76). "Europe would no longer be Europe if this fundamental nucleus of its social edifice were to vanish or be changed in an essential way" (76-77). Benedict cites here the problems of cohabitation and the increasing demand for recognition of marriage between homosexuals.

"The final element of the European identity is religion" (78). The Pope stresses that fundamental to all cultures is "respect for that which another group holds sacred, especially respect for the sacred in the highest sense, for God, which one can reasonably expect to find even among those who are not willing to believe in God" (78). When this respect, this religious sense that is natural to humankind, "is violated in a society, something essential is lost" (78).

But here Benedict turns to the problem of multiculturalism, and in this context to the problem of the West's peculiar self-hatred, and lack of love for its own values (78f.). He stresses that "multiculturalism cannot survive without common foundations, without the sense of direction offered by our own values" (79). "It definitely," he says, "cannot survive without respect for the sacred. Multiculturalism teaches us to approach the sacred things of others with respect, but we can only do this if we, ourselves, are not estranged from the sacred, from God" (79). "With regard to others, it is our duty to cultivate within ourselves respect for the sacred and to show the face of the revealed God, of the God who has compassion for the poor and the weak, for widows and orphans, for the foreigner; the God who is so human that He Himself became man, a man who suffered, and who by His suffering with us gave dignity and hope to our pain" (79).

In short, "unless we embrace our own heritage of the sacred, we will not only deny the identity of Europe, we will also fail in providing a service to others to which they are entitled. To the other cultures of the world, there is something deeply alien about the absolute secularism that is developing in the West. They are convinced that a world without God has no future. Multiculturalism itself thus demands that we return once again to ourselves," that is, to our own roots (79-80).

In his subsequent letter to Pera, which makes up his second contribution to *Without Roots*, Benedict takes up clarification of the notion of civil religion, in particular of the relation between a religion that reaches beyond the limits of denominationalism, on the one hand, and the faith of the Catholic Church, on the other (108f.). And here he makes reference to the example and distinct contribution of America. "American society was built for the most part by groups that had fled from the system of state churches that reigned in Europe, and they found their religious bearings in free faith communities outside of the state church" (110). Thus "there is a much clearer and more implicit sense in America than in Europe that the religious and moral foundation bequeathed by Christianity is greater than any single denomination" (109). At the same time "you could say that American society is built on a separation of church and state" (110). This separation was vastly different from that imposed in Europe by the French Revolution (110). In America, it is in the nature of the state "to recognize and permit these [different religious] communities to exist in their particularity and their non-membership in the state," and the separation of church and state is thus "conceived positively" in terms of the freedom of religion to be and fulfill itself (110-11).

Now Benedict points out that the Catholic principle, rightly understood, does not at all involve a state church system; and he notes as well the complications, the strengths and the weaknesses, of the Protestant kinship with the Enlightenment (117) and its "profound intertwining with modern culture" (118). Regarding the latter, he notes in particular that its "fatal tendency to conform to the times — which led Protestantism to the brink of dissolution during the Enlightenment — is alive and well today, as the traditional Protestant churches in the United States demonstrate" (118). The point, says Benedict, is that, although Protestantism can help us in the matter of the development of a civil religion, "its current crisis . . . demonstrate[s] that 'de-confessionalization' does not automatically," in and of itself, resolve the problem (119).

Regarding the notion of civil religion, the Pope thus says in summary: "an ambiguous light is . . . cast upon the concept of civil religion: if it is no more than a reflection of the majority's convictions, then it means little or nothing. If instead it is a source of spiritual strength, then we have to ask what feeds this source" (119-20).

Benedict's answer to what can serve as this source of spiritual strength is expressed in a single fundamental principle, which he explains in four corollary theses. The principle is that "[s]omething living cannot be born except from another living thing" (120). "This is why it is so important to have convinced minorities in the Church, for the Church, and above all beyond the Church and for society: human beings who in their encounters with Christ have discovered the precious pearl that gives value to all life (Matthew 13:45ff.)" (120-21). "There is nothing sectarian about such creative minorities. Through their persuasive capacity and their joy, they reach other people and offer them a different way of seeing things" (121).

The four corollary theses are as follows:

First, "a civil religion that truly has the moral force to sustain all people presupposes the existence of convinced minorities that have 'discovered the pearl' and live it in a manner that is also convincing to others. Without such motivating forces, nothing can be built" (121).

Second, "we all need forms of belonging or of reference to these communities, or simply of contact with them" (121).

Third, "these creative minorities can clearly neither stand nor live on their own. They live naturally from the fact that the Church as a whole remains and that it lives in and stands by the faith in its divine origins. It did not invent these origins but it recognizes them as a gift that it is duty-bound to transmit" (122-23).

Fourth, "both secular people[2] and Catholics, seekers and believers . . . must move toward each other with a new openness. Believers must never stop seeking, while seekers are touched by the truth and thus cannot be classified as people without faith and Christian-inspired moral principles. There are ways of partaking of the truth by which seekers and believers give to and learn from each other" (123).

In light of the foregoing reflections, Benedict asks why it is that the Christian faith is struggling so much today to convey its great message to people in Europe. His answer is twofold:

The first reason is expressed by Nietzsche, who says that, "as long as one does not perceive Christian morality as a capital crime against life, its defenders will always have an easy game" (125). The decisive issue, in other words, is whether Christianity provides a convincing model for life: "the decisive reason for the abandonment of Christianity," says Benedict, is that "its model for life is apparently unconvincing. It seems to place too many

---

2. Benedict explains that *laici*, translated here as "secular people," means "to belong to the spiritual current of the Enlightenment" (pp. 115-16). It can also "[mean] free thinking and freedom from religious constrictions," "the exclusion of Christian contents and values from public life," which leads to a "tendency on the part of modern conscience to treat the entire realm of faith and morals as 'subjective'" (p. 116).

restraints on humankind that stifle its *joie de vivre*, that limit its precious freedom [and so on]" (125).

"The second reason for the crumbling of Christianity [is] that it seems to have been surpassed by 'science' and to be out-of-step with the rationalism," or the conception of reason, of the modern era (126).

The principles of Benedict's response to these two failings of or objections to Christianity have already been indicated: "[T]he Christian model of life must be manifested as a life in all its fullness and freedom, a life that does not experience the bonds of love as . . . limitation but rather as an opening to the greatness of life" (126). Thus the importance again of the creative minorities already referred to. But, further, these minorities need to enter into dialogue with people in the broader secular culture, engaging them in the basic questions of our time, such as: "Does matter create reason? Does pure chance produce meaning? Or do the intellect, *logos*, and reason come first, so that reason, freedom, and the good are already part of the principles that construct reality?" (127). "A valid civil religion," he says, "will not conceive of God as a mythical entity but rather as a possibility of reason" (127).

Benedict then introduces the problem of relativism, of the intolerance and dogmatism spawned by an increasingly widespread relativism in Western democracies (127f.). Recalling an earlier comment of the Pope, we see that this growing relativism is bound up with the "tendency on the part of modern conscience to treat the entire realm of faith and morals as 'subjective'" (116). Which is to say, this dogmatism is expressed in the tendency to treat all claims to truth as equal, to reduce all such claims equally to matters of merely subjective preference. This increasing dogmatic tendency to reduce all claims of truth to expressions of subjective preference includes the essential truths that Benedict says lie at the roots and hence identity of European society: the inviolable dignity of each human being from the natural beginning to the natural end of life, monogamous marriage between a man and a woman, and respect for the natural religious sense of humankind. I will return to this problem of dogmatic relativism below.

First we turn to a final observation by Benedict, which bears on a fundamental problematic running through all the foregoing reflections. Our modern cultural situation is characterized by the presence of many different faiths, different forms of theism and indeed of atheism. In such a situation, Christians, says Benedict, "can only reclaim that which belongs to the human foundations accessible to reason and therefore essential to the construction of a sound legal order" (129). (Recall the three essential truths mentioned above.) It is just here, he says, that

> the dilemma of human life emerges fully. . . . The Christian is convinced that his or her faith opens up new dimensions of understanding, and above all that it helps reason to be itself. There is the true heritage of the faith (the Trinity, the divinity of Christ, the sacraments, and so on), but there is also the knowledge for which faith provides evidence, knowledge that is later recognized as rational and pertaining to reason as such, and thus also implying a responsibility toward others. The person of faith, who has received help in reason, must work in favor of reason and of that which is rational: this, in the face of dormant or diseased reason, is a duty he or she must perform toward the entire human community. (130)

Benedict then cites again areas where this issue has especially important significance today, the related questions such as the beginning of life, artificial reproductive technologies, and the institution of marriage (129-32). He stresses the importance of exhibiting a "rationality of argument" in such cases that will lead to an "ethics of reason" that somehow bridges the gap between a strictly secular ethics on the one hand and a strictly religious ethics on the other, or again between the empirical and the philosophical. An example of where development of such an ethics of reason might be expected is the question of when human life begins. In this case, says Benedict, an ethics of reason entails "a deduction for the legislator: *If this is the way things are,* then the authorization to kill the embryo means that 'The state is denying the equality of all before the law'" (132; emphasis added).

On the other hand, there are areas where it may not be possible today to reach a consensus on the basis of such an ethics of reason. For example, though the Church rejects both homologous and heterologous artificial insemination, it may not be possible, given today's society, to achieve a consensus regarding prohibition of the former (132-33).

Affirming, then, that Christians cannot simply impose their morality on the political order, Benedict says that there will be times when it will be necessary for them to claim from legislators the right to conscientious objection (134). Failing recognition of even this right, Christians should claim "the right to passive resistance and thereby offer a testimony of conscience that could somehow make people reflect and lead to the formation of a new conscience" (134-35). In all of this, the creative minorities to which

Benedict referred earlier will play a central role. Indeed, following the road to conscientious objection and passive resistance "will become less necessary the more we succeed in developing a civil Christian religion that can shape our conscience as Europeans and — bridging the separation between secularists and Catholics — manifest the reasonable and binding value of the great principles that have edified Europe and can and must rebuild it" (135).

III.

Let us return now in conclusion to the problem of relativism, and frame the issue with particular attention to the separation of Church and state that has been a distinct contribution of America to the problematic of Europe's heritage and identity. The issue is that of a growing intolerance and dogmatism: the increasingly widespread public imposition of the idea that claims of truths — such as those regarding the inviolable dignity of the human being, monogamous marriage, and respect for the natural religious sense of humankind — are expressions of merely "subjective" preferences rather than genuinely "objective" truths, indeed truths indicative of the "human foundations accessible to reason and therefore essential to the construction of a sound legal order" (129).

In his Angelus message on 4 December 2005, commemorating the fortieth anniversary of *Dignitatis Humanae* (1965), Benedict stated that "religious liberty derives from the special dignity of the human person"; that it "is in accordance with their dignity that all men, because they are . . . endowed with reason and free will . . . , are both impelled by their nature and bound by a moral obligation to seek the truth, especially religious truth" (*DH*, n. 2). In light of this, Benedict goes on to say that "the Second Vatican Council reaffirms the traditional Catholic doctrine which holds that men and women, as spiritual creatures, can know the truth and therefore have the duty and the right to seek it" (referring to *DH*, n. 3). "Having laid this foundation, the Council places a broad emphasis on religious liberty, which must be guaranteed both to individuals and to communities with respect for the legitimate demands of the public order. . . ." "Religious liberty is indeed very far from being effectively guaranteed everywhere: . . . [sometimes,] although it may be recognizable on paper, it is hindered in effect by political power or, more cunningly, by the cultural predomination of agnosticism and relativism."

Note how Benedict approaches here the problem of religious liberty, and indeed, by implication, of pluralism and multiculturalism. In the face of the problem of multiple claims to truth, especially religious truth, his response is to defend freedom and rights and respect for difference by way of appeal to *truth itself*. According to Benedict, genuine respect for others in society, for "secular" people and people of other religious faiths or of no religious faith at all, is safeguarded most properly and profoundly, not by detaching the right to freedom, especially religious freedom, from the truth, but on the contrary by situating that right to freedom within the truth that alone can in the end really liberate: the *truth* of freedom *as love*. Benedict anchors the problem of respect for cultural and religious and moral differences in our society, not in a rationality or freedom conceived neutrally, but rather in a definite notion (content) of the truth itself.

Benedict, in the text cited, says that *Dignitatis Humanae*, in tying the right to religious liberty to the duty and the right to seek the truth, thereby affirms the traditional Catholic doctrine. This of course is true, though we should recognize with Benedict how this Gospel- and Creed-founded understanding of *truth as love* has been developed in the pontificate of John Paul II (in the latter's emphasis, for example, on *Gaudium et Spes* [1965], n. 22, as the key to the teaching of the Council; on a *communio* ecclesiology and the "communion of persons"; and on the "nuptial" meaning of the body), a development carried further in Benedict's first encyclical, *Deus Caritas Est* (2005).

The point, then, is that Benedict does not speak of freedom here first or most properly in terms of "immunity from coercion," which is to say, he does not adopt the primarily juridical interpretation of *DH* that has prevailed among Catholics in Western democracies, certainly in the United States. In a word, the legitimate separation of state and Church affirmed by Benedict in the name of a rightly understood Catholic principle, to which understanding the United States has made a distinct contribution, does not entail for him a detachment of the state *from the question of truth*. This does not mean, of course, that the sense of freedom as an immunity from coercion does not remain an essential feature of freedom in its (primary) sense as truth. The point is to *make explicit* the non-relativistic *truth* that alone can *ground*, and provide the proper inner form and condition *of*, freedom as entailing immunity from coercion.

The importance of the issue raised here becomes clear when we recall the reference by Benedict to the growing tendency of democratic societies to impose the view that truths such as those he cites as essential for the construction of a sound legal order are matters merely of subjective preference. The question I mean to press, in light of Benedict's concerns and his comments regarding *Dignitatis Humanae*, is whether this dogmatic imposition of relativism is not bound up in a fundamental way with the adoption by Western states — for example, by the majority of Americans in their interpretation of the First Amendment of the United States Constitution — of the juridical notion of freedom as primarily an "immunity from coercion." By definition such a judicial notion of freedom protects freedom as an act of choice conceived first and most properly in abstraction from the truth, or order, to be chosen. The order chosen in the exercise of that act, in other words, becomes now, *eo ipso*, *"private"*: a matter of the preference of this or that individual subject or group in society. To be sure, an individual subject or group might well insist that the truths it defends make reasonable and objective demands on others, indeed, make a universal demand on the community. However, given the juridical reading of the public (legal or constitutional) order, these truths will and can only be treated in the public sphere as private preferences among which the state is to referee but the substantial content of which the state can in no way judge and toward which it must remain officially indifferent.[3]

3. Pera is quite right to insist that "the modern democratic ... state is especially protective and moral. In its desire to care for its citizens (from cradle, if not sooner, to grave), it must necessarily adopt and safeguard within its own public sphere many values that are widespread in the private sphere of individuals, groups, or categories" (p. 97). And Pope Benedict is likewise right to say that some moral truths make demands on the legislator (precisely *qua* legislator, not merely *qua* member of society) because of their inherent reasonability ("this is the way things are ..." [p. 132]); and that there are "human foundations that are accessible to reason and [are] therefore essential to the construction of a sound legal order" (p. 129). What I am suggesting here is that these important claims can be sustained in their required substantial sense only insofar as their implied recognition of the state as more than and distinct from a purely juridical entity is drawn out. To draw out this implication, I am proposing, one must defend freedom as a truth along the lines indicated by Benedict apropos of a proper interpretation of *Dignitatis Humanae*. One must, in other words, clarify how a state with a properly truthful-moral purpose — and hence with a freedom that is always already an order of truth (e.g., as love) — differs from a state whose constitutional order is conceived in purely juridical terms as "articles of peace" (John Courtney Murray), and hence whose freedom is properly an empty or neutral act of choice the truthful-moral content of which is always and in principle something yet to be (privately) chosen. As indicated earlier, this latter sense of freedom as an act of choice entailing immunity from coercion remains essential for Benedict, though it does so now as ontologically consequent upon, and expressive of, freedom as an order of truth — the truth of love.

In a word, we can see the peculiar if paradoxical way in which, given a primarily juridical notion of freedom, democracy tends to invert into totalitarianism, in which democratic relativism tends to become dogmatic. Insofar as they adopt the juridical notion of freedom as first and properly an immunity from coercion, or, again, insofar as they confuse the necessary and legitimate separation of Church and state with an embrace of the purely juridical state, Western democracies thereby, however unwittingly and paradoxically, cannot but affirm as their sole "truth" in the official-public arena that all claims to truth are merely the expressions of private or individual or "subjective" preferences. It is this sole "truth" of relativism that the juridical democratic state now increasingly imposes on society.[4]

The simple summary proposal I wish to make, then, in light of Benedict's argument, is twofold: first, any adequately conceived civil religion, at whose heart lies the energy of what Benedict calls "creative minorities," will need to witness to, and thus also to give a reasonable account of, freedom as the truth of love. This truth is expressed most basically in the inviolable dignity of the human being, in monogamous marriage, and in re-

---

4. Again, as made clear above, this does not mean that the juridical state would not (or does not intend to) defend the right/freedom of various groups (religions, etc.) to conceive and preach their moral values as matters of an objective truth that in principle makes a reasonable claim on all human beings. Indeed, that it does so is the burden of the distinction between "society" and "state," rightly understood. The problem is that the purely juridical state, notwithstanding this objectivity claimed by various societal groups, can consider such claims, for legal-public purposes, *only as matters of private subjective preference* — again, insofar as it would remain consistent with its purely juridical notion of freedom. The problem, in other words, is that the state, conceived juridically, necessarily implies a dualistic relation between society and state: the state (legal-constitutional order) opts for a purely procedural form, as though this form itself embodied no substantive, objective content; while society alone claims substantive content, but now only as this has been reduced to a merely subjective preference. Such a juridical state necessarily imposes this disjunction in all of its official-legal actions, insofar as it acts consistently with an exclusively juridical purpose.

For an interesting discussion of the problematic identified here, see Alasdair MacIntyre's *Whose Justice? Which Rationality?* (Notre Dame: University of Notre Dame Press, 1988), chapter 17, "Liberalism Transformed into a Tradition," especially pp. 335-46. The burden of MacIntyre's argument is to show how the liberal state's denial of any conception of the common good proper to itself, inevitably, however unwittingly and paradoxically, implies "enforcement" of *endless, inconclusive debate* among various subjectively *preferred* goods as its single permissible common good. He shows how and why the liberal state — in its purely juridically conceived form, in the terms adopted here — must therefore be "severely limited" in its (legal) capacity to tolerate any non-procedural, non-relativistic or substantive, goods or truths in the public arena (p. 336).

spect for the native or natural religious sense of humankind. Creative minorities, certainly in North America, will need to witness to the distinction between freedom *qua* the truth of love and freedom *qua* an ontologically empty, primarily juridical, exercise of choice.

Second, insofar as "creative minorities" fail in their efforts to convince the broader culture of this substantive truth of freedom as love, which is to say, insofar as Western civilization continues its drift in the direction of a purely juridical order, the witness of these minorities to the true roots of our civilization will increasingly need to take the form indicated by Benedict: first conscientious objection, then if necessary passive resistance.

Benedict's reflections in this book surely move us to ponder in all its depth and breadth the question regarding the truthful ordering of freedom, a question that goes to the roots of the identity of Western democracies in the face of the problem of relativism.

Civil Community Inside the Liberal State: Truth, Freedom, and Human Dignity

By the liberal state I mean the modern state conceived as an essentially juridical order: a state taking its purpose to be the protection of rights even as it understands rights primarily in terms of immunity from coercion. The juridical state understands itself to be about procedures necessary for adjudicating fairly between competing exercises of freedom by individuals in society, as distinct from defending, or calling to mind in an explicit way, metaphysical truths to which these individuals might be anteriorly bound by virtue of their common humanity. Such a state tends of its inner logic toward displacing the notion of a substantive common good with that of a procedurally fair public order.

My purpose is to examine the nature of this juridical state in terms of its ability to secure authentic civil community, in a sense that promotes authentic dialogue and argument and protects especially the weakest and most vulnerable members of society. I begin by setting out the nature of the problematic to be addressed.

I.

It is important to see that, at least on the Anglo-American version of the juridical state, this displacement of metaphysical truth or a substantive common good does not intend a rejection of the idea of truth or the establishment of a "secularist" state. On the contrary, this state simply declares itself incompetent in matters of truth bearing on the nature and destiny of the human person. In the phrasing of John Courtney Murray, America's constitutional order embodies "articles of peace" in contrast to "articles of faith."[1] According to Murray, the First Amendment of the United States Constitution, with its religious clauses, contains "only a law, not a dogma." The Amendment bears "no religious content," and answers "none of the eternal human questions with regard to the nature of truth and freedom or the manner in which the spiritual order of man's life is to be organized or not organized." "The highest value of law" is thus "rationality," not "sanctity" (*WHTT,* 48-49). The First Amendment, in a word, implies neither any particular ecclesiology, nor any kind of religious philosophy (*WHTT,* 53).

According to Murray, America's liberal state thus intends not at all to eliminate the question of truth. On the contrary, this state means merely to transfer truth claims beyond the sphere of the *state,* in order to ensure the unencumbered freedom of citizens to engage the search for truth in the distinct sphere of *society.* The professed intention of the juridical state at its best is not to exclude truth claims from society but only to see to it that those that prevail do so by virtue of free inquiry, hence in accord with fair procedures and thus with the method most respectful of the dignity of every citizen.

Murray's point, then, is that this state is peculiarly able to promote genuine freedom, or is most able to secure *all* persons' rights, because, *de jure,* it advances *no* person's truth, *no substantive truth about the person at all.* In sum, while (rightly) insisting that no human government is the source of truth, Murray interprets this to mean that the government has no *intrinsic concern* with truth *qua government or constitutional order.* To be sure, he affirms that, if government is over time to sustain its purpose of securing freedom and rights for its citizens, it will need a natural law consensus and moral virtue among its citizens. But that is the function of society and its private institutions, not of the state.

In a word, given the pluralism in modern American society with respect to "articles of faith," or ideas regarding man, God, and religion, the *"unum" ("e pluribus unum")* to be sought in this society must be "civil" or "peaceful," not metaphysical or theological, in nature.

In a similar vein, the late American political theorist John Rawls insists on a distinction between a liberalism that is "political" in nature, and liberalism as a "comprehensive doctrine." "Political liberalism" affirms a conception of "justice as fairness," without implying endorsement of any particular set of metaphysical truths. As Rawls puts it, "in public reason, ideas of truth or right based on comprehensive doctrines are replaced by

---

1. *We Hold These Truths* (Kansas City: Sheed & Ward, 1988 [originally published 1960]), pp. 48-49. Abbreviated here as *WHTT.*

an idea of the politically reasonable addressed to citizens as citizens."[2] "In political liberalism, . . . we try to avoid natural or psychological views . . . , as well as theological or secular doctrines" (482). Politically reasonable conceptions thus underwrite a "constitutional democratic society" (482). That is, such conceptions involve affirmation of political institutions that recognize "equal basic rights and liberties for all citizens, including liberty of conscience and the freedom of religion" (483).

Rawls insists that this idea of political liberalism does not imply "pure liberal proceduralism." On the contrary, it allows for comprehensive doctrines, as long as these doctrines are consistent with a democratic polity (482-84): that is, as long as they do not undermine justice, understood as fairness. Although liberal political principles "can be presented independently from comprehensive doctrines of any kind," they may "be supported by a reasonable overlapping consensus of such doctrines" (453). What is crucial is that any "transcendent" values that might be affirmed by these comprehensive doctrines not override "the reasonable political values of a constitutional democratic society" (483). In sum, "a *reasonable* comprehensive doctrine is one in which these latter political values are not overridden; it is the unreasonable doctrines in which reasonable political values are overridden" (483).

Murray and Rawls, then, may both be said to hold variants of the modern idea that, in the order of politics, the political has primacy over the metaphysical, or that *"auctoritas non veritas facit legem"* ("authority, not truth, makes law": Hobbes). Contemporary Catholic theologian Martin Rhonheimer defends this primacy in terms of what he calls "Christian secularity."[3] Suggesting that "the Catholic Church has come to fully ac-

---

2. "The Idea of Public Reason Revisited," in *Political Liberalism*, Expanded Edition (New York: Columbia University Press, 2005), p. 481. For critical studies of Rawls, see George Parker Grant, *English-Speaking Justice* (Notre Dame: University of Notre Dame Press, 1985), especially Part II; Allan Bloom, "Justice: Rawls versus the Tradition of Political Philosophy," in Bloom's *Giants and Dwarfs: Essays 1960-1990* (New York: Simon & Schuster, 1990), pp. 315-45; and Michael J. Sandel, *Liberalism and the Limits of Justice* (Cambridge: Cambridge University Press, 1982).

3. My remarks here are based primarily on his 2006 lecture, "Christian Secularity and the Culture of Human Rights," delivered in Vienna at a symposium entitled "A Growing Gap — Living and Forgotten Christian Roots in Europe and the United States" (26-29 April 2006). Citations are from the text posted at http://www.pusc.it/fil/p_rhonheimer/. For Rhonheimer's qualified defense of the framework of Rawls, see his "The Political Ethos of Constitutional Democracy and the Place of Natural Law in Public Reason: Rawls's 'Political Liberalism' Revisited," in *The American Journal of Jurisprudence* 50 (2005): 1-70.

knowledge the secularity of the state and the political principles of constitutional democracy" (p. 1), he says that, though long in coming, this acknowledgment in fact reconciles the Church's own cultural heritage, which affirmed the dualism of spiritual and temporal power and thereby the intrinsic secularity of the latter (1). At the Second Vatican Council, the Church acknowledged "the secular, religiously neutral state as a positive value and as a cultural achievement, and with this also the modern idea of human rights" (2).

According to Rhonheimer, however, an important question still remains unanswered: What does it mean for Christians to participate *as Christians* "in a political culture which is defined by secular values, pluralism and neutrality regarding [their own religious truth] and the moral claims depending on it" (2)? In response, he says that the challenge of multiculturalism makes clear that "at the root of occidental pluralism lies a common foundation of values" (3). "Citizenship itself, which is a basic political and public value, must be defined on a common ground of shared cultural values; it cannot be defined in a multicultural way" (3).

> In the European understanding, the nature of such a common ground is the idea of liberal-democratic citizenship — "liberal" in a broad sense — which is closely related to basic liberties and rights which define the status of citizens independently from their religious, cultural or ethnic identities. "Multiculturalism" or pluralism on *this* level is impossible. (3)

"Christian secularity" in this light, says Rhonheimer, means to realize one's Christian identity and vocation

> in the context of a society — and an international community — the public institutions of which are defined in secular ways, by fully accepting . . . this secularity as a political value and . . . as an integral part of one's self-understanding as a Christian. To use a Rawlsian term, "Christian secularity" means for Christians to enter into an "overlapping consensus" which may be epistemologically supported and nourished by one's proper religious and moral convictions as a Christian, but is neither identical *with* them nor derived *from* them. (3)[4]

---

4. My own position as proposed in this chapter presupposes with Rhonheimer that the "common ground of shared cultural values" required for an "overlapping consensus" is neither identical to nor simply derived, in the sense of deduced, from what are one's prop-

Prior to the Council, Rhonheimer suggests, such a "Christian secularity" was viewed with ambivalence, in the sense that Catholics "did not accept as a political value the fundamental reciprocity of political rights' claims independent from their being used in conformity with truth" (4).

Secularity as thus defined has consequences above all in terms of "public reason and public justificatory discourses" (4). There are different kinds of discourse, for example, with respect to human rights: "exclusively political," on the one hand, and "religious and metaphysical," on the other (4). According to Rhonheimer, rooting discourse in metaphysical truth "would provide a very weak political basis for human rights" (5).

> If their effective *political* recognition and *juridical* validity needed to depend on shared metaphysical assumptions about the nature of man or on a shared acknowledgment of the theological truth on his being created in the image of God, the political standing of human rights would be rather uncertain and fragile. (5)

Indeed, in this view, metaphysical and theological truths, far from providing a common ground, serve instead mostly as sources of dispute and disagreement.

Here Rhonheimer follows Canadian political scientist Michael Ignatieff,[5] stating that, "though we cannot agree on *why* we have rights, we can all see what they actually *do* for us and why we need them" (5). Such functional grounds are much more secure: "secular modernity . . . is in need of a minimal foundation in order to achieve a maximum consensus" (5). "The more . . . public justification [of human rights] becomes linked to metaphysical and religious premises, the less ability it has to politically assert itself and become universally implemented" (5). Nonetheless, Rhonheimer at the same time insists, contrary to Ignatieff, that it is "not necessarily idolatry" to recognize that "politics do actually exist from sources they did not create" (5).

In other words, "reductive political justification is a *political* necessity," even though politics needs "categorical foundations which are not themselves pluralistic or merely political, or at least are able to base the lat-

---

erly Christian convictions. What I deny is that the relation between such a "common ground" and one's Christian convictions, rightly conceived, is exhaustively accounted for in terms of either identity or simple derivation (deduction). But what this means will be sorted out in the argument that follows.

5. Michael Ignatieff, *Human Rights as Politics and as Idolatry* (Princeton: Princeton University Press, 2001).

ter on firm moral convictions and on the kind of rational discourse on the basis of justice which we call 'natural law'" (5-6). On this level of discourse, as distinct from the properly political level of discourse, Christians know that "only a foundation rooted in metaphysical truth about man can provide for a culture of human rights the ultimate and stable *cognitive* basis" (6). Rhonheimer says that it is just the distinction between these two discourses that John Paul II highlights in *Centesimus Annus*, thereby making a decisive contribution to "the reconciliation of secular political modernity (constitutionalism, democracy, the priority of freedom, human rights) with a transcendental, metaphysical and ultimately religious foundation of the moral basis of modern secularity" (6).

Thus "Christian secularity" involves a double presupposition: on the one hand, pluralistic societies need "minimalist political justification of human rights and political justice," while on the other hand these societies need "a metaphysical-ethical anchoring" that both goes beyond political justification and supports the latter (6). This paradox, he says, proves "the ineluctable validity of the modern — in its original Hobbesian form one-sided — principle *Auctoritas non veritas facit legem*" (6). In a word, we arrive at "the principle of the institutional, legal, and practical primacy of the political over the metaphysical" (6). Rhonheimer summarizes:

> I am far from pleading for the Hobbesian solution of this problem, which submits truth claims and the norms of justice entirely to the factuality of positive law. But I subscribe to the maxim in the sense of the need of recognizing the democratic legitimacy and legal validity of the law even though it is considered to be, in certain limits, unjust, untruthful and in need of being overturned by equally legal and democratic means. This is the price we have to pay for peaceful social and international cooperation, prosperity, justice — always imperfect — and, mostly, political and civil freedom. Yet, this price is rather low and certainly a reasonable one to pay. As we know from history, the alternatives are the continuous threat of civil war or, in other cases, authoritarian or even totalitarian repression in the name of some truth-claiming ideology, and on the international level, unjust domination and war. (7)

A final point: because "*political* freedom on the national level and rights of participation in international organizations are defined and legitimized not by their relation to moral and religious truth, but to *political* values like peace, liberty, equality, [and] economic efficiency . . . ," Rhonheimer says that "the consciousness of the relation of freedom to truth must be reinforced on the non-political or pre-political level. It must be primarily cultivated in the family and, generally, in educational practice" (7). Thus, for example,

> to legally grant a right to abortion and support corresponding choices by the public health system is certainly a great evil and opposes the common good of society, but it is not the fault of the democratic political culture or the secularity of the state, but rather the problem of civil society and its predominant value system which renders such laws or jurisprudence possible. (7)

It is in the realm of civil society, and not in terms of the state and its constitutional order, that, according to Rhonheimer, "Christian ferment is called to come to bear" (7). Here Rhonheimer recalls Wolfgang Böckenförde's dictum that "the modern secular state lives from presuppositions which it itself cannot create and guarantee" (7). The point is that the Church finds its legitimate role by forming the consciences of citizens, but not by participating directly in politics itself, which is the task of the laity (7-8).

Despite differences, each of the three thinkers treated here affirms, with respect to the liberal-democratic constitutional order, a primacy of the political over the metaphysical (and *a fortiori* over the theological), and again of "positive" authority over truth. In so doing, each at the same time expressly rejects the purely procedural idea of the state. Each of them, in other words, makes a double appeal: on the one hand, to a political order that defines itself only in terms of publicly reasonable values that are "political" in nature and conceived in terms such as peace, liberty, equality, rights, economic efficiency, and the like; on the other hand, to a distinctly non-political or pre-political order which, in the name of a particular metaphysics or religion, provides "articles of faith" (Murray), or a "comprehensive doctrine" (Rawls), or "categorical foundations" (Rhonheimer) that support these politically reasonable values characteristic of the modern constitutional-democratic order.

What is decisive for all three thinkers is thus a clear distinction between two kinds of discourse: a "political" discourse proper to the constitutional democratic state and public order, and a "pre-political" discourse proper to individuals and groups who may appeal to "natural law" or Christian revelation as a foundation for their exercise of "public reason" in political matters.

For all three thinkers, public-political discourse must be as free as possible from metaphysics, from ideas regarding the nature of man and his destiny, or indeed regarding the whole of reality in relation to God. The pluralism of modern societies regarding the meaning of man and his destiny is such that civil unity can be achieved only around ever fewer and less substantive claims of truth. Civil discourse and civil dialogue and debate should concern itself with man in as "formal" a sense as possible: with a freedom conceived, for example, primarily in terms of an exercise of choice, and rights conceived first in terms of immunity from coercion. This sort of discourse is rightly termed "formal" because it intends, relative to such ideas of freedom and rights, to avoid as far as possible any substantial metaphysical claims of truth regarding the nature of man and his relation to God. Metaphysical, or theological, claims of truths may — and for Murray and Rhonheimer should — provide foundations for what is affirmed in the constitutional-political order, as long as these claims are not understood themselves to take a properly "political" form.[6] As a matter of principle, such claims remain properly "pre-political," and just so far "private," expressions of a particular individual or group in society. Or better: these "private" metaphysical claims of truth can indeed enter the "public-political" realm, but only insofar as they coincide with what has already been adopted in this realm as merely "political" ideas of freedom,

---

6. I am thus terming "formal" any position that deems it possible to assign *political* meaning to peace, liberty, equality, economic efficiency, and the like, without thereby implying a metaphysics already in the constitution of this political meaning. My presupposition, in other words, is that terms like peace and liberty cannot but imply some idea of the being of man and his destiny, of man in relation to God, an idea that shapes decisively, even if unwittingly, the original political meaning of such terms. One of the main burdens of this chapter is to demonstrate how this is so, especially in terms of Murray's formal-juridical conception of political order: to show the sense in which this would-be purely formal conception entails, contrary to Murray's own express intentions, a fragmented metaphysics of man that may be properly termed instrumentalist.

The twentieth-century Catholic philosopher Etienne Gilson, in his *The Unity of Philosophical Experience* (New York: Scribner's, 1965), argued that metaphysics always "buries its undertakers" (p. 306). By this he meant that tacit judgments regarding the meaning of being operate in our specific judgments about man, cognitional theory, and the like; and that ignorance that this is so entails, not that the judgments cease to operate, but only that they operate now in a hidden and just so far controlling way. What I am suggesting is that Gilson's dictum regarding the undertakers of metaphysics holds also when the "undertaking" in question is done in the name of liberal political strategy and order. Even the *juridical-political* "undertakers" of metaphysics get buried — by a bad, albeit mostly unconscious, metaphysics of instrumentalism. Showing how and why this is so is the burden of the rest of this chapter.

rights, equality, peace, economic efficiency, and the like. What a "pre-political" metaphysics cannot legitimately do is enter the "public-political" realm in a way that would undercut these "political" ideas, by calling for their transformation in some significant sense. This must be so because, once again, were such "pre-political" claims of truth explicitly to inform these "political" ideas, there would ensue a risk of violence among those civil groups, or churches, or states, holding different "pre-political" claims of truth.

Thus we have, according to Murray, Rawls, and Rhonheimer, the hallmark achievement of the politically liberal constitutional order: it resolves things (or intends to resolve them) publicly-legally with recourse not to a *metaphysical content* of justice, but only to what is, as far as possible, a *metaphysically empty form* of justice. For all constitutional purposes, the state government, qua government, intends to remain open to and hence neutral toward *all* metaphysical claims, because, *de jure*, it would espouse *no one* metaphysical claim. Or rather: the state remains open to all metaphysical claims insofar as they are consistent with and provide support for "political justice."

Needless to say, this argument in defense of liberalism's constitutional democratic state contains much that is compelling. Indeed, let me emphasize that my purpose in raising questions about the argument is to secure, and not to reject, the distinct achievements promoted by modern liberalism in its development of the juridical state, as argued by Murray and Rawls and Rhonheimer. I mean this in the sense that we should embrace without reservation the liberal intention to protect all human beings in their dignity as free and rational subjects, above all in matters of conscience and of religious belief, and especially those human beings who are least able to protect themselves. Furthermore, liberalism is correct that realization of this intention, and of liberalism's intention generally of promoting peaceful dialogue and genuine civil community, requires a limited state and thus a distinction between state and society. Liberalism is also right that the state is not the ultimate or proper source of truth, and that the institutions of church and state must therefore be kept separate, and that the state accordingly must have a distinctly "secular" purpose.

My critical argument calls none of this into question. The burden of the argument is simply that the liberal-juridical state, in its putative purely political or formal meaning, bears a hidden metaphysical logic that *undermines the good that is intended in the key ideas involved in bringing this state into existence in the first place.*

Indeed, I believe there is warrant for raising significant questions regarding the juridical state only because the inner logic of this state can be shown to undercut this intended good. Such a demonstration contains essentially two parts. First, it must be shown that the supposed purely formal justice administered by this state unwittingly enforces definite metaphysical claims of truth. Second, it must be shown that these metaphysical claims lead of their inner dynamic to an undercutting of the juridical state's intention, which is to overcome violence and promote peace, by fostering genuine dialogue and communication and civil peace among its citizens and by securing the equal protection of all, especially those who are weakest and most vulnerable.

It is the burden of what follows to argue these two points. First, relative to the terms assumed by the authors introduced above, my contention is that the assertion of the priority of the "political" over the "metaphysical" presupposes and expresses a metaphysics, even as the assertion of the priority of "positive" authority over (metaphysical) truth in the making of law presupposes and expresses a claim of (metaphysical) truth. The liberal-constitutional state, however unwittingly and contrary to its own intentions, sanctions a metaphysics of human being and action. It assumes that it has successfully avoided such a metaphysics by virtue of its appeal to what it understands as purely formally or politically conceived freedom, rights, conscience, and religion. But in point of fact these would-be purely formal ideas of freedom and rights are not *simply formal* at all, in the sense of lacking a metaphysical content or order. On the contrary, they are *abstract fragments* of freedom and rights: they signal not the absence of metaphysical order but rather the presence of *fragmented* metaphysical order. They exhibit precisely the fragmented metaphysical character that I will show is appropriately termed "instrumentalist."

My contention, secondly, is that this *instrumentalist metaphysics* which is unwittingly adopted by the juridical state in fact does violence to the kind of truth-centered argument and communication necessary for authentic civil community, even as, in so doing, it fosters a peculiar kind of violence with respect to the most vulnerable members of society.

My argument thus attempts to bring into relief what is a dangerous set of paradoxes at the heart of the liberal-juridical state. That state's peculiar defense of freedom at once really does (in one sense) maximize the spread of freedom even as, at the same time (and in another sense), it covertly promotes a deep and pervasive unfreedom. The juridical state's peculiar defense of limited coercive power at once really does (in one sense) result in the restriction of such power even as, at the same time (and in another sense), it covertly promotes the ever-increasing expansion of this power. In a word, the juridical state, *by virtue of its inner logic as such,* albeit *unintentionally,* inclines toward what is at once an ever-more fragmented state *and* an ever-more monolithic state, and embodies what is at once a dualistic distinction *and* a confused and reductive unity between state and society and state and church.

These paradoxes can be summarized in more concrete terms. The liberal state with its formally-politically conceived freedom and rights embodies an instrumentalist metaphysics, in its inmost order as a state. And this metaphysics undermines the state's own intention to protect equally the freedom and dignity of all human beings: it embodies a hidden dynamic for a relativism that undoes genuine dialogue and civil community, a dynamic for what may be termed a peculiar and paradoxical "dictatorship of relativism";[7] and it thereby creates a vulnerability for what John Paul II highlights as a paradoxical tendency in liberal democratic societies toward inversion into a "totalitarianism" marked by "the supremacy of the strong over the weak" (*Evangelium Vitae,* n. 20, 23).

This critical argument raises the obvious question of whether there exists an alternative metaphysics of human being and action that can meet the just intentions of the liberal state, including its legitimate demand for reasonableness and thus for accessibility in principle on the part of all members of society. Although the purpose of this chapter is focused primarily on showing the meaning and implications of the metaphysics tacitly enforced by the juridical state, it will also indicate the main lines of this alternative metaphysics, suggesting how this alternative meets in principle the legitimate demand for reasonableness and hence universal accessibility. The key, given the problems as framed above, is to see that truth and freedom, rightly conceived, are mutually inclusive. They are in their deepest and original meaning neither opposed nor merely juxtaposed to each other. On the contrary, they form an ontological unity, in and through the reality of being as gift.

Or, to anticipate, freedom is at root a natural, ultimately God-centered, personal *act* of love, even as love properly understood is a natural, ultimately God-centered, personal *order of truth.* Freedom and truth are therefore united in what is at once an *act* and an *order* of love.

---

7. Joseph Ratzinger, Homily at the Mass "Pro Eligendo Romano Pontifice," 18 April 2005.

The burden of my task in the present chapter, in sum, is to show that *the ends rightly intended by political liberalism can be realized properly only on non-liberal terms,* and thus in ways that demand transformation of formally conceived, and hence (as I will show) instrumentalist, freedom, rights, and intelligence. Only a radical criticism of liberalism's mostly unwitting instrumentalist metaphysics renders it possible to secure in their most proper meaning liberalism's own best intentions.

II.

The problem I am suggesting is characteristic of liberalism is thus bound up with the fact that its juridical state harbors an assumed claim of metaphysical — with implications of theological[8] — truth about freedom and reason *inside* what is its announced public or constitutional *incompetence* in matters of truth. As already noted, the state is not the proper *source* of the truths by which men ought to live. That source is God, the truth about whom Catholics believe is discoverable above all in his revelation in Jesus Christ, as recorded in Scripture and embodied historically-sacramentally in his Church. That truth is also in a significant sense discoverable in the nature of every human being, hence in a naturally reasonable way, by virtue of creation itself. In this sense the often-cited dictum is right: the state presupposes truths of which it is not the source.

A crucial ambiguity can nonetheless be seen in this dictum when it is viewed in light of the problematic of the juridical state as indicated. On the one hand, the dictum can (rightly) mean that the truth exists and that it transcends the state. Consistent with this understanding, the state would understand itself as *limited* precisely because it is *subordinate to* the truth about man and indeed finally to the Creator, or to some transcendent order, as source of that truth. The state would see that it had an *intrinsic responsibility qua state* to foster conditions — institutions and forms of community — embodying and favorable to seeking the truth, including about God and

---

8. Metaphysics rightly understood opens of its inner nature into some judgment regarding the meaning and existence of God, and thus into (natural) theology. Insofar as this is the case, metaphysics can never remain indifferent, or neutral, with respect to the meaning of God as developed also in revealed, or Christian, theology. My argument that the state is shaped inevitably by a metaphysics thus entails that the state is shaped by a natural theology, with implication as well regarding a (possible) revealed theology. This will become clear in our treatment of the church-state distinction in section VI.

religion. In a word, the state's "negative" relation to the truth, so to speak, as implied in the state's distinction from society, would, on this reading, be conceived rather as an intrinsic sign and expression of man's "positive" relation to the transcendent order of truth. This indeed seems to me the understanding implied by the New Testament, in Jesus' statement that what is Caesar's ought to be rendered unto Caesar and what is God's unto God. In this case, what is rightly judged to be the state's incompetence in matters of truth would signal, not that the state is agnostic regarding the question of truth (finally about God), but that it is inherently respectful of that truth: that it is genuinely open to, and indeed somehow *a participant in,* the truth that it does not *create* but nevertheless in some significant sense *reflects,* already *in its limited nature as a state.* On this reading, consistent for example with the classical Greek philosophical view, the constitutional order of the state as a matter of principle implies a pedagogy in the nature of truth.[9]

The liberal-juridical state on its best understanding, on the other hand, does not see itself properly as a pedagogue in the matter of truth.[10] It claims to be respectful of the truth, and not at all to deny that truth exists. Its task as state, however, is limited to making space for each citizen to make his own arguments on behalf of truth. What is relevant is to ensure that every citizen has equal freedom to pursue the truth and live it as he or she understands it, *within the bounds of justice as fairness.* The state thus brackets the question of truth in its administration of legal power, in favor of juridically conceived freedom and rights. This state's (would-be) incompetence in the matter of truth, consequently, is understood to mean that the state officially acknowledges itself, and can acknowledge itself, only as a (metaphysically neutral) *instrument* for securing fairness among citizens in their exercise of freedom and rights in the pursuit of truth, that is, as the guarantor of a fair process of debate among the multiple private "factions" making up society.[11] The state is an *instrument* of the *process*

---

9. The idea of the state as properly pedagogical presupposes that it is a matter of *meaning* before it is a matter of technical or "coercive" management. See the *Catechism of the Catholic Church,* n. 2244, on institutions as embedding a view of the human being.

10. The idea of state power as primarily "coercive" rather than pedagogical presupposes that government has its origin more basically in man's sin than in his nature as social and inherently good. Thus government arises by means of a "contract" among human beings, the purpose of which is to check their bad behavior, preventing each from interfering with the rights of others.

11. I take the term "faction" here from James Madison. When speaking of "faction," Madison uses the language of "interest." A faction is a group organized around interest:

whereby citizens themselves, as members of particular social or ecclesial groups, arrive at and make their own case for the ideas they think should

---

around what, from the perspective of the government, expresses a private or self-interested claim, and not a truth (see *The Federalist*, No. 10), even if the governors might themselves, as private persons, take it to be true. But we should qualify further here: Madison himself believed that virtue was necessary if America's republican way of government were to survive, and he was confident, for example, that "'true' religion would triumph of its own merits if its advocates were free to pursue it without coercion" (Frank Lambert, *The Founding Fathers and the Place of Religion in America* [Princeton: Princeton University Press, 2003], p. 4). As Michael Sandel points out, the framers of the Constitution adhered to republican ideals in that they "continued to believe that the virtuous should govern and that government should aim at a public good beyond the sum of private interests"; and "they did not abandon the formative ambition of republican politics, the notion that government has a stake in cultivating citizens of a certain kind" (Michael J. Sandel, *Democracy's Discontent: America in Search of a Public Philosophy* [Cambridge, MA: Belknap Press of Harvard University Press, 1996], pp. 130-31). The relevant point, however, in anticipation of the argument I intend to make apropos of John Courtney Murray, is that Madison's response to this problem remains more "procedural" than "formative" (Sandel's terms): Madison interpreted the Constitution to be an effort not so much "to elevate the moral character of the people" as to provide the "institutional devices that would save republican government by making it less dependent on the virtue of the people" (p. 129). "Liberty would depend not on civic virtue but instead on a scheme of mechanisms and procedures by which competing interests would check and balance one another: 'Ambition made to counter ambition' [Madison]" (p. 130). Sandel, I think, is right to insist that Madison wanted government to transcend interests. But the point is that Madison conceived this in terms of multiplying the factions that would cancel interests out, rather than shaping them through virtue (p. 131). My argument with respect to Murray will be that, whether or not Murray emphasizes the necessity of virtue for sustaining republican government more strongly than Madison, he insists, like the latter, on a primarily "procedural" role for the state, and this primarily procedural understanding leaves Murray — as well as Madison — still vulnerable logically to the four paradoxes discussed in section VI, for reasons to be developed below. The issue, in other words, is precisely the primacy of "procedural" freedom and reason in securing what would be a common *good*.

The difficulty with respect to America, then, in sum, is that those who insist that the American Founders realized that virtue (and moral truth or even the religious truth that man is created) are necessary for sustaining republican government invariably end up equivocating vis-à-vis the terms of the problematic as framed in this chapter. That is, these interpreters typically fail to clarify adequately whether the necessity for virtue or truth is a matter of what is "pre-political" and thus of proper concern only to civil society as distinct from the state (in the sense of Rhonheimer and Murray); or whether on the contrary such virtue or truth is a matter of intrinsic concern also for the state and "political" discourse as such. If the necessity is a matter only of what is "pre-political," interpretations that would defend virtue and truth as necessary for sustaining America's republican government are *eo ipso* subject to the critical argument — and dangerous paradoxes — set forth in this chapter. If, on the contrary, virtue and truth are understood to be of intrinsic concern to the state

prevail in the public-constitutional order. And the state finally adjudicates competing claims among the various factions only in terms of their aptness qua justice as fairness: in terms of their aptness for securing peaceful public order, and not what is classically understood as the common good of man.

The state on such a reading is thus as a matter of principle never permitted *itself* to *end* in any metaphysical truth about a natural or transcendent order of being as true and good, or about the openness of this order to God as the creative source of being in its truth and goodness. The juridical state can never, qua state, recognize transcendental truth and goodness in *their givenness qua being*,[12] and hence as *ends in themselves* that serve in some significant sense to bind the civil community as such. To be sure, the individuals and groups making up civil society might well claim truth and

---

and "political" discourse, those who hold this interpretation are just so far committed to defending America's *novus ordo seclorum* not simply in terms of freedom, but in terms of freedom *as tied intrinsically to virtue and the truth about man*. But, lest we judge this to be an obvious and hence trivial assertion, we should be aware that such an interpretation contradicts John Courtney Murray's "political" or "juridical" reading of both the American constitutional order and the Second Vatican Council's *Dignitatis Humanae*. And this reading remains dominant, one still virtually uncontested in America. Indeed, the main implication of making freedom-*as-tied-to-truth* intrinsic to America's constitutional order is that the question of truth becomes, *eo ipso*, proper to "political" discourse as such.

Thus, for example, in his recent book, *We Still Hold These Truths* (Wilmington, DE: ISI Books, 2010), Matthew Spalding says — rightly — that "the American founders were practical and constructed a new constitutional order that was based on the traditional concept of a fixed human nature" (p. 21); and that "the American Founders understood Locke in light of classical political reason and biblical revelation, as part of the English Whig republican thinking and the natural law tradition in which they understood themselves" (p. 23). And he insists in this context that "we must restore America's principles — the truths to which we are dedicated — as the central idea of our nation's public philosophy" (p. 4). From the point of view of the present chapter, however, these assertions leave unaddressed and thus unclarified two crucial questions: Is this natural law, or public philosophy, a matter only of the "pre-political," or does it enter into the "political" as such? And how precisely is the content of this natural law/public philosophy to be assessed in terms of the anthropology of love, of being as gift — which is to say, the anthropology characterized by "constitutive relations" — developed in the pontificates of John Paul II and Benedict XVI, in the name of the Second Vatican Council?

12. Cf. Joseph Ratzinger, *Introduction to Christianity* (New York: Seabury Press, 1969), pp. 31ff., on the role played in modernity by the shift in the notion of truth from what is *verum qua ens* (true qua being) to what is *verum quia factum* (true because made [by man]). The point, in other words, is that the juridical state logically recognizes "truth" only in the latter sense.

goodness as ends in themselves. But the pertinent point is that the sole function of government, juridically interpreted, is to secure the justice that guarantees fairness in the process of dialogue and the exercise of freedom among these individuals and groups. The only legitimate "end" of government consists in fostering this (would-be) fair-formal *process,* hence in recognizing truth and goodness only as *instruments* of *justice as fair process,* which, *eo ipso,* from the point of view of the state, must remain precisely an end-less process relative to metaphysical truth or goodness. In a paradoxical way, therefore, the liberal-juridical state *does* in the final analysis become an (unwitting) pedagogue, on behalf of *an instrumentalist understanding* of truth and goodness and indeed of God and religion as the transcendent source of truth and goodness.

Again, members of society may take to be intrinsically reasonable and truthful what they propose as a possible foundation for the "political-peaceful" justice affirmed by the state. As Rhonheimer points out, occidental pluralism requires at its root a common metaphysical foundation of values. But here is the point: however inherently true this metaphysical foundation may appear to the citizens themselves, and however much such a foundation may appear to be necessary for sustaining "political" justice, this foundation is logically permitted to serve only as an *instrument* in the promotion of what remains, and must remain, on the juridical understanding of the state, a (putatively) merely *formal-political* justice. This "truth" can properly enter the public or political order of liberal constitutional democracy only qua *procedural instrument* of a justice conceived formally: not as intrinsically true or good, but only as an effective instrument in the securing of this formal justice.

Indeed, in light of the foregoing, we can also say: for all public-political or constitutional purposes, freedom as fostered by the juridical state will be understood as essentially voluntaristic — a matter of (would-be) purely formally-conceived choice; reason, as essentially "calculative" or "technical" — a means of enabling freedom to be more effective in the exercise of choice; and religion, as essentially positivistic — an expression of what can only be an originally indifferent exercise of choice, and just so far arbitrary option, for God. In a word, the human act, in its exercise of freedom, intelligence, and religious concern, will be of public or constitutional relevance only in its formal, hence purely instrumental, character.

Thus the juridical state, for all of its insistence on incompetence in matters of truth regarding the nature and destiny of man, does in fact embed a claim of competency[13] regarding the primary meaning of freedom, reason, and religion, though the "substance" of each of these is, paradoxically, formalist and instrumentalist. And this formalism cannot be rightly construed as a matter simply of strategic political *methodology,* as distinct from *ontology.* For the point is that any such would-be merely methodological deferral *eo ipso* conceives the *reality* of freedom, for the purposes of democratic political culture and the public-constitutional ordering of society, to be an act of choice disjoined from an anterior order providing objective metaphysical content, an act of choice that is thereby already understood, however unwittingly, to bear the metaphysical structure of formalism: freedom is treated as a purely formal-instrumental, and thus indifferent, act.[14]

But we need now to show in metaphysical terms how this is so, and the ways in which it is significant.

III.

We will approach the question in the terms set by John Courtney Murray. As we have seen, Murray says that the constitutional order of America's juridical state contains only articles of peace, not of faith. Indeed, he says that, if these articles of peace were articles of faith, in the sense that they carried answers to "the eternal human questions with regard to the nature of truth and freedom or the manner in which the spiritual order of man's life is to be organized," these answers, given the historical circumstances of the American Founding, would reflect an amalgam of Protestant and Enlightenment presuppositions. The condition that alone allows Catholics to accept the juridical order of this state, in other words, is not that this state

---

13. From the Latin, *com-petere:* to come together, be suitable; hence to have adequate abilities or qualities to function in a particular way.

14. It is important to underscore that the indifference indicated here is "logical" or "ontological," as distinct from psychological or moral. The relevant point, in other words, is not whether a person, in the exercise of freedom, intends to choose truth, but whether freedom itself in its original structure already implies an order of truth: whether freedom, already in its nature as a spontaneous act, participates in truth. On this point, see David C. Schindler's "Freedom Beyond Our Choosing: Augustine on the Will and Its Objects," *Communio: International Catholic Review* 29, no. 4 (Winter 2002): 618-53. See also the discussion on "Freedom of Indifference" in Servais Pinckaers, *The Sources of Christian Ethics* (Washington, DC: Catholic University of America Press, 1995), pp. 327-53.

implies the right sort of "truthful" answers, so to speak, but that it implies no answers at all — Enlightenment, Protestant, or Catholic — to the eternal questions regarding truth and freedom. The state is simply incompetent in such matters.

Later, following the Second Vatican Council, Murray says that the Council's affirmation of the right to religious freedom in *Dignitatis Humanae* is "identical" in "object or content" to that affirmed in the United States Constitution.[15] He thus emphasizes that the right to religious freedom is a matter of formal recognition of religious freedom in *political-juridical*, as distinct from metaphysical or theological, terms (*DRF*, 568). In a word, this right is to be conceived in the first instance as "negative, namely an immunity from coercion in religious matters" (*DRF*, 568).

Nonetheless, Murray has reservations regarding *DH*. He says that it may be questioned "whether the Declaration [*DH*] manifests sufficient awareness that [the] *political* [dimension of the rights question] is the crucial issue" (*DRF*, 569, emphasis added), as the American or Anglo-Saxon approach clearly does. In the American approach, freedom is "simply juridical," not "ideological." In both the nineteenth-century continental laicist and the American understanding, freedom is an "instrumental concept" (*DRF*, 569-70). However, on the American reading, freedom is instrumental, not to "an ideological negation of the public status of religion," but on the contrary to the "freedom of religion as a public phenomenon, whose manifestations are of a transcendent order" (*DRF*, 568-69).

Given this distinction between the continental-laicist and American liberal traditions, Murray puzzles over "the prominence given [in *DH*] to man's moral obligation to search for the truth, as somehow the ultimate foundation of the right to religious freedom" (*DRF*, 570). In the same vein, he questions the emphasis of *DH* (e.g., n. 3) on the need for government to foster the religious life of the people. As he puts it, the right to religious freedom is "simply an immunity" (*DRF*, "Discussion," 580), and "I don't see how you can promote an immunity — making someone more and more immune. This just doesn't make any sense to me; it never has" (580). Hence Murray concludes that the demand that government show religion favor is actually tied, not to the logic of the right to religious freedom,

---

15. John Courtney Murray, "*Declaration on Religious Freedom:* Commentary," in *American Participation at the Second Vatican Council*, ed. Vincent A. Yzermans (New York: Sheed & Ward, 1967), pp. 668-76, at 668. See also Murray's "Declaration on Religious Freedom" [=*DRF*], in *Vatican II: An Interfaith Appraisal*, ed. John Miller (Notre Dame: Associated Press, 1966), pp. 565-76, at 568. Citations in the text are from this second article.

properly speaking, but rather to the fact that "society itself may benefit from [such favor] in terms of justice and order" (580), or indeed to what is otherwise at best a legitimate pastoral as distinct from strictly theoretical-political concern (*DRF,* 571). In short, Murray contends that *DH*'s emphasis on the moral obligation to seek the truth, and on the state's need to foster conditions favorable to religion, is due primarily to the Council Fathers' failure to appropriate fully the distinction between the continental-laicist and American liberal traditions, and hence to appreciate the properly juridical nature of the American liberal idea of rights.

Indeed, tying the right to religious freedom to man's duty to search for the truth, according to Murray, leads to problematic tendencies he says are evidenced in both Catholic and contemporary communist governments: namely, "that they already have the truth; that they represent the truth, which is also the good of the people; that, consequently, they are empowered to repress public manifestations of error" (*DRF,* 571).[16]

Further in this context, Murray says that, in conceiving rights and freedom as juridical in nature, we understand that the purpose of government is best expressed now in terms of maximizing freedom, and of securing the public order that enables each person to exercise his freedom equally. Thus, although the common good includes much more than public order, it is this latter that is the specific function of government for Murray (*DRF,* 575-76).

As a proper foundation for the distinctly political-juridical meaning of the right to religious freedom, and indeed of rights generally as he conceives them, Murray then offers his own argument, which he says can be constructed from "the principles of the Declaration [*DH*] itself, assembled into an organic structure" (*DRF,* 571). Given the argument's concise and comprehensive formulation, I quote it at length:

> The argument begins from the dignity of man as a moral subject. Man is intelligent. Therefore he is capable of, and called to, an understanding of

---

16. The problematic tendency cited here by Murray is of course a very real one. The difficulty, or so I mean to show, is that Murray's rejection of the duty to search for the truth as an adequate foundation for religious freedom presupposes notions of both truth and freedom that can be shown to be defective by an adequate metaphysics, and indeed by the anthropology developed by the Second Vatican Council itself. It is instructive in this light that Murray sees no need to differentiate between Catholic and Communist in the matter of truth and the sense of the duty to seek it. I address briefly, later in this chapter, the question of how best to interpret the meaning of truth and freedom in *DH*.

his own existence — its meaning and purpose. Man is free. Therefore he is called personally to realize, in love and through a lifelong process of choice, the sense of his own existence. Hence the mark of man as a person is his personal autonomy. Inseparable, however, from personal autonomy is personal responsibility. This is twofold. First, man is responsible for the conformity between the inner imperatives of his conscience and the transcendent order of truth. Second, man is responsible for the conformity between his external actions and the inner imperatives of conscience. These responsibilities are moral and altogether stringent. Man bears them as a moral subject, as he confronts, so to speak, his vertical relationship to the transcendent order of truth. However, on the horizontal plane of intersubjective relationships, and within the social order, which is the order within which human rights are predicated, man's fulfillment of his personal responsibilities is juridically irrelevant. The major reason is that no authority exists within the juridical order that is capable or empowered to judge in this regard. . . .

What is juridically relevant, however, and relevant in the most fundamental sense, is the personal autonomy that is constituent of man's dignity. More exactly, resident in man's dignity is the exigence to act on his own initiative and on his own responsibility. This exigence is of the objective order; it is simply the demand that man should act according to his nature. And this exigence is the basic ontological foundation, not only of the right to religious freedom, but of all man's fundamental rights — in what concerns the search for truth, the communication of opinions, the cultivation of the arts and sciences, the formation and expression of political views, association with other men for common purposes, and, with privileged particularity, the free exercise of religion.

All these rights are immunities from coercion. Given the exigence of the person to act on his own initiative and responsibility, coercion appears as a thing of no value to the person. (*DRF,* 571-72)

Finally, concluding this argument, Murray says that to speak thus of a right "is to imply a juridical relationship, within which to the right of one there corresponds a duty on the part of others with regard to whatever the object of the right is — in our case, immunity from coercive action" (*DRF,* 572-73).

Murray's argument is both subtle and powerful. The point on which I wish to focus concerns the link between what Murray takes to be a purely juridical notion of freedom and rights on the one hand, and the metaphysical idea of the human person that he takes to undergird and warrant this political-juridical notion on the other. More precisely, I wish to show how Murray's juridical notion of freedom and rights expresses his particular metaphysics of the person. As Murray himself acknowledges, the (putative) purely juridical conception of rights involves understanding rights primarily in terms of immunity from coercion, *even as this understanding is demanded by that particular metaphysics of man according to which primacy is granted to man's exigence to act on his own initiative and in this sense to a definite sense of man's autonomy.*

To be sure, Murray emphasizes that this metaphysics of the person only provides a *foundation* for the juridical rights that remain simply political and procedural in their properly conceived "content and object" as concerns of the state. The point I am making, however, is just this: a (putatively) purely juridical conception of rights, and a metaphysics that grants priority to the human being's formal exercise of choice, or to the self's exigence to act on its own initiative, *mutually demand and presuppose one another.* Each signifies and expresses in different, respectively political and philosophical, ways what is a *single understanding of the human person.*

But this observation is significant only if it can be shown that such a metaphysics of the human person is problematic, and that some reasonable alternative exists. And indeed the first thing to be acknowledged is that the idea of the person affirmed by Murray appears to bear a kind of self-evident truth. Surely freedom and intelligence and the exigence to act on one's own initiative, and thus personal autonomy, are all basic to man and expressions of his nature. Likewise, rights in a basic sense are matters involving an immunity from coercion which, in a juridical context, suggest a corresponding duty on the part of others with regard to the recognition of such immunity. Further, man is responsible for the conformity between his conscience and the transcendent order of truth — for his "vertical" relation to this order — and between his external actions and his conscience, and there is a crucial sense in which no governmental authority can or should enter within the domain of personal conscience. Finally, it is true that freedom is of the very essence of political method rightly understood in its goal of achieving equality of rights.[17]

Nevertheless, in the form conceived by Murray, all of these claims

---

17. Murray states that "[f]reedom . . . is the political method par excellence." Indeed, it "is not only the primary method of politics; it is also the highest political goal" (*DRF,* 574). As I clarify below, I agree with Murray here, but only coincident with reconceiving freedom as an intrinsic feature of truth understood as an order of love.

bear only a partial truth, and in fact remain seriously defective. Missing from Murray's metaphysics of the person is recognition of the category of *relation* as *constitutive* of the human being and of the human act in its freedom and intelligence. Missing is recognition of the fact that man's exigence to act on his own initiative, hence his personal autonomy, is *originally* and *abidingly given* to him. The exigence to act on one's own initiative is through and through a *response to,* indeed as at once a *participation in,* what is always ontologically *first initiated in us* by God, and in a significant sense also by other creatures — our parents, the human community, the natural environment — under God.

Human freedom, in other words, is not in the first instance merely a capacity to choose *(liberum arbitrium),* a choice which then first effects an order of relations to God and others. On the contrary, freedom *chooses* relations to God, family, others, and the world only as it is itself already a participant in the *naturally given order of these relations.*

Freedom, then, is never a merely formal or procedural act whereby the self first contracts relation with others, and thus never merely an instrument of this order of relations.[18] It is an instrument only in the sense of *re*-enacting, as it were, in the unique manner proper to itself as a *responsive* spontaneous act, this *order* of relations which precedes it and in which it is always already an *integral participant,* and of which it is thus itself always a sign and expression.[19]

It is in light of the idea of constitutive relations that we begin to see the sense in which Murray's conception of human freedom, and rights, is problematic. The only thing that is truly juridically relevant, according to Murray, is man's exigence for acting on his own initiative, which is to say, his sheer or purely formal capacity to choose for himself, and thus rights

---

18. For a treatment of the distinction between freedom as a mere capacity for choice and freedom as a matter of form and actuality, see D. C. Schindler, *Freedom and Form in Schiller, Schelling, and Hegel* (forthcoming), Introduction. See also Schindler's article, "Freedom Beyond Our Choosing."

19. Thus, as conceived in the present chapter, an instrumental act rightly conceived is understood to realize truth and goodness only as itself already participating in this truth and goodness; while an instrumentalist act is understood as the means by which truth and goodness are (supposedly) produced but which itself remains extrinsic to this truth and goodness. An act of freedom conceived instrumentalistically, in other words, tends logically, if unintentionally, to drain its objects of their truth and goodness *in se,* of their *inherent* truth or goodness. Cf. here Schindler, "Freedom Beyond Our Choosing," pp. 650-53, regarding the link between an empty freedom and a world without intrinsic value, and the fact that there is no political freedom except in the presence of goods that are nonnegotiable.

are essentially immunities. The purpose of government is limited essentially to protecting each person from the encroachment of the other, and rights thus veer of their inner logic toward what is often called "entitlement": I have a right to as much freedom as possible, and this means that your essential political duty is dispatched in giving me as much space as possible. This maximization of freedom as understood by Murray is of course "politically" circumscribed, but by the demands of public order rather than of the common good, and this public order is itself conceived primarily in terms of securing space for each to exercise free choice equally. Duty in the sense of responsibility to a given transcendent order of truth and goodness is juridically pertinent only as a necessary instrument for maintaining public order in this sense.

Thus, in a word, relative to the problematic of the present chapter, the state according to Murray is properly concerned with freedom only in terms of the *empty space* necessary for the *exercise of choice* to take place in *uncoerced, autonomous* fashion: in terms, thus, of what he calls public order. The state does not concern itself properly with freedom in its original meaning *also as an order of truth-ful relations:* with freedom as *already participant, qua free act, in the order of relations constitutive of man in his reality as a creature.* Indeed, if the state did concern itself with freedom in its relation to truth, there would, for Murray, remain the risk that the state thinking itself to be in possession of truth would short-circuit freedom in order to hasten citizens' arrival at the truth.

Note that the criticism of Murray introduced here does not deny but on the contrary presupposes that, as he says, freedom is the "primary method of politics," and indeed in a basic sense is also "the highest political goal." The point is simply that this assertion demands a crucially important qualifier: freedom is a *spontaneous act* only as at once an *originally given order of relations* to God and others, an act that is thus itself a *sign and expression of the truth* carried in this given order. Freedom is the primary method of politics, in other words, only as *itself an integral feature of the truth about man,* even as the truth about man essentially presupposes and indeed contains freedom. It therefore cannot be the case that the constitutional democratic state, rightly understood, should concern itself with the equal right of each citizen to the exercise of formally conceived freedom, to the exclusion of the question of truth: should concern itself with freedom while, for example, society alone concerns itself with truth.[20] On the contrary, what the

---

20. See Benedict XVI's *Caritas in Veritate,* which affirms that civil society has the

modern democratic state, rightly understood, must be about is not the deferral of truth in favor of freedom, but the *integration* at a basic level of *freedom and truth,* in such a way that each bears *the essential and deepest meaning* of the other *within* its own distinct integrity as such.[21]

IV.

We will say more later about the implications of these issues raised in connection with Murray. First, we should say more about what is meant by "constitutive relations," with its implied idea of being as gift, and about what serves as the foundations for such relations. These relations, as indicated, invoke the idea of God and indeed of creation. Given the nature of my proposed criticism of the juridical state, therefore, it is especially important to show that the idea of constitutive relations and of being as gift is in principle reasonable and thus accessible to both believers and nonbelievers. The following grouping of texts, several of them cited and discussed in other chapters of this book, articulate the key features and foundations of constitutive relations as presupposed in my critical argument.

The encyclical *Evangelium Vitae* says, for example, that our main cultural problems stem from a failure to understand that "freedom possesses an inherently relational dimension" (quae *essentialem necessitudinis rationem* secum fert) and an "essential link with the truth *(constitutivum*

---

most proper, but not exclusive, care for solidarity, which is a responsibility also of the state and the economy (see especially n. 38-40).

21. As noted elsewhere, the claim introduced here presupposes a reading of *Dignitatis Humanae* different from Murray's reading, but I will take this up in the conclusion to section VI. Needless to say, there is much to be elaborated regarding what it would mean for the democratic state to embody in some significant sense the integration of truth and freedom as indicated here, and indeed regarding how this integration could come about, given the dominant liberal conception for this state. The present argument, in this connection, is limited to showing the sense in which liberalism, in its intended denial of any intrinsic relation or unity between truth and freedom, itself embodies a particular sense of the relation between metaphysics and freedom, however much this is rendered invisible by virtue of liberalism's would-be purely juridical order. In terms of how an authentic integration of truth and freedom in the political order could be brought into existence within a liberal cultural context, my argument is limited largely to suggesting that a dialogue must begin by making defenders of the liberal-juridical state aware of the claims of truth carried in their own intended avoidance of such claims (for all purposes of public reasonableness and constitutional order).

veritatis vinculum)" (n. 19).²² The encyclical speaks further of man's "inherent condition as a creature *(originalem perspiciat suae condicionis evidentiam qua creaturae)* to whom God has granted being and life as a gift and a duty *(donum et munus),"* and then says that "only by admitting his innate dependence *(innatam dependentiam in propria existentia)* can man live and use his freedom to the full and at the same time respect the life and freedom of every other person [from his roots]" (*EV,* n. 96). Regarding this dependence, the encyclical states that, "[b]ecause he is made by God . . . , man is naturally drawn to God. When he heeds the deepest yearnings of the heart, every man must make his own the words of truth expressed by St. Augustine: 'You have made us for yourself, O Lord, and our hearts are restless until they rest in you'" (*EV,* n. 35).

Again, the *Compendium of the Social Doctrine of the Church* states that human beings have a "constitutive social nature" (n. 37), and that *"the essence and existence of man are constitutively related to God. . . ."* This relationship "is not something that comes afterwards and is not added from the outside. The whole of man's life is a quest and a search for God. . . . [M]an of his inmost nature is a capacity for God *('homo est Dei capax')"* (*CSDC,* n. 109). Pertinently, this document says further that the freedom proper to creatures is one that is "given to us as a gift" which is "to be received like a seed to be cultivated responsibly" (*CSDC,* n. 138; cited from *Veritatis Splendor,* n. 86). Finally, and consistent with these affirmations, John Paul II says in *Go in Peace* that "God inscribed in . . . man and woman the vocation, and thus the capacity and responsibility, of love and communion. Love is therefore the fundamental and innate vocation of every human being."²³

The central idea carried in these texts is articulated in a summary way in a recent book by Joseph Ratzinger, in which he cites the great monastic rule of St. Basil: "The love of God is not based on some discipline imposed on us from outside, but as a capacity and indeed a necessity it is a constitutive element of our rational being." Ratzinger discusses in this context the phenomenon of conscience:

---

22. As the Vatican summary of *Evangelium Vitae* puts it: democracy's peculiar inversion of rights stems from a notion of freedom "which is seen as disconnected from any reference to truth and objective good, and which asserts itself . . . without the constitutive link of relationship with others" (n. 1).

23. John Paul II, *Go in Peace: An Enduring Gift of Love* (Chicago: Loyola Press, 2003), p. 211.

> [T]he first level, which we might call the *ontological level,* of the phenomenon "conscience" means that a kind of *primal remembrance of the good and the true* (which are identical) is bestowed on us. There is an inherent existential tendency of man, who is created in the image of God, to tend toward that which is in keeping with God. . . . This anamnesis of our origin, resulting from the fact that our being is constitutively in keeping with God, is . . . an inner sense, a capacity for recognition, in such a way that the one addressed recognizes in himself an echo of what is said to him. If he does not hide from his own self, he comes to the insight: *this* is the goal toward which my whole being tends, *this* is where I want to go.
>
> This *anamnesis of the Creator,* which *is identical with* the *foundations of our existence,* is the reason that *mission* is both *possible* and *justified.* The Gospel may and indeed must be proclaimed to the pagans, because this is what they are waiting for, even if they do not know this themselves (see Isa. 42:4).[24]

The view expressed here by Ratzinger is echoed in other authors of the Christian tradition. Thus Augustine says that God is "more inward than my inmost self [*intimior intimo meo*] and higher than my topmost height" (*Confessions,* 3:6). In the words of Aquinas, "God is in all things *(intime),* and innermostly *(magis intimum)* (*ST* I, q. 8, a. 1). This is the ground for Aquinas's view that "all cognitive beings know God implicitly in whatever they know" and tend implicitly toward God in every end they seek or desire (*De Veritate,* q. 22, a. 2).

In sum, man is rightly understood in his deepest reality as *capax Dei et alterius,* and this creaturely capacity "can be ignored or even forgotten or dismissed, but . . . never . . . eliminated" (*CSDC,* n. 109). The human act of freedom and intelligence, in a word, is never, even for a moment, empty of or neutral to this basic ordering of man to (and from) God and others.

Regarding constitutive relations, then: what this means most basically is that man is constituted in his innermost reality as a *gift from the Creator.* His being is a being-given, by God and indeed in some way also by other creatures in relation to God. My being and acting, precisely in their active character and indeed in their nature as free, bear a memory of this order of relations initiated in me by God and by other creatures in God. I truly participate in their giving from the beginning, but always first as a receiver, as

---

24. Joseph Cardinal Ratzinger, *Values in a Time of Upheaval* (New York/San Francisco: Crossroad/Ignatius Press, 2006), pp. 91-93.

one whose essential spontaneity is re-sponsive. My most basic act is to give, but always through recuperation of my anterior being-given, a givenness that implies giftedness.[25] Or better, my most basic act is to receive myself *as participant in the givingness of another;* and this act of self-reception thus already itself indicates the first and basic form of creaturely generosity.

In a word, the truth of my being is this givenness by another of myself "in itself," and this givenness, or giftedness, establishes at once the truth of my being as "in itself" good.

What I am proposing relative to Murray's metaphysics, then, is that the human subject is originally constituted as a subject only as one whose being is given by another. The subject-self is exigent for exercising his own initiative, for determining himself, only from inside this anterior relation of being given by another, hence as a gift from another. The point is both that the subject is truly constituted in himself, in a way that is essentially ordered to and already involves his own act of self-possession, and that the subject is so constituted only as *at the same time,* anteriorly, *given to himself by another*.[26]

---

25. In a word: every being is inherently good, good-in-itself, because it is always-first loved by God (see 1 John 4) and by others, indeed by others by virtue of their common responsive participation in God's act of love. Being given by another, a relation that is inscribed within the creature even as, in and through this relation, God makes each individual creature be ("autonomously") in the first place, signifies the truth of being as also good, because the basic truth about being is now, *eo ipso,* that it is lovable. This order of being as lovable qua true and true qua lovable is called transcendental (in a Thomistic, not Kantian, sense), because it is an order of being that is *given* as *in itself* true and lovable. Here is the root reason why "facts" in their most radical sense are at once "values," in the modern parlance. The fact-value dichotomy of modernity, in other words, has its roots in a forgetfulness of being and ultimately of God.

Cf. in this connection the statement of philosopher Ferdinand Ulrich: "The fundamental act, which is *'super-fluous'* because it is not a desire to have, consists in self-surrender. This is the new beginning of freedom. In this new beginning, being oneself consists in receiving oneself, and to bear fruit is to be the receiver of another's gift. Thanks is the fundamental act of finite freedom. It is the only adequate form in which being livingly brings to birth the gift of its own release into freedom. . . . The fundamental act of the creature accrues to itself as the gift of the Other. Therefore, it can be taken up by another (creature) in a communion which gives him room to be free. In one and the same movement the gift is given and I am in it both as myself — because the gift is present in me — *and* as one who has been given away and distributed. To pray is to ponder this event" ("A Dangerous Reflection on the Fundamental Act of the Creature," *Communio: International Catholic Review* 23, no. 1 [Spring 1996]: 36-46, at 45-46). On the above, see the note that follows.

26. See here the helpful article by Adrian Walker, "Personal Singularity and the *Communio Personarum:* A Creative Development of Thomas Aquinas's Doctrine of *Esse*

What I am proposing therefore does not deny the principle of an autonomous subject, or the freedom and rights tied to an autonomous subject. It merely begins with a subject who is already, in his very constitution as a subject, a responsive participant — that is, an *active qua responsive* participant — in a community initiated by another, by the Creator, *ex nihilo*. It follows that the subject's primitive act of self-possession cannot but be already a participatory sign and expression of the subject's *being given* in community. In a word, the subject, in the exercise of his own proper and just so far spontaneous subjectivity, bears a memory of the order of all those to whom he is constitutively related: God, family, other persons, the world. The truth of this order of relations is never first or simply an **object** of choice but always operates objectively *within* the *free subject* of choice and his very *act* of choosing, and thus in a significant sense co-constitutes the act of the subject.[27]

The foregoing comments contain only an outline of the fuller argument that needs to be made, but they will suffice to indicate the terms of the presuppositions informing my criticism of the juridical state. The crucial issue, in light of the texts cited and given the nature of that criticism, concerns what is the link of my ontology with the idea of God and indeed the Christian doctrine of creation. The ontology presupposed in my criticism requires faith and revelation for its full and proper understanding.

The question thus is whether this provenance of my argument as a matter of principle undermines what I take to be the argument's distinctly philosophical hence reasonable character. My response, consistent with the positions of the authors of the texts cited in this section, is that it does not: that the Christian doctrine of creation, rightly understood, bears a definite

---

Commune," *Communio* 31, no. 3 (Fall 2004): 457-79; and also his unpublished statement, "The Unity of *Esse Creatum*." Needless to say, there is much that must be further unpacked here. The burden of my argument is simply that we must avoid, in our basic understanding of human being, juxtaposing being a subject in itself and being given by another, in such a way that what Walker calls communionality, and my chapter calls relationality, can only follow upon and thus be simply-originally the expression of a person's conscious acts of love, or exercise of freedom. As I intend to show later, such an understanding of human being implies precisely the ontological self-centeredness and indeed "ontological pelagianism" that lie at the root of liberalism's vulnerability to a "dictatorship of relativism" and a "totalitarianism" of the strong over the weak. On the issues raised here, see also Martin Bieler's "*Analogia Entis* as an Expression of Love According to Ferdinand Ulrich" (unpublished manuscript); D. C. Schindler, "What's the Difference? On the Metaphysics of Participation in Plato, Plotinus, and Aquinas," *Nova et Vetera* 5, no. 3 (2007): 583-618.

27. See D. C. Schindler, "Freedom Beyond Our Choosing," pp. 639-40.

ontological, hence distinctly philosophical, meaning, which is therefore in principle accessible to reason. The pertinent point, in other words, is that being as such can be shown *reasonably* to carry the implication of a giver and just so far to reveal itself as a participatory sign of this giver, and thus of God, *even if this God is only grasped implicitly or confusedly.*[28]

Indeed, we should take note here of Benedict XVI's recent emphasis on secularity.[29] For Benedict, the *secular as such* already implies a sense of being as gift. That is the implication of the *anamnesis* of God built into the foundational structure of our being. Contrary to what some may surmise, this emphasis on secularity does not signal a departure from Ratzinger's earlier work, for example, his commentary on the anthropology of *Gaudium et Spes*. On the contrary, it merely renders explicit a new accent of the truth that is fundamental for his argument in this commentary: that the order of gift and love which is fully and most properly revealed only in Jesus Christ, and fully realized only by Christ's supernatural gift of grace, finds an echo in the heart of every human being, Christian or non-Christian. In other words, human reason is understood adequately only when reason takes account somehow of all that is implied in the human being's *givenness:* his reality as gift, his call to generous love, his constitutive-natural love of God.[30] As we will see, this affirmation is crucial relative to any idea of "Christian secularity" that would assert a clean line between a religious-metaphysical reason and a properly public or "political" reason, such that political reason could be adequately understood in abstraction from the metaphysical-religious roots of reason. But I will come back to this important point later.

V.

Let us then return to Murray's argument. The metaphysics of constitutive relations we have sketched helps to bring further into relief the fact that his putative purely formal sense of rights, with its foundations in man's exigence to act on his own initiative, expresses a metaphysics that differs significantly from this metaphysics of constitutive relations. What does Murray's understanding of the self and its rights imply with respect to instrumentalism?

---

28. See Henri de Lubac's recovery of the tradition on this point: *The Discovery of God* (Grand Rapids: Eerdmans, 1996).

29. For further discussion of secularity, see section VI.

30. See Benedict XVI's encyclicals *Deus Caritas Est* (2005) and *Caritas in Veritate* (2009), as well as his 2006 lecture at the University of Regensburg.

Certainly we must be careful in imputing instrumentalism in a facile way to Murray. As indicated, he is unequivocal in stressing that man bears a transcendent relation to God, that there is a transcendent order of truth, and that man's conscience is bound to the moral order. Further, it is axiomatic for him that some form of a natural law consensus in civil society is necessary if the justice of the juridical state is to be sustained. At the same time, he says that all of this is, strictly speaking, juridically irrelevant. What alone is juridically relevant is man's exigence to act on his own initiative. It is this truth about man that alone founds rights in their properly juridical sense, as immunities: as demands above all for *protection from* others and their possibly intrusive behavior.

What is juridically relevant, in a word, does not properly include man's *given order of relations* to God and others, but only the freedom or free space to enact these relations: not freedom as at once an order *already naturally given and received*, but freedom *as a formal exercise of choice*, and order thus as something logically *yet-to-be-enacted* by freedom.

The point is that Murray takes this metaphysics of the human person, of freedom and relation, to be true. That is, it is because this is the most basic natural structure of the person that rights for him are correctly conceived as essentially formal or juridical in nature. The enforcement of justice as the securing of rights in this sense affords maximum freedom to all members of society because the most obvious and all-inclusive thing one can say about a human being is that he is exigent to act on his own initiative. This argument of Murray's is adequate, however, only if the difference between a constitutively given relation, on the one hand, and a first self-enacted relation, on the other, affects little or not at all the nature of either the self's freedom or the self's relation to God and others, or indeed the nature of the self, God, and others.

Let me then qualify further. Murray, as we have seen, clearly affirms that a transcendent relation to God is something *given to, not first created by* man. However true, even axiomatic, this is for him, the pertinent question is whether he takes adequate account of the fact that this relation, given to the self *in its original constitution*, is thereby presupposed in the self's original act, in a way that makes a difference to the nature of that act.

Thus a self that remembers its constitutive givenness, or being-given by another, bears a movement outward that is anteriorly patient and marked by interiority. It is this ontologically rooted patience and interiority, this primitive "letting be," that logically enables the self's seeing the other first *as genuinely other*, as true and good qua *given in itself*, and not first as merely the object of the self's formally conceived human agency. A self understood first as the *original enactor* of relation, on the other hand, bears a movement outward that, *eo ipso*, lacks the ontologically rooted patience and interiority that derive from the self's original being-given in relation. The difference is crucial: a constitutively related self is creative only as anteriorly responsive — creative only in a *filial* manner; a self understood as the first giver of relation, on the contrary, is by definition creative in an *originate* manner. The former self's relating to the other begins in a "letting be" of what has always already been initiated by another, while the latter self's relating begins in a constructing of what is always logically yet-to-be-initiated by the self.

It is the self understood in this latter sense that stands at the heart of what I have termed instrumentalism.[31]

But let me amplify the meaning of this instrumentalism in more technical terms. First of all, a relation to others that is not first enacted by the self *responsively* is wrongly ontologically "ego-centric":[32] such a relation is, *eo ipso*, precipitously centered in the agency of the self. But this is to say, secondly, and for the same reason, that the movement of the self toward the other is also precipitous. Such a self, in other words, is at the same time wrongly ontologically "ex-centric." In a word, the self is *simultaneously* wrongly weighted toward itself ("introverted"), and thus wrongly self-interested; and "extroverted," and thus turned too quickly outward, with the consequence that this outward movement becomes of its inner logic manipulative of the other in the interests of the self.

Of course, the very notion of an acting self cannot but presuppose some significant sense of ontological self-centricity, or self-centeredness,

---

31. Let me be clear: a constitutively given relation is always also a self-enacted relation. As indicated above, the human being is an *order of relations* as at once, in itself, a *free agent*. Indeed, a constitutive relation rightly understood implies a circumincessive unity of being-given and enacting. The crucial issue turns on what is taken as the most basic (ontological, not chronological) *order* within this circumincessive unity. Only an enacting that remembers its anterior being-given suffices for a giving or acting that would be legitimately autonomous, in the manner proper to a creature. A constitutive relation rightly understood thus presupposes, indeed demands, the self's exigence for acting freely and with its own initiative, *albeit in a responsively creaturely* way; while an originally self-enacted, or contracted, relation presupposes a freedom that cannot logically recuperate the constitutively responsive relation entailed by creatureliness: because this latter relation is *eo ipso* precipitously creative.

32. Again, it is important to see that the point here bears primarily on the logic as distinct from the conscious intention of the self, however much an ontological self-centeredness disposes one toward a psychological self-centeredness.

and ex-centricity, or other-centeredness. The relevant point is that, on a reading of relation as first contracted, the self is ego-centric and ex-centric in a way that is prematurely *self-interested and constructive* or *technologistic* in its relations. On a reading of relation as constitutively given, on the contrary, the ego-centricity and ex-centricity are formed first in *letting be:* the self receives both the other and the self as they are in themselves, inside their anteriorly given relation to each other. On a contractual reading, the self's acting is thus *first restless* for relation; on a constitutive reading, the self's acting is *first restful* in the relation that has always already been initiated.[33]

The point, then, in a word, is that only an acting that recuperates God's originally creative act in and through which the self and the other are in the first place is able to receive both the other and the self as truly and radically *given*, hence in terms of what each really is *in itself*. Only such an acting, as originally *patient*, is able thus to be *generous* simultaneously with respect to the other and to one's self, *as* the self goes out toward the other. In contrast, an acting conceived first in would-be purely formal terms, as simply spontaneous in nature, can never begin restfully in a relation between the self and the other that is already given; it can on the contrary only be always, at root, restless for and engaged in the ongoing process of constructing this relation. In a word, on this latter reading, the self and the other have their most basic reality, each in relation to the other, not as they *are given in themselves*, but only as *precipitously self-interested instruments of mutual construction*. It is here, once again, that we arrive at the ontological meaning of what we are terming instrumentalism.[34]

---

33. To be sure, on a constitutive reading of relation, the self remains restless for deepening this relation that has always already been initiated. In this case, however, a rest-filled *stasis* abides, providing stability for what is also this relation's always *ec-static* movement toward God and others. Or better, recalling the restlessness for God affirmed by St. Augustine, the self's ec-static movement toward God is structurally patient: it is a movement that generously awaits and precisely does not demand the revelation of the other. This point is of fundamental importance for entering reasonably into the debate regarding the relation between nature and grace.

34. Once again, however, it is crucial to take note of the qualifiers. It is not the case that generosity itself does not permit and even demand a kind of "instrumentalizing," or usefulness, in the relations between the self and others. On the contrary, generosity is *diffusivum sui*: of its inner logic, generosity demands that the self be available to others and share itself with others, in *service* to them. An acting rooted in memory of an already given order of relations, in contrast to a contractual acting, springs from and is informed by an anterior letting be of the other and the self and above all of God. And only the former acting

I know of no version of liberalism that integrates the idea of constitutive relations adequately into its sense of human being and acting, and thus would argue that no version of liberalism can logically avoid the problem of instrumentalism in this sense.[35]

Regarding Murray himself, then: it would be irresponsible to accuse him of this instrumentalism in any obvious or vulgar sense. On the contrary, as we have emphasized, he is unequivocal in his affirmation of a transcendent order of truth and goodness having its origin in the creator God. The critical claim I am making is a fine but decisively important one: Murray's privileging of man's formal exigence for initiative as alone relevant to the juridical order of society leads him logically, contrary to his own best intentions, to a collusion with the instrumentalism characteristic of liberal public order.[36] His idea of the human act, and of the juridical or-

---

is logically able really to rest *in* the other and the self as they are first given in themselves, and thereby to respect the root meaning of the other (and the self) in a truly generous way that properly integrates the dimension of usefulness. The point, then, in sum, is that acts of the self in relation to the other (and vice versa), on a contractual view of relation, are marked by a mutual usefulness that is onto-logically premature: because lacking the patient interiority necessary to see and rest in the other (the other, the self, and the Creator) *as given* and thus as true and good *in themselves*.

35. It is worth noting in this connection that liberalism as conceived in these ontological terms stands not only at the heart of modernity, but also at the juncture of modernity *and* what is termed postmodernity. A false ego-centricity (modernity) implies a false ex-centricity (postmodernity), and vice versa. The two are in the end but variant expressions, albeit from opposite directions, of the same onto-logic of instrumentalism. Modernity in its proper meaning is already a movement logically into postmodernity: modern self-centeredness and postmodern "self-lessness" are each presupposed dialectically in the original meaning of the other. It will be important to remember this in our discussion of the paradoxes of the liberal state.

36. It is sometimes said that the Catholic Church in the nineteenth century was too harsh in her criticisms of liberalism, and that the Second Vatican Council has adopted a more nuanced and indeed favorable position in this regard. Although this matter can scarcely be treated adequately in the present context, I would say that I agree that the Church was too harsh, but only insofar as the terms of her criticisms were too moralistic. What I would say, in other words, is that when and insofar as the terms are ontological (the ontological terms presupposed in an adequate view of creation as developed at Vatican II and the pontificates of John Paul II and Benedict XVI), what we should see, rather, is a deeper acceptance by the Church, in the documents of the Council and these pontificates, of the emphasis on freedom and rights that emerges in modernity, *simultaneous with* a radical critique of the liberal reading accorded freedom and rights. In this connection, we might recall that the problem of "Americanism" raised by the Church at the turn of the twentieth century was widely dismissed as a "phantom heresy." What the present argument implies, on the con-

der bound up with this idea, lacks an adequate sense of man's constitutive relationality to God and others, and of the human act's constitutive participation in the order implied in this relationality. The unintended result is an ontological vulnerability to the defective notions of freedom, rights, intelligence, and indeed religion in the public order that I have noted above and that are essentially tied to a lack of this constitutive relationality and participation.

Let me again stress: Murray would surely insist here that, however much instrumentalism might in fact characterize the juridical order on his conception, the relevant point is that he has distinguished between the orders of the state and civil society. And, in this context, he presupposes that the latter bears proper responsibility for developing the theological, metaphysical, and moral habits of life and mind necessary to protect society from an instrumentalist way of life. Now, as I pointed out already at the outset of this chapter, the distinction between state and society embodies an important truth. The problem, nevertheless, is that Murray's understanding of this distinction is tied to an essentially juridical idea of the state, even as the juridical idea of the state is tied to a formalist conception of human action, a conception that Murray is defending as a member of civil society. *Murray's distinction between state and civil society is mediated by a single metaphysical claim of truth: his appeal to the idea of the juridical state is but one — the political-constitutional — expression of what he takes to be the metaphysical truth about man. Which is to say, the state-society **distinction** as understood by Murray itself signifies and expresses, and is thus given **unity** in terms of, the sort of metaphysical claim of truth that his own juridical idea of statecraft demands be left to society, however much the formalistic nature of this claim tends to obscure the fact that the claim is properly metaphysical. And, once again, it is just this formalism that we have seen lies at the root of an instrumentalist conception of human action.*

In the next section, I will discuss the dangerous paradoxes that ensue when and insofar as the distinction between state and society is mediated, mostly unwittingly, by a formalist-instrumentalist metaphysics. Murray himself would, to be sure, vigorously resist the patterns of life and mind embodied in these paradoxes. The burden of my argument is simply that

---

trary, is that at the heart of the problem of Americanism lies the profoundly serious problem of liberalism with its instrumentalist ontology (anthropology), a problem that needs to be addressed in terms of the ontology of love carried in the Christian doctrine of creation. Of course, as indicated, the point introduced here presupposes a reading of Vatican II and the recent pontificates, the main lines of which I indicate briefly later in this chapter.

the formalism of his own understanding of the state, mediated by the formalism of his understanding of the metaphysics of human action, affords him no way of mounting a *consistently reasonable* challenge to these patterns of life. Given a formalist metaphysics, attempted challenges to the problems of an instrumentalist culture come *logically too late*. Which is to say, they provide what can now be only, at best, moralistic resistance.

Recall, then, in light of the above, that Murray reads the religious articles of the First Amendment of the United States Constitution as "articles of peace," as distinct from "articles of faith." He contends that these religious articles contain no doctrine of truth and that, if they did, this doctrine would likely be some amalgam of the Enlightenment and (Puritan) Protestantism. What we have shown is that his interpretation of these "articles of peace" in fact assumes a definite claim of truth about the nature of human being and acting in relation to God, and thus "articles of faith." Although this cannot be demonstrated adequately here in historical terms, I would suggest, in terms of Murray's own options as indicated, that the ontology implied in his reading of America's official conception of freedom and rights coheres more readily with the ontology of modernity as expressed in the Enlightenment, or indeed in America's peculiar mixture of Puritan and Enlightened thought,[37] than it does with the relational ontology set forth above.[38] In the absence of such a demonstration, it will suffice here simply to say that Murray's defense of a (putatively) purely formal human act, an autonomous and spontaneous act construed as devoid of any ordered content deriving from anteriorly given relations, echoes metaphysical tendencies paradigmatically expressed in Descartes, who stands at the core of modern thought as realized in America.[39]

---

37. For a classic statement regarding how the theology of the Calvinist tradition in America (Puritanism) leads to a "rationalizing" of worldly activity, and thus to a sense of autonomy, one that draws heavily on thinkers like Descartes and Bacon, see Max Weber's *The Spirit of Protestantism and the Rise of Capitalism* (Oxford: Routledge, 1987). As Weber shows, this rationalizing tendency emerges as a way not of securing but of signifying salvation. Perhaps it should be mentioned here that, contrary to a frequent misinterpretation, Weber does not claim that Puritanism is the exclusive cause of capitalism, but only that there exists an inner logic between Puritanism and capitalism in its distinct modern sense. Apropos of the Puritans' rationalizing of worldly activity, see also Robert K. Merton's "classic" study of the Puritans' embrace of seventeenth-century science: "Science, Technology, and Society in Seventeenth Century England," *Osiris* 4 (1938): 360-532, at 414-95 (Chapters 4 through 6).

38. See the concluding part of section VI for indications of the developments in and since the Second Vatican Council, pertinent to this relational ontology.

39. On the Cartesian tendencies of American culture, see, for example, Alexis de

But let us turn now to consider what we termed at the outset the paradoxes bound up with the liberal state's unintended instrumentalist metaphysics.

VI.

It is important first of all to emphasize again that the following criticisms call attention to what are termed paradoxes because of what I presume to be a serious ambiguity resident in the heart of liberalism. In other words, it is true that the intentions and achievements of liberalism and its juridical state embed truths signaling various advances relative to premodern societies, even as it is true also that these achievements are deeply flawed in their inner logic and thus remain highly ambiguous with respect to the ideas of (religious) freedom, rights, and reason lying at the heart of such achievements.

In our approach to the criticism that seems indicated, then, there are two tendencies that must as a matter of principle be avoided. On the one hand, there can be no question simply of rejecting liberalism. This is so because each of its achievements continues to embed important truths of the natural order, however distorted in their liberal meaning and realization.[40] On the other hand, because criticism of liberalism rightly conceived is not a matter of simple rejection, it does not follow that the needed criticism is therefore merely "partial" in character, as though it were possible simply to isolate one or another aspect of liberal freedom (for example) in its distortion, and correct things by removing that aspect and *adding* something

---

Tocqueville's well-known judgment: "America is . . . the one country in the world where the precepts of Descartes are least studied and best followed. That should not be surprising. Americans do not read Descartes's works because their social state turns them away from speculative studies, and they follow his maxims because this same social state naturally disposes their minds to adopt them" (*Democracy in America,* trans. Harvey C. Mansfield and Delba Winthrop [Chicago: University of Chicago Press, 2000], Part One, Chapter 1, "On the Philosophic Method of the Americans," p. 403).

40. The root assumption is thus that the integrity of nature and the natural order is not destroyed by sin, even as nature is always in the actual order of history profoundly affected by sin, including sin in its structural sense as developed in the pontificate of John Paul II. This assumption holds as well with respect to the order of being in its convertibility with truth and goodness. Such a claim is basic to a metaphysics consistent with Catholicism. For a limited discussion on nature and history that is pertinent here, see "The Significance of World and Culture for Moral Theology: *Veritatis Splendor* and the Nature of the Body," pp. 219-41 in this volume.

else in its place. This is so because the whole of freedom is not the sum of fragmented parts, nor does the nature of freedom exist apart from its history, and thus from the sin that is inevitably present in all human and cosmic history. To be sure, there is much presupposed here regarding the relation between wholes and parts and between nature and history that cannot be dealt with thematically in the present context. I wish merely to highlight the fact that criticism with respect to liberalism, adequately conceived, is both subtler and more radical than often assumed.

My presupposition, then, is that the very freedom and rights and reason that have generated and expressed the unique achievements of modernity bear within them, in their liberal articulation, a logic of instrumentalism tending toward nothing less than a peculiar kind of nihilism. My purpose in the remainder of this chapter is to outline the sense in which this is so.

It is thus precisely inside liberalism's highest achievements that we discover the ontological roots of its dangerous paradoxes. I will treat the paradoxes under the following four headings, the meaning of each one of which is fully understood only in relation with all the others: the state-society distinction; the problem of relativism; the problem of totalitarianism; and finally, the church-state distinction.

(1) The State-Society Distinction

The achievement secured by this distinction is that of a limited state. The *state*, on a liberal reading, is not the source of and intends not to impose the truth, but only to protect the equal freedom of all members of *society* to make their own best argument for what they hold dear and would like to see enshrined in public policy. It is up to institutions like the church, the family, and education to ensure that truth and virtue maintain a public presence in society, in a way supportive of constitutional democratic justice.

The civil unity promoted by the juridical state, in a word, is intended to be minimal, in order to permit a maximum freedom, and hence pluralism, among its citizens.

The problem is that the state harbors an unwitting claim of truth that undermines both the rightful unity and the rightful pluralism necessary for a genuinely "peaceful" civil community.[41] How so?

41. It should be pointed out, though the point cannot be adequately treated here, that

As we have indicated, the liberal state sanctions a would-be merely formal understanding of human freedom that cloaks its metaphysical "substance" of instrumentalism. This formalist instrumentalism has its roots in liberal "doctrine." The juridical *state*, in other words, expresses the formalist conception of human agency which liberal members of *society* have institutionalized qua state, and which this state thus enforces in its turn, as the governing institution of liberalism. The juridical state, *in* its very hallmark intention of a *dualistic distinction between* state and society, therefore hides its *own identity with* a liberal society, via the latter's formalist ontology. In its very separation of the function claimed to be proper to itself, which is the enforcement of "articles of peace," the juridical state hiddenly absorbs into itself, and thereby enforces, liberal society's "articles of faith." The civil community promoted and protected by the juridical state thus, in a word, tends always and only to be a liberal civil community, the nature of which is essentially instrumentalist.

This of course does not mean that non-instrumentalist communities cannot and do not exist inside the juridical state. It means merely that they arise *per accidens* relative to the logic of this state and its liberal doctrine. Such communities are free to exist; the point is that they have public-reasonable or constitutional relevance only insofar as they project themselves into the public order in "peaceful" or "political" terms: only insofar as they defend their activities in terms of freedom and rights in the dominant liberal, or formal-juridical, sense.

Note, however: the problem raised here regarding the juridical state is not that it bears a metaphysical "substance" in terms of which it tends to foster a certain kind of civil society. Indeed, this is a main presupposition of my own argument: *every state* will foster such a unity, in the sense

---

the idea of being as gift defended in the present argument, with its hallmark affirmation of a mutual coinherence of truth and freedom, in and through love, itself demands not only a unity but a pluralism within civil society. Such a mutual coinherence, in other words, implies that truth itself, as free, bears within it a principle of novelty: the very "uni-versality" of truth (its "turning toward unity") just so far bears a logic of "di-versity" ("turning away from one," hence toward a plurality). Understanding that this is so is crucial for my criticism, which is not that modern liberal societies harbor too much pluralism, or not only that; but that they harbor at the same time too much unity: they are too monolithic. Indeed, that is just the point: the mostly hidden metaphysical assumptions of modern liberal societies, sanctioned by the modern liberal-juridical state, force these societies into a unity that is too closed, while *simultaneously* fracturing them into a pluralism that is too dispersive, and the result is a tendency toward a totalitarian logic of nihilism. On this last point, see also the following note.

that it will mediate its constitutional authority to civil society via some metaphysical claim of truth which in fact has already been embodied in members of society. The relation between state and society, in other words, can never be rightly conceived dualistically, or extrinsically, but only as a distinction within some anterior metaphysical unity. The problem I am raising regarding the juridical state thus concerns rather the *nature* of this state's metaphysical claims coincident with the *hiddenness* of those claims.

Thus, on the one hand, the metaphysical "truth" that mediates its exercise of authority and sets the criteria for public reasonableness is that of the formalist instrumentalism which, *eo ipso*, always displaces the truth about man in his constitutively given order in favor of man as a prematurely self-interested agent of construction. Again, this does not mean that the state does not permit or indeed even encourage members of society to think and act however they wish, including in ways they take to express the intrinsic truth about man in his original givenness. The point, rather, is that only prematurely self-interested and constructive agents, exercising what are logically now a voluntaristic freedom and a calculative, technical intelligence supported where helpful by a positivistic religion, will be recognized as publicly reasonable and thus as capable of making a legitimate demand on the body politic as such.

At the same time, liberalism's formalist metaphysics is peculiar in that it renders itself invisible as a substantive truth claim, as a matter of its inner logic. This metaphysics shifts attention away from its own implied substantive claim of truth toward what liberalism claims to be, and what indeed *appears* to be, the *purely formal* acts and *open process* whereby each member or group of society develops its own claims, consistent with the requirements of justice as fairness.

The upshot is that the juridical state, through its "peaceful" political order and canons of public reasonableness, blindly and just so far "coercively" imposes unity on civil society in terms of a formalist-instrumentalist conception of the human being, even as this formalist unity unfolds of its inner logic into a pluralism involving an endless deferral of the truth about man as he is *in himself*, as a *naturally given order* (of a substantial-person-in-itself, in-relation). The juridical state fosters a civil society whose community is "closed" by virtue of its hidden metaphysical unity ("truth" *as formalistically conceived human act*), even as this formalistic "unity" logically promotes a "pluralistic openness" consisting in end-less process ("truth" *as deferral of the naturally given order of the human being "in itself" and as at once related intrinsically to God and others).*

Hence, in sum, the paradox: citizens of the juridical state remain, so to speak, procedurally free without limit, even as a hidden formalist-instrumentalist unity "closes" their freedom by virtue of its reductive idea of freedom, thus rendering the "openness" characteristic of this freedom just so far repressive. The juridical state's maximum freedom, which in one sense is a real maximization of freedom (as formal act), gives way simultaneously to paradoxical closure: to what is at once the "closed unity" ("presence") characteristic of modernity *and* the "repressive deferral" ("absence") characteristic of postmodernity.

The content of the juridical state's metaphysical truth, with its implicit way of "imposing" unity and pluralism in civil society, thus renders that state "competent" in the wrong sense with respect to the truth. The juridical state and liberal civil society bind themselves invisibly into an *a priori* unity around formalist-instrumentalist "truth," even as the invisibility of this unified truth is such that it logically disposes members of civil society to think that they are affirming a clear separation between state and society and thus permitting maximal freedom on the part of each member of society to develop his or her own truth, subject only to the demands of public order. Indeed, this invisible *a priori* unity between the juridical state and liberal civil society around formalist-instrumentalist "truth" covertly involves the state itself in arrogating to itself the role of *originating source* of truth.[42]

---

42. Thus, once again, we need to subject to scrutiny any interpretations of modern liberal societies that begin by assuming that these societies are pluralistic, in simple contrast to what such interpretations take to be the more "monolithic" character of premodern societies — a claim which is a staple in the works of Catholic thinkers like Michael Novak, for example. It is rather the case that premodern and modern societies are monistic and pluralistic in different ways. Evidently, premodern societies make their metaphysical unity more explicit in terms of political order, whereas modern liberal societies, assuming what they take to be purely formal conceptions of human being and action, deny that their political order bears any such metaphysical unity. The question arising from my argument is whether the invisibility of liberalism's formalist-instrumentalist metaphysical unity is in the end less "repressive" in its imposition of "unity" on society, for all of that imposition's hidden character. The implication of my argument is in fact that modern repressiveness is in crucial ways more virulent than in earlier societies. But, to see how this is so, we need to look further into the peculiar violence promoted by the liberal democratic state with respect to the truth, in its "dictatorship of relativism," and with respect to the weakest members of society, in its inversion into a "totalitarianism of the strong over the weak." On this, see the argument that follows in the text.

But, to see the further, concrete implications of the paradox asserted here, we turn to the problem of relativism.

(2) The Problem of Relativism

The logic just described implicates the juridical state in relativism. Key again is the unity of metaphysical "truth" that hiddenly informs this state in its conception and administration of justice as fairness: a unity provided by the single ontological "truth" of instrumentalism. The public-political order is properly concerned with justice only in terms of securing equal space for each person to *exercise an agency conceived in terms of formalistic freedom and intelligence.*

The juridical state thus grants maximum political freedom to citizens to make public-legal arguments, even as it tacitly ensures, by virtue of its covert instrumentalism, that all substantive-truthful contents of those arguments will be treated merely as expressions of a would-be purely formally understood human act: as instruments of a freedom conceived in voluntaristic terms, supported by an intelligence conceived in reductively technical terms. The juridical state can never of its inner logic end in anything claiming to be true or good *in itself* or *for its own sake*, qua *naturally given*. To be sure, citizens are free to claim things as intrinsically true and good, but such claims, from the perspective of what is publicly reasonable or constitutionally relevant, can logically be treated only as competing expressions of self-interest by purely formally and constructively conceived agents. Thus the relative "truth" or "goodness" of these expressions will be judged only on the basis of their *effectiveness* — in strategic or rhetorical terms, for example, as distinct from their cogency in terms of inherent reasonable substance.

The liberal state thus tends to turn all "publicly reasonable" arguments into matters of dialogue and discussion, the logic of which is to generate more dialogue and discussion, without end: without resolving itself

---

Needless to say, I do not mean by the foregoing to deny the pluralism of liberal societies, which is genuine and indeed obvious at one level: one need only note the existence within liberal nations of a great multiplicity of ethnic groups. I mean only to direct attention to the unity hiddenly operative within such groups, insofar as they would realize a publicly reasonable presence in society. The point, in other words, is simply that the issue of pluralism in modern liberal societies can be addressed in non-question-begging fashion only by coming to terms simultaneously with the tacitly assumed metaphysical unity of liberal societies.

in any significant sense in terms of the truth in itself. Dialogue on liberal terms presupposes a prematurely extroverted and egocentric self whose arguments cannot but tend of their inner nature to be manipulative for reasons indicated in the previous section. It is no accident that "publicly reasonable" arguments in a liberal society rely primarily on political strategies and cosmetic marketing techniques, on forms of communication and knowledge that enhance speed and surface interaction, and on instruments that facilitate efficient information gathering and control of data.

Regarding the peculiar relativism fostered inside the juridical state, then: it is important to see first of all that the fair-formal process of liberal justice bears a universality that is the opposite of relativism, insofar as every member of society is in principle equally protected in the formal exercise of his freedom and intelligence. The problem lies in the formalist-instrumentalist character of this universality. Justice involving a substantive, non-instrumentalist order of the truth of man as given in itself and for its own sake is *always relativized in advance* to justice as (would-be) merely fair-instrumental "form." This *a priori* relativizing through instrumentalist fairness, *eo ipso*, does "violence" to this *order of truth* as *given-in-itself* and to *substantively reasonable* arguments on its behalf.

It is just this universal justice as formal fairness, coincident with the covert closure and hence "violence" of this justice to man as a *naturally given order* of truth and goodness, which involves the liberal-juridical state in what Joseph Ratzinger has termed a "dictatorship of relativism." The very "truth" that is publicly-politically affirmed and protected in the liberal-juridical state disperses of its inner logic into an endless deferral of any metaphysical "truth" but the empty, paradoxically nihilistic "truth" of metaphysical "formalism." (Again, liberal-*modern* justice is the ontological beginning of what ends in liberal-*postmodern* justice.)

But note the peculiar nature of "dictatorship" as thus realized in the liberal-juridical state. Such a "dictatorship," with its attendant "violence," is of its inner dynamic not overt. It is to be properly enforced, in other words, not by tanks, but by lawyers: by those whose responsibility it is to protect the equal right of all citizens to the exercise of freedom and intelligence.[43] It is a "dictatorship" resulting in the first instance in the dispatch

43. Cf. in this connection Tocqueville's interesting discussion of what he takes to be America's peculiar vulnerability to a "tyranny of the majority," in *Democracy in America*, Part One, Chapters 7 and 8 (Mansfield translation, pp. 235-64). Apropos of this vulnerability, Tocqueville states that he does "not know any country where, in general, less independence of mind and genuine freedom of discussion reign than in America" (p. 243). In Chapter 8 he

of citizens who publicly contradict the instrumentalist view of truth and goodness, not to prison, but to the margins of the culture, all the while protecting the right of these citizens to a due formal process.

Hence the paradox peculiar to the liberal-juridical state in the matter of truth: such a state protects the virtually unlimited freedom and right (which are limited politically only by the demands of public order) of each citizen equally to seek his own truth and argue publicly on its behalf. This unlimited freedom, however, is mediated covertly to society via an instrumentalism that *eo ipso* does violence to the truth and goodness of things in their defenseless givenness, as well as to the arguments made in terms of truth and goodness so understood. The liberal-juridical state promotes a human conscious act understood to consist most basically, for all public-reasonable purposes, in extroverted, self-interested movement which by definition is unable to see and rest in the meaning of things as *given in itself:* a movement which thus signals a drift toward meaninglessness, and hence toward the frenetic boredom that inevitably fills space vacated by meaning.[44]

---

notes characteristics of America that temper this vulnerability, notably the country's absence of "administrative centralization." (Briefly: Tocqueville distinguishes between "governmental," which indicates the right to command things, establish the right principles of government, and regulate the great interests of the country; and "administrative," which involves the executing of the details of application, and descending to the limit of individual interests [p. 250].) From the perspective of our own argument, it needs to be asked whether this distinction between "governmental" and "administrative" centralization can be sustained as meaningful, at least over time, given the formal-technical nature of public reason and institutional authority as conceived in liberalism. For the point is that the formal-technical nature, or what may be called the technological form, of America's public reason and institutional authority bears an inner dynamic for the multiplication of procedures and rules and laws, precisely as distinct from the formation of virtue and other interior habits of the mind, in response to problems of civil order. The technological form of America's liberal public reason, that is, unfolds of its inner logic into more and better machinery in terms of which citizens can be governed more efficiently. In a word, it seems to me difficult to exaggerate the extent to which technology, in form and content, has homogenized American patterns of life and thought as embodied in its dominant public institutions, not only political but also economic and educational. The work of twentieth-century Canadian philosopher George Grant is important for showing how this is so in the liberal culture of North America.

44. We may therefore also say that habits of the patient interiority necessary to see and judge things for what they truly are, and of the wonder that demands leisure and leads toward worship, will occur only *per accidens* relative to the dominant logic of culture as fostered by the liberal-juridical state. Indeed, patterns of thought and behavior formed in such habits will be perceived as unserious, tending to obstruct career advancement in the public professions of politics, economics, law, science, medicine, and the academy.

The paradox of the liberal-juridical state, in sum, lies in what may be termed that state's virtually unlimited *"political"* freedom of thought and expression, which is nevertheless always undermined in advance by a formalism that covertly "dictates" a violence toward truth, thus blindly limiting freedom to only instrumentalist choices, and just so far enslaving freedom.

(3) The Problem of "Totalitarianism"

Human rights as conceived and defended by the liberal-juridical state are intended to be universal, extending equally to all members of society, and are conceived primarily in terms of immunity from coercion. Recognition of such rights is an important achievement of the liberal state. Once again, however, a problem arises in connection with this intended universality, by virtue of this state's understanding of the subject of rights: the human being conceived as formal-instrumental agent. Rights are considered to be essentially immunities because and insofar as the human being is viewed first as a "bare center" of initiative. In a word, as shown in connection with Murray, the demand for freedom understood primarily as an immunity from "coercive" or intrusive influence by others, an immunity that thus precedes responsibility toward others, flows from the self *qua formal-effective agent*.

The problem therefore has the same ontological roots as the liberal state's relativism. Rights conceived primarily as immunities presuppose a self who, as a would-be purely formal agent, is a wrongly self-interested constructive agent. The self is therefore a proper subject of rights, but only insofar as subjectivity elides with *enacting one's self*. Missing, in other words, is the crucial note of interiority, or interior worth, implied in the self's original *givenness* qua *being*-a-self, and thus being-*in-itself,* anterior to, albeit simultaneous with, its *acting* as a self.[45]

---

45. To be sure, there is no dualism of being and acting implied here: to be is to act. The point is simply that, although being and acting are circumincessive, being-given retains an absolute priority, even as the generosity inherent in being given my being implies my participation in this act of being-given, from the beginning of my existence. The problem regarding rights on their liberal reading, then, is not that my dignity is rooted in my exigence for initiative, but that this exigence itself needs to be seen as ontologically consequent upon, and thus intrinsically bound up with, my being given *to* myself. It is this being given to myself that constitutes me at once as a being *in* itself and as having my basic worth already in

The point is thus that the self, on the view presupposed in the justice of the liberal-juridical state, remains barren and thus without intrinsic worth except in terms of the exercise of initiative. The self's legitimate demand to be allowed space to exercise this initiative, which is to say, the implied original worth or goodness of the self that warrants this demand, turns first on the self's spontaneous effectiveness qua agent, not on what the self *is in* itself.

Rightly understood, this being-in-itself spontaneously enacts itself only insofar as it is also anteriorly *being-given* by God and others, and thus insofar as it receives itself from others. This enacting, in other words, implies of its inmost nature a responsive relation to others: the interiority of each self *in itself* is characterized at once by *receptive responsiveness to others*. It follows that recognition of the right of each self in itself to *immunity from coercion* by others, rightly conceived, needs to be tied from the beginning to the immanent demand within each self *to be responsive toward* others: rights are protections of the self from intrusive action by others inside what is an anterior responsibility of each self to serve the others.

Needless to say, there is much more to be said regarding the nature of rights. However, this suffices for my purpose here, which is to draw attention to the grave limits in the idea of rights guiding the juridical state's administration of justice. The liberal state's enforcement of justice as fairness presupposes the self as a logically self-interested effective agent:[46] the self as effective instrument of the demand for immunity. The danger here should be obvious: to the extent that a human self is not yet, or is no longer, manifestly given as an effective agent, capable thus itself of demanding immunity from coercive action, that self is not a full subject of rights. The instances where this is the case are not hard to ascertain: embryonic life in its earliest stages, the severely disabled, the terminally ill. Such human beings tend to become by definition invisible as proper subjects of rights. Indeed, looked at from the point of view of those who *are* properly subjects of rights in a liberal society, these "invisible" human beings risk becoming, especially to those closest to them, burdens that threaten the latter's own rights to immunity from "coercive" activity by others. Indeed, the technological mind-

---

my self *as so given.* Needless to say, further, we must have criteria whereby we can judge whether and when a self — a complete human being — exists. On this, see the several articles in *Communio: International Catholic Review* 31-32 (2004-2005) by myself, Adrian Walker, Robert Spaemann, and Roberto Colombo on the nature and beginning of human life and the ANT-OAR controversy.

46. Again, this self-interest is not necessarily intentional.

set, together with the technological capacity, of a liberal society tends of its inner logic to dispose those thus burdened to resolve the problem "compassionately," that is, via technically efficient acts of intelligence and in a way that enhances the ease and comfort, and reduces the pain and suffering, of themselves and the others who *are* acknowledged to be subjects of rights in a liberal society. A liberal society will be logically disposed, for example, to harvest early embryonic life in an effort to ensure that future disabled and seriously diseased human beings will be fully effective agents, or again to encourage the technical designing of babies for the same end.

Consistent with the logic of the liberal-juridical state's rights, then, and despite its universalist intention, only the "strong" (or "effective") human beings are unconditionally ruled in as proper subjects of rights, while the weakest of the weak human beings tend logically to be ruled out. Hence the paradoxical inversion of a liberal democratic state into totalitarianism: in its universal intention of securing equally the life and safety of all members of its civil community, this state by virtue of its hidden, largely unthematic, ontology imposes a logic of the power of the "strong" over the "weak." Human rights as affirmed by the juridical state thus are not, and as a matter of the inner, instrumentalist logic of liberalism can never be, universal.[47]

Hence the third paradox characteristic of the juridical state: on the one hand, its core achievement lies in the fact that it recognizes in principle the equal rights of all members of society, in a way that intends inclusion especially of those who are without power and influence. At the same time, this recognition is tacitly guided by a formalist instrumentalism that renders this state logically blind to those who truly *are* the weakest human

---

47. Some thinkers would insist that a sound argument against the state's permitting of abortion can be consistently made within the logic of liberal self-interest on its own terms, by pointing out what is claimed to be the logical inconsistency in supporting such legal permission. It is argued, in other words, that, did such permissive laws exist at the time prior to one's own birth, one's own life may have been at risk. The problem is that this argument begs the relevant point, which is that I already exist. The point, in other words, is that the ground for a legitimate appeal to self-interest on its liberal understanding has already been removed: the risk of loss of life by someone in a future generation carries no risk at all with respect to my own existence, and my own self-interest, here and now. On the contrary, the consistency of such an argument demands precisely a *transcendence* of self-interest to include generosity, and this not in a way that rejects self-interest (and hence not in the manner of altruism), but in a way rather which understands that acting toward an other for his own sake precisely *fulfills self*-interest while being simultaneously centered firmly and distinctly in the other who transcends the self.

beings: human beings who are not yet, or are no longer, manifestly acting subjects, subjects who thus exercise initiative on their own behalf.

In a word, the liberal state's peculiarly subtle violence against truth and goodness in their originally given "defenselessness," expressed in this state's instrumentalist relativism, is seen here to take its most virulent form in a logic of violence toward the truth and goodness of human beings in their originally given defenselessness: human beings simply as they are *given in themselves.*

We may say, therefore, in sum, that the juridical state's distinctive achievement regarding rights hides what is its most serious disorder: its peculiarly invisible violence against human beings in their original, defenseless givenness qua being.

Note in light of these remarks: to say as defenders of the juridical state are often wont to do, that the problems regarding innocent life indicated here are a function of civil society as distinct from the state is to beg the question. As shown above, the juridical state and its liberal civil society are indissolubly linked via the same liberal doctrine regarding the nature of the self, and this state and civil society are therefore mutually reinforcing. The liberal-juridical state enforces in its own constitutional-political way the very notion of the self that is generated by liberal doctrine.

Once we see this, we understand also that acceptance of the "peaceful-political" justice of the modern state is not, or at least not obviously, a "small price to pay" (Rhonheimer) in terms of moving beyond the overt violence of premodern societies with their explicit concern for the (religious, metaphysical) truth about man and his destiny. The violence we have noted in the case of the liberal state is not merely a moral aberration with respect to the logic of this state and its instrumentalist "truth." It is rather an expression of the heart of that logic, even as it contradicts this state's express intentions. It seems difficult, *prima facie,* to maintain that this violence of the liberal state, which to be sure is peculiarly quiet and "compassionate," is, in quantitative terms, less than that perpetrated in earlier societies.

But we turn now to the final paradox of the liberal-juridical state, that regarding its idea of the church-state distinction and the problem of secularity and secularism.

(4) The Distinction between State and Church

As indicated, the instrumentalist ontology implied by the juridical state presupposes a voluntarist idea of freedom and a technical, or technologistic, intelligence, and thus what becomes, in the matter of religion, a positivist approach to God and the church. My argument, then, apropos of the distinction between state and church, is that the juridical state in fact, however unwittingly, *fuses* the state with churches of a particular type, even as it thereby promotes a secularistic, as distinct from legitimately secular, civil society. How so?

In its administration of justice and in the public reasonableness presupposed by this justice, the juridical state favors those churches that assume religion to be most basically a *voluntary matter,* a sect, for example, rather than also, and more basically, an *order between man and God already given to man in his original constitution as a creature.*[48] The juridical state thereby, of its proper logic and in the name of non-establishment, implies "establishment," not of this or that particular church, but of churches of a definite kind, and just so far unwittingly constitutes itself as a competent source in determining, for all public-political purposes, how God is first encountered by human beings, and indeed thereby also the nature of the God that is so encountered.[49]

---

48. This of course does not mean the exercise of freedom is not essential also in the churches for whom man is naturally religious: a *homo religiosus.* Nor does it mean that those who conceive the church as an essentially voluntary society would deny the primacy of God as revealed in Jesus Christ in the original foundation of the church. The point rather is the ontological one concerning the sense in which relation to God, and hence the origin of religion, is already implied in man's nature. Insofar as this is the case, the church as it appears in history, precisely in its newness, its supernatural character as such, is understood as a fulfillment of that which the human heart seeks by nature. Insofar as relation to God is not implied in man's nature as created, the church as it appears in history becomes *ipso facto* a purely "positive" addition to what the human heart seeks by nature. The present section of this chapter explores the significant consequences of the difference indicated here, in terms of how the temporal and the secular are to be conceived in relation to God.

49. Lest the terms of my discussion in this section be misunderstood, let me note the following. Frank Lambert argues in *The Founding Fathers* that we must distinguish between what he terms, on the one hand, America's "planters" — those seventeenth-century New England Puritans and Chesapeake Anglicans who conceived America as a Christian nation, and who were through the founding period disposed toward an "established" church in the individual states — and, on the other hand, America's founders — those late-eighteenth-century men like Madison and Jefferson who conceived America as a haven of religious liberty. Lambert makes this distinction in the context of arguing that the founders' view prevailed as the "official" view of America. Again, Alexis de Tocqueville says that America was the product of two perfectly distinct elements that combined marvelously: "the *spirit of religion* and the *spirit of freedom*" (*Democracy in America,* Part One, Chapter 2; trans. Harvey C. Mansfield and Delba Winthrop [Chicago: University of Chicago Press, 2002], p. 430). My argument does not call into question the accuracy of these claims. The presupposition of my

Furthermore, the juridical state, in unwittingly privileging voluntaristic, hence positivistic, churches, enforces what is for all public-political purposes an instrumentalist view of the relation between the temporal and the eternal, thereby sanctioning also its own definite, even if unspoken, sense of the rightful secularity of the world in relation to God (in the language of the Second Vatican Council: *iusta autonomia*).

But let us take note immediately of the familiar objection: the genius of the juridical state is that, however much this state may happen to favor positivistic churches, all churches are nevertheless in principle left their freedom to construe man's relation to God as they wish, and this includes their freedom to understand this relation as given naturally rather than first simply voluntary. They are left free to understand this relation as naturally given for purposes of their own inner teaching and practice. The problem I am introducing, however, is that, relative to the demands of the liberal constitutional order and its particular notion of public-peaceful reasonableness, this self-understanding of religion as natural to man can be treated logically only as a matter of these churches' preference, or exercise of choice. Which is to say, only positivist churches will be truly free to take up public reason and interface with the constitutional order of the state in a way consistent with their own inner ecclesial self-understanding. Churches have juridical relevance only insofar as they are, or for public-constitutional purposes behave like, positivist churches.

---

argument, rather, is that Americans' self-understanding of religion vis-à-vis government, in terms of either its support for or its opposition to "established" churches, embeds a notion of freedom and (religious) truth that leaves each in its natural roots extrinsic to the other, such that the relation between them invariably breaks into a dialectical opposition, an opposition that is indeed tied to an originally reductive view of each in relation to the other. Lambert is of course right that the Puritans' overt "establishment" tendency gave way eventually to the "founding" conception of governmental protection of religion only by way of protecting religious freedom. What he fails to notice, however, is that the dominant view of governmental protection of religious freedom does not so much resolve the problem of "establishment" as it now repeats it dialectically, from the opposite direction, in its covert "establishment" of what I am terming a "positivistic" view of freedom in its relation to religion or religious truth. The burden of my argument in what follows, in other words, is that we can break out of the dialectic that sets the terms of the historical debate in America regarding religious truth and freedom vis-à-vis the public-constitutional order only by reconceiving religious truth and freedom in their ontological roots, in a way that recognizes the inner unity of the two, such that each is seen to have its own integrity only as at once, albeit in asymmetrical ways, an expression of the other.

According to the creaturely ontology I have outlined above, man is naturally religious. He is most basically a religious animal, anterior to, though essentially inclusive of, his being a rational animal,[50] or even, as assumed so often in liberal societies, a *homo economicus*. This affirmation of man's natural religiosity is implied in some significant sense in all the major religious cultures of the world. My focus here is on natural religiosity as affirmed in Christian sacramental churches, and especially in the Roman Catholic Church with which I am most familiar.

Sacramental churches presuppose the natural integrity of things, an integrity that is inclusive of ordering toward God. Things bear a constitutively given order to God, and thus image God, from the moment of their creation. They bear a kind of "pre-sacramentality": a "pre-sacramental" sign and expression of God's love which as such is open to, though it can never demand or even explicitly anticipate, the true and proper sacrament of God's love revealed uniquely by Jesus Christ. And this presupposes in turn that Jesus Christ, in and through his Eucharist, assumes and fulfills, rather than preempts, the original creaturely integrity of things, or again their natural "pre-sacramental" reality as signs and expressions of God-centered love.[51]

These few remarks suffice to point toward the deep differences between a natural or "pre-sacramental" religiosity and a positivist religiosity. On the relational ontology sketched earlier, seen now in its "pre-sacramental" nature as affirmed in Christian sacramental churches, time of its inner nature bears an openness to and indeed an image of eternity, even as eternity is shown — already in the act of creation, but fully and properly in God's act of revelation in Jesus Christ — to be open to time. The integrity of time, in other words, is disclosed only in its naturally given relation to eternity, and indeed in this relation only as itself ordered in turn to God's further gratuitous revelation of eternity in his Son, who enters time in Jesus Christ and in his Eucharistic Church. On a contractualist ontology of relation, on the other hand, as expressed in positivist religious bodies, time bears no naturally given image of eternity, nor is time naturally open to God's ultimate revelation of eternity in Jesus Christ.

Consider the "classical" liberal political theory of John Locke.[52]

---

50. See "The Embodied Person as Gift and the Cultural Task in America," pp. 242-74 in this volume.

51. See *Gaudium et Spes*, n. 22: "Cum in Eo natura humana *assumpta*, non *perempta* sit, eo ipso etiam in nobis ad sublimem dignitatem evecta est" (emphasis added).

52. I follow here Locke's *Letter on Toleration* (New York: Library of Liberal Arts/ Macmillan, 1950). Patrick Romanell is right in his introduction to note the Cartesian dual-

Locke distinguishes between the political commonwealth (state) and religious bodies (church) after the manner of two "perfect" societies, in the sense that each is complete in its own order. The political commonwealth is essentially concerned only with the temporal ends of human existence, and religious bodies only with the eternal end. Each body, so to speak, devotes itself exclusively to one part of the human being's whole existence: the temporal part is understood as a public matter coming properly within the purview only of the state's authority, the eternal part as a private matter of the soul coming properly within the purview only of the church's authority. Locke links the purposes of the commonwealth and religious bodies through their concern for morality. But even here what appears to be a common concern is in fact not so common. On the contrary, the commonwealth is concerned with morality only in terms of the external behavior necessary for *public civil order*, while religion is concerned with morality only in terms of its purely inner dimension as pertinent to the *private order* of an individual's eternal salvation.

The implicit endorsement by the juridical-liberal state of positivistic churches with their dualistic sense of the relations between temporal (public, outer, and earthly) and eternal (private, inner, and heavenly), as indicated by Locke, thus bears profound consequences. It entails transformation of what is meant by *both* the temporal-public *and* the eternal-private. It is no accident that today's liberal juridical state, having disjoined the former pair from the latter in a way consistent with that of Locke, officially favors a public societal life whose characteristic acts are outward or extroverted acts of power and consumption and whose primary exchange is an exchange of commodities, and which indeed relies on technology as the most effective mediator of power and (consumerist) acquisition and (commercial) relation. It is no accident that such a state logically pushes to the margins of society the interior-spiritual, now understood to be merely the inner-private and hence arbitrary dimension of life; and, likewise, marginalizes questions regarding the meaning and destiny of man, except insofar as this meaning might serve as moral inspiration for the more effi-

---

ism of body and soul implicit in Locke's understanding of the distinction between the political-temporal and public on the one hand, and the religious-eternal and private on the other (p. 9). It is surprising how little the Cartesian character of liberal institutions is generally remarked upon: Cartesian in the sense that such institutions are conceived most basically in terms of technically organized structures and procedures which, strictly, embody no inner human form or meaning. Murray's understanding of liberal political institutions in terms of "articles of peace" is Cartesian in this sense.

cient execution of what, consistent with Locke's positivistic view, remain the proper ends of public-societal life qua constitutionally sanctioned order: namely, more effective power and better commerce and consumerist comfort — and less physical pain and suffering — via more and better science and technology. All of these together are understood to yield a greater, more "peaceful" civil justice; and they are thus driven by the juridical state's single purpose, which is to enforce each individual person's claim of rights to these things that alone are "officially" recognized by that state to be essential to the earthly dignity of all and thus as matters of legitimate public-reasonable interest. The constitutional order of the liberal-juridical state, in a word, thus implies official endorsement of the view that heaven is a reality arriving *only after* life on earth, as distinct from a reality to which earthly life has been opened and ordered already in the act of creation, and in which earthly life thereby is already intended to participate, even if it is only beyond life on earth that heaven is fully realized.

This conception of the temporal or earthly, on the one hand, and the eternal or heavenly, on the other, turns the relation between these into an essentially instrumentalist relation, simultaneously in both directions. Earth, as it concerns religion, reduces simply to what is a *means* of getting to heaven; and heaven, as it concerns worldly affairs, reduces simply to what provides support for what is taken to be the right (moral) functioning of worldly things on their own and in abstraction from relation to heaven. The two reductions both imply that religion can only have what is at best a *moral* presence in the earthly or public order. Religion has no public *form qua religion;* on the contrary, it plays the role only of providing a hidden, and thus merely "private,"[53] support for the morality which alone can take public form. Which is to say, in turn: earthly-public life can be but a moral instrument for attaining heaven in the next life. As indicated above, however, even this is somewhat deceptive, since, on the juridical view, morality is of concern to the state only *as an instrument* for the maintenance of external-public order, and thus only as an externally conceived pattern of acting.

Thus religion, strictly speaking, given the juridical state, is in the end of no intrinsic importance *as religion* for the body politic. It is purely instrumental vis-à-vis what that state takes to be its exclusive proper function: securing formally conceived freedom and rights, and indeed the

---

53. "Private," that is, in the Cartesian sense, thus not in the sense of what has inner *form,* but what is on the contrary hidden and a-formal movement.

health and abundance, which enable the space for each citizen to choose, and thereby include the space to choose religion. To be sure, some of these citizens will understand religion rightly in its natural givenness as ordered to sacrament, and thus as indicating a transcendent-eternal order of truth and goodness that ought to inform human affairs from within. Once again, however, the problem is that, relative to the juridical logic of public reasonableness and political order, such an understanding of religion will be treated as a matter simply of a person's *choosing* to conceive religion that way, and of the implications of so choosing for the externally conceived public moral order. The integrity of the human being and of the action of citizens will continue to be conceived in instrumentalist terms, relative to God and the eternal or heavenly meaning of things.

Regarding the problem of secularity, then: for the juridical state and its unwittingly "established" positivist churches, liberalism's extrinsic conception of the relation between the temporal and eternal defines the meaning of the secular in its rightful autonomy vis-à-vis religion; for sacramental churches, this extrinsic relation, on the contrary, defines what is already the false autonomy that collapses secularity into secularism.

Consider here, for example, Orthodox theologian Alexander Schmemann's definition of secularism:

> Secularism, I submit, is above all a *negation of worship*. . . . It is the negation of man as a worshipping being, as *homo adorans:* the one for whom worship is the essential act which both "posits" his humanity and fulfills it. It is the rejection as ontologically and epistemologically "decisive," of the words which "always, everywhere and for all" were the "epiphany" of man's relation to God, to the world and to himself: "It is meet and right to sing of Thee, to bless Thee, to praise Thee, to give thanks to Thee, and to worship Thee in every place of Thy dominion. . . ."
>
> [W]orship implies a certain idea of man's relationship not only to God, but also to the world. . . . [I]t is precisely this idea of worship that secularism explicitly or implicitly rejects.[54]

Thus we can say, in light of this definition, that Christian sacramental churches, with their constitutive relationality and "pre-sacramental"

---

54. Alexander Schmemann, *For the Life of the World* (Crestwood, NY: St. Vladimir's Seminary Press, 2000 [1963]), pp. 118-19. I would want to elaborate Schmemann's definition here further in terms of the order of being and the natural, but in a way that, rightly understood, would not at all attenuate the profound and true burden of that definition.

natural order, entail that no human act can be without an implicit religious meaning. No human act can be logically formless, hence neutral, with respect to God. Every human act, indeed every entity in the cosmos, rightly analogically understood in terms of its naturally given integrity, is in search of God and made for worship of God. Every human act bears in its depths a natural love for God, indeed for God above all. This presupposition is thus radical, as indicated above: it implies nothing less than that every entity in the cosmos bears within it a call to holiness meant finally, via the agency of human beings, to take Eucharistic form, a form that precisely *assumes* and *fulfills*, rather than preempts or short-circuits, each entity's integrity as natural and as human. All of this I take to be implied in Ratzinger's claim regarding the memory of God built into the foundations of creaturely being. *Anamnesis*, the creaturely activity that corresponds to God's abiding active-immanent presence, expresses the very form of creaturely autonomy, for it belongs wholly to the creature, as his own act, at the same time as it acknowledges and transpires within and because of God's presence within him.

The decisive difference between sacramental and positivistic churches, then, lies in the fact that, on a "pre-sacramental" understanding of the human being, in contrast to a positivist understanding, the secular, or the this-worldly, is naturally inclusive of the relation to God and the eternal. The earthly-temporal dimensions of life have their proper integrity as such, precisely as implicit signs and expressions of God and the eternal. The point bears emphasis: on a "pre-sacramental" understanding of things, the secular *as secular* bears an implicit reference to God.[55] This contrasts radically with the dominant positivist understanding that the secular remains structurally silent with respect to God, that the relation to God is logically *always-yet-to-be-added* (by virtue of God's grace as revealed in Jesus Christ, for example), in a way that thereby makes that relation into something un-natural and un-worldly. An original-logical silence with respect to God thus signifies, not a simple *lack* of relation to

---

55. This implicit reference to God at the heart of the secular as secular receives insufficient attention in the scholastic tradition within which Murray undertakes his argument regarding America, and indeed I think the same problem plagues the Americanists' attempt to interpret the meaning of America vis-à-vis Catholicism. Such an implicit reference to God as bound up with the legitimate autonomy of the secular seems to me to lie at the root of what Pope Benedict XVI had in mind when he said, in the opening address of his apostolic visit to France: "I am firmly convinced that a new reflection on the meaning and importance of 'laïcité' is now necessary" (12 September 2008).

him, but already a *fragmented* relation. Such a logical silence indicates what is from the point of view of sacramental churches already a secularistic notion of man and nature's relation to God.

The criticism here, once again, does not deny but on the contrary presupposes that the juridical state as a matter of principle encourages religious bodies each to propose its own views of what kind of religion is necessary for a full human life and indeed for the healthy functioning of civil community. Non-positivistic, sacramental religions inside the liberal state remain constitutionally free to affirm an intrinsic relation between temporal (world, earth) and eternal (God, heaven), attempting to show what this different relation implies with respect to public community life, and regarding the rightful meaning of the secular. The problem is that these religious bodies will have to do so in their constitutionally sanctioned status only *qua sects:* as bodies which, from the point of view of the juridical state and its demand for public reasonableness, express voluntary religious preferences that can as a matter of principle provide only private-subjective moral inspiration, and not objective form, for public action. In order to be recognized publicly as reasonable, sacramental churches, with their naturally religious sense of man and the cosmos, will have to make their arguments in the same terms as positivist religious bodies: in terms of temporal realities from which any constitutive implication of openness to eternity has been removed. Only such terms will be received as effectively reasonable, and truly audible, within the public ethos of that state.

Let me emphasize: my remarks apropos of secularism are intended to protect the distinction between state and church, albeit while reconfiguring the nature of that distinction. Indeed, the burden of my criticism is that the juridical state itself, in the very way it distinguishes state and church, unwittingly collapses that distinction, blindly *uniting* the state with positivistic religions, and thereby imposing a secularistic, as distinct from legitimately secular, conception of the earthly-temporal reality of man. My own view is not that the state and the church do not have distinct roles with respect to the temporal and the eternal — they emphatically do — but only that, from the point of view of churches that recognize man's constitutive relationality to God, such distinctness can never be rightly construed in terms of a temporal order that is structurally *indifferent* to the eternal. Ignorance of the implication of a constitutive relation to God scarcely means that the implication dissolves. A so-called indifferent or "negative" relation to God, in other words, is logically not an absence of relation to God but, again, already a *fragmented* relation.

The burden of my argument, in a word, is that no state, not even the liberal-juridical state, can avoid taking a stand relative to the whole of the human being as ordered toward God in both the temporal and eternal, earthly and heavenly, public and "private," spheres of existence.[56] Every state, in its exercise of authority, will of necessity embed judgments with respect to the nature of religion in its implications for the destiny of man and the cosmos.

Needless to say, the fact that every state, willy-nilly, implies judgments regarding the religious, heavenly-eternal, meaning of man does not yet clarify for us the form these judgments would most appropriately take in public and in the constitutional order; and I will return to this point in a moment. Let me only first recall that my argument is limited primarily to demonstrating the paradox of the liberal-juridical state in matters of religion and the truth about God. This state, in its *ex officio* neutrality toward churches or indeed toward the phenomenon of religion as such, really does secure a kind of unlimited political freedom and space whereby each citizen or group can express its own convictions about the relation between the temporal order and God. In this sense, the juridical state defends what is virtually an absolute distinction between state and church. At the same time, the demands of constitutional order and public reasonableness in the juridical state covertly force this unlimited political freedom into a civil ontological unity consisting in positivist "truth" regarding the nature of God and religion.

This paradox is especially significant in light of the "exceptionalist" claim regarding religion in America: the claim that the liberal-juridical state, in its distinctly American version, has succeeded in fostering an enduring religiosity. But that has been just my point: this enduring religiosity, whose significance we surely do not deny and which we can surely grant is sincere, represents what, from the point of view of sacramental churches, expresses not legitimate creaturely secularity but already, logically if not intentionally, the first and most basic meaning of secularism.[57]

---

56. The church and the state, in other words, both take stands relative to the whole of the human being, but they do so *differently:* the church bears intrinsic concern for both the temporal and the eternal, from the perspective properly of the eternal; the state bears concern for both from the perspective properly of the temporal.

57. See Will Herberg's *Protestant–Catholic–Jew: An Essay in American Religious Sociology* (Chicago: University of Chicago Press, 1983) for a discussion of how America's Puritan ethos gives rise to a peculiar coincidence between secularism and religiosity in America, in a way that differs from Europe.

Let us then return briefly to the question of the unavoidable implication of God and the innately religious sense of man in state and civil society, as demanded by a sacramental or "pre-sacramental" understanding of religion. How is it possible for sacramental churches to maintain a principled distinction between state and church, or, more concretely, to promote the religious sense of man, without denying human freedom and thereby doing violence to the rightful pluralism that is inextricably bound up with the exercise of freedom?[58] I limit myself here to a statement of principle drawn from Roman Catholic ecclesiology, especially as developed in the pontificates of John Paul II and Benedict XVI, and in the name of the Second Vatican Council.

First, it is often said today, rightly, that, in light of the developments at Vatican II, the Church understands better that she enters properly into the worldly-political order in the persons of her lay members and not *qua* institution. A correct understanding of this truth, however, presupposes recognition that the laity themselves participate in the inner sacramental-eucharistic reality of the Church, and thereby bear within themselves, and hence bear also into the public order, the deepest *form* of the institution of the Church. Indeed, this integration of the laity into the full reality of the *communio* of the Church is one of the key developments of the Council. What this integration implies is that the sacramentality of the Church bears a dual dimension: lay or Marian, on the one hand, and "official," priestly-institutional, or Petrine, on the other.[59] Such integration implies no attenuation in the distinct importance of the Petrine, sacramental-institutional-priestly, dimension of the Church.[60] On the contrary, the point is simply the Church's renewed awareness of the Marian (and, I would add, Johannine)[61] meaning of the Church. As developed in the the-

---

58. Cf. the discussion of pluralism at the beginning of section VI.

59. To state the matter more completely: each of these shares in the other in its own way. Thus the lay or Marian Church shares in the priesthood shared by all believers via Baptism, even as the Petrine Church presupposes its always anterior participation in the Marian Church (on this, see the discussion regarding Vatican II later in this section).

60. See the Congregation for the Doctrine of the Faith's 1992 letter to Catholic bishops, "On Some Aspects of the Church Considered as Communion."

61. Briefly, by Marian here I mean the participation in Baptism that takes the form of the *fiat*, the *Magnificat* and the *Theotokos;* by the Petrine, I mean the objective participation in sacramentality that takes the form of office and institution; by the Johannine, I mean the participation in Baptism that takes the form of a love that abides, and stays in the world in unity with the Church, thereby uniting Marian and Petrine love. Each of these presupposes the others in its own subjective/objective way.

ology of John Paul II and Benedict XVI, the sacramental church as *communio* is a unity within distinctness of Mary and Peter, with each having a distinct priority.

The burden of these ecclesiological developments, pertinent to the present question, seems to me twofold. On the one hand, the Church, on innerly ecclesial grounds, unequivocally affirms the lay character of the state with its worldly-political responsibilities. The Church can never rightly seek unity with the state *qua official-institutional or jurisdictional authority:* she must never seek to unite Peter and the secular state. On the other hand, and at the same time, the Church's sacramental mission to the worldly-political order remains intact, *in its Marian-Johannine form.* The Church, through its lay dimension understood as properly Marian and Johannine in character, still bears her essentially missionary task, which is to penetrate every aspect of worldly order, attempting to recuperate its integrity as natural and as at once open to the generous love of God as disclosed in the whole of being and every being, as created and as called to re-creation (redemption) in Jesus Christ.

Needless to say, these brief statements of principle raise many difficult issues that nevertheless cannot be adequately treated in the present context. The statements simply highlight a twofold principle: on the one hand, the Church's *communio* ecclesiology requires affirmation of the inherently secular-lay character of the state, and this not for reasons of politically necessitated compromise, but on grounds rather of her own inner self-understanding as Church. On the other hand, and at the same time, this same *communio* ecclesiology demands that the laity who properly enter into the heart of the state and its worldly-political order do so in terms of their inner sacramental reality, and not simply as a "sociological" presence. This latter point is crucial: the rightful secularity of the laity is not a positivist secularity that fragments the relation between the temporal and the eternal.[62] On the contrary, the point, consistent with what was said above, is that the laity are to enter into community with all created persons and things, to enter *within* all worldly orders and professions — political, economic, academic, cultural — drawing everything forth in patient freedom toward its realization in generous love, as open ultimately to the generous love of God embodied in Jesus Christ.

---

62. Herein lies, then, what seems to me the core problem with Rhonheimer's idea of "Christian secularity." What his idea lacks is an adequate sense of man as constitutively religious *(homo religiosus)* and of the Christian layman as a Marian-Johannine participant in the sacramental-eucharistic reality of the Church.

But again here the lay, or Marian-Johannine, character of this intended entry into all things, including the public political community, is crucial. This entry, always and everywhere, is meant to be formed in the *fiat*: in the anterior "letting be" of the other in his natural integrity as other. Such "letting be" is thus of its essence respectful of the freedom of the other. This respect, in other words, is not a matter of compromise relative to the truth of God's love as revealed in creation and indeed by redemption in Jesus Christ. On the contrary, it is from within the very heights of this truth that the laity discover the properly Marian-Johannine way of entering into relation with others, which is by way of respect for the inmost depths and mystery of the other in his freedom.[63]

In a word, one cannot, consistent with a *communio* ecclesiology, oppose, or even merely juxtapose, the truth about man in his relation to God, on the one hand, and man's freedom in appropriating this truth, on the other. On the contrary, rightly understood in terms of such an ecclesiology, this truth and this freedom mutually imply one another, and members of the laity's approach to non-members will be informed by recognition of this mutuality.[64] Rightly understood, lay members' approach to non-members of the church, to the whole world and everything within it, will take the anterior form of letting the other be as he is in his concrete historical reality. *This letting be will bear an inner dynamic for recuperation of the full natural integrity of the other as open to the truth of God's love, precisely in and through the patient generosity of the self which is presupposed by that same truth.* Directly physical or overtly political force, and even the more subtle manipulation that often characterizes commercial transactions, are not part of the laity's proper approach to secular culture, as a means of (supposedly) hastening secular culture's arrival at truth.[65]

Again, these brief statements of principle leave implicit many impor-

---

63. The language of "from below" and "from above" is used often today. With respect to the present context, then, which concerns the difference between a lay and an "official" Petrine approach to the world, we can say that both the lay and the Petrine are properly concerned with the world simultaneously from above and from below, albeit in different ways: the laity qua from below, the Petrine qua from above.

64. Here it may be helpful to call attention to the emphasis by both John Paul II and Benedict XVI on ecumenical dialogue rightly understood, not merely for the sake of the ecclesial community and as a matter of inner churchly concern, but *in terms of the intrinsic significance of such dialogue for secular — including political — society and order itself.*

65. To be sure, this does not deny the necessity of concern for natural justice, and for a legitimate use of coercive power by the state when this justice is seriously violated.

tant questions needing clarification and sustained argument: questions, for example, regarding when reference to God is rightly to be made explicit in the public-constitutional order and in what form.[66] It nevertheless suffices, given the limits set by the present chapter, only to stress here that the missionary-sacramental task of the Church in her lay meaning is genuinely to seek to open all of natural-secular reality, hence including also the political order, to the love that expresses the natural-secular order's own deepest integrity as natural-secular, doing so all the while in a manner consistent with the patient and respectful freedom characteristic of that love in its ecclesial-lay form as embodied in Mary and John.

In pondering these brief statements of principle, it is crucial that we keep in mind the burden of our earlier argument: namely, that the liberal-juridical state, despite its claims to avoid substantive claims of religious truth in favor of a purely formal freedom and rights, itself fosters such claims of its own inner logic, albeit unwittingly. Indeed, it fosters such claims in a way that "enslaves" more than it liberates religious freedom. Taking account of this fact is a necessary condition for dealing reasonably and critically with the understanding of the relation between religious truth and freedom as suggested in my brief statements of principle.[67]

VII.

Since the introductory context of this chapter was set by authors claiming the authority of Vatican II in their defense of the juridical state with its formal-political justice, I wish before concluding to take account of this claim. The argument I have advanced, to be sure, implies a different reading of the Council. The question of the juridical state and of formal-political freedom and rights is engaged most directly at the Council in *Dignitatis Humanae*. As pointed out earlier, John Courtney Murray him-

---

66. Even if this reference to God takes a public form, which is in principle legitimate on the basis of a *communio* ecclesiology, and in light of the fact that no constitution can be innocent of the implication of some definite religious form, this public form would be properly actualized in and through lay members of the church, and indeed qua lay (Mary, John). What is precluded is that this public form take a jurisdictional-institutional form qua church (Peter).

67. It would be interesting, in connection with the foregoing paragraphs, to show how the liberal idea of institution might be understood as a secularized version of a clericalist idea of institutions: i.e., in the sense of a managerial organization that is without genuine interior form.

self was not satisfied that *DH* had successfully articulated the primarily juridical notion of the state and of rights.[68] He was nevertheless convinced that this was the view toward which the document had moved in the course of its different drafts, and which in any case represented its most adequate reading. Indeed, disciples of Murray often assume that this would likely have been made clearer in the final drafts, had Murray not been absent at crucial periods due to his heart problems.

In connection with Murray's primarily juridical reading of *DH*, Father Hermínio Rico, in his book *John Paul II and the Legacy of* Dignitatis Humanae, is right to see a difference between Murray and John Paul II regarding the relation between freedom and truth as intended in *DH*.[69] However, the terms in which he conceives this opposition are inadequate. Rico takes John Paul II's insistence on a priority of truth to involve in principle a move away from, hence an attenuation of, *DH*'s commitment to freedom. Indeed, Rico interprets this insistence as an effort on John Paul II's part to "restore" the Church's earlier emphasis on truth as a protection against a growing secularism in liberal societies.[70]

What Rico's interpretation fails to consider, however, is the "new" understanding of truth itself that is arguably one of the great achievements of the Council. Truth is at root an order of love, indeed, finally the order of love disclosed as a *person* in the revelation of Jesus Christ; and truth itself is thus of its inner *ratio* an order inclusive of freedom. The problem, in other words, is that Rico assumes the more conventional understanding of truth and freedom, such that standing in the truth would, *eo ipso,* entail a proportionate constriction of freedom. Indeed, as we have seen, such a view seems basic to Murray's argument regarding *DH*. It is why he insisted that the right to religious freedom could never be properly rooted in the duty of each person to seek the truth: because, if the state understood itself to be in possession of the truth, as he said the Communist and some Catholic states did, such states would logically be tempted to short-circuit citizens' freedom to seek it. Such a search, in other words, would no longer be necessary, or protected, as a matter of principle.

68. For an account of the interpretation of *DH* and the matter of the Americans' proposed juridical reading of religious freedom, a reading not fully accepted by the Council Fathers, see Walter Kasper, "Die 'Erklärung über die Religionsfreiheit' des II. Vatikanischen Konzils" (Heidelberg: Carl Winter Universitätsverlag, 1988).

69. Hermínio Rico, S.J., *John Paul II and the Legacy of* Dignitatis Humanae (Washington, DC: Georgetown University Press, 2002).

70. See Chapter 3, especially pp. 147-82.

Having assumed this extrinsic relation between truth and freedom, Rico and Murray understand the achievement of the Council, as expressed in *DH*, in terms of the enshrinement of freedom to the exclusion of truth as the proper concern of the state now conceived juridically. Emphatically: not to the exclusion of truth in the way expressed in the French Revolution and post-revolutionary continental liberalism, which were direct and aggressive in imposing their own secularistic version of truth. To the exclusion of truth, rather, in the Anglo-American way, which would render the state incompetent in the matter of truth precisely for the sake of securing the freedom and right of every citizen to conduct his own search for truth.

Rico's interpretation of *DH*, which indeed expresses the dominant interpretation, at least in America, therefore misses what has been one of the main burdens of the pontificates since the Council to argue: namely, that the human person is an order of truth qua love, an order, thus, that is in principle inclusive of freedom. The development in the matter of (religious) freedom that occurred at the Council (in *DH*), in this light, is not simply, or most properly, that the Church has learned a new appreciation for freedom, *alongside* her traditional appreciation of truth. On the contrary, she has developed a new appreciation for *truth itself as inclusive of freedom*, and for freedom as also an order of truth, precisely by virtue of and concomitant with a new understanding of the human person in terms of an anthropo-logic of love. That this is so is confirmed, for example, in the centrality accorded paragraph 22 in the reading of *Gaudium et Spes* by John Paul II and Benedict XVI: that Jesus Christ, in his revelation of the Father and his love, interprets the meaning of man to himself.

This text, repeatedly emphasized in the encyclicals of John Paul II, implies no reduction in the consistency of man in the integrity of his own human nature, as some critics have argued. On the contrary, as paragraph 22 itself states, Christ *assumes* and precisely *does not preempt* human nature. This paragraph, indeed, provides the right context for understanding properly the "legitimate autonomy" of earthly affairs and thus of the secular affirmed in *GS*, n. 36 and 59. The burden of *GS*, n. 22 relative to the latter texts is not that it absorbs this autonomy precipitously into relation to Christ and the order of grace. Rather, what *GS*, n. 22, rightly interpreted, does is bring into relief the fact that man, created in the image of God, is most basically an order of love *already in his integrity as a human-natural being*, even as this truth-filled order of love is disclosed fully and finally only in God's own self-revelation in Jesus Christ.

This understanding of the human person as an order of love is supported further by *Lumen Gentium*'s *communio* ecclesiology, with its integration of Mary into the inner reality of the Church, and indeed the *Catechism of the Catholic Church*'s affirmation of the primacy of Mary over Peter in the order of holiness,[70] a primacy that thereby also integrates the lay dimension of the Church more fully and properly into the Church's inner sacramental reality. There is also John Paul II's hallmark development regarding a theology of the body, in which the order of the human being and the body, and thus by implication of the entire physical-natural world in its "flesh," is an order of God-centered love. There is, finally, the Council's renewed emphasis, in *Ad Gentes Divinitus*, on the theological nature of the Church's inner mission to reach out to all peoples and the whole world. Indeed, the first chapter of this document may best be read as an exploration of the missionary implications of *GS*, n. 22, and indeed of the Christ-centered understanding of Scripture developed in *Dei Verbum*.

To be sure, further argument is needed to defend these interpretations of the various documents cited, and indeed of the developments in recent pontificates in their regard. But these comments suffice to show, *prima facie*, that the most basic achievement of the Second Vatican Council lies arguably in its development regarding the meaning of man and indeed the world as an order of love, and of freedom itself as an integral feature of this truthful order of love.

In his encyclical on the social teaching of the Church, *Caritas in Veritate*, Benedict XVI emphasizes the importance of the category of relation understood metaphysically, and of relation to God above all (n. 53). He likewise emphasizes the importance of "renewed reflection on how *rights presuppose duties*" (n. 43), and of how development, "if it is to be authentically understood, must make room for the principle of gratuitousness" (n. 34). Further, in a striking passage (n. 38), the encyclical refers explicitly to John Paul II's *Centesimus Annus*, which, as many are aware, has often been cited in terms that lend support to Murray's primarily juridical rendering of the meaning of the modern state. *CA* states that modern societies are systems comprised of three sectors or "subjects": the market, the state, and the civil society (or culture). In accord with Murray's juridical rendering of political order, each of these "subjects" has often been interpreted to have its own proper logic, such that the civil society or culture alone is properly concerned with the truth regarding man. Consistent with the dominant liberalism of many societies, in other words, the state is un-

---

70. *Catechism of the Catholic Church*, n. 773.

derstood to be properly concerned with rights conceived in terms primarily of immunity, and the market with mutually self-interested freedom in pursuit of profit. The state and the market are thus interpreted essentially as "juridical" orders concerned with formally conceived freedom and rights in the sense developed in this chapter, which civil society then, from outside the logic proper to the state and the market, undergirds with its own metaphysical truth and social morality. *CIV* corrects such a reading, stating that gratuitousness and fraternity have a place also *in* the State and the market, that normal economic activity "cannot prescind from gratuitousness" (n. 38).

CIV seems thus to provide a profound summary of the main teaching of the Council as expressed in its development of a God- and Christ-centered anthropology of love, now stated in the framework of the Church's social teaching.[72]

VIII.

The upshot of the foregoing argument is that the starting point of discussion in matters of political order and justice, even with respect to the liberal state, is not *whether* metaphysical truth is necessary for realizing civil peace and community, but rather *which* metaphysical truth can realize these most adequately as a matter of principle: not whether truth, but which truth, is needed to realize fully and properly the burden of modernity's political freedom and rights, adquately conceived.

The point, in other words, is that the question of metaphysical, and indeed also by implication theological, truth cannot be avoided in statecraft, even in the case of the liberal-juridical state. The would-be deferral of metaphysics attempted in liberal-juridical statecraft is mediated by metaphysical assumptions: those of a technological instrumentalism that leads unwittingly to a paradoxical inversion of liberalism's fundamental goals and purposes.

The significance of this point can scarcely be exaggerated. The hallmark assumption of liberal societies is that metaphysical claims of truth must be deferred as far as possible for purposes of juridical order and public reasonableness: for the purpose of avoiding violence, of realizing a

---

72. See "The Anthropological Vision of *Caritas in Veritate* in Light of Economic and and Cultural Life in the United States," pp. 430-49 in this volume.

peaceful society respectful of dialogue and protective of the dignity of all human beings, especially those most vulnerable to oppression. The problem, however, is that liberalism's would-be deferral of truth itself signifies and expresses, within its inner dynamic as an intended deferral, a formalist metaphysics which, as we have shown, leads logically to a violence of an extraordinarily virulent sort, with respect to both authentic reasonable dialogue and the truly weakest human beings.

The minimal burden of the present argument as it affects liberals, then, is that they cannot reasonably delay the question of metaphysical truth. On the contrary, they can either beg it, with the pernicious paradoxical consequences we have noted; or they must consider alternative metaphysical claims, precisely in order to secure their own rightful intentions of a peaceful, reason-informed civil community. The burden of my argument, in a word, is that modern liberal societies are no less metaphysical, and by implication theological, in nature than premodern societies. They are on the contrary merely metaphysical and theological in a less overt manner. Liberal societies, furthermore, are not without violence, although this violence is cloaked within liberalism's professed and laudable intentions of reasonableness, tolerance, and compassion. Moreover, this violence is *systemic*, tied to the peculiar metaphysics and theology that liberalism unwittingly presupposes.

The patterns of life and thought characteristic of liberal societies are shaped in profound ways by a largely unthematized and indeed unconscious idea of the relation between God and the world and between be-ing (*esse*) and being (*ens*) or essence (*essentia*). This idea may be termed in different respects an ontological Pelagianism, by virtue of liberalism's precipitous sense of man's creative initiative in relation both to God and to the whole of being and all beings; and nominalist, by virtue of liberalism's lack of a genuinely ontologically rooted, analogically conceived worldly community. It is crucial for my argument to see that the violence peculiar to liberal societies derives from patterns of life and thought informed by metaphysical presuppositions such as those named here. Indeed, a basic implication of my argument is that metaphysical and theological errors such as those named are not matters simply of abstract propositional truths. On the contrary, they are assumptions regarding the nature of our being in the world and before God, and they thus articulate by implication an entire way of life — in the case of liberalism, a way of life disposed to violence of a peculiarly subtle and virulent sort.

My argument in this light is that the alternative view needing especially to be considered is that presupposed by the doctrine of creation *ex nihilo*, understood to bear a distinctly ontological meaning. The problem, as we have seen, is that liberalism's primarily formal-political conception of reason as a matter of principle precludes any public-reasonable recognition of the truth of being as constitutively given by a transcendent Giver and thus as gift.[73] The present chapter has been limited primarily to the critical task of exposing the assumptions that drive this tendency of liberalism. Let me then conclude by offering some brief comments regarding what I take to be implied for a rightly conceived public reason.

The most basic task of a public reason consistent with an ontology of being as gift from God is to recover the roots of public reason itself in an understanding of *being as given*, in all the depth and breadth of what is implied in this *givenness*. It is thus to seek to recuperate as far as possible the original and most basic meaning of all being, including public institutions in their being as constructed by man, inside the givenness of all being as gift.

It is crucial to note, with respect to this task, that it involves transformation. The point is to enter into reason in its dominant public-institutional forms, in order to retrieve what is reason's own deepest and most comprehensive intention *as reason*, and thus to *fulfill* reason even while integrating it into its deeper and broader logic. The point is not to reject reason in its different customary forms as exercised in the public institutions of politics, the economy, and the academy. Rather it is to enter into these forms and show from within how the *logic proper to reason in each case* is *fulfilled* when inserted into the logic of God-centered love, even as this insertion will require reason to recognize more fully its own hidden depths and comprehensiveness.[74]

The transformation in liberal social-political life indicated by an ontology of gift must begin by entering into the heart of public life and thought as conceived in its dominant logic by liberal culture, even as it repatterns that life and thought from the inside out. The intended transformation is thus radical (from *radix:* root). And this raises the question of "realism": In what sense is the required transformation "realistic" with re-

---

73. The upshot is that being in its inmost character as love, and love in its inmost character as being, can have no principled place in the public order: reality, for all public-constitutional purposes and from the perspective of public reason, is not properly a matter of love; and love is not properly a matter of reality.

74. See Pope Benedict XVI's Regensburg lecture. See also "Modernity and the Nature of a Distinction: Balthasar's Ontology of Generosity," pp. 350-82 in this volume.

spect to the juridical state with its formal-political justice and its conception of public reasonableness? This question is dealt with in other chapters in this study. Here I wish to focus only two points.

The heart of my argument, first of all, is that gift indicates the basic *ratio* of being as naturally given, by God as Creator. The transformation indicated in all facets of public-reasonable life inside the liberal-juridical state is therefore a transformation that in principle *fulfills the innermost naturally given meaning* of freedom and rights and reason, even as it liberates this meaning into an (analogically) differentiated historical form. The change, in other words, is one that freedom and rights, in their properly conceived natural onto-logic as such, "want" for themselves.

The universality implied here is critical: in recovering freedom and rights in their own deepest natural reality as such, one is thereby liberating what is sought at the most profound level, even if unconsciously, by everyone in his or her exercise and affirmation of freedom and rights. Which is to say, in recovering freedom and rights in their natural meaning as given by God, one does not as a matter of principle, as the liberal juridical view of freedom and rights does, do violence to any man's, or any particular group's, freedom and rights.

This is so because what is sought implicitly by every person in every act of freedom and every claim of rights is *to be loved* and *to love:* to be loved for *what he is in himself* and to love the other (and his own self) for *what each is in itself,* all of this inside the desire at once to be loved above all by God (forever) and to love God above all (forever).

The point, then, is that this desire resonates more profoundly and comprehensively, and *universally,* in the heart of man than does liberal freedom in its character as a would-be purely formal act empty of an order of love, or liberal rights in their character as negative demands for immunity from coercive action by others, as distinct from positive demands for liberation into relationship with others. The point, in other words, is that liberal freedom and rights resonate only with a fragment of one's being; gifted freedom and rights with the whole of one's being.

All claims regarding the relative *"realism"* of liberalism's instrumental ontology of freedom and rights, and indeed reason, and a gifted ontology of freedom and rights need to reckon with the nature of the *reality* of man as indicated here.

To be sure, every exercise of freedom is weighted by personal sin, including personal sin extended into the institutional structures of society, and therefore consciousness of the desire for love and for God is often overwhelmed, and realization of this love often obstructed. What is important to see, however, is that this desire itself, however obscured and short-circuited, is never eliminated. It always remains, at least in the form of an unconscious restlessness to be loved and to love, above all in relation to God as giver of my being.

The upshot is that the desire for love, in the face of the sin that is omnipresent (because "original"), will always involve suffering. The question of suffering is also taken up in other chapters of this study. Here I wish only to point out that suffering can never be absent from any human life, and indeed that the juridical state, with its formal-political freedom and reason and rights, promotes of its inner logic suffering of the most profound sort: the suffering that consists in a meaninglessness induced by this state's implied instrumental-technological ontology. Suffering in society is thus scarcely reduced by settling for more "modest" public versions of freedom and rights and reason. No way of public life, not even inside the institutions of a liberal culture, will be free of the need to suffer a kind of crucifixion resulting from sinful relations among men. Which is to say, the Cross has implications for man's public life in every human society, including liberal society.

Given that there will inevitably be suffering in every human culture, what becomes key is to see that suffering bears an *intrinsic meaning*. Here an instrumentalist freedom and rights and reason are of no help. On the contrary, instrumentalist freedom and reason serve precisely to deflect from meaning and thus to destroy inner peace: to promote a boredom that often expresses itself in withdrawal or in violent acts of desperation. Living the reality of freedom and reason as orders of gift, on the other hand, can lead to the discovery of suffering as a participation, in the face of man's inveterate injustices toward man, in love's patient affirmation of the other. However difficult it may be to live the reality of love, what an attempt to do so can do, in a way that living an instrumentally reduced reality cannot, is to release joy into the heart of our suffering, a joy that derives from being *what one truly is* in one's inmost depths before God.

Charity, Justice, and the Church's Activity in the World: A Reflection on *Deus Caritas Est*

My task is to reflect on the Church's charitable mission to the world as understood in *Deus Caritas Est* (2005). Following a look at Benedict's own overview of the encyclical (Part I), I will discuss some key principles of the encyclical that inform its understanding of this mission (Part II). I will then discuss how the Church in her missionary task is to be present in the world, giving particular attention to issues most likely to arise in the current circumstances of the West (Part III).

I. The Love That "Moves the Sun and Stars" and Has a Human Face and Human Heart

Pope Benedict presents his new encyclical with Dante's words about the light that is at the same time the love that "moves the sun and the other stars."[1] This light and love in their unity "are the primordial creative powers that move the universe."[2] Though these words reveal the thought of Ar-

---

1. Dante, *Paradiso* XXXIII, 145.
2. Benedict XVI, Address of His Holiness Benedict XVI to the Participants at the Meeting Promoted by the Pontifical Council "Cor Unum," 23 January 2006. All subsequent citations in this section are from this address.

A first version of this chapter was prepared as part of *The Way of Love: Reflections on Pope Benedict XVI's Encyclical Deus Caritas Est,* presented to Benedict XVI on the occasion of the twenty-fifth anniversary conference celebrating the founding of the Pontifical John Paul II Institute for Studies on Marriage and Family at the Lateran University in Rome, May 2006. My assignment was to treat the topic of charity and the Church's activity in the world.

istotle, who "saw in *eros* the power that moves the world," Dante perceives something "completely new and inconceivable for the Greek philosopher": the revelation of God as a "trinitarian circle of knowledge and love" (1).

Even more, Dante saw that this Trinitarian God of love has a human face and indeed a human heart in Jesus Christ. Dante thus shows the "continuity between Christian faith in God and the search developed by reason and by the world of religions," while at the same time he shows the novelty of a love that has led God "to take on flesh and blood, the entire human being." God's *eros*, in a word, is not only a "primordial cosmic power" but also the "love that created man and that bows down over him, as the Good Samaritan bent down to the wounded and robbed man" (1).

Although love has become a much-abused word today, Benedict insists that we must take it up again and purify it, showing how faith in this love "becomes a vision-comprehension that transforms us." In an age in which "hostility and greed have become superpowers," and in which religion has been abused "to the point of deifying hatred," the burden of the encyclical is to show that a "neutral rationality alone" can no longer protect us; that, on the contrary, we "need the living God, who loved us even to death" (2).

Benedict says that the encyclical welds together the subjects "God," "Christ," and "Love," in order to show the humanity of faith. This is to be done above all by showing how *eros* is transformed into *agape*, the "love for the other which is no longer self-seeking but becomes concern for the other, ready to sacrifice for him or her and also open to the gift of a new human life" (3). This *eros* that is ordered to the self-transcendence of *agape* — that is, in such a way that these two loves bear an inner unity with each other — is "in the first instance" manifested "in an indissoluble matrimony between man and woman [that] finds its form rooted in creation" (3). It is in this relation between man and woman that we see above all that "man is created to love." With this foundation, says Benedict, the encyclical shows that "the essence of the love of God and neighbor as described in the Bible is shown to be the center of Christian existence, the result of faith" (4).

The second part of the encyclical underlines how "the totally personal act" of *agape* cannot remain "as something isolated," but must on the contrary "become an essential act of the Church as community." "[I]t also requires an institutional form which is expressed in the communal working of the Church" (4). This communal action is more than "a form of social assistance . . . that is casually added to the Church's reality, an initiative that could be left to others." In its communication of love of neighbor, the Church's charitable activity must "make the living God in some way visible." "In the charitable organization, God and Christ must not be foreign words; in reality, they indicate the original source of ecclesial charity" (4). Thus, in a word, "charitable commitment has a meaning that goes well beyond simple philanthropy" (5). God himself moves us "interiorly to relieve misery," and in this way "it is he himself whom we bring to the suffering world." In sum: "the more consciously and clearly we bring him as a gift, the more effectively will our love change the world and reawaken hope: a hope that goes beyond death" (5).

II. God, Man, and the Integrity of Love: On the Unity of *Eros* and *Agape*

With this overview, we turn to the first part of the encyclical and highlight four points in anticipation of discussion of the Church's charitable activity.

(1) The Unity of Eros and Agape

The encyclical takes note of the vast semantic range of the word "love" today, and then singles out one in particular: "love between a man and a woman, where body and soul are inseparably joined."[3] This would seem to be "the very epitome of love" (n. 2). The question in this connection, then, is whether love "in its many and varied manifestations" can be "basically one" or "ultimately a single reality" (n. 2). The Greeks called the love between a man and a woman ("which is neither planned nor willed but somehow imposes itself on human beings") *eros*. The New Testament, however, does not use the term *eros* at all, preferring for its vision of love the term *agape*, which "points to something new and distinct about the Christian understanding of man" (n. 3). Here, then, arises the issue that has become especially acute since the Enlightenment: Does not the Christian faith entail rejection of *eros*? Nietzsche poses the question with particular force: Does not Christian-agapic love, with its negative prohibitions and commandments, involve checking human *eros* and thereby evacuating

---

3. Benedict XVI, *Deus Caritas Est (DCE)* (2005), n. 2.

human life of its joy and its passion (n. 3)? *Deus Caritas Est* rejects this charge, and the opposition between *agape* and *eros* that it presupposes.

The Greeks as well as other cultures linked *eros* with a kind of "divine madness" or intoxication — see the fertility cults with their sacred prostitution, for example — and thus celebrated *eros* "as divine power, as fellowship with the divine" (n. 4). The Old Testament firmly opposed this form of religion, "combating it as a perversion of religiosity" (n. 4). But the Old Testament did so, not because it rejected *eros*, but on the contrary because "this counterfeit divinization of *eros* actually strips it of its dignity and dehumanizes it" (n. 4) — the prostitutes in the temple, for example, were used as instruments and thus exploited. The point, then, is that an "intoxicated and undisciplined *eros* . . . is not an ascent in 'ecstasy' toward the divine but a fall, a degradation of man" (n. 4).

The lessons, therefore, are two: there is indeed "a certain relationship between love and the divine," inasmuch as love "promises infinity, eternity — a reality far greater and totally other than our everyday existence" (n. 5). But this promise is not realized simply "by submitting to instinct," but only through a "purification and growth in maturity" that pass also "through the path of renunciation" (n. 5). This is due to the fact that "man is a being made up of body and soul" (n. 5). Only when these two dimensions are truly united can man attain the full stature that includes an appropriately mature *eros*. The call for purification is not to be confused with opposition to the body (though there have been such mistaken tendencies among Christians in the course of history). Indeed, the fact that purification is construed as implying opposition to the body stems from the tendency today to reduce the body to a biological sphere wrongly disjoined from the soul, which leads either to an exaltation of the body apart from its spiritual significance, or to a degradation of the body as reduced to a mere "material part" of man. In either case the body becomes a commodity to be bought or sold; which is to say, man himself becomes such a commodity.

How, then, concretely, can the path of ascent and purification be said to realize its human and divine promise? *DCE* turns again to Scripture, referring to the Old Testament book the Song of Songs, which was "perhaps intended for a Jewish wedding and meant to exalt conjugal love" (n. 6). Noting the two different words used for love in this book (*dodim* and *'ahaba*), Benedict points out how *dodim*, with its "indeterminate" or "searching" meaning, is gradually replaced by *'ahaba*, with its sense "of a love which involves a real discovery of the other, moving beyond the selfish character that prevailed earlier" (n. 6). No longer is love "self-seeking, a sinking in the intoxication of happiness; instead it seeks the good of the beloved: it becomes renunciation and it is ready and even willing for sacrifice" (n. 6). This love seeks to become definitive in the sense both of being exclusive (for one person alone) and of being forever. "Love embraces the whole of existence," including "the dimension of time," and "it could hardly be otherwise, since its promise looks forward toward its definitive goal: love looks to the eternal" (n. 6).

Thus, says *DCE*,

> Love is indeed an "ecstasy," not in the sense of a moment of intoxication but rather as a journey, an ongoing exodus out of the closed inward-looking self toward its liberation through self-giving and thus toward authentic self-discovery and indeed the discovery of God: "Whoever seeks to gain his life will lose it, but whoever loses his life will preserve it" (Luke 17:33). (n. 6)

With these words, "Jesus portrays his own path, which leads through the Cross to the Resurrection" (n. 6), and he thereby also portrays "the essence of love and indeed of human life" (n. 6).[4]

These "somewhat philosophical reflections," as *DCE* terms them, thus lead by their own inner logic "to the threshold of biblical faith" (n. 7). The question that launched the reflections was that of how the *eros* referring to a "worldly" love relates to the *agape* referring to the love grounded in and shaped by faith. These two loves are "often contrasted as 'ascending' love and 'descending' love" (n. 7), or again by distinctions such as that between "possessive love and oblative love *(amor concupiscentiae — amor benevolentiae)*" (n. 7) — with human love typically referring to ascending and covetous or possessive movement and Christian love to descending or oblative movement. *DCE* stresses, however, that, were this distinction to be hardened into a separation, "the essence of Christianity would be detached from the vital relations fundamental to human existence and would become a world apart" (n. 7). On the contrary, "the more the two in their different aspects find a proper unity in the one reality of love, the more the true nature of love in general is realized" (n. 7).

The point, then, is that "even if *eros* is at first mainly covetous and ascending, a fascination with the great promise of happiness, in drawing near to the other it is less and less concerned with itself, [and] increasingly

---

4. Cf. *Gaudium et Spes* (1965), n. 22.

seeks the happiness of the other" (n. 7). Indeed, if *agape* does not enter into this ascending movement toward happiness, *eros* itself is impoverished and "loses its own proper nature" (n. 7). On the other hand, "anyone who wishes to give love must also receive love as a gift" (n. 7), and thus man cannot live by descending, oblative love alone. As the Lord says, "one can become a source from which the living waters flow (cf. Jn 7:37-38)," but this presupposes that "one must constantly drink anew from the original source, which is Jesus Christ, from whose pierced heart flows the love of God (cf. Jn 19:34)" (n. 7). "[T]he fathers of the Church saw this inseparable connection between ascending and descending love, between *eros* which seeks God and *agape* which passes on the gift received" (n. 7). Gregory the Great, in a particularly striking interpretation of the patriarch Jacob's vision of the ladder to heaven, "tells us that the good pastor must be rooted in contemplation" (n. 7). "'Within [the tent Moses] is borne aloft through contemplation, while without he is completely engaged in helping those who suffer'" (n. 7).

With this, Benedict says that "an initial but still somewhat generic response" has been reached: love is indeed a single reality, but with the double dimension of *eros* and *agape*. Biblical faith thus "accepts the whole man," intervening "in his search for love in order to purify it and to reveal new dimensions of it" (n. 8).

(2) The Newness of Biblical Faith

The newness of biblical faith is shown chiefly in two elements: the image of God and the image of man. (a) First of all, the Old Testament teaches us that there is "only one God, the Creator of heaven and earth, who is thus the God of all" (n. 9). This means that "all other gods are not God, and [that] the universe in which we live has its source in God and was created by him" (n. 9). Secondly, "this God loves man" (n. 9), indeed loves him with a personal and elective love. Citing Dionysius the Areopagite's *The Divine Names*, Benedict says that this personal and elective love "may certainly be called *eros*, yet it is totally *agape* [*prorsus* agape]" (n. 9). "The prophets, particularly Hosea and Ezekiel, described God's passion for his people using boldly erotic images. God's relationship with Israel is described using the metaphors of betrothal and marriage [*sponsalium coniugique*]; idolatry is thus adultery and prostitution" (n. 9). But this love is also totally *agape*, "not only because it is bestowed in a completely gratuitous manner, without any previous merit, but also because it is love which forgives" (n. 10).

"The philosophical dimension to be noted in this biblical vision, and its importance from the standpoint of the history of religions, lies in the fact that on the one hand we find ourselves before a strictly metaphysical image of God: God is the absolute and ultimate source of all being; but this universal principle of creation — the *Logos*, primordial reason [*primordialis ratio*] — is at the same time a lover with all the passion of a true love. *Eros* is thus supremely ennobled, yet at the same time it is so purified as to become one with *agape*" (n. 10).

DCE notes how the Song of Songs in the canon of Scripture came to be interpreted ultimately as a description of "God's relation to man and man's relation to God," and indeed "an expression of the essence of biblical faith: that man can enter into union with God," a union which is no mere fusion but a unity that "creates love, a unity in which both God and man remain themselves and yet become fully one" (n. 10). Spousal imagery, in other words, shows us how there can be a genuine unity between two persons that not only permits but fosters the integrity of each.

(b) The second novelty of the biblical faith consists in its distinct image of man. Genesis speaks of "the solitude of Adam, and God's decision to give him a helper" (n. 11). None of the other creatures is capable of being the helper that man needs, and so God "forms the woman from the rib of man" (n. 11). Man is by nature somehow incomplete, and "only in communion with the opposite sex can he become 'complete'" (n. 11). The Genesis account, says Benedict, implies especially two things: first, "*eros* is somehow rooted in man's very nature": "Adam is a seeker who 'abandons his father and mother' in order to find woman; only together do the two represent complete humanity and become 'one flesh'" (n. 11). Second, "from the standpoint of creation, *eros* directs man toward marriage, to a bond which is unique and definitive, and only thus does it fulfill its deepest purpose" (n. 11). In a word: "Corresponding to the image of a monotheistic God is monogamous marriage. Marriage based on exclusive and definitive love becomes the icon of the relationship between God and his people and vice versa. God's way of loving becomes the measure of human love" (n. 11).

(c) The foregoing account of the newness of biblical faith, however, has been developed thus far mainly in terms of the Old Testament. In the New Testament, we see how God's "divine activity now takes on dramatic form when, in Jesus Christ, it is God himself who goes in search of the 'stray sheep,' a suffering and lost humanity" (n. 12). Examples such as that of the father who goes to meet his prodigal son are not merely words. On the contrary, they "constitute an explanation of [Jesus'] very being and activity. His death on the Cross is the culmination of that turning of God against himself [*contra se vertit Deus*] in which he gives himself in order to raise man up and save him. This is love in its most radical form" (n. 12). Indeed, it is from here "that our definition of love must begin" (n. 12). It is in the contemplation of this love that "the Christian discovers the path along which his life and love must move" (n. 12).

Further, then, Jesus gave "this act of oblation an enduring presence through his institution of the Eucharist" (n. 13).

> The ancient world had dimly perceived that man's real food — what truly nourishes him as man — is ultimately the *Logos*, eternal wisdom: this same *Logos* now truly becomes food for us — as love. The Eucharist draws us into Jesus' act of self-oblation. More than just statically receiving the incarnate *Logos*, we enter into the very dynamic of his self-giving. The imagery of marriage between God and Israel is now realized in a way previously inconceivable [*quae antea concipii non potuit*]. It had meant standing in God's presence, but now it becomes union with God through sharing in Jesus' self-gift, sharing in his body and blood. (n. 13)

According to *DCE*, then, we see the unity of love in the mutual-asymmetrical inclusion of *eros* and *agape* that is disclosed uniquely in the created order in spousal love, and the Bible shows us how this spousal love images for us God's relation to man and man's relation to God. Finally, we see in the New Testament how this spousal imagery deepens inconceivably in the incarnate *Logos*'s becoming food for us, such that we now share truly in his very body and blood.

(3) The Sacramental "Mysticism" of the Eucharist Is Social in Character

Union with God entails "union with all those to whom he gives himself. I cannot possess Christ just for myself; I can belong to him only in union with all those who have become, or will become, his own. Communion [thus] draws me out of myself toward . . . unity with all Christians. We become 'one body,' completely joined in a single existence. Love of God and love of neighbor are now truly united" (n. 14).

The transition Jesus makes to the twofold commandment of love of God and of neighbor "is thus not simply a matter of morality — something that could exist apart from and alongside faith in Christ and its sacramental realization. Faith, worship and ethos are interwoven as a single reality which takes shape in our encounter with God's *agape*" (n. 14). Hence "the usual contraposition between worship and ethics simply falls apart. 'Worship' itself, eucharistic communion, includes the reality both of being loved and of loving others in turn. A Eucharist which does not pass over into the concrete practice of love is intrinsically fragmented. . . . The 'commandment' of love is only possible because it is more than a requirement. Love can be commanded because it has first been given" (n. 14).

"This principle is the starting point for understanding the great parables of Jesus" (n. 15). For example, the parable of the good Samaritan teaches us that "[a]nyone who needs me, and whom I can help, is my neighbor. The concept of neighbor is now universalized, yet it remains concrete. Despite being extended to all mankind, it is not reduced to a generic, abstract, and undemanding expression of love, but calls for my own practical commitment here and now" (n. 15). Further, we see that Jesus identifies himself with those most in need: the hungry, the thirsty, the stranger, the naked, the sick, and those in prison. In a word, "[l]ove of God and love of neighbor have become one: in the least of the brethren we find Jesus himself, and in Jesus we find God" (n. 15).

(4) The Saints and Mary, Mother of the Lord and Mirror of All Holiness

It is the saints who best exhibit the inseparability of the love of God and the love of neighbor. The saints "constantly renewed their capacity for love of neighbor from their encounter with the eucharistic Lord, and conversely this encounter acquired its realism and depth in their service to others" (n. 18). The double commandment to love God and to love one's neighbor both "live from the love of God, who has loved us first" (n. 18).

Benedict says that "prayer, as a means of drawing ever new strength from Christ, is concretely and urgently needed" (n. 36). As Mother Teresa wrote to her lay co-workers, "'We need this deep connection with God in our daily life. How can we obtain it? By prayer'" (n. 36). The Pope stresses "the importance of prayer in the face of the activism and the growing secularism of many Christians engaged in charitable work" (n. 37).

It is Mary especially who reveals the unified meaning of this double commandment and the significance of prayer. In her great words — "My soul magnifies the Lord" — "she expresses her whole program of life: not setting herself at the center, but leaving space for God, who is encountered both in prayer and in service of neighbor — only then does goodness enter the world" (n. 41). Mary's "only desire is to be the handmaid of the Lord (cf. Lk 1:38, 48). . . . [R]ather than carrying out her own projects, she places herself completely at the disposal of God's initiatives. Mary is a woman of hope" (n. 41). In "her quiet gestures," "in the delicacy with which she recognizes the need of the spouses at Cana and makes it known to Jesus," we see that she is a woman who loves (n. 41).

In a word, the saints make one thing clear: "Those who draw near to God do not withdraw from men but rather become truly close to them. In no one do we see this more clearly than in Mary. The words addressed by the crucified Lord to his disciple — to John and through him, to all disciples of Jesus, 'Behold, your mother!' (Jn 19:27) — are fulfilled in every generation" (n. 41).

III. The Relation between Justice and Charity and the Distinctiveness of the Church's Charitable Activity in the World

As Benedict said in his presentation of *DCE*, the two parts of the encyclical can be rightly understood only if they are seen as a single thing [*solo se visti come un'unica cosa, sono compresi bene*].[5] This unity is evident immediately in Benedict's placing of the Church's mission to charitable activity in the light of the Trinity and of the Father's sending of his Son in the Spirit. The Church's charitable activity, in its most fundamental meaning, is a participation in the missionary love of the Son (n. 19). "The entire activity of the Church is an expression of a love that seeks the integral good of man: it seeks his evangelization through word and sacrament . . . ; and it seeks to promote man in the various arenas of life and human activity. Love is therefore the service that the Church carries out in order to attend constantly to man's sufferings and his needs, including material needs" (n. 19). It is on this aspect, "the service of charity," that Benedict proposes to focus in the second part of *DCE*.

---

5. Benedict XVI, Address to Participants at the Meeting Promoted by the Pontifical Council "Cor Unum."

(1) The Church's Responsibility for Charity

Love of neighbor, says the Pope, is first of all "a responsibility for each member of the faithful, but it is also a responsibility for the entire ecclesial community at every level" (n. 20). This "constitutive relevance" of the love of neighbor in the Church was manifest from the beginning, for example, in the early believers' common possession of goods (Acts 2:44-45).

In time, the Church put this fundamental ecclesial principle into practice through the establishment of the diaconal office (cf. Acts 6:5-6). A group of seven persons was entrusted with the daily distribution to widows and the like. Benedict points out that these persons were not to carry out this task in a purely technical manner [*tantummodo technicum ministerium*]. On the contrary, they were to be men "full of the Spirit and wisdom" (cf. Acts 6:1-6). Which is to say, the concrete social service they were to provide was at the same time "a spiritual service" (n. 21).

Benedict discusses several examples of how, in the course of Church history, this charitable service is seen as essential to her "ministry of the sacraments and the preaching of the Gospel" (n. 21). Justin Martyr (d. c. 155), for example, "in speaking of the Christians' celebration of Sunday, also mentions their charitable activity linked with the Eucharist as such" (n. 22). Benedict then adduces further examples of how the Church understood this link, and of the legal structures associated with the service of charity in the Church (n. 22-24).

The foregoing considerations point toward two essential facts: first, "[t]he Church's deepest nature is expressed in her threefold responsibility: of proclaiming the Word of God *(kerygma-martyria)*, celebrating the sacraments *(leitourgia)* and exercising the ministry of charity *(diakonia)*. These duties presuppose each other and are inseparable." Second, "[t]he Church is God's family in the world. In this family no one ought to go without the necessities of life. Yet at the same time *caritas-agape* extends beyond the frontiers of the Church" (n. 25).

We must remain mindful of these two essential facts if we are to understand properly *DCE*'s discussion of the central issues of the relation between justice and charity, and of the distinctiveness of the Church's charitable-social activity in the world, to which issues we now turn.

(2) Justice and Charity

The Pope begins his discussion of this issue by noting the objection that has emerged since the nineteenth century with respect to the Church's charitable activity: "The poor, it is claimed, do not need charity, but justice" (n. 26). "Instead of contributing through individual works of charity to maintain the status quo, we need to build a just social order in which all receive their share of the world's goods and no longer have to depend on charity" (n. 26). Benedict acknowledges that there is some truth to this argument but "also much that is mistaken" (n. 26). He emphasizes that "the pursuit of justice must be a fundamental norm of the state and that the aim of a just social order is to guarantee to each person, according to the principle of subsidiarity, his share of the community's goods" (n. 26). He notes that the issue of social justice has taken on a new dimension "with the industrialization of society in the 19th century" (n. 26).

Though, admittedly, "the Church's leadership was slow to realize that the issue of the just structuring of society had to be approached in a new way," a growing number of groups, associations, and the like, especially new religious orders, were founded to combat poverty and disease and promote better education (n. 27). Then there were the social encyclicals, beginning with Leo XIII (*Rerum Novarum,* 1891), and followed by Pius XI (*Quadragesimo Anno,* 1931), and then later by John XXIII (*Mater et Magistra,* 1961), Paul VI (*Populorum Progressio,* 1967), and the trilogy of social encyclicals by John Paul II (*Laborem Exercens,* 1981; *Sollicitudo Rei Socialis,* 1987; and *Centesimus Annus,* 1991).

In light of the above, and in light further of the complexity of today's situation due at once to the collapse of the collectivist revolution of the twentieth century and to the growth of a globalized economy, Benedict says we need to consider anew the relevance of the Church's social doctrine even beyond the confines of the Church. In so doing, he says, two fundamental points must be considered: (a) that "the just ordering of society and the state is a central responsibility of politics" (n. 28); and (b) that "[l]ove — *caritas* — will always prove necessary even in the most just society" (n. 28). There has been much commentary on these two principles, and it is therefore important to examine them carefully. How are these principles to be understood, in light of the unity of the encyclical as affirmed by Benedict and in light as well of the changed social situation in the world?

(a) Regarding the statement that the just ordering of society and the state is a matter properly of politics, the Pope begins by affirming as "fundamental to Christianity"

> the distinction between what belongs to Caesar and what belongs to God, in other words, the distinction between Church and state or, as the Second Vatican Council puts it, the autonomy of the temporal sphere [*Gaudium et spes*, 1965, 36]. The state may not impose religion, yet it must guarantee religious freedom. . . . For her part, the Church . . . has a proper independence and is structured on the basis of her faith as a community which the state must recognize. The two spheres are distinct, yet always interrelated. (n. 28)

It is important, especially in light of tendencies in Western liberal societies, to see that the distinction between Church and state affirmed here by *DCE* does not entail an embrace of a purely juridical state. That is, justice remains "both the aim and the intrinsic criterion of all politics. Politics is more than a mere mechanism for defining the rules of public life; its origin and goal are found in justice, which by its very nature has to do with ethics" (n. 28). The necessary distinction between Church and state, in other words, does not entail a separation between (moral) truth and the state. The purpose of the state is not simply a matter of refereeing among various individuals and groups claiming immunity from coercion by other individuals or groups. On the contrary, as just stated, it is a matter of the positive pursuit of a justice that is intrinsically bound up with the ethical good.

Furthermore, recognition of the fact that pursuit of the just ordering of society is properly the function of the state, and not the Church, does not mean that the Church's role in this pursuit is merely negative, or purely "accidental" with respect to her own mission. On the contrary, the issue of justice is a matter of practical reason, and this reason needs constant purification, "since it can never be completely free of the danger of a certain ethical blindness caused by the dazzling effect of power and special interests" (n. 28). It is here, then, says Benedict, that "politics and faith meet" (n. 28).

> Faith by its specific nature is an encounter with the living God — an encounter opening up new horizons extending beyond the sphere of reason. But it is also a purifying force for reason itself. From God's standpoint, faith liberates reason from its blind spots and therefore helps it to be ever more fully itself. Faith enables reason to do its work more effectively and to see its proper object more clearly. (n. 28)

On the one hand, then, the Church's social doctrine gives the Church no power over the state: that is, the two must remain institutionally-juridically separate. "The formation of just structures is not the immediate duty [*statim officium*] of the Church, but rather belongs to the order of politics, the ambit of reason itself [*ad ambitum scilicet rationis sui ipsius consciae*]" (n. 29). On the other hand, this social doctrine aims "to help purify reason and to contribute, here and now, to the acknowledgment and attainment of what is just" (n. 28). "The Church has an intermediate duty [*officium intermedium*], in that she contributes to the purification of reason and the reawakening of those moral forces without which just structures are neither established nor prove effective in the long run" (n. 29).

It is helpful to note here the significance of Vatican II's *communio* ecclesiology, which, while essentially including the institutional (Petrine) dimension of the Church in fidelity to Vatican I, nevertheless draws out the distinct meaning of the Church as a communion of christological-eucharistic love made possible through Mary's *fiat*. This ecclesiology helps to clarify further the crucial distinction being made by *DCE*: although the institutions of Church and state each have their own proper end, reason, the reason shared by all human beings, retains its ultimate finality in the love whose sacrament is the Church. "[T]he Church's social teaching argues on the basis of reason and natural law, namely, on the basis of what is in accord with the nature of every human being" (n. 28). And, in so doing, it is not the responsibility of the Church — that is, the Church *qua* juridical institution — "to make this teaching prevail in political life" (n. 28). But this does not mean that she can or should "remain on the sidelines in the fight for justice. She has her part to play through rational argument, and she has to reawaken the spiritual energy without which justice, which always demands sacrifice, cannot prevail and prosper" (n. 28).

DCE's assigning the just ordering of society properly to the state thus implies no withdrawal whatsoever of the Church from a commitment to social justice, a commitment, for example, to the elimination of "structures of sin" in the sense developed by John Paul II.[6] The issue, rather, concerns the manner in which this commitment is to be executed. And the pertinent point is that, consistent with Vatican II's ecclesiology of *communio*, *DCE* is insisting that the Church must carry out her commitment to social justice

---

6. Cf. *Sollicitudo Rei Socialis (SRS)* (1987), n. 37; *Centesimus Annus* (1991), n. 38; *Evangelium Vitae* (1995), n. 12. See also "The Significance of World and Culture for Moral Theology: *Veritatis Splendor* and the Nature of the Body," pp. 219-41 in this volume.

through means that are not directly juridical-institutional, but on the contrary a matter properly of her missionary communion-love. The commitment to social justice and to the elimination of unjust social structures is to be carried out properly by the Church *qua* communion of saints, a communion first constituted as a *sacramental gift* from God in Christ and which, as such, is not reducible to community in a "sociological-democratic" sense. It is in and through this missionary love, with its Eucharistic origin and form, mediated through Mary, that the Church forms the consciences of the faithful with respect to the political order, and "stimulate[s] greater insight into the authentic requirements of justice as well as greater readiness to act accordingly, even when this might be contrary to individuals' own gain [*etiam cum contrarium est singulorum lucri*]" (n. 28).

(b) This leads to the second principle emphasized by Benedict: "[l]ove — *caritas* — will always prove necessary even in the most just society. There is no ordering of the state so just that it can eliminate the need for a service of love" (n. 28). Thus if, in accord with the principle just discussed, Christian faith/love assists rational ethical argument and social justice to be "more fully [themselves]" (n. 28), we should see that Christian love also goes beyond the justice properly realized by the state. "There will always be suffering which cries out for consolation and help. There will always be loneliness. There will always be situations of material need where help in the form of concrete love of neighbor is indispensable" (n. 28).

What the suffering person most needs, in other words, is something that the machinery of the state as such cannot provide: namely, "loving personal concern" (n. 28). Indeed, as the great contemporary saints of charitable activity today, such as Mother Teresa, Madeleine Delbrêl,[7] Dorothy Day,[8] and others, have emphasized, the suffering that runs deepest is that caused by the absence of meaning, especially of ultimate meaning. And in this they echo the words of *DCE:* "[o]ften the deepest cause of suffering is the very absence of God" (n. 31). In and through her saints, the Church "is alive with the love enkindled by the Spirit of Christ," a love that "does not simply offer people material help, but refreshment for their souls, something which often is more important than material help" (n. 28). To deny this is to presuppose an unacceptably "materialist conception of man" (n. 28).

---

7. Cf. Madeleine Delbrêl, *We, the Ordinary People of the Streets,* trans. David L. Schindler, Jr., and Charles F. Mann (Grand Rapids: Eerdmans, 2000).

8. Cf. Dorothy Day, *On Pilgrimage* (Grand Rapids: Eerdmans, 1999).

"The proper-particular duty [*proximum operandi officium*] for the just ordering of society" thus falls to the lay faithful who, as citizens of the state, must work for the common good in legislative as well as cultural areas (n. 29). Again, this implies respecting the "legitimate autonomy" [*legitimam autonomiam*] of social life and "cooperating with other citizens according to their respective competences," that is, while recognizing that it "remains true that charity must animate the entire lives [*pervadere vitam*] of the lay faithful and also their political activity, lived as 'social charity'" (n. 29).

As the final phrase here suggests, it is important, apropos of a proper understanding of the relation between justice and charity, to recall again the unity of the two parts of *DCE* as stressed by Benedict. The reason and natural law to which the lay faithful must properly appeal in their efforts to secure justice in the political order bear an inner relation, already *qua* human-natural, to love, a love understood as an *eros* that cannot but move toward its fulfillment in *agape* — that cannot be fulfilled *as eros* outside of a dynamic for transformation toward and in *agape*. Were this not true, "the essence of Christianity would be detached from the vital relations fundamental to human existence and would become a world apart" (n. 7). Were this not true, Jesus, in his path that "leads through the Cross to the Resurrection," would not portray "the essence of love and indeed of human life" (n. 6). Further, *ethos*, ethical reason, would not be interwoven with faith and worship "as a single reality which takes shape in our encounter with God's *agape*" (n. 14), as is implied in the Church's reality as sacramental *communio*.

In a word, then, the reason to which the lay faithful are to appeal in their public pursuit of justice is never "neutral" with respect to man's destiny.[9] Rather, reason itself is ordered to love (cf. n. 10), a love which has its most basic meaning in the created order in marriage, and in the Eucharist of the Incarnate *Logos*.

It is from within this ever-present dynamic for love and for the encounter with the living God in Christ and his Church that the lay faithful are to carry out their proper mission of ethical formation, of purifying reason and of being ready to act in the pursuit of social justice. To be sure, the very nature of this love itself precludes "what is nowadays considered proselytism" (n. 31). Christians living this love will "never seek to impose the

---

9. Benedict XVI, Address to Participants at the Meeting Promoted by the Pontifical Council "Cor Unum."

Church's faith upon others. They realize that a pure and generous love is the best witness to the God in whom they believe and by whom we are driven to love" (n. 31). "A Christian knows when it is time to speak of God and when it is better to say nothing and to let love alone speak: he knows that God is love (cf. 1 Jn 4:8)" (n. 31).

In a word: the laity's necessary appeals to reason and the natural law when cooperating with other citizens in politics, appeals to the "legitimate autonomy" of social life, that is, must not be taken to imply, even for a moment, that the reason of *every human being*, even in modern multicultural societies, is not restless for the *Logos*, the "primordial reason" who "is at the same time a lover" (n. 10), and who is eucharistically-sacramentally present in the Church. It is the call to love, or to fulfill human *eros* in *agape* in *this* sense, that must animate the lives [*pervadere vitam*, cf. DCE, n. 29] of the laity here and now and in their common pursuit of public justice with other citizens, even as we know that this call to *agape*-inspired and -formed justice will never be completely realized in the present life, and in any case can never be imposed or forced on others.

(3) The Distinctiveness of the Church's Charitable Activity

DCE reaffirms John Paul II's insistence (in *SRS*) on "the readiness of the Catholic Church to cooperate with the charitable agencies of other churches and ecclesial communities, since we all . . . look toward . . . a true humanism which acknowledges that man is made in the image of God" (n. 30). *DCE* also affirms the fruitfulness of the "many forms of cooperation between state and Church agencies" that have come about (n. 30). The increase in diversified organizations devoted to meeting the various human needs, says Benedict, is "due to the fact that the command of love of neighbor is inscribed by the Creator in man's very nature [*a Creatore in ipsa hominis natura est inscriptus*]" (n. 31). But the development of these organizations is also the "result of the presence of Christianity in the world," and thus we see "how the power of Christianity [can] spread well beyond the frontiers of the Christian faith" (n. 31). "For this reason," says Benedict, "it is very important that the Church's charitable activity maintain . . . all of its splendor and . . . not become just another form of social assistance" (n. 31). And so he asks: "[W]hat are the essential elements of Christian and ecclesial charity?" (n. 31). What is it that Christian faith and love "add" to "secular" charitable activity? The question is an increasingly significant one in Western societies. *DCE* answers with three comments.

(a) First of all, Christians who engage in social work need to be professionally competent, and this generally implies civil training that is not the peculiar prerogative of Christians. While professional competence and training are "a primary, fundamental requirement, however, they are not of themselves sufficient [*facultas professionalis prima est fundamentalis necessitas, sed sola non sufficit*]" (n. 31). On the contrary, in addition to this necessary professional training, Christian charity workers require also and "before all else a 'formation of the heart' [*ante omnia, 'cordis formatio'*]" (n. 31). "Technically proper care [*cura simpliciter technice apta*]" is not enough (n. 31). Charitable workers need to be rooted in "that encounter with God in Christ which awakens their love and opens their spirits to others" (n. 31).

(b) Second, "Christian charitable activity must be independent of parties and ideologies [*factionibus et doctrinis*]. It is not a means of changing the world ideologically [*secundum quandam doctrinam*], and it is not at the service of worldly strategies [*neque adstat in ministerio mundanorum consiliorum*], but it is a way of making present here and now the love which man always needs" (n. 31). *DCE* takes special note in this context of the "various versions of a philosophy of progress" that have dominated the modern age since the nineteenth century, citing in particular Marxism (n. 31). Such philosophies reject charity because they judge that the exercise of charity obstructs the dynamic for overturning the unjust structures of society, thus thwarting the progress of history.

(c) Third, and as already noted, charity cannot be understood as a means of what is today considered "proselytism."

> Love is free; it is not practiced as a way of achieving other ends. . . . But this does not mean that charitable activity must somehow leave God and Christ aside. For it is always concerned with the whole man. Often the deepest cause of suffering is the very absence of God. Those who practice charity in the Church's name will never seek to impose the Church's faith upon others. (n. 31)

Earlier we noted the Pope's reference to "the activism and growing secularism of many Christians engaged in charitable work" (n. 37). In light of *DCE*'s concern that Christian charity maintain its distinctiveness, on the one hand, and indeed of these dominant tendencies among Christians in Western societies, on the other hand, it is worthwhile to underscore how, in relying necessarily on technical training and professional competence in carrying out his work, the Christian social worker must take care to avoid slipping, however unwittingly, into the activist-secularist mindset that *DCE* decries (n. 37).

Thus, in the texts just cited, *DCE* emphasizes that Christian social work necessarily presupposes professional competence, that is, because such competence is a matter of human reason and nature. At the same time *DCE* stresses that "before all else" a "formation of the heart" involving encounter with God in Christ must accompany and penetrate this social work, because human reason and nature in their concrete history always stand in need of purification and (re-)formation. A prevalent "ideology" in our time, unspoken and largely unconscious, would reduce the sense of this formation to an *intention* that (otherwise) leaves the methods and content of social assistance untouched, such that secular and Christian charitable activities and organizations are then conceived to be more or less identical insofar as they are engaged in feeding the hungry, caring for AIDS patients, providing loving homes for children, and the like. In such a framework, the specificity of Christian love is conceived largely (albeit often unconsciously) "moralistically," as a matter of a good will that simply takes over the logic of conventional professional-secular training and methods and puts the latter to a good use, by situating that logic within a new intentional horizon. This new intentional horizon is necessary, of course, but it is not yet sufficient.

DCE's position is rather more substantial than this. It is the very activity of social work itself that becomes different upon being assumed by Christians, different, that is, in its inner form and not merely by virtue of an intention that is "superadded." Again, this is seen above all in the saints of "social work" like Mother Teresa (who did not like the term "social work") in our own age. In these persons the very "how" and "what" of social work, the very meaning of "competence," takes on a transformed quality, a different sense of time and space and presence. Such saints make clear above all that the whole of social work, its every aspect, has to do intrinsically with *meaning:* ultimately, the meaning of man before God that alone can breathe enduring joy into suffering and hope into forsakenness. Only in this way does Christian faith/love become a "vision-understanding that transforms,"[10] as dis-

---

10. Benedict XVI, Address to Participants at the Meeting Promoted by the Pontifical Council "Cor Unum."

tinct from merely a new-good intention that continues to presume a conventional technical or secular logic.

This does not mean that Christian social charity cannot and should not, for example, also take on institutional forms similar to other, secular social agencies. The point is that, even in these cases, the formation of the heart demanded of Christians will make a claim affecting not only their intention but the inner order or "rationality" of how they participate in and govern such institutions, requiring a distinct sort of "planning, foresight, and cooperation with [these] other . . . institutions" (n. 31). Christian workers in these institutions will realize that, to be "workers of . . . justice, [they] must be workers who are *being made just* by contact with him who is just: Jesus of Nazareth"; that "the place of this encounter is the Church, nowhere more powerfully present than in her sacraments and liturgy."[11] Christian workers will realize that their institutions must be concerned for justice when issues and problems arise that the broader culture "no longer sees as bound up with human dignity, like protecting the right to life of every human being from conception to natural death, or when the Church confesses that justice also includes our responsibilities to God himself."[12] For example, Catholic charities seeking to find loving homes for abandoned or abused or orphaned children will understand that social justice, rightly understood, requires placing such children as far as humanly possible inside monogamous marriages between a man and a woman. Catholic social agencies will understand that their commitment to feeding the poor or assisting AIDS patients must be integrated into the whole of the Church's teaching, and must entail the freedom, for example, to witness to that teaching in the "benefits" the agencies provide to workers (such as distinct support for married couples, exclusion of contraceptive devices from insurance benefits, and the like). Catholic hospitals will understand that their care cannot include abortions and the "morning-after" pill.

What *Deus Caritas Est* makes clear is that these distinct practices demanded of Catholic social institutions are not at all, rightly understood, a matter of a failure to recognize the dignity of all human beings or indeed to be sensitive to the suffering, for example, of homosexuals or of women seeking abortions. On the contrary, it is a matter — and it can be justified finally only as a matter — of protecting what Christians believe is the deepest *eros* of *every human being,* including especially those who suffer

---

11. Cardinal Joseph Ratzinger, "Homily," St. Peter's Basilica, 18 March 2005.
12. Cardinal Joseph Ratzinger, "Homily," St. Peter's Basilica, 18 March 2005.

the most, who are the weakest and most vulnerable and most rejected by society: of protecting the *eros*, that is, whose deepest search is for a happiness liberated into the generosity of *agape*, an *agape* that in Jesus takes the form of sacrificing himself, suffering with all of us and for all of us, unto death. It is a matter of seeing that *eros* and all of its passion can be realized in the end only by being somehow integrated in and through what is given by God in human nature, hence "objectively," as the way to share in the truth of his love and life.

At any rate, professional-social skills and conventional-managerial social service methods combined with generous intentions do not suffice to account for the love that "is the light . . . that can always illumine a world grown dim" (n. 39). Man is created in the image of God who is *Logos* and Love. All Christians, and in a special way Christian charity workers, are called to form every phase and aspect of their activities in the image of this God. "To experience love and in this way to cause the light of God to enter into the world — this is the invitation [that Benedict] extend[s] with the present encyclical" (n. 39).

Does the Free Market Produce Free Persons?

Exercise of economic freedom, private ownership of property, earning a profit, and realizing wealth are all goods to be affirmed in any adequate vision of man, and hence in any economy. The relevant issue is that of determining the precise meaning to be accorded these, and on the basis of what anthropology.[1] I begin with a summary of the principles informing my own judgment regarding the proper sense of these goods.

I. Toward an Anthropology of Gift and Gratitude

(1) An adequate anthropology, on the grounds at once of faith and human reason, recognizes a restlessness for happiness at the core of every human being that is resolved only through a life integrated into the truth that "we are not our own."[2] We possess ourselves fully only through recuperation of

---

1. In his recent encyclical letter *Caritas in Veritate* (2009) Benedict XVI teaches that the economic order must be structured in accord with the truth about man — his identity as a creature who is a gift to himself and to others and a steward of creation — in order to facilitate the achievement of an authentic common good. This encyclical appeared only when the final corrections were being made to this chapter and therefore its argument could not be fully taken into account in the framing of the argument.

2. See George Grant, "Conversation: Intellectual Background," in Larry Schmidt, ed., *George Grant in Process: Essays and Conversations* (Toronto: Anansi, 1978), pp. 62-63.

This chapter is a revised version of my contribution to a debate between Doug Bandow and myself titled "Economic Freedom and Moral Virtue: Does the Free Market Produce Captive Souls?" co-sponsored by the Intercollegiate Studies Institute and the Tocqueville Forum at Georgetown University on 1 April 2009, as part of the "Cicero's Podium Debate Series."

relations that are first *given to* us ("constitutive"), not first *constructed by* us ("contractual"). The human self is most basically a gift: from the Creator, and from our parents and indeed from all other creatures inside relation to the Creator. The basic act elicited from the self in response to its being-as-gift is therefore gratitude.

In a word, the self's desire for happiness is at root a desire to be loved and to love; and to respond to things first intrinsically, in terms of their natural truth and goodness and beauty, and not first merely as instruments.

(2) The fact that this desire for grateful giving is built into the core of our creaturely being does not imply that it is fully conscious or easily realized in the concrete order of history, which is always marked by sin. It means simply that, though its fulfillment demands sacrifice and suffering, this desire expresses our *inmost reality as human*. It is not merely a supererogatory "ideal," best set aside as unrealistic in our public, here economic, activity.

(3) Comfort and pleasure, adequate food, clothing, and property are inherently good. Indeed, material abundance in its root meaning is a continuing sign of the extravagance characteristic of God's original act of creation (Annie Dillard).[3] Relative abundance of material things is thus itself already a matter of "quality" and not merely of "quantity." And of course one can scarcely exercise the fullness of freedom and intelligence if one is starving to death, and thus food and shelter retain a certain obvious priority.

At the same time, it is crucial to see that economic activity addressing the human want for adequate food and shelter, and the abundance accruing from this activity, must be integrated all along the way into what is the human being's *radical* need for *meaning:* for the love borne in the self's constitutively given relations to others. Wealth adequately conceived includes above all richness in one's relations to God (Luke 12:21), to a father and a mother and a family, to one's natural civil community, and to the world of nature (all of which also presuppose sufficient material wealth, precisely for the sake of and as integral to these relations). Poverty in its deepest sense thus consists in the poverty of *meaning* resulting from brokenness in these relations.[4] It is this poverty of meaning that signals what the question of the original title assigned this paper calls "captive souls."

---

3. See also Joseph Cardinal Ratzinger/Benedict XVI, *Credo for Today: What Christians Believe* (San Francisco: Ignatius Press, 2009), p. 15.

4. See *Caritas in Veritate*, n. 53.

The dominant historical forms of socialism and liberal capitalism both foster this poverty of meaning as a matter of their inner logic, albeit in unequal and asymmetrical ways.[5]

II. Smith and the Logic of "Self-interest, Rightly Understood"

What this means in terms of the logic of the liberal free market can be illustrated briefly in terms of the famous principle expressed by Adam Smith in his *Wealth of Nations*.[6] Smith states:

> [I]t is in vain for man to expect [the help of his brethren] from their benevolence only. . . . It is not from the benevolence of the butcher, the brewer, or the baker, that we expect our dinner, but from their regard to their own interest. We address ourselves, not to their humanity but to their self-love, and never talk to them of our own necessities but of their advantages.[7]

First of all, Smith is right to insist that what he terms benevolence alone cannot account for economic activity, indeed for any human activity, rightly understood. What is often termed "altruism" never accounts adequately for the logic of human activity. The very idea of a self, with its presupposition of an inner consistency *as a self,* just so far entails an abiding self-interest or self-love.

But this leads to my second point: Smith in this passage expresses a *reductive* view of self-interest or self-love. As stated earlier, what I love most basically, what interests me at the deepest level, even if only implicitly, is my self *as a participant in the gift-giving of God and others.* My deepest desiring love, which bends back toward the self, is ordered at once toward generous love centered in others.

Smith's argument presupposes a dualistic separation of self-love and other-centered love: self-love turns in on itself such that the other can

---

5. For a more extensive elaboration of this argument, see "Market Liberalism and an Economic Culture of Gift and Gratitude," pp. 166-218 in this volume.

6. There is much discussion today regarding how best to understand Smith's idea of human action, when viewed for example also in light of his *Theory of Moral Sentiments*. I limit myself here, however, to consideration of his statement in terms of what I take to be its meaning as received in the dominant liberal understanding.

7. Adam Smith, *The Wealth of Nations* (Hamburg: Management Laboratory Press, 2008), pp. 21-22.

only be conceived first primarily as an instrument. Other-centered love, on the other hand, then becomes a kind of supererogatory, and more or less arbitrary, additional activity, to be enacted privately if one wishes, because one is a Christian believer, for example. In any case, it is not an activity for which the human self is made already in its originally constituted desire *as* a self, an activity that belongs intrinsically to the fulfillment of every human being. My own view of the matter, contrary to that of Smith, follows a tradition of thought recently articulated in Pope Benedict XVI's encyclical *Deus Caritas Est* (2005): self-love and other-centered love bear a unity within their abiding distinctness, such that the self loves itself truly *as a self* only from within its love as at once ordered toward and centered in others. The self truly loves itself, but only from within a self that "knows" itself to be from and for others, even if this knowledge is not reflexive or explicit.

Nor is Smith's reductive sense of self-interest adequately corrected when one insists, as many thinkers do today in defending Smith, that he understands self-interest, *rightly conceived,* to involve mutuality. For an instrumentalizing become mutual is still an instrumentalizing, and is not yet inclusive of a mutual generosity. The point, in other words, is that mutual self-interest demands an opening into mutually generous love, precisely as the inner condition and form of its own realization as mutual *self-interest,* because only such an opening takes into account the deepest meaning of the self as from and for others.

What may seem an arcane technical matter here makes all the difference in terms of our judgment regarding the question posed in our title. Smith's statement, as generally interpreted, implies that the bread, and indeed the producer and the consumer of the bread, will all be made better by virtue of the harnessing of the self-interest of the consumer with that of the bread's producer. In fact, the logic of Smith's argument bears a dynamic, strictly, not for the baking of the best bread, but only for what *appears* to be the best bread, and in a way that instrumentalizes the meaning of the selves of both the producer-baker and his consumer-customer. The baker's end, for Smith, is to be profitable as a baker, and insofar as this is the case, the quality of the bread is strictly a means.[8] The best-case sce-

---

8. Competition is often seen nowadays as an antidote to this problem, since competition "compels" the different persons or companies making a product to improve its quality, for the sake of survival. This, of course, is true to a certain extent. However, the problem is that, as long as the logic of self-interest remains in place, competition will tend, rather, to "compel" each person or company to improve the cosmetic *appearance* of the product

nario would thus be one in which the baker could devise ways continuously to lower the costs and the time that it takes to produce bread, which entails lessening the qualities of the ingredients that go into the bread, all the while retaining what as far as possible *appears* to be bread of the same high quality. There is nothing in the logic of Smith's argument requiring the baker to make bread that is *intrinsically* of the highest quality, made for the sake of its own inner quality. In a word, on Smith's reading the bread has its worth strictly as a means to an end, and means by definition have their worth conditionally to their end. The quality of the bread and indeed all the "virtues" that might be involved in the making and selling of the bread, are *instruments* of profit, which alone is the end of such activity.

Note that my argument here does not deny the legitimacy of profit, or indeed of mutual usefulness in the process of realizing profit. It merely insists that profit and usefulness be seen as *intrinsic features of,* and thus *in subordination to, service to the other in his integrity.* Indeed, we should recall here the classical understanding of (human) being, whereby the *goodness inherent* in being in its natural givenness as such includes its "usefulness" for other beings: it is of the essence of what is good to share itself *(bonum est diffusivum sui)*. Further, service to the other in his integrity, needless to say, is not to be understood in terms of an abstract-utopian perfection. On the contrary, such service rightly conceived always acknowledges the real limits and material constraints that must mark every generous love in the finite and indeed sinful world. The point is simply that the demand to order profit and usefulness prudently in terms of generous service can never be rightly set aside in the name of some putatively more adequate worldly "realism."

III. Objections

Let me now clarify the meaning of this necessarily abbreviated criticism, in terms of some common objections.

(1) First, it is often asserted, rightly, that sin is present in every society, and thus that there is nothing peculiar about its being present in the functioning of the liberal market. The problem, however, is that Smith,

---

through advertising: demonstrating the quality of athletic shoes, for example, not in terms of how they are actually made, but by putting Michael Jordan's feet in them.

having in the name of "realism" removed the dynamic for generosity from the inner meaning of self-love, reduces the latter to what can now only be selfishness in the form of the reduction of the other primarily to an instrument. Smith thus effectively inverts sin itself into a kind of virtue, albeit now a virtue of "realistic" necessity: mutual self-interest in his sense is the best we can do in history, and so this becomes the only realistic public "virtue." Virtues such as honesty and service and the like thus tend toward the *appearance* rather than the full reality of these virtues.[9]

What follows from my own argument, on the contrary, is that we must continue to affirm selfish instrumentalism as (objectively) sinful, even as we recognize its always pervasive presence in human society. We can rightly understand man in the "realism" of his actual-sinful historical condition only insofar as we understand this simultaneously in light of what is the deeper *realism* of man as always already, in his actual historical condition, called to generosity. In a word, rather than marginalize the call to generosity as historically unrealistic, we need on the contrary to continue to affirm it as realism of the most profound sort, even as we need now, in view of the actual-sinful historical human condition, to include within the realism of the call to generosity the need to sacrifice: the need to suffer the call to generosity into realization in history.[10]

The distinction here is of crucial importance. The upshot of the Smithian reductive reading of self-interest is that it makes virtue *accidental* to the public-economic order. Or better, genuine virtue, insofar as it involves self-transcendence, becomes essentially a private matter. In any case, Smith's reading eliminates among economic agents any intrinsic teleology toward a genuinely common good.

(2) A second objection is that the market economy based on the liberal idea of self-interest has worked: it has generated an abundance of free-

---

9. Thus, for example, we have all heard flight attendants say, at the conclusion of a flight: "Thank you for flying with us; we are happy to have had the opportunity to serve you." I do not mean to say here that there is no truth in what the attendants are saying, only that self-interest of its inner logic tends to render this truth into a merely surface phenomenon, an *appearance* of gratitude.

10. This does not demand the practice of perfect virtue on the part of the baker as a condition of his bread-making. Perfect virtue can never be achieved in this life. My point is simply that what we need to do, on a rightful understanding of man in his economic activity, is not to declare the exigence for generosity practically unrealistic, but rather to insist on the utter and basic practical realism of this exigence, all the while now incorporating the need for self-sacrifice and indeed suffering into what is meant by realism — again, apropos of man in his concrete reality as given in history.

dom, through its creation of an abundance of wealth in the form of material capital, property, money, technology enabling greater physical comfort and less physical pain, and indeed more effective means of communication through travel and electronic media.

Of course I do not deny the obvious regarding the free market's realization of abundance as indicated. My argument merely insists that assessment of abundance in all of its realizations take its measure from man in his wholeness as human, and not from man the material needs and desires of whom have already been conceived in abstraction from this wholeness. Indeed, the obvious abundance of commodities realized by the liberal market economy has coincided with an increase in poverty of meaning; and that this economy, paradoxically, has expanded freedom conceived as exercise of choice only at the expense of the liberation of freedom into its true meaning as an inclination of the self toward God and others.[11] This economy's inner dynamic has in fact reinforced an enslavement of freedom through a tyranny of instrumentalism.

(3) I pass immediately to a third objection: that, even if the liberal market economy has been attended by this poverty of meaning and paradoxical reduction in freedom, responsibility for these problems lies primarily in the failures of cultural institutions such as church, family, and education. The economy, in other words, *reflects* the habits of the culture, according to this objection; it is not their primary agent. The market is, to be sure, in need of a moral environment, but this is to be supplied from outside the market. The market as such neither advances human virtue nor corrects human vice. That is the job of these cultural institutions. Furthermore in this light, the church, or the Bible, while responsible for the development of human virtue, endorses no particular system of economics.

My response is that, if the economy really reflects and is thus a sign of a disordered, because fragmented, logic of self-love, then the economy itself cannot but be, *eo ipso,* a carrier of that logic. It cannot but itself influence culture in turn, in the direction of the false notions of freedom and wealth that are a function of this logic. The influences of the economy on the one hand, and of ecclesial, domestic, and educational institutions on the other, are, in other words, always *mutual:* the institutions of church,

---

11. See *Caritas in Veritate,* n. 55 and 79, which insists, in the words of *Populorum Progressio* (1967), that the criterion of culture, religion, and authentic development is "the whole man and all men."

family, and education form the culture only in and through their members who are always-also participants in the economy's logic of producing, consuming, using, and possessing commodities (and vice versa).

The point, in a word, is that economic agents have to come to terms with the anthropology that is always concretely embodied, even if often unwittingly, in the very logic of their activity as economic agents; even as the church or Bible thereby in turn has an intrinsic stake in how the logic of this activity is to be understood, and is thus never simply neutral with respect to economic systems.[12]

To see what is meant here, consider the inner dynamic of the liberal market economy for increasing the speed and efficiency of communication. Development of instruments such as the computer and the cell phone is integral to this dynamic. I do not wish to demonize technology, but merely to propose an argument for the proposition that technology in its very hardware always embodies a *meaning*, to which we need to attend. The computer, for example, reinforces experience as instant acquisition and manipulation of useful information. The cell phone enables listening to someone on the way to doing something else, to the detriment of the patient attention characteristic of true personal communication. Each of these gives us experience without a sensorium, in a way that promotes movement along the surface as distinct from into the depths of whatever is the object of one's concern. Each of these turns time into what is as it were a "bad eternity" of endlessly successive moments lacking depth, interiority, and transcendence. Again, my intention is not to reject these instruments out of hand, but only to point out that, insofar as our patterns of communication take shape through their use, we dissolve the patient capacity necessary to see and appreciate genuinely — in other words, to love — partic-

---

12. See *Caritas in Veritate*, n. 38, and its reference to *"civilizing the economy."* Clarifying the teaching of John Paul II's encyclical letter *Centesimus Annus* (1991), Benedict notes that John Paul II "saw civil society as the most natural setting for an *economy of gratuitousness* and fraternity, but did not mean to deny it a place in [the market and the state]. Today we can say that economic life must be understood as a multi-layered phenomenon: in every one of these layers, to varying degrees and in ways specifically suited to each, the aspect of fraternal reciprocity must be present. In the global era, economic activity cannot prescind from gratuitousness, which fosters and disseminates solidarity and responsibility for justice and the common good among the different economic players.... While in the past it was possible to argue that justice had to come first and gratuitousness could follow afterwards, as a complement, today it is clear that without gratuitousness, there can be no justice in the first place."

ular persons and things in their naturally given truth, goodness, and beauty. In a word, we instrumentalize them.

In sum, the liberal free market with its inner logic of commodification fosters an *incapacity to pay attention* — to God, to other persons, and indeed to the things of nature: fosters an incapacity *truly to rest in anything for its own sake.* The logic of the market reinforces an incapacity for interior stillness, or again dissipates the *patient relations* necessary for giving depth of meaning to the concrete time and space and place in which alone our humanity really exists: to what is *here* and *now.* But if we are not able to give meaning to *this* time and *this* place, we will lack the capacity for meaningful memory of who we are, and hence for a meaningful future.

To repeat what I've said elsewhere, the most basic problem of liberal society may be rightly described as a massive Attention Deficit Hyperactivity Disorder (ADHD). The liberal market economy is a significant, though scarcely the exclusive, agent of this disorder, which, again, is both a sign and an expression of liberalism's relentless logic of instrumentalism. (It is this logic, for example, that informs at its root our distinctly liberal-technological form of "compassion," which inclines us toward manufacturing babies to the design desired by parents, or for the purpose of killing them to harvest their genetic parts for easing the pain and suffering of others.)

IV. An Alternative?

But there remains a final and overarching question: What alternative can be proposed?

In response, I offer three brief points: what is demanded first by this critique is not a new economic *system*, but a "new" anthropology. This anthropology to be sure entails a radical transformation (from *radix,* root) of the market economy in its dominant liberal understanding, but only as a sign and expression of what must be an anterior transformation of our selves in the relations that most profoundly define us. A proposed systemic change in the market economy that gets out ahead of this call to the inner self-transformation will result in what is merely another version of *homo economicus,* albeit now dressed in a different costume.

Second, the alternative demanded by the critique does not in the first instance invite increased intervention by the government, for two reasons. The purpose of government rightly understood is service to the common good through the promotion of solidarity, in adherence to the principle of subsidiarity — promotion thus of a solidarity that is first realized locally.[13] Furthermore, the government is scarcely the first place to turn for redressing the problems identified because it is run today largely by technicians. Contemporary liberal democratic government is best described as a "tyranny of bureaucrats" (Solzhenitsyn), led mostly by lawyers and academic experts and other secular clerics: which is to say, by those who are least capable of recognizing commodification as a reduction of reality.

Third, and in positive terms, the burden of my critique is that each of us should begin simply by pondering his or her own way of life in light of the principles enunciated above. The recommended alternative, in other words, is not primarily to be *imposed* via the machinery of a new system of government, but rather to be *proposed* through the inner transformation of our particular persons, which transformation will involve our participation as citizens in effecting realization of a deepened understanding of the common good in the political order. We do not need to make an abrupt change in our profession, place of living, and the like. Rather, we can, and must, begin precisely from where we are, here and now and from within our concrete reality. All of us are already in various ways "havers," producers, and consumers. What we must do first of all is simply pay better or more patient attention, to God, family, our local (civil) community, to natural things, relations to all of which reach to the heart of our being as creatures. It is this attention alone that orders our self-love simultaneously toward other-centered love, in a way that makes both ourselves, as subjects, and the objects of economic activity into matters of gratitude and gift, in a way that *affirms* while *transforming the meaning of* self-interest and profit and wealth.

The limits of the present forum preclude any detailed development of what this means. What is crucial is that we recuperate the habits of patient consciousness and freedom proper to our being as creatures, as from and for God and others. Two examples will help illustrate what this implies.

First, we can try to recuperate a sense of our reality as children: of God, of our parents and the generations of parents before them, of the entire creaturely world that has preceded us and remains the anterior condition of our own being. To be a child is to be from-others, for-others. We

---

13. See the *Compendium of the Social Doctrine of the Church,* published in the pontificate of John Paul II, e.g., n. 181-88 on subsidiarity, and n. 192-96 on solidarity. These themes also run through *Caritas in Veritate.*

teach children to say "please" and "thank you." But, properly understood, this is not a matter merely of manners but of teaching them the truth of their being, which lies in the child's reality as a gift calling forth gratitude. Recuperation of childlikeness in this sense is the first step in realizing that the relations that give us our deepest meaning are not those first *contracted by* us but *given to* us, in the very constitution of our being.

Second, we can try to live freedom in its truest sense as ordered from its inmost depths to saying forever, to vocation. God's act of creation bears the structure of a covenant: he promises unfailing fidelity to his creation, inviting unfailing fidelity to God in return on the part of creatures. This implies saying forever, which normally takes the form of a vow, either in consecrated virginity or in marriage.[14]

Saying forever enables an entry of the whole of our being into each of our actions and productions, a patient drawing of eternity into each moment and each place of our existence, affording each moment and place a literally infinite depth and fullness of meaning.

Here, it seems to me, we touch the foundation for the ineliminable truth of what is termed Distributism:[15] that we must learn truly to indwell time and to stay in place, by indwelling the organic communities into which we are born: the community with God through this particular family and generation of families, in a particular time and place and natural environment. This community reaches, in and through these particularities of family and time and place and environment, to the whole of the creaturely world of all times and all places. It is through indwelling community in this way that we realize the sense in which "property" is at root a matter simultaneously of cultivation, culture, and cult (Josef Pieper), and in which an authentic economy is rightfully a matter of capitalizing only as it is a matter more basically of promoting genuine human sufficiency and completeness.

Realization of the alternative vision of economic life implied by my argument, in sum, does not require that we move from the city or from urban professions to, say, farming (though survival of local, family-owned farms is an urgent matter for the health of civilization). The point, rather,

---

14. Cf. "Living and Thinking Reality in Its Integrity: Originary Experience, God, and the Task of Education" and "Modernity and the Nature of a Distinction: Balthasar's Ontology of Generosity," pp. 310-27 and 350-82 in this volume.

15. For discussions of what is meant by Distributism, see, *inter alia*, the work of G. K. Chesterton, as well as the several collections of source essays on Distributism published by IHS Press in Virginia. See also the related work of Wendell Berry and Allan Carlson.

is that each of us is already involved in economic activity in some way: in the professions, as homemakers, as laborers and business executives; all of us in various ways as owners, producers, purchasers, and consumers of things. We all can begin living more profoundly our reality as from-and-for God and others, pondering how, from inside our economic activity in all of these ever-present concrete ways, we can deepen this freedom as ordered to saying forever, in a way that draws eternity into every moment and place of our life and gives grateful and generous form to each of our activities. It is in this way alone, which is only apparently "small," that we can truly transform economic freedom, private ownership of property, earning a profit, and realizing wealth as these are conceived and practiced in the dominant liberal market economy.

Market Liberalism and an Economic Culture of Gift and Gratitude

In debates among Christians regarding market systems, the conventional assumption is that the contested issues are first economic in nature. Beginning with the idea that the purpose of economic exchanges is to produce wealth, we assume that properly economic questions are about how to realize that wealth most effectively, within the limits set by our common Christian eschatological and ethical framework. In a word, we understand an economic system as something conceived first on its own terms, to which theological or philosophical or cultural substance is then added.[1]

This conventional approach to market debates, however, begs what we will see are crucial questions: those questions, namely, that concern the original nature and purpose of "economic exchanges" and of "wealth." The conventional way of approaching these debates, in other words, begs the prior question of how man's *telos* anteriorly shapes (or should shape) the meaning of economics and wealth as such, and therefore ignores the sense in which an economic system itself already embeds, indeed also is, a theol-

---

1. On the nature of the economy, see Pope Benedict XVI's encyclical letter *Caritas in Veritate* (2009), particularly n. 11, 30, 36, and 38. Regarding the definition of wealth, or "authentic development" see in particular n. 17, 21, 25, 52 and 76. Note that this chapter was written prior to this encyclical and thus does not integrate Benedict's argument in a comprehensive manner.

An earlier version of this chapter was written in connection with a joint project undertaken by the John Templeton Foundation and the Intercollegiate Studies Institute. The collection of essays making up the project was published as *Wealth, Poverty and Human Destiny*, ed. Doug Bandow and David L. Schindler (Wilmington, DE: ISI Books, 2002). As a co-editor of the book, I was asked to respond to various of these essays. Hence the particular authors and essays engaged by me in the present chapter.

ogy and an anthropology and a culture. The burden of my reflections is to show how this is so, and why it is crucial for us to understand how it is so as we engage the urgent problems, increasingly global in reach, regarding the market economy and its approaches to wealth and poverty.

It is of course beyond the scope of a reflection such as this to mount a full-scale argument regarding the nature and destiny of the human being. Instead, Part I provides an outline of what I take to be an adequate anthropology. Part II indicates what this anthropology implies for an economy of gift and gratitude, in contrast to a liberal economic culture. Part III offers a technical review of the assumptions that establish liberal anthropology as "instrumentalist." In light of the argument of Parts I-III, and drawing on the writings of Pope John Paul II and also on an argument by Jennifer Roback Morse, Part IV describes and assesses our contemporary cultural problematic in terms of its underlying "instrumentalist" or "utilitarian" logic. Finally, Part V illustrates how certain economic proposals of several Christian thinkers embody the substance of a liberal anthropology: how what are otherwise the genuine goods defended in those proposals — efficiency, creativity, freedom, productivity, and indeed things in relative abundance — express and contribute to this instrumentalism, despite what are these thinkers' clear intentions to the contrary.

Before we begin, a methodological note: as indicated, this chapter presupposes a background of Christianity, and my own argument unfolds within a definite reading of Christianity. Essential to my reading of Christianity, however, is that Christianity makes ontological claims about how things are. That is, the claims I make regarding the nature and destiny of the human being are meant to be in some significant sense accessible and indeed convincing, in their ontological meaning, to readers who do not share the Christian faith, even as I take Christian faith to be required for the claims to be fully accessible and convincing. The following text from Pope John Paul II indicates, in form and content, the relation between Christian faith and ontology (anthropology) I am presupposing here:

> Man cannot live without love. He remains a being that is incomprehensible for himself, his life is senseless, if love is not revealed to him, if he does not encounter it and make it his own, if he does not participate intimately in it. This . . . is why Christ the Redeemer "fully reveals man to himself."[2] If we may use the expression, this is the human di-

---

2. The text cited here is that of *Gaudium et Spes*, n. 22, which is referred to in a

mension of the mystery of the Redemption. In this dimension man finds again the greatness, dignity and value that belong to his humanity. . . .[3]

What is crucial for the integrity of the Pope's statement is that its claim about love finds an echo, a resonance, in every human heart, not just in explicitly Christian hearts; and that his claim does so even as it retains its intrinsically Christian character, that is, even as the love about which the Pope speaks is fully revealed only in Jesus Christ. My argument unfolds in terms of man's encounter with love in the fact of his creation, hence in man's original reality as gift-eliciting-gratitude. And it presupposes with John Paul II that this creative love finds its full realization in the redemptive love of God revealed in Christ.

Clearly, the relation presupposed here between faith and philosophy/culture demands justification on its own terms.[4] The foregoing statement nevertheless suffices for the limited purposes of the present forum.

I. The Idea of "Home": Toward an Anthropology of Gift and Gratitude

"Homelessness" seems to me the fundamental problem of a liberal economy. The term "homelessness" is taken here in its root sense as a matter of man's relation simultaneously to earth and to heaven. "Homelessness," in other words, refers to a lack of one's proper place in the cosmos, and not in the first instance to the condition of a discrete group of people living in the streets (though my argument presupposes that these two senses of "homelessness" are intrinsically related).

The dictionary defines "home" as "one's place of residence," "a familiar or usual setting," "a place of origin." To be "at home" is to be "relaxed and comfortable or at ease," as well as to be "in harmony with one's surroundings." The Latin term for "home" is *domus*, and "to domesticate"

---

significant way in nearly every one of John Paul II's encyclicals. Indeed, the Pope states that the relation between Christology and anthropology affirmed in this text indicates what is perhaps the most important teaching of the Second Vatican Council (cf. *Dives in Misericordia*, n. 3).

3. *Redemptor Hominis*, n. 10.
4. See my "God and the End of Intelligence: Knowledge as Relationship," *Communio: International Catholic Review* 26, no. 3 (Fall 1999): 510-40.

thus means to "bring into domestic use," or "to fit for domestic life." "Home" and its attendant terms here receive their most proper meaning in terms of man's creation and destiny, of man's ontological beginning and *telos*. "Home" and "homelessness," in other words, refer most basically to the sense in which man is made to be in harmony with his earthly surroundings, in relation to God as his origin and end.

In a word, man is rightly said to be at home insofar as he realizes the relations that most profoundly constitute his being as a creature.

We can state this in more technical terms. First, each man is an individual. But each man is constituted in his individuality precisely in and by virtue of his relation to the creator — and redeemer — God. In the words of John Paul II, "relation to God is a constitutive element of [one's] very 'nature' and 'existence': it is in God that we 'live and move and have our being' (Acts 17:28)."[5]

The relevant point is thus that each man has his meaning as an individual only *from within this original and abiding ontological community with God*.

Second, this relation to God that is constitutive of the individual person includes relation to other persons: "The human person has an inherent social dimension which calls a person from the innermost depths of self to *communion* with others and to the *giving* of self to others. . . . Thus *society* as a fruit and sign of the *social nature* of the individual reveals its whole truth in being a *community of persons*."[6]

In contrast to a common view in liberal societies, therefore, individuality and community in their primary meanings do not oppose but on the contrary presuppose each other. Individuality emerges *from within* commu-

---

5. John Paul II, Apostolic Exhortation, *Christifideles Laici* (CL), n. 39. Of course, the Pope's affirmation of the individual's constitutive relation to God does not obviate the need for baptism and hence for the Church for the fulfillment of this relation that is given in and with creation: the "already" remains essentially a "not yet," needing the redemptive grace of baptism. But here is not the place to sort out the twentieth-century debate within Catholicism regarding nature and grace. Cf., for example, Henri de Lubac, *The Mystery of the Supernatural* (New York: Crossroad Herder, 1998) and *The Discovery of God* (Grand Rapids: Eerdmans, 1996). See also Nicholas J. Healy, "Henri de Lubac on Nature and Grace: A Note on Some Recent Contributions to the Debate," *Communio: International Catholic Review* 35, no. 4 (Winter 2008): 535-64.

6. John Paul II, *CL*, n. 40. The *Catechism of the Catholic Church* (*CCC*) amplifies this by stating that the "divine image is present in every man. It shines forth in the communion of persons, in the likeness of the union of the divine persons among themselves . . ." (n. 1702).

nity and is always already an expression of community, even as individuality itself conditions and is presupposed by the original meaning *of* community.

Third, "The first and basic expression of the social dimension of the person . . . is the married couple and family. . . . [The] partnership [*consociatio*] of man and woman constitutes the first form of the communion of persons." "The family is the basic cell of society."[7] These assertions imply that familial or nuptial relations — that is, (aptness for) paternity or maternity, and filiality — are intrinsic to the original and hence abiding identity of the person.[8]

Finally, each entity of the world, as created, is intrinsically related to God and thereby in some intrinsic sense also to all other entities of the world. This original relation, or "community," of cosmic entities is meant to be lifted up and transformed into the service of human and indeed finally liturgical-eucharistic community, in and through the "flesh" and labor of man (St. Maximus the Confessor). It follows that space, time, matter, and motion are themselves, in their original and proper — i.e., creaturely — nature, apt for expressing and "containing" community.[9]

I said above that man is at home when he realizes the relations that constitute his being as a creature. We now see that these relations include relations both to God above all and in some significant sense to all creatures, and that they pass through and are mediated by familial relations. Man is at home, therefore, when he is rightly related to God, to others, and to the world in and through a family.[10] It is within these relations and in their right ordering that he finds his basic place of residence, or truly comes to rest.

---

7. *CL*, n. 40.

8. See "The Embodied Person as Gift and the Cultural Task in America," pp. 242-74 in this volume.

9. On the cosmic dimension of the Incarnation and of the Church and sacrament, see John Paul II, *Dominum et Vivificantem*, n. 50, and Alexander Schmemann, *For the Life of the World* (Crestwood, NY: St. Vladimir's Seminary Press, 1973 [1963]). On the (cosmic) community implied in creation, see Wendell Berry, *The Art of the Commonplace*, ed. Norman Wirzba (Washington, DC: Counterpoint, 2002).

10. The present chapter does not develop the idea of the Church as the historical-sacramental place, or home, of man's community with God, and indeed of his community with others, the world, and the family in relation to God. This idea, however, serves as the presupposed horizon for all that is argued. For elaboration of this horizon, see Henri de Lubac, *Catholicism: Christ and the Common Destiny of Man* (San Francisco: Ignatius Press, 1988); and Émile Mersch, *The Whole Christ: The Historical Development of the Doctrine of the Mystical Body in Scripture and Tradition* (London: Dennis Dobson, Ltd., 1938).

Now, it is difficult to see how anyone, certainly any Christian, would object to these assertions in the schematic form in which they are expressed here. Certainly no Christian thinker who wishes to defend the liberal market economy would want to dispute the centrality of right relations to God, others, the world, and the family for realization of a person's health and wholeness, his fundamental "at-home-ness." And yet I propose to argue that the very conceptions of wealth and poverty prevalent in today's liberal market economy tend to prevent realization of this fundamental at-home-ness. The liberal market economy, in its very efforts to produce wealth and reduce poverty, tends of its inner logic to fragment a person's relations to God, others, the world, and the family, thus rendering man "homeless" in the deepest sense.

To justify these assertions, which may at first appear to be extreme, I must now explain how I am conceiving these relations of each individual man to God, others, the world, and the family.

The crucial point is to see what is implied in saying that these relations are *constitutive*. They are constitutive in that they are first given to man: they are entailed in the fact of his creation, his very constitution as a creature. The relations are not first *chosen by* man.

In a word, the relations, and the original communities implicit in these relations, are *gifts* "before" they are *constructions*. The priority indicated here is an ontological, not temporal priority. That is, the relations that are constitutively given to man are also, at once, essentially matters of freedom. My point, whose sense is yet to be properly qualified, is simply that these relations are *objects* of free choice only as already operative in the *subject* of free choice.

Clearly, there are significant differences among the types of community indicated in man's relations to God, others, the world, and his family. The community a man shares with his family, for example, differs in fundamental ways from the community he shares with all other human beings. The pertinent point is simply that these communities, despite and within what are their important differences in other respects, all share the fact of first being given *to*, and not *by*, man.

Furthermore, insofar as these relations are constitutive of man's being, they are necessarily presupposed in any and all of his actions. But this is just to say that man is structurally dependent *in* the very independence that characterizes his activity as an individual: he is dependent on the others to whom he is constitutively related in the very independence, or creativity and self-determination, of his actions as entailed by his individuality.

These features of gift and dependence are essential to the idea of home rightly understood, and hence for the realization of man's at-home-ness.

A phrase drawn from the writings of Canadian philosopher George Grant puts the matter nicely. "We are not our own," he says, in words offered in response to our cultural problematic.[11] In other words, we belong to others. This of course does not mean that we do not belong also, and fundamentally, to ourselves, but that we belong to ourselves only in our original and continued belonging to God, and, after God, to our parents and indeed in some sense to the world as a whole. We truly "possess" ourselves, but only as we are also gifts from Another (and others). This is what it means ontologically to be a creature: to discover that we come to ourselves only *in* and *through* our selves' constitutive belonging to others (God, and other creatures in God).

Thus, it is not as though we start out dependent upon and belonging to others, and then grow eventually into an autonomy that leaves this dependent belonging behind. On the contrary, the fact of our createdness implies that we bear this relation of dependent belonging in the core of our being, however much, as we move from infancy to adulthood, there is a progressively deeper capacity for recuperating this relation in freedom.

Contemporary theologian Hans Urs von Balthasar sums all of this up well when he suggests that a creaturely ontology is best approached through reflection on the mother's smile.[12] A child's first experience of being comes through the smile and embrace of the mother, hence through the radiant presence of the goodness of another. The child's first experience of existence, then, is of being loved. It is an experience of existence itself as generous: as gift from another.

To be sure, the child is scarcely aware of this in any explicit fashion at the moment of birth! The relevant point, however, is that in time the child smiles back at the mother. Note what is happening here. The child's eventual smile is a *response* to the *generosity* of the mother: the mother's loving smile becomes effective in the child, evoking the child's smile in return, just as the rays of the sun penetrate the flower and evoke its bloom.

Hence, the child comes into existence and begins to realize his own existence only in and through the abiding, anterior presence of another, a

---

11. See "George Grant and Modernity's Technological Ontology," pp. 277-87 in this volume.

12. Hans Urs von Balthasar, *The Glory of the Lord: A Theological Aesthetics*, vol. 5 (San Francisco: Ignatius Press, 1991), pp. 615-17; cf. also 613-37, 646-56, *passim*.

presence that, precisely *because and insofar as it is generous,* reveals to the child *his own worth.*

We discover here the primitive structure of a creaturely ontology. We see that creaturely being, as gift-from-another, is defined most properly in terms of *being-as-response.* In its own proper being and activity, in its very independence and autonomy and individuality, the creature is anteriorly receptive of, dependent on, and in intrinsic community with, another.[13] Thus, receptivity and dependence are positive, not negative, features of our being.[14]

But we can take this further. For what the foregoing implies is that the most basic disposition of the created being in relation to the other (the world) is that of an *obedient and patient and contemplative wonder,* evoked by what may be called the *beauty* of the other. An obedient wonder: that is, a wonder that listens *(oboedire, ob-audio).* A patient and contemplative wonder: that is, not in the sense of "passivity," but rather in the sense of an activity that is anteriorly responsive. Wonder, insofar as the being of the other, and of one's self, comes unexpectedly and surprisingly, or, in more traditional language, contingently. A wonder evoked by the beauty of the other, insofar as it is the attractiveness of the other that always first elicits and indeed in a significant sense continues to bear the active response of the self both to itself and to the other.

In short, an ontology of being as gift-from-another entails, on the part of the being who is inescapably from his depths a receiver, a dependence taking the form of a contemplative wonder born of and sustained by the beauty of the other. I believe these features are accurately summed up in the word *gratitude.*

My contention, therefore, is that the ontology proper to a creature is an ontology of *being-as-gift* that elicits and is completed in *being-as-gratitude.*

Such an ontology of gift and gratitude enables us, in the face of the ever-present brokenness and evil in the world, to find a positive meaning even in *suffering.* Again, consider the mother in relation to her child. In conceiving and giving birth, she makes space for the other, in his otherness. This entails risk and vulnerability: in "letting the other be," she allows

---

13. Cf. "Liturgy and the Integrity of Cosmic Order: The Theology of Alexander Schmemann," pp. 288-309 in this volume.

14. For a philosophical recovery of a positive sense of dependence, see Alasdair MacIntyre, *Dependent Rational Animals: Why Human Beings Need the Virtues* (Chicago: Open Court, 2001).

for the possibility that the child will abuse his freedom and reject or disappoint her, or indeed, more broadly, that the child himself will be subject to abuse and rejection and disappointment at the hands of the world. This possibility of suffering, or this anterior willingness to suffer, is inherent in the original *positive* meaning of being as gift and gratitude.

For Christians, the highest creaturely expression of this ontology of gift and gratitude that is from the beginning disposed to suffer is Mary in her *fiat* ("let it be done unto me"). Mary, in contemplatively-actively responding to God's initiative in grace, makes space for the incarnate Other, a space that is ready to endure, in the face of evil and with a gratitude eventually full of sorrow, even his crucifixion and death.

I have proposed that man is rightly said to be at home when he realizes the relations that constitute his being as a creature. We can now see, in more concrete terms, that man is truly at home insofar as he finds his identity inside the *constitutive belonging to others* — God, other creatures — summed up in gift and gratitude. Obversely, he becomes homeless, in the root sense, insofar as his identity falls outside of or is abstracted from this belonging, that is, insofar as his relations to God and others become fragmented.

There is a common expression in English that "a man's home is his castle." The term "castle" adds to "home" the notion of wealth or riches, and with this we can now resume our larger theme. For I wish to suggest that home is rightly understood as a "castle" because and insofar as home is where the creature most truly *belongs,* where the creature comes to realize the richness of the relations that most profoundly and intimately constitute his being as a creature.

Wealth and poverty in their deepest and most proper meaning, in other words, signify being in relation and not being in relation, respectively, in the sense indicated by "home" and "homelessness."

This notion of wealth and poverty will no doubt appear arcane to some, but I invite the reader to ponder the ontological nature of the argument. For the precise point has been that the creature is understood in his truest *reality* as gift (from God above all, but also from others in relation to God), and that this reality can therefore be realized *as such* only through an abiding grateful receptivity that, *eo ipso,* enables proper participation in reality in its character as gift.

Wealth in its truest sense thus consists in participation in reality-as-gift, a participation enabled and indeed always first constituted by gratitude; and poverty in its truest sense, consequently, consists in the failure to participate in reality so understood, a failure that stems finally from an absence of gratitude (whatever its various causes).

This ontological rendering of wealth by no means excludes the more immediate and obvious sense of wealth as consisting in having, producing, and exchanging things, food, clothing, property, and the like. On the contrary, it insists merely that having, producing, and exchanging things be from the beginning formed and thus integrated in and by grateful receiving and giving. Without this anterior formation and integration, having or producing things even in great abundance will contribute, not to the deepened participation in reality as gift that we are calling wealth in the truest sense, but on the contrary to the reduced participation in reality that we are calling poverty in its root sense.

II. Toward an Economy of Gift and Gratitude

I come now to a critical turn in the argument. For the argument concerns not simply the ontological idea of wealth, however "realistic" we may now see that it is on its own terms, but the bearing of this idea on wealth in its specifically economic context, or on the nature of economic exchanges themselves. This requires that the ontological idea of wealth as a matter primarily of gift and gratitude be shown to carry its own way of producing and exchanging and possessing things. It must be shown that the things produced, exchanged, and possessed will themselves differ *in their very character as things,* depending on the extent to which their production, exchange, and possession are integrated into a grateful sense of reality as gift — that is, such that the things themselves take on the nature of gift.

I refer to this as a critical turn in the argument because of the conventional insistence that it is the task of economics in the proper sense to show how best to produce, possess, and exchange things, while it is up to theology, philosophy, and culture to order this production and exchange and these things to a good end, or to give them a moral intention. Economics, in a word, tells us how to produce and exchange things efficiently, while theology, philosophy, and culture tell us how to *order* or *use* this production and exchange rightly in terms of man's *telos,* an ordering or use that, however important in moral terms, leaves essentially intact the meaning of "efficient" as supplied by economics on its own terms.

The burden of my argument is to challenge the extrinsicism indicated here: to show that the order given in man's *telos* itself partially but decisively shapes what it means to produce, exchange, and possess things efficiently, in the properly economic meaning of these terms. How so?

As a first example, let us turn again to the mother, and to the meal she prepares for her family. Notice that we always refer spontaneously and warmly to a "home-cooked" meal, or again, to a dish prepared the way Grandma used to make it. Even restaurants characteristically advertise their food in this way: never do they recommend themselves on the grounds that the food they serve is store-packaged and mechanically prepared. What is the difference that is implicitly recognized here?

An obvious answer is that the mother prepares her family's food with love. But, however true, such an answer remains both vague and question-begging. For it could mean that love adds an intention that otherwise leaves the dinner unchanged in its intrinsic nature or order. But that is just the view I am challenging. My proposal, in other words, is that the love of the mother affects the dinner precisely in its reality as food. A mother builds into the food a distinctive sense of time, space, matter, and motion. She takes time, and she knows that taking time, however burdensome, is necessary for care and attention to detail. She measures with a sense of proportion, but not mechanically and not without some sense of "extravagance." She keeps in mind all along the way the health needs and peculiar tastes of these particular familial others, especially the infirm and most helpless, for whom she is making the meal. She prepares and presents the food with a sense of its aesthetics. And so on.[15]

The mother's love, in brief, is not merely a matter of an intention remaining external to the food. On the contrary, her love *takes form* in the food, such that the food itself now takes on the form of love, somewhat in the way that John Paul II says that the human body is and must become "nuptial": that the body as body, the body in its very structure and physicality, expresses and is meant to express love for another.[16]

To take another example, consider the difference between Mother Teresa and a caretaker performing duties primarily for the sake of making

---

15. For reflections helpful for setting the larger context of the argument here, cf. Wendell Berry, "The Pleasures of Eating," in *The Art of the Commonplace*, pp. 321-27, and Leon Kass, *The Hungry Soul: Eating and the Perfection of Our Nature* (Chicago: University of Chicago Press, 1999 [1994]).

16. See John Paul II, "Christ Appeals to the Beginning," in *Man and Woman He Created Them: A Theology of the Body*, trans. Michael Waldstein, pp. 131-223, at 181-85 and passim. See also "The Embodied Person as Gift and the Cultural Task in America," 242-74 in this volume.

money. Both provide health care, but we spontaneously recognize the difference in the way in which the care is ordered. Some of this difference is quantitative in nature: Mother Teresa would certainly do more things for the patient. But the point to which I am drawing attention bears intrinsically on the manner or order of the discrete acts of care themselves. Mother Teresa's very manner of touching the patient, of looking at the patient, of dressing the patient, of arranging the bedding of the patient are all different. The difference is similar to the difference in the case of the mother's home-cooked meal: all of these acts by Mother Teresa are changed in their very form as health- and care-giving acts. Anyone who has spent time in a contemporary hospital knows intuitively the difference to which I am referring here, however much he or she might not be able to articulate with precision the nature of that difference.

Before attempting myself to characterize that difference, let us consider a third case. Adam Smith has famously asserted that we really do not need to appeal to the beneficence or generosity of the baker if we want good bread. On the contrary, we need merely to appeal to the baker's own self-interest: to point out to him that making good bread is the best way to ensure that he makes a profit. In light of the previous two examples, however, we are able to see that a generous way of making and selling bread will be different in its nature and order from a primarily profit-motivated way of making and selling. The former way of producing bread takes on the form of love, in the sense that it is undertaken for the sake of making what is intrinsically a good loaf of bread and for the sake of the person who will consume it. As with the home-cooked meal, a different sense of time and measurement and aesthetics, a different sensitivity to concerns of health and taste, and the like, enter intrinsically into the act of producing and selling, and thereby into the thing produced.

Producing bread primarily for profit, on the other hand, by definition entails instrumentalizing toward the end of profit everything that goes into that production, with the consequence that it is the *appearance* of a certain quality of bread and bread-making with which the baker is most properly concerned. The baker, on the reading recommended by Smith, wants his bread-making to embody the qualities of good bread and bread-making, *not* for their own sake, but *only insofar* as embodying these qualities is necessary for and promotes his profit-making. The best possible situation for the baker on such a reading, therefore, is that he find a way to reduce his costs, a way which, however much it might entail reducing the qualities proper to good bread and bread-making, would see to it that the bread and bread-making nevertheless remain *effectively,* that is, for all practical intents and purposes, the same.

The import of Smith's proposal, in a word, is that it makes no significant difference whether the baker bakes for love or for profit. In the end, it will come to the same thing: what is more or less the same loaf of bread will be produced.

What must be said first in response is that things cannot finally be *effectively* the same unless they in fact *are* the same. Things can be *effectively* the same finally only insofar as they are *intrinsically* the same, or better, the same in terms of their *inner,* or *interior,* reality. To claim otherwise is, however unwittingly, to slip into a Cartesianism that alone would warrant the disjunction presupposed on a Smithian account, a disjunction between a thing in its external or outward effect (the thing *quoad nos*) and a thing in its internal meaning (the thing *quoad se*).

In other words, those who claim that the act of making bread is the same, irrespective of whether that act is performed intrinsically in love or instrumentalistically, invariably employ what is an extroverted or mechanical (and just so far Cartesian) standard of judgment. They ignore the possibility of what I am arguing here: that love as a "motive" already and as a matter of principle gives interior form, hence order or structure, to the thing made; that the thing made therefore itself takes on the interior form of love, precisely in its character as a thing, as an artifact. In a word, such thinkers, in their claim of effective sameness and as a condition of the force of this claim, overlook or discount, *a priori,* exactly the differences introduced by love: those differences, namely, that involve interior movements affecting and indeed already in some significant sense constituting the time, space, and matter "congealed" in and as the thing. Unless one already assumes (however unwittingly) a Cartesian criterion for judgment, the examples I have adduced above suffice to illustrate these differences, at least in brief.[17]

---

17. The differences between artifacts produced on an assembly line and artifacts crafted in personal love are perceptible to those whose criteria for judging do not dispose them already to miss the subtle "irregularities" introduced by *organic form.* Cf. in this connection the interesting recorded interview of violin-makers Peter and Wendy Moes in "Tacit Knowing, Truthful Knowing: The Life and Thought of Michael Polanyi," produced by Ken Myers (Charlottesville, VA: Mars Hill Audio, 1999).

In connection with my argument here, I should make mention of Anglo-American culture's tendency to confuse the "empirical" with the "concrete." "Empirical" in its conventional understanding indicates what is already an extroverted reduction of perception and experience to the terms of abstractly quantified (sense) data.

But I need now to highlight the further burden of the proposal here, given my intention of indicating how an anthropology of gift and gratitude transforms the original meaning of an economy and indeed of *homo economicus* as such.

The baker who works for the sake of love, however much he may or may not conceive what he is doing explicitly in theoretical terms, approaches the making of bread, the bread made, the other for whom the bread is made, and indeed himself as invested in the process and the thing, as gift. He makes the bread, which is to say, he gratefully gives himself over to the making of the bread, simultaneously for its own sake and for the sake of another.

In contrast, the baker who works primarily for profit, and insofar as he works primarily for profit, approaches the making of bread, the bread made, and the other for whom the bread is made, merely as instrument. He does not make the bread intrinsically for itself or for the other (the consumer). Rather, he utilizes, for the sake of himself, i.e., primarily out of self-interest, the process of bread-making, the bread made, and the person who eventually buys and consumes the bread. It might seem that the baker, in so doing, thereby enhances at least the reality of his own self. But this is deceptive. For in so instrumentalizing the bread-making process, the bread, and the other for profit, he just so far reduces the reality of each of them, and thereby the reality also of what each has to offer him, to a reality-primarily-for-profit. But this entails a reduction thereby *also in the bread-maker's own reality*. For the point is that all of these — the bread-making process, the bread, and the intended consumer — are by definition now seen to enhance the bread-maker himself only (or primarily) in the mode of profitability. In reducing these things to instruments of and for profit, therefore, the bread-maker, in that very act, makes his own reality also into an instrument of and for profit.

The simple but crucial point I wish to make here, then, is that an economy of love deepens the reality, which is to say, enhances the worth, of *everything* and *everyone involved in the production and exchange of goods: self, thing, and other*. Granting that this may be obvious with respect to the other person as consumer, the suggestion is surprising with respect to conventional views of the self and of things. For the pertinent point is that the self and things now become deeper and "better" in their very reality as self and as things. Things: because and insofar as the baker bakes the bread for its own sake and not simply as instrument, or more exactly, intrinsically for its own sake and for the sake of the other as other, rather than simply as an instrument for profit and for the other as a means to profit. And the self for the same reason: in acting for the enhancement of the bread as such and of the other as such, he thereby transforms his own self into the gift that he himself was created to be. The point, in other words, is that, once we ponder the meaning of love along the lines indicated above, we see that the conventional Smithian, self-interested approach to producing and selling bread sets in motion an intrinsic dynamic, not for the enhancement of the thing and the other and (consequently) the self in their *truest reality* as such, which is their reality as gift, but on the contrary for the promotion of these now only in their *reduced reality as and for profit*.

It should go without saying that baking for love as understood here by no means excludes baking also for profit: the crucial point, that is, the crucial difference from the Smithian account, is that profit now is put into the service of and thereby integrated into the good of the person and of the thing in their proper created and artifactual reality as gift.[18]

We turn now to a common equivocation, and objection, associated with the foregoing argument. The equivocation: those who follow Smith with respect to his defense of self-interest ("rightly understood") often imply that acts of self-interest, when they are harnessed into a self-interest that has become mutual, thereby become, for all practical (or public) intents and purposes, the same as acts of mutual generosity. The objection: acts of self-interest harnessed into mutuality are in any case the best we can generally hope to achieve, given the "realistic" conditions of human history.

What has been said already suffices to show that a self-interested act in a Smithian sense does not become generous simply because it is now hooked up with the self-interest of the other: a self-interest become mutual does not thereby become inclusive of mutual generosity. Nevertheless, making explicit the feature of mutuality enables us to clarify further. My argument does in fact affirm an intrinsic mutuality between the self and the other in the producing and selling of bread. More pertinently, the self is not eliminated but in fact *fulfilled* precisely *as a self* in acting for the other as other, in acting for love. However, it is crucial to notice the asymmetry of the order in the mutual relation between self and other. In other words, the self does serve or enhance itself, but only insofar as this self-

---

18. Concerning this point, cf. the relevant discussions on the chapters "Civil Community Inside the Liberal State: Truth, Freedom, and Human Dignity" and "Does the Free Market Produce Free Persons?" The argument is not that it is never legitimate to "use" or "instrumentalize" things or even persons, but that this "use" be tied intrinsically to and give expression to the inherent analogical worth of these things and persons.

service or self-enhancement is already placed inside and ordered to the service and enhancement of the other as other.

Thus, we need not eliminate self-centeredness in acting for another in a truly other-centered way, in accord with the conventional reading of "altruism," which requires an acting for the other that is to the exclusion of the self. On the contrary, we need to recuperate self-centeredness, but *from within the self's simultaneous, anterior centeredness in the other.* The radical difference between Smithian self-interest and genuine love, in sum, lies in the asymmetrical ordering, and not in the mutuality (which is granted), of the relation between the self and the other.

Once this is seen, we recognize the striking equivocation harbored in statements such as the following, which are offered by way of defending a Madisonian self-interest, "rightly understood": "self-interest of a sort is the propellant of a mother's love even unto death for her child."[19]

In Christian terms, the above qualification enables us to see the ontology implicit in the relation between two important statements of Jesus pertinent to neighborly love. He says, on the one hand, that we ought to love our neighbor as ourselves; and on the other, that we ought to love each other as "I have loved you." Thus we truly ought to love ourselves, but only at once as we, in the manner of Jesus, give ourselves away to the other. We will indeed find ourselves, but only in losing ourselves, and in no other order.

Once again, the creaturely archetype for proper "self-love" as indicated here is Mary, in her *Magnificat.* In Mary's *fiat*, in her "letting it be done according to the Word" of Another, Mary's self is not effaced but is on the contrary magnified, precisely in her magnification of the Other.

However, we still need to address an objection that, if legitimate, would render the foregoing argument moot, *tout court.* The objection concerns the "realism" of the argument in practical terms, a "realism" that is the further burden of arguments such as those offered by Smith, and in political terms by James Madison, for example. However much it is the case that love is the ultimate or "ideal" truth of things, it seems fruitless to try to build an economy around such an anthropology. The fact of the matter is that most people in the world as we know it act primarily for reasons of profitable self-interest, and it is this self-interested motivation that has enabled the market economy's productivity and abundance. The best we can and ought to do, in recognition of the abiding sinfulness of the

---

19. Michael Novak, *Free Persons and the Common Good* (Lanham, MD: Madison Books, 1989), p. 49.

world, is thus to harness self-interest into mutuality, in the manner indicated by Smith and his successors.

My ontological argument, in a word, so the objection goes, leaves unanswered the question about its "worldly realism."

My response is threefold. First, however prevalent profitable self-interest is in a person's engagement with the economy, this self-interest never exhausts a person's motivation. On the contrary, man is in fact most fundamentally characterized by his desire for God, even if this desire remains for the most part unthematic. Augustine and Aquinas both affirm that man knows and wills God implicitly in everything he or she knows or wills, and in this sense "naturally" loves God above all else.[20] According to Augustine, it is the restlessness for God, evoked by the relation to God established in and with creation, that most deeply inspires man's choices. Given this fact, and in light of the creaturely ontology set forth earlier, we can say that man's deepest desire is for the community implied in his originally given relations to God and others — is, in short, his original, natural love for God and others.

Thus, the desire for God, for community and love, is precisely *not* "unrealistic," and God, community, and love, consequently, are *never* merely "ideal." The desire for these does not arise sometimes and in some people alongside the self-interested desire for profit, or only after this desire has been satisfied or after material abundance has been achieved. On the contrary, the desire for God, community, and love operates at the core of the desire for profit and material abundance.[21] It is crucial to see this: any economy that fails to take account of this constitutive desire operating at the heart of man's being, hence always and everywhere at the heart of man's actions, fails thereby to be realistic in its truest and most basic sense.

Indeed, it is only in light of this realism that we can understand sin for what it truly is: that is, sin. What may seem obvious, however, typically gets lost in the (Smithian, Madisonian) argument on behalf of "worldly realism." What starts out as a defense of profitable self-interest in the name of man's historical sinfulness slides quickly into what is a defense in the name of "virtue," if to be sure only a "virtue of necessity." Taking God and love to be more or less utopian "ideals," the best we can do, given our sinfulness, becomes the best we "realistically" *ought* to do. God and love are realities to be attended to only alongside our more immediate concerns for

---

20. See the discussion in Aquinas, *De Veritate*, q. 22, a. 2.
21. Cf., e.g., the text from John Paul II's *Redemptor Hominis*, n. 10, cited earlier.

profit and abundance — realities attended to, that is, mostly in our "private" or "eschatological" moments.

What realism in an integrated sense requires, rather, is that self-interest or desire for profit in Smith's sense be recognized always and everywhere as a vice indicating a need for conversion, however much it is also simultaneously recognized that this vice will never, in the present condition of the world, be entirely removed from the heart of man.[22] Realism in the proper sense likewise requires that the acquisition and indeed very nature of material abundance be measured intrinsically, from the beginning and at every point along the way, in terms of man's always deeper, anterior desire for God, community, and love.

Realism properly conceived thus leads, secondly, to a crucial qualification in the conventional claim on behalf of the market's effectiveness in producing a high material standard of living. Of course, in an obvious and important sense the market is effective in this way. The needed qualifier, however, arises when we recall the burden of our earlier argument in connection with an economy of gift, which is that both the process of production itself and the artifact produced are of higher quality when formed in love and indeed as love than they are when formed primarily in profitable self-interest (assuming here equal abilities in the respective agents of production!). Furthermore, the persons of both the self and the other are enhanced more fully and truly in the former case than in the latter. Defense of the market economy's productivity typically begs this question of the quality of the process of production itself, the artifact produced, and the self and other engaged in the production. That is, it comes attached almost invariably to the extroverted, instrumentalist criteria of quality that take production and artifacts to be effectively the same irrespective of whether they are formed integratively in love or reductively in profitable self-interest.

The preceding two points, however, still leave unaddressed what is the crux of the conventional appeal to "realism": that production driven by a Smithian self-interest has in fact generated artifacts in ever-greater abundance and with ever-greater technological efficiency. I will address the matter of technology at greater length below in connection with an essay

22. Conservative liberals typically misread John Paul II's *Centesimus Annus* (see n. 25 and 35) on this point, as though the fact that a wrongly ordered desire for profit cannot be eliminated from history (as the Pope acknowledges) implies that we need only — consequently — harness that desire into mutuality, in the way indicated, and criticized, above. Regarding profit, see also *Caritas in Veritate*, particularly n. 21 and 37.

by Max L. Stackhouse and Lawrence M. Stratton. Regarding abundance, let me make two observations.

First, man's bodiliness is a good implicit in the good of his creaturely nature and destiny. Adequate food, clothing, and property, with the abundance implied therein, are inherently good. Indeed, as the writer Annie Dillard has pertinently, and beautifully, stated, extravagance is the characteristic gesture of the Creator himself.[23] Relative abundance of material things is thus already a matter of "quality" and not merely "quantity." Such relative abundance is to be sought as an integral part of man's destiny as an embodied creature, and the productivity of the liberal market is just so far an important good needing to be acknowledged as such.

Secondly, however, the qualifier introduced with "relative" invites the pertinent question: *What sort of abundance is both necessary and truly enhancing of man's dignity as an embodied person, relative to his here-and-now creaturely call to love and glorify God, to love others, and to value the world itself intrinsically in relation to God?*

In response, we must recognize that the love implied in our creatureliness carries its own distinctive notions of the acquisition and indeed proper nature of material abundance — in all of its forms: property, power, position, technological efficiency, money — and that these notions differ from the way in which they are conceived in their prevalent liberal sense. Rightful material abundance involves dynamic integration of the self into the fullness of the truth, goodness, and beauty of the others (including God and all others in relation to God) to whom the self is constitutively related. More radically, all that is implied in relative material abundance finds its true meaning in terms of Mary's *Magnificat,* which is to say, in the magnification of the self in and through the magnification of others, most especially the innocent and vulnerable others named in the Beatitudes,[24] in their embodied reality and in service of their full reality as true and good and beautiful before God.

In sum, abundance is to be integrated in terms of the need "to be rich toward God" (Luke 12:21).

This large assertion, however, raises again, perhaps even more sharply, the problem of "worldly realism." Yet it also makes clear that we

---

23. Annie Dillard, *Pilgrim at Tinker Creek* (New York: Bantam Books, 1974), pp. 9 and passim. See also *Caritas in Veritate,* particularly n. 34.

24. Cf. Matthew 5:3-12. See also the discussion of the Beatitudes in *CCC,* n. 1716-19, where it is stated that the "Beatitudes respond to the natural desire for happiness," and again that the "Beatitudes reveal the goal of human existence, the ultimate end of human acts. . . ."

must ultimately come to terms with the fact that the love proper to creatureliness is made in the image of God as revealed in Jesus Christ, that the "realism" characteristic of creaturely love therefore finds its ultimate meaning within the life of Jesus himself. Jesus *incarnated* himself in the world, and thereby affirmed the reality of the world in its deepest and most comprehensive, or embodied, abundance. Nevertheless, because of his love and affirmation of the world, integrated in terms of his hypostatic relation to the Father, Jesus was crucified.

It is, in sum, precisely Jesus' *integrated love* for, and not "sectarian" denial of or withdrawal from, the world in its abundance that evokes rejection by those who would conceive worldly abundance — power, property, position, technical efficiency, money — in a fragmented and extroverted form.

This by no means implies that we ought not to enter the economic world and seek to participate effectively in its institutions, or that we ought not to seek to make our presence in the world as productive of abundance as possible. This misunderstanding misses the point of both creation and the Incarnation. Rather, we must, given "worldly realism" in the sense indicated in the one historical order not only by sin but also by the incarnate-crucified love of Jesus, expect to experience reversal precisely at the heart of what it means to be "productive," and indeed relative to material abundance in all its forms as conceived in the dominant liberal understanding.

Any understanding of "worldly" realism and success that would be adequate must finally measure itself by the historically irreducible tension indicated here.

Having offered a sketch of what we have termed an economy of gift, and having criticized in this light what may be termed the instrumentalist economic culture implied in a liberal anthropology, let us now summarize in technical terms what is the deepest ontological source and meaning of that instrumentalism.

III. Liberal Anthropology as an Instrumentalist Anthropology

Anglo-American liberalism, I wish to suggest, presupposes what may be termed an "abstract" identity of the person. "Abstract" signifies an identity of the person conceived first and most basically *in abstraction from the relations constitutive of the creature.* This does not mean that liberalism necessarily denies the importance of man's relations to God, others, the world, and the family, or that liberalism fails to see the obvious ways in which man is born into these relations. Rather, insofar as liberalism recognizes the importance or indeed "naturalness" of these relations, as in fact it does on its best reading, it nonetheless fails to grasp what is implied in their constitutive character. It fails to recuperate the community that anteriorly conditions, and thus helps intrinsically to form, self-identity in its original and abiding meaning.

In its abstract notion of the self, liberalism thereby leaves self-centeredness in the objectionable sense intact. Indeed, that is just what an abstract self is: a self that has been stripped of the original relation to the others that alone could give the self's identity an originally other-centered orientation. But note what this then implies for the rightful meaning of human action. Typically, a liberal account of human action emphasizes self-determination or creativity. This may seem innocent enough, since we all affirm the worth of such features: after all, the passivity implied when these features are absent would empty human freedom of its legitimate power. The problem arises, however, when we notice that liberalism, in its emphasis on self-determination and creativity, fails to take account of the implications of the effective presence of the other in the abiding structure of these.

The receptivity and dependence entailed in the self's ontological status as a gift from Another must form anteriorly, from the beginning and all along the way, what it means to be self-determinative and creative. Further, this receptivity and dependence imply an obedient and patient and contemplative wonder evoked by the *attractiveness* of the Other, i.e., as *giver*. All of these features together indicate a grateful response, which, in forming self-determination and creativity from the beginning, transforms these latter into what are now acts of self-giving.

In a word, self-determination and creativity, understood in their rightful creaturely structure, are grateful-responsive acts of self-giving; and the freedom of the self, accordingly, is first not simply an option or act of choice, but an act of love. Human action is thus most properly a "co-act": an act that recuperates the always already effective and attractive presence *of the Other* (others) in itself as the anterior condition for being *its own action*.[25]

---

25. See D. C. Schindler, "Freedom Beyond Our Choosing: Augustine on the Will and Its Objects," *Communio: International Catholic Review* 29, no. 4 (Winter 2002): 618-53, at 640. The present chapter draws much from this article regarding human action and freedom. Pertinent to my discussion of liberalism's "indifferent" action/freedom is also Servais Pinckaers's *The Sources of Christian Ethics* (Washington, DC: Catholic University of America Press, 1995), pp. 327-53.

It is just here, then, that we can see the ontological source of instrumentalism, or of the other as instrument. The point becomes clear as soon as we notice the original *indifference* of the self to the other implied in the foregoing. This indifference *eo ipso* renders the self, in its abiding constitution as such, wrongly self-centered, and thereby also removes all of the features noted above that are necessary for the self's action to be at its origin other-centered. It follows that the self's engagement with the other, the self's doing, having, and producing relative to the other, cannot but be wrongly centered in the self and the self's interest: the other by definition becomes primarily a function or instrument of the self and the self's interest.

In a word, instrumentalism is logically avoided only if the self-determination, creativity, and freedom of the self are conceived most basically as acts of love, and this requires recognition of the constitutive relation of the Other in the self that is denied in liberalism's congenital abstract self-identity.

The structural indifference of the self to the other that founds liberal instrumentalism can best be summarized technically in terms of an ontological "unitarianism," coincident with what consequently may be called an ontological "pelagianism." *Unitarianism:* the self is originally-ontologically indifferent to relation with the other; and *pelagianism:* the self's relation to the other is consequently first an enactment or construction by a self not yet formed by the effective presence of the other in the self. Unitarianism and pelagianism get expressed differently in each of the areas of community indicated in our creatureliness. Thus the liberal self is, in turn, *a-theistic:* the self in its original constitution is unrelated, or only extrinsically related, to God (cf. deism or religious positivism generally, according to which religion is in the first instance a "voluntary" society). It is also *a-social,* in that the self in its original constitution is unrelated, or only contractually related, to other persons; *a-cosmic,* in that the self is originally extrinsically related to the world, and the world, accordingly, is first a "dumb" (mechanistic) instrument; and *a-familial,* in that the self is conceived first in abstraction from the relation of filiality that is partially constitutive of one's being, and from the aptness for either fatherhood or motherhood that originally *differentiates* one's being into male (masculine) or female (feminine).

It goes without saying that liberalism on its best reading means to avoid the negatives indicated here. The point is that it can consistently do so only insofar as it relinquishes the abstract logic of self-identity that renders the self's creativity and freedom ontologically indifferent toward the other. Liberalism cannot consistently avoid these negatives, in other words, simply through an *option* to embrace community with God, others, world, and family, when it is precisely the notion of "option" in its original structure as conceived in liberalism that is in question.

In sum: my contention is that it is liberalism's (often unwitting) abstract self-identity that sets in motion the logic of self-centeredness operative in Smith's instrumentalist self-interest, and indeed that it is this logic of self-centeredness that lies at the heart of what Pope John Paul II terms a "culture of death" and what Jennifer Morse calls a culture of "utilitarianism." But to see the sense in which this is the case, we must now describe these two cultures more fully.

IV. Instrumentalism and the "Culture of Death"

Recognizing many positive developments in contemporary society, John Paul II nonetheless characterizes our situation in terms of a "dramatic clash between good and evil, death and life, the 'culture of death' and the 'culture of life.'"[26] Identifying the "culture of death" as a "structure of sin" (*EV*, n. 12), the Pope describes the main features of this culture. "The criterion of personal dignity — which demands respect, generosity and service — is replaced by the criterion of efficiency, functionality and usefulness: Others are considered not for what they 'are,' but for what they 'have, do and produce.' This is the supremacy of the strong over the weak" (n. 23).

The Pope speaks of "a certain Promethean attitude" in the culture that "leads people to think that they can control life and death" (n. 15); of an attitude that views suffering as "the epitome of evil, to be eliminated at all costs" (n. 15). He speaks of "a self-centered concept of freedom" (n. 13), and again of a false autonomy that fails to see that freedom "possesses an inherently relational dimension" and is essentially linked with truth (n. 19). Corresponding to this view is a mentality that "recognizes as a subject of rights only the person who enjoys full or at least incipient autonomy and who emerges from a state of total dependence on others" (n. 19). Man becomes "concerned only with 'doing,' and using all kinds of technology," busying "himself with programming, controlling and dominating birth and death" (n. 22). "Nature itself, from being *mater* (mother), is now reduced to being 'matter,' and is subjected to every kind

---

26. *Evangelium Vitae* (=*EV*), n. 28.

of manipulation" (n. 22). However paradoxically in light of the intention of democracy, the "supremacy of the strong over the weak" (n. 23) "effectively moves toward a form of totalitarianism" (n. 20), in the sense that the "state arrogates to itself the right to dispose of the life of the weakest and most defenseless members, from the unborn to the elderly, in the name of a public interest which is really nothing but the interest of a certain group" (n. 20).[27]

John Paul II locates the source of the primacy accorded the criteria of efficiency, functionality, and usefulness ultimately in the culture's loss of the sense of God. "By living 'as if God did not exist,' man not only loses sight of the mystery of God, but also of the mystery of the world and the mystery of his own being" (n. 22).[28] "He no longer considers life as a splendid gift of God, something 'sacred' entrusted to his responsibility and thus also to his loving care and 'veneration.' Life itself becomes a mere 'thing,' which man claims as his exclusive property, completely subject to his control and manipulation" (n. 22).

The Pope's description and criticism of the "culture of death" do not imply a denial that persons in such a culture often seek to "program . . . and control birth and death" out of motives of compassion (cf. embryonic stem cell research, for example), motives that are indeed often supported by sincerely held religious beliefs. In the United States, for example, polls indicate that more than 90 percent of the people believe in God.[29] The Pope's description and criticism bear rather on the *order* (onto-*logic*) carried (often unconsciously) in a culture's way of life, action, and thought, *despite and within* what may otherwise be the compassionate, religious intentions motivating this way of life. That is why the Holy Father refers to the "culture of death" as a "*structure* of sin" (emphasis added) (*EV*, n. 12: *peccati institutum; EV*, n. 24: *structuras peccati*). He means that, in order to understand the nature of this "culture" properly, we need to extend the reality of "personal" sin to include the structures generated by, but not re-

---

27. See also "The Dramatic Nature of Life: Liberal Societies and the Foundations of Human Dignity," pp. 34-52 in this volume.

28. "[W]hen the sense of God is lost, the sense of man is also threatened and poisoned, as the Second Vatican Council concisely states: 'Without the Creator, the creature would disappear. . . . But when God is forgotten, the creature itself grows unintelligible' [*Gaudium et Spes*, n. 36]" (*EV*, n. 22).

29. Pew Forum on Religion and Public Life, U.S. Religious Landscape Survey, "Religious Affiliation: Diverse and Dynamic" (Washington, DC: Pew Research Center, 2008). See "Religion and Secularity in a Culture of Abstraction," pp. 328-49 in this volume.

ducible to, sin in this "personal" sense, that is, to personal intentions and acts of choice.[30]

The nature of the "culture of life" that the Pope calls for in response to the "culture of death" is implicit in the foregoing description: a culture rooted in a sense of community and relationship ordered ultimately from and toward the love of God revealed in Christ and inclusive of all of life and of the body itself.

> It is the proclamation of a living God who is close to us, who calls us to profound communion with himself and awakens in us the certain hope of eternal life. It is the affirmation of the inseparable connection between the person, his life and his bodiliness. It is the presentation of human life as a life of relationship, a gift of God, the fruit and sign of his love. It is the proclamation that Jesus has a unique relationship with every person, which enables us to see in every human face the face of Christ. It is the call for a "sincere gift of self" as the fullest way to realize our personal freedom. (*EV*, n. 81)

Jennifer Morse's description of our current cultural problematic in "Making Room in the Inn: Why the Modern World Needs the Needy" echoes the Pope's in striking ways.[31] She begins by stressing the importance of the fact of dependency in human society: "Human beings are born as helpless babies and our species has a long period of dependency. In fact we might say that dependency is the one truly universal human experience" (180). Indeed, the "ubiquity of unavoidable helplessness [of infancy, illness, old age, and the like] points to the possibility that dependency is not peripheral to the social order, but somehow central to it" (181). Morse then describes how modern America "marginalizes" the dependent or needy:

---

30. What John Paul II understands as structural sin thus is always rooted in personal sin, but this personal sin nevertheless has a social and indeed objective-intellectual dimension that reaches beyond individual persons and into the structures of society. As he puts it in *Dominum et Vivificantem*, n. 56, sin as a "subjective" rebellion against God can take the ("external") form of a philosophy or ideology shaping a program or indeed the institutions of civilization, giving those institutions their original shape and meaning, precisely *as* institutions. Such a philosophy or worldview of course need not be explicitly thought out or thematized as such. On the contrary, it often operates more or less unconsciously and invisibly in the original order and consequent functioning of institutions, which is the case especially in liberal societies. Benedict XVI affirms and develops John Paul II's concept in *Caritas in Veritate*, particularly n. 34.

31. In *Wealth, Poverty, and Human Destiny*, pp. 179-212.

Market Liberalism and an Economic Culture of Gift and Gratitude | 191

> First, we define them out of existence, . . . [changing] the terms of the discussion so that those who are apparently dependent are really just as autonomous as everyone else. Second, we commercialize their care. . . . Finally, we have developed elaborate justifications for ending the lives of those who are dependent on us. In other words, if all else fails, we kill them. (182)

She continues: "care of children becomes one more commodity" (189). Though there is a difference between market child care and government child care, the more significant difference is between "personal care by a family member and impersonal care provided by a paid stranger"(191). "The logic of dependence and independence means that the dependent appear to have no value" (192). Often, the unspoken claim in our culture is "that a person's dignity depends on the ability to think, choose, and make and keep commitments," but Morse notes critically that such a defense of personal dignity "cannot take account of situations in which recognizably human creatures are unable to choose and behave rationally" (195). Humans without these capacities "have no rights at all" (196). Morse describes the needed response to the cultural patterns indicated here in terms that again are strikingly similar to those of John Paul II. She writes that the answer to these problematic patterns ("impersonal bureaucracy and atomistic individualism") is "the law of the gift" (201). "To put it simply, we need love" (201).

> The gift perspective . . . preserves the universality principle that is so important to the Western philosophical and legal tradition. Not only am I a gift to myself, so is every other person a gift to him or herself. There is still a powerful egalitarian impulse in the gift approach. Although we may differ in our gifts and talents, each one of us is still a gift as much as any other. . . . There is a level at which no one really has reasonable bragging rights. I didn't create my intellect, my health or my family background, any more that I created my own life. The gift perspective helps us to see that each of these talents and endowments was entrusted to us, and is not of our own creation.
>
> Thus, the gift perspective maintains crucially important features of our Western system of legal rights and obligations. But at the same time, it provides us with several unique advantages. (202)

For example, "viewing the person as a gift helps us to have a more realistic understanding of human dependency" and "inspires an attitude of gratitude" (202-3). "The helpless person," says Morse, "invites us to enter into the realm of unconditional love" (205). Indeed, "[w]e work harder when our work is motivated with love" (207).

Morse then concludes her essay by reinforcing all of the above in light of a Christian vision, with its deepened sense of the meaning of suffering, its hallmark attentiveness to the weak, and its expansion of "the definition of neighbor to include anyone in need" (208). She sums up by saying that the contribution of the dependent to the rest of us ultimately is that "they teach us how to love, and be loved" (210).

John Paul II and Morse describe in similar ways the deeply problematic patterns of contemporary cultural life, and both link these patterns with an "instrumentalist" or "utilitarian" view of the human person. Both identify the marginalization of the weak and dependent as lying at the heart of our culture's troubling patterns. Finally, both propose the renewal of community, or what Morse calls "the gift perspective," in response to these patterns, and they both, albeit in different ways, appeal to Christianity in support of this gift perspective.

The anthropology of creaturely being as gift as I have developed it here is fundamentally in harmony with what John Paul II affirms as a "culture of life" and Morse as the "law of the gift." I wish here, however, to recall the logical link suggested above between liberalism's abstract notion of the self (self-identity) and contemporary culture's dominant logic of instrumentalism, as manifest in what the Pope terms a "culture of death" and Morse, "utilitarianism" — a link that Morse nevertheless does not make, indeed that she denies.

I do not mean to suggest that liberal anthropology *necessarily* leads to extreme expressions of utilitarianism, or indeed that it is liberal anthropology in an explicit conceptual form that brings us to these extremes. The point, simply, is that the liberal idea of man, operating however unwittingly and unthematically in Americans' patterns of life, creates an ontological vulnerability to such extremes. In short, I am conceiving liberal anthropology after the manner of what John Paul II terms sin in its "structural" sense: namely, a dis-*order* that conditions and disposes toward, but never exhaustively or wholly accounts for, sin in its properly personal reality, in the sense that it requires and expresses an exercise of freedom.[32]

---

32. To say that liberalism is a "structure of sin" is not to say that every participation in or furtherance of a liberal institution (e.g., voting) constitutes a personal sin. Every Christian is born into a culture and thus cannot help but be already enculturated; and he or she is

Now, Morse affirms the benefits of capitalism, which, she says, "has given millions of people a far higher standard of living than they could have obtained under any other economic system" (194). She does acknowledge that the "system of free enterprise, constitutionally limited government and culturally sanctioned individualism" rests on an inadequate sense of the content of human dignity, one that omits any affirmation of the dependent as such. However, she also states, "Of concern is not the economic system per se, but the wider philosophical framework of individualism within which capitalism is most often defended" (194).[33]

But implicit in my argument thus far is the claim that this "wider philosophical framework of individualism" has in fact been endemic to the very structure of the economic system, in its historical origin and in its only historically dominant forms. Capitalism from the beginning has been embedded (however unconsciously) within what may be called the philosophical tradition of liberalism, and it thereby shares in the defects of that philosophical tradition, *already as an economy.* How can we hope to humanize the vision of a free society in and through a gift perspective, how can we hope to avoid the free society's drift toward a utilitarian "culture of death," if our economic culture — the entire world of producing and exchanging things that pervades our patterns of life, thought, and action — has been handed over without logical resistance to the primacy of instrumentalized self-interest?

I turn, then, to consider the implications of my own argument regarding liberal economic culture in terms of several other Christian authors. My treatment of their arguments will have to be highly selective, relying for its fuller meaning on the more extensive constructive analysis developed thus far. My comments are organized around the issues of liberalism, anthropology, and globalization. I hasten to emphasize that the ar-

---

thus called to transform the culture from within. The point is that institutions, including liberal institutions, are never neutral with respect to the meaning of man in relation to God (see the *Catechism of the Catholic Church*, n. 2244), and Christians therefore need to be attentive to this meaning when they participate in the public-institutional life of society, seeking to re-form such meaning where necessary.

33. The issue here is not whether there ought to be a *distinction* between economic order on the one hand and philosophical or cultural order on the other: that is granted. (John Paul II, for example, makes just such a distinction in *Centesimus Annus*, n. 39.) What I deny is that the relation between these orders is or can ever be merely extrinsic, such that we are empowered to speak of an economic system or order without already, in that very act, importing an anthropology. For the significance of the point raised here, see the related discussion in note 38 below. See also *Caritas in Veritate*, n. 11, 30, 36, and particularly 38.

gument to follow by no means intends simply to reject the achievements of what Morse terms the "free society" of Western modernity. My intention is not to deny but to recuperate freedom, albeit a freedom now conceived in its proper nature as *creaturely*. Within a freedom so conceived, my intention is to retrieve the important features Morse identifies as characteristic of the modern West, namely, its "powerful egalitarian impulse" and the rightful aspects of its sense of autonomy — as well as the creativity, self-determination, and similar features noted by other authors. However, as we will now see in more detail, the differences between their, and indeed Morse's, arguments and my own lie in the extent of the transformation required of these features for the rightful ordering of market exchanges as such.

V. Liberal Economics as Instrumentalist Economics and Culture

Liberalism The late Father Richard Neuhaus begins his essay "The Liberalism of John Paul II and the Technological Imperative"[34] by emphasizing the importance of distinguishing among liberalisms. There are corrupt versions of liberalism that ought to be rejected and benign versions that ought to be defended, or at least are defensible. Neuhaus insists in this context that the differences between him and me are chiefly not over matters of Catholic theology (anthropology), but over how we interpret liberalism, and that my criticism presupposes liberalism in an already reduced version. This matter, however, can be quickly put to rest by making it clear that the liberalism I have in mind is what I and presumably he take to be liberalism at its most benign. It is liberalism already in its putatively benign sense that is subject to deep criticism from the point of view of a creaturely anthropology of gift. Contra Neuhaus, the differences between him and me are thus rooted in our respective (Christian) anthropologies. It is from within an anthropology of gift that his liberalism, assumed by both of us to be "benign" as liberalism, is nevertheless judged by me to be "corrupt," that is, defective, as an anthropology. How so?

Neuhaus is basically right when he says that:

> [i]t is a mistake to pit . . . modern individualism against a more organic Catholic understanding of community. Rather should we enter

34. In *Wealth, Poverty, and Human Destiny*, pp. 289-306.

into a sympathetic liaison with the modern achievement of the idea of the individual, grounding it more firmly and richly in the understanding of the person destined from eternity to eternity for communion with God. (296)

He then goes on to qualify this as follows:

The problem with the contemporary distortion of the individual as the autonomous, unencumbered, sovereign Self is not that it is wrong about the awesome dignity of the individual, but that it cuts the self off from the source of that dignity. The first cause of this error . . . is atheism. (296-97)

Neuhaus's positive point, with which I am not in substantial disagreement, is that we should seek to uncover, within the "autonomous, unencumbered, sovereign Self" of modernity, the truth of the "awesome dignity of the individual" that is somehow struggling to come to expression therein. The problem, says Neuhaus, is that modernity "cuts itself off from the source of that dignity," and that the "first cause of this error is atheism." Elsewhere he says the problem consists in a lack of freedom's obedience to transcendent truth.

The anthropology of gift outlined earlier, however, prompts us to ask just what is meant here by the individual's being cut off from God and transcendent truth as the source of his dignity. For the pertinent point, given that anthropology, is that the relation of God and hence of transcendent truth to the individual self always already reaches to the core of the individual self, such that the self and its freedom are always, at their deepest level, other-centered. This implies a primitive, largely implicit, movement of the self toward the other that is quite distinctive, one which I take to differ significantly from that apparently accepted by Neuhaus.

What that difference is can best be seen in Neuhaus's discussion of America's Declaration of Independence. The theistic references in that document, Neuhaus says, are not merely "crowd-pleasing asides, but are integral to [its] moral argument" (297). The liberty enshrined in that document is an "ordered liberty," because it is meant to be anchored in "self-evident truths" (297). I quite agree with both assertions. The crucial issue nevertheless comes into relief when we link these two assertions, as the Declaration does, with the individual's "rights": each of us as an individual has a right to life, liberty, and the pursuit of happiness.

To be sure, we do have such rights. But it does not suffice for an adequate understanding of these simply to tether the individual self to its transcendent source, for this tethering can still be too "extrinsically" conceived. And it is so conceived insofar as the self's rights are not given their first form in the self's anterior call to respond in love to the other (God, others). Nor does a variant of Neuhaus's appeal — an appeal which Jefferson himself makes, namely to rights as *natural* rights — suffice here. For nature can be understood merely as a "fact" from which we spring to claim rights, exactly in the sense given them by Jefferson. That is, in what is otherwise a necessary appeal to nature, we can fail to grasp the anterior relation to God that is constitutive of nature, failing thereby to grasp the implications of a relation so understood for a reordering of rights in the Declaration sense.[35]

The heart of this needed reordering, then, lies in recognizing that rights, in their true creaturely structure, bear from the inside out an order centered in the self, to be sure, but in the self only as centered simultaneously-anteriorly in God, others, the world, and the family. Rights, in a word, because and insofar as they are created, need to be recuperated in their original ontological structure as gifts. This implies a priority of the other (giver), even as this priority, in the way indicated earlier, is always already inclusive of the self.

The upshot of the reordering indicated here is thus that generosity is folded into the original meaning of rights. This implies two things. First, I claim my rights before the other only *inside of* and as *anteriorly ordered by* the claim of the other on me. This anterior claim of the other, with its note of "obligatoriness," is not to be interpreted after the manner of a duty in the modern (e.g., Kantian) sense. The claim, rather, takes the form of a *call to community with God and all other creatures that is inscribed at the core of my being as a creature*. It is a being-bound *(ob-ligo)* in God's creative love that always presupposes my now-responsive freedom.

Second, this original binding of rights to an anterior love for an Other does not thereby reduce rights merely to "instruments," such that, if one refused to give primacy to the service of God and others, one would thereby forfeit one's rights. Quite to the contrary, such an interpretation overlooks the crucial fact that the existence of the self, and consequently of self-interest, is itself already a matter of God's own created community.

---

35. See "Civil Community Inside the Liberal State: Truth, Freedom, and Human Dignity," pp. 65-132 in this volume.

What it is crucial to see, in other words, is that my rights remain irreducibly good, not merely good as a *means* (say, to truth) because, as created, they participate in God's own abiding generosity as creator and thus are themselves already matters of truth. Truly understood, and precisely as claims *of the self*, they are meant to participate anteriorly in God's *other-centered giving*.

In sum, my "claim" upon God and others is *mutual with*, even as it is *anteriorly-asymmetrically ordered by*, the "claim" of God and others on me.

Now it is typically asserted by liberalism in its benign or "conservative" reading that the Declaration's affirmation of rights bears a certain innocence, in the sense that it permits those making this affirmation to continue to hold the truths of the premodern Western tradition (the best of classical Greek and Christian thought, for example). What the Declaration adds to the tradition, in other words, is merely the form of freedom that leaves otherwise in place the tradition's substantial content. But this assumes that, as long as we affirm both the rights of the self and the rights of the other — as long, that is, as we affirm both the self and the other in their mutuality — we need not fuss over the issue of their relative priority. This assumption, however, begs the question of the asymmetrical order between self and other indicated in creatureliness, as argued in section II above, and indeed as is necessarily evoked in any attempt to harmonize liberal modernity and classical (Christian) thought. In any case, without this qualified asymmetry of order within the mutuality of rights (self) and goods (other), rights by definition become wrongly self-centered or selfish, and not generous.[36]

Neuhaus fails to differentiate sufficiently between self-centered and other-centered rights, in the way demanded here, in his defense of the Declaration of Independence's recognition of the transcendent source of individual dignity. But before considering significant related points, let me

---

36. For an interesting reading of the difference between liberal modernity and classical (Christian) thought on the matter of rights, see Ernest L. Fortin, "On the Presumed Medieval Origin of Individual Rights," *Communio: International Catholic Review* 26, no. 1 (Spring 1999): 55-79. Apropos of my own argument, I would emphasize that, if the classical (premodern) tradition rightly insists on the asymmetry necessary for a true understanding of the relation between the self and the other — insists, that is, on the priority of the other — it is also the case that that tradition itself now needs to expand, in order to incorporate a legitimate sense of the self-centeredness entailed in modernity's recognition of the mutuality of that relation, a self-centeredness that, rightly conceived, is demanded by God's very act of creation itself.

note some of the concrete transformations in the content of rights as reordered here, in contrast to the content of rights as construed in their more conventionally liberal terms.

Relation to God (religious freedom) The original right to freedom in religion emerges from within the always anteriorly given élan for God, or, again, the always anterior claim of God on us. This implies two things. First, the right to religious freedom is not primarily an immunity from coercion, after the manner argued by John Courtney Murray, for example, but on the contrary emerges intrinsically from, and as formed by, this always anterior call to be for God.[37] And, for the reasons given, this right is not forfeited if a person either fails to recognize or refuses to follow this call. Second, religion is a "natural" community before it is a freely chosen community. Or better, the movement toward God that essentially involves freedom is itself always elicited first by God himself in the very act of creation. This implies a transformation of the conventionally liberal sense of religion as primarily a voluntary society (cf., e.g., Locke, Madison).

The foregoing, then, exposes the non-neutrality of any appeal to religious freedom in terms primarily of freedom of choice, or immunity from coercion. A freedom that is originally "full" of a dynamic order toward God is different from a freedom that is originally empty of that order.

Neuhaus stresses the importance for a free society of a limited state and, in this connection, also of a distinction between state and society, and he is right to do so. The preceding two paragraphs of our discussion, however, imply that Neuhaus's argument here needs to be further differentiated. For the state's "limitedness," on the Murrayite reading that Neuhaus follows, is conceived as constitutional "silence" about God: hence Murray's interpretation of the religious articles of the First Amendment as "articles of peace" rather than "articles of faith." The state, in other words, affirms religious freedom as a putatively neutral immunity from coercion, leaving it to private individuals (society) to choose their own religion. The only demand on the state is that it protect the right of each individual to choose or to "confess" God in his or her own way.

But notice the (unintended) deception here: the state, on this read-

---

37. See the chapter on Murray ("Religious Freedom, Truth, and Anglo-American Liberalism: Another Look at John Courtney Murray") in *Heart of the World, Center of the Church* (Grand Rapids: Eerdmans, 1996), pp. 43-88. See also "Civil Community Inside the Liberal State."

ing, favors a notion of religious freedom whereby freedom's "negative" moment in relation to God (its silence or indifference) ontologically precedes its "positive" moment (its constitutive élan or restlessness for, or implicit affirmation of, God). Which is to say, the state favors a notion of religion the positive meaning of which emerges first as a matter of private choice, a notion that is properly termed positivistic. On a positivistic conception of religion, man is viewed not as "naturally" religious, as he is by Augustine and Aquinas and the entire patristic-medieval Christian tradition, but as primarily voluntarily religious. The upshot, then, is that the liberal state, on Murray's and Neuhaus's reading, in fact officially confesses a "positivist" or "voluntarist," as distinct from "natural," religiosity.

It follows that Murray's and Neuhaus's desired distinction between a non-confessional state and a confessional society is not, and in fact cannot be, as neat as they characteristically insist.[38] Once this becomes clear, we see how the liberal state, with its privileging of religious freedom as immunity, becomes in its own way unlimited: the only religion the liberal state officially supports, always and everywhere in "public," is one that keeps its contents "private," a religion, that is, that construes its "public" role to be, not that of *forming*, but only of *inspiring*, life, thought, and moral action. The liberal state just so far officially favors a fragmented, as distinct from integrated, idea of religion.[39]

Once again, there are very difficult and subtle issues raised here that need further sorting out on another occasion. However, in a sense that is just my point. We need to differentiate the issues further, precisely in order to understand, for example, the distinctive way in which America's consti-

---

38. As mentioned in an economic context above (note 33), the issue here is not whether we need a distinction between "state" and "society" (we do), but how we are best to conceive this distinction. What we need is a distinction that affirms a unity between state and society coincident with their distinction. The significance of the qualifier here can be illustrated with respect to the soul-body distinction. On a Cartesian reading, the soul and body are distinguished in terms of an external relation, such that the body in its physical nature as such is empty of *human-spiritual* meaning. On a Thomistic reading, the soul and the body are, on the contrary, distinguished in terms of an internal relation, such that the body in its physical nature as such is always already "full" of human-spiritual meaning. Descartes, if you will, offers an "articles of peace" rendering of the body in its relation to the soul. To be sure, these comments leave much to be sorted out in terms of the distinctly political character of the state-society distinction. I wish simply to highlight how the rightful appeal to the necessity of this distinction needs itself to be articulated further in terms of the difference between an internal and an external relation.

39. See "Civil Community Inside the Liberal State."

tutional defense of religious freedom as a matter of principle favors America's peculiar kind of secularization.[40]

In sum, we need to exhibit an understanding of religion and the state that moves us beyond the conventional terms of liberalism on the one hand and the old confessionalism on the other. Such an understanding seems to me exactly the intention of the Second Vatican Council's *Dignitatis Humanae*, rightly interpreted. Neuhaus's argument, following that of Murray, leaves us locked within these conventional terms, which John Paul II and Benedict XVI have both challenged in their writings.[41]

Relation to others ("subjectivity of society" and "solidarity") What needs to be highlighted here is how the constitutive nature of the self's relation to the other alone yields the full integrity, and indeed novelty, of the meaning of the terms "subjectivity of society" and "solidarity" as used by their author, John Paul II. In "Catholic Social Teaching, Markets, and the Poor,"[42] Michael Novak is concerned to distinguish the Pope's understanding of these terms from a socialist understanding. Novak emphasizes the personal responsibility and initiative of the human subject, and he opposes this to what socialists imply in collectivization. He is concerned also to emphasize the subjectivity of the human person over against the non-subjectivity of animals, who cannot choose for themselves. But such emphases, however necessary, do not get us to the nub of the crucial difference between liberal, or originally contracted, community and genuinely creaturely, or originally given, community as articulated throughout this chapter. For what the latter as distinct from the former community demands is precisely an *order* of community that already partially but decisively structures the meaning of individual freedom. It demands an order, that is to say, that transcends the individual even as it already itself essentially includes the individual's freedom.

This suggestion is best clarified in relation to what John Paul II refers to as a "structure," a social order, as it were, of sin, an order that is brought into being by personal choice but which nevertheless does not reduce to sin in the sense of personal choices. The Pope's notions of the "subjectivity

---

40. See "The Dramatic Nature of Life," in addition to "Religion and Secularity in a Culture of Abstraction."

41. Regarding Benedict XVI and *Dignitatis Humanae*, see "Truth, Freedom, and Relativism in Western Democracies: Pope Benedict XVI's Contributions to *Without Roots*," pp. 53-64 in this volume. See also "Civil Community Inside the Liberal State."

42. In *Wealth, Poverty, and Human Destiny*, pp. 51-75.

of society" and "solidarity" refer to what are the positive correlatives to sinful structures or order. That is, they indicate an order, for example, a "civilization of love" or "culture of life," that, precisely as a matter of social or cultural *order*, expresses the good of community in a way that cannot be accounted for in terms of the sum of the personal choices of individuals, even as it presupposes and includes those choices.[43]

The distinction indicated here is important not least of all because it implies that any renewal of culture in accord with what is meant by "subjectivity of society" and "solidarity" on the Pope's terms requires a dynamic for *social-structural* transformation that presupposes even as it "transcends" the sum transformation of individual persons. (It is notable in this connection that neither Neuhaus nor Novak has ever undertaken, or to my knowledge even mentioned, a critique of contemporary society in terms of "structural sin" in the way that John Paul II repeatedly has, indeed in the way the Pope says we must if we are to provide the needed critique.)[44]

---

43. See "The Significance of the World and Culture for Moral Theology: *Veritatis Splendor* and the Nature of the Body," pp. 219-41 in this volume.

44. The importance of taking account of the "structural" dimension of sin in our engagement with contemporary culture is indicated, *inter alia*, in John Paul II's *Dominum et Vivificantem*, n. 56, and *Sollicitudo Rei Socialis*, n. 36-37, as well as in the Sacred Congregation for the Doctrine of the Faith's "Instruction on Christian Freedom and Liberation" (*Libertatis Conscientia*: AAS 79 [1987]: 554-99 at n. 74-75). Neuhaus's essay, to which we are responding here, is meant to provide an interpretation of the Pope's *Centesimus Annus* (*CA*). Given this, and relative to the issue of "structural sin," we should call attention here to the abridgment of this encyclical that Neuhaus published on several occasions, for the purpose, as he says in his *Doing Well and Doing Good* (New York: Doubleday, 1992), p. 13, of testing his (Neuhaus's) own reading of that encyclical. Noting that we need to move beyond all that was short-lived in earlier, often too Marxist-driven attempts at liberation, *CA* states nevertheless that "present circumstances are leading to a *reaffirmation of the positive value of* an authentic theology of integral human liberation" (n. 26, emphasis added), referring to the CDF's "Instruction" above. Notably, Neuhaus's abridged version of this passage reads, without indication of omission: "present circumstances are leading to an authentic theology of integral human liberation." The encyclical's effort explicitly to integrate what was positive in the "old" liberation theology — its concern for "structural sin," for example — thus disappears in Neuhaus's restatement, which instead simply points ahead to what Neuhaus takes to be the now-required form of liberation, namely, the free market. Lest this criticism seem heavy-handed, we should note further, for example, that Neuhaus omits, again without any indication of omission, the statement in n. 52 of *CA*, which says that promoting development "may mean making important changes in established lifestyles, in order to limit the waste of environmental and human resources. . . ." Indeed, Neuhaus interprets this statement elsewhere as "most likely a vestigial rhetorical fragment that somehow wandered into the text

Relation to the world ("stewardship") The constitutive relation of the individual self to the world that is given with his creation implies, most basically, that the world, or the entire natural environment, is a home for man before it is his instrument. Or better, it is an instrument, but only as it is always more basically a gift. This truth does not imply that man ought not to use the world, but only that his use needs to be ordered to the world's fundamental reality as gift, its reality as a gift from God that is for God, for others, and for one's self in relation to God. The natural environment must always be seen first in its givenness as inherently ("transcendentally") true, good, and beautiful. Thus, work, and the artifacts of work, ought always finally to be ordered to community, to friendship with others, and to the worship of God.[45] Though much of what I affirm here is implicit in my earlier comments apropos of liberalism's instrumentalist view of work and artifacts, I have yet to highlight what is termed "stewardship." Man is meant to care for the non-human cosmos, and indeed to use it for his own purposes. But this care and use must be ordered intrinsically toward human and divine love, an aptness for the containment and expression of which is *already present* in the original order of things and is given with their creation. What this implies for Western modernity's science and technology is of course a vast question, which I address more extensively in Part II of this book.

Relations of family and gender ("mediating institutions") Catholic social teaching refers frequently to the notion of "subsidiarity," and many Catholics rightly affirm the need for "mediating institutions" in this regard. Human society rightfully conceived requires intermediate communities between the state and the individual. Paramount among such mediating institutions is the family. The creaturely anthropology defended in this

---

and is notable chiefly for its incongruity with the argument that the Pope is otherwise making" (*Doing Well and Doing Good*, p. 224). I note all of this by way of calling attention to what seems to me the significance of Neuhaus's failure to engage "structural sin," and indeed to see with John Paul II and the "Instruction" how key elements of the "old" liberation theology (properly qualified) need to be taken over, so that the free market itself might be realized as "an authentic theology of integral human liberation." The nature of this "authentic theology" of liberation is sketched for us in the Congregation for the Doctrine of the Faith's 1986 Instruction on Christian Freedom and Liberation, *Libertatis Conscientia*. Cf. also in this connection, apropos of how properly to read *CA*, Pope Benedict XVI's *Caritas in Veritate*, particularly n. 34.

45. See Benedict XVI, *Caritas in Veritate*, n. 50-51.

chapter understands familial relations as intrinsic to the substantial identity of the individual. The crucial implications of this come into relief when we contrast this sense of individual identity with the originally abstract individual identity of liberalism. As a matter of its own inner logic, liberalism tends to invest rights in the individual independent of his relations to family. A genuinely creaturely ontology, on the contrary, invests rights in the individual *at once as a member of a family*. It is the individual as always and already ordered to (and from) his most immediate natural community who is properly the subject of rights.

Furthermore, creaturely ontology as I have conceived it, for example, in light of Genesis, entails recognition of gender difference as intrinsic to man's original identity.[46] It just so far recommends a notion of rights that would accord these to individuals precisely *in* this *difference* that at once expresses the unity, or equality, of man and woman. This approach contrasts, again, with the tendency of liberalism, which insists on abstracting from this difference, precisely as a condition of defending its own abstract, or egalitarian, notion of equality.

The burden of the foregoing brief descriptions is to amplify what is entailed in a generous conception of rights. Rights in their true creaturely understanding are intrinsically ordered to, even as they are themselves already and in principle inclusive expressions of, community in each of the four ways outlined here: with God, others, the world, and the family. The breakdown of community in each of these areas in contemporary society, accordingly, I take to be a function *logically* of liberalism's insufficiently generous, or wrongly self-centered, conception of rights, an insufficiency that emerges by virtue of ambiguity within the Declaration of Independence itself.

My argument thus indicates a distinct approach to the interpretation of current cultural problems relative to the (liberal) founding documents of America. Father Neuhaus sees in the Declaration sound principles to which we need to be called back in order to overcome our current difficulties. In other words, he locates the roots of the present cultural difficulties in the moral-political departure from America's founding principles that is evidenced, for example, by various decisions of the Supreme Court since the 1940s. Thus, he argues, to take but one example, that legalized abortion indicates an "abandoning [of] the first [i.e., 'founding'] liberalism that has sustained all that is hopeful in the American experiment" (293). The bur-

---

46. See also "The Embodied Person as Gift and the Cultural Task in America."

den of my own argument, on the contrary, is that present-day legalized abortion exposes what is a crucial ambiguity regarding the self and its rights already resident in the implicit anthropology of the "first liberalism," whatever its express *intentions* to the contrary.[47]

We can now comment briefly on other pertinent claims of Neuhaus. First, in connection with his defense of the Declaration of Independence, Neuhaus suggests that the American experiment as constituted by a Puritan-Lockean synthesis "has been bowdlerized to fit the secularist prejudices of our academic elites" (298). And he insists in the same vein that the religion indicated in this synthesis is not a mere "civil religion," because it acknowledges "the transcendent source and end of human existence" (298). But these assertions miss the a-theism peculiar to American liberalism, as we outlined it above, and as in fact it is well described by Will Herberg in his "classic" book, *Protestant–Catholic–Jew,* which expresses itself primarily not in an overt denial of God's existence, but in an implicit affirmation of God's irrelevance to the *form* of our daily acting, producing, and thinking.[48]

Furthermore, Neuhaus insists that liberalism in any case is not "the content of the Church's message. It is simply the condition for the Church to invite free persons to live in the *communio* of Christ and his Mystical Body, which communion is infinitely deeper, richer, and fuller than the liberal social order — or, for that matter, any social order short of the right ordering of all things in the kingdom of God" (298). The fault then, if we fail to propose the Church's message in a way that is sufficiently persuasive, "is not with liberalism but with ourselves" (298).

Neuhaus's suggestion here (liberalism is a "condition," not a content) expresses the characteristic claim of liberalism that its freedom, that is, freedom of choice, is in principle empty of an anthropology. But we have seen that liberalism's freedom of choice already and essentially *is* an anthropology, one indeed that misses the implications of the originally given

---

47. For a discussion of the relationship of mother and child as the "basic figure of human freedom," in light of the problem of abortion as an expression of the Enlightenment's claim of liberty without relationality, see Joseph Ratzinger, "Truth and Freedom," *Communio: International Catholic Review* 23, no. 1 (Spring 1996): 16-35, 26f. Rights, properly understood, need to be able to take account of the human being in the womb, and this *qua* dependent. On this, see the discussions in "Civil Community Inside the Liberal State" and "The Dramatic Nature of Life."

48. Will Herberg, *Protestant Catholic Jew* (Chicago: University of Chicago Press, 1983 [1955]). On America's peculiar secularization, see "Religion and Secularity in a Culture of Abstraction."

creaturely order. Indeed, Neuhaus's assertion here betrays an extrinsicism in his defense of America's experiment in "ordered liberty." For the crucial issue, in light of all we have written, lies in differentiating the sense in which "order" toward God and transcendent truth *anteriorly forms* freedom *in its first act* relative to God and truth.

Further, then, the "fault" regarding our inability to be persuasive in proposing *communio* to the broader culture is not only in ourselves, so to speak. Our ability to be persuasive, rather, is seriously hindered by liberal claims — such as that freedom is a condition and not a content — which, in the name of putatively empty "process," hide what is already, *eo ipso*, a definite liberal conception, or content, of freedom. Liberalism, in other words, in its appeal to freedom, hides the *order* implicit in that appeal. The point is thus that to be persuasive in the broader culture, we need to expose liberalism not just as the sum of (bad) personal uses of freedom, but as an *order* of freedom. Which is to say that we have to come to terms with liberalism also as a "structure of sin."

Finally, it is of course true that the right ordering of things, of the self and its love, is never complete except in the kingdom to come. The relevant point, however, is that the Son of God came to earth in order that the earth, in him and already here and now, might begin bearing heaven. The eschatological kingdom, in other words, finds its rightful meaning only in Jesus' incarnational kingdom. The fact that the right ordering indicated in the latter is to begin now scarcely means that it ought to be "imposed" rather than "proposed," despite many errant past practices of the Church in this regard. As Neuhaus says, the Church's communion is infinitely more than the liberal social order. The crucial points, however, are whether and in what sense the transformation toward this communion is to begin already now and "publicly," and not merely in the future and "privately"; and whether this dynamic transformation is to originate from within the core of the social order or only by way of addition to it.

Neuhaus concludes that the would-be liberalism of John Paul II is "commensurate with the American liberal tradition, and in critical continuity with the great work of John Courtney Murray" (306). At any rate, he says, he "hope[s] that is the case, for we have not the luxury of imagining the reconstitution of this social and political order on foundations other than the liberal tradition" (306). What I have said suffices to indicate why I think Neuhaus is mistaken in his claim that the thought of John Paul II is commensurate with American liberalism. Regarding the "luxury" of reconstituting America's social and political order on terms other than those of liberalism, I fail to see why things are so different with respect to American culture from what they have been with respect to dominant cultures throughout history. We are called to attempt to transform whatever culture we live in, hence including that of America, in accord with the truth about man and God as we understand it in light of reason illuminated by revelation. On the question of the "realism" of such an attempt, I recall the reader to the discussion at the end of Part II above.

If I may summarize: (1) for the reasons given, I believe that America's characteristic notion of rights, the "benignly" liberal notion defended by Neuhaus, for example, needs to be transformed at its roots ("radically"); and (2) I believe that it is this transformation alone that finally permits, indeed demands, a legitimate sense of America's "exceptional" achievements. It is the very radicality of the transformation, in other words, that enables us to retrieve the historically significant goods that are intended in and by the Declaration but are nevertheless undermined by the Declaration's own ambiguous logic.

Anthropology Michael Novak, in "Catholic Social Teaching, Markets, and the Poor," argues that "liberals" in the best sense are not materialists "concerned solely with market processes, profits, and efficiency, to the neglect of the human spirit, human values, and human rights" (53). On the contrary, he insists, "[i]n the new economy of today . . . it is very difficult to be a materialist, strictly understood" (53). Why? Because in an age characterized by computers and the like, "*matter* matters less and less, and *intelligence* (or spirit) matters more" (53). What matters, in other words, is rather the "information . . . created by human intelligence," "the fruit of the human spirit" (53). "[A]n increasing proportion of production today lies in its 'spiritual' rather than its 'material' components. Industries are becoming cleaner; through miniaturization, physical products are becoming smaller, more powerful, and (usually) cheaper" (63). Furthermore, Novak appeals to the "growing immateriality of what people are actually willing to buy," reflected not only in their demand for information, but also in their increasing demand for entertainment, sport, music, theatre, and literature, as well as their increasing preference for intellectual and aesthetic delight, all of which "place much smaller demands on materials and energy" (63).

The burden of my earlier argument, however, is that liberalism is "materialist" in the objectionable sense, not because it is concerned more with "matter" than with "spirit," but because of its characteristic instrumentalism, which embodies and contributes to dehumanizing patterns of having and producing and indeed of thinking and acting. Viewed in this light, Novak's suggestion becomes scarcely credible: liberals are no longer materialistic because they now collect information instead of Rolls Royces! His suggestion ignores the sense in which the human "spirit" itself can remain — and, given liberal presuppositions, characteristically does remain — *consumeristic*, precisely in its alleged increased interest in entertainment, sport, music, literature, and the like. It is beyond the scope of the present chapter to show this in any detail. I will, however, return to the important question of an age characterized by technology, below, and in more sustained fashion in Part II of this book.

Under the heading "Breaking the Chains of Poverty," Novak states that the task of this century "is to arrange our institutions so that all the poor of the world may exit from poverty" (59). He then goes on to describe, by way of defending the market economy, some of the key conditions necessary for creating wealth. Here he makes a sustained appeal to John Paul II's emphasis on the "acting person" (64). The Pope's argument, he says, rests "on the doctrine of creation and a longstanding Christian interpretive tradition associated with the Book of Genesis" (65). Despite this theological provenance, the argument still implies much about the creation of wealth: notably, for example, in terms of how the cause of wealth lies not primarily in land or the ownership of the means of production, but rather in the "human wit, discovery, invention, the habit of enterprise, foresight, skill in organization" (66). "Creativity by any other name causes wealth, as natural resources alone do not."

Indeed, "the pope sees that the market is, above all, a social instrument":

> [M]ost economic activities in the modern environment are too complex to be executed by one person alone; nearly all of them require the creation of a new type of community, not organic but artifactual, not natural (as the family is natural) but contractual, not coercive (as was "real existing socialism") but free and voluntary, not total like a monastery but task-oriented and open to cooperators, even ones of different belief systems and ultimate commitments. In short, the distinctive invention of capitalist societies is the business firm, independent of the state. (67)

Novak then summarizes as follows:

> [T]he pope has advanced two new arguments in support of his proposal that market systems shed practical light on Christian truth and advance human welfare. The first is that markets give expression to the creative subjectivity of the human person, who has been created in the image of the Creator of all things, and called to help complete the work of creation through sustained historical effort. His second argument is that markets generate new and important kinds of community, while expressing the social nature of human beings in rich and complex ways. (69)

I have already spoken much about the need for creativity to be anteriorly formed in and through the gratitude, or grateful receiving, that alone suffices to integrate creativity into what is an act truly of *giving or loving*, hence humanly enhancing in the proper sense. Novak's assertions, however, help to highlight the central connection between creativity and the nature and origin of wealth. In emphasizing how wealth is a function of invention, habits of enterprise, organizational skills, and the like, Novak in fact brings more sharply into relief the significance of my earlier argument regarding how a creativity conceived in instrumentalist terms gives rise to and itself already participates in a reductive sense of wealth. His failure to qualify creativity in terms of an adequate anthropology of creatureliness backs him into just the wrongly self-centered, instrumentalist creativity that is the bane of liberalism, and indeed informs liberalism's reduced and (in light of the foregoing argument) question-begging notion of wealth. Not surprisingly, Novak defends Smith's notion of self-interest, "rightly understood," in the equivocal form noted earlier. And not surprisingly, therefore, Novak's defense of creativity ignores the potentially serious consequences of a creativity not clearly differentiated in terms of the distinction between a Smithian account and what I have argued is a genuinely creaturely account of creativity.

This critique may seem unfair, since Novak claims to be interpreting John Paul II in his appeal to creativity. He appeals to creativity, in other words, exactly in its character as an image of the Creator. However, his interpretation of the creature's imaging of God does not take sufficient account of the individual's *original constitution in a communion of persons*, a failure manifest in his failure to see how this anterior community affects the original meaning of creativity, wit, invention, enterprise, and the like. In other words, he does not come to terms with the crucial issue: the relative ordering of self-centeredness and other-centeredness in such acts.

My point here, it should go without saying, is not that creativity should in any way be attenuated. The point, rather, is to see that an anterior gratitude (listening, patience, contemplativeness, wonder) is necessary, if the initiative toward the other inscribed in creativity is to become a genuinely *loving* — which is to say, a genuinely self-within-other-centered — response to the other. Without these anterior implications of community within creativity, creativity as a matter of its inner logic will generate just the instrumentalized abundance, the instrumentalized having, producing, and exchanging of things, that is characteristic of the culture of utilitarianism.

But a likely rejoinder by Novak would be, compared to what? However incomplete or deficient the abundance produced by capitalist creativity, he asks in his essay, what system has done better? He answers: "In comparing which system is more likely to bring about universal opportunity, prosperity from the bottom up . . . the historical answer is clear: for the poor, market systems provide far better chances of improving income, conditions, and status" (75). Novak is indeed right to demand that criticism of the market system be undertaken in comparison with other economic systems realized in history. I would insist only that this comparison between systems *itself* always be compared to the human destiny that Christian faith and indeed the nature of reality itself call us to embody here and now on earth, however much that call will be fully realized only eschatologically. In light of this destiny, we see that Novak's arguments as they bear on wealth and poverty beg the question of the extent to which the very creativity and abundance embodied in and produced by capitalism themselves contribute to a "culture of death." To put it another way, his arguments beg the burden of what Mother Teresa meant when she insisted that the "poverty" characteristic of the West was, in the deepest sense and in its own way, as bad as the poverty characteristic of India.[49] Here is a comparison that must become part of any argument comparing economic systems in the matter of wealth.

The second contribution of John Paul II that Novak highlights is the Pope's recognition of how the market generates new senses of community, such as that found, for example, in the business firm. This new community, he points out, is "artifactual" rather than "organic" or "natural." To be sure, the business firm has and must have legitimate "contractual" dimensions not proper to communities like the family. The radical, constitutive

---

49. See also *Caritas in Veritate*, n. 53.

nature of creaturely community, however, requires that voluntary communities themselves be integrated into the more radical sense of community entailed in creation. Which is to say, there is no community anywhere in the creaturely universe that is purely, or first, voluntary in character, because relation to all creatures is already *given* in the act of creation.

The upshot is that even communities like the business firm are subject intrinsically to the criteria given in the call to generous gratitude and grateful giving, with all that this implies in terms of solidarity, the subjectivity of society, and stewardship as outlined with respect to our discussion of Neuhaus, and in contrast with these terms as Novak interprets them.[50]

Globalization Finally, I wish to comment on a single but significant passage from Stackhouse and Stratton's "Capitalism, Civil Society, Religion, and the Poor: A Bibliographical Essay."[51] The passage concerns globalization, with the threat of homogenization which some see to be built into the globalization process.

> There has been a great fear, in some quarters, that [the globalized economy] would bring about a homogenization of culture, and that people would lose their distinctive identities. Such dire predictions remind one of the widespread anxiety in the 1910s and 1920s that factory work would turn persons into mere cogs in machines, and of the 1950s and 1960s lament that computers, mass communication, and suburbanization would so standardize everything that all diversity and personality would be lost. There has been some loss of cultural particularity, certainly. Peoples from tribal cultures and peasant peoples from societies essentially feudal in structure, especially, have been drawn into complex cultures where their traditional patterns of life are severely compromised and their hereditary forms of status less valued — both in the dominant culture and among their own youth. And it is often the case that when such folk seek to join the dominant, more complex society, they must often struggle mightily simply to find a place on the lower rungs of the economic ladder.
>
> However, commissioned, independent studies by the *Economist* converge with data collected by the World Bank and my own studies in

---

50. See *Caritas in Veritate*, ch. 3.

51. Max L. Stackhouse with Lawrence M. Stratton, "Capitalism, Civil Society, Religion, and the Poor: A Bibliographical Essay," in *Wealth, Poverty and Human Destiny*, pp. 431-63.

this regard: Confucian/Maoist China, Hindu/Democratic India, Islamic/technocratic Malaysia and Indonesia, Christian/Iberian-influenced Brazil and Mexico are all preserving quite distinctive cultures, each with ethnic, religious, and social pluralism continuing under the mantle of these dominant patterns. To be sure, minorities and dissidents frequently encounter human rights violations and cultural disadvantages in these regions, and international legal, political, and economic regulatory and developmental agencies will surely continue to put pressure on these societies to conform to international standards. Those cultures with authoritarian patterns of leadership often resist this pressure — speaking rather romantically, for example, of "Asian values" — yet some of them such as South Korea, Thailand, and Taiwan in Asia, and Chile in Latin America, have recognized that such patterns are economically dysfunctional, and each of these regions is adopting technological, economic, and corporate practices that allow them to interact more easily with the wider human community. Simultaneously, these standards and patterns are being integrated into deeper cultural traditions. . . . The growth of the conditionalities of civil society, to be sure, modifies cultures, but no culture has ever been static or entirely closed to extrinsic influence, and the changes they must adopt to foster economic growth are unlikely to destroy them, even if they modulate these cultures so that they can become more fully interactive with other cultures and societies. (441-43)

Stackhouse and Stratton thus insist that the data support the conclusion that traditional or peasant cultures are not losing their distinctive identities in the face of globalization. At the same time, however, these authors acknowledge the influence of dominant societal patterns, coincident with this persistent distinctiveness. This influence is due to international pressure to conform by ending human rights violations, authoritarian patterns of leadership, and economic dysfunctionality. To counter these signs of backwardness, many of the cultures in question are integrating the dominant practices of first-world, liberal societies in order to reap the perceived benefits of globalization.

In sum, Stackhouse and Stratton argue that the various religious and ethnic cultures named above need to be brought into line with international standards and practices, which means basically with the standards and practices of the democratic capitalist culture of liberalism, with its technology and science. Adoption of such standards and practices nevertheless permits these cultures, in principle and in fact, to retain their distinctiveness in crucial respects.

The authors' argument here, however, is in significant ways rigged. It is guided *a priori* in its observations and conclusions by a certain understanding of the nature and worth of the standards and practices of liberal democracy and capitalism. This may seem to be stating the obvious. But the importance of the point comes into view upon recalling what was said earlier, for example, about freedom, and about the possession, production, exchange, and indeed nature of things (artifacts) themselves, as characteristically conceived in liberalism. None of these is without a definite anthropology. Each embodies a definite anthropological form that just so far inclines toward the displacement of contrary anthropological forms.

Again, it is unlikely that the authors would deny this, or that they would claim that liberal freedom and modes of production and exchange are neutral with respect to different possible anthropologies. Rather, what they apparently mean to argue is that liberal anthropological forms — freedom of choice, "rights," efficiency of production, and the like — are more or less what reasonable persons would take as evidently good; that "neutrality" therefore is a matter of what is *effectively* neutral, because and insofar as it is (more or less) transparently good to and for all reasonable persons. Such forms provide what might be considered the surface machinery proper to civilized life as such, and otherwise leave intact the deeper anthropology proper to indigenous ethnic and religious groups.

But liberal freedom of choice, "rights," and the like are not so transparently good and reasonable. However genuine the advances that these liberal forms represent in certain important respects, liberal freedom of choice, rights, and economic structures in fact serve already to change our notion of the human being in crucial, albeit often subtle, ways. As I have argued, they assist in bringing about, and indeed themselves already express, liberalism's characteristic instrumentalism. Insofar as traditional cultures become more rational and free on liberal terms, then, they already will have transformed their basic view of the human being and indeed of the nature of the cosmos as created, and in so doing they will have reshaped the cultural and religious meaning in and through which all aspects of their cultures are ordered.

To be sure, Stackhouse and Stratton are correct that these cultures will remain pluralistic, not monolithically liberal. The question I am posing concerns the nature, not the denial, of pluralism among non-Western cultures. Stackhouse and Stratton suggest that homogenization will be a relatively superficial phenomenon leaving intact deep religious-anthropological differences. But this judgment imports a reading of liberalism as a surface phenomenon. The problem is that, if liberal standards and practices embody an anthropology that tends to displace indigenous religion and anthropology, then, given enough time[52] and global pressure, these cultures will, *eo ipso*, change in deep — i.e., religious, anthropological — ways. This does not mean that there will no longer be any pluralism, but merely that that pluralism will take the form increasingly of *varieties of liberalism*.[53]

I would like to illustrate my point here further in terms of the concept of technology that is so important for Stackhouse and Stratton. Technology, they say, "is enormously powerful in contemporary globalization," although the view that people have "some ultimate duty to reshape, invent, revise, reform, or transform the world" is today "largely secularized" (453). Nonetheless, it was not always so. On the contrary, technology and science, properly understood, have a theological origin. Following Nancy Pearcey, Stackhouse and Stratton argue for the biblical belief that, because the world is created by God, it has "a rational, intelligible order." They then note three further religious principles. First,

> [t]he universe is contingent and can be changed, a principle that fundamentally challenges the ontocratic assumption that nature (as it is by itself, or as it is created by God) is teleological and imbued with inherent rational purposes, as was taught by Aristotle and Thomas Aquinas. Instead, the expectation of a future transformation, the arrival of a "new heaven and new earth," indicates that nature as it is will collapse and is less to be contemplated and followed than to be intentionally altered and used. (451-52)

---

52. The vagueness of this phrase of course opens it up to a charge of question-begging: Just how long before the changes might be evident? I would only underscore here, in keeping with what was argued in section II above, how significant differences in being and action and things can be missed precisely because of their subtle nature; how, consequently, it can take long periods of time, even centuries, for the full implications of such differences to come into view. And, indeed, the extroverted ("empirical," cf. note 17) criteria in terms of which cultural judgments are characteristically rendered in a liberal culture further complicate our ability to discern these differences. For further discussion and examples of problems in liberal culture, see "The Dramatic Nature of Life" and "Civil Community Inside the Liberal State."

53. Regarding cultural pluralism in relation to globalization, see *Caritas in Veritate*, particularly n. 26.

Second, "Humans find their primary kinship not with nature but with a transcendent God and with other humans created in God's image. This generates a perspective that gives permission for humans to have an active role in engaging nature and a denial of the view that humans are so embedded in nature that they can only conform to it," a perspective that they claim was "widespread among the Puritans" (452). And third, "[h]umans have a duty to shape and intervene in the world; indeed, we are commissioned by God to have dominion" (452).

Furthermore, Stackhouse and Stratton cite the work of David Noble as evidence that "the striking acceleration and intensification of technological development in . . . [medieval] Europe ['the dynamic project of Western technology,' which is 'the defining mark of modernity'] emanated from contemplative monasticism" (452). The thirteenth-century theologian-scientist Roger Bacon, for example, saw "the mechanical arts as a means of anticipating and preparing for the kingdom to come. . . . Technology might well help restore humankind by recovering the knowledge lost in the Fall, and such knowledge would be most useful for moving humanity, as an ally and servant of God, closer to a new kind of perfection" (453).

These are indeed striking claims, to which I will respond in three stages. First, the argument that Christian theology underpins technology in its hallmark modern sense is made here in a way that sets aside without discussion an entire stream of historical Christianity. I refer to the theology of thinkers like Maximus, Aquinas, and Bonaventure, to mention only a few. Or again, in the contemporary period, we might recall Henri de Lubac, whose work sought to recuperate the social and cosmic meaning of the Church and the Eucharist;[54] or Alexander Schmemann, who sought likewise to recuperate the liturgical-sacramental-symbolic meaning of the cosmos, of space and time and matter and motion in their originally destined meaning as such;[55] or John Paul II, who insists on the "cosmic dimension of the Incarnation," how Christ unites himself with "the entire reality of man," and "in this reality with all 'flesh,' with the whole of creation," "with the whole of the visible and material world."[56] All of these theologians affirm some form (though not the reduced form characterized

---

54. Cf., inter alia, *Corpus Mysticum: The Eucharist and the Church in the Middle Ages* (London: SCM Press, 2006); and *Catholicism* (San Francisco: Ignatius Press, 1988).

55. See, for example, his *For the Life of the World*, cited in note 9.

56. *Dominum et Vivificantem*, n. 50.

by Pearcey) of the "ontocratic assumption" rejected by Stackhouse and Stratton. All of them would continue to affirm a primacy of the contemplative, even and precisely within the active engagement with the cosmos that they would simultaneously affirm. None of them would disjoin their kinship with a transcendent God from a simultaneous (albeit, to be sure, subordinate) kinship with nature. Much more needs to be said to show what is implied by each of these assertions relative to the claim of Stackhouse and Stratton. It suffices for my intention here, however, to call attention to what seems to me the *a priori*, and thus question-begging, nature of their neglect of such theologians.

Second, Stackhouse and Stratton assert a simple continuity between the medieval monks and modern technological development, for example, in terms of the monks' exact organizing, and hence rationalizing, of time. Drawing on David Landes's book *Revolution in Time*,[57] the authors mention how "timing was essential to the assembly line, to industrial efficiency experts, and now to the speed of the microchip — all a direct result of the monastery's adoption of technology for rational ends" (454).

It will suffice, relative to the simple continuity asserted here, to call attention to the (*prima facie* significant) contrast between the sense in which Calvinism/Puritanism understands the world as an "instrument" of salvation and the sense in which, for example, a Bonaventure, an Aquinas, or an Ignatius of Loyola understands the world as an "instrument" of salvation. Again, Descartes's (re-)conceiving of the physical in mechanistic terms needs to be taken into account. There is Francis Bacon's reconfiguring of knowledge into a matter first of power, and his distinctive sense, consequently, of how science is already itself a matter of technology, albeit for the betterment of humankind. Finally, there is the movement in both Descartes and Bacon toward the elimination of inner causes such as form and finality in their respective accounts of nature.[58] Can we really argue for a simple continuity between what the monks meant by order and by time and by the world as *instrument*, without taking account of what are *prima facie* the large differences introduced by Calvinism/Puritanism, Descartes, and Bacon, relative, say, to Maximus, Bonaventure, Aquinas, and Ignatius?

Third, consider the nature of modern technology in relation to what

---

57. David Landes, *Revolution in Time: Clocks and the Making of the Modern World* (Cambridge, MA: The Belknap Press of the Harvard University Press, 2000).

58. For further discussion of this loss of causality and the Cartesian/Baconian revolution in thought, see Hans Jonas, *The Phenomenon of Life* (Evanston, IL: Northwestern University Press, 2001), particularly "The Practical Uses of Theory."

might be called the more "ontocratic" theologies of these latter thinkers. Recall the obvious point that technology is an artifact, nature as changed or transformed by man. This may seem simple enough, but the problem occurs when, as is customary in liberal cultures, we overlook the human meaning that is thereby (partially) constitutive of the thing made. The point, in other words, is that technology is not "dumb," after the manner of a "Cartesian" thing, such that its first human significance comes in and through a use that is *subsequent* or *external* to the thing in its original constitution *as* a thing. Rather, technology, or things as artifacts, already bears an anthropology. Further, the anthropology carried in modern technology is mechanistic in nature. Modern technology characteristically fails to take integrated account of the teleology, or destiny, of man and nature as conceived by the "ontocratic" theologians, or indeed as discussed earlier apropos of an economy of gift.[59] Insofar as this is the case, we cannot but view globalization's potential for homogenization with much greater concern than do Stackhouse and Stratton.[60]

Conclusion

As has become evident, it is a common claim among Christian writers that Christianity has made its peace with liberalism, at least as a matter of principle and in terms of liberalism on its best reading. My contrary claim is that liberalism, even at its most benign, presents Christianity with what is arguably its most profound challenge in engaging the contemporary world. To be sure, there is the global threat of terrorism linked with Islamic extremists, and any argument that would attenuate the evil of terrorism lacks credibility. Still, it is not unequivocally clear that the violence of liberal cultures is any less in quantity, only that it is subtler. Liberalism proposes itself in benign terms that cloak its capacity for violence, terms like "freedom" and "rights" and indeed "tolerance" and "compassion." But it is precisely these terms that enable liberalism to direct its violence characteristically at those who can say or do nothing in response, who cannot *themselves* claim rights: the unborn, the infirm, the elderly, the harvested human embryos. Liberalism's violence takes the subtle form enacted, for

---

59. In connection with the general argument here, cf. "The Given as Gift: Creation and Disciplinary Abstraction in Science," in this volume.

60. Regarding the ambiguity of technology, see also chapter 6 of *Caritas in Veritate*.

example, in the designer children that will likely soon come, or in the widespread replacement of natural gender identity with constructed gender identity, with a consequent loss of the paradigmatic *difference* necessary for the first, that is, familial, community of love in the world. And all of this violence comes in the name of "freedom of choice" and rights, understood as immunities.[61]

The rejoinder will be that these features of a liberal culture are a function of liberalism at its most corrupt and not at its best. We have seen, however, that the instrumentalist logic disposing our culture to these features resides in the original meaning of liberalism. The problem is congenital: it lies in liberalism's original abstract sense of personal self-identity. Recognition that this is so does not warrant rejection of what are the genuine goods struggling to come to expression in liberalism, as I have noted time and again. The point is that we need now to go to the roots of those goods, reconfiguring them from the inside out for the purpose of giving them their truer and ampler form: the form of gift and gratitude.[62] My argument regarding the difference between constitutive relational identity and abstract identity exposes the grave ambiguity inherent in all the positive achievements of liberal societies: the "rights" of the individual, freedom of choice, equality, the power of self-determination, the creativity of the self, community as mutual and enlightened self-interest, the capacities of modern science and technology, the institutionalized freedoms of market economics and democratic politics, and so on. Each of these achievements — and each *is* a genuine achievement — insofar as it presupposes, however unconsciously, an onto-logic of abstract self-identity, *eo ipso* bears within it the seeds of its own undoing and indeed reversal. Each of these achievements bears within it a logic of inversion whereby the "powerful" and "productive" and "independent" and "functional" displace the "weak" and "unproductive" and "dependent" and "useless" (see *EV,* n. 23), contrary to what are the original and abiding best *intentions* of liberalism.

The increasing global influence of modern Western socioeconomic institutions, viewed in light of the West's ever-advancing biotechnological manipulation of birth and death, thus intensifies the need for clarifying, in relation to liberalism, the distinction between relational-personal identity

---

61. For further discussion see "Civil Community Inside the Liberal State" and "The Dramatic Nature of Life."

62. For a brief discussion of how to think about an alternative way of life informed by gift and gratitude, see the final section of "Does the Free Market Produce Free Persons?" pp. 162-65 in this volume.

and abstract-personal identity, not as a matter of "academic" speculation but for the sake of living the truth of our creatureliness at the heart of the world. This clarification is necessary insofar as we believe that the world continues to have a self-centered destiny only inside a God- and other-centered destiny, even within the democratic capitalistic societies of modernity. Certainly John Paul II, in his repeated call for a "civilization of love," and more recently Benedict XVI, in his call to open economics to the "principle of gratuitousness," believe the world still has such a destiny. What I have attempted to make clear is the sense in which such a civilization requires the "domestication" of man and his economic culture: requires, that is, recuperation of the relations to God, others, the world, and the family that most deeply and intimately constitute man's being as a creature.

The Significance of World and Culture for Moral Theology: *Veritatis Splendor* and the Nature of the Body

John Paul II's 1993 encyclical *Veritatis Splendor (VS)* says that the problems facing Christian morality today have to do not only with specific teachings but with the foundations and nature of the moral life itself. The encyclical states that these problems have their origin in patterns of thought "which end by detaching human freedom from its essential and constitutive relationship to truth" (n. 4). Paragraphs 46-50 discuss this detachment in terms of an extrinsicism, or division, between freedom and nature or, more precisely, between freedom and human nature in its bodiliness. This extrinsicism entails a denial that the order of freedom and hence of morality is anticipated in the person's physical-biological reality, and in fact involves a conception of the "finalities of [bodily] inclinations [as] merely 'physical' goods, called . . . *premoral*" (n. 48).

Veritatis Splendor, in contrast, by virtue of the intrinsic relation between freedom and human-bodily nature, understands the body in a significant sense always to *anticipate* the order of freedom and of morality. The body, in its physiology as such, is not "premoral" but always already "moral": it bears an order characterized by "the anticipatory signs, the expression and promise of the gift of self, in conformity with the wise plan of the Creator" (n. 48).

This argument of *VS* seems to me to contain, *in nuce*, an important development for moral theology. When placed in the light of other writings of John Paul II, for example, his catechesis on the body, the argument implies rejection of a "physicalist" or "premoral" understanding, not only of the body, but also, in and through the body, of the world and culture.

Thus *VS* argues that recovery of the foundations of moral life involves restoring freedom to its constitutive or intrinsic relationship to human-bodily nature. My proposal is that recovery of this intrinsic relationship, and thereby of the "moral" meaning proper to the body, entails recovery of a "moral" meaning proper to both the physical world and human culture. If we are to recover the foundations of morality as conceived by VS, we must, as an anterior condition of this recovery, (re-)awaken the sense in which the cosmos and culture, each in its own way and in its original structure as such, bear the "anticipatory signs, the expression and promise of the gift of self." We can recover the rootedness of morality in nature-as-gift only in and through a simultaneous *trans-formation of world and culture* into the analogically conceived gifts they are meant to be.

My purpose is to indicate how and why this is so. I begin with a summary of the encyclical's theological and indeed ontological anchoring of morality, which establishes the larger framework within which (bodily) nature is considered. Sections II-VI explore the mutual immanence of freedom and (bodily) nature, in its implications for the Pope's notions of the body, the physical world, and freedom as gift. Sections VII-VIII extend the argument of I-VI in terms of the intrinsic relation between nature and culture, and of the consequent "moral" meaning of culture as gift, in light of the challenge of liberalism.

I. *Veritatis Splendor* and the Moral Life

I wish to highlight five points in connection with the moral life as developed in VS. First, the moral life in its largest sense originates in a religious and indeed ontological quest: a quest for the meaning of life that is prompted by and has its fulfillment in a movement initiated by God himself. It is a search for meaning that, from beginning to end, is comprehended by relationship: by God's original invitation to relationship with him which itself is already the first sign of that relationship; and by a fulfillment that is the realization of that relationship, through the following of Jesus made possible by the power of the Holy Spirit.

Second, the Church is the sacrament of this "encounter" or relationship with God in Jesus, restlessness for which inspires the moral life.

Third, the moral life involves not only man's will, but the whole of his being, recapitulated in a creative way through his will. Human freedom remains unsatisfied until it realizes its destined relationship with the infinite good, in a way that comprehends man's being in all of its depths. The infinite good that is "the mystery of the Father and the Father's love" is revealed in Jesus Christ, who is "the last Adam" (*Gaudium et Spes* [GS], n. 22): in "assuming human nature," Christ reveals the Father's love to be the ultimate meaning and destiny of human nature. Since Christ's *assumption* of human nature is not an *absorption* (*assumpta non perempta*: GS, n. 22), the perfection that consists in participating in the Father's love through Jesus does not short-circuit the order of human virtues and the laws of human nature but on the contrary presupposes even as it fulfills them. The Word of God's love took human flesh in Jesus (John 1:14), and it is his very flesh that Jesus offers for the life of the world (John 6:51). Jesus' gift of love, in other words, penetrates and thus comprehends the whole of his bodily existence, fulfilling the latter in its *natural integrity as bodily*.

It is important thus to see that the comprehensive Trinity- and Christ-centered context indicated here does not signify merely an extrinsic "condition" for the norms of moral life, even as it also does not destroy the content of those norms in their natural integrity. God's invitation in Jesus Christ to share in his life, rooted in the heart of man's moral consciousness, establishes an openness and restlessness inside all human decisions and actions, thereby giving order to every decision and action. Moral norms, therefore, in their original nature as such in the one concrete order of history, cannot but be formed by this inner openness to and restlessness for the divine life embodied in Christ.[1]

Fourth, VS makes it clear that human freedom *is set in motion*. The élan characteristic of human freedom in its primitive structure is an echo of, indeed a response to, a call from God who is the origin and goal of our being. The movement proper to freedom is a response to the initiative of an other — absolute good — which is evoked and sustained by the attractiveness, or splendor, of that good. It follows that human freedom is not, in its basic constitution as such, a simply self-initiating and formless move-

---

1. On the question of Christian ethics, see the following divergent points of view: on the one hand, in Josef Fuchs, "Is There a Specifically Christian Ethics?" in *The Distinctiveness of Christian Ethics*, ed. Charles E. Curran and Richard A. McCormick (New York: Paulist Press, 1980), p. 319; Fuchs, "Christliche Moral: Biblische Orientierung und menschliche Wertung," *Stimmen der Zeit* 205 (1987): 671-83; John Langan, "The Christian Difference in Ethics," *Theological Studies* 49 (1988): 131-50. And, on the other, in Joseph Ratzinger, "Magisterium, Faith, Morality," in Curran and McCormick, eds., *The Distinctiveness of Christian Ethics*, pp. 174-89; Angelo Scola, "Christologie et Morale," *Nouvelle Revue Théologique* 109 (1987): 382-409. And, generally, see Livio Melina, *Sharing in Christ's Virtues: For a Renewal of Moral Theology in Light of Veritatis Splendor* (Washington, DC: Catholic University of America Press, 2001).

ment or act. Freedom is not a choice originally empty of content: the "content" of freedom is not in the first instance simply an *object* of choice. Human freedom on the contrary is an ordered desire. The movement proper to freedom from its beginning comes filled with "in-*form*-ation" given through the call of God, through the attractiveness of God as good. This always-in*form*ed desire is what may be termed love: human freedom is by nature love, a natural love.[2]

In a word, human freedom is creative *in* and *as* response to the splendor of the good; and human freedom is an *act* only at once as an *order*.

Finally, it is Mary who is a sign and model of the moral life (n. 120). She is so because she "lived and exercised her freedom precisely by giving herself to God and accepting God's gift within her" (n. 120). She "became the model of all those who hear the word of God and keep it (cf. Lk 11:28) . . ." (n. 120).[3] As St. Augustine says, hearing the word means having it implanted in us, while doing the word shows that the seed has borne fruit.[4] Through Mary's active *fiat,* the Word takes flesh. Which is to say, in and through her flesh and blood, Mary contributes to and bears the life of God in Jesus *(Theotokos),* a life that comprehends both the human and the divine natures in their integrity, that is, in their distinctness-within-unity.

In sum, we may say that the moral life, understood in its fullness, implies a double gratuitousness on God's part. On the one hand, in the very act of creation itself, God freely grants an invitation to share in the good that is finally God's own life, an invitation that implies an initial orientation toward that good life given with the beginning of one's existence. This invitation touches the inmost depths of each person (n. 117), and indeed evokes the aspiration lying at the heart of every human decision and action (n. 7). At the same time, the following of Christ that alone fully responds to this invitation presupposes the further gift of God's grace. In both senses, the moral life is a response to, and indeed is sustained by, the always anterior and gratuitous initiative of God. Thus we may say that "the moral life presents itself as the response to the many gratuitous initiatives

---

2. See D. C. Schindler, "Freedom Beyond Our Choosing: Augustine on the Will and Its Objects," *Communio: International Catholic Review* 29, no. 4 (Winter 2002): 618-53.

3. Cf. the Congregation for the Doctrine of the Faith's *Instruction on Christian Freedom and Liberation* (1986): "Mary is totally dependent on her Son and completely directed towards him by the impulse of her faith; and, at His side, she is the most perfect image of freedom and of the liberation of humanity and of the universe" (n. 97).

4. Cf. *Sermo* 23A: *CCL* 41, 321-23: *Office of Readings,* Twenty-Second Sunday in Ordinary Time.

taken by God out of love for man" (n. 10); and that "the moral life, caught up in the gratuitousness of God's love, is called to reflect his glory" (n. 10).

We turn now to consider how *VS*'s integration of freedom and (bodily) nature, and John Paul II's notion of the "nuptial body," specify and extend concretely the meaning of the moral life as described here.

II. Freedom and Nature

Having criticized those who effectively deny freedom through their emphasis on "physicochemical constants, bodily processes, psychological impulses and forms of social conditioning," *VS* considers those thinkers who, in order to stress the distinctive importance of human values, would conceive "freedom as somehow in opposition to or in conflict with material and biological nature, over which it must progressively assert itself" (n. 46). Such a view

> ends up treating the human body as a raw datum devoid of any meaning and moral values until freedom has shaped it in accordance with its design. Consequently, human nature and the body appear as presuppositions or preambles, materially necessary for freedom to make its choice, yet extrinsic to the person, the subject and the human act. Their functions would not be able to constitute reference points for moral decisions, because the finalities of these inclinations would be merely "physical" goods, called by some *premoral.* (n. 48)

This framework leads to a rejection of the traditional conception of natural law as physicalist and naturalist. The encyclical points out, however, that this approach misses

> the unity of the human person, whose rational soul is *per se et essentialiter* the form of his body. . . . [I]t is in the unity of body and soul that the person is the subject of his own moral acts. The person, by the light of reason and the support of virtue, discovers in the body the anticipatory signs, the expression and the promise of the gift of self, in conformity with the wise plan of the Creator. (n. 48)

Indeed,

> [a] doctrine which dissociates the moral act from the bodily dimensions of its exercise is contrary to the teaching of Scripture and tradi-

tion. Such a doctrine revives in new forms certain ancient errors which have always been opposed by the church, inasmuch as they reduce the human person to a "spiritual" and purely formal freedom. This reduction misunderstands the moral meaning of the body and of kinds of behavior involving it. (n. 49)

The natural law . . . understood [in terms of the person's "unified totality"] does not allow for any division between freedom and nature. Indeed, these two realities are harmoniously bound together, and each is intimately linked to the other. (n. 50)

Note, then, how decisively paragraphs 46-50 of *VS* break with the modern mechanistic or Cartesian understanding of biology. The paragraphs break with the notion that bodily-physical reality is dumb and mute, acquiring anthropological or theological significance only insofar as it is subjected to use by human will; and thus also break with the notion that natural "facts" in this sense are simply without "value" until such value is conferred upon them through an exercise of human freedom.[5]

In positive terms, paragraphs 46-50 recall the "premodern," Aristotelian biology according to which "the soul is the cause [αἴτιον] or source [ἀρχή] of the living body," in the threefold sense of being the body's end and form and source of movement.[6] That is, the soul gives the body its first order or meaning, even as the body then simultaneously, in its very nature *as* a body, enters into and is partially constitutive of the original order of freedom itself. What this means concretely is already hinted at in the suggestion above that the body carries "anticipatory signs, the expression and the promise of the gift of self, in conformity with the wise plan of the Creator."

To be sure, in saying that the body and its order are not merely "premoral," *VS* does not mean to deny the distinctness of the moral order as such, which is a function of an exercise of spiritual freedom. The point is simply that the original unity of body and soul implies the body's always-actual participation in human order. Such unity implies that the body itself is already ingredient in the *subject* of freedom, hence that the

---

5. The Pope's assertion does not deny but on the contrary presupposes a distinction between ontological "value" and moral "value": see the discussion that follows in the text.

6. *De Anima*, bk. II, ch. 4, 415b8-415b28. Cf. also here Leon Kass, *The Hungry Soul: Eating and the Perfecting of Our Nature* (New York: Free Press, 1985), and Hans Jonas, *The Phenomenon of Life: Toward a Philosophical Biology* (New York: Harper & Row, 1966).

body in its original structure is never *neutral toward,* never first or most properly an *object* or *instrument* of, human freedom.[7]

VS's point, in short, is not that an exercise of "practical" human intelligence and freedom is not necessary for the constitution of moral order properly speaking, but that any such exercise itself presupposes an anterior order and goodness already *given* to freedom in the body's original human-created constitution. In light of *VS*'s references to the soul as the form of the body and to the body as an "anticipatory sign, the expression and the promise of the gift of self," we may describe this bodily-physical order as "organic" and "creational" and involving the notion of gift. But let us take note of how John Paul II's notion of the "nuptial attribute" of the body deepens and broadens the meaning of "organic" and "creational" and "gift."

III. John Paul II and the "Filial-Nuptial and Sacramental" Meaning of the Body

The main points for our purposes are two: first, the Pope links the image of God with the communion of persons, in a way that includes the corporality of man within that image; and he does this while developing a notion of the body as "nuptial."[8] Secondly, and in this framework, John Paul II indicates the sense in which the world and man in his bodiliness are "primordial sacraments," that is, visible signs of the invisible mystery of

---

7. See, for example, Maurice Merleau-Ponty: "An Unpublished Text by Maurice Merleau-Ponty: A Prospectus of His Work," in Maurice Merleau-Ponty, *The Primacy of Perception* (Evanston, IL: Northwestern University Press, 1964), pp. 3-11: "The perceiving mind is an incarnated mind. I have tried, first of all, to re-establish the roots of the mind in its body and in its worlds, going against doctrines which treat perception as a simple result of the action of external things on our body as well as against those which insist on the autonomy of consciousness. These philosophies commonly forget in favor of a pure exteriority or of a pure interiority the insertion of the mind in corporeality, the ambiguous relation which we entertain with our body and, correlatively, with perceived things" (pp. 3-4). "[T]he body is no longer merely *an object in the world,* under the purview of a separated spirit. It is on the side of the subject; it is our *point of view on the world,* the place where the spirit takes on a certain physical and historical situation" (p. 5).

8. It is important to see that man's filial relation to God, implied in man's "original solitude," precedes even as it unfolds into and is further expressed by man's nuptial meaning. On the relation between and mutual inclusion of man's constitutive filial and nuptial meaning, see "The Embodied Person as Gift and the Cultural Task in America," pp. 242-74 in this volume.

holiness ultimately hidden in God.[9] The world and the body, in other words, as revealed in and as revealing man, are structurally destined, in and through man, to enter into and thus (partially) themselves to constitute the subject of holiness.

(1) "The body reveals man. This concise formula already contains all that human science will ever be able to say about the structure of the body as an organism, about its vitality, about its particular sexual physiology, etc."[10] Man "as a person . . . [is] a being that is, also in all its bodiliness, 'similar' to God."[11] "We find ourselves, therefore, within the very bone marrow of the anthropological reality whose name is 'body,' human body. Yet, as can easily be observed, this marrow is not only anthropological, but also essentially theological. The theology of the body . . . is linked from the beginning with the creation of man in the image of God."[12] Furthermore, the Pope says, man "is, in fact, not only an image in which the solitude of one Person, who rules the world, mirrors itself, but also and essentially the image of an inscrutable divine communion of Persons."[13]

What is termed the nuptial meaning of the body thus arises in terms of how the original understanding of "the meaning of the body is born at the very heart, as it were, of [man and woman's] community-communion."[14] John Paul II describes the "nuptial attribute" of the body as its "*power to express love: precisely that love in which the human person becomes a gift* and — through this gift — fulfills the very meaning of his being and existence."[15] "The body has a 'spousal' meaning because the human person, as the Council says, is a creature that God willed for his own sake and that, at the same time, cannot fully find himself except through the gift of self."[16] By virtue of creation by God who is love, "every creature bears within itself the sign of the original and fundamental gift."[17] "Man appears in creation as the one who

---

9. Clearly the Pope does not mean to imply that bodiliness is a sacrament in the strict sense. Rather, the body is created as a visible sign *ordered toward* revelation of the mystery of divine holiness carried properly sacramentally in the Church.

10. John Paul II, *Man and Woman He Created Them: A Theology of the Body*, trans. Michael Waldstein (Boston: Pauline Books and Media, 2006), p. 164.

11. John Paul II, *Man and Woman He Created Them*, p. 164.

12. John Paul II, *Man and Woman He Created Them*, p. 165.

13. John Paul II, *Man and Woman He Created Them*, p. 163.

14. John Paul II, *Man and Woman He Created Them*, p. 178.

15. John Paul II, *Man and Woman He Created Them*, pp. 185-86 (emphasis original).

16. John Paul II, *Man and Woman He Created Them*, p. 189.

17. John Paul II, *Man and Woman He Created Them*, p. 180.

The Significance of World and Culture for Moral Theology | 227

has received the world as a gift, and vice versa, one can also say that the world has received man as a gift."[18]

(2) Further, the nuptial body indicates the "primordial sacramentality" of man and the world:

> Thus . . . a primordial *sacrament* is constituted, understood as a *sign that* efficaciously *transmits in the visible world the invisible mystery hidden in God from eternity.* And this is the mystery of Truth and Love, the mystery of divine life, in which man really participates. . . . The sacrament, as a visible sign, is constituted with man, inasmuch as he is a "body," through his "visible" masculinity and femininity. The body, in fact, and only the body, is capable of making visible what is invisible: the spiritual and the divine. It has been created to transfer into the visible reality of the world the mystery hidden from eternity in God, and thus to be a sign of it.
>
> In man, created in the image of God, the very sacramentality of creation, the sacramentality of the world, was thus in some way revealed. In fact, through his bodiliness, his masculinity and femininity, man becomes a visible sign of the economy of Truth and Love, which has its source in God himself and was revealed already in the mystery of creation. . . . The sacrament of the world, and the sacrament of man in the world, comes forth from the divine source of holiness and is instituted, at the same time, for holiness.[19]

Returning to paragraphs 46-50 of *VS*, we can now see the fuller implications of these paragraphs' recovery of the unity of soul and body and indeed of freedom and nature. The soul is the finality and form as well as the source of the movement of the body. The body, in other words, in its first actuality *as* a body, is human. In its primitive order as body, it bears, contains, and expresses a human end, form, and movement, all of which are anticipatory signs and expressions of the gift of self. The Pope's notion of the nuptial-"sacramental" body amplifies what is meant by the body as an anticipatory sign of the gift of self: namely, that the human body is ordered intrinsically to the communion of persons expressed paradigmatically in the "original unity of man and woman"; and that this communion of persons at once images God and points toward participation in the divine communion of persons. The body, in other words, in its very nature as

---

18. John Paul II, *Man and Woman He Created Them*, p. 181.
19. John Paul II, *Man and Woman He Created Them*, pp. 203-4 (emphasis original).

body, is apt for the containment and expression of the sacrament of God's holiness in which man is called from his creation to participate, and which is properly-historically realized in the Church.

IV. The Body as Organic Gift

Thus, the person is the subject of moral acts in the unity of soul and body, and it is this unity that grounds the mutual relatedness of bodily nature and freedom. The mutual relatedness between bodily nature and freedom does not imply a symmetrical relation between the two. It does not deny but on the contrary presupposes that nature and freedom each contribute something distinct to the unified human subject, and that human freedom, as properly spiritual, transcends nature. Secondly, although the mutual internality, hence unity, of nature and freedom coincides with the ontological unity of soul and body, the two unities nonetheless presuppose a distinction between "first act" and "second act": they presuppose at once a unity and a distinctness between the soul as the act constitutive of the human composite and freedom as the proper act of the soul.

The consequence, in any case, is that the body is best understood as an organism and not as a machine. In other words, the body as such bears an interior order characterized by what may be termed form and finality. The body is not dumb stuff pushed and pulled about by (efficient) acts simply external to itself. The body is not first or most properly an *instrument* of freedom.

The body, apt for expressing the order proper to human freedom, is thus apt for embodying and expressing gift. The body, in its distinct constitution as such, is a participation in the giftedness, or gift of self, characteristic of the human spirit in the latter's deepest meaning. The gifted nature of both body (nature) and spirit (freedom) in the unity of the human person derives most fundamentally from the fact of creation: created being is a being-given, a being-from Another that is thereby also a being-for Another (and others). This created reality of being-from-and-for Another and others is completed and transformed through the holiness consisting in participation in the life of God himself, in and through the ecclesial-eucharistic sacrament of divine life.

The order of organic gift indicated here thus has an ultimately theological origin and meaning. It nonetheless bears, precisely from within this theological provenance, a distinctly ontological meaning. Creation renders nature *(what-is)* as a matter of its original and inmost structure, into *what-is-from* (Another). Being-from, which in some significant sense already implies being-given,[20] is *in* the thing, and is thus accessible in principle to reason. In short, the meaning of reality as gift is not exclusively a function of supernatural faith, even if faith is necessary to disclose the full and final meaning of reality as gift.

V. Physical Nature as Gift

Given these premises, what are we then to say about the nature of the physical world, of freedom, and of culture?

By "physical" here I mean nature not as actually formed in the human body but in its proper meaning as such: that is, space, time, matter, and motion in their original and proper constitution. It follows from the premises stated above that physical nature bears an intrinsic openness to the order proper to human being, hence to the order indicated in organism and gift.[21]

That this is so follows from the nature of the community affirmed in *VS* and implied in the nuptial meaning of the body. The body and soul are substantially "communified" in the human person. This implies that the physical "elements" taken up into the person's substantial body-soul unity are themselves already open to the "higher" integration indicated in this body-soul unity. Notice, for example, such simple processes as breathing and human metabolism. Were the physical "elements" involved in these processes structurally closed to higher integration in the human organism, these "elements" could be assimilated by the human organism only by way

---

20. See Hans Urs von Balthasar, *The Glory of the Lord,* vol. 5: *A Theological Aesthetics* (San Francisco: Ignatius Press, 1983), pp. 613-56. See also "The Embodied Person as Gift and the Cultural Task in America."

21. In its 1988 document, "Faith and Inculturation," the International Theological Commission (ITC) defines nature as "what constitutes [a being] as such, with the dynamism of its tendencies towards its proper ends. It is from God that natures possess what they are, as well as their proper ends. They are from that moment impregnated with a significance in which man, as *the image of God,* is capable of discerning the 'creative intention of God' [*Humanae Vitae*]" (*Irish Theological Quarterly* 155 [1989]: 142-61, at 144). What I am arguing is that physical nature, in its very physicality, shares in nature in the sense defined here. I leave aside the difficult question of the sense in which nature in any given instance possesses a wholeness qualifying it as an individual existent in the proper sense.

of either addition or violence, that is, only mechanically. But a mechanical "assimilation" entails reduction of the body to a mechanism that *eo ipso* fractures the body's substantial unity with the soul and at once the body's own organic nature.

But if physical nature is open in principle to the "higher" integration indicated in the human person's substantial union of body and soul, it is thereby open in principle to integration into the order proper to the human spirit, or freedom.

The theological-ontological warrant for the community indicated in this aptness for integration, already sketched in the preceding sections, is summarized in a particularly comprehensive way by John Paul II in *Dominum et Vivificantem* (1986):

> The Incarnation of God the Son signifies the taking up into unity with God not only of human nature, but in this human nature, in a sense, of everything that is "flesh": the whole of humanity, the entire visible and material world. The Incarnation, then, also has a cosmic significance, a cosmic dimension. The "first-born of all creation," becoming incarnate in the individual humanity of Christ, unites himself in some way with the entire reality of man, which is also "flesh" — and in this reality with all "flesh," with the whole of creation [*cum omni "carne," cum universa creatura*].[22]

Creation and the Incarnation thus imply a genuine *community* established freely by God in Jesus Christ that reaches all the way down through the "flesh" of the entire created cosmos.

The community indicated here between the physical and the organic-human, and, in and through the human, also between the physical and the holy, is analogical in nature. The inherent openness of the physical to the organic-human and the holy, in other words, signifies neither that physical nature as such does not have essentially mechanical properties, nor that it has essentially personal or spiritual properties. It means rather that physical nature bears an *interior order* (e.g., form and finality)[23] rendering nature, precisely from within what are its essential,

---

22. John Paul II, *Dominum et Vivificantem* (1986), n. 50.
23. See, for example, Kenneth L. Schmitz, "Immateriality Past and Present," in *The Texture of Being: Essays in First Philosophy*, ed. Paul O'Herron (Washington, DC: Catholic University of America Press, 2007), pp. 168-82; and his *The Gift: Creation* (Milwaukee: Marquette University Press, 1982). The key, of course, is to recognize that interiority as con-

hence, abiding mechanical properties, apt for integration into the organic-human and in turn sacramental-holy.[24]

The community affirmed between the physical ("lower") and the human-spiritual and the sacramental-holy ("higher") thus is conceived in terms that recognize the proper, even infinite, differences between the physical and the spiritual and the holy, simultaneous with a real unity coincident with these differences.[25]

Physical nature in its original and abiding constitution thus has a worth or "value" deriving from its interior order as apt for integration into the organic-human and in turn the sacramental-holy. This interior order indicates an initial, *proportionately-analogically conceived*, participation in the giftedness proper to all being created by God in Jesus Christ.

In saying that the physical world is *gift*, of course, I do not mean that the physical world does not also and at the same time bear an *instrumental* character. Recognition of the intrinsic worth and goodness of material things does not entail that they may not legitimately be *used*. On the contrary, such use is just what the foregoing argument implies, when it insists that the interior order according the physical world its worth and goodness is already as such *apt for integration into and by the higher orders* of the organic, the human, and the holy. The very notion of the physical-as-gift, in other words, rightly-analogically conceived, bears within it a necessary and legitimate sense of the physical-as-instrument: of the latter, however, as now situated inside and subordinate to, and thus containing and ex-

---

ceived here is metaphysical (not only anthropological), which is to say, again, that it is analogically conceived.

24. See in this connection Emile Mersch's argument in *Morale et Corps Mystique* (Paris: Desclée de Brouwer, 1955), ch. 1-3, regarding the way in which some genuinely analogous sense of "religion," e.g., "worshiping" and giving glory to God, is structured already into nature, even as this sense is then properly realized in humanity and in turn finally fulfilled in Catholicism.

25. The argument here thus recognizes essential differences between levels of being, so long as these essential differences are conceived in terms of an intrinsic analogy. And it is important to keep in mind, relative to the question regarding the "special" creation of man as a spiritual being, that all of being requires creation, or participation in God's creative act, all the time, by virtue of the "ontological difference" between *esse* and *ens*.

On the continuity coincident with discontinuity between human and non-human animals, see the argument of Alasdair MacIntyre, *Dependent Rational Animals: Why Human Beings Need the Virtues* (Chicago: Open Court, 1999). For an interesting discussion of Darwinism and creation, see Michael Hanby, "Creation Without Creationism: Toward a Theological Critique of Darwinism," *Communio: International Catholic Review* 30, no. 4 (Winter 2003): 652-92.

pressing, the physical-as-gift. The *world-as-gift*, in a word, is at once also the *world-as-instrument*, even as the world's instrumentality can now be rightly understood only in terms of its intrinsic aptness for integration into the *gift of self* proper to the human person in his body-soul unity as created (and redeemed) by God.

The burden of what I mean to suggest here is summarized well in a 1977 lecture by Karol Wojtyla:

> [C]ulture . . . forms a kind of organic whole with nature. It reveals the roots of our union with nature, but also of our superior encounter with the Creator in the eternal plan, a plan in which we participate by means of reason and wisdom. . . . There exists in nature, or the world, an anticipation of . . . human activity and . . . a radiation of humanity through praxis. There is also in nature, or the world, a kind of readiness to put itself at our disposal: to serve human needs, to welcome within it the superior scale of human ends, to enter in some way into the human dimension and participate in human existence in the world.[26]

Wojtyla introduces the section in which this statement appears with a citation from the Polish poet Cyprian Norwid, who says that "beauty exists that we might be enticed to work / And work, that we might be resurrected."[27] Wojtyla thus fittingly insists that an organic relation of culture to nature, or nature's radiation of humanity through praxis, requires a "nonutilitarian" disposition consisting in enticement, wonder, contemplation, and awe before the reality of the cosmos.[28] Employing the terms of St. Thomas, Wojtyla emphasizes that this "intransitive" or "immanent" activity "does not take place beyond work, beyond human activity" or praxis.

---

26. Karol Wojtyla, "The Problem of the Constitution of Culture Through Human Praxis," in *Person and Community* (New York: Peter Lang, 1993), pp. 232-75, at 269-70. Cf. Isaiah 55:10-11: "Thus says the Lord: As the rain and the snow come down from the heavens and do not return without watering the earth, making it yield and giving growth to provide seed for the sower and bread for the eating, so the word that goes forth from my mouth does not return to me empty, without carrying out my will and succeeding in what it was sent to do." See also in this context Adolf Portmann's *Animal Forms and Patterns: A Study of the Appearance of Animals* (New York: Schocken, 1967), which proposes, *inter alia*, that flowers in some significant sense bloom in order to be seen.

27. Wojtyla, "The Problem of the Constitution of Culture," p. 269. The text is cited from Norwid's Dialog I, *Prometheus*.

28. Wojtyla, "The Problem of the Constitution of Culture," pp. 270-71.

On the contrary, the point is that "human activity . . . has the dual character of being both transitive and intransitive."[29]

The Pope's affirmation that the physical world is ready to put itself at the disposal of the human, or again that the world is a gift apt for participation in (human) giving, thus does not imply that the physical world as such participates in the *self*-gift proper only to spiritual, or spiritually reflexive, beings, that is, persons. The affirmation of the physical-as-gift does not collapse the distinction between what may be termed physical good on the one hand and moral good on the other, which would indicate a fall into a "naturalistic" sense of the foundations of morality. The burden of his argument is merely that this distinction, understood in light of VS and the notion of the nuptial body, precludes a reading of the physical as empty of intrinsic worth in its primitive structure *as* physical, or of the physical as structurally *indifferent* to participation in a giftedness apt for appropriation in spiritual, holy giving.[30] In short, as described by Kenneth Schmitz in his *The Gift: Creation*, there is a kind of generosity proper in an analogical way to being at all levels.[31]

It is in this sense, then, that VS's rejection of the idea that the body is "physicalist" or "premoral" in nature entails rejection also of the idea that the world or cosmos in its most proper meaning is "physicalist" or "premoral" in nature.

VI. Freedom as Gift

In my earlier highlighting of five salient points of the moral life as conceived in VS, I noted that freedom is an act of choice only as at once an order. The intervening sections have clarified crucial features characteristic of this order. Freedom derives its proper meaning in and through the person's substantial body-soul unity, his creation by God, and his nuptiality.

---

29. Wojtyla, "The Problem of the Constitution of Culture," p. 271.

30. See also David S. Crawford, "Recognizing the Roots of Society in the Family, Foundation of Justice," *Communio: International Catholic Review* 34, no. 3 (Fall 2007): 379-412; and "Natural Law and the Body: Between Deductivism and Parallelism," *Communio: International Catholic Review* 35, no. 3 (Fall 2008): 327-53; Martin Rhonheimer's response, "Rawlsian Public Reason, Natural Law, and the Foundation of Justice: A Response to David Crawford," *Communio: International Catholic Review* 36, no. 1 (Spring 2009): 138-67; and "The Embodied Person as Gift and the Cultural Task in America."

31. That is, through the generosity of *esse*. See Schmitz, *The Gift: Creation*.

The act of choice characteristic of freedom thus bears from the inside out a form and purpose shaped by relation to the body, to God, and to other persons. Freedom discovers its primitive and proper meaning as a free and spiritual act only *from within these relations.* John Paul II, in affirming the nuptial attribute of the human person, states that the person discovers "his true self only in a sincere giving of himself." The spiritual-free act proper to the human person thus consists in giving himself. What is important, in light of all that has been said, is to see the sense in which this *giving* of self proper to freedom is always-anteriorly a *being-given* by God, at once in and through the gift of the body and of others. In a word, freedom properly acts, gives, or creates only as inside the order *anteriorly given* in these relations. We may say, then, that the person's free *giving* of self is anteriorly a *gift* from Another. What is crucial to notice is the ontological patience or contemplative interiority indicated in the notion of gift, that is, implied in what-*is-given.* Freedom can properly *give,* and thus realize its proper nature and dynamism as such, only by taking over what has *always-already been given* to it, hence by first[32] listening and seeing, even as such listening thereby itself becomes an active participation in the giving that is being given.[33]

The point here can be made in terms of modernity's characteristic "freedom of indifference."[34] "Indifference" refers to an act of choice conceived without an intrinsic reference to the good, such that the good is then construed primarily as an object of choice rather than as an anterior condition *for,* hence an order already operative *in,* choice. What I am signaling is the contemplative "moment" of freedom implied in recognizing freedom's *anterior ordering by* the good: by God, in and through the body and the other. It is this contemplative moment that alone enables an overturning of freedom's putative "indifference."

In the terms proper to *VS,* then, my proposal is that freedom remains "premoral" insofar as its act of choice is conceived as primitively empty of the order given in the person's relation to God through the body and the other. Freedom is understood in its true nature as a *giving* of self only insofar as freedom recuperates the *structural patience* inherent in self-giving's

---

32. "First," that is, in an ontological not chronological sense.

33. See Hans Urs von Balthasar, *The Glory of the Lord,* vol. 1: *Seeing the Form* (San Francisco: Ignatius Press, 1983).

34. See D. C. Schindler, "Freedom Beyond Our Choosing." See also Servais Pinckaers, *The Sources of Christian Ethics* (Washington, DC: Catholic University of America Press, 1995), pp. 327-53.

always-anterior giftedness. It is with this qualifier that one can, and must, affirm that freedom is a gift.

VII. Culture as Gift

As we have seen, the human soul, in its distinct human specificity, is the first end, form, and source of movement of the body, hence of the body's physical-chemical-biological "elements." But if this is so, then acts of freedom and intelligence, as acts *of* the soul, become themselves somehow, as a matter of principle, internal to the end, form, and movement of the body's physical-chemical-biological elements. I take this to entail that culture thus becomes internal to nature.

The suggestion that acts of freedom affect the whole of the body from within does not imply a denial of the distinction between the soul and freedom as, respectively, the first and second acts of the human person. It merely signals the unity between the soul and freedom implicit in this distinction, as noted earlier. What I am now proposing is that this unity, *eo ipso*, implies an internal relation of culture to (bodily) nature. Bodily nature as such is dynamically ordered toward the order of freedom and thereby of culture, and at any given actual moment this dynamic relation has already been realized.

In short, given the unity within distinctness of first act and second act, it follows that bodily nature at any given moment is an inculturated nature.

That this is so is confirmed, for example, in the Report to the Nation from the Commission on Children at Risk, "Hard-Wired to Connect: The New Scientific Case for Authoritative Communities," which adduces evidence of the mutual relation of human action ("nurture") and brain development and even genetic dispositions;[35] or again in Leon Kass's *The Hungry Soul*, which shows an intrinsic link between the social relations intended in human action and the development of the physiological structure and processes of eating and metabolism.[36] Claims such as these con-

---

35. Commission of Children at Risk (Principal Investigator: Kathleen Kovner Kline), "Hard-Wired to Connect: The New Case for Authoritative Communities," YMCA of America, Dartmouth Medical College, Institute for American Values (New York: Institute for American Values, 2003).

36. Leon Kass, *The Hungry Soul: Eating and the Perfecting of Our Nature* (Chicago: University of Chicago Press, 1999).

firm in their own way what is already implied in principle in the mutual ordering of physical-biological nature and freedom indicated in *VS* and John Paul II's notion of the nuptial body.

Thus, nature is never neutral to freedom, and nature and culture are never neutral to each other. The internality of culture to nature leads, not to the dissolution of nature, but on the contrary to recognition of nature's internally historical character. Nature itself in any of its actual moments has a cultural history. It follows that the recovery of nature carries an immanent demand for cultural trans-formation: recuperation of a *nature-always-become-culture* carries an intrinsic dynamic for discernment of a nature-always-become-*culture*. This discernment is required, of course, because a nature affected from within by acts of human freedom and intelligence, a nature that is thus always historically conditioned, is weighted *eo ipso* with a meaning distorted in some significant sense by sin.

The fact that nature-in-history involves some distortion does not mean that nature ever loses its inner consistency *as* nature. Indeed, it is nature itself that serves as the immanent criterion for discernment. The criterion for cultural discernment lies within the bodily nature of which culture is at once an extension and, in any given instance, a distortion. The criterion is bodily nature in its organic order (form-finality) as sketched earlier, understood in light of its nuptial-sacramental origin and destiny: bodily nature as organic gift calling forth gratitude. Comprehensively stated: culture needs to be judged and transformed in terms of its proper meaning and finality as an *analogically- and organically-conceived* nature-become-*human*-artifact, in light of the deeper and basic reality of this whole — organic nature *cum* human artifact — as *God's* artifact.[37]

The burden of the argument here can be clarified in terms of John Paul II's notion of "structural sin." The Pope says in *Sollicitudo Rei Socialis* (1987), for example, that "sin" and "structures of sin" are categories "seldom applied to the situation of the contemporary world," though we "cannot easily gain a profound understanding of the reality that confronts us unless we give a name to the root of the evils which afflict us" (*SRS*, n. 36). Of course, he emphasizes that structures of sin are "rooted in personal sin, and thus always linked to the concrete acts of individuals" (n. 36, citing *Reconciliatio et Paenitentia*, n. 16). These concrete acts of individuals, introduced into "structures," become "consolidated" and "hard to remove." Having become "structural," they "grow stronger, spread, and become the

---

37. See ITC, "Faith and Inculturation," n. 3-11.

source of other sins, and so influence people's behavior" (*SRS*, n. 36). Indeed, *Reconciliatio et Paenitentia* (1984) speaks of "a communion of sin [in contrast to a communion of sanctity/saints], whereby a soul that lowers itself through sin drags down with itself the church and, in some way, the whole world" (*RP*, n. 16).[38]

In *Dominum et Vivificantem* (1986), the Pope gives an important indication of how he understands it to be possible, and what it means, for sin, personal in origin, to assume a communal, social, structural-institutional dimension:

> [T]he resistance to the Holy Spirit which Saint Paul emphasizes in the interior and subjective dimension as tension, struggle and rebellion taking place in the human heart finds in every period of history and especially in the modern era its external dimension, which takes concrete form as the content of culture and civilization, as a philosophical system, an ideology, a programme for action and for the shaping of human behavior. It reaches its clearest expression in materialism, both in its theoretical form: as a system of thought, and in its practical form: as a method of interpreting and evaluating facts, and likewise as a programme of corresponding conduct.[39]

The Pope's insistence on the importance of the category of "structures of sin," then, is linked with his distinctive understanding of sin as not only "subjective" but also "external," hence "objective," and thus able to be carried "socially" in and as culture and civilization.

The pertinence of this reference to "structures of sin" becomes clear when we recall how nature, as it is taken up into and by freedom, becomes culture, for example, in the form of institutions. Institutions, in other words, viewed in light of the Pope's argument, are properly conceived as embodied, shared "logics," or inculturations of nature, which become "structures of sin" insofar as they are distorted by misuses of freedom.

What the notion of "structural sin" makes clear, relative to the pres-

---

38. For further discussion of "structures of sin," see "Market Liberalism and an Economic Culture of Gift and Gratitude" and "Religion and Secularity in a Culture of Abstraction," pp. 166-218 and 328-49 in this volume.

39. *DV*, n. 56. The Pope goes on to speak of Marxism following the statement cited, but it is clear that this is but one important example illustrating the more general point he is making about philosophy or ideology as the "external" or "objective" dimension of sin needed to complete the idea of sin as an interior and subjective phenomenon.

ent argument, is that sin, as an act of human freedom and intelligence, is a matter not only of bad subjective will but of objective meaning: sin is a dis-*order*, involving an objective distortion of nature or natural order. The notion of "structural sin" thus reinforces and completes our argument regarding the importance of the need for discernment of culture, that is, of bodily-natural order as extended "outward" into cultural institutions and the like.[40] This need for cultural-institutional discernment, again, arises *coincident with nature in each of its actual moments* as penetrated by human freedom and intelligence. Such discernment, in other words, consists most properly, not in *applying* a nature understood simply ahistorically *to* new historical circumstances, but rather in discerning nature itself *from within* what is always already its internally differentiated cultural history.

Discernment of nature-in-history takes the form of attending to patterns that are *universally* and *analogously* present. These patterns manifest a certain type of natural, hence universal, order, viz., "free-organic" in the sense outlined above, even as, given this order's always new historical inculturation, its universality is analogous. Because the order is universal, it yields a non-arbitrary criterion for cultural discernment; because that universality is analogous, it includes a novelty showing forth a development within the unity of nature itself. Further, then, this novelty, or always-new inculturation of natural order, will involve some distortion, because of the misuse of freedom. Tradition thus becomes important, not only as an ongoing argument about its own content, but also as a natural order that shows its analogous universality over time to those who know how to read it (Newman), which is to say, to those who know how to discern that universality from within nature-become-culture's ever-present "structural sin."

In sum: recuperation of nature-in-history implies a dynamic for ongoing transformation, or trans-*ordering*, of culture away from a "community of sin" and into a "community of sanctity." It implies a dynamic for transforming the *created giftedness* proper to nature and freedom, and proper to the culture that is the fruit intrinsic to these in their unity, into the *redeemed giftedness* whose sacrament is the ecclesial communion of saints.[41] It is in this sense that all of human culture both is and is called to be a *gift*.

---

40. On culture as the extension of nature, see ITC, "Faith and Inculturation," n. 34.

41. See the important study of Giorgio Buccellati, "Sacramentality and Culture," *Communio: International Catholic Review* 30, no. 4 (Winter 2003): 533-80.

VIII. The Significance of World and Culture for Moral Theology: The Challenge of Liberalism

The foundations of moral theology, adequately conceived in light of *VS* and the notion of the nuptial body, thus carry a dynamic for cultural trans-formation rooted in rejection of "premoral" notions of the physical world, of freedom, and of culture itself. In positive terms, this signifies a dynamic for trans-forming the world, freedom, and culture into the gifts that they, each in its own proper-analogical way, already are and are called to become by virtue of their creation and their nuptial and sacramental-eucharistic destiny.

Therefore we may say, in summary: retrieval of the foundations of moral theology, adequately conceived in light of *VS* and John Paul II's idea of nuptiality, demands that we recuperate a cosmology rooted in an ontology of giftedness, and a physics and biology integrated by and into such a cosmology;[42] and that we recuperate simultaneously an anthropology likewise rooted in an ontology of giftedness, and a politics, an economics, an academy, and a science, medicine, and technology integrated by and into such an anthropology.

Such conclusions, in their comprehensive character, may appear startlingly bold. However, the fact that the conclusions likely strike us as bold leads me to the final part of my argument, which is that it is just our dominant culture's different assumptions about the nature of the world, of freedom, and of culture that incline us *a priori* to be skeptical. Our dominant culture's would-be modesty in the face of comprehensive claims such as I have proposed, in other words, carries, however unconsciously and paradoxically, an equally comprehensive meaning regarding the nature of the world, freedom, and culture. Understanding the nature of this paradox seems to me a condition *sine qua non* for retrieving what I have argued are the adequate foundations for moral life as conceived by *VS* and implied in John Paul II's idea of a nuptial body.

Characteristic of liberal societies, and I am thinking here especially of Anglo-American societies, is the assumption that we as a public culture can avoid ontological views regarding the world, freedom, and culture. In

---

42. For an account of modernity's recasting of cosmology, and technological science, see Hans Jonas, "Seventeenth Century and After: The Meaning of the Scientific and Technological Revolution," ch. 3 of *Philosophical Essays: From Ancient Creed to Technological Man* (Englewood Cliffs, NJ: Prentice Hall, 1974), pp. 45-80.

our use of the physical world, that is, in our technology or *technē*, in our appeal to the exercise of free choice, and in the building of our cultural, political, economic, and academic institutions, we can, or so we think as a matter of official-public principle, delay an ontological view of the nature and final destiny of the universe before God and indeed the ontological question regarding the nature and foundations of morality. In fact, the very heart of the liberal achievement is seen to lie in just its ability to do this.[43]

Liberalism, in other words, claims to have developed notions of the world, freedom, and institutions that are in their constitutive structure empty of and thus neutral toward any ontological view of the nature of the universe and of morality. Rather than offering us an ontology, liberalism claims merely to have cleared space for each of us to choose our own ontology, with the assumption that this choice might well include, for example, the very ontology of creation and redemption, and of moral foundations, developed above in the name of *VS*. The hallmark claim of liberalism, in short, is that it does not displace any particular ontological and moral content relative to how we should best approach the world, freedom, and culture; that, on the contrary, it merely changes the *strategy* or *means* by which this content is to be arrived at: that is, not via public-constitutional order, but rather via individual free choice and thus through the free exchange of ideas among (private) individuals and groups.

My contention is that liberalism's putatively empty, and consequently neutral, notions of the world, freedom, and cultural institutions are in fact *not* neutral; they are, on the contrary, *premoral*. What liberalism defends as *empty* notions are in fact but a species of the *"indifferent,"* hence *"premoral,"* world, freedom, and culture whose rejection is entailed by an adequate reading of *Veritatis Splendor* and of the nuptial body. Liberalism's would-be "openness" to all conceptions of the nature of morality, which conceptions are always yet to be chosen privately, is, *eo ipso*, weighted toward what may, in light of all we have written, be termed an ontological *instrumentalism*, or again a *moralism*, both of which consist precisely in a failure to recuperate morality's original rootedness in the *intrinsic order and worth* (truth, goodness, and beauty) of *what is anteriorly given*, or *gifted*.[44]

---

43. See "Civil Community Inside the Liberal State: Truth, Freedom, and Human Dignity," pp. 65-132 in this volume.

44. For further development, see "Civil Community Inside the Liberal State." See also the article "Is Truth Ugly? Moralism and the Convertibility of Being and Love," *Communio: International Catholic Review* 27, no. 4 (Winter 2000): 701-28.

Liberalism, in short, of its inner logic and despite what are its hallmark intentions to the contrary, delivers a world, a freedom, and a culture all of which imply "premoral" foundations for morality as conceived by *VS* and as carried in John Paul II's notion of nuptiality.

*   *   *

Once we recognize the sense in which the liberal cultural tradition has rendered us unduly timid in the matter of the inclusion of the cosmos and culture in the foundations of morality — the sense, that is, in which the liberal cultural tradition itself invokes a comprehensive view of the cosmos and culture — we see the urgency of resuming the horizon repeatedly insisted upon in the history of Christianity. This horizon is summarized well by the International Theological Commission:

> The apostolic writings and the patristic witness do not limit their vision of culture to the service of evangelisation but integrate it into *the totality of the Mystery of Christ*. For them, creation is the reflection of the Glory of God: man is its living icon and it is in Christ that the resemblance with God is seen. Culture is the scene in which man and the world are called to find themselves anew in the glory of God. The encounter is missed or obscured insofar as man is a sinner. Within captive creation is seen the gestation of the "new universe" [*Gaudium et Spes*, n. 53]: the Church is "in labour" [*Slavorum Apostoli*, n. 21]. In her and through her, the creatures of this world are able to live their redemption and their transfiguration.[45]

---

45. ITC, "Faith and Inculturation," n. 30. The article by Buccellati cited in note 41 is a profound reflection on the sense of inculturation implied here by the ITC.

The Embodied Person as Gift
and the Cultural Task in America

The body in its physical structure as such bears a vision of reality: it is an anticipatory sign, and already an expression, of the order of love or gift that most deeply characterizes the meaning of the person and indeed, via an adequately conceived analogy, the meaning of all creaturely being. This is the burden of John Paul II's seeing in the body a theology, which indeed implies an anthropology or, better, a metaphysics rooted in the personal.[1]

Cardinal Joseph Ratzinger, in his *God and the World*, says that

> man is constructed from within, in the image of God, to be loved and to love.... In the Trinity, Love's own essence portrays itself. Man is in

---

1. See John Paul II, *Man and Woman He Created Them: A Theology of the Body*, trans. Michael Waldstein (Boston: Pauline Books and Media, 2006). See also in this connection Joseph Ratzinger's statement: "It is said that the spiritual meaning, not the biological fact, can alone be of importance for theology, and the biological is to be considered only a symbolic means of expression. But however plausible this exit appears, it only leads to a dead end. Closer scrutiny reveals the illusion. The cavalier divorce of 'biology' and theology omits precisely man from consideration; it becomes a self-contradiction insofar as the initial, essential point of the whole matter lies precisely in the affirmation that in all that concerns man the biological is also human and especially in what concerns the divinely-human *nothing* is 'merely biological.' Banishment of the corporeal, or sexual, into pure biology, all the talk about the 'merely biological,' is consequently the exact antithesis of what faith intends. For faith tells us of the spirituality of the biological as well as the corporeality of the spiritual and divine" (*Daughter Zion: Meditations on the Church's Marian Belief* [San Francisco: Ignatius Press, 1983], pp. 52-53; and see also 34-35). Cf. also Ratzinger, "Thoughts on the Place of Marian Doctrine and Piety in Faith and Theology as a Whole," *Communio: International Catholic Review* 30, no. 1 (Spring 2003): 146-60, especially 156-58.

God's image and thereby he is a being whose innermost dynamic is likewise directed toward the receiving and giving of love.[2]

Elsewhere Ratzinger, referring to the scholastic understanding of conscience in terms of the two levels indicated in *"synderesis"* and *"conscientia,"* suggests that *synderesis* be replaced with the Platonic concept of *anamnesis* (recollection), which, he says, "harmonizes with the key motifs of biblical thought and the anthropology derived from it."[3] He says this term "should be taken to mean exactly that which Paul expressed in . . . his letter to the Romans" regarding the law written on the hearts of the Gentiles and on their conscience that also bears witness (31). The same idea, according to Ratzinger, is also "strikingly amplified in the great monastic rule of Saint Basil. Here we read: 'The love of God is not founded on a discipline imposed on us from outside, but is constitutively established in us as the capacity and necessity of our rational nature'" (31).

Ratzinger goes on:

> This means that the first so-called ontological level of the phenomenon of conscience consists in the fact that something like an original memory of the good and true (they are identical) has been implanted in us, that there is an inner ontological tendency within man, who is created in the likeness of God, toward the divine. . . . This anamnesis of the origin, which results from the god-like constitution of our being, is not a conceptually articulated knowing, a store of retrievable contents. It is, so to speak, an inner sense, a capacity to recall, so that the one whom it addresses, if he is not turned in on himself, hears its echo from within. (32)

And this suggests the ground for mission:

> The possibility for and right to mission rest on this anamnesis of the Creator, which is identical to the ground of our existence. The gospel may, indeed must, be proclaimed to the pagans, because they themselves are yearning for it in the hidden recesses of their souls (see Isaiah 42:4). . . .

---

2. Joseph Ratzinger, *God and the World,* trans. Henry Taylor (San Francisco: Ignatius Press, 2002), p. 189 (translation modified).

3. Joseph Cardinal Ratzinger/Pope Benedict XVI, "Conscience and Truth," in *On Conscience* (San Francisco: Ignatius Press/NCBC, 2007), pp. 11-41, at 31. The same essay appears as "If You Want Peace . . . Conscience and Truth," in *Values in a Time of Upheaval* (New York/San Francisco: Crossroad/Ignatius Press, 2006), pp. 75-99.

In this sense Paul can say that the gentiles are a law to themselves — not in the sense of the modern liberal notions of autonomy, which preclude transcendence of the subject, but in the much deeper sense that nothing belongs less to me than I myself. My own "I" is the site of the profoundest surpassing of self and contact with him from whom I came and toward whom I am going. (32-33)

Ratzinger says that Paul's proclamation thus "encountered an antecedent basic knowledge of the essential components of God's will, which came to be written down in the commandments, which can be found in all cultures, and which can be all the more clearly elucidated the less an overbearing cultural bias distorts this primordial knowledge" (33).

This chapter first (I-VI) shows the sense in which this love and anamnesis of God is reflected in the embodied person and implies a metaphysical anthropology of being as gift. It then (VII) considers a different interpretation of the relational logic carried in this anthropology of being as gift, and (VIII) concludes by reflecting on the nature of the Church's cultural mission to America, in light of the anthropology of being as gift.

I

First principle. The soul is "the principle of unity of the human being, whereby it exists as a whole — *corpore et anima unus* — as a person" (*Veritatis Splendor*, 1993, n. 48). "*It is in the unity of body and soul that the person is the subject of his . . . acts*" (n. 48). "The human person cannot be reduced to a freedom which is self-designing, but entails a particular spiritual and bodily structure" (n. 48).

These statements, first of all, affirm the unity of the human being as a dual, or differentiated, unity of body and soul.

But, secondly, in light of the teaching of St. Thomas (following Aristotle), this unity, rightly understood, presupposes the *primacy* of the soul within the mutual relation of body and soul. The soul gives the body its first meaning *as a body,* although, given the unity of soul and body, the causal relationship between them is always mutually internal, albeit asymmetrical.[4]

---

4. Note, then, the statement by Edith Stein in her *Self Portrait in Letters, 1916-1942* (Washington, DC: ICS Publications, 1994), pp. 98-99 (Letter of 8 August 1931): "The insistence that sexual differences are 'stipulated by the body alone' is questionable from various points of view. (1) If *anima = forma corporis,* then bodily differentiation constitutes an in-

The body accordingly is never, after the manner of Descartes, simply physicalist "stuff" that somehow has its own "organization" prior to and independent of the order provided by the soul.[5] Thus the body, in its very

---

dex of differentiation in the spirit. (2) Matter serves form, not the reverse. That strongly suggests that the difference in the psyche is the primary one." An important truth is affirmed here that nevertheless demands further qualification. Given the unity coincident with distinctness between soul and body, each contributes to the meaning of the other, in their respective differences *as* soul and *as* body: the soul contributes to the meaning of the body qua body, even as the body, in a subordinate sense, contributes to the meaning of soul qua soul. The important truth affirmed by Stein is that the soul as form has an absolute priority over matter; nevertheless, for the reason given, it is the case that matter at the same time, within the absolute priority of form, maintains a relative priority over form. The "service" between form and matter, therefore, while thus radically asymmetrical, is nonetheless mutual.

Apropos of the above, see the argument of Adrian Walker regarding Aquinas's understanding of the soul as the substantial form of the body, which he integrates into a larger context via John Paul II's theology of the body. Walker states: "the substantial unity of the intellectual soul and the body, grounded in the *actus essendi* that encompasses both but is identifiable with neither, includes a kind of reciprocal though asymmetrical interpenetration of the two components without separation or confusion. In other words, the unity of the human composite includes a circumincessive *communicatio idiomatum* thanks to which the body and the intellectual soul can each enter into the inmost core of the other without destruction or mingling" ("'Sown Psychic, Raised Spiritual': The Lived Body as the Organ of Theology," *Communio: International Catholic Review* 33, no. 2 [Summer 2006]: 203-15, at 207, footnote 8). Further, citing 1 Corinthians 15:44 ("it is sown a soul-body [*soma psychikon*] and raised up a spirit-body [*soma pneumatikon*]"), Walker recalls what Henri de Lubac called the "tripartite anthropology" of "body, soul, and spirit," which Walker says expresses the sense of spirit he wishes to defend (p. 210). He says, however, quite rightly in my opinion, that "it is a mistake to draw too sharp a contrast between a 'Hebrew' tripartite anthropology and a 'Greek' dual one. Aristotle, for example, makes a sort of tripartition between the body, the soul-as-form-of-the-body (roughly Paul's *psyche*), and the soul-as-intellect-transcending-the-body (roughly Paul's *pneuma*). . . . This 'tripartition' in Aristotle's account of body-soul-intellect passes over into Aquinas's attempted reconciliation of Aristotelian anthropology with the Christian doctrine of the Resurrection" (pp. 211-12). The point here, relative to my argument, is simply that, in the human soul, the spiritual takes on a corporeal meaning, even as the corporeal *in its very distinctness as such* thereby gives new meaning to the spiritual.

5. Cf. *Veritatis Splendor*'s rejection of such a "premoral" conception of the body, which implies that the body is simply "matter" with respect to the exercise of human freedom and intentionality (n. 48), and does not embed what Joseph Ratzinger has called "moral reason" already in its nature as a body. See Ratzinger's "Bishops, Theologians, and Morality," in *On Conscience*, p. 67. See also Benedict XVI, Address to the Participants of the International Congress on Natural Law, organized by the Pontifical Lateran University of Rome (22 February 2007), available online at http://www.zenit.org/article-18989?l=english.

bodiliness, can participate in the *imago Dei*. The body in its distinctness as a body indicates a new way of being in the world, a distinct way of imaging God and love.[6]

In sum: the soul, as it were, lends its spiritual meaning to the body as body, even as the body simultaneously contributes to what now becomes, in man, a distinct kind of spirit: a spirit whose nature it is to be embodied.[7]

II

Second principle. In the *Compendium of the Social Doctrine of the Church* [*CSDC*] we read: "*The likeness with God shows that the essence and existence of man are constitutively related to God in the most profound manner.* This ... relationship ... is therefore not something that comes afterwards and is not added from the outside" (n. 109, emphasis original; see *CCC*, n. 356, 358). And further: "*The relationship between God and man is reflected in the relational and social dimension of human nature.* Man ... is not a solitary being but 'a social being....'" [cf. *GS*, n. 12]" (n. 110, emphasis original).[8]

(1) Thus the social dimension of human nature, or again the communion of persons toward which each person is ordained, is a matter of constitutive order. It is an order that is first *given to* the creature, and *enacted by* the creature only and always qua anteriorly given.

What the constitutive relatedness among human beings implies, in sum, is that I am in my original and deepest meaning as such a *substantial individual* who is *ordered at once from and toward* God and others.

(2) My being thus bears the character of gift: of a "what" that is given and received. Indeed, my reception is a response to the gift, a response that, in its very character as receptive-responsive, already participates in the generosity proper to gift-giving. I bear a constitutive order *toward* generos-

---

6. For a discussion of how the body images God in its own distinct and proper way, that is, qua body and not merely as that which enables the revelation of the light (soul) behind it, see José Granados, "Embodied Light, Incarnate Image: The Mystery of Jesus Transfigured," *Communio: International Catholic Review* 35, no. 1 (Spring 2008): 6-45, at 19ff.

7. The implications here for the resurrection of the body and the nature of the beatific vision — and of theology — are discussed in Walker, "'Sown Psychic, Raised Spiritual.'"

8. Cf. here also the Congregation for the Doctrine of the Faith's "Letter to the Bishops of the Catholic Church on the Collaboration of Men and Women in the Church and in the World" (2004): "The human creature, in its unity of soul and body, is characterized therefore, from the very beginning, by the relationality with the other-beyond-the-self" (n. 8).

ity that always anteriorly participates in the generosity I *have received* and am *always already receiving* — from God and other creatures in God.

Note that this constitutive order of generosity bears a dual meaning, characterizing both what is proper to man in his being qua natural and his call to share in the Trinitarian life of God himself in Jesus Christ. The constitutive creaturely order of generosity, in other words, bears a properly natural meaning even as it also always is open, however unconsciously, to participation in God's own generosity. Although sin weighs down and profoundly skews the constitutively generous order of being, sin can never destroy the integrity of this order as naturally given. The upshot, in sum, is that I cannot but always, in some significant sense, implicitly and from my depths, tend toward generosity and desire to be generous, and this tending already manifests a natural generosity that is in search of participation in God's own generosity as revealed in Jesus Christ.

(3) It is important to see, thirdly, that constitutive relatedness does not undermine the traditional notion of the person as an individual substance of a rational nature.[9] For it is the very relation to God, which rela-

---

9. Cf. in this connection the *Compendium of the Social Doctrine of the Church*:

108. *The fundamental message of Sacred Scripture proclaims that the human person is a creature of God* (cf. Ps 139:14-18), *and sees in his being in the image of God the element that characterizes and distinguishes him:* "God created man in his own image, in the image of God he created him; male and female he created them" (*Gen* 1:27). God places the human creature at the center and summit of the created order. Man (in Hebrew, *"adam"*) is formed from the earth *("adamah")* and God blows into his nostrils the breath of life (cf. *Gen* 2:7). Therefore, "being in the image of God the human individual possesses the dignity of a person, who is not just something, but someone. He is capable of self-knowledge, of self-possession and of freely giving himself and entering into communion with other persons. Further, he is called by grace to a covenant with his Creator, to offer him a response of faith and love that no other creature can give in his stead" [*CCC*, n. 357].

109. *The likeness with God shows that the essence and existence of man are constitutively related to God in the most profound manner* [cf. *CCC*, n. 356, 358]. This is a relationship that exists in itself, it is therefore not something that comes afterwards and is not added from the outside. The whole of man's life is a quest and a search for God. This relationship with God can be ignored or even forgotten or dismissed, but it can never be eliminated. Indeed, among all the world's visible creatures, only man has a "capacity for God" *("homo est Dei capax")* [*CCC*, Title of Chapter 1, Section 1, Part 1. Cf. *Gaudium et Spes* (1965), n. 12; *Evangelium Vitae* (1995), n. 34]. The human being is a personal being created by God to be in relationship with him; man finds life and self-expression only in relationship, and tends naturally to God [cf. *Evangelium Vitae*, n. 35; *CCC*, n. 1721].

tion always already includes relation to all other creatures, that establishes each person *in his individual substantiality.*

The crucial point, in a word, is that the relation to God, and to others in God, that establishes the individual substance in being is *generous.* The relation itself makes and lets me *in my substantial being be.* This "letting be" implies a kind of primordial, ontological "circumincession," or "perichoresis," of giving and receiving between the other and myself.[10] What I am in my original constitution as a person has always already been given to me by God and received by me in and as my response to God's gift to me of myself — indeed, has also, in some significant sense, been given to me by other creatures and received by me in and as my response to their gift to me.

The substantial unity characteristic of the traditional notion of the person, therefore, while reaffirmed, is nevertheless now conceived from within the order of love. Each individual substance possesses a substantial unity *(esse in)* while bearing from its beginning and in its depths a dynamic reference from *(esse ab)* and toward *(esse ad).* This dynamic reference, given already with the being *(ens: esse habens)* of the person, indicates the *ontological* beginning of the receiving-giving that characterizes the primitive meaning of human action and is thereby meant to be realized in every human action. In the words of Cardinal Ratzinger cited above: man "is a being whose innermost dynamic is . . . directed toward the receiving and giving of love."

(4) The logic of gift characteristic of creaturely being is best described as *filial.* My being in its substantial unity is constitutively dependent on God and on others in God. It is for this reason that Cardinal Ratzinger has stated that the child in the womb provides the basic figure

---

10. This "Marian" dimension of being is thus essential for a relationality that would remain truly generous and not slip, for example, into a kind of "dialectical" relationality that would indeed undermine the "substantial" consistency of the person. But this important point requires sustained development on another occasion. See, in this context, Benedict XVI's encyclical letter *Caritas in Veritate* (2009), n. 54: "The Trinity is absolute unity insofar as the three divine Persons are pure relationality. The reciprocal transparency among the divine Persons is total and the bond between each of them is complete, since they constitute a unique and absolute unity. God desires to incorporate us into this reality of communion as well: 'that they might be one even as we are one' (Jn 17:22). The Church is a sign and instrument of this unity. Relationships between human beings throughout history cannot but be enriched by reference to this divine model. In particular, *in the light of the revealed mystery of the Trinity,* we understand that true openness does not mean loss of individual identity but profound interpenetration."

for what it means to be a human being.[11] And indeed it is important to recall in this connection what is perhaps the central emphasis in his Christology, summed up in the claim that "Son" is the highest title of Jesus Christ.[12] Thus the basic logic of our being as creatures is disclosed in the child: the obedience, humility, and dependence characteristic of the child disclose creaturely being's deepest and most proper symbolic nature.

In a word, each of us as originally constituted is a sign and expression of the relation to God that is always first granted to us by God in and through the order of being: a sign and expression, in other words, of God's relation to (in difference from) the world that is mediated through

---

11. See Joseph Ratzinger, "Truth and Freedom," *Communio: International Catholic Review* 23, no. 1 (Spring 1996): 16-35, at 27: "For what is at stake here? The being of another person is so closely interwoven with the being of this person, the mother, that for the present it can survive only by physically being with the mother, in a physical unity with her. Such unity, however, does not eliminate the otherness of this being or authorize us to dispute its distinct selfhood. However, to be oneself in this way is to be radically from and through another. Conversely, this being-with compels the being of the other — that is, the mother — to become a being-for, which contradicts her own desire to be an independent self and is thus experienced as the antithesis of her own freedom. We must now add that even once the child is born and the outer form of its being-from and -with changes, it remains just as dependent on, and at the mercy of, a being-for. . . . If we open our eyes, we see that . . . the child in the mother's womb is simply a very graphic depiction of the essence of human existence in general."

12. "Let us not forget that the highest title of Jesus Christ is 'the Son' — the Son of God. The divine dignity is specified by means of a word that describes Jesus as a perpetual child. His existence as a child corresponds in a unique way to his divinity, which is the divinity of the 'Son.' And this means that his existence as a child shows us how we can come to God and to deification. This also explains the meaning of his words: 'Unless you turn and become like children, you will never enter the kingdom of heaven'" (Joseph Ratzinger, "Ox and Ass at the Crib," in *The Blessings of Christmas* [San Francisco: Ignatius Press, 2007], pp. 65-85, at 76).

Also: "A fundamental word in the mouth of 'the Son' is 'Abba.' It is no accident that we find this word characterizing the figure of Jesus in the New Testament. It expresses his whole being, and all that he says to God in prayer is ultimately only an explication of his being (and hence an explication of this one word); the Our Father is this same 'Abba' transposed into the plural for the benefit of those who are his" (Joseph Ratzinger, *The Feast of Faith: Approaches to a Theology of the Liturgy* [San Francisco: Ignatius Press, 1986], pp. 26-27).

See also Ratzinger's commentary on *Gaudium et Spes*, "The Dignity of the Human Person," in *Commentary on the Documents of Vatican II* (=*CDVII*), vol. 5, ed. H. Vorgrimler et al. (New York: Herder & Herder, 1969), pp. 115-63, especially his comments on articles 12 and 22; and Benedict XVI, *Jesus of Nazareth* (New York: Doubleday, 2007), pp. 335-44. It is worth recalling here that if Christ is the first-born of all creatures, then Mary is the protomother of all creatures.

the "ontological difference" indicated in the distinction between *esse* and *ens (essentia)*. What this means concretely is that I am always first *granted entry into the generosity* of God and of the order of being in relation to God. I am never the absolute origin or source of generosity but always a participant in generosity: I am an *origin* of generosity but *only always qua recipient* of generosity, a generous giver but *only always qua receiver* of generous giving.[13]

In sum: the relationality of the human person introduced by love is first the relationality characteristic of the child as the one who is absolutely *from* the Other — God — and from other beings in God, even as he is thereby *simultaneously also for* the Other, and for other beings in God. For this reason, worship and service most basically characterize the order of creaturely being, with worship of God providing the anterior form of what is meant by service, to God and to others.

(5) It is important to take note of the structure of human-creaturely being implied in the foregoing: a unity that is differentiated, a dual unity. Each substantial being at once possesses *its own substantial unity* and does so coincident with relationality to God and to other creaturely beings, and this constitutive relationality at once presupposes and always already "causes" a reference *within each person* to God and others.

The relationality characteristic of each person in his substantial unity as a creature, in other words, signifies and expresses what is the triplex unity-in-duality of the person already, as it were, in his "original solitude," his filiality, before God. In his original substantial "aloneness" as *one*, the human person bears a double reference *from* and *toward* God.[14]

---

13. It may be interesting here to note the etymological link of the meaning of "nature" with *being born* (Latin, *nascor;* Greek, φύω): thus with what originates — bears within itself the source of activity, of movement and rest — but does so only as always already *given* by another. The roots of this understanding of nature lie in Aristotle (cf. *Physics,* Bk II, ch. 1), though it is only in the context of the Christian doctrine of creation that the full implications of such a link can be adequately seen.

14. Cf. here the statement by John Paul II: "The account of Genesis 1 does not mention the problem of man's original solitude: in fact, man is 'male and female' from the beginning. The Yahwist text of Genesis 2, by contrast, authorizes us in some way to think first only about man inasmuch as, through the body, he belongs to the visible world while going beyond it; it then lets us think about the same man, but through the duality of sex. Bodiliness and sexuality are not simply identical. Although in its normal constitution, the human body carries within itself the signs of sex and is by nature male or female, *the fact that man is a 'body' belongs more deeply to the structure of the personal subject than the fact that in his somatic constitution he is also male or female.* For this reason, the meaning of original solitude,

(6) Further then, as already suggested, this substantial unity *cum* double dynamic reference to God is at once, albeit consequently, a substantial unity *cum* double reference also to other beings. As Genesis makes clear, the relationality implied in this double reference to other beings is first relationality with another being who is fully human while at once embodying a different way of being human. Thus the text cited from the *CSDC* states that "the relationship between God and man is reflected in the relational and social dimension of human nature." And, as Joseph Ratzinger points out in his commentary on *Gaudium et Spes* (1965),

> the sexual differentiation of mankind into man and woman is much more than a purely biological fact for the purpose of procreation but unconnected with what is truly human in mankind. In it there is accomplished that intrinsic relation of the human being to a Thou, which inherently constitutes him or her as human. . . . The likeness to God in sexuality is prior to sexuality, not identical with it. It is because the human being is capable of the absolute Thou that he is an I who can become a Thou for another I. The capacity for the absolute Thou is the ground of the possibility and necessity of the human partner. Here too, therefore, it is most important to pay attention to the difference between content [*Inhalt*] and consequence [*Folge*].[15]

The point is that the content of the doctrine of the *imago Dei* is, in the first place, that man is *capax Dei:* it is the relation to God that originally constitutes each person, and this relation immediately expresses itself in and as relation also to others, which is realized in a privileged way through rela-

---

which can be referred simply to 'man,' is substantially prior to the meaning of original unity; the latter is based on masculinity and femininity, which are, as it were, two different 'incarnations,' that is, two ways in which the same human being, created 'in the image of God' (Gn 1:27), 'is a body'" (John Paul II, *Man and Woman He Created Them*, p. 157).

My colleague, Father José Granados, first drew my attention to the link of original solitude, as understood by John Paul II, with the absolute priority of the whole man's being ordered to God in a relation of prayer and adoration. It is just this priority of the whole man as originally made for God alone that forms the priority of virginity already in the order of creation. It is important to see that this original "virginal" relation to God must be recuperated in all relations between spouses — even as the spousal relation can then deepen the meaning of virginity itself. On this "circumincession" of the inner meaning of the two states of life (consecrated virginity and marriage), see David Crawford, "Christian Community and the States of Life: A Reflection on the Anthropological Significance of Virginity and Marriage," *Communio: International Catholic Review* 29, no. 2 (Summer 2002): 337-65.

15. Ratzinger, "The Dignity of the Human Person," p. 122.

tion to another who is the *same* kind of being as myself, *differently:* through the relation of two beings who share a *common humanity* in the different ways termed male/masculine and female/feminine.

Thus there is in the structure of the human person a second dual unity latent within the person as he stands in his original "solitary" unity before God, and that is the one expressed in the ordering of each person toward a *unity between* persons, between a *one* and an *other*. In the substantial (differentiated-)unity of my own person, I am ordered simultaneously toward *unity with* an other, toward what may be called a communion of persons. I am ordered toward a unity of two — a dual unity. But a unity of two implies transcendence into a "we" that is more than simply the sum of parts; this differentiated unity indicates in some significant sense a new "third" beyond myself and the other.[16] This unity of two that transcends itself into a "third" is, according to Genesis and the text from Ratzinger cited above, expressed in the spousal relation that presupposes the common filial relation of the partners to God[17] and that is fruitful, most concretely in the procreation of the child.[18]

III

Third principle. The constitutive order of human being as gift or love, according to John Paul II, is signified and expressed *in the body*. "Human na-

---

16. This double triplicity, one *within* each person, the second *between* persons, echoes the two traditions seeking analogies of the Trinitarian image in the human being: Augustine and Aquinas on the one hand, with their indications of triplicity within each human being, and Richard of St. Victor on the other hand, with his argument that love, or the unity of two, requires a third.

17. Cf. in this connection Ephesians 5:21, where Paul affirms the common obedience of both spouses to Christ. It is the common submission of both spouses to Christ that grounds their mutual submission to each other as affirmed by John Paul II in *Mulieris Dignitatem* (1988), n. 24 — a mutual submission that is expressed differently in the man and the woman.

18. It is the dimension of filiality at the root of their love for each other (each spouse's acknowledgment of the other as a gift from God and as *capax Dei*) that actually grounds their fruitfulness, that is, the transcendence of their union beyond the "two" — and this may be blessed by God (in and through the order of nature) in the gift of a child that symbolizes the transcendent union. The interesting thing is that this is all written into the order of the body, so that "literal fruitfulness" does not depend only on our actually behaving like or acknowledging the other as a gift or "son." The order of nature itself is structured filially, structured to crown filiality with fruitfulness.

ture and the body [are not merely] presuppositions or preambles, materially necessary for freedom to make its choice, yet extrinsic to the person, the subject and the human act. [On the contrary,] their functions ... constitute reference points for moral decisions, because the finalities of these inclinations [are not] merely 'physical' goods, called by some *premoral*" (*VS*, n. 48). The body bears "the anticipatory signs, the expression and the promise of the gift of self, in conformity with the wise plan of the Creator" (*VS*, n. 48). It exhibits a "primordial *sacrament*[ality] ... understood as a *sign that* efficaciously *transmits in the visible world the invisible mystery hidden in God from eternity.*"[19]

The body, always-already informed by soul or spirit and actualized by *esse*, thus exhibits an order of love. But what is crucial to see here is that this sign of the creature's constitutive relation to God and others takes a *new form qua body*. The body, in other words, indicates *a distinctive way* of imaging God and love, in its very order *as a body*, as personal-creaturely flesh.

IV

Fourth principle. As the *CSDC* says, "the fact that God created *human beings as man and woman* is significant" (n. 110). "Man and woman have the same dignity and are of equal value, not only because they are both, in their differences, created in the image of God, but even more profoundly because the dynamic of reciprocity that gives life to the 'we' in the human couple is an image of God" (n. 111). The human body, marked with the sign of masculinity or femininity, "contains 'from the beginning' the 'spousal' attribute, that is, *the power to express love: precisely that love in which the human person becomes a gift* and — through this gift — fulfills the very meaning of his being and his existence. In this, its own distinctive character, the body is the expression of the spirit. . . ."[20] "Sexuality characterizes man and woman not only on the physical level, but also on the psychological and spiritual, making its mark on each of their expressions."[21]

19. John Paul II, *Man and Woman He Created Them*, p. 203.
20. John Paul II, *Man and Woman He Created Them*, pp. 185-86.
21. Congregation for Catholic Education, *Educational Guidance in Human Love* (1983), p. 4.

By the nuptial or spousal attribute of the body, then, John Paul II refers to the body's capacity for expressing love, as realized in and through the body's sexual difference.

But let me emphasize: the importance accorded by John Paul II to the sexual-gender difference, and thus to what he terms the "nuptial" or "spousal" *body,* does not overturn the traditional emphasis on the human *spirit* as the primary locus of the image of God in the human being. The human person is, qua embodied, a new image of what it means to be a person conceived in terms of God's creational love: an image which, as at once *new* and *of the person,* enriches and deepens *in its very difference as a body* what is *in some significant sense* already, and indeed more basically and properly-analogically, *inherent in the reality of person-spirit as such.*[22]

John Paul II's theology of the body, in a word, is about God and being as love, and about the body and the sexual difference insofar as these are a sign and expression of this theologically-ontologically-anthropologically prior love, even as the body precisely in its sexual difference provides a *new and just so far enriched and deepened* understanding of this prior love.

Aptness for fatherhood and motherhood thus is not "accidental" to the human person conceived as a substantial unity constitutively related to others. On the contrary, fatherhood and motherhood specify in a unique way the aptness for receiving and giving characteristic of the human, embodied person's relationality; they are a realization *in the flesh* of the *imago Dei* that originates and abides in the person's filial relation to God.

---

22. Note here Fergus Kerr's sardonic criticism of the Congregation for the Doctrine of the Faith's "Letter on the Collaboration of Men and Women in the Church and in the World," which he interprets as follows: "According to the Congregation document . . . [t]he human creature, as 'image of God', . . . is 'articulated in the male-female relationship.' It is not in our rationality but in sexual difference that we image God — in our genitalia, not in our heads, so to speak" (*Twentieth-Century Catholic Theologians: From Neo-Scholasticism to Nuptial Mysticism* [Malden, MA: Blackwell, 2007], p. 194). Such a criticism misses the point that sexuality is understood in this document — and by Ratzinger — as a *consequence (Folge)* of the *capax Dei* and thus filial love (hence spirituality/rationality) which are the *content (Inhalt)* of the image of God: thus "likeness to God is prior to sexuality, not identical with it" (cf. Ratzinger, "The Dignity of the Human Person," p. 122). It must be said, however, that there are interpretations, for example, of John Paul II's theology of the body, which, failing to take note of what is implied by the distinction made here by Ratzinger, give credibility to criticisms such as Kerr's.

V

It is important to note that man and woman each contain the *whole meaning* of the person, but *in a different order*. It is from within the *substantial wholeness* of each as human that the man and woman bear *a dual reference* from and toward others that is ordered differently in each. Needless to say, even with its rejection of a fragmentary understanding of the sexual-gender difference, the unified polarity of man and woman indicated here, along with the filial meaning of both indicated earlier, meets with strong resistance in the current cultural situation. It is important to take note of the assumptions that drive this resistance. These seem to me above all three, involving, first, the role of the biological in interpreting the meaning of the personal; second, the nature of unity and distinction and hence equality and difference; and, third, the idea of receptivity, with its related ideas of obedience and dependence.

(1) Following John Paul II, I have proposed that the physical-sexual difference, precisely in and as physical-sexual, symbolizes an ontological-spiritual and also psychological difference. The language of giving and receiving and fruitfulness, for example, in their physical meaning as instantiated in the body — in the *consummatum*, conception, and the like — signify and express *qua body* what is characteristic of a spiritual act or activity in its most basic meaning as an order of love. This language, in other words, symbolizes *in bodily form* what is termed the giving and receiving, and indeed just so far what may be termed the "transcendence" and "immanence," necessary for personal love in its full and proper meaning. A common contemporary objection is that this use of terms characteristic of the sexual or physical weights the latter with a human or spiritual and indeed ontological significance all out of proportion to what is typically today viewed as simply biological. It suffices here simply to note that this objection presupposes, however unwittingly, a Cartesian idea of the body: the very mechanistic notion of the body that John Paul II's anthropology means to call into question.

(2) Regarding the second: using language that indicates a unity *within* difference creates difficulties because the dominant culture is accustomed, again, to making distinctions in an unwittingly Cartesian manner: if x is truly distinct from y, x must just so far share nothing in common with y.[23]

---

23. Note Descartes's fondness for the straight lines of (abstract) geometry: *x* and *y* lie

It seems to me difficult to exaggerate the significance of this modern- "Enlightened" idea of unity and distinctness. Such an idea precludes *a priori* any unity between x and y that is inclusive, precisely *qua unity*, of real difference between x and y, and hence of any asymmetry in the mutual relation of the two. And it precludes any difference between x and y that is inclusive, precisely *qua difference,* of any real unity hence equality between x and y. In a word: insofar as x and y are equal, they are necessarily the same; and insofar as they are different, they are necessarily unequal, lacking the unity that would render them equal.

(3) Regarding the third assumption: human agency as typically conceived in modern culture, after the manner, say, of Francis Bacon (and Descartes), is characterized by a primacy of *originary power.* This idea of human agency, in other words, precludes the possibility of any kind of power in which the agent is essentially a participant, and thus is anteriorly receptive and dependent and indeed obedient, *in* his original power. On this dominant post-Enlightenment understanding, an original receptivity in the agent would indicate a passivity that is *eo ipso* defective.[24]

---

on opposite sides of the line from each other, in a way that ensures that *x* is only *x* and is entirely exclusive of *y*, and vice versa. The first consequence is that what is distinct from *x* must be simply different from *x*. But this first consequence needs to be seen immediately in terms of a second, more paradoxical consequence. For Descartes's mechanistic way of distinguishing between *x* and *y*, which would render each wholly different from the other, hiddenly imports its own new sense of unity. In their would-be simple difference from each other, *x* and *y* in fact remain hiddenly the *same* as each other, that is, in the still mechanistically distinguished identity of each. The Cartesian idea of unity and distinctness, in other words, which on the one hand *separates in an equivocal manner* what it would distinguish, at the same time unwittingly, at a deeper level, *unifies in a univocal manner* what it would distinguish. Cf. the discussion of Descartes on unity and distinctness in "The Given as Gift: Creation and Disciplinary Abstraction in Science," pp. 383-429 in this volume.

24. It should be pointed out here, however, that the understanding of receptivity as properly negative, a sign simply of an imperfect agent, has roots in a significant sense already in the classical tradition of Christian philosophy as well. It must be said nonetheless that the classical tradition has resources countering a purely negative idea of receptivity or patience that "Enlightened" thought does not have: its primacy of the contemplative or the "theoretical" or indeed of leisure and worship, its cognitional realism, its convertibility of the true, the good, and the beautiful with being (i.e., in its givenness as such: *verum et bonum qua ens* and not *quia factum*), and so on. (The work of Josef Pieper is very helpful on these points.) There nevertheless remain many — significant — difficulties in the classical tradition of philosophy, in terms of integrating the patient-receptive (or indeed the childlike and the "poor") into the proper meaning of act or activity, which ultimately becomes possible only insofar as one (re-)conceives the primary meaning of act or activity in terms of love. Here the work of Hans Urs von Balthasar, Ferdinand Ulrich, and Joseph Ratzinger is espe-

The understanding of the human person-body developed in this article in the light of creation and the "ontological distinction" demands receptivity and dependence for its integrity. A person who is constitutively from God is "rich" *in* the very "poverty" of the receptiveness that enables his *full and substantial being* as a creature; and his obedient dependence is itself always already a *creaturely* participation in God's generosity and thus

---

cially helpful. See also Kenneth Schmitz's remarkable article, "Created Receptivity and the Philosophy of the Concrete," in *The Texture of Being,* ed. Paul O'Herron (Washington, D.C.: The Catholic University of America Press, 2007), pp. 106-131.

For a limited discussion of this problem in terms of Thomism, see *Heart of the World, Center of the Church:* Communio *Ecclesiology, Liberalism, and Liberation* (Grand Rapids/Edinburgh: Eerdmans/T. & T. Clark, 1996), pp. 292-309; and also the articles by Steven Long and Father Norris Clarke, which develop two strong but different interpretations of Thomism on the above matters. See Steven A. Long, "Divine and Creaturely 'Receptivity': The Search for a Middle Term," *Communio: International Catholic Review* 21, no. 1 (Spring 1994): 151-61; and W. Norris Clarke, S.J., "Response to David Schindler's Comments," *Communio: International Catholic Review* 20, no. 3 (Fall 1993): 593-98, and "Response to Long's Comments," *Communio: International Catholic Review* 21, no. 1 (Spring 1994): 165-69. Available at communio-icr.com/person.htm. See also in particular Fr. Clarke's concluding statement in the matter:

> I had not thought of this profound dimension of receptivity, hence relativity, in all of us, even preceding any action on our part. Hence I am quite willing to broaden my description of all — at least finite — being to include a triadic aspect: being from another, being in itself, being toward others, or in the luminous terseness of the Latin, *esse ab, esse in, esse ad.* That is why the first appropriate response of a conscious being should in principle be gratitude for its own being as a gift from. . . .
>
> Can we go further and assert that this relation of primordial receptivity of its own being is proper not only to created being but to all being, including the divine? We could not affirm this on the basis of philosophical inference about the divine, hidden in mystery from our limited concepts, extrapolated from our experience of finite beings. But the Christian revelation of God as triune opens up to us a vision of the interior life of God as containing receptivity within it as part of its very being as divine life, i.e., it is of the very nature of the supreme divine being that the Second and Third Persons within possess the one, whole, and complete divine nature as gift *received from* the First Person through the eternal processions of the Son from the Father and the Holy Spirit from both. Thus this primordial relation of receptivity is somehow present in all being, though in a highly analogous way in God, freed from all limitation and imperfection.
>
> I might add that in created beings this primordial relation of receptivity in being extends not only to God but also to many other preexisting beings, such as our parents, and indeed to the whole supporting environment of our tightly interwoven material cosmos. We are indeed *from* this whole material world in some significant way and should extend our gratitude appropriately to it. (W. Norris Clarke, S.J., "To Be Is to Be Substance-in-Relation," in *Explorations in Metaphysics: Being, God, Person* [Notre Dame: University of Notre Dame Press, 1994], pp. 102-22, at 119-20)

at once *an image of that generosity*.[25] Joseph Ratzinger/Benedict XVI deepens the point here in Christological terms, stressing repeatedly in his work that Christ's *unconditionally obedient* fidelity to the will of God is an integral sign and expression of his being united with God — his being *Son* of God.[26] Obedience and receptivity at their root are thus "perfections" of what it means to be human, indeed of what it means to *be* in a filial sense. And unity and equality, while affirmed, are nevertheless now differentiated into an order of service and just so far "subordination" to an other. This "subordination" is not dehumanizing, but on the contrary humanizing in the fullest sense, given the constitutive reality of human being as created in love and for love. In a word, unity on a Christian understanding is never the mono-unity required by Descartes's logic of the machine, but always the dual unity (which, as fruitful, is in fact a tri-unity) required by the constitutively creaturely logic of love.

The errors carried in the above "Enlightened"-liberal assumptions can be given names: for example, gnosticism, which fails to recognize the giftedness proper to creation and its penetration down through the order of the body, such that the body is good already *qua ens* (intrinsically good) and not only *quia factum* (good qua instrument of humans), and that the body thus participates in the "transcendental" meaning of being as at once true, good, and beautiful. Deism and pelagianism, both of which fail to recuperate divine-fatherly origin as an immanent presence informing the original-constitutive meaning of human being and acting. Nominalism, which denies the singular being, in its very singularity, any inherent symbolic reference to another; or again which permits no complex or differentiated unity and thereby reduces the singular always and everywhere to a "mono-unity" exclusive of a dual unity that is fruitful. And so on.

---

25. See here the work of Ferdinand Ulrich, *inter alia*: *Der Mensch als Anfang. Zur Anthropologie der Kindheit* (Einsiedeln: Johannes Verlag, 1970); *Homo Abyssus. Das Wagnis der Seinsfrage* (Einsiedeln: Johannes Verlag, 1998); and "A Dangerous Reflection on the Fundamental Act of the Creature," *Communio: International Catholic Review* 23, no. 1 (Spring 1996): 36-46. See also Martin Bieler's "The Analogia Entis as an Expression of Love According to Ferdinand Ulrich" (paper given at the conference "The Analogy of Being: Invention of the Anti-Christ or the Wisdom of God? A Symposium," Washington, DC, 4-6 April 2008). The burden of Ulrich's argument is implicit in what we stated earlier: namely, that the primordial act of reception ("poverty") that constitutes the creature is at once a participation in God's own giving ("wealth"), expressed in what is now the creature's own autonomy as a creature.

26. Cf., *inter alia*, Benedict XVI, *Jesus of Nazareth* (New York: Doubleday, 2007).

Such errors, again, entail denial of the distinctly ontological meaning of the human being as a creature. Having abstracted from the concrete, filial-spousal order of love established by God in the act of creation, the dominant "Enlightened" vision of reality eliminates adoration and service as the fundamental order of man's being — an order that is inclusive of his body — even as it tends of its inner logic to reduce the body to a merely "empirical" reality, freedom to a purely formal exercise of choice, sexual-gender difference to a more or less inconsequential physical difference, and receptivity and obedience to dehumanizing passivity. It is important, in light of the foregoing argument, to see that, though the fullness of what is meant by adoration and service as the fundamental order of man's being can be understood finally only in light of God's revelation in Jesus Christ, this order is manifest in principle, in some significant sense, in the creature already in his being as a thing of "nature," and is just so far accessible in principle to reason *(anamnesis)*.

VI

My argument, in sum, is that being, viewed at once in light of creation and of the "ontological" or "real" distinction between *esse* and *ens (essentia)* that gives creation its first and basic "natural" meaning, is gift, and that this giftedness is signified and expressed in a uniquely privileged way in the body: in the filial and spousal-fruitful relations that constitute marriage and family. The suggestion that being is gift or love does not indicate the invention of a new "transcendental" called love, in addition to unity, truth, goodness, and beauty. On the contrary, it affirms these latter anew, understanding them now analogically in terms of the filial-spousal-fruitful relationality constitutive of human persons vis-à-vis God and others. It is the love proper to persons in this sense, in other words, that properly realizes the depth and breadth of being as such in its "transcendental" truth and goodness: realizes fully, in a truly analogical way, what it means for cosmic entities to be and to act and indeed to interact. In a word, it is in persons so understood that metaphysics takes its proper form as at once meta-anthropology.[27]

What all this implies for our cultural-"worldly" task can be put in terms of Maximus the Confessor's understanding of the order of crea-

---

27. Cf. Balthasar's *Epilogue* (San Francisco: Ignatius Press, 2004).

turely being as a "cosmic liturgy,"[28] which we might amplify, in light of our argument, in terms of a cosmic liturgy unfolding at once into "cosmic service." Every creaturely being is a gift from and toward God and other creatures in God, a gift that is as such ordered constitutively to worship and to service of God and others. Every cosmic entity is a gift that participates, via its creaturely receptivity and each in its own (analogical) way, in the gift-giving of God and in the generosity of being itself.[29] According to Maximus, the human being is the mid-point, as it were, of the order of creation. In the human being, physics and biology become personalized, even as the person takes the shape of a body. Thus the human person, after Christ and in Christ, becomes the mediator *(analogatum princeps)* for the whole of creation. In and through the human being, the cosmos itself *properly* realizes its destined participation in worship of God and fruitful service to God and others.[30]

---

28. Pope Benedict XVI, in his weekly audience of 25 June 2008, dedicated to Maximus the Confessor, said, "God entrusted to man, created in his image and likeness, the mission of unifying the cosmos. And just as Christ reunified the human being in himself, the Creator unified the cosmos in man. He showed us how to unify the cosmos in the communion of Christ and thus truly arrived at a redeemed world. Hans Urs von Balthasar, one of the greatest theologians of the twentieth century, referred to this powerful saving vision when . . . he defined Maximus's thought with the vivid expression *Kosmische Liturgie,* 'cosmic liturgy.' . . . We must live united to God in order to be united to ourselves and to the cosmos, giving the cosmos itself and humanity their proper form." (For an English translation of the work in question, see Balthasar's *Cosmic Liturgy: The Universe According to Maximus the Confessor* [San Francisco: Ignatius Press, 2003].)

29. See Karol Wojtyla, "The Problem of the Constitution of Culture Through Human Praxis," in *Person and Community* (New York: Peter Lang, 1993), pp. 263-75, at 269-70:

> Culture forms . . . a kind of organic whole with nature. It reveals the roots of our union with nature, but also of our superior encounter with the Creator in the eternal plan: a plan in which we participate by means of reason and wisdom. . . . There exists in nature, or the world, an anticipation of . . . human activity and a radiation of humanity through praxis. There is also in nature, or the world, a kind of readiness to put itself at our disposal: to serve human needs, to welcome within it the superior scale of human ends, to enter in some way into the human dimension and participate in human existence in the world.

30. It is helpful to recall in this connection the original, comprehensive meaning and order of the sin of Adam and Eve. Their sin consists most basically in actualizing in freedom a privation of their creaturely-filial relation to God (Gen. 3:5); the sin results immediately in a rupture of their spousal relationship, in a way expressed differently with respect to Adam and to Eve (in terms respectively of control and of desire: Gen. 3:16); and this double rupture of filial and spousal relations immediately results in a third rupture: that between the hu-

VII

Let us now consider an alternative interpretation of the theology of the body and gift: that provided by Professor Michael Waldstein in the long introduction to his fine translation of John Paul II's discourses on the theology of the body. My intention is to propose a friendly line of criticism, inviting mutual clarification relative to issues that seem to me crucially significant for our conception of the Church's cultural task in contemporary America. I raise the issues, not simply because of their relevance to Waldstein, but because he articulates in an especially clear and sophisticated manner what I believe is a dominant reading of the theology of the body.

Waldstein rightly emphasizes John Paul's rejection of a Cartesian in favor of an Aristotelian-Thomistic understanding: "the purpose of TOB as a whole," he says, "is to defend the spousal meaning of the body against the alienation between person and body in the Cartesian vision of nature."[31] My question, however, is whether his argument suffices to give us more than Aristotle's human-organic body, in other words, whether what this line of argument gives us in the end is truly a filial-spousal body or indeed person: a body or person understood as gift or love already in its constitutive order *qua body* and *qua person*. This assertion may seem strange, since the explicit intention of this argument is to affirm that the body is meant to express the logic of gift: "*the Incarnation shows that the meaning of the body is spousal. . . .* Christ's gift of self is . . . the goal that most deeply explains God's original intention in creating the body" (97). Nonetheless, I take his argument in its entirety to harbor an ambiguity. What is this ambiguity, and why is it significant?

Consider what is the first and basic assertion of the argument: "To love is to give oneself" (24). Waldstein links this assertion with "the spousal love between a man and a woman," which he understands as the "paradigmatic case of a total gift of self in our experience" (24), and he

---

man couple and the rest of creation, and among all of created-cosmic entities themselves (Gen. 4:12). It is important here, then, to note the order (filial, spousal, cosmic) and comprehensive effects of sin in its original meaning: both the order and the effects are somehow recapitulated in every sin. It is sin in just this comprehensive sense that the human person, as integral to Maximus's "cosmic liturgy," is meant to address, that is, in and through the Son of God, Jesus Christ, and his Petrine-sacramental Church that is brought into being in and by the immaculate *fiat* of Mary.

31. Michael Waldstein, "Introduction" to John Paul II, *Man and Woman He Created Them: A Theology of the Body* (Boston: Pauline, 2006), pp. 1-128, at 107.

then links the latter in turn with the "Trinity as the exemplar of love and gift" (24). Thus "the gift of self is present with particular completeness in the spousal love between man and woman"; and "Love and Gift take place in complete fullness in the begetting of the Son and the procession of the Spirit" (24). Citing *Gaudium et Spes*, n. 24:3, a text he says is key for John Paul II's theology of the body and gift, Waldstein emphasizes the fundamentality of the principles contained in the last sentence of this text: "First, God wills human beings for their own sake, for their good.... Wojtyla calls this principle 'the personalistic norm.' Second, persons can only find themselves in a sincere gift of self" (23).

This text from *GS*, and the two principles stated here, are indeed essential for John Paul II's theology of the body and gift. But their proper meaning needs to be seen in light of the whole of his theology. As emphasized repeatedly earlier in this chapter, the giving of self is always, anteriorly, a being-given of the self by another. I give only qua being-given, as a participant in a generosity originating in the Creator God and carried consequently, always already, in the generosity of other creatures, the generosity inherent in the universal community of creaturely being as such. Love is something I *do* only as always, anteriorly, a *being-done to (fiat)*. In the words of philosopher Robert Spaemann, the fundamental act of freedom is "letting be":[32] the letting be of the being-given of myself to myself by God and others — the letting be of the effectiveness of God and others *in* me that originally constitutes my being as a gift that *itself* gives. My freedom at its core and thus in each of its acts actively-receptively recollects my being-given as gift and thus as apt for gift-giving (cf. Ratzinger's discussion of *anamnesis*): it recuperates the relation to God and others in which I find myself always already a participant and of which, consequently, I am *never simply first the origin.*

The point, in a word, is that I *enact* generosity only insofar as my *being* is always already effectively generous by virtue of the presence *in* me of the generosity of God and others. I am an *agent* of love only as one whose *being* is always already constituted *by* love and *in* love.

Note that there thus can be no disjoining of *esse* (being) and *agere* (acting): *esse* and *agere* are each inside the other, and just so far presuppose a unity inside their distinctness. They nevertheless bear an order within

---

32. Robert Spaemann, "Natur," in *Philosophische Essays,* 2nd ed. (Stuttgart: Reclam, 1994), pp. 19-40. A translation of this essay will be published by ISI Books in a forthcoming translation of a selection of Spaemann's writings.

The Embodied Person as Gift and the Cultural Task in America | 263

their co-extensiveness. My acting in its primordial meaning bears a memory of the relation to God and others in God that is constitutive of my very *being* as an agent. My being to be sure presupposes in some significant sense an act of receiving on my part, even if this act is not yet a fully reflexive act of freedom. The point is that this act is just that: an act which, precisely in its form at once as act and as act of receiving, presupposes the being-given of my self, or the gift of my being. It is an act precisely qua active reception of my being as gift-from-another.[33]

The point here can be clarified in terms of the way in which Waldstein conceives the relation between *GS*, n. 24, and *GS*, n. 22 (a text that is cited in significant ways in nearly every one of John Paul II's encyclicals). He says these two texts are closely connected:

> According to *GS* 22:1, Christ reveals man to himself through the very revelation of the mystery of the Father and his love. According to *GS* 24:3, the trinitarian exemplar of union between the divine Persons shows that man can only find himself through a sincere gift of self. These two formulations seem to aim at one and the same thing: for man to be fully revealed to himself and to find himself are at least closely connected, if not identical. . . . (96)

Waldstein then says, further: "From the Father's love and the Trinity of Persons, through the creation of the world, all the way to the body, there is a single logic of gift" (97).

All that Waldstein says here is true. My argument, nevertheless, is that there still is lacking the crucial qualifier which comes with recognition of the distinctly filial dimension of self-giving. It is this *filial* dimension of self-giving that is brought into relief in the phrasing of *GS*, n. 22: it is in his revelation of the Father and the Father's love that Christ, the second Person of the Trinity, the Son-Word of the Father from all eternity, reveals the meaning of man to himself as ordered toward the giving of self. That is: creatures image the Father as unoriginate origin of self-giving only in and through the Son, the one who gives what he is given, who is *for* another only and always as *from* another.

The point here is clarified further in light of Colossians 1:15-18, which says that Christ is the firstborn of creatures, that we are all created in him and for him, as sons and daughters in the Child-Son. And again in light of

---

33. Cf. Schmitz, "Created Receptivity and the Philosophy of the Concrete."

the First Letter of John, which tells us that "in this is love, that God has first loved us" (1 John 4:10).

The text of *GS*, n. 22, in other words, together with scriptural texts such as these, helps us see the fuller implication of the principle emphasized in *GS*, n. 24, that God wills human beings for their own sake. God gives us our being for our own sake, and this means generously: he gives us our being such that, in this *being-given*, we are at once exercisers of our own being as *responsive givers.*

In a word, Jesus gives of himself only as the one who has always already and from all eternity received all that he is as divine Son from the Father, even as he has always already and from all eternity returned all that he is as divine Son to the Father. And it is only in this Sonship, this filiality, that creatures image the Father.

This, then, in a word, is what it means for God to will creatures for their own sake: he grants them their own generosity, their own *intrinsic participation* in generosity, in and through the *filial generosity* characteristic of sons and daughters in the Son.

Further, then, it is this filiality constitutive of the creature that lies at the root and informs the first meaning of the constitutive community of all creatures in and under God. This constitutive community takes its primordial form as a creaturely *communio personarum* in the spousal, fruitful relation of Adam and Eve. The spousal community characteristic of the human person is given to Adam and Eve inside their filial community with God, as a sign that expresses this anterior filial community: a sign that expresses in a new creaturely and personal way the generous, fruitful love between the Creator God and his creaturely world that is properly termed a filial-spousal relation. Any failure to incorporate filiality within the constitutive meaning of the human being logically entails a failure also to incorporate nuptiality, and filial-nuptial fruitfulness, within the constitutive meaning of the human being.

It is this *constitutive* filial-spousal-fruitful relationality that alone, in my opinion, gets us to the root meaning of John Paul II's theology of the body. As I read that theology, especially in light of *Gaudium et Spes* and indeed in interpretation of the fundamental meaning of the Second Vatican Council, its burden is that creaturely being is gift; that this order of gift is disclosed above all in the human person; and that this order reaches down through the body of the human person, such that the sexual-gender difference, and the filial-spousal relation presupposed and expressed in this difference, play a privileged analogical role in symbolizing (in a primordially "sacramental" way) the meaning of creaturely being in its relation to God and to the community of creatures under God.

Waldstein himself notes the father-son relation as the normative image for the Trinity in the teaching of Jesus (33). My question, simply, is whether the creature's constitutive being-as-memory of God and others has been integrated into the logic of gift in the way required by creation in Christ, in the sense indicated. That was the burden of my suggestion above that his appeal to the organic-personal body of Aristotle and St. Thomas as decisive in Wojtyla's rejection of Descartes is necessary but not yet sufficient. On Waldstein's reading, it seems to me, the human person really becomes a matter of love first via his own enactment of the gift of self (*agere*). On such a reading, however, it is more the case that we make the body into a gift than that we re-enact in freedom — to be sure, in a new way — what the body itself already signifies and expresses in its very givenness, or giftedness, qua body. Again, for Waldstein, it seems, it is more the case that we first bestow a spousal meaning on the body in its sexual difference than that we re-enact in freedom, in reflexive awareness and with new and deepened meaning, what the sexually differentiated body always already symbolizes in its original constitution as a body. The qualifier indicated here indeed reveals what is a significant ambiguity in Waldstein's sense of "completeness," as in his statement cited above that "the gift of self is present with particular completeness in the spousal love between man and woman." It makes all the difference whether the human-spousal act that completes the gift of self is understood as a recuperation in a new and reflexive way of what is the *already given* meaning of the body as spousal, or on the contrary as a *simple addition* of spousal meaning, *via human intention*, to a body conceived to be sure as an organism rather than a machine, but not yet as a matter of spousal meaning, already qua body.

There is to be sure much to be argued further with respect to the issues I have raised relative to Waldstein's reading of John Paul II's *Man and Woman He Created Them*.[34] My limited purpose in the present article is to

---

34. There are for example many hermeneutical issues that arise relative to the question of the various sources of Wojtyla/John Paul II's thought, among which sources St. John of the Cross is certainly central, as Waldstein argues. Here I would only insist that an adequate interpretation of that thought needs to take integrated account of what was basic to Wojtyla's life experience as a pastor and indeed as a participant in the Second Vatican Council: the centrality of love in his understanding of the human person, and his clear recognition of the Council's (re-)centering of its understanding of the human person and indeed of creation in Christ, and, in this connection, John Paul II's repeated singling out for emphasis

bring into relief what is perhaps the most fundamental constructive question raised by Waldstein's reading: that regarding the original source and nature of the *givenness* or *giftedness* or *givingness* characteristic of the body-person. When and on what terms does generosity or gift-giving first emerge in the (human) creature? In what sense does this gift-giving presuppose an always anterior being-given by another, a given-giving that is reflected in the human body thus as a *constitutive* filial-spousal order? Answers to these questions, in the end, demand distinct but interrelated theological and philosophical accounts of the relation and distinction between God and the world and of the relation and distinction between be-ing *(esse)* and essence or substance *(ens)*, and indeed between each being and all other beings *(esse commune)*.

It is in terms of these issues, in a word, that the question of how best to conceive the theology of the body must finally be framed and argued.

The significance of the issues I have raised comes into view when we recall our earlier references to the problems of deism, pelagianism, nominalism, and gnosticism. Each of these problems turns on the nature of creaturely being as gift from God and indeed of the creaturely community of being established in this gift. The filial-spousal relations of the human person rooted and reflected in the sexually differentiated human body indicate the *most basic and concrete logic* of the being of the creature as gift. Conceiving this giftedness sufficiently radically in light of creation demands the primacy of the features of being from another and (thereby) being symbolic of another: the primacy of a generosity or gift-giving that is always already a *being-given*, hence a *received* or *participated* generosity. An adequate sense of creaturely giftedness demands the affirmation, again, of being as constitutive memory of God and others, already in its original constitution *in* and *as* a substantial self. It is the absence of this being as memory that most basically defines deism and pelagianism. It is this absence of memory in a different sense — this fail-

---

Gaudium et Spes, n. 22, with its linking of man to love in and through Christ's revelation of the love of the Father. Cf. in this connection, *inter alia:* Cardinal Karol Wojtyla, *Sources of Renewal* (San Francisco: Harper & Row, 1980), p. 75, and John Paul II, *Dives in Misericordia* (1980), n. 1: regarding the integration of Christology and anthropology as perhaps the central teaching of the Council. Needless to say, the historical-methodological issues raised here are complicated, and need more discussion elsewhere. My limited purpose has been to try to draw attention to "systematic" or "constructive" issues that seem to me of crucial importance for a right understanding of the theology of the body and gift and that are very much bound up with these methodological questions.

ure to recapitulate analogically the universe of being in which an entity is always anteriorly a participant — that defines nominalism in its most primitive meaning.[35] Finally, it is in this absence of being as constitutive memory and constitutive relatedness to other creatures that we find the primitive roots of what is meant by gnosticism in its distinctly modern sense, by gnosticism's failure to see the body as good already in its givenness as such *(verum et bonum qua ens),* and not good only insofar as it is acted upon or "re-made" by the human being *(verum et bonum quia factum).* Each of the foregoing errors then becomes in the end but a different violation of the logic of freedom as most fundamentally a "letting-be," which is to say a deficient expression of freedom as forgetful of its being-given.

My presupposition, in a word, is that, in order to understand the idea of the embodied person as gift in the radical sense needed properly to identify, and respond to, these fundamental errors, we need to recover relationality in its *constitutive* roots in being as created by God.

These errors are not merely "theoretical" problems. More properly understood, they are rather articulations of entire ways of life: they indicate the root meaning of the dominant contemporary patterns of life.

VIII

I conclude, then, with an overview of what all of the foregoing implies for the Church's cultural task specifically in America.

(1) Writing on the hundredth anniversary of Leo XIII's *Testem Benevolentiae* at the end of the twentieth century, many Catholics on both the left and the right insisted that history had borne out the truth of the judgment that the so-called "Americanist heresy" criticized in Leo's encyclical was a phantom heresy.[36] Framing the issue of Americanism in terms

---

35. Indeed it is in deism, pelagianism, and nominalism as summarily defined here that we find the primitive roots of the liberal conception of human *agere* as purely formal agency, an agency abstracted from the inner reference to another carried in the sexually differentiated body with its filial-spousal meaning.

36. In his 1899 encyclical, *Testem Benevolentiae,* Leo XIII highlighted some problematic tendencies in America that he thought were becoming influential among Catholics. Notable among these were a sense of freedom that risked drawing men "away from conscience and duty"; a certain primacy of the natural over the supernatural virtues; a division of the virtues into passive and active, with the former viewed as "better suited for . . . past times"; a

of the relation between Catholicism and distinctly Anglo-American liberalism, these Catholics argued that the Church of the Council and the post-Conciliar period, reflected in such documents as *Dignitatis Humanae* (1965), *Centesimus Annus* (1991), and indeed *Gaudium et Spes* (1965), had now come to see more clearly an inner harmony between her own tradition and the juridical-"political" liberalism present in the history of America, in contrast to the doctrinaire liberalism present in post-revolutionary Europe. The Church had come to accept Anglo-American liberalism's juridical conception of public — political and economic — institutions, with their (so-called) "negative" rights and formal freedom; and had come to a greater appreciation for the "legitimate autonomy" of human-natural being and action — a double claim that has its "classical" expression in the work of Father John Courtney Murray.

The presupposition of my argument, relative to those who have insisted that the problem of the relation between Catholicism and American liberalism has been put to rest especially with the Council and in the pontificate of John Paul II, is that in fact the Council, and John Paul II and now Benedict XVI as interpreters of the Council, give us the terms in which this problematic can be properly taken up, for the first time, we might say. My limited purpose in the present chapter has been to frame the historical problematic in the constructive terms provided by the theology of body and gift as articulated in John Paul II and developed further in Benedict XVI's Christological anthropology of sonship. What is developed in the work of these men is nothing less than a renewed understanding of what it means *to be*, in light of creation, an understanding that is theological while bearing also a distinctly *metaphysical* anthropology.

What I am arguing is that at the heart of the controversy regarding the meaning of Catholicism relative to American culture is the meaning of the ontological generosity of man as rooted in his constitutive being-given. It is this question which also lies at the heart of how one is to understand, vis-à-vis American culture, liberty in its relation to conscience and duty, the distinction between natural and supernatural virtues, the nature of the virtues in their so-called passive as distinct from active meaning, and so on. These are all issues given a first formulation in *Testem Benevolentiae*

---

conception of the evangelical virtues as passive, with a consequent sense of the life of religious vows as "out of keeping with the spirit of the age"; and so on. As is well known, many leaders of the Church at the time, while acknowledging that in principle such tendencies were aptly seen as errors, said nevertheless that such errors did not characterize Catholic life in America; hence the term, "phantom heresy."

(1899). The meaning of each of the issues has to do with how one conceives the self in its relation to God and to other beings, with the sense in which that relation is first given by God and by others to the self — or better, in the case of creatures, is mutually given by each to the other in radically asymmetrical ways. John Paul II's theology of the sexually-and-gender-differentiated nuptial body as gift and Benedict's theology of sonship in Christ and of conscience as constitutive *anamnesis* of God and others are more ample articulations of this sense of the self's relation to God.

Filial-nuptial fruitfulness, in other words, understood at once in light of the doctrine of creation (and redemption) in Christ, and of the family as the first and most basic "secular" *communio personarum*, does not indicate just one particularly important, or "complete," way of expressing the meaning of the human being as gift. On the contrary, it is the *most basic and concrete content* of human being as gift. It is not as though the human being were a gift ordered to giving who happened to be male and or female and whose being born was merely a necessary biological condition for the free and intelligent acts of giving to come later. On the contrary, being born, and being born as male or female and apt for paternal- or maternal-nuptial fruitfulness, indicate the original and abiding *order* of gift-receiving and gift-giving as actualized qua embodied persons. Filial and gender-differentiated nuptial relationality is never first simply "contractual" in nature. It is rather a "primordially sacramental" sign and expression of the ordered relationality that is always first given by God and by other creatures in God. It is because of this constitutive filial and nuptial relationality, of this being first a child of God and indeed of the universe of being itself, in and through one's own parents, that each one in each of his acts cannot but recuperate his being — in a basic if not wholly conscious way — as a generous-responsive "letting be" of oneself, and thus of God and of others, relation to whom is always already generously effective in one's self.

My basic point with respect to the relation between Catholicism and America's "exceptional" liberalism is thus that "letting be," as the original-anterior form of creaturely being and action, is the key enabling us to go to the root of the criticisms first identified by Leo XIII. "Letting be," as generous-responsive participation in being as gift, is the key enabling us to appropriate the primitive meaning of conscience and duty with their implication of being bound to God and others; to see the unity within distinction of the so-called passive and active virtues, and to understand thus that "passivity" and "activity" each give primitive form to the other in each's basic meaning as such; and, finally, to perceive the originally positive character of the obedience and poverty proper to the consecrated life of virginity — indeed to perceive why the consecrated life of virginity in obedience and poverty fulfills the original creaturely meaning of man as man, hence including also modern man, in his destined covenant with God.

It is only in light of this that we can interpret properly the "legitimate autonomy" and indeed legitimate natural secularity of man; and only in this light can we see how and why the putative purely formal freedom and intelligence presupposed by juridical liberalism is, *eo ipso*, however paradoxically, "full" of ontological (and implicitly theological) form. Thus is the hidden ontological-theological form revealed to be of its inner dynamic deistic, pelagian, nominalist, and gnostic in nature, bearing an unwitting logic of violence toward being in its defenseless givenness and "transcendental" truth, goodness, and beauty.[37]

My summary argument, then, is that the problems of America in our time can be identified and addressed properly only through recuperation of generous "letting be" as constitutive of our being and acting, and this as a matter not of mere "theory" but of the concrete logic of our being, of our entire way of life. Which is to say, we can address these problems only through recuperation of our basic and abiding reality as children of God and of our parents, and as participant, via our sexually differentiated, spousal fruitfulness, in the *always anteriorly given* generosity of the creaturely universe of being itself. Our mission to the culture of today, in a word, is most basically *to be* in this sense, and to extend this logic of being, in all of its analogical forms, into all aspects of natural-cosmological and cultural life.

Insofar as we fail to embrace being in its constitutive (filial-nuptial) relation to God and others as the basic logic of our lives, we will, *eo ipso*, lack the capacity to transform our culture in the required Christian and human sense.

(2) As we conclude, however, we must take special note of the political question. In urging the above as our main cultural task, we must reckon with the question of how much of the content of what we have proposed can or should become part of the public-constitutional order, and by what means, that is, in light of the distinction between society and state and the

---

37. Cf. "Civil Community Inside the Liberal State: Truth, Freedom, and Human Dignity" and "Modernity and the Nature of a Distinction: Balthasar's Ontology of Generosity," pp. 65-132 and 350-82 in this volume.

Gospel-indicated distinction between Church and state, and indeed in light further of America's pluralism and of every human culture's need for a legitimate secularity.

Since it is impossible for a state actually to avoid a truth claim whether it intends one or not,[38] the only finally reasonable approach to statecraft involves taking seriously the question of truth, in order to secure in its fullest form the best intention of the liberal democratic state itself: which is to secure the dignity, the equality and liberty, of every human being, including those who hold views different from ours and indeed the weakest and most vulnerable among us. It is not the absence of truth that enables the most comprehensive civil peace and community. Nor is it the presence of truth that destroys peace, but only a lack of truth in its integrity that causes the breakdown of civil peace and community.

It is in this light that we can and must consider whether, or how much of, the ontology-anthropology of gift I have outlined can legitimately be proposed for the public or constitutional order of society. I limit myself here to a statement of principles. Note again, first of all, that what we are proposing affirms the separation of church and state, but in accord with a Gospel-coherent, as distinct from a liberal-juridical, reading of this separation. Further, our proposal entails accepting what is often termed "public reason," and indeed "Christian secularity," but only in terms of an understanding of these that sees that "public reason" will always reflect some ontology and that "secularity" always bear some ontological sense of relation to God. Thus members of the Church should understand that their engagement with the culture of its inner logic includes engagement with the political, or public-constitutional, order, in a way that respects the distinctness of the latter.[39] Members of the Church should take up the cul-

---

38. See "Multiculturalism and Civil Community Inside the Liberal State: Truth and (Religious) Freedom," *Revista Española de Teologia* 67 (2007). For a much more complete statement of the argument, however, see "Civil Community Inside the Liberal State."

39. Thus the issue for a Catholic is not *whether* the cultural, political, and economic orders should be distinguished, as affirmed for example in *Centesimus Annus* (1991), but how the distinction is properly to be conceived (see, *inter alia*, n. 39, 47, and 51). The burden of my argument is simply that, given the fundamental unity of the human person indicated in the person's constitutive relation to God, hence in what is the person's constitutive memory (conscience as *anamnesis*) of God, it follows that these three orders can never be cleanly separated, or rightly construed as merely extrinsic to each other: since they all involve the reality of man whose most profound structural feature is this *anamnesis* of God that never goes away even if ignored or left unconscious. There can be no political or economic order that, in its very constitution qua political or economic, is simply "formal" or juridical, hence

tural task in a way that proceeds with prudence and is committed to showing the *inherent reasonableness* of the God- and other-centered, filial-nuptial relationality implied in the Christian doctrine of creation. Indeed the foregoing argument presupposes that this reasonableness is always already implied by the experience and deepest intentions even of those who ignore or reject Christianity, or who would reject substantive justice in favor of purely procedural justice. Christians should take up the cultural task in a way that thus respects the equal freedom and dignity of every human being; and they should do so in a way, finally, that affirms that the state is neither the source nor the sacrament of God's truth about man and God, thus distinguishing the Church and state and radically limiting the power of the state.

It is crucial for our argument to see that the requirements noted here arise not from outside but from within the truth of man's constitutive, God- and other-centered, filial-nuptial relationality as affirmed in the Christian doctrine of creation. We need not, and indeed must not, go outside of the ontological truth of God and man in order to make a reasonable claim on the public-constitutional order (even if this truth in its supernatural fullness is revealed only in Jesus Christ and need not, as such, always be explicitly invoked). We need not and should not conceive public reason and Christian secularity in terms of the liberal state's formal-procedural justice and formal freedom, which in any case are already "full" of a "contractual" relationality and thus never realize their intention of metaphysical neutrality. The necessary distinction of citizen and believer will always invoke some sense, positive or negative, and however unconsciously and hence hiddenly, of the constitutive relation to God and others that unifies man *within* all the diverse aspects of his being and that alone can give this diversity its final, rightful meaning. The proper, and most truly reasonable, form of this distinction, accordingly, can be realized only by coming to terms with the implications of this ever-present, always at least implied *anamnesis* of God and others that is constitutive of my being.

The burden of my argument has been, in a word, that it is precisely the rightly conceived ontological truth about God and man that both guarantees a proper sense of creaturely autonomy and secularity and sustains the legitimate idea of church-state separation, and secures protection for the equal freedom and dignity of all human beings, all of which liberal-

---

neutral, with respect to the metaphysical (and finally theological) question of the meaning and existence of God.

ism intends but which the logic of its would-be purely procedural-juridical state radically undermines.

Attention is often called today, and rightly so, to the fact that Benedict XVI has highlighted the importance of the separation of Church and state. It is nevertheless crucial to see that his understanding has its roots in the Gospel sense of this separation, and does not entail embrace of this separation as expressed in the liberal-juridical idea of the state. Thus he has insisted that "law needs to be a fundamental image of justice,"[40] that the inviolable dignity of the human being, monogamous marriage, and respect for the natural religious sense of humanity represent "human foundations . . . accessible to reason and . . . essential to the construction of a sound legal order."[41] Further, he says that "the legal enactment of the value and dignity of man, of freedom, equality, and solidarity . . . entails an image of man, a moral option, and a concept of law that are not at all self-explanatory";[42] and that "politics is not the sphere of theology but of ethics, which . . . can only be given a rational basis in theology."[43] All of this reflects what is basic to Benedict's theology, and is summed up in a basic way in the quotations cited at the outset of this chapter: regarding man's constitutive *anamnesis* of relation to God and by implication to other creatures in God;[44] by Benedict's insis-

---

40. Joseph Ratzinger, *Church, Ecumenism and Politics* (Slough, UK: St. Paul Publications, 1988), p. 210.

41. Joseph Ratzinger, "Letter to Marcello Pera," in Joseph Ratzinger and Marcello Pera, *Without Roots* (New York: Basic Books, 2006), p. 129; cf. 74-78.

42. Joseph Ratzinger, "Europe's Identity," in *Values in a Time of Upheaval* (New York: Crossroad, 2006), pp. 129-50 at 147.

43. Ratzinger, *Church, Ecumenism and Politics*, p. 216. Cf. *Caritas in Veritate* (2009), n. 56: "*Reason always stands in need of being purified by faith:* this also holds true for political reason, which must not consider itself omnipotent."

44. Cf. in this connection the following statement by Ratzinger: "And this brings us back to the two controversial points in the preamble to the European Constitution. The failure to mention Christian roots is not the expression of a superior tolerance that respects all cultures in the same way and chooses not to accord privileges to any one of them. Rather, it expresses the absolutization of a way of thinking and living that is radically opposed to all the other historical cultures of humanity. The real antagonism typical of today's world is not that between diverse religious cultures, rather, it is the antagonism between the radical emancipation of man from God, from the roots of life, on the one hand, and the great religious cultures, on the other. If we come to experience a clash of cultures, this will not be due to a conflict between the great religions, which of course have always been at odds with one another but, nevertheless, have ultimately always understood how to coexist with one another. The coming clash will be between this radical emancipation of man and the great historical cultures. Accordingly, the refusal to refer to God in the Constitution is not the expres-

tence, taken up and emphasized again in his first encyclical, *Deus Caritas Est* (2005), that man is made to love and be loved, made in love and for love.

What I am contending is that this *anamnesis*, reflective of man's constitutive relationality, is presupposed in, and lies at the heart of, all that Benedict proposes regarding political-constitutional order. His proposal of natural law and its public reasonableness is not simply formal but is always already metaphysical, in a way that is itself always open to the theological. His proposal of natural law and public reasonableness, and indeed legitimate "secularity," always implies, and is thus shaped from within by, memory of man's constitutive relationality to God and others.

In sum, then: the cultural task of our time in America must involve an effort to tie the political-constitutional order intrinsically to a natural law the public reasonableness of which is always already metaphysical (and open to the theological) and not — as a matter of principle not ever — first simply formal or merely "political"-juridical. Precisely as a necessary condition for securing the most comprehensive civil community, for protecting the weakest members of society and respecting those who differ most from us in their beliefs, we need to recover a sense of the truth of being in its defenseless givenness as good: of the unity of the true and the good qua *ens* and not only *quia factum*. We need, in a word, to recuperate, in its relevance also for the constitutional order, the *anamnesis* that Benedict XVI proposes: the awareness that *we are not our own*, that belonging to ourselves at its root is always inside a belonging to God and to others, to the entire community of being, a belonging whose basic (indeed, in light of Christian revelation, whose primordially sacramental) form is given in filial-nuptial relationality. Only such an awareness will enable us to bring to fruition the positive meaning of America, her generosity and achievements, while transforming these from within toward a genuine civilization of love and culture of life.

---

sion of a tolerance that wishes to protect the non-theistic religions and the dignity of atheists and agnostics; rather, it is the expression of a consciousness that would like to see God eradicated once and for all from the public life of humanity and shut up in the subjective sphere of cultural residues from the past. In this way, relativism, which is the starting point of this whole process, becomes a dogmatism that believes itself in possession of the definitive knowledge of human reason, with the right to consider everything else merely as a stage in human history that is basically obsolete and deserves to be relativized. In reality, this means that we have need of roots if we are to survive and that we must not lose sight of God if we do not want human dignity to disappear" (Joseph Ratzinger, *Christianity and the Crisis of Cultures* [San Francisco: Ignatius Press, 2006], pp. 43-45).

PART II

THINKING AND ACTING
IN A TECHNOLOGICAL AGE

George Grant and Modernity's Technological Ontology

The Second World War had already shaken Canadian philosopher George Grant from his comfort with "progressive liberalism."[1] But it was only in the 1960s that he began to ponder the thought

> that the Western experiment, the experiment that had gone on since the seventeenth century in both natural science and political science, had been a mistake. That is the great central thought that I have tried to think; and it's very hard to think... because we're all brought up within the idea that the Western experiment is supremely good and something that has to be taken out to the whole of the world. This doubt of the Western experience has certainly been the central idea of my thought.[2]

Grant constantly acknowledged his appreciation for the genuine achievements of modernity, as well as his hesitancy in posing this radical question about modernity.[3] He was nonetheless deeply concerned with what he saw as the West's mostly unrecognized sense of "technology as ontology."[4] By this he meant that the modern West has ever-more pervasively conflated knowing — that is, conflated the human being's original pres-

---

1. George Grant (1918-1988) is increasingly recognized as one of the most significant cultural critics of the twentieth century in North America. For what is perhaps his best summary statement of how he understands the United States, see "In Defense of North America," in *Technology and Empire* (Toronto: Anansi, 1969).
2. David Cayley, *George Grant in Conversation* (Toronto: Anansi, 1995), pp. 74, 75.
3. *George Grant in Conversation*, p. 75.
4. See George Grant, *Technology and Justice* (Toronto: Anansi, 1986); also, Grant, *Lament for a Nation* (Princeton: Van Nostrand, 1965), p. 11: "As Heidegger has said, technique is the metaphysic of the age."

ence to and in the world — with making. Missing from this presence-as-making, we may anticipate with our own terms, is an anterior sense of presence-as-being-given: of being, ours and the world's, as gift.

It is the conflation of knowing and making that, according to Grant, resulted in a disjunction he takes to be central in modern civilization: the disjunction between truth and beauty.[5] Seeing civilizations "as dominated by particular paradigms of knowledge," Grant takes the modern paradigm to be aptly expressed in Bacon's "putting nature to the question."[6] The heart of modern technology is that it "summons rather than . . . leading forth": it "sees everything around it as an object which is summoned forth to give its reasons."[7] Again, in construing the world, or nature, as originally indifferent to worth and purpose, the modern technological approach to knowledge has transformed that world into something like what Heidegger termed a "standing reserve": something that is always yet to acquire its worth through its being-used or being-available-for-manipulation. This transformation empties love of any intrinsic relation to the order or intelligibility of things, even as it renders beauty incapable of bearing any intrinsic reference to truth.[8] Thus, Nietzsche, in saying that "truth is ugly," merely brought out into the open what had been implied from the beginning in the modern conception of knowledge.[9]

In ways reminiscent of Heidegger, Grant therefore thinks we must find our way again into the "Nearness of Being." This means that we must find a way to see again, a seeing that has its origin in contemplation. But,

> [t]o say contemplation "tout court" is to speak as if we lacked some activity which the Ford Foundation could make good by proper grants to the proper organizations. To say philosophy rather than contemplation might be to identify what is absent for us with an academic study which is pursued . . . under that name. Nevertheless, it may perhaps be

---

5. *George Grant in Conversation*, p. 43.

6. *George Grant in Conversation*, p. 135. Grant refers to Heidegger, noting the latter's view that, for the reasons already indicated in Bacon's statement, "technology is *before* science." See pp. 131-43 for a fuller discussion of Grant's sense of technology as the particular paradigm of knowledge in modernity: his discussion of the ancient Greeks, of the roles of Descartes, of Puritan Protestantism (in the United States), and of Heidegger. Grant also discusses the difficult issue of Christianity's "demystification" of nature itself, which made possible the false shifts of Bacon, and the like.

7. *George Grant in Conversation*, p. 134.

8. "Faith and the Multiversity," in *Technology and Justice*, pp. 35-78.

9. *George Grant in Conversation*, p. 38.

said negatively that what has been absent for us is the affirmation of a possible apprehension of the world beyond that as a field of objects considered as pragmata — an apprehension present not only in its height as "theory" but as the undergirding of our loves and friendships, of our arts and reverences, and indeed as the setting for our dealing with the objects of the human and non-human world. Perhaps we are lacking the recognition that our response to the whole should not most deeply be that of doing, nor even that of terror and anguish, but that of wondering or marvelling at what is, being amazed or astonished by it . . . ; and that such a stance, as beyond all bargains and conveniences, is the only source from which purposes may be manifest to us for our necessary calculating.[10]

However, according to Grant, the more or less tacitly assumed technological ontology of our age always blocks in advance this seeing that alone might generate and begin to form adequate economic, political, or moral responses to our cultural problems.

As he points out, "we live . . . in the most realized technological society which has yet been; one which is, moreover, the chief imperial centre from which technique is spread around the world."[11] Given that this is so, one might expect that it is we above all who would be the best able to "comprehend what it is to be so."[12] But that is just the problem: our pervasive ontology tends of its inner dynamic to place technology outside ourselves, and thereby to hide from us what it really is.[13] It is of the essence of the technological worldview that it perceives technology more or less simply as the *sum of things that are made* — televisions, computers, automobiles, and so on, but also economic and political institutions — and that it then begins to assess these only in terms of how they are *used*. The order of these in their original constitution as "artifacts" is deemed "neutral," and they acquire their "meaning" and "value," or "disvalue," first in the ends to which we choose to put them.

Grant argues that this very act of placing technology outside us al-

---

10. *The George Grant Reader*, ed. William Christian and Sheila Grant (Toronto: University of Toronto Press, 1998), p. 406. Cf. also George Grant, "In Defense of North America," in *Technology and Empire* (Toronto: Anansi, 1969), which is perhaps Grant's best summary statement of how he understands the United States.
11. *The George Grant Reader*, p. 407.
12. *The George Grant Reader*, p. 407.
13. See *George Grant in Conversation*, pp. 27, 55.

ready changes the nature of ends and of choice, the nature of artifacts, morality, and freedom, and indeed, finally, the nature of cosmic order and human destiny. He therefore concludes that "the very substance of our existing which has made us the leaders in technique [in fact] stands as a barrier to any thinking which might be able to comprehend technique from beyond its own dynamism."[14]

It is under such circumstances that Grant counsels that we learn to "sense our dispossession" by listening for "intimations of deprival"[15] through "intimations of perfection": that we retrieve the inner stillness that alone might allow the ultimate meaning of being, hence original order and measure of *technē*,[16] again to become manifest. But this retrieval is gravely misconceived if we do not see that it is a matter not only of "theory" but of an entire way of life, a truth Grant sees embodied in especially significant ways in Plato and Simone Weil. Weil, Grant notes, rightly stressed that "[h]uman nature is so constituted that any desire of the soul, in so far as it has not passed through the flesh by means of action and attitudes which correspond to it, has no reality in the soul. It is only there as a phantom."[17] Further, Grant pointed to Weil's insistence that, "when you contemplate God, you should have in mind the seventy thousand slaves that Crassus crucified when he put down the slave rebellion in Rome."[18]

Still, the way of life to be retrieved presupposes as its anterior condition and form a distinctive way of seeing. Given the nature of our present predicament, our first task is not that of adding new content to our doing, or indeed of making new and better things or erecting new institutions. While such tasks remain important, unless imbued with a deep ontological patience they all risk begging the question of technology that sets the terms of our predicament in the first place. Unless rooted in a perception of being as being-given, hence of being-as-gift, all efforts to renew actions

---

14. *The George Grant Reader*, p. 407.

15. *George Grant in Conversation*, p. 28; *Technology and Empire* (Toronto: Anansi, 1969), p. 139.

16. *The George Grant Reader*, p. 410: regarding the Greeks.

17. See George Grant, "Notebook: Zarathustra," cited by William Christian, "Editor's Introduction," in George Grant, *Time as History* (Toronto: University of Toronto Press, 1995), p. xxv.

18. *George Grant in Conversation*, p. 178. Grant emphasizes elsewhere that it is precisely "the division between contemplation and charity" that is "central to the Western world" and that needs to be overcome. The point of the statement from Weil, then, is that truth and contemplation must be tied to a love that is moved by suffering.

or reform institutions will inevitably serve at a deeper level only, all along the way and however unconsciously, to "re-ontologize" technology: to re-actualize the view that the meaning and worth of humans and non-humans arise first in terms of a human *making* (doing, acting, producing) that fails to recognize both humans' and non-humans' originally-abidingly *being-given-to-themselves*.[19]

According to Grant, then, the dualism of an originally indifferent world awaiting an originally creative human freedom describes the characteristic flaw of modernity.[20] We live in an era defined mostly by "a mixture of technological progressivism and personal self-assertion — all that is left of official liberalism in the English-speaking world."[21] Cosmos and culture stand before us as the sum of (neutral, mechanical) tools awaiting the human mastery and control that will turn these tools to "compassionate," comfort-bringing ends. Grant insists that this dualistic horizon can be overcome only through retrieval of the truth that we and the world "are not our own."[22]

That "we are not our own" means for Grant that we belong to ourselves only as we belong more basically to God. The centrality of this conviction evokes the question of the place of Christianity in terms of its influence on Grant and indeed of his understanding of its own role in the emergence of our cultural predicament. Two texts help summarize Grant's sense of this place.

> It seems to me that Western Christianity is now going to go through a great purging of its authority because it was in the civilization where it was dominant that the worst form of secularity has arisen and is now likely to become worldwide. Both Roman Catholicism and Protestantism are going to pay terrible prices . . . for the ultimate relation they maintained with that progressive materialism. This kind of historical remark has no relation at all to the truth of Christianity which is just given for me in the perfection of Christ, which to me can only be thought in terms of Trinitarianism. . . . My particular function . . . is to try to understand just a small amount of what was at fault in this par-

---

19. *George Grant in Conversation*, p. 41. Cf. also *Evangelium Vitae*, n. 83, on the need to foster a contemplative outlook.
20. *George Grant in Conversation*, pp. 27-28; *Technology and Empire*, p. 137.
21. *Lament for a Nation*, p. 14.
22. "Conversation: Intellectual Background" in Larry Schmidt, ed., *George Grant in Process: Essays and Conversations* (Toronto: Anansi, 1978), pp. 62-63.

ticular manifestation of Christianity, so that one plays a minute part in something that will take centuries — namely, the rediscovery of authoritative Christianity. I have no doubt that that will, slowly and through very great suffering, occur — because Christianity tells the truth about the most important matter — namely the perfection of God and the affliction of human beings. . . .[23]

It would be foolish to judge that thought has much immediate influence on events in any era, let alone in ours when a particular destiny of knowing and making moves to its climax. Our paradigm of knowledge is the very heart of this civilization's destiny, and such destinies have a way of working themselves out — that is, in bringing forth from their principle everything which is implied in that principle. Most scientists seem so engrossed within this paradigm (and at a lower level, seem so engrossed, like everybody else, with their own advancement within their community) that they seem unable to care to think beyond the unfolding of the paradigm, let alone to think about it as a particular aspiration of human thought and to relate it to the highest human aspiration — knowledge of good. Yet in the presence of the obvious disregard of thought in our era, the demand to think does not disappear.[24]

The burden of Grant's remarks here is to highlight the collusion of Christian theology with the paradigm of knowledge lying at the heart of our predicament (of our particular "secularity"). This collusion may be judged, with Hans Urs von Balthasar, to have its roots already in an earlier historical failure to understand our knowledge of the world — to understand both the method of our knowledge and the content of worldly order — in terms of sanctity.[25] The point is simply that Grant, in the spirit of Balthasar, sees how deeply the modern paradigm of knowledge is a function of developments within Christian theology itself,[26] even as Grant, again like Balthasar, presupposes that these developments themselves are corruptions of the truth of Christianity that remains a constant.[27] The consequence of this collusion is

---

23. "Letter to Derek Bedson," 2 February 1978, in *The George Grant Reader*, pp. 434-35.
24. "Knowing and Making," in *The George Grant Reader*, p. 417.
25. See in this connection the discussion in "Religion and Secularity in a Culture of Abstraction," pp. 328-49 in this volume.
26. See Hans Urs von Balthasar, "Theology and Sanctity," in *Explorations in Theology I: The Word Made Flesh* (San Francisco: Ignatius Press, 1989), pp. 181-209.
27. Balthasar is clearer and more explicit than Grant that this constancy of the truth is a characteristic of the Church, given its sacramental nature.

that Christians will have to suffer, if and insofar as a new paradigm of knowledge is going to be truly thought through and lived into being.

The truth of Christianity for Grant, while a fundamental given for him, bears not a trace of "triumphalism," because of his abiding sense of the mystery of what is given, which always entails that "we know that we do not know"; because of his conviction that the true Christian always recognizes his or her own sin in that of the "other," and indeed knows that he or she must always remain solidary with the (suffering, vulnerable) other; and because of his recognition that justice must transform itself into love, in order to realize its proper meaning *as* justice.[28] On all of this, again, the witness of Weil is decisive for Grant.

The radicality of Grant's probing of modernity raises the question of whether his approach is not too pessimistic and "unrealistic," indeed utopian, in its implications. This question, however, typically takes the form of a dilemma that sets in advance the terms of, hence the range of possible responses to, our cultural predicament, and in so doing begs precisely what Grant argues is the depth and seriousness of the predicament: Either one accepts the benefits of modernity, with its technological science, in which case one cannot legitimately pose radical (i.e., ontological) questions regarding the meaning of modern technique, or one poses radical questions about the meaning of modern technique, in which case one cannot, with consistency, appreciate electricity and the benefits of Western medicine. The burden of Grant's work is to deny that these are exhaustive alternatives, indeed to show how dangerous it may be for the future of world culture to assume that these alternatives *are* exhaustive. For what the two alternatives exactly preclude, *a priori*, is that an *ambiguity* might reside *within* what are in other respects good developments, an ambiguity significant enough that it could over time lead to a disastrous subversion even of these readily acknowledged goods.

Pointing out how a distinctly modern notion of an opposition between "ideal" and "real" often operates in the charge regarding pessimism,[29] Grant nonetheless stresses at every point both his own hesitancy in the face of the magnitude of the issues, and his belief that retreat from the world — except in order to live better *in* the world — is in any case never a legitimate response.[30] Grant summarizes in 1965 what is the finely differentiated spirit of his radical questioning of modernity:

28. *George Grant in Conversation*, p. 179.
29. *George Grant in Conversation*, p. 79.
30. *George Grant in Conversation*, p. 75.

It can only be with an enormous sense of hesitation that one dares to question modern political philosophy. If its assumptions are false, the age of progress has been a tragic aberration in the history of the species. To assert such a proposition lightly would be the height of irresponsibility. Has it not been in the age of progress that disease and overwork, hunger and poverty, have been drastically reduced? Those who criticize our age must at the same time contemplate pain, infant mortality, crop failures in isolated areas, and the sixteen-hour day. As soon as that is said, facts about our age must also be remembered: the increasing outbreaks of impersonal ferocity, the banality of existence in technological societies, the pursuit of expansion as an end in itself. Will it be good for men to control their genes? The possibility of nuclear destruction and mass starvation may be no more terrible than that of man tampering with the roots of his humanity. Interference with human nature seems to the moderns the hope of a higher species in the ascent of life; to others it may seem that man in his pride could corrupt his very being. The powers of manipulation now available may portend the most complete tyranny imaginable. At least, it is feasible to wonder whether modern assumptions may be basically inhumane.[31]

---

31. *Lament for a Nation*, pp. 104-5. Peter C. Emberley, in his 1994 Foreword to this book, gives a good summary of the content of Grant's proposals, as well as of the nuanced spirit in which he makes those proposals:

> What we are, Grant explained, is ... constituted by a milieu whose logic and direction had been unfolding since the beginning of modernity, with the American empire as its most expressive manifestation: being as technology. Grant, indebted here to Heidegger, was later to call the technological spirit of modernity a "complete ontological package," meaning that our institutions, our programs, our laws, our behaviours, our amusements and our self-understandings were all fundamentally echoing its logic. A philosophy of reason as domination over nature, a politics of imperial, bureaucratic administration, a public discourse of efficiency, and a sociology of adjustment and equilibrium were forging, as so many specialized arts of modern technology, a new way for us. Grant's short-hand version of how technology was reshaping us was to speak of its "universalizing" and "homogenizing" effect. Contained within these terms were complex reflections on the modern dream of universal liberation and the prospect of universal tyranny, and on the moral hopes associated with equality and the reality of creeping sameness. Taken together, he was to demonstrate, technology involved a fundamental reshaping of the human spirit and the gradual eclipse or transformation of human experiences that in the past had provided us with moral and intellectual ballast.
>
> An assessment of this ... destiny was not as easy as one might expect. It would be otiose, Grant never tired of reminding, to overlook the moral promise and concrete achievements of modern technology. It had made possible, in a way never believed

Now, even if we concede the grave defects in modernity as pointed out by Grant, one might object that the distance between modern political, social, and cultural realities and the "ideal" (if you will) realities sought by Grant still remains too great actually to be traversed. One might object, in other words, that, even if, indeed especially if, with Grant, we are impressed with the gravity of the present predicament, we should for this very reason also be impressed with the utopian implications of his critique. Precisely *if* Grant's diagnosis is accurate, there would seem to be nothing that we can really — practically, effectively — do about it.

Alasdair MacIntyre, in responding to such an objection with respect to his own proposals regarding the modern liberal university, captures,

---

possible, the actualization of the duty of charity and the extension of individual freedom. . . . While no one should deny this was progress, the question remained, At what cost?

As Grant argues . . . , technological progress could not be separated from an accompanying transformation of the human spirit; a transformation which made it impossible to unite the new social controls with traditional moralities and politics. Universalizing and homogenizing, technology's driving principle of "efficiency" demanded the suppression of local differences, particular loyalties, and credible resistances. Whatever lingering pockets of "autochthony" might declare opposition, the spirit of the regime — sustained by its . . . ruling class of technicians and administrators, and the officially sanctioned discourse of instrumentality and efficiency — regarded their opposition as nothing more than folly or sentimentality. The new regime, whatever value the fruits of its technical arts and sciences, was a universal tyranny. . . .

The fate of Canada was a microcosm of the confrontation of all peoples with the powerfully transforming forces of the West. The expectation that Canadians might recall what within their "primal" constituted a "precious good" worth preserving, or what might be testimony to a spiritually more profound way of being human, had been annulled in the realization that any distinctiveness in Canada's way of life, its skills, and practices, could only appear now as stylized, abstract images circulating through the homogenizing processes of technological efficiency. The same would be true around the globe. The conservative and communitarian strands in our heritage, once understood as containing enduring concepts of what is good for humanity, could now only be seen as mere political ideology or a set of values.

Against this, no simple appeal to the spirit or rootedness of our past sense of belonging to this land could be relevant. To think of containing and embalming the distinctive virtues of that time would be to condemn oneself to antiquarianism or romanticism, if not worse. There could be no return to a past, nor should the spirit of modernity be dampened by willing away what had come to be. Grant, following Nietzsche, had continually warned of the poisonous "resentment" that lay at the heart of wishing away time's "it was" — a poison that could deprive life of vitality and confidence. (pp. 18-20)

with customary trenchancy, also the reply implicit in the whole of Grant's undertaking:

> Those most prone to accuse others of utopianism are generally those men and women of affairs who pride themselves upon their pragmatic realism, who look for immediate results, who want the relationship between present input and future output to be predictable and measurable, and that is to say, a matter of the shorter, indeed the shortest run. They are the enemies of the incalculable, the skeptics about all expectations which outrun what *they* take to be hard evidence, the deliberately shortsighted who congratulate themselves upon the limits of their vision. Who were their predecessors?
> They include the fourth-century magistrates of the types of disordered city which Plato described in Book VIII of the *Republic*, the officials who tried to sustain the pagan Roman Empire in the age of Augustine, the sixteenth-century protobureaucrats who continued obediently to do the unprincipled bidding of Henry VIII while Thomas More set out on the course that led to his martyrdom. What these examples suggest is that the gap between Utopia and current social reality may on occasion furnish a measure, not of the lack of justification of Utopia, but rather of the degree to which those who not only inhabit contemporary social reality but insist upon seeing only what it allows them to see and upon learning only what it allows them to learn, cannot even identify, let alone confront, the problems which will be inscribed in their epitaphs. It may be therefore that the charge of utopianism is sometimes best understood more as a symptom of the condition of those who level it than an indictment of the projects against which it is directed.[32]

Sheila Grant, Grant's widow, insists in a 1997 postscript to Grant's *Lament for a Nation* that the positive core of his response to the charge of pessimism and utopianism lay in the simple statement that he repeated throughout his life, "It always matters what each of us does." For one who believes, as he did, that "the spiritual life is open to all," pessimism and unrealism can never be the last word.[33]

---

32. Alasdair MacIntyre, *Three Rival Versions of Moral Enquiry* (Notre Dame: University of Notre Dame Press, 1990), pp. 234-35.

33. Sheila Grant, "Afterword," in *Lament for a Nation*, p. 110. Cf. in this connection the comment of Gabriel Marcel in a similar context:

MacIntyre indicates how the conventional charge of utopianism presupposes just the instrumentalized and fragmentary mode of rationality, the very notions of practice and practical, of ideal and real, whose meaning and truth Grant's radical inquiry means to probe. Sheila Grant points us simply but profoundly toward what in the end can be the only "credible" positive response to the charge of unrealism: namely, each one's entire way of life, as carried in the whole of one's countless concrete acts, thoughts, and gestures. Such a response can be otherwise identified, in the words of the Second Vatican Council, as the universal vocation to holiness. Of course, to demonstrate that this response indicates something more than a naïve, voluntaristic piety that would, *ipso facto,* miss the depth, magnitude, and complexity of what is at stake, we would need to unfold the theology and ontology and distinctive sense of cosmic order and worldly engagement implied by this vocation — which is a main burden of the present book as a whole.

I am, of course, not unaware of the disquieting and superficially even discouraging character of such a diagnosis. But it has, I think, the great advantage of helping us, by the very strength of the reaction it evokes in us, to choose the only path that is open to us if we want to avoid complicity, not merely in a catastrophe, but in the greatest crime which mankind has ever committed against itself.

Let me make myself clear. There can be no question here of my attempting to define anything at all resembling a political line of action. What we have to do with is rather an inner attitude; but this inner attitude cannot remain at the stage of a mere attitude, it must find expression in deeds, and that according to the situation in which each of us finds himself: I mean by that, that this is not a matter, as is unfortunately so often the habit of intellectuals, of our thrusting ourselves into fields in which we are wholly without authority, by signing appeals, manifestos, and so on. I am not giving a distorted emphasis to my own point of view when I say that this sort of thing is too often at the moral level of the petty confidence trick. But on the other hand it is within the scope of each of us, within his own proper field, in his profession, to pursue an unrelaxing struggle for man, for the dignity of man, against everything that threatens to annihilate man and his dignity. (Gabriel Marcel, *Man Against Humanity* [London: Harvill Press, 1952], p. 184)

Liturgy and the Integrity of Cosmic Order: The Theology of Alexander Schmemann

The debate over secularism — over what it is and the sense in which it is a good or a bad thing — hinges on the nature of the distinction between religion and the secular, or God and the world.

Presuming not at all to deal with the full range of issues evoked here, my proposal is that secularism in the "bad" sense, at least as found in Western (e.g., American) liberal patterns of thought and life, consists above all in a false abstraction from God in our first and most basic understanding of the world: secularism consists in an abstract notion of the cosmos. The purpose of this article is to give a preliminary indication of the meaning of some of the key terms of this proposal.

I.

Alexander Schmemann, in his *For the Life of the World*, defines secularism as "above all a *negation of worship*."[1]

> It is the negation of man as a worshiping being, as *homo adorans*: the one for whom worship is the essential act which both "posits" his humanity and fulfills it. It is the rejection as ontologically and epistemologically "decisive," of the words which "always, everywhere and for all" were the true "epiphany" of man's relation to God, to the world and to himself: "It is meet and right to sing of Thee, to bless

---

1. Alexander Schmemann, *For the Life of the World* (Crestwood, NY: St. Vladimir's Seminary Press, 1998 [1963]), p. 118.

Thee, to praise Thee, to give thanks to Thee, and to worship Thee in every place of Thy dominion. . . ." (118)

What is crucial here, says Schmemann, is that we see that "the very notion of worship implies a certain idea of man's relationship not only to God *but also to the world*" (emphasis added); and that we see also that it is "the idea of worship that secularism explicitly or implicitly rejects" (119).

Schmemann's argument hinges on what he calls the *sacramental* or symbolic character of the world — that is, of space and time and matter and body and motion — and of the human being's place in the world (cf. 120, 139). Worldly realities find their true meaning precisely as worldly in their character simultaneously and intrinsically as epiphanies of God. Schmemann, in this book and again in his *Journals*,[2] stresses how Christian theology, by virtue of a certain longstanding understanding of sacrament, has itself contributed to draining the world of its structurally symbolic character, and this notwithstanding what is often an intense piety in other respects. He explains thus:

> At the end of the twelfth century a Latin theologian, Berengarius of Tours, was condemned for his teaching on the Eucharist. He maintained that because the presence of Christ in the eucharistic elements is "mystical" or "symbolic," it is not *real*. (128)

Unfortunately, Schmemann says, the Lateran Council that condemned Berengarius largely reversed the formula:

> It proclaimed that since Christ's presence in the Eucharist is *real*, it is not "mystical." What is truly decisive here is precisely the disconnection and the opposition of the two terms *verum* and *mystice*, the acceptance, on both sides, that they are mutually exclusive. (128-29)

The consequent assumption is that

> that which is "mystical" or "symbolic" is not real, whereas that which is "real" is not symbolic. This was, in fact, the collapse of the fundamental Christian *mysterion*, the antinomical "holding together" of the reality of the symbol, and the symbolism of reality. It was the collapse of

---

2. *The Journals of Alexander Schmemann 1973-1983* (Crestwood, NY: St. Vladimir's Seminary Press, 2000).

the fundamental Christian understanding of creation in terms of its ontological *sacramentality*. (129)

Since then, Christian thought has continued the tendency "to oppose these terms, to reject, implicitly or explicitly, the 'symbolic realism' and the 'realistic symbolism' of the Christian world view. . . . [T]he world ceases to be the 'natural' sacrament of God, and the supernatural sacrament ceases to have any 'continuity' with the world" (129). "[B]y denying the world its natural 'sacramentality,' and radically opposing the 'natural' to the 'supernatural,' [this dualistic tendency] make[s] the world *grace-proof*, and ultimately lead[s] to *secularism*" (130).[3]

Schmemann summarizes as follows what he means by the "ontological *sacramentality*" of the world:

> We *need* water and oil, bread and wine in order to be in communion with God and to know Him. Yet conversely — and such is the teaching, if not of our modern theological manuals, at least of the liturgy itself — it is this communion with God by means of "matter" that reveals the true meaning of "matter," i.e., of the world itself. We can only worship in time, yet it is worship that ultimately not only reveals the meaning of time, but truly "renews" time itself. There is no worship without the participation of the body, without words and silence, light and darkness, movement and stillness — yet it is in and through worship that all these essential expressions of man in his relation to the world are given their ultimate "term" of reference, revealed in their highest and deepest meaning.
>
> Thus the term "sacramental" means that for the world to be means of worship and means of grace is not accidental, but the revelation of its meaning, the restoration of its essence, the fulfillment of its destiny. It is the "natural sacramentality" of the world that finds expression in worship and makes the latter the essential ἔργον [work] of man, the foundation and the spring of his life and activities as man. Being the epiphany of God, worship is thus the epiphany of the world; being communion with God, it is the only true communion with the world; being knowledge of God, it is the ultimate fulfillment of all human knowledge. (121)

---

3. Schmemann's argument here echoes and explicitly appeals to that made by Henri de Lubac, especially in his *Corpus Mysticum: The Eucharist and the Church in the Middle Ages* (Notre Dame: University of Notre Dame Press, 2007).

In sum, for Schmemann the movement toward God in Christ is not something tacked on, as it were, to a space and time and matter originally constituted in abstraction from this movement. On the contrary, the movement toward God in Christ lies at the core of these in their original constitution, and hence in their original meaning precisely *as* space and *as* time and *as* matter.[4]

It is important to see that the "continuity" of the Christian *leitourgia* with the whole of man's natural worship and indeed with what Schmemann terms the "ontological sacramentality" of creation "includes in itself an equally essential principle of *discontinuity*" (122). To use my own language, the orders of redemption and of creation remain distinct; but the pertinent point emphasized by Schmemann is that the Church and the cosmos are nonetheless still brought into being *from their beginning with the same end*.[5] Hence, although the world, as distinct from the Church, is not yet a sacrament in the proper sense, it remains dynamically ordered, precisely in its original ontological creatureliness, toward sacrament in the proper sense.

The sacramental or symbolic nature of the world-cosmos presupposes this simultaneous, albeit paradoxical, continuity within discontinuity of the Church-sacrament and the world.

Schmemann emphasizes how the discontinuity between sacrament and world is intensified by the world's rejection of "its own destiny and fulfillment" (122). Thus he says that,

> if the basis of all Christian worship is the Incarnation, its true content is always the Cross and the Resurrection. Through these events the new life in Christ, the Incarnate Lord, is "hid with Christ in God," and made into a life "not of this world." The world which rejected Christ must itself die in man if it is to become again means of communion,

---

4. See Psalm 104 and the Canticle of Daniel 3:52-90. See also Emile Mersch, *Morale et Corps Mystique,* 4th ed. (Brussels: Desclée de Brouwer, 1955): "Every being in itself and through its structure is a limitless submission. It is created; that is to say, its very existence, being a relation, is a dependence and a homage. The universe is only cult and religion. . . . But, it must be carefully noted, [the] ordinary sense [of religion] runs the risk of dwarfing the real meaning. Religion is not merely a human phenomenon; it is but the new and infinitely more elevated expression taken in us by a manner of being which is necessarily the manner of being of all things. So, the different aspects which it assumes in us are in continuity with the constitution of the universe" (p. 28).

5. Cf. Colossians 1:15-18; *Gaudium et Spes,* n. 22; John Paul II, *Dominum et Vivificantem,* n. 50.

means of participation in the life which shone forth from the grave, in the Kingdom which is not "of this world," and which in terms of this world is still to come. (122)

Hence his summary conclusion:

> It is only because the Church's *leitourgia* is always cosmic, i.e., assumes into Christ all creation, and is always historical, i.e., assumes into Christ all time, that it can therefore also be eschatological, i.e., make us true participants of the Kingdom to come.
>
> Such then is the idea of man's relation to the world implied in the very notion of worship. Worship is by definition and act a reality with cosmic, historical, and eschatological dimensions, the expression thus not merely of "piety," but of an all-embracing "world view." (123)

Thus, to resume the problem of secularism: "[a] modern secularist quite often accepts the idea of God. What, however, he emphatically negates is precisely the sacramentality of man and the world" (124).

II.

Elsewhere in *For the Life of the World*, Schmemann indicates the centrality of the nuptial relation, or the sacrament of matrimony, in understanding the biblical idea of God's relation in Christ to the world, and in turn the liturgical relation of the world to God (84). Schmemann suggests that, provided we understand this nuptial mystery in its properly theological terms, i.e., in terms of the relation between Christ and the Church, we can see that it bears "cosmic and universal dimensions," indeed, reveals itself "as the all-embracing mystery of being itself" (82). The cosmic dimension of the liturgical-nuptial love emphasized here by Schmemann is, in my opinion, captured nicely by what Pope John Paul II terms the "nuptial attribute" of the (human) body.[6]

The notion of "nuptiality" or "nuptial body" entails, in light of the foregoing, that the space, time, matter, and motion ingredient in the body

---

6. John Paul II, *Man and Woman He Created Them: A Theology of the Body*, trans. Michael Waldstein (Boston: Pauline Books and Media, 2006), pp. 131-225, at 183. In this notion of the body as nuptial, we see the root of the Pope's rejection of those moral theories that view the body as simply "premoral." See also here *Dominum et Vivificantem*, n. 50, on the "cosmic-flesh" implications of the Incarnation.

somehow themselves already, in their original structure as space, time, matter, and motion, bear an aptness for sacramental-nuptial love.

Schmemann emphasizes the link of the sacrament of matrimony, not with an "abstract theology of love," but with "the one who has always stood at the very heart of the Church's life as the purest expression of human love and response to God — Mary, the Mother of Jesus" (83).

> [I]n her love and obedience, in her faith and humility, [Mary] accepted to be what from all eternity all creation was meant and created to be: the temple of the Holy Spirit, the *humanity* of God. She accepted to give her body and blood — that is, her whole life — to be the body and blood of the Son of God, to be *mother* in the fullest and deepest sense of this world, giving her life to the Other and fulfilling her life in Him. She accepted the only true nature of each creature and all creation: to place the meaning and, therefore, the fulfillment of her life in God.
>
> In accepting this nature she fulfilled the *womanhood* of creation. This word will seem strange to many. In our time the Church, following the modern trend toward the "equality of the sexes," uses only one-half of the Christian revelation about man and woman, the one which affirms that in Christ there is neither "male nor female" (Gal. 3:28). The other half is ascribed again to an antiquated world view. In fact, however, all our attempts to find the "place of woman" in society (or in the Church) instead of exalting her, belittle woman, for they too often imply a denial of her specific vocation.
>
> Yet is it not significant that the relation between God and the world, between God and Israel, His chosen people, and finally between God and the cosmos restored in the Church, is expressed in the Bible in terms of marital union and love? . . . This means that the world . . . is the bride of God and that in sin this fundamental relationship has been broken, distorted. And it is in Mary — the Woman, the Virgin, the Mother — in her response to God, that the Church has its living and personal beginning. This response is total obedience in love; not obedience *and* love, but the wholeness of the one as the totality of the other. (83-84)

Schmemann goes on:

> [I]n the "natural" world, the bearer of this obedient love, of this love as response, is the woman. . . . This acceptance is not passivity, blind submission, because it is love, and love is always active. It gives life to the

> proposal of man, fulfills it as life, yet it becomes fully love and fully life only when it is fully *acceptance* and *response*. This is why the whole creation, the whole Church — and not only women — find the expression of their response and obedience to God in Mary the Woman, and rejoice in her. She stands for all of us. . . . For man can be truly man — that is, . . . the priest and minister of God's creativity and initiative — only when he does not posit himself as the "owner" of creation and submits himself — in obedience and love — to its nature as the bride of God, in *response* and *acceptance*. (85)

Indeed, recalling the tradition that refers to Mary as the "new Eve," Schmemann locates the first Eve's sin precisely in her failure "to be a woman" (85). That is, in words that are bound to "scandalize" today, and which will be treated in sustained fashion below, Schmemann says that Eve "took the initiative" and thereby, paradoxically, "made herself, and also the man whose 'eve' she was, the slaves of her 'femininity'": she was now to be "ruled over," "possessed," and made into an "instrument of procreation" by man (85). The first Eve, then, contrasts exactly with Mary, who, in her *"fiat,"* in obedient love and loving obedience, awaited "the initiative of the Other" (86).

> The light of an eternal spring comes to us when on the day of annunciation we hear the decisive: "Behold the handmaid of the Lord, be it done unto me according to thy Word" (Lk 1:38). This is the whole creation, all of humanity, and each one of us recognizing the words that express our ultimate nature and being, our acceptance to be the bride of God. . . . (86)

III.

Needless to say, and as already suggested, the terms of Schmemann's argument here are difficult and controversial in our contemporary cultural setting. My proposal, however, is that this is so above all because of the long tradition in the West that has generated and continues to sustain an abstract notion of the cosmos, a tradition that has its origin in a decisive sense in Christian theology itself. The crucial point is that it is a secularizing tendency within Christian theology itself (as indicated by Schmemann, and by Henri de Lubac and indeed Hans Urs von Balthasar) that has led in decisive ways to the failure to see that the cosmos is destined for holiness, precisely in its original-constitutive *order*.[7]

The core of the problem is a theology — and in turn an ontology, an anthropology, and a cosmology — from which the liturgy, nuptiality, and Mary have been originally abstracted, that is, *separated*. Given this separation, any relationality that entails the asymmetry indicated in obedience and feminine responsiveness can (rightly) appear now to be little more than a "romantic" or "moralistic," not to say arbitrary and even dehumanizing, *imposition* on reality. This, in a word, is the consequence of the dualism between sacrament and world discussed above (or, in Balthasar's terms, between theology, or intelligent order, and sanctity). By definition, this dualism, from the side of both the Church and the world, makes these features entailed in liturgy, nuptiality, and Mary into "private," "pietistic," "positivistic" matters from which the realism of the cosmic order of things has always already been removed.

Here, then, is the overarching point: continued or renewed insistence (e.g., by Christians) on a piety that is without an intrinsically liturgical, nuptial, and Marian sense of cosmic-cultural order is in the end little more helpful in resolving the crisis of our time than is continued insistence (e.g., by "secularists") on an order that is not intrinsically oriented toward a liturgical, nuptial, and Marian *piety*. For, again, the point is that moralistic-voluntaristic *piety* and formalistic-mechanistic *order* are but different expressions of the same abstract understanding of the cosmos that lies at the source of current difficulties.

This is what is meant by the suggestion, following Schmemann, that the problem of our time, as it affects both religion and secularity, originates in the loss of the inherently symbolic dimension of the creaturely order of things and persons. The task of Christians today is thus to recover an ontology bearing an intrinsic openness to liturgy, nuptiality, and Mary (symbolic ontology), and simultaneously to understand liturgy, nuptiality, and Mary in their full ontological sacramentality. The task is to recover an

---

7. Regarding Balthasar, see his "Theology and Sanctity," in *The Word Became Flesh* (San Francisco: Ignatius Press, 1989), pp. 181-209, which discusses the growing divorce, beginning in the epoch following St. Thomas and St. Bonaventure, between the *order* of things (of intelligence and the cosmos) as revealed in and through the Church, and the *life of piety* (cf. the *devotio moderna*). See also Michael Buckley, *At the Origins of Modern Atheism* (New Haven: Yale University Press, 1987), which makes this case in a more "Rahnerian" manner.

ontological sense of the *relation* between the one and the Other disclosed in liturgy, nuptiality, and Mary.

IV.

But we need now to define more precisely what is meant by symbolic, and indeed to show how Mary, in her concrete historical reality as Virgin-Mother of God, reveals the deepest meaning of "symbolic." And we need to show further how this symbolic ontology meets some of the serious issues of our age, for example, those raised by feminism.

(1) Regarding the symbolic character of created being: in light of the above, I take this to mean that being is always a being-*with* that presupposes a *mutual but asymmetrical relation between the one and the Other*.

(2) This relation that structures creaturely being has its archetype in Mary — not Mary as an "accidental" occasion or illustration, but rather as the unique mother of the unique Son of God, who, precisely as such, as the second Eve, is herself the singular symbol in which history (being) has its proper symbolic meaning. Mary, in her concrete *fiat* and *Magnificat* and in her unique reality as *Theotokos*, bears the destined meaning of the created universe already in its original creaturely order, in the one concrete order of history.

In sum, the symbolic nature of creaturely being signifies that the original character of being is a *being-given;* and that the singular historical person, thus Mary of Nazareth, is the one in whom the meaning of this being-as-gift is, in the order of creatures, first and most fully, or archetypically, realized.[8]

It will suffice in the present chapter to present schematically some main implications of these assertions relative to what was identified earlier as our problematic "culture of abstraction."

---

8. Of course, in another and still more basic sense, Jesus Christ, the child of God, the "first-born of creatures" (Col. 1:15), is the one in whom being-as-gift is first and most properly revealed. And yet, in the "economic" order, since the "permission" (free *fiat*) of a woman is the anterior condition for the incarnation of the Son of God, her nuptiality takes a certain precedence even over Christ's filiality in this order. However, it is beyond our purposes to sort out thematically here this question of the relative priority of nuptiality and filiality in the basic revelation of (creaturely) being-as-gift. Mary's fruitfulness is a consequence of her obedience, even as her capacity for radical obedience (immaculate conception) is a gift ordered to fulfillment in sponsality and motherhood.

(3) As already indicated throughout the foregoing discussion, the term "abstraction" signals an absence, or inadequate sense, of relation, that is, of relation in its original asymmetrical meaning. This inadequate sense of relation has typically taken the form in modern Western culture of an emphasis on individual autonomy and freedom, initiative and creativity, self-determination, self-reflexivity, and indeed self-love: all of these are taken to indicate the dignity and worth of the individual human person. My proposal presupposes that all of the features noted here are essential to any adequate understanding of creaturely being. It is emphatically true that, without individual initiative and autonomy and the other features noted, creatures would not and could not, finally, have any genuine dignity. The intention of my proposal is not at all to deny this, but on the contrary simply to insist that we need to insert *an asymmetrical "with"* within the original structure of creaturely initiative and autonomy (freedom, self-determination, self-love, and so on), an asymmetrical "with" whose meaning is disclosed to us symbolically, in the manner realized most properly in liturgy, nuptiality, and Mary.

My task, then, is both to indicate what this means, and to show how this symbolic rendering of creaturely initiative and autonomy in the end recuperates initiative and autonomy, indeed deepens these, albeit *while transforming the basic meaning typically given them in the West.*

Let me begin by recalling what was said above regarding Mary. Mary lets God be effective in her *(fiat);* she herself magnifies God, becoming effective, simultaneously albeit "subordinately," *with* God *(Magnificat);* and this simultaneous, mutual, but asymmetrical relation with God, this filial and nuptial relation, is fruitful: it results in Mary's unique virginal motherhood of the Son of God *(Theotokos).*

Key here is the intrinsic link between Mary's *Magnificat* and her becoming the *Theotokos* on the one hand, and her utterance of the *fiat* on the other. That is, we need to see the "perichoretic" unity among these *that is coincident with the order that begins with the fiat.* Mary's *fiat* expresses the *response* that reveals God's *initiative* as *gift.* As a consequence (ontological, not temporal) of this obedient, contemplative-active response, she *shares immediately* in this *initiative-gift.* She becomes a giver *simultaneously in subordination to,* and *with,* the divine Giver: she magnifies the Lord, and immediately begins herself to be magnified in and with the Lord. Mary becomes what, on her own, she was not: a mother, the co-creator of new life. Indeed, she becomes the co-creator of the divine-incarnate Son of God himself.

All of this is richly expressed in the Gospel of Luke:

Behold, I am the handmaid [δούλη] of the Lord; let it be to me according to your word. (Luke 1:38)

Blessed [εὐλογημένη] are you among women, and blessed is the fruit of your womb! (Luke 1:42)

My soul magnifies [μεγαλύνει] the Lord, and my spirit rejoices in God my Savior, for he has regarded the low estate [ταπείνωσιν] of his handmaiden. For behold, all generations will call me blessed; for he who is mighty has done great things for me [ἐποίησέν μοι μεγάλα ὁ δυνατός], and holy is his name. . . . He has shown his strength with his arm, he has scattered the proud in the imagination of their hearts, he has put down the mighty [δυνάστας] from their thrones, and exalted those of low degree; he has filled the hungry with good things, and the rich he has sent empty away. (Luke 1:46-53)

Mary, as interpreted in these texts, reveals archetypically at least three features indicating the original symbolic structure of creaturely being. To use the language of ontology, Mary reveals the original and abiding asymmetry in the creature's relation to God *(fiat)*; she reveals the ontologically *consequent-but-simultaneous* mutuality in that asymmetrical relation *(Magnificat)*; and she reveals the (inherent) fruitfulness of this asymmetrical-mutual relation *(Theotokos)*. To be sure, Mary reveals these in a singular way, utterly unlike that of any other creature: her responsiveness is sinless, wholly transparent to God's initiative; her mutuality with God involves a literal unity with the divine person within her; and her fruitfulness consists literally in giving birth to the divine Son of God himself. My assumption, with Schmemann and Pope John Paul II, among others, is that Mary nonetheless is archetypical for all creaturely being, male and female. God offers to all creatures, from the beginning of their existence, a genuine participation in what takes place uniquely in Mary.

Presupposing this analogy — real unity within greater difference — between Mary and all other creatures, our proposal is that the symbolic-nuptial structure of creaturely being, that is, the peculiar "with" that structures the creature, signifies an asymmetrical-mutual relationality that is inherently creative and fruitful. In a word, Mary reveals to us the paradox that it is precisely in subordination to the Other that one *assumes the power of* the Other enabling one to be *genuinely creative and fruitful with the*

Other in a way utterly beyond what one can create or produce on one's own — that is, to be creative and powerful in some significant sense with the generativity and power of God himself![9]

V.

What, then, does all this imply with respect to the original meaning of the initiative and autonomy and self-determination that are proper to the creature?

The urgency of this question is already clear from what was said above about the (rightful) emphasis on these features in contemporary thought and culture. But the urgency is of course intensified when, as indicated above in Schmemann's reference to the "*womanhood* of creation," we assign the "subordination" implied in asymmetry primarily to the feminine. The "subordinate" asymmetry indicated in the symbolic-nuptial structure of creaturely being is seen by many both to threaten any genuine *partnership* between the creature and God in carrying on the work of creation, and, further, insofar as this asymmetry is disclosed first in reference to women, also to undercut any genuine *equality* between men and women. How does our interpretation of Mary above help to address the quite legitimate concerns voiced here? Again, given present limits, we can answer this question only schematically.

Perhaps it is best to begin by stating the obvious: namely, that the only adequate way, finally, to deal with the concerns raised is to go to the heart of what it means for a creature to be and to act. And the crucially relevant point in this connection is to see that, for a creature, being a self, an individual substance, is also, from the beginning, a *being-given-by-Another*, hence a *being-from-Another;* and to see consequently that creaturely individual initiative and autonomy are *originally and constitutively gifts-by-and-from-Another.* The paradox here is fundamental and ineliminable. All of the things dear to myself — my individual autonomy and singular freedom and creativity — are due, originally and constitutively, to the effective presence of the Other in me. The paradox, then, con-

---

9. I should perhaps add here, for greater precision and completeness: it does not suffice to say merely that the creature participates subordinately in God's "power." For the point, left implicit here, is that God's power *itself* includes a "subordination," albeit a different, asymmetrical one, insofar as he brings something about, and at that instant *presupposes* what he brings about as a factor in then giving a *more,* a *plus* beyond even the original gift.

sists in the fact that the "*self*-centeredness" implied in individual autonomy and freedom, self-determination, self-love, and creativity remains in place, but with a transformed meaning, such that it is at the same time, anteriorly, an *Other*-centeredness.

The "asymmetrical-mutual with" at the heart of the self, then, signifies a relation of the self to the Other that grants absolute primacy to the Other even as it simultaneously includes a *relative* primacy of the self within that absolute primacy. The self-centeredness characteristic of legitimate autonomy is retained even as it is turned on its head. In short, the creaturely self, precisely as its own individual self, is constitutively also anteriorly a reference to Another.

All that I want to say concerning the recuperation of the self's initiative and autonomy is expressed in the paradox indicated here. The crucial point is that this initiative and autonomy are genuinely recuperated, but only simultaneously *in reference to Another*. Creaturely initiative always and everywhere bears within it a *relation to the Other* that makes that initiative, from the beginning and all along the way, an initiative *from, in, and with the Other:* makes creaturely initiative originally and constitutively symbolic.[10]

But further, and the point is decisive, this original creaturely initiative, which is always an initiative-in-reference-to-Another, just so far becomes creative and powerful beyond what is possible for it on its own: beyond what individual initiative is capable of *without* the creativity and power of the Other. In sum, as already stated above, creaturely initiative, in its symbolic-nuptial understanding, becomes creative and powerful in some significant sense with the generativity and power of God himself.[11]

Let me now note briefly some important implications of these general assertions.

---

10. Cf. note 24 of "The Embodied Person as Gift and the Cultural Task in America," pp. 256-57 above, for an extended discussion concerning the receptive or responsive creativity of the creature.

11. Again, recalling note 9, it may be useful to emphasize that it is not a question here simply of a shared power in the creature versus "sheer" power in God. Rather, God's "sheer" power is *also* affected (without loss of integrity!) by its being-shared. The *fruit* is more than what the creature can do alone and, *in a certain sense,* more than what God does alone. The fruit is the fruit of the gift as one with the Giver *in* its (the gift's) *givenness.* For a helpful discussion, and abundant sources, pertinent to the issue raised here, cf. Gerard O'Hanlon's *The Immutability of God in the Theology of Hans Urs von Balthasar* (Cambridge: Cambridge University Press, 1990).

VI.

(1) Perhaps most fundamentally, the constitutive "addition" of asymmetrical-mutual reference to Another in the original meaning of creaturely initiative entails a re-definition of that meaning in terms of a primacy of love, of beauty, and of drama.

Love signals the *relationality* that is constitutive of creaturely initiative. Relationality is something always already immanent within creaturely initiative and not something first simply effected by creaturely initiative. *Beauty* signals the primacy of the Other as giver, of the Other thus as attractive in a way that is inclusive of the attractiveness of the self as gifted. *Drama* signals the irreducible *polarity* in the creature's original relationality with God. Drama indicates the intended simultaneous, albeit always asymmetrical, deepening of the participatory and the creative character of the creature's initiative in relation to God.

(2) Creaturely power begins in wonder and gratitude before the inherent beauty of the Other. The power of creaturely being originates and consists primarily in the beauty of the Other: it is *the attractiveness of the Other become effective in me* (the self). The paradox indicated here is staggering. Creaturely power begins in and presupposes all along the way precisely "littleness" (δούλη, ταπείνωσιν), but the pertinent point is that this littleness turns immediately into genuine power (δυνατός). It does so by virtue of the beauty that is made effective in me, and immediately-also now *with* me and *through* me, paradoxically by that very littleness, by the littleness that constitutes me as a "handmaid," one whose being is structurally subordinate to the Other.[12] What this implies, further, is that the creature becomes powerful, in the authentic loving sense, precisely through obedience, which, as the foregoing makes clear, is thus ontological before it is moral.

(3) Here, then, we can see the intrinsic link between creaturely power and the poor and vulnerable ones of the Gospel, those who are exalted in Mary's *Magnificat* and in the Beatitudes. And we can see as well the original and deepest meaning of creaturely-cosmic "liberation": "Mary is totally dependent upon God and completely directed towards him, and, at the side of her Son, she is *the most perfect image of freedom and of the liber-*

---

12. Once again: "littleness" simultaneously guarantees and transforms the meaning of *creaturely* power, and, in so doing, *also* reveals the authentic nature of God's power as including "kenosis" — again, without loss of integrity (cf. notes 9 and 11 above).

ation of humanity and of the universe. It is to her as Mother and Model that the Church must look in order to understand in its completeness the meaning of her own mission" (*Redemptoris Mater*, n. 37).

Authentic liberation, in other words, begins in the *fiat*, and is intrinsically ordered to the power of the *Magnificat* that enables the vulnerable and the poor, the weak and the suffering, to become themselves creative and powerful precisely *with the power of God*, which is to say, with the power of a love that is intended to be inclusive-transformative of the poor and the vulnerable in the whole of their embodied, cosmic-cultural reality. Here is indicated the relevant criticism of the "worldly" liberations of both the left and the right: of socialism which, lacking the depth-giving patience (not passivity) of Mary, would liberate economic-political structures precipitously and "violently," through external, and just so far superficial, manipulation; and also of neoliberal capitalism which, lacking the same Marian patience as a matter of original creaturely *order,* invariably inclines toward the commodifying and moralizing of economic-political liberation.

VII.

But let me now illustrate the significance of the foregoing argument in terms of the work of an important figure in American feminist theology, Elizabeth Johnson of Fordham University. I will proceed simply by citing several texts at length, since I believe the texts themselves bring effectively into relief the critical issues raised by her work relative to my argument.

> In what sense can it be claimed that God has "dimensions," let alone dualistically conceived dimensions of masculine and feminine? Such an idea extends human division to the godhead itself. It actually ontologizes sex in God, making sexuality a dimension of divine being, rather than respecting the symbolic nature of religious language.[13]

> Not just Mary's vocation but that of every woman — and man — is to partner Holy Wisdom in bringing about the reign of mercy and peaceful justice. Relieved of her historical burden as complement to the patriarchal divine and positively signaling the depth of women's dignity vis-à-vis God, Mary becomes free to rejoin us in the communion of saints. (319)

13. Elizabeth Johnson, *She Who Is* (New York: Crossroad, 1992), p. 54.

Mary is a friend of God and a prophet within the communion of saints.[14]

Hans Urs von Balthasar takes this approach, arguing that in the church there is a Marian principle of holy obedience complementary to the Petrine principle of orderly hierarchical rule. This Marian principle indicates that women ought to divest themselves of self-will in order to be obedient to the word of God as articulated by male authority figures. . . .

Perhaps the most widely-heard proponent of this view is Pope John Paul II. . . . Like Mary, he [says], all women are oriented toward giving love without measure once they have received it. Like Mary, all women are to be mothers, either physically or spiritually (virgins). In Mary, women see mirrored the highest virtues to which they are called, which the Pope delineates as "the self-offering totality of love; the strength that is capable of bearing the greatest sorrows; limitless fidelity and tireless devotion to work; the ability to combine penetrating intuition with words of support and encouragement."[15]

As these examples demonstrate, the notion of Mary as the ideal feminine inevitably leads to the subordination of women and the privileging of men spiritually, psychologically and politically. Much of women's negative reaction to this image of Mary stems from the realization that this feminine ideal functions as an obstacle to personal growth, preventing the development of a critical intellect, capacity for righteous anger, and other characteristics of a mature personality. Living "femininely" can even be dangerous to one's health and life, inculcating passivity in abusive and violent situations. The rigid definition of the feminine, when applied to social roles, also blocks women from functioning in the public order, for by nature they are designed for domestic auxiliary roles. (319-20)

An adequate theology of Mary for the third millennium must be clear on this point: there is no eternal feminine; there is no objective, essen-

---

14. Elizabeth Johnson, "Mary, Friend of God and Prophet: A Critical Reading of the Marian Tradition," *Theology Digest* 47, no. 4 (Winter 2000): 317-25, at 317. This is the annual Aquinas Lecture of the Aquinas Institute of Theology, Saint Louis University, given by Johnson in January 2000. All subsequent citations in the text are from this lecture.
15. *Redemptoris Mater*, n. 46. Johnson also refers to *Mulieris Dignitatem* in her argument here.

tial feminine nature; there is no ideal woman. The very notion of the feminine is a product of patriarchal thinking intended to keep women in their so-called proper "place." In contrast to dualistic anthropology that so separates head and heart, a liberating view of Mary grows out of an egalitarian anthropology of partnership. In no way does this stance negate differences between women and men, but it refuses to make sex the sole primary marker of personal identity or to use sex to stereotype a person's characteristics. Rather, it affirms that sex combines with race, class, ethnicity, sexual orientation; historical, geographical, and social location; and cultural makeup to define each person as unique. We all exist as human persons with multiple differences. Indeed, differences among women as a group can be even greater than differences between some women and some men.

Relieved of the burden of being the ideal feminine woman, Mary can be simply herself. A poor woman singing her Magnificat about the downfall of tyrants and full bellies for the hungry, she takes another step toward rejoining us in the communion of saints. (320)[16]

Further, regarding the *Magnificat*, Johnson says that "Mary's faith-filled partnership with God in the work of liberation is underscored in her *Magnificat*. . . ." She concludes by saying that

[i]t does no honor to reduce [Mary's] faith to a privatized piety or, worse yet, a doting mother-son relationship. . . . Interpreting this Jewish village woman of faith as friend of God and prophet allows her dangerous memory to inspire our own lives. . . . To relate to Miriam of Nazareth as a partner in hope in the company of all the holy women and men who have gone before us; to reclaim the power of her memory for the flourishing of suffering people . . . — these results of a critical reading of the Marian tradition are of immeasurable benefit. When the Christian community remembers like this, our eyes are opened to sacred visions for a different future. (324)

---

16. Thus Johnson suggests a new understanding of the communion of saints based on a "companionship" as distinct from "patron-client" model, whereby those who have died remain "friends and colleagues of the living in one Spirit-filled community" (pp. 320-21). Note here, she says, "the mutual give and take that recognizes difference but shares the same call to faithful discipleship" (p. 321). "This is not to say that we no longer call upon saints to pray for us; but this prayer occurs in a context of mutual sharing in the project of the reign of God" (p. 321).

Liturgy and the Integrity of Cosmic Order | 305

Given present limits, I restrict myself to two comments in response to Johnson's argument. (1) First and above all, her argument turns us back to the question of the nature and most proper meaning of creaturely love and indeed of beauty. In terms of our proposal as developed above: How deeply within the structure of the self do we root reference to Another, and how are this reference and its implications best to be understood? Johnson's answer, defended in terms of an interpretation of Mary, is given the name of partnership: Mary "partners Holy Wisdom in bringing about the reign of mercy and peaceful justice." The term "partnership," of course, suggests equality, or simple symmetry, between the partners. And it suggests further a primacy of a certain sort of "autonomy."[17]

As indicated in our earlier argument, these features mentioned by Johnson, insofar as they all signal a basic sense of independence, are surely legitimate indicators of what she calls the "mature personality." However, this still leaves the question, raised earlier, concerning the basic terms in which this maturity or independence is best to be conceived. In scriptural terms, the question concerns the meaning of what is traditionally translated as "handmaid" (δούλη): How does one translate this into a "partner" who is without inner "subordination" or indeed "low estate" (ταπείνωσιν), unless one begins by assuming that the "lowliness" indicated in the Greek is simply a function of the social-historical conditions of the time — which assumption of course presupposes exactly what is in dispute, and indeed begs the following question?[18] In theological-ontological terms, the question concerns the implications of creation *ex nihilo* as understood in Christianity. What does it mean for a being to be in its origin *wholly from-Another,* even as it simultaneously thereby comes into its *own* being? How are we to understand the rightful autonomy or "self-ownership" of such a being?

My own answer has been given: the rightful autonomy or independence of the creature indicates an "asymmetrical with," and indeed "subordination," implicit in the creature's original and abiding *being-given:* requires, that is, an original and abiding *symbolic* structure.

Clearly, the issue raised here is a difficult one, but it is hardly arcane.

---

17. See the interrelation among the various features of the person privileged by Johnson as marks of the "mature personality" who is apt for the "public" realm: for example, critical intellect, assertiveness, independence, ability to make decisions, righteous anger, and so on.

18. Johnson does refer to Mary as a "poor and common woman," but the relevant point is that "poor and common" are not integrated into the basic meaning she accords to partnership.

What is at stake is the question of how deeply in the human person *service* and *gratitude* to the Other, and *wonder* before the (inherent) beauty of the Other — all of which are essential features of love — are to be found. The issue in the end comes down to the question of whether love is something first *given to* the creature, and just so far present already in the creature's original structure, or whether love is rather *something first chosen* or *effected by* the creature.[19]

In short, if I may so put it, what is risked in the idea of a partnership that is not innerly qualified by "handmaidship" is a slip into a kind of ontological "pelagianism" that removes the Other-centeredness that lies at the core of, and accords the original and abiding meaning to, the creature's rightful *self-centeredness*.[20]

(2) But, secondly, it is important to see the paradox that emerges here. For it should be clear that the line of criticism introduced with respect to Johnson in fact echoes the criticism offered by Schmemann with respect to the secularizing trend within "traditional" theology itself, in the latter's failure to integrate liturgy, nuptiality, and Mary, hence symbolism, sufficiently into its original understanding of cosmic and cultural *order*. Johnson's argument, in other words, itself continues in significant ways the dualism between sacrament and the world, intelligent order and sanctity that Schmemann and Balthasar have insisted is characteristic of much of modern Western Christian theology. In coming to terms with Johnson's argument, therefore, we need to take account of at least two consequences of this paradoxical fact.

On the one hand, this paradox implies that an adequate assessment of Johnson's feminist theology just so far invites a renewed scrutiny also of the "traditional" theology criticized by Schmemann. Viewed from the fundamental theological-ontological perspective sketched earlier, we should see that this theology itself does not so much oppose as actually make ready the road taken in Johnson's feminism. What is taken to be traditional theology in the modern period in fact, in its failure to order things intrin-

---

19. Cf. David C. Schindler, "Freedom Beyond Our Choosing: Augustine on the Will and Its Objects," *Communio: International Catholic Review* 29, no. 4 (Winter 2002): 618-53.

20. Again, this does not involve self-alienation, because the creature is a gift having an inner order in which self-centeredness is anchored in Another who is so "selfless" as to give me selfhood as a gift to be given — the original meaning, then, of creativity! Note that "handmaidship," shown in its perfection in Mary, is a creaturely paradigm that properly characterizes the being of men and women alike, though in distinct ways. In this connection, see "The Embodied Person as Gift and the Cultural Task in America."

sically toward and from the symbolism indicated in liturgy, nuptiality, and Mary, *just so far* inclines *ontologically* toward an inadequate sense of creaturely autonomy, and indeed toward an inadequate sense of the masculine as the privileged carrier of this autonomy. We must acknowledge, therefore, that there has existed in recent centuries an ontological disposition toward what Johnson identifies as "patriarchy," "paternalism," and "clericalism." Her criticisms here are not without foundation.

To be sure, the theology criticized by Schmemann typically contains a deep sense of liturgical and indeed Marian piety. But that is just the burden of Schmemann's criticism: Mary and the liturgy, and the nuptiality implied in these, were not integrated sufficiently into the *intelligent-cosmic order* of things.[21] The neuralgic point is that this tradition failed precisely to understand the *legitimate autonomy* of *creaturely reality* from the beginning in its inherently *symbolic* structure.

The point, in sum, is that a merely "pious" response to Johnson, a response, in other words, that remains only moral or positivistic rather than genuinely theological and ontological in character, in the end only begs the seriousness of the questions raised by her concerns.

But the paradox indicated here also cuts the other way. For Johnson herself, on the above reading and however unwittingly, continues to assume exactly the wrong elements in the tradition. Rather than challenging the false sense of autonomy, and indeed of the abstract masculinity as generated and sustained by this false sense of autonomy, she moves instead now simply to "democratize" this autonomy. This false autonomy, which was formerly largely restricted, as a matter of theological-ontological *order*, to men, and indeed often checked by an accompanying liturgical-nuptial-Marian piety, now becomes unrestricted and unchecked: it is available to all, women *and* men. All of us are now equal partners in our autonomy; none of us is a "handmaid."

The problem, of course, at least from the point of view argued earlier, is that such a way of proceeding prevents us from reaching all the way to the source of the older ontologic of clericalism. Indeed, this way of proceeding succeeds for the most part only in democratizing the problem. Formerly restricted largely to the "right," the logic of clericalism, which,

---

21. The point here of course is quite relevant to the decision at the Second Vatican Council to place its reflection on Mary within its ecclesiology (ecclesial order) *(Lumen Gentium)*. Cf. in this connection the article by Joseph Ratzinger, "Thoughts on the Place of Marian Doctrine and Piety in Faith and Theology as a Whole," *Communio: International Catholic Review* 30, no. 1 (Spring 2003): 147-60.

again, consists in a juridical-male power insufficiently integrated in and by liturgical-Marian love, beauty, and drama, now becomes a "prerogative" of both the "right" and the "left." The centralized authority of the old clericalism gives way to the decentralized authority of the new clericalism of a Church governed by "experts," commissions, committees, procedures, media strategies, computers and technology (emails, cell phones, social networking websites), multiple assemblies, and much chatter.[22] As Balthasar once put it, the decentralization of the Roman curia has led directly to the "curialization" of the diocese.[23]

The upshot of Johnson's failure to challenge much of modern-traditionalist theology's inadequate ontology of autonomy, in sum, is that she offers what in the end appears to be little more than a democratic "feminist" version of precisely what is most objectionable in the older ontology: its logic of autonomy. In a word, her manner of proceeding assumes just the dialectical opposition between subordination and autonomy that lies at the heart of that earlier logic.

My own response to Johnson and her many legitimate concerns has been indicated. We need to challenge more radically the modern sense of ontological and cosmic order, by recuperating this order more fully in light of liturgical, Marian symbolism. Johnson's "egalitarian" or symmetrical approach to the question of the relation between women and men, however paradoxically, retains a significant aspect of the dualism rejected, at

22. All of which, without life- and depth-giving (liturgical, nuptial, Marian) patience, produce only more *mechanisms*, not *organisms*. In connection with the general point made here, see Eugene McCarraher, "Smile, When You Say 'Laity': The Hidden Triumph of the Consumer Ethos," *Commonweal* (12 September 1997), pp. 21-25; and the symposium in response to McCarraher, "Smile, When You Say 'Starbucks,'" *Commonweal* (21 November 1997), pp. 12-19. McCarraher, however, does not describe in terms of clericalism the phenomenon of what he refers to as the new authority-style of the "Church Mellow." I should perhaps emphasize that I offer my criticism of clericalism here in what I take to be the spirit of Georges Bernanos, Charles Péguy, Madeleine Delbrêl, and Dorothy Day, in addition to Balthasar. Consistent with the criticisms of these persons, my own criticism does not intend to blur or attenuate the essential distinction between ordained and common priesthood in the Church, but only to argue for a new sense of the whole Church as integrated into an adequately liturgical, nuptial, Marian order, as the larger unified context within which this ineliminable distinction receives its proper and in fact deeper legitimacy. Regarding this integration, see the *Catechism of the Catholic Church*, n. 773: "Mary goes before us all in the holiness that is the Church's mystery as 'the bride without spot or wrinkle.' This is why the 'Marian' dimension of the Church precedes the Petrine.'"

23. Cf. Balthasar's *The Laity and the Life of the Counsels* (San Francisco: Ignatius Press, 2004).

least by implication, in Schmemann's symbolic understanding of space, time, and matter, an understanding that is recapitulated in John Paul II's notion of the "nuptial body." On Johnson's reading, the differences between women and men can have no natural significance. The different bodies of women and men cannot serve in an intrinsic way as bearers, precisely *in* their physiological character, of any different symbolic meaning. It is difficult to see how such a notion of the body can avoid reducing in the end to the dumb-mechanical body of Descartes, whose dualism is a paradigm of the non-symbolic understanding[24] that it has been our burden to reject.

---

24. According to which the body reveals only itself and nothing else.

Living and Thinking Reality in Its Integrity: Originary Experience, God, and the Task of Education

Genuine thinking in today's culture occurs mostly *per accidens*. Contemporary thought, for example, theology, is often criticized for its uncritical appeal to experience. But this criticism is misguided insofar as it implies that thought today roots itself too deeply in experience. The problem, rather, is that contemporary thought presupposes too little experience: it is forgetful of experience in its original, most basic and catholic, meaning, and needs to be criticized above all for just this forgetfulness.

My purpose is to discuss what is meant by original or "originary" experience, and how it is bound up with thinking and living reality in its integrity, with a word about what this implies for education. The task is a daunting one. For originary experience, rightly understood, must be seen as open from its roots to the whole of reality, in terms not merely of the *sum* of things in their singularity, but also of the *integrated relation* among things that establishes them as an ordered whole and hence as a cosmos. Any essential aspect of experience that is ignored or left unaccounted for at the outset cannot simply be added later without risk of diminishing reality. Such ignorance or omission, in other words, disposes us toward, even as it presupposes, what is already a fragmented and reductive sense of reality, at once as a whole and in each of its "parts."

My argument is that the idea of originary experience implies engagement of the whole of our being with the whole of reality, with God at its center. More specifically, originary experience embeds a desire of man to say forever: to give the whole of himself irrevocably to the whole of God, in a way that involves the whole of creation.

I will begin by offering some preliminary observations and premises regarding the nature of experience, and follow this with an outline of the main philosophical and theological presuppositions operative in originary experience, rightly understood. I will then discuss the main terms of my argument. Finally, I will conclude with a reflection on the cultural and educational implications of the argument.

I.

(1) Every experience bears a universal meaning, in a singular way. By this I mean that experience is never meaningful only for myself in my individual subjectivity, and hence is never nominalistic in nature. Nor does experience ever bear a universal meaning in such a way that my individual subjectivity indicates what is merely an example of a universal meaning to which my individual subjectivity is "accidental." Experience, rather, bears meaning as a kind of *universale concretum et singulare*. Experience is a concrete whole whose meaning bears a universality *in* its singularity, and *qua* singular.

(2) "Experience" comes from the Latin term *experior*, to try, or to learn by trying. In one of its definitions, the dictionary states that experience is "the fact or state of having gained knowledge through direct observation or participation in events or particular activities." The German term for experience is *Erfahrung*, from *fahren*, to drive or travel; and thus *erfahren*, "to come to know, discover, suffer, undergo." My suggestion, then, is that experience in its root meaning involves anticipation, even as this anticipation presupposes a preliminary undergoing of a reality that is already initiated in me by another. It presupposes a reality *given to* me that is simultaneously *operative in* me. Indeed, experience in its originary structure anticipates the whole of reality — God and the order of being — even as that anticipation is always already mediated in and through encounter with singular others.

(3) Experience is a gaining of knowledge that always involves a surprise, but does so through an anterior *anamnesis*, or recollection, of the objective other, relation to whom has first been given to me. I thus always discover myself as already participating in this relation. Experience is a matter of the self's *having* relations only as a matter simultaneously and anteriorly of the self's *being* in relation.

Note that this notion of experience involves no "ontologism." That is, reality is not drawn out of or deduced from experience, as though it were simply a function of experience. Experience indeed involves anticipation of the whole of reality, but, again, only from inside an encounter with an other. Experience thus always incarnates a new historical event, via an analogical and not nominalist singularity.

As Balthasar puts it, experience is "not man's entry into himself *(Einfahren)*."[1] Rather, it is an entry into one's self only as the self has always already entered into, through being entered into by, the objectively given reality of the other.

(4) The foregoing implies that experience at its root is beyond the distinction between active and passive in the conventional sense. Experience is receptive, but in a way that involves active participation in the reception. It involves participation in the initiative of the other who has become effective in one's self. As the German verb *Empfangen* nicely captures, to receive is also to conceive (from the Latin, *con-cipere*: to take in, or *with;* to become pregnant). Experience involves "consciousness," which is to say, a "knowing with." Here we can note the French term *connaissance* which, as Paul Claudel suggests, is a *"con-naissance,"* a being born together with.[2] Further, as Balthasar points out in his interpretation of Aquinas, what is involved in experience is attunement to the whole of Being,[3] an ontological disposition that is most basically a *cum-sentire*, a "feeling with," or, in the Greek, a *sympatheia*, "feeling, undergoing, or indeed 'suffering,' with."

All of this implies that a "letting be" forms experience in its inmost structure. Experience is at root a matter of patient agency.

(5) Experience involves objectively informed subjectivity. Experience is a newly subjective event *of* an objective form or *logos*, an event that thus never occurs beneath or prior or "accidental" to this objective *logos*. (It is the failure to see this that characterizes the "modernist" conceptions of experience still prevalent today.)

It therefore falsifies the nature of both the subjective reality of the self and the objective reality of the other to talk of the self's experience in abstraction from the reality of the other objectified in that experience; or, from the opposite direction, to speak of the other primarily as a function, or simply as an *object*, of the self's own conscious activities and desires.[4]

---

1. Cf. Hans Urs von Balthasar, *The Glory of the Lord,* vol. I: *Seeing the Form* (San Francisco: Ignatius Press, 1982), p. 222.

2. Paul Claudel, *Poetic Art* (New York: Philosophical Library, 1948), p. 40.

3. Cf. *The Glory of the Lord,* vol. I, pp. 220ff.

4. That is, as though something of the thing in itself, the thing as its own subject, is not disclosed in the object. Such a view implies rejection of the "transcendental" meaning of being as true and good *in itself,* in its Thomistic sense. Which is to say, it signals the origin of an instrumentalist view of being and its truth and goodness.

II.

The foregoing sketch of originary experience presupposes a definite understanding of the ontological order of things, as open to the theological. All of being is a community that is first given to us, and established in us, by God as Creator. This ontological community is best conceived in terms of a relation of love, which consists most basically in the love of God for the world: "In this is love, not that we loved God but that he loved us . . ." (1 John 4:10).

The fact that an ontology is presupposed in our account of originary experience does not entail that experience is a matter of deduction from ontology. On the contrary, it is of the essence of ontology that its first principles, precisely by virtue of being first, are operative always and everywhere. The result in the present case is a kind of paradox. If these principles, as first, are operative in every time and place, then it follows that we do not have to *deduce* them from an objective account of being. On the contrary, *they will themselves always already be exercised in* our originary experience. Their truth will be operative, however unconsciously, in every experience by the subject. Experience itself, in other words, bears an ontology *in its distinctness as subjective.*

The key to my proposal, then, lies in pondering the ontological implications of the *givenness* of things as originally experienced. Three comments will help indicate these implications.

(1) First, human experience at its root is a matter of an inchoative knowing and seeking of God. God, as Aquinas says, is known implicitly in whatever is known, and loved implicitly in whatever is loved. This implies that relation to God has always already been initiated in me by God, in the very act of creating me, and that my seeking of God is at root already a "finding." This relation reaches to the inmost core of my being, and I participate from the beginning in the actualization of the relation as its subject in the created order. Being constituted in relation to God first by God, and being a substantial being in my own right, are not at root opposed. On the contrary, the two features together signify and express the generosity of God implied in his creating me.

This inchoative, implicit sense of God does not contain an intuition of God, and thus again it does not imply the kind of *a priori* knowledge that would warrant a charge of "ontologism."

The idea of our implicit knowledge of God is, in sum, captured well in the statement of Joseph Ratzinger that memory *(anamnesis)* of

God is "identical with the foundations of our being."[5] And it has its objective foundation in Aquinas's statement that "God is in all things, innermostly."[6]

(2) Second, the creature's constitutive relation to God implies a constitutive relation also to the whole of created being and to all created beings.[7] Key here is Aquinas's distinction between *esse*, or act of being, and *essentia*, or what being is. Creaturely *esse* is at once common to all created beings and itself substantially existent only in each individual being. Every creaturely being is related from within to the whole of being, always in and through a singular subject encountering other singular subjects.[8]

---

5. Cardinal Joseph Ratzinger, *Values in a Time of Upheaval* (New York: Crossroad, 2006), p. 92.

6. *ST* I, q. 8, a. 1.

7. Cf. the Pontifical Council for Justice and Peace, *Compendium of the Social Doctrine of the Church*, which, in n. 37, referring to the foundations of Christian anthropology, refers to "the constitutive social nature of human being, the prototype of which is found in the original relationship between man and woman, the union of whom 'constitutes the first form of communion between persons.'" See also the following statements: "The likeness with God shows that the essence and existence of man are constitutively related to God in the most profound manner. This is a relationship that exists in itself, it is therefore not something that comes afterwards and is not added from the outside" (n. 109); "[t]he relationship between God and man is reflected in the relational and social dimension of human nature" (n. 110). Regarding the meaning of "constitutive" relations, then: the act whereby each reality is at all, the act of *esse*, whose subject is always an individual substance, nonetheless remains "common" to all individual substances, in a way that mediates the relation of each to the Creator. Thus it is the very act by which each substance is created *in its singularity* that simultaneously establishes a *relation* among all substances. It follows, given a rightly conceived notion of the distinction between *esse* and substance, and of the fact of creation, that each individual substance's being *in itself* and being *in relation* always presuppose each other. These features are never in principle or at the deepest level a threat to each other. Again, this is so by virtue, not of a *dialectical* understanding of being (Hegel), but of a properly *analogical* understanding of being rooted in a "real distinction" between *esse* and substance that mediates the *"common"* relation of creation *uniquely* to each individual substance (Aquinas).

8. See Adrian Walker, "Personal Singularity and the *Communio Personarum*: A Creative Development of Thomas Aquinas's Doctrine of *Esse Commune*," *Communio: International Catholic Review* 31, no. 3 (Fall 2004): 456-79. Regarding relationality, see Pope Benedict's statements in *Caritas in Veritate* that "the development of peoples depends, above all, on a recognition that the human race is a single family . . ." (n. 53); and that "the Christian revelation of the unity of the human race presupposes a *metaphysical interpretation of the 'humanum'* in which relationality is an essential element" (n. 55).

(3) Third, the "real distinction," or difference, between *esse* and *essentia* or *substantia* mediates the generosity of the Creator to the creature. The creature in its basic structure is thereby disclosed as gift. This means that the creaturely giver, or actor, is always first *given*. Creaturely giving occurs first *as* and *through* an *active reception* of what has been given.

The "real distinction," which accounts for the reality of creaturely being as gift, is implicitly affirmed in our *originary experience* of the world. The self is given to itself at once *in itself* and *by another*. The human-personal experience on which Balthasar draws to show this is helpful. The child discovers the truth of his own being as good, or again the beauty of his being as given, through the radiation of the beauty of the mother become effective in the child. The child thus discovers his own reality as gift *in response* and *as actively responsive* to the attractiveness of the other that has been communicated to him and in which he simultaneously participates.

The experience of the self as gift, therefore — and note again the receptive or responsive character implied in the idea of gift as something *given* — lies most basically in a "letting be" of the self in relation to the other, in wonder. I experience the world most primitively not as something to be grasped at or possessed but to be gratefully received, something to which I myself am "owed," in love. My activity toward an other is inherently responsive, always "co-generated" in its roots by the attractiveness of the other become effective in me.[9] The self's originary experience rightly understood thus undercuts at its root any pelagian disposition toward the world, even as it affirms in non-reductive fashion the distinctness of my own agency.

In sum, we recuperate originary experience in its catholicity only in terms of a God-centered ontological order, appropriated via a grateful and wonder-filled letting be.

III.

But further, as announced at the outset, my thesis is that originary experience, rightly understood, implies a dynamic in the creature for saying for-

---

9. See in this connection David C. Schindler, "Freedom Beyond Our Choosing," *Communio: International Catholic Review* 29, no. 4 (Winter 2002): 618-53.

ever. The sense in which this is so can be seen by pondering further the radicality of that experience and its implied ontology. The "real distinction" undergirds what is our primitive experience of the whole of ourselves as gift. I experience the whole of myself as "owed" to an other, finally to an other who is inchoatively known as God. And I experience this owing as good, as a thing of attractiveness and beauty, hence as something relative to which I am spontaneously, even if at first not fully consciously, grateful and full of wonder. The crucial point is the wholeness implicit in this originary experience. It is the whole of my self that I experience implicitly as owed to another, finally to the Creator, in gratitude and wonder. I experience the whole of my natural life as owed to the giving, hence the love, of another.

To be sure, originary experience in its natural ontological roots as sketched is, in the one order of history, profoundly obscured by sin, and is restored in unexpected form in Jesus Christ. It is only in light of God's revelation in Jesus Christ that we can see the depth and breadth of what is involved in experiencing oneself as a gift from, and thus as owed to, another. What I mean to stress here is simply that God's invitation to a generous *fiat* toward him as Creator, which is realized in radically new form through Christ's granting us graced participation in his own divine *fiat* toward the Father, is planted in the roots of our being from creation. That this is so I take to be implied by Ratzinger's idea of an *anamnesis* of God lying at the foundations of our being.

But before indicating how the wholeness of being gifted by and of owing oneself to another gets expressed in saying forever, we need to take note of the duality implied in our reference to a relation that is at once to God and to other creatures inside this relation to God.

This duality is treated by John Paul II and also by Joseph Ratzinger in relation to Genesis. In light of this text, John Paul II discusses man's imaging of God in terms of his "original solitude" and "original unity," as well as in his dominion over the rest of creation. First of all, man's "original solitude" means not only that man is different from all other creatures of the visible universe, but that man's relationality begins most radically in his "aloneness" before God. The point is not that man is originally without relation, but that man's relationality, his original being-with, is a being-with God (ontologically) before it is a being-with other human beings. This being-with God, as creaturely, is first a *being-from*, in the manner of a child. It is a filial relation.

Second, simultaneous with man's "original solitude" is man's "original unity," which refers to the spousal communion between man and woman. Ratzinger, in his commentary on *Gaudium et Spes,* refers to this spousal communion between a man and a woman as the immediate consequence *(Folge)* of the content *(Inhalt)* of man's imaging of God that lies first in man's "unitary" being as child of God.[10] This aptness for spousal union, established inside man's and woman's common filial relation to God, is given with creation and is in this sense constitutive of the human being. But the point is that Ratzinger stresses the *capacity for worship* as the primary content of man's imaging of God. He does so because human beings are most basically "sons and daughters in the Son." As Ratzinger says succinctly elsewhere, "the center of the Person of Jesus is prayer."[11]

Third, Genesis affirms man's dominion over the rest of creation, linking this with God's command that the man and woman be fruitful and multiply.

Thus, as indicated earlier, man's basic experience bears an order of God-centered gift-receiving and gift-giving. But we can now see more clearly, in light of the further specifications by John Paul II and Joseph Ratzinger, that this order of God-centered receiving and giving enfolds the twofold form of original solitude and original unity, and thus of filiality and nuptiality. This originary experience with its dual form occurs inside the first covenant. God's gift of creation bears from the beginning a promise of enduring fidelity to his creation in its integrity. And this promise of enduring fidelity to the creature embeds an invitation to the creature to promise enduring fidelity to God in return. This call to enduring fidelity to God, in other words, is implicit in the creature's original self-reception of himself as gift-from-God. There is built into the creature a "primordially sacramental" or "pre-sacramental" sign and expression of God's love which says forever to the creature in the act of creating him, and this unending fidelity on God's part invites, and thereby initiates, a call to unending fidelity to God in return, on the part of the creature.

In sum, what the creature really wants, what lies most basically at the heart of his originary experience, is to love God above all things, and to

---

10. See Joseph Ratzinger, "Introduction and Chapter I: The Dignity of the Human Person," in *Commentary on the Documents of Vatican II*, vol. 5, ed. Herbert Vorgrimler (New York: Herder & Herder, 1969), Article 12 *("Erster Hauptteil: Kommentar zum I,"* in *Lexikon für Theologie und Kirche* 14: *Der Zweite Vatikanische Konzil,* vol. 3, ed. H. Vorgrimler et al. [Fribourg: Herder & Herder, 1968], Artikel 12).

11. Cardinal Joseph Ratzinger, *Behold the Pierced One,* trans. G. Harrison (San Francisco: Ignatius Press, 1986), p. 25.

love other creatures inside this love of God, *forever*.¹² Further, in light of John Paul II's and Ratzinger's thought, this love that desires to say forever finds its objective mediation in the dual form of filiality and sponsality. This love that desires to say forever to God involves fidelity to all of God's creatures, especially human but also subhuman. It exercises dominion over these latter and thereby renders the whole of creation into a participatory sign and expression of man's call to be faithful in relation to God and in service to the human community.

Of course I do not mean to suggest here that the sense of a vocation to what we term a state of life is explicitly present in its full or Christian meaning already in originary experience. Nor, *a fortiori,* that the duality in states of life as conceived in Christianity — expressed in consecrated virginity on the one hand, and sacramental marriage on the other — is unambiguously implied in that experience. What I am saying, simply, is that originary experience embeds an implicit sense, an ontologically rooted memory, of a desire or "exigence" to say forever to God, which unfolds via the double relation of the creature in his original "aloneness" with God coincident with the original unity between man and woman, in a way that implies inclusion of the whole of created being within the ambit of the creature's faithful, God-centered generosity. My argument is that the self's originary experience carries this ontological memory, not in a complete and explicit way, but inchoatively.

I mean to suggest further that this inchoative "exigence" to say forever implies the desire to give one's whole self, thus including one's possessions, body, and mind, and that such a gift can be offered only once. But why only once? Why can't this gift of the self in its entirety be given simply in and as the *sum* of an ending series of discrete acts over time? Such indeed is the dominant view of our contemporaries, which insists, for example, that marriage can be adequately understood as just such a sum of discrete subjective acts of freedom exercised by the spouses. But this overlooks what is implied in giving the whole of oneself. If an act truly bears the promise of being a gift of one's whole self, it implies inclusion, not only of one's present but also of one's past and one's future. It follows

---

12. Regarding the desire for God, it should perhaps be emphasized, in light of what has been said, that this desire is always more basically a responsive participation in God's desire for me already expressed in his creation of me, and is thus but the form that objective being as gift takes in the subject, that is, in and as subjective activity. As a participation in God's desire for me, in other words, *my desire for God is at the most basic level already an act of service to God.*

that any subsequent act of self-giving can only, *eo ipso,* be a renewed taking up and reaffirming in freedom of a gift that has already been accomplished in principle, in its wholeness. And indeed the original vow of one's whole self now calls for, even as it opens up the space for, a literally unending series of such free acts of renewed memory of what is already implicitly contained in the vow.[13]

According to the dominant view, in contrast, the sum of free acts of self-giving can add up to a total gift of self, provided they *continue to be exercised.*[14] But such a set of free acts of self-giving without a singular all-at-

---

13. The point here is nicely summed up in the words of David C. Schindler:

Marriage is not the end of personal disclosure, but rather provides in its completeness a space for the development of intimacy, for the mutual self-manifestation of one person to another over time and in principle without end. . . . In taking vows, the couple has already *implicitly* realized the whole. When one pledges oneself, one hands over not simply one's present being, but in the very same act one includes both one's past and one's future. The future is, so to speak, anticipated in advance. . . . But this embrace of the whole *a priori* does not replace the future, it does not eliminate the graduality of time. Instead, it is a pledge precisely to live out that future in all of its temporal "unvordenklichkeit." In this case, we have a filled infinity, a form that is closed, and indeed perfectly, exclusively closed, but which for that very reason is now "ready for anything" (*Freedom and Form in Schiller, Schelling, and Hegel* [forthcoming]).

Schindler goes on to note that "the American writer Wendell Berry is right to compare the form of marriage with poetic form: there is, indeed, a powerful analogy here. Just as the closed form of poetry gives it an inexhaustible wealth of meaning, a depth of possibility that would be lacking in simply the aimless jotting down of thoughts, so too the ethical form of marriage opens up an endless source of personal gift, an infinite potential of spirit. In this case, insofar as it represents a super-actuality that embraces but does not exhaust possibility, we may point to marriage once again as a paradigm of freedom." See Wendell Berry, "Poetry and Marriage," in *Standing by Words: Essays,* paperback reprint edition (Berkeley, CA: Counterpoint, 2005), pp. 92-105.

14. In this light I recall that, when I was living in California some four decades ago, there was much agitation for the idea of trial marriages, say for three years, at which time couples could part ways with no legal implications — an idea that seems oddly old-fashioned from today's perspective. The objection, which one might expect to have been obvious, is that it is impossible to practice on an explicitly temporary basis a promise the nature of which is determined by its implication of unending endurance. What the idea of a trial marriage overlooks, in other words, is that a vow that promises forever changes the character of all the acts that follow, giving them, objectively and from within, a participation in eternity. Indeed, the dominant contemporary view, which thinks that a permanent promise of fidelity can be given *simply over time,* renders consistent the common judgment of the culture that, whenever one or the other of the partners stops exercising his or her subjective acts of self-gift, the marriage has, *eo ipso,* come to an end.

once inclusion of past and future in a permanent vow gives us, even if these acts are exercised for the rest of one's life, the sum of what can only, logically, be partial or fragmented gifts of self.

Indeed, the idea that a vowed state, for example, between a man and woman in marriage, is synonymous with the sum of the spouses' subjective acts of freedom, is truly a bane of our culture. It goes to the heart of modernity's inability to grasp what is implied most basically in the act of freedom, which is its inner dynamic for saying forever with the whole of one's being.[15]

What I am proposing, again, demands completion in a theology that places all that has been said within the framework of God's self-revelation as the God of creation and redemption in Jesus Christ, and of the Church as the continuing Christological sacrament of that revelation. What is meant by the wholeness of the gift of self and its definitive and irrevocable nature, and thus by a vow, can be understood and realized in the full and proper sense only when incorporated, through the grace of Christ, into Christ's own Eucharistic and crucified love unto death and rising from the dead, and into the Church's Christological sacrament of this love. The argument begun here wants only to say, ultimately, that the vow that establishes a state of life, either as consecrated virginity or as marriage, is ordered intrinsically to martyrdom: to the witness of the gift of one's self unto the end, even to the point of including (possibly) the sacrificial gift of one's own life. But again, the unexpected depth and breadth of what this means is disclosed only in terms of God's own gift of self embodied in Christ. A state of life, finally, is but the "existential" image, actualized in and through the grace of Christ, of the love expressed in Christ's Eucharist, crucifixion, and resurrection. And a state of life on this understanding is best conceived as the distinctly Marian, as distinct from Petrine, form of participation in the Eucharistic gift of self that passes through suffering and death to eternal life.[16]

---

15. Indeed, there is an important further point implied here, which is that I enact the wholeness of my promise of fidelity only through the *fiat* of my active reception. Such enactment, in other words, is at the most basic level a "co-enactment" on my part enabled by God's goodness become effective in me, and taken over by me *in* my letting be. My act of unconditional fidelity is evoked and anteriorly "co-borne" in me by God's act of fidelity to me in creating me, an act of fidelity in which I become an originary participant in the very act of being created. But the full implications of this important point cannot be developed in the present forum.

16. There is much that needs to be sorted out here. A state of life, properly under-

The present argument in this light is limited to directing attention to the echoes of Christ's love stirring already in the deepest recesses of the creature's originary experience, with the intention of drawing toward its inconceivable fullness all that is implicitly "recalled" in this originary experience. My argument is best understood as a laying down and clarifying, in terms at once of the object and subject of experience, of the ontological premises that serve as necessary but insufficient conditions for the ampler theological argument that is needed.

IV.

I conclude by addressing some implications of the foregoing for education and culture.

My overarching theological presupposition is that a state of life, as the distinctly "existential" image of Christ's Eucharistic love, discloses in a unique and decisive way the truth of our being as creatures. A state of life, constituted by a vow of either consecrated virginity or sacramental marriage,[17] discloses, in objective form, the true relation between eternity and

---

stood, gives objective form to an "existential" (as distinct from "office-bearing") participation in Christ's Eucharistic love. Each of the baptized participates in Christ's Eucharist both existentially and "officially," in the sense that ordained priests are always first members of the Church, and that all members of the Church, by virtue of their Baptism, exercise a priestly office, manifest, for example, in the capacity themselves to baptize in certain circumstances. This emphatically need not, and does not, imply attenuation of the clear and profound difference between the laity and the ordained priesthood. What I mean to emphasize here is simply that a state of life, for example, consecrated virginity, is as such not a clerical state. It seems to me that an awareness that this is so opens the way to a deepened appreciation for the state of consecrated virginity as a distinctly lay state, recognized already officially by the Church in Pius XII's *Provida Mater*, and indeed in Vatican II's renewed teaching regarding the laity and their "worldly" vocation. My statement is also meant to carry the implication that the vowed life of the three evangelical counsels, which express the gift of one's whole self — possessions, body, and mind — indicates the most objectively fitting existential form for the priest's office-bearing participation in the Eucharist and sacramental life of the Church. But again, all of this needs more sustained development than can be offered in the present forum. For a reflection on the relation of the life of the evangelical counsels and the vocation of the laity, see Balthasar, *Laity and the Life of the Counsels* (San Francisco: Ignatius Press, 2004).

17. The suggestion here that there are only two states of life raises many questions within the Church today. On the one hand, there is the common perception that the priesthood as such is a state of life, which in the proper sense it is not. On the contrary, it has its

time, heaven and earth. Each state does so in its own way, virginity by disclosing the meaning of eternity and time in light primarily of eternity, marriage by disclosing the meaning of eternity and time in light primarily of time.

To be sure, all of our actions can and should disclose the truth of this relation throughout the whole of our lives, and not only upon entering one of these states. The point is that a state of life gives the disclosure of this mutual asymmetrical relation between eternity and time, heaven and earth, its existentially *objective integration as the form of my life as such, in its wholeness*. All of our actions, rooted in our originary experience, are ordered toward the gift of self in its entirety, even as this total gift of self realizes its full and objective integration finally only in and as a state of life.

---

sacramental-ontological reality as an office, indeed as an office that, as I have suggested in the previous note, bears an objective fittingness for a vowed life of the three evangelical counsels. On the other hand, there is also an increasing tendency today to affirm that singleness as such can qualify as a state of life. But neither is this properly so, because a state of life requires saying forever to God, in a vowed form. The character of this vow that constitutes a state of life has its ultimate foundation in the dual character of the human being's original experience, in original solitude and original unity, or filiality and nuptiality, both of which have their center in God. A state of life, properly speaking, is the mature person's recuperation in freedom of the creature's call to fidelity to God forever, which occurs either through consecrated virginity (thus remaining "alone" with God), or through marriage (thus promising fidelity to God through another human being). It is nevertheless crucial to see here that the single life, if not (yet) actualized by either of these vows, does not thereby remain merely a kind of neutral place where one remains suspended in a mode of inaction and unfulfillment. On the contrary, as we have indicated, there is a call for the gift of one's whole self implicit already in the act of being created, and thus in originary experience, and this call is immeasurably deepened in the act of being baptized. The point, then, is that this call is actualized in the tacit and mostly unconscious *fiat* which, in receiving creation, and in turn new creation in Christ, already begins one's participation in a promise of the gift of one's self to God. The call to be faithful to God forever with the wholeness of one's life is implied, and is already initially realized, in a natural form at one's conception, and again in a supernatural form at one's Baptism. As long as one remains single, then, the relevant point is that one can already begin living the *fiat* of total availability to God, and, in this sense, realize the fundament of what becomes a state of life when recuperated in the maturity of one's freedom in the form of a vow of consecrated virginity or marriage. What one is meant to do as long as one is single, in other words, is to live one's total availability: to wait with active availability for God's will. Of course, it has to be recognized that humanity, and the cosmos as a whole, exists in a deeply disordered condition by virtue of sin. And therefore it has to be recognized as well that the call to a consecrated state of celibacy or to marriage may never be historically realized, as it is the case that everything in the cosmos exists in a broken condition, sometimes a seriously disordered condition that must be accepted, even with much suffering.

My proposal is that the primary purpose of education should be understood in this light. Education, which can be rightly understood only in terms of the whole person, has as its most basic purpose, in terms of method and content, the liberating of experience in this comprehensive ontological sense. The end of education thus lies in forming habits of thought and freedom that assist students to integrate the whole of worldly time in terms of heaven and eternity, and to understand that such integration takes objective form in a "perfect" way in a state of life.[18]

But let me say more about what is meant concretely by patterns of thought that integrate eternity and time.

The relation between eternity and time is given its first form in the creature by God in the act of creation, and this form is implicitly affirmed in man's originary experience as a creaturely subject. This form is expressed in the Creator's commandment to "be still and know that I am God" (Ps. 46:10). It is only through such patient activity that the creature truly remembers the reality of God. Otherwise, in the words of Job, we know God "only by hearsay" (42:1-6). As Pope Benedict has affirmed, we recognize a presence only through silence.

Contemplation and silence are not matters of inactivity. It is not as though contemplation signals a contrast with creative action, such that

---

18. The language of perfection has to be carefully qualified. (1) Historically, the state of perfection has been identified with the life of the three evangelical counsels. This is fine, as long as it is understood thereby that this "perfection" refers to the objective state and not necessarily the subjective condition of the persons living in the state, who may of course live more imperfect lives than those not living the life of the three evangelical counsels. (2) Secondly, my argument has referred to a state of life as such, hence including both consecrated celibacy and marriage, as objectively "perfect." This in fact must be the case, insofar as marriage is understood itself also to embody, in its own way and *qua state*, a call to holiness. Both consecrated celibacy and marriage witness to the relation between heaven and earth, eschatology and incarnation, *differently*. It seems to me that the theological work of John Paul II, which recovers marriage as a call to holiness *qua state of life*, and the work of Balthasar, which develops the lay and "worldly" sense of the state of consecrated celibacy ("secular institutes"), share a deep unity in terms of the point proposed here. Balthasar develops the meaning of consecrated celibacy in its lay character. John Paul II develops marriage as a call to holiness, and thus as a participation, *qua state of life*, in eternity and heaven. (On marriage as a call to holiness, *qua state of life*, cf. David S. Crawford, *Marriage and the* Sequela Christi [Rome: Lateran University Press, 2003].) This does not mean that the hierarchy between consecrated celibacy and marriage as states of life is eliminated. On the contrary, as indicated above, consecrated celibacy witnesses to heaven and earth, *in terms primarily of heavenly existence;* marriage witnesses to heaven and earth, *in terms primarily of earthly existence.* And therein lies sufficient ground for continued affirmation of a hierarchical relation between the two states.

these are at root two different kinds of acts meant at best to alternate with one another. On the contrary, contemplative letting be is the inmost form of creaturely activity as such. Patience is not the absence of activity but, in the words of T. S. Eliot, the still point of the turning world, where the dance begins, and is. It is the presence of God liberated into my being through my letting be that enables me to participate, in a creaturely way, in the power of God's love.

Charles Péguy once said that the integrity of man and his work demands "staying in place," suffering and silence.[19] Just as the right relation between eternity and time demands silence, in other words, so too does it demand "staying in place." "Staying in place" in the first instance does not mean simply not moving around in a physical sense. For if God as Creator can be found anywhere in his creation, then he can surely be found when one moves from one place to another. However, we must avoid confusing the finding of God anywhere with finding him nowhere in particular. We do so only by truly *being* in a place, through the interior stillness that alone permits depth of presence. "Staying in place," in a word, is but stillness now expressed in the form of space: it signals the depth of presence, hence its genuine incarnation, which occurs only in singular persons in singular times and places, in the opening of these singularities to eternity. There is no access to heaven except by sinking proportionately more deeply into the earth, taking on its flesh *here* and *now*.

Another French author, Georges Bernanos, often used the term "imbecile" as an appropriate way to describe peculiar tendencies of our time. By "imbecile" he meant, roughly, one who moves quickly through life not seeing anything. Such a person cannot "enter within himself," but only "explores the surface of his own being." One effort of which such a person is seriously incapable is thinking. Bernanos says that "the intellectual is so frequently an imbecile that we should always take him to be such until he has proved to us the contrary. He is particularly at home in the modern world of technology and numbers. In such a world he can climb to very high positions without giving away his half-culture." The imbecile is "informed about everything and hence condemned to understand nothing." He shows up at one's door every morning, "his pockets stuffed with newspapers."[20] Needless

---

19. Cf. Charles Péguy, *The Portal of the Mystery of Hope* (Grand Rapids: Eerdmans, 1996), p. 156 (Chronology). Cf. also Charles Péguy, " On Money," *Communio: International Catholic Review* 36, no. 3 (Fall 2009): 534-64.

20. For the sources of the quotations from Bernanos, see Balthasar, *Bernanos: An Ecclesial Existence* (San Francisco: Ignatius Press, 1996), pp. 358-68.

to say, Bernanos could have enriched his examples abundantly in this day of communication by cell phone and via the Internet, showing the link between such phenomena and a world dominated by imbecilic politics, economics, and academics. These phenomena foster an ability to be anywhere at any time and therefore in no place or time in particular; they thereby mediate a perception of the world as primarily an instrument.[21]

Bernanos says, in sum, that man has created technology and technology is now creating man, "by a sort of demonic inversion of the mystery of the Incarnation."[22] The peculiar "misery and odium of the modern world . . . is that it disincarnates everything it touches by accomplishing in reverse the mystery of the Incarnation."[23] Already in the first half of the twentieth century, Bernanos saw the coming in the West of what Pope Benedict has termed a "dictatorship of relativism," understanding it to be driven most basically by a tyranny of technicity and expertise.[24]

The burden of my argument has been that there is an inner causal relation between the ills of modernity and the overlooking of the originary experience at whose heart lies a forgetfulness of God and of being as gift; and that this forgetfulness obscures the relation between time and eternity, or secular reality and the reality of heaven, that gives our human existence its most basic creaturely form. The fragmentation, technologism, and activism of our time are all signs and expressions most basically of a wrong relation between time and eternity, between heaven and earth. My proposal is that it is only in learning to say forever that we become able finally to address these tendencies at their root. Only in saying forever in a vow do we give "perfect" and objective form to the presence of eternity and heaven in our creaturely time and flesh. Only such a vowed promise of forever permits eternity objectively and as a way of life to fill every moment of time, and stillness objectively and as a way of life to form every motion and place.

As I said at the outset, the problem today is not too much experience

---

21. Bernanos' point is not that technology is to be condemned *tout court*, but that we need to recognize its non-neutrality with respect to the order of human consciousness and to the nature and destiny of the human being. His view, in other words, is entirely consistent with what Benedict XVI suggests when he says, in *Caritas in Veritate*, that "technology is never merely technology" (p. 69).

22. Cited in Balthasar, *Bernanos: An Ecclesial Existence*, p. 545.

23. Balthasar, *Bernanos: An Ecclesial Existence*, p. 545.

24. Joseph Ratzinger, Homily at the Mass "Pro Eligendo Romano Pontifice," 18 April 2005.

or too much thought based on experience. The problem, rather, is that there is virtually no experience at all in its proper depth and breadth as rooted in the search for God and for the whole of being, and therefore no thought or life rightly based on experience. The "experience" that prevails among our contemporaries, on the contrary, is best termed a distraction from experience, stemming from our inability to be still, and thus to know anything in its full presence.

* * *

Benedict XVI says in *Caritas in Veritate* that "integrated human development" involves a "broadening [of] our concept of reason and its application" (n. 31). "Intelligence and love are not in separate compartments: *love is rich in intelligence and intelligence is full of love*"(n. 30), and love must therefore inform the disciplines as a whole marked by unity and distinction (n. 31). The problem today, he says, is an "excessive segmentation of knowledge" that results in an inability to "see the integral good of man in its various dimensions" (n. 31). Benedict thus affirms that the recovery of the place of metaphysics and theology, especially in their integrative capacities in the realization of wisdom and as themselves integrated by love, "is indispensable if we are to succeed in adequately weighing all the elements involved in the question of development . . ." (n. 31).

I have attempted to show some of the root implications embedded within the God-centered unity of truth and love urged in *Caritas*. I have not attempted to show how these implications are to take form in the disciplines of the academy. My purpose, rather, has been to suggest that the academy should above all, in its methods and contents, serve human experience in its originary form, at the heart of which lies the "exigence" for saying forever to God, and to all of being as God's gift, in wonder and gratitude and with the whole of one's self. To be sure, education is ordered to the acquisition of the information and expertise necessary for careers in economics, politics, academia, and the like. Adequately understood, however, education is ordered to information, expertise, and career training only as these are integrated in light of the basic human vocation to live truly the relation between time and eternity as revealed in God's creative and redemptive love.

As we consider our ecclesial and cultural situation today, it seems to me impossible to exaggerate the need for deepening our awareness of experience in its originary meaning. Only through such awareness are we truly able to realize the destiny of our embodied, intelligent and free human acts — which destiny, to paraphrase Eliot again, is to arrive finally at where we started and to know and love the place (God, self, and other in their objective wholeness) as if for the first time.

Religion and Secularity in a Culture of Abstraction: On the Integrity of Space, Time, Matter, and Motion

I.

The Pew Forum on Religion and Public Life's 2008 U.S. Religious Landscape Survey, "Religious Affiliation: Diverse and Dynamic," found that for all the complexity and fluidity of Americans' contemporary relations to institutional churches, 92 percent of adults believe in God or a universal spirit. "Despite predictions that America would follow Europe's path toward widespread secularization, the U.S. population remains highly religious in its beliefs and practices, and religion continues to play a prominent role in American public life," writes Luis Lugo, director of the Pew Forum.[1]

Responding to earlier studies with similar findings, Wendy Kaminer has argued that the problem regarding religion in America is not, as is often lamented, that we have too little of it, but that we have too much of it.[2] While advocates of religiosity extol the moral habits that religion is supposed to instill in us, she says they need to pay more attention to the intellectual habits it discourages in us. Religion sanctifies bad thinking, preempting the inner dynamic of intelligence through arbitrary appeals to authority — scriptural or clerical or mystical — that issue in premature closure. What America needs, therefore, is not more religion but more secularism.

---

1. Pew Forum on Religion and Public Life, U.S. Religious Landscape Survey: "Religious Affiliation: Diverse and Dynamic" (Washington, DC: Pew Research Center, 2008).

2. Wendy Kaminer, "The Last Taboo," in *The New Republic* (14 October 1996), pp. 24-28, 32.

Now in fact I agree with Kaminer that there is a significant sense in which contemporary America has too much "religion." But I also agree in a significant sense with those she criticizes, who insist on the contrary that contemporary America "suffer[s] from an excess of secularism." To put it another way: I believe (with the "left") that American religiosity typically harbors an inadequate sense of and appreciation for the secular; and I also believe (with the "right") that American secularity has wrongly emancipated itself from religion, has emancipated itself in ways that presuppose, however unconsciously, an inadequate sense of religion. How is it possible to hold both of these positions simultaneously?

In attempting to answer this question, we need first to take note of the profound, if ironic, sense in which the left and the right agree regarding religion in America, coincident with the disagreement signaled by Kaminer's article. For both sides apparently accept the polls indicating that "almost all Americans . . . profess belief in God or some universal spirit," that "seventy-six percent imagine God as a heavenly father who actually pays attention to their prayers" (Kaminer, 24), and other such data. That this is so for "liberals" like Kaminer is a relatively straightforward matter: the data provide empirical support for her lament about the pervasiveness of religion.

For "conservatives" the matter is more complex. On the one hand, thinkers on the right are likewise often quick to appeal to such data, to confirm their judgment that America is a "nation with the soul of a Church," and thus to decry the myth of a secularistic America. On the other hand, these same thinkers are equally quick to identify a growing relativism or indeed nihilism in contemporary culture, calling attention to widespread support for legalized abortion, gay marriage, and the like. Such thinkers, then, explain the apparent discrepancy between what they regard as an innate American religiosity and growing signs of secularism largely by regionalizing the phenomenon of secularism, restricting it to what they regard as the left-leaning "knowledge class," in contrast to the ordinary mass of Americans who, in the ways suggested by the polling data, persist in their religiosity. These thinkers, moreover, are inclined to conceive the secularism of this left-leaning knowledge class primarily as a sign of bad will, as a moral falling-away from what they regard as an originally structurally sound American religion.

It is just here that I wish to focus our discussion. In their interpretation of the polling data indicating widespread religiosity, neither the so-called secular left nor the so-called religious right in their prevalent forms notice the profound ways in which religion and secularism in America, in their original logic, grow from the same soil.[3] On the contrary, however much they differ in other (important) respects, the left and the right both commonly assume that American religion, in its original and historically dominant forms, Protestant and Catholic, stands in fundamental opposition to contemporary secularism. Both sides assume that religion and secularism in America are essentially separate and discrete phenomena, such that where one is present the other is just so far absent; and where one increases, the other just so far diminishes. They assume, in a word, that the division between religion and secularism is clean and fundamental.

My proposal is that the division between religion and secularism in America is not so clean and fundamental, that these phenomena are rather more like two different branches of the same tree or, to change the metaphor, like two quarreling siblings unaware that they are born of the same parents.

Let me stress that I do not mean by this to suggest that the polling data regarding religion in America are insignificant, or that the religiosity indicated by these polls is insincere. Nor do I mean to suggest that the conflicts — what some term the "culture wars" — between the secular left and the religious right are not very real, that moral issues are not an important part of these conflicts, or that the two sides in the conflicts are worthy of equal and symmetrical criticism. My proposal is simply that there exists an original and indeed continuing coincidence between religion and secularism in America, and that, unless we understand the nature of this coincidence, we remain incapable of interpreting properly the polling data indicating religiosity, or of developing an adequate response in the face of our so-called "culture wars."

Thus my argument, as it concerns Christians, is that the problem of secularism in America begins in a significant sense within the Protestant and Catholic churches themselves and their theology and religious practices. To put it in its most radical and indeed what seems to me also most precise terms, the disappearance or indeed death of God is a phenomenon occurring not only in the 8 percent of Americans who do not profess belief in God, but also and more pertinently in the 92 percent who do. Nietzsche's "diagnosis" holds in this sense not only for nineteenth-century Europe but also for twenty-first-century America.

---

3. Cf. the now "classic" argument of Will Herberg, in his *Protestant–Catholic–Jew* (Chicago: University of Chicago Press, 1983).

My general proposal, then, in light of the above, is that America's defective religiosity has largely set the terms for America's defective sense of secularity, or secularism, and that the relation between these is mutual. We can therefore respond constructively to today's cultural situation as it concerns religion and secularity only by re-conceiving both, *simultaneously.*

This chapter takes the form mostly of entering a series of qualifiers, followed by examples, intended to clarify the meaning of these assertions.

II.

A statement by Wendell Berry, one of America's most thoughtful and imaginative writers, brings us immediately to the heart of the matter: "Perhaps the great disaster of human history," he says, "is one that happened to or within religion: that is, the conceptual division between the holy and the world, the excerpting of the Creator from the creation."[4] "The churches . . . excerpt sanctity from the human economy and its work just as Cartesian science has excerpted it from the material creation. And it is easy to see the interdependence of these two desecrations: the desecration of nature would have been impossible without the desecration of work,

---

4. Wendell Berry, "A Secular Pilgrimage," in *A Continuous Harmony: Essays Cultural and Agricultural* (New York: Harcourt Brace, 1972), pp. 3-35, at 6. This dualism "between Creator and creature," which unravels into a series of further dualisms — between "spirit and matter, religion and nature, religion and economy, worship and work, and so on" — "is the most destructive disease that afflicts us" ("Christianity and the Survival of Creation," in *Home Economics* [New York: North Point, 1987], p. 105). Although the religion Berry has most in mind here is a Puritan Protestantism, modern Catholicism has had its own version of the dualisms to which he refers. It suffices to note the work of Henri de Lubac, and recall the great resistance that greeted de Lubac's attempts to recover the social-cosmic dimension of Catholicism and of the Eucharist (in *Catholicisme* and *Corpus Mysticum*, for example), and to retrieve a more organic and concrete sense of the God-world relation (in his work on grace and nature in *Le mystère du surnaturel*, for example). De Lubac's concern, not unlike that of Berry, was to draw attention again to what had been largely lost from view in the modern era, namely, God's original and intrinsic, if wholly unearned and unexpected, invitation to the world to share in his own life and hence holiness. De Lubac understood this invitation in terms of the sacramental mediation of the Church in a way that Berry does not address. The point is only that de Lubac and Berry are, notwithstanding, in profound agreement regarding the need for Christianity to reject the dualism that undergirds a conception of salvation as individualistic and, as it were, world-less. For an overview of the problematic here as it concerns de Lubac, see my "Introduction to the 1998 Edition," Henri de Lubac, *The Mystery of the Supernatural* (New York: Crossroad/Herder & Herder, 1998).

and vice versa."[5] In a word, the excerpting of the Creator from his creation prevents creation — the world *(saeculum)* — from being understood as a destined dwelling place for holiness.

What I wish to propose, in light of this statement by Berry, is that there is an intrinsic connection between a religion originally reduced by its dualistic reading of the relation between God and the *saeculum*, and a sense of secularity that is thereby itself originally reduced by virtue of the same dualism. This original "secularizing"-through-dualistic-reduction of the *saeculum* remains hidden and appears harmless so long as relation to God continues to be added to the world, an addition that has been readily forthcoming throughout most of America's history. Today, however, this "secularizing" reduction of the secular has taken a more overt and aggressive form, turning more explicitly *against* religion. My point is that this should really come as no surprise. A secularity that has been given its original meaning in abstraction from God already and in principle conceives relation to God as an arbitrary addition to itself. It is a small logical step to construe this arbitrary addition, over time, as an imposition from without, something to be kept at a distance or indeed removed altogether from the secular, precisely to safeguard secularity's original integrity *as secular*.[6] Thus is an anti-religious hostility born from the heart of an original secularizing dualism for which religion itself also bears responsibility.

At any rate, that is what I wish to propose. The oppositions in today's dialectic in America between religion and secularism, or religionists and secularists, are oppositions originating from different sides of the same coin of theological-ontological dualism identified by Berry. However significant their differences in assessing our current cultural situation — and these differences are significant — religionists and secularists alike begin by accepting, albeit from different directions and however tacitly and unwittingly, the separation, or extrinsic relation, between God and the *saeculum* that is a hallmark of American religion's original, and still dominant, self-understanding.

---

5. Berry, "God and Country," in *What Are People For?* (New York: North Point, 1990), pp. 96-97.

6. It should be stressed that religious believers intended this separation to be itself an expression of religious devotion, one that protected the gratuitousness of God's creation and guaranteed God's transcendence. The problem is that they construed this rightful gratuitousness and transcendence of God, of the God of Revelation, in terms of a "superadded" relation that presupposed an original extrinsicism.

III.

Of course, there is much about the claim that American religion begins in an original separation between God and the world that strikes one as immediately counterintuitive, and thus we need to qualify. Surely the evidence of history, confirmed again in today's polls, suggests that Americans are inveterately pious. From the beginning until today they have been abundantly inclined to relate events in the world to God's will or providence. In any case, it would seem odd indeed to try to convict the Puritans, for example, of not doing this. In my discussion of dualism above, I used the term "abstraction," referring to an original abstraction of secularity from relation to God, but this seems only to make my claim less tenable. Surely the Puritans, as well as present-day Christians, do not intend to abstract the things they do in this world from the provident will of God.

Here, then, is the needed and crucial qualifier. The dualism we are alleging is twofold. It consists in an extrinsic relation between the will or volition on the one hand, and intelligence or cognitive order, on the other, in our original engagement with God and the world. And it consists at the same time in an extrinsic relation between God and the world, or a false abstraction from God in our original understanding of the concrete world. This abstraction is not from a simply transcendent monopolar God but ultimately from the transcendent-immanent Trinitarian God hypostatically united to man in Jesus Christ. The abstraction between will and cognitive order that we are calling false, in other words, itself presupposes a double extrinsicism: between the God of natural reason and the God of supernatural faith, and hence between the orders of reason and revelation.

The abstraction of the world or secularity from God to which I have referred is therefore a matter not primarily of volition but of intelligent and cosmic order. The will, in the form of supernatural faith, maintains (or intends to maintain) real relation to God as it engages the world, even as the intelligence engages that same world in terms of an order that has been first abstracted from the Trinitarian God incarnate in Jesus Christ, and thus abstracted from a creation made in the image of this Trinitarian God and destined already in its original created structure to share in God's Trinitarian love and beauty, in and through Jesus Christ (Col. 1:15-18).[7] We might say that Christians have been careful watchdogs of morality and inner-churchly piety even as they have largely given away the orders of

---

7. See note 4 regarding de Lubac and the sacramental mediation of the Church.

space, time, matter, and motion, and indeed the entire realm of the body and bodiliness, and of the artifacts and institutions in and through which space, time, matter, and motion become human culture. The dualism I am alleging in America, in a word, may be described as an originally moralized and "voluntarized" *religiosity* coincident with an originally "mechanized" cosmic *order*.

Thus, regarding Americans' proclivity for relating their secular or "worldly" lives to God: the giving away of the orders of space and time and matter and motion to which I refer does not mean that Christians do not still see these realities as subject to a proper *use:* see them, that is, as instruments in and through which the will of God is to be faithfully executed. The relevant point, rather, is that this appeal to a moral or faithful *use* of things, in its conventional understanding, typically begs the set of questions I mean to be raising. It presupposes and reinforces just the voluntaristic piety we are insisting is the nub of the issue. A cosmos originally understood as "neutral" or "dead" stuff, hence as essentially blind and dumb until appropriated as an instrument of moral or pious choices, indicates a cosmos that is originally indifferent to God.[8] And such a cosmos itself already and as a matter of principle maneuvers piety, the pious use of the cosmos, into what now becomes mostly a moralistic, because arbitrary, imposition on the cosmos.[9] The point, in short, is that an appeal to the moral or pious use of the world, as conventionally understood in America, expresses just the defective conception of both holiness and secularity that, in the way indicated by Berry, lies at the root of current difficulties.

Here we can see the response also to the view which assumes that the rationalized and mechanized world or cosmos is harmless, because neutral, except at those critical junctures where this world challenges religion

---

8. See Joseph Ratzinger's treatment of Italian philosopher Giambattista Vico in *Introduction to Christianity* (San Francisco: Ignatius Press–Communio Books, 1990), pp. 31ff.

9. Cf. here the statement of Luigi Giussani: Genuine morality occurs when "one's behavior flows from the dynamism intrinsic to the event to which it belongs"; moralism, on the contrary, is "an arbitrary and pretentious selection of affirmations among which the choices most publicized by power will dominate" ("Religious Awareness in Modern Man," *Communio: International Catholic Review* 25, no. 1 [Spring 1998]: 132 and *passim*). The point is that an authentic morality cannot flow from a cosmos that is originally dumb and blind, hence not open in its intrinsic structure to the destiny intended in authentic moral choices. For the full meaning and consequences of these suggestions, see the discussion below, especially that concerning Romano Guardini. Cf. also "Is Truth Ugly? Moralism and the Convertibility of Being and Love," *Communio: International Catholic Review* 27, no. 4 (Winter 2000): 701-28.

or morality on specific issues and in explicit ways, for example, in the matter of abortion, or the cloning of human beings, and so on. But such a view fails to notice that the rationalized and mechanized world itself already presupposes American religion's positivistic self-understanding. And, again, it is just this self-understanding that reinforces the secular climate within which morality and religion are now perceived as arbitrary additions to the inner logic of the secular world's own order, and experienced just so far as intrusions upon that order.

Thus, to return to my opening remarks: Why should we be surprised if Americans today are increasingly disposed to dismiss religion, together with its attendant morality, as arbitrary and irrelevant, when religion in its dominant American Christian form has defined *itself* as irrelevant: irrelevant, that is, to the world, the integration of the *secular order* of which religion has conceded already to have occurred on that order's own terms, in abstraction from the world's constitutive relation to God? Why should we be surprised if Americans increasingly experience Christianity as alien to their secular experience, when their Christianity has already defined *itself* as alien to secular experience, to experience *in its integrity as secular*?

America's culture of increasing secularism, in a word, is today largely in the process of simply turning inside out America's own religious self-understanding.

IV.

These are strong words, to be sure. Let me now back up and clarify the nature and key elements of the proposal, which I will then illustrate in terms of the contemporary situation, particularly as discussed in my own Roman Catholic tradition.

Earlier I introduced what may seem to some an extreme claim regarding the disappearance of God also among the 92 percent of Americans who profess belief in God, and not only among those who are explicit in their denial of God's existence. I have qualified that claim to signify the disappearance of God, not primarily in the moral will or religious intentions of Christians in America, but in Christians' sense of the intelligent ordering of things, in the cosmos. And I have suggested that this disappearance is brought about by an abstraction from God in one's original understanding of the cosmos, resulting in an original rationalizing and mechanizing of the cosmos. My argument, then, hinges decisively on the nature of a distinction: between will and intelligence and between God and the world.[10] It may, however, still seem a mouthful, not to say a trifle intellectualist, to hang the death of God and an entire cultural crisis on the nature of a distinction. Let me therefore first describe briefly how I understand the historical origin of what I am suggesting to be a false, because dualistic, distinction, and how, in this light, I understand the nature of this distinction, as it pertains to the matters at hand.

(1) Theologian Hans Urs von Balthasar locates the origin of the West's dualistic religious sense decisively in what he terms the split between theology and sanctity, or again between theology and "Christian life."[11] Up until after the time of the great Scholastics, the great theologians, he says, were, mostly, great saints. "Their . . . lives reproduced the fullness of the Church's teaching, and their teaching the fullness of the Church's life" (181). The unity of knowledge and life was the canon of truth for these thinkers. "But as theology increasingly took on a 'scholastic' form," through the advent of Aristotelianism, "the naive unity hitherto accepted was gravely shaken" (184). "Philosophy began to emerge as a discipline alongside theology, with its own concept of philosophical truth" (185). It is emphatically not the case for Balthasar that this concept of truth did not have a certain, important legitimacy. The point is rather that philosophy, as it developed, tended to focus one-sidedly on truth conceived in abstraction from its concrete and ultimately personal-divine origin. The issue, in other words, is not whether a distinction between philosophical truth and theological truth is necessary — Balthasar is unequivocal that it is — but how it is to be understood.[12] Thus, as he puts it:

> The intimate connection was seen, and indeed emphasized, between the true and the good as the transcendental properties of the one be-

---

10. See "Modernity and the Nature of a Distinction: Balthasar's Ontology of Generosity," and "The Given as Gift: Creation and Disciplinary Abstraction in Science," pp. 350-82 and 383-429 in this volume.

11. "Theology and Sanctity," in *The Word Became Flesh* (San Francisco: Ignatius Press, 1989), pp. 181-209.

12. See, for example, Balthasar's positive comments regarding the influence of Aristotelianism in the emergence of the rightful independence of the modern sciences of nature and mind, and the gain in enormous clarity and insight from this development: "Theology and Sanctity," pp. 184-85. For Balthasar's view regarding the distinct, positive contribution of Scholasticism, cf., *inter alia*, his "The Fathers, the Scholastics, and Ourselves," *Communio: International Catholic Review* 24, no. 2 (Summer 1997): 347-96.

ing, but it was looked at more from the human standpoint, in the mutual presupposition of intellect and will . . . , than in their objective mutual inclusion. . . . Philosophy, as a doctrine of natural being and excluding revelation, could not know that the highest mode of interpreting that philosophical definition of truth must be a trinitarian one, corresponding to the passages on truth in St. John. . . . (185)

According to Balthasar, it took the greatness of a Bonaventure or a Thomas "to irradiate and transfigure [this] self-subsisting science of nature, raising it to the plane of the sacred, and so to impart to the secular sciences a real Christian ethos, one affecting the whole outlook of the scientific endeavor" (186). The difficulties began to emerge when the

philosophical propaedeutic [in the guise, for example, of a natural theology antecedent to biblical theology] came to be considered a fixed and unalterable basis, whose concepts, without the necessary transposition, were used as norms and criteria of the content of faith, and therefore set in judgment over it. Teachers behaved as though man knew from the outset, before he had been given revelation, knew with some sort of finality what truth, goodness, being, light, love and faith were. It was as though divine revelation on these realities had to accommodate itself to these fixed philosophical concepts of philosophy and their content, before going on to their application in theology. (186)

Thus there emerged a double movement: a separation of philosophy from theology (dualism), coincident with what then became the pressure to reduce theological truth to philosophical truth (rationalism), especially as students were eventually required to familiarize themselves with the concepts of philosophy and their content, before going on to apply these concepts in theology (180).[13]

The epoch following Bonaventure and Thomas, says Balthasar, saw the completion of the split between theology and spirituality. "Spiritual men were turned away from a theology which was overlaid with secular

---

13. It should be pointed out here that it is not the case for Balthasar that philosophy does not retain a *relative* priority over theology, or that philosophy may never precede theology. The issue, rather, turns on whether and in what sense philosophy, if and insofar as it is studied prior to theology, nonetheless remains intrinsically open to revelation. For further argument in the context of natural science's openness to mystery, see "The Given as Gift."

philosophy — with the result that alongside dogmatic theology, meaning always the central science which consists in the exposition of revealed truth, there came into being a new science of the 'Christian life,' one derived from the mysticism of the Middle Ages and achieving independence in the *devotio moderna*" (187).[14]

There are, to be sure, enormously complex developments distilled here.[15] My purpose in offering this brief historical sketch is simply to indicate the sense in which the dualistic distinction with which I have been concerned — between will and intelligence, or again between voluntaristic religiosity and mechanistic secular order — has an "existential" origin and meaning. This distinction, in other words, in its original historical form, represents what was a failure on the part of Christians *to carry through in their lives the integration of all aspects of being, here especially the mind and intelligent order, in terms of the relation to God that is the heart of the call to holiness.* What we have been describing in conceptual terms as a dualistic distinction first appeared not outside of but within lived experience, precisely as the logic of that experience. Christians' relation to God became increasingly voluntaristic in nature, even as Christians' understanding of the order of the cosmos became increasingly abstract.[16] The logic of that experience, in sum, consisted in the double abstraction to which we have referred, of intelligent order both from the God of revelation and from will and affectivity. As is well known, Balthasar identifies this abstraction in terms of a displacement of the centrality of glory in our understanding of God and of beauty in our understanding of the secular order of things. We will return to this important question of beauty later. First, two comments about the nature of the distinction about which I am arguing, in light of Balthasar's overview.

(2)(a) Returning to the question of American culture: when I say that America's current problems regarding religion and secularism turn

---

14. See, for example, the discussion by Balthasar in *The Glory of the Lord*, vol. V: *The Realm of Metaphysics in the Modern Age* (San Francisco: Ignatius Press, 1991), pp. 9-47. Cf. also in this connection Graham Ward, "Introduction, or, A Guide to Theological Thinking in Cyberspace," in *The Postmodern God* (Oxford: Blackwell, 1997), pp. xv-xlvii, esp. at xxiii-xxiv.

15. See, for example, Michael Buckley's *At the Origins of Modern Atheism* (New Haven: Yale University Press, 1987); and my discussion of this book in "The Catholic Academy and the Order of Intelligence: The Dying of the Light?," *Communio: International Catholic Review* 26, no. 4 (Winter 1999): 722-45, at 730-33.

16. Cf. Buckley, *At the Origins of Modern Atheism*.

decisively on the nature of a distinction, I do not refer in the first instance to a conceptual distinction consciously and explicitly formulated as such, an idea from which our current cultural problems are supposed then to have deductively unfolded. It is not the case that there was first simply an idea which then produced an experience, but rather that the original, and dominant, American experience itself contained, as one of its distinct but not exhaustive features, an intelligent *order:* a "logic." To be sure, this logic has, from the beginning and all along the way, also been given explicit theological formulation, which in turn has reinforced and guided the original experience. The point is that the logic, or the nature of the distinction, upon which I take our religious-cultural situation so decisively to hang, is a matter first and fundamentally of a logic *implicit in a way of life.*

The consequences of this organic relation of logic and way of life, then, are two. Insofar as the logic is always already inside the experience, it cannot but influence and direct that experience. At the same time, insofar as this logic is itself but one element of the total experience — because, as Balthasar's historical analysis indicates, the total experience includes not only intelligence but also will and affectivity and the like — this logic never wholly determines the content or direction of the experience, but is in fact partially determined itself *by* this experience.

What my argument is asserting, in short, is that the logic of dualism in crucial ways shapes even as it does not exhaustively account for today's cultural situation. What I am urging in response, therefore, is an entire way of life, but one *that essentially includes a new and distinct logic.*

(2)(b) But there is a more radical question regarding whether our insistence on the importance of the nature of a distinction for our cultural situation, even with the foregoing qualification, is still not too academic or intellectualist. To put it in its most trenchant form: Does my argument mean to imply that this situation can be accounted for without recourse, for example, to the reality of sin?

I raise this question to make clear that of course I have no intention of attenuating the reality of sin as a source, indeed the most fundamental source, of our current troubles. My argument, rather, merely implies a challenge to the moralistic-voluntaristic reduction of sin that is the obverse of what I have identified as the moralistic-voluntaristic piety of Americans. In other words, my argument implies an expansion of the notion of sin, along the lines indicated in what Pope John Paul II calls sin's structural dimension. Perhaps the best definition of what he means by this is given in his encyclical *Dominum et Vivificantem:*

> Unfortunately, the resistance to the Holy Spirit which Saint Paul emphasizes in the *interior and subjective dimension* as tension, struggle and rebellion taking place in the human heart finds in every period of history and especially in the modern era its *external dimension,* which takes concrete form as the content of culture and civilization, *as a philosophical system, an ideology, a programme* for action and for the shaping of human behavior. (56)

And again in *Sollicitudo Rei Socialis*:

> Sin and structures of sin are categories which are seldom applied to the situation of the contemporary world. However, one cannot easily gain a profound understanding of the reality that confronts us unless we give a name to the root of the evils which afflict us. (36)

Thus sin bears not only a subjective but also an external or "objective" dimension. It takes the form of an idea or a philosophy informing a program or institution or indeed civilization. To be sure, as the Pope insists,[17] sin in this "structural" sense is always finally personal, that is, originates in someone's personal, or subjective, act. The point is simply that this subjective (voluntary) dimension of sin itself extends "beyond" subjectivity, expressing itself in an objectively disordered meaning. Personal sin, in a word, has not only a voluntary or subjective but also a cognitive or objective dimension, an objective dimension which is social, extending into, and embodied in and informing, social-political-cultural institutions. In other words, as I indicated above, every experience contains a distinct *logos* or claim about objective order that makes the experience at once personal and social.[18]

The burden of my argument, therefore, in light of the Pope's analysis, is not that America's religious-cultural problems have nothing to do with sin in the subjective sense, which would be ludicrous, but that these problems have to do in a particularly significant way with the structural-objective sin that reaches beyond even as it remains intrinsically connected with, "subjective" sin. If my argument does not emphasize the "personal" or subjectively sinful dimension of America's problems, this is only because this dimension is hardly unique to Americans. Presumably Ameri-

---

17. In *Reconciliatio et Paenitentia,* n. 16, and *Sollicitudo Rei Socialis,* n. 36.

18. For further exposition of the notion of "structures of sin," see "The Significance of World and Culture for Moral Theology: *Veritatis Splendor* and the Nature of the Body," pp. 219-41 in this volume.

cans' lives are a mixture of moral viciousness and moral virtue much like the lives of all people in the infralapsarian period. What I wish to emphasize, in short, is that what is most peculiar about America is the way in which its religion and liberal tradition have from the beginning dissociated questions of will and morality from questions of intelligence and cosmological and ontological order, and the way in which, accordingly, America's moralized-voluntarized religion has persisted coincident with a secularized cosmic-intelligent order.

The further crucial point, as already hinted, is that America's distinctive piety, presupposing as it does a moralized or voluntarized notion of sin, thereby renders invisible what, following John Paul II, I have identified as the objective, or structural or intellectual, dimension of sin. That is, the peculiar nature of American religion is that it renders sin invisible precisely as a matter of distinctly *cognitive dis-order*. But the point is that it is sin in just this cognitive or structural sense that needs above all now to be brought into relief, as the condition *sine qua non* for a proper understanding of America's current cultural situation.

However, it is time to illustrate the content of my argument directly in terms of this cultural situation. I have suggested that America's abstraction of intelligent order from will and affectivity and from the Trinitarian God expresses and generates reduced notions of space, time, matter, and motion, a reduction that is properly termed at once a fragmentation and a secularization.[19] And I have suggested further that these fragmented and secularized notions of cosmic order in fact constitute structural sin. What does all of this mean concretely?

V.

I will respond primarily in terms of the project of Anglo-American modernity, as engaged especially by my own Roman Catholic tradition. The

---

19. Cf. here the pertinent comment of Graham Ward in his introduction to *The Postmodern God*, relative to the problem of what may be termed "postmodernity": "modernism is linked to specific conceptions of space, time, and substance, and . . . postmodernism explodes the myths and ideologies constructing these conceptions" (p. xvii). And again: "If we wish to apprehend the postmodern God," he says, "we have . . . to investigate the project of modernity with reference to the shapes it gave to time, space, and bodies. For these shapes portrayed the face of modernity's god — the god whom Nietzsche (following a suggestion by Hegel) pronounced dead" (p. xvii).

concern, again, in light of the foregoing argument, is to identify how and where the dead cosmos — the mechanistic, hence dumb and blind, order of space and time and matter and motion, which make up nature and indeed culture — manifests itself in this project.

(1) To do this, we can look at the reading of American institutions — political, economic, academic — prevalent among Catholics in recent decades, a reading that has indeed been justified increasingly in terms of Vatican II and in the name of the pontificate of John Paul II. For example, in the political realm, we have John Courtney Murray's "articles of peace" reading of the First Amendment, which maintains that America's official political institution (the state) is, as such, empty of any notion of human destiny, until members of society, in the course of a free market exchange of ideas, put some such notions there.[20] In the economic realm, we have disciples of Murray arguing, in the name of John Paul II's *Centesimus Annus*, that that encyclical's distinction between culture and economics should be read in the same Murrayite, "articles of peace," vein: insisting, to wit, that the economic system as such is empty of any theology or anthropology, and that religious or moral evaluations of that system turn first on how the system is used or on the ends to which it is instrumentalized.[21] Finally, in the realm of the academy, and again in a Murrayite spirit, prominent American Catholic educators have claimed, in accord with the Land O'Lakes statement and indeed also in the name of Vatican II, that the Catholic university is substantially a university and only adjectivally Catholic: that the modern university, in its original definition as a university, indicates first an order of critical-disciplinary methods, procedures, and categories (university as a noun), to which a Catholic or Buddhist or Islamic or Jewish worldview or ethics is to be added (adjectival qualification). The pertinent point, once again, is that the order of the university as such is conceived to be originally empty of, hence neutral toward, any definite notion of the ontological destiny of man and cosmos.[22]

---

20. Cf. "Civil Community Inside the Liberal State: Truth, Freedom, and Human Dignity," pp. 65-132 in this volume.

21. Cf. "The Anthropological Vision of *Caritas in Veritate* in Light of Economic and Cultural Life in the United States," pp. 430-49 in this volume.

22. For further argument about the nature of the university, see "The Catholic Academy and the Order of Intelligence: The Dying of the Light?," *Communio: International Catholic Review* 26, no. 4 (Winter 1999): 722-45, as well as "Catholicism and the Liberal Model of the Academy in America: Theodore Hesburgh's Idea of a Catholic University," in *Heart of the World, Center of the Church: Communio Ecclesiology, Liberalism, and Liberation* (Grand

My simple suggestion is that all of these readings of the world as ordered into institutions share a common view of order as first and most basically dumb and blind, which is to say, mechanistic and instrumentalist. To put it another way, the distinction between "institution" and "ideology" as accepted here by Catholic thinkers[23] in fact presupposes and reinforces just the dualism of moralism and voluntarism, on the one hand, and mechanism and instrumentalism, on the other, that I have insisted is the bane of American culture.[24] More precisely, the liberal distinction between institution and ideology subscribed to by Catholics, now in the name of the Second Vatican Council and the pontificate of John Paul II, expresses exactly the reduced sense of both God and secularity implied by the positivistic sense of religion lying at the root of our present difficulties.

In a word, we have first the empty mechanisms of institutions whose order is dead, which are then to be instrumentalized in and through what can now only be arbitrarily or voluntaristically introduced religious, anthropological, and ontological substance. In the parlance of today, the problem identified here as mechanism can alternatively be termed the problem of "proceduralism," in accord with which appeals to the formal mechanisms of the institution always arrive in advance of any substantive content, thereby always-already making that content over into what is, from the perspective of the order of the institution as such, an extrinsic addition.

Let me be clear: the Catholic thinkers in question here all insist that the three respective institutions function properly only when guided by the substance of an adequate anthropology, in the form, for example, of the practice of natural law or of natural or civic virtue. It is obviously true that these thinkers believe that the order of political, economic, and academic institutions needs the addition of a substantive philosophy and morality to avoid corruption. My argument bears rather on the logical "lateness" of this addition as they conceive it. It bears precisely on the nature of a distinction, here between the order of the institution as such and the "ideology" or destiny to which it is put in service.

Rapids: Eerdmans, 1996), pp. 143-76. Cf. also "On Meaning and the Death of God in the Academy," in *Heart of the World, Center of the Church*, pp. 189-202.

23. Joseph Komonchak, among others, has affirmed, rightly in my opinion, that this distinction is a hallmark feature of Anglo-American liberalism. See his "Vatican II and the Encounter Between Catholicism and Liberalism," in *Catholicism and Liberalism: Contributions to American Public Philosophy*, ed. R. Bruce Douglass and David Hollenbach (Cambridge: Cambridge University Press, 1994), pp. 76-99.

24. See "Civil Community Inside the Liberal State."

The main point, then, is that the addition of ideological substance as conceived by these Catholic thinkers is mediated by a modern, liberal sense of distinction that itself, as a matter of principle, fragments the sense of distinction indicated by Catholicism.

That this is so can be illustrated briefly, for example, in terms of the difference between Aquinas and Descartes in their respective understandings of the order of the body. Both thinkers distinguish between soul (or human meaning: "psychics") and body (physical matter: "physics"). But the point is that Aquinas, unlike Descartes, does so all the while presuming an anterior unity between the two, with the important consequence that the human meaning is not arbitrarily and just so far mechanically added to the body, nor is the original body sheer — which is to say morally and anthropologically empty — mechanism. Aquinas gives us the body as originally an organism, a body whose very physical order as body is intrinsically related to, hence just so far also "images," spiritual meaning.[25] This is quite unlike Descartes, who gives us the body as originally machine, a set of dumb and blind procedures to which spiritual meaning is always yet to be added, instrumentally and arbitrarily, from outside. The point is that spirit and body both become profoundly different by virtue of how they are originally distinguished relative to one another, an intrinsic relation between the two yielding an organic space and time and matter (Aquinas), an extrinsic relation yielding a mechanistic space and time and matter (Descartes).

At any rate, my suggestion is simply that, in insisting that institutions, *in their original order as such,* are empty of spiritual or moral substance, the Catholic thinkers noted above are just so far committed, not to a neutral sense of order, but, however unwittingly, to a Cartesian — in contrast, for example, to a Thomistic — sense.

Again, let it be emphasized: the burden of my argument concerns not the simple denial but the late addition of anthropological-spiritual meaning. A Cartesian sense of worldly institutions implies a mechanized order juxtaposed to a human or religious meaning, which meaning can now be introduced to that order only arbitrarily or voluntaristically.

In a word, the liberal distinction between institution and ideology

---

25. See "The Significance of World and Culture for Moral Theology" and "The Embodied Person as Gift and the Cultural Task in America," pp. 219-41 and 242-74 in this volume, for elaboration of the significance of John Paul II's theology of the body. Cf. also "Liturgy and the Integrity of Cosmic Order: The Theology of Alexander Schmemann," pp. 288-309 in this volume, on the need for a "symbolic" or sacramental understanding of physical reality.

that many Catholics take to be sanctioned if not embraced by the Second Vatican Council is in fact a precise embodiment of the reduced sense of religion coincident with the reduced sense of the secular that bedevils contemporary American culture.

(2) But let me approach in another way the point urged here, drawing on George Grant's perceptive book, *Technology and Justice*.[26]

In a chapter called "Thinking About Technology," Grant considers the extent to which "technology" has become "the pervasive mode of being in our political and social lives" (17). He proceeds by reflecting on a statement by a computer scientist that "the computer does not impose on us the ways it should be used" (19). This claim and the warrant offered for it, Grant says, are familiar to us. Computers "are instruments, made by human skill for the purpose of achieving certain human goals. They are neutral instruments in the sense that the morality of the goals for which they are used is determined from outside them" (20).

Grant's argument is that this claim presupposes the "prevalent 'liberal' view of the modern situation," which, he says, "is so rooted in us that it seems to be common sense itself, even rationality itself. We have certain technological capacities; it is up to us to use those capacities for decent human purposes" (20-21). Indeed, he insists that such a claim asserts nothing less than "the essence of the modern view, which is that human ability freely determines what happens" (31).[27]

Against this claim regarding the computer as neutral instrument, Grant indicates the ways in which the computer embodies a certain conception of knowledge, an implied view of the relation between subject(ivity) and object(ivity), and between knowing and making, and a definite sense of the nature and place of "abstraction" and indeed information in human consciousness. The computer, further, carries an implied judgment about the nature of the other that is the object of knowledge, in a way that presupposes a particular view of the relation between knowledge and love and indeed of the nature of the other as beautiful (38ff.). Grant's point therefore is that the computer, far from being a neutral instrument, is in fact bound up finally with a whole conception of human destiny. The computer tends to homogenize its users just so far in terms of that destiny.

---

26. Notre Dame: University of Notre Dame Press, 1986. For a summary presentation of Grant's understanding of technology, see "George Grant and Modernity's Technological Ontology," pp. 277-87 in this volume.

27. Cf. what I have called voluntarism.

Regarding the claim that the computer does not impose a particular substantive form upon us, then, Grant responds: "Common sense may tell us that the computer is an instrument, but it is an instrument from within the destiny which *does* 'impose' itself upon us, and therefore the computer *does* impose" (23). Grant summarizes thus:

> When we represent technology to ourselves as an array of neutral instruments, invented by human beings and under human control, we are expressing a kind of common sense, but it is a common sense from within the very technology we are attempting to represent. The novelness of our novelties is being minimized.... The coming to be of technology has required changes in what we think is good, what we think good is, how we conceive sanity and madness, justice and injustice, rationality and irrationality, beauty and ugliness.
>
> ... [The] changed conception of novelness ... entails a change in the traditional account of an openness to the whole, and therefore a quite new content to the word "philosophy." A road or a sparrow, a child or the passing of time come to us through that destiny. To put the matter crudely: when we represent technology to ourselves through its own common sense, we think of ourselves as picking and choosing in a supermarket, rather than within the analogy of the package deal. We have bought a package deal of far more fundamental novelness than simply a set of instruments under our control. It is a destiny which enfolds us in its own conceptions of instrumentality, neutrality and purposiveness. It is in this sense that it has been truthfully said: technology is the ontology of our age. (32)

What I wish to suggest, in light of this argument by Grant, is that the distinction between ideology and institution developed in the areas of politics, economics, and the academy by American Catholic thinkers in the ways indicated above is a variant or analogous expression of just this sense of ontology as technology: of order as mechanistic and instrumentalist, hence as dumb, blind, and neutral; and consequently of morality, which Grant discusses in terms of justice, as voluntaristic. This ontology represents, in short, what seems to me American Catholicism's distinctive contribution to secularism, to the secularized order characteristic of the increasingly globalized Anglo-liberal culture.

VI.

Let us now attempt a summary of the positive import of our proposal. If I have interpreted matters accurately, what is most fundamentally at issue in our current religious-cultural situation is the nature of the cosmos in its creatureliness. At issue is the integrity of creation, in light of its constitutive relation to God. I have suggested that American religion characteristically fragments that integrity, through an abstraction of the mind or intelligent order or truth from the concrete Trinitarian God of revelation and from the will and the good. The result is a defective sense of religion, but also a defective sense of the secular. What I wish now to propose is that this defective sense of both religion and the secular can be identified best in terms of the displacement of beauty, for reasons already indicated briefly in our references to Balthasar and Grant. I wish now to conclude by bringing into relief this intrinsic link between religion and beauty, in its implications for an integrated view of secularity, of cosmos and culture.

I turn to two texts for assistance. The first is drawn from Grant's argument regarding the paradigm of knowledge he takes to be implied in the development of modern technology and indeed in the liberal academic institutions characteristic of our technological age. Grant suggests that this paradigm turns on what is meant by objective knowledge and hence by the nature of the world as object.[28] He discusses this in terms of the meaning of faith, whose definition he takes from Simone Weil: "Faith is the experience that the intelligence is enlightened by love" (38). Grant says that this statement implies that "love is consent to the fact that there is authentic otherness" (38). That is, we love otherness; and we do so because and insofar as we perceive the other to be beautiful.

Thus for Grant the fundamental claim implied in Christian faith is the link between intelligent order and love. And beauty is the proper name for this link or integration. Grant's point, then, is clear. The modern world, insofar as it would be understood in light of faith, needs above all to re-center objective knowledge — which is to say, the world as object, the world in its objective order and meaning — in the beautiful. Those who would, in light of faith, have an adequate notion of secularity must overcome the disjunction between the intelligent order or truth of things and beauty, a disjunction summed up sharply in Nietzsche's dictum that "truth is ugly" (66).

---

28. Grant, *Technology and Justice*, pp. 36-37.

To see the radical and comprehensive meaning of this assertion, in light of the integrated view of creation that is needed, we turn finally to another text, from Romano Guardini. "In the experience of a great love," he says, "all that happens becomes an event inside that love."[29] This statement is to be viewed first of all in terms of the revelation of God himself. The whole of creation, everything in the cosmos, is an "experience" of God's great love. And the whole of creation thereby becomes an event inside that love. It follows that the world, and everything in the world — its space, its time, its matter, and its motion: in a word, every aspect of the order of cosmic being and activity — is most basically a gift. The point, in other words, is that the world reflects not only the will but the mind of God, of the Trinitarian God of love whose *logos* is revealed in Jesus Christ. The world reflects not only God's loving *will* but God's loving *order*.

Consider, for example, how even the material elements of the food prepared by the mother for her children take on the character of gift. They are not only neutral instruments of her loving will. On the contrary, her love enters into the very space and time and matter and motion in and through which she prepares the food. These are no longer neutral, blind, and dumb instruments manipulated from outside by her will. On the contrary, this time and space and matter and motion now become the very form of her love. Which is to say, these so-called instruments rather become intrinsic features, an intrinsic part, of the event of her love. They reveal, by virtue of their own order now transformed by love, the very face and figure of the mother.

What I am proposing is that this holds true, by way of analogy, for the entire cosmic order in its relation to God. Every last bit of cosmic and cultural space, time, matter, and motion reveals the face of God, the order of the event of God's great act of creative love.[30] Beauty, then, is the proper term for the *order* proper to what is *given* by God. Beauty, in short, is cosmic *order* understood as *gift*.

Thus, in sum: Nietzsche and Dostoevsky, in their very different ways, are right about the crisis of modernity, even in America. Our crisis above all is a crisis of the death of God *simultaneous with* the death of beauty in the secular order of things.

With this, we return to our original set of questions regarding the prevalence in America of a voluntaristic religion and a mechanistic

---

29. Cited by Giussani, "Religious Awareness in Modern Man," p. 137.
30. Cf. note 4 above.

saeculum. The key to this dualism, we can now see more amply, is Christians' original detachment of the world's *giftedness from God* from the world's *order*. It is the uncoupling of the notions of *gift* and *order*, with a consequent moralizing of gift and rationalizing of order.

What is therefore demanded in response is twofold. On the one hand, in terms of religion, what is needed is a deeper and more comprehensive sense of God, now understood to include the world, in and through Jesus Christ and the Church, in a way that makes the world into the "sacrament" of God's presence.[31] And this sense of the world as the sacrament of God's presence demands, from within its own inner logic as religious, a re-centering of the whole of worldly logic, precisely as worldly or natural, in beauty.

On the other hand and at the same time, in terms of secularity, what is needed is a re-centering of the whole of the world, precisely in its own inner logic as natural and worldly, in beauty. This re-centering of the world in beauty finally demands, by virtue of its own creaturely dynamism as given gratuitously by God, the world's transformation into the "sacrament" of God's glory.

These assertions also indicate the method by which the renewal of culture, what Christians call "evangelization," is to be accomplished. The means whereby all of this is to be realized, simply, is the whole of one's life ordered by the love, friendship, and communion whose sacramental home is the Church and the primary sense of which is aesthetic. This is so because, as Balthasar reminds us, "[t]he exchange of love that takes place within God is now open to the world in the form of an exchange between heaven and earth." In this exchange "the creature is not confronted with anything 'alien' but the innermost truth about the being and destiny of things and himself."[32] "This is what is meant by saying that the entire created universe has come into being in, through, and for the Word" (106).[33]

---

31. Cf. Alexander Schmemann, *For the Life of the World* (Crestwood, NY: St. Vladimir's Seminary Press, 1998), p. 17, and "Liturgy and the Integrity of Cosmic Order."

32. Cf. *Gaudium et Spes*, n. 22: "The truth is that only in the mystery of the incarnate Word does the mystery of man take on light. For Adam, the first man, was a figure of Him Who was to come, namely Christ the Lord. Christ, the final Adam, by the revelation of the mystery of the Father and His love, fully reveals man to man himself and makes his supreme calling clear."

33. Citing Adrienne von Speyr, in *Theo-Drama*, vol. 5 (San Francisco: Ignatius Press, 1998), pp. 105-6.

Modernity and the Nature of a Distinction: Balthasar's Ontology of Generosity

The question to be treated bears on the nature of Balthasar's intellectual achievement and of my own indebtedness to that achievement. In order to be able to state this adequately, it seems best to describe something of the history and constellation of issues and concerns that were part of my life leading up to my encounter with him. The historical narrative to follow is of course highly selective and fragmentary. Certainly such a brief retrospective suggests a synthetic clarity about things that was not accessible at the beginning or even along the way, and brings with it an inevitable reduction and oversimplification. I offer the narrative, then, only to help clarify why that encounter was so significant for me.

I.

(1) Immediately upon graduation from high school (in 1961), I entered the Jesuit seminary of the Oregon Province in Sheridan, Oregon. After two years of novitiate, my formation entered the phase of humanistic studies, consisting especially in the study of ancient Greek and Latin culture and literature. I began early in this Juniorate phase of studies (as it was called then) to read Christopher Dawson and Cardinal Newman, occupying virtually every minute of my extracurricular time over the next two years

---

A longer version of this essay was originally published in *How Balthasar Changed My Mind: 15 Scholars Reflect on the Meaning of Balthasar for Their Own Work*, ed. Rodney Howsare and Larry Chapp (New York: Crossroad, 2008), pp. 224-58.

reading their works.¹ This exercise led to the theme I chose for the "senior essay" that capped our Juniorate studies: the educational theories of Dawson and Newman.

The burden of the essay was to show the unity of vision that inspired these two men despite obvious differences in the character of their work. Both struggled with the question of the truth of religion, coincident with how best to read religion and culture, especially in ancient and modern Western civilization. Both were led into the Catholic faith for reasons not unrelated to the integrity of human culture generated by this faith: by the capacity, that is, of the Catholic faith to take account of humanity in all its dimensions. Dawson, with his immense historical erudition, showed that the question of God and religion lay at the heart of every human culture, and that religion and culture were thus bound up with one another from their origin and in their deepest roots. Newman demonstrated in his life and his thought that the "method" adequate for reaching truth in the matter of religion and with respect to the culture had to be catholic in every sense of the word: a passionate opening with the whole of one's being, including both mind and heart, to the whole of reality, in light of the whole God and the whole of his Church. Both men turned their attention in sustained fashion to the problem of education in the modern university, and both recognized the grave failure of the latter to educate in the Catholic and catholic manner necessary to sustain a truly human civilization. Both recognized the failure, that is, to form men and women in the integrated and indeed God-centered habits of mind that enable intelligent resistance to the fragmentation and secularization that they perceived as the looming problem in the West.

(2) Following the Juniorate, I entered the three-year phase of studies devoted to philosophy (1965-1968). Two things stand out during this period. First, there was my course in Metaphysics, taught by Jesuit Father Gordon Moreland. This class, more than any other class in my life, transformed how I approached reality. Moreland conducted the class by way of weekly lectures that are perhaps most appropriately termed "metaphysical meditations." The lectures were centered on texts from Thomas Aquinas, often supplemented by long passages from Joseph de Finance's *Être et Agir dans la Philosophie de St. Thomas*. Moreland had also been deeply influ-

---

1. The two-volume biography by Meriol Trevor, *The Pillar of the Cloud* (New York: Doubleday, 1962) and *Light in Winter* (New York: Doubleday, 1963), was especially helpful in guiding me in the reading of Newman.

enced by Gabriel Marcel. At any rate, in the lectures he advanced fourteen Thomistic theses over the fourteen weeks of the course, beginning with the Thomistic distinction between act and potency, and focusing above all on the "real distinction" between *esse* and *essentia*. From the first "lecture" of this great teacher, I began to sense a new and strangely profound way of thinking about things, about the meaning of culture and indeed everything else in relation to God. It was as though my entire life was changing. For the first time I felt that a truly "explanatory" account of what was missing from modernity's picture of life was beginning to settle in upon me.

At about the same time, I began to read several other philosophers, including especially Etienne Gilson (above all *The Unity of Philosophical Experience, The Spirit of Medieval Philosophy,* and *Being and Some Philosophers*). I have always been particularly conscious of having learned from Gilson three main principles, which indeed guided me in basic ways through subsequent studies in philosophy and theology: (i) ontological judgments — one's notion of being, of what fundamentally makes reality real, so to speak, and hence makes life meaningful and truly worth living — operate within and thus shape one's (penultimate) judgments about *this* or *that* thing, and thus the method and content of one's thought. Gilson's point, of course, was not that everyone has deliberately appropriated or indeed is even conscious of such judgments, but that they remain operative, whether one is aware of them or not, indeed in a sense all the more so when one is unaware of the implication of their presence in one's conscious acts. In a word, for Gilson, man "by his very nature . . . is a metaphysical animal," and it is only in retrieving being in its wholeness *qua* being that one can take adequate account of the whole of reality.[2]

A proposition that has always stayed with me in this connection is Gilson's famous statement in *The Unity of Philosophical Experience* that "Philosophy [i.e., metaphysics] always buries its undertakers." If one denies metaphysics, or thinks one can make claims about this or that aspect of reality without somehow implying metaphysical claims about the nature or logic of reality as a whole, the result will be, not that one successfully avoids such claims, but only that one is now being controlled by presuppositions of which one remains unaware.

(ii) But this teaching of Gilson was tied to a second judgment, re-

---

2. It was just this openness to being in its wholeness, grounded above all in Aquinas's distinction between *esse* and *essentia,* that indicated for Gilson the singular greatness of Aquinas's achievement: see point (iii).

garding the significance of the "real distinction" between *esse* and *essentia*, and indeed, in this connection, of the primacy of *esse*. Herein lay the heart of Gilson's sustained criticism of the "essentialism" he took to be characteristic of the dominant tradition of modern (i.e., Cajetanian) scholasticism. *Esse* is not merely the act that actualizes essence, simply signifying the fact that essence exists. On the contrary, *esse* is the act of acts, the perfection of act that, as such, has primacy in accounting first or absolutely for the richness and density of the thing in its "transcendental" truth, goodness, and beauty.[3]

(iii) Thirdly, the question of the distinction between *esse* and *essentia* for Gilson at once presupposed and evoked the question of God and creation. Gilson resolutely insisted on the enduring distinction between faith and reason. At the same time, his historical studies revealed to him the ways in which, for example, the philosophy of the great thinkers of the Middle Ages differed from that of the Greeks, by virtue of the intervening historical revelation of God in Jesus Christ, and of the articulation of that revelation in the Creed and its doctrines of creation and redemption. Gilson argued that Aquinas's sense of the distinction between *esse* and *essentia*, and his introduction thereby of a significantly new meaning into Aristotle's duality of act and potency, could not be properly understood except in light of Aquinas's faith in the Christian God of creation. Gilson argued, in a word, for a distinctly Christian philosophy, a philosophy that remains essentially or formally philosophy even as it acknowledges the internal influence of faith on philosophy in the concrete order of existence or exercise.[4]

Here is not the place to enter into the controversy that arose around these distinctive claims of Gilson. It suffices simply to emphasize how Gilson's Thomistic philosophy opened up for me being and the intelligibility of being — the intelligibility of being in its inner constitution and its inner rationality as such — to what may be called their historical and transformal dimensions. Mystery, for example, is not merely the unknown lying beyond or "underneath" what is known, but the excess of intelligibility implicit in every act of knowing and in every cognitive content of being. Furthermore, Gilson showed how, through the "real distinction" of

---

3. See section V for a discussion of how this Gilsonian understanding of Thomism was modified and deepened for me by Balthasar and, more indirectly, by philosopher Ferdinand Ulrich. The development of my understanding was also helped immensely by an abundant reading of the works of Kenneth Schmitz.

4. Gilson's notion of Christian philosophy is clearly affirmed in John Paul II's encyclical *Fides et Ratio* (see n. 74 and 76).

Aquinas, the question of God and creation was implicitly present at the heart of all other questions about the nature of things.

Among the many things I learned from Gilson, then, was that the questions of being and its intelligibility as such are deepened within the life of faith and thus within the call to holiness. Man is at once, most basically, a metaphysical and a religious animal, and this teaching has common roots in Augustine and Bonaventure and Aquinas, despite significant differences in the philosophical articulations of each of these thinkers. In language I became more accustomed to using later on, Gilson's position as expressed in the foregoing three points showed how and why being in its structural roots is a matter of gift and love in relation to God.

(3) In 1970, having left the seminary, I began doctoral studies at Claremont Graduate School in southern California, enrolling in a program called Philosophy of Religion and Theology. My time at Claremont was dominated above all by an encounter with the person of John Cobb, a Methodist theologian deeply influenced by Alfred North Whitehead and Charles Hartshorne. Cobb, a man of remarkable simplicity, humility, and generosity, took up theology with a deep and concrete passion for the truth and concern for the crisis he saw developing in modern Western culture. My classes with him and our conversations together over four years constantly gravitated back toward discussion of what he was convinced was modernity's affliction by dualisms (between God and the world, the soul/mind and the body, the mind and reality, etc.) and consequent reductionisms (as inspired, for example, by Descartes and seventeenth-century philosophy and science generally).

Cobb insisted that what lay at the heart of the modern West's liberal culture was a lack of a truly relational understanding of reality, one that at its core implied a centeredness in God. In this insistence, of course, Cobb had been influenced by Whitehead and Hartshorne, and so it was not surprising that he took the notion of substance — substance as such, that is, already beginning with Aristotle and not only with the seventeenth century — to be a major source of the problem. This became a matter of friendly but vigorous discussion between us over four years, because it seemed to me then, as it still does today, that Whitehead and Hartshorne had conflated what were in fact fundamentally different ideas of substance: Aristotle's substance is simply not static in the way that, say, the Lockean substance is. Aristotle understands the human being, likewise, as naturally social, and naturally-dynamically inclined to seek the truth about being (metaphysics) and God (natural theology). I defended Aristotelian substance against Whitehead's criticisms, supported by Gilson and in light also of Thomist philosophers such as Fr. Norris Clarke and especially Frederick Wilhelmsen (for example, his *The Paradoxical Structure of Existence*); and I thus defended Aristotle in terms of the philosophical deepening provided by Aquinas. Above all, it was Aquinas's metaphysical distinction between *esse* and *essentia*, conceived in light of the Christian doctrine of creation, that enabled me to see how every being is fundamentally related to God and to other beings in God, in a way that does not attenuate but on the contrary presupposes the notion of substance.[5]

Through the sustained discussions with Cobb, it became ever more profoundly clear to me that Aquinas's "real distinction" is the key to coming to terms both reasonably and Christianly with the dualisms and reductionisms, and consequent fragmentation, that Cobb took to be the greatest threat to the future of Western civilization, and indeed to Christianity itself. This four-year period of study ended with my writing a dissertation, under Cobb, on the "methodological" aspects of the issues raised here, that is, on how Christian faith deepens the metaphysical understanding necessary to deal adequately with theological-cultural problems.

(4) Cobb's criticisms of modernity, with Whitehead in the background, were much involved with issues in modern science and technology. As a consequence, my conversations with Cobb prompted much reading in the philosophy of physics and biology and indeed psychology.[6] It was some years after leaving Claremont, when I began (in 1979) to teach in the University of Notre Dame's Program of Liberal Studies, and offered a course called "Concepts of Man," that I read an article by theoretical physicist David Bohm.[7] What immediately interested me was Bohm's concern to recover a "realistic" or ontological sense of physical order in the uni-

---

5. That is, the substantial identity granted to each creature in the act of creation is the necessarily presupposed term (the *"what"*) *of* the constitutive relation to God established in and by that act.

6. Most important here were probably the writings of philosopher–physical chemist Michael Polanyi and my introduction, through Cobb, to the person and work of Hans Jonas (for example, his *The Phenomenon of Life*). From Polanyi I learned to appreciate, *inter alia*, what he terms the "tacit dimension" of human cognition, the act by which we grasp the implication of what is not abstracted, or "pulled out" for focus, in the act of cognition. This feature of the implicit is indispensable for any theory of cognition that would be adequate to the ontology of generosity indicated in what follows: cf. "The Given as Gift: Creation and Disciplinary Abstraction in Science," pp. 383-429 in this volume.

7. "The Implicate Order," in a collection of essays edited by Cobb (and David Griffin) titled *Mind in Nature* (Lanham, MD: University Press of America, 1978), pp. 37-42.

verse. Bohm saw that this order, rightly understood, requires some version of interior causes such as Aristotle's form and finality, some significant sense of a simultaneity of necessity and non-necessity in causality, and some non-reductive version of the wholeness of things, indeed a version of relationality among cosmic entities that would permit us truly to affirm a universe (i.e., a *uni-verse:* a genuine turning of the many toward unity). The burden of Bohm's work, in a word, was to challenge the mechanistic patterns of thought that he took to characterize modern physics, which, as the basic science of modernity, played a fundamental role in modern culture generally. Bohm insisted that an adequate sense of physical order entailed recuperation of an adequate notion of eternity and infinity, in order to understand time and the finite properly.

After reading this article, I wrote a review of Bohm's just-published book, *Wholeness and the Implicate Order.* I sent a copy of the review to him, while inviting him to a conference to be sponsored by *Communio* and held at Notre Dame.[8] Bohm sent a response to my review,[9] and accepted the invitation for the conference, and this began a conversation between us that continued with some regularity until the time of his death in the early 1990s. At the heart of our discussions was the question, from his side, of how to develop an ontological interpretation of modern physics (e.g., quantum theory), the problem of deterministic versus non-deterministic order in the physical universe; and, from my side, of how the Thomistic notion of being, rooted in the distinction between *esse* and *ens,* and opening dynamically into the Christian understanding of the God-world relation, could account for all that Bohm wanted to correct in the modern conception of order in the physical universe, while enabling one to avoid what seemed to me the problems involved in Bohm's proposed idea of the "implicate order."[10]

---

8. The conference, "Beyond Mechanism: The Universe in Recent Physics and Catholic Thought," took place March 29-31, 1984, and the proceedings were published under the same name (Lanham, MD: University Press of America, 1986).

9. The two articles, my "David Bohm on Contemporary Physics and the Overcoming of Fragmentation" and Bohm's "Response to Schindler's Critique of My *Wholeness and the Implicate Order,*" were published in the *International Philosophical Quarterly* 22, no. 4 (December 1982): 315-27, 328-39.

10. Perhaps chief among these problems is an inadequate sense of the analogy of being, which would, for example, afford a more satisfactory view of finite entities in their singular integrity. See, in addition to the review cited above, *Heart of the World, Center of the Church* (Grand Rapids/Edinburgh: Eerdmans/T. & T. Clark, 1996), pp. 173-75, n. 51. Some years later Bohm, in a conversation he and I had at a meeting in Zurich, said that he had de-

During a sabbatical from Notre Dame spent in France during the fall semester, 1983, and while beginning to write a book on modernity and the metaphysics of love,[11] I read Balthasar's book on de Lubac and books by de Lubac himself. When I returned to Notre Dame, I set aside this manuscript, judging now, in light of the reading of Balthasar and de Lubac that I had begun, that the argument on which I had embarked needed more explicit and comprehensive theological integration.

II.

Although my reading of Balthasar had thus begun in the early 80s, it was only in the time immediately following his death in 1988 that I began to study his work in sustained fashion. My experience in reading him at this time was much like that undergone in my course in metaphysics, except that the reading continued steadily over several years. I was being drawn into a "new" vision of reality, one that gathered up and restored in radically deepened and transformed ways all that I had learned to that point, with respect to the basic and abiding question: What does it mean to live, simultaneously and with integrity, the truth of reality, of the Church, and of God, *at the heart of the world*?

But the problem, again, as it continued to seem to me, was that modernity in its pervasively liberal articulation rendered living the truth in this comprehensive way impossible. Reality and reason were one thing; the Church and God, and indeed the love associated with both, were something else. Modernity had its way of distinguishing — or, better, separating, and at the same time reducing — these. Science as conceived in its

---

cided to replace the term "implicate order" with the term "generative order," but I am unsure whether this change was made anywhere in print. The term "implicate order" is still used in his last book, *The Undivided Universe: An Ontological Interpretation of Quantum Theory* (co-authored with B. J. Hiley), which appeared posthumously (London: Routledge, 1993).

11. Based on the Thomistic metaphysics of *esse* and the distinction between *esse* and *ens*. Interestingly, I suggested in a letter to Bohm during this time that it seemed to me that the argument he was making could be summed up as an effort to interpret the basic order and activity in the (physical) universe in terms of love. He replied (roughly): "Yes, of course, but I can't use such language with physicists." I should say about Bohm that he was a man of profound humility and gentleness and compassion, and in fact quite shy, though his being and manner exuded a genius and passion for inquiry after the truth in all of its mystery that were the equal of any man I have ever met.

dominant academic disciplinary modes gives us the meaning of reason, and of reality as accessible to reason. Politics and economics in their dominant liberal democratic-capitalist mode circumscribe for us what counts as a legitimately *public* exercise of reason, and hence as public "realism." Fundamental to reason and reality as conceived in both science in its dominant modern disciplinary form, and politics and economics in their dominant Anglo-American liberal form, is abstraction from God, Church, and love. Not that these latter, to be sure, might not be granted by scientists and persons in liberal institutions to have even decisive importance in their lives. But such importance is granted only in terms of piety, moral intentionality, or faith, now conceived voluntaristically, and for life in "private," not in terms of what is judged reasonable or realistic in the proper sense, or meant for life in "public."

After years of formative guidance by Christian thinkers like Dawson and Newman and Gilson, as well as Augustine and Aquinas, it seemed to me that this abstraction of scientific-public reason and reality from God, Church, and love cannot be squared with the God of the Bible and Christian revelation. If God is truly the Creator of all things, if all things are made through the Word (John 1:3); if all things are created in Christ, the image of the invisible God (Col. 1:15-16); if we know and love God implicitly *(implicite)* in all that we know or love (cf. Aquinas, *De Veritate*, q. 22, a. 2, ad 1); if it is in his very revelation of the Father's love that Christ reveals the meaning of man, and through man, of all flesh and hence of all the matter of the cosmos (*Gaudium et Spes* [GS], n. 22; *Dominum et Vivificantem*, n. 50); if this Christian revelation of God's fatherly-trinitarian love abides sacramentally in the Church — then God and the love of God revealed in Christ through the Church must make a difference to everything, to every entity and every act, including every human cognitive and voluntary act, all the time. Nothing in the cosmos is or can be indifferent to God or indeed to love, ultimately to the love of God as revealed in Jesus Christ through the Church. The point, then, vis-à-vis modernity with its fragmented and reductionistic patterns of thought, is that God and love carry *their own way of making distinctions among, and unifying or integrating, all creaturely entities.*

Here, then, is the heart of what Balthasar communicated to me with an unequaled comprehensiveness and depth: *God in his creative and redemptive love — in his love as imaged in creation, as embodied hypostatically in the person of Jesus Christ, and as present sacramentally in the Marian-Petrine Church — reveals the most basic terms of all distinctions and all uni-*

ties in the cosmos. In a word, God and love penetrate to the innermost meaning and form of all "worldly" being and cognition.

To be sure, "worldly" being and knowing and acting and making have their own autonomy, a lawful "logic" of being proper to themselves as distinct natural entities. Indeed, that is just the crucial point to be made relative to modern patterns of thought: not that this autonomy is to be denied or short-circuited, but that creaturely autonomy is on the contrary preserved and deepened, albeit now precisely *from within* and *by virtue of* the relation of generous love by which God gives the creature being and sustains the creature in being in the first place. After all, human nature was not absorbed *(non perempta)* but assumed *(assumpta)* by the Son of God (*GS*, n. 22), and thus the Incarnation presupposes the integrity of nature as created. Creaturely being and knowing and acting, to realize their rightful autonomy or distinctness or difference, need not, and indeed finally cannot, remain indifferent toward God or the love that images God, even for a moment.

This, it seems to me, is the burden of Balthasar's lifelong emphasis on the relation between theology — or, more comprehensively stated, the order of reason and reality — and sanctity, expressed emblematically in his 1948 article of that title.[12] It also lies at the core of his lifelong work regarding the lay state of consecrated life and of his decision, with Adrienne von Speyr, to begin the Community of St. John: namely, to go to the heart of the world in order to take every thought and action, every aspect of every reality, captive to Jesus Christ (2 Cor. 10:5), so that God might be "all in all" (1 Cor. 15:28), beginning here and now on earth, and hence including "worldly," public order.[13]

It is this catholicity, coincident with Catholicity, of Balthasar's life and theological work that led to reconfiguring in new, more profound and

---

12. "Theology and Sanctity," in *Explorations in Theology I: The Word Made Flesh* (San Francisco: Ignatius Press, 1989), pp. 181-209. This translation of the article includes Balthasar's 1960 revision and expansion.

13. Perhaps it should be stated in this connection that love rightly understood carries its own answer to the problem of political integralism — that is, its own way of distinguishing state and society — a problem that may be suggested by the reference to public order. But treating this falls outside the scope of the present article (cf. in this connection "Civil Community Inside the Liberal State: Truth, Freedom and Human Dignity," pp. 65-132 in this volume, and "The Way of Love in the Church's Mission to the World," in *The Way of Love: Reflections on Pope Benedict XVI's Encyclical* Deus Caritas Est, ed. Livio Melina and Carl A. Anderson [San Francisco: Ignatius Press, 2006], pp. 29-45. An expanded version of the latter article appears in *Communio: International Catholic Review* 33, no. 3 [Fall 2006]: 346-67).

comprehensive ways all that I had learned from the authors and teachers mentioned earlier. For present purposes, I will limit myself to sketching only the basic contours of how Balthasar reconceives the nature of distinction and unity within and among all cosmic entities, in the orders of both being and of cognition; how he does so, that is, vis-à-vis modern culture's fragmented, reductionistic way of distinguishing and uniting, and in terms of the call to sanctity that is formed in the love that says forever in response to God.

III.

From within the dominant liberal-modern patterns of thought (which are operative both outside of Catholic institutions and often within them), this formulation of the problem of modernity, and of how I understand the center of Balthasar's thought in relation to modernity, may seem too general or simplistic, academically unserious, or even politically dangerous, and in any case an invitation to confusion. The characteristic achievements of modernity, with its affirmation of the autonomy of the creature that is itself taken to be the fruit of the Christian idea of creation,[14] seem to presuppose and demand just the proliferation of distinctions within and among things, as well as the need for specialized forms of study and methodological abstraction, that Balthasar at once objects to and reconfigures. But what Balthasar proposes is not fewer or less precise distinctions, but rather distinctions made differently, that is, in the manner of one who loves and in terms of the thing itself understood as a matter innermostly of love. In other words, Balthasar accepts the real contributions of modernity while transforming them in terms of God-centered love.

This objection, then, goes to the heart of concerns that need to be faced, precisely to avoid the kind of reductionism ruled out by the catholicity of Catholicism. Let me say initially only that the God- and love-

---

14. The claim regarding the rightful autonomy of the creature, and the disciplinary method by which the creature is properly to be studied, as entailed by the Christian doctrine of creation, is a more complicated and subtle matter than is typically assumed. How one interprets this autonomy, in other words, differs significantly depending on how one understands the creature (especially the human person) to be made in the image of God: whether and in what sense the creator God who is imaged is the God of trinitarian love revealed in Jesus Christ. The significance of this point is made clear in the argument that follows in the text. See also "The Given as Gift."

centered understanding of reality developed by Balthasar does not collapse distinctions into premature unities. On the contrary, he conceives cosmic-creaturely distinctions and unities in terms of a God-, Christ-, and Church-centered (and also, so to speak, being-centered) *analogy of love*. In contrast, modernity conceives cosmic-creaturely distinctions and unities in an equivocal way that in fact expresses a kind of inverted univocity, a paradoxical equivocity-cum-univocity that is informed by a forgetfulness of God and being and that consequently drains the reasonable and real universe of love. To put it another way, Balthasar conceives cosmic-creaturely distinctions and unities in terms of a universal-catholic *community* of being and reason, while modernity conceives these distinctions and unities in a way that leads at every turn to a reduction of community to an aggregate of individual entities, logically, even if typically unintentionally. Let me now attempt a brief sketch of what is meant by modernity's fracturing of authentic community, first in terms of modernity and then in terms of Balthasar's thought.

Consider the various dualities that are commonly invoked in one way or another in accounting for our experience of things: God and the world; the order of reality and the order of knowing; the soul, or mind, and the body; the self as individual and the self as social; rights and duties; the private and the public; state and society; the human and the subhuman; object (or objective) and subject (or subjective); freedom and necessity; love, or freedom, and intelligence; faith and reason; obedience and creativity; the holy and the secular; the inner-ecclesial (for example, liturgy and sacrament) and the inner-worldly; experience and idea; the living and the non-living; analysis and integration, or synthesis; part and whole; singular and universal; the theoretical or contemplative and the practical; fact and value — the list goes on and on. Needless to say, each of these dualities raises issues specific to itself. Nevertheless, each at the same time invokes the problem of relation in some way, the problem of a distinction between a one and an other, between x and non-x.

Modern culture's approach to this problem of relation and distinction is exposed paradigmatically in the work of René Descartes. The clarity and distinctness sought by Descartes as the condition for an idea's reasonability, and hence for something's being affirmed as certainly present in reality or in the objective world, require that there be no trace of an implication of non-x in x. The straight lines of abstract geometry serve the important function for Descartes of indicating the way in which x and non-x, lying on opposite sides of the line from each other, are thus cleanly outside of one another, and hence indicating that there is no implication of non-x in x, and vice versa. The clarity and distinctness required for the intelligibility and reality of the one demand the closure of its identity to that of the other. Again, clarity and distinctness demand conceiving x and non-x first in terms of each's *externality*, relative to the other. And, lacking any order *from within itself toward* the other, the identity of x cannot but be logically weighted toward itself, even as non-x then appears to x first as available-for-use in x's own interests.

All of this bears profound consequences for how one can then reasonably conceive any subsequent relation between x and non-x. The key is the original mutual indifference between the two. Given this indifference, the relation between them remains external in nature and hence a matter merely of *addition,* and thus remains just so far what is properly termed a dualistic relation. On the other hand, insofar as the relation becomes "real," that is, insofar as x truly reaches inside non-x, that relation cannot but be forceful and intrusive, because any relation between the two, given the original indifference just indicated, is *eo ipso* adventitious: the relation is one for which there is no already-given interior order in x or non-x. The significance of this can be stated in various terms: any "real" relation of x to non-x entails an *external* movement that can only be *outward* and *without a center* — without an anterior-interior centering in either the one or the other — a movement, therefore, that is simply *dispersive* in nature. Again, the adventitious and thus forceful character of any "real" relation of x to non-x entails that this relation, always and everywhere, be a matter most basically of coercive power and thus of violence.

This understanding of reason and reality, mediated as it is by the presupposition of an originally indifferent relation of x to non-x, and vice versa, lies at the root of modernity's characteristic ways of conceiving the various dualities mentioned above. Thus we have modernity's dominant religious positivism, whereby relation to God is not so much given to man, and thus constitutive of man's being, as initially posited by man. We have social contractualism, whereby the relation between the self and the other is first contracted. We have a human dignity founded on self-determination, or what one achieves, and not (also) on one's being as constitutively *given and received.* We have constitutively self-interested rights, whereby responsibilities of the self toward the other, and vice versa, tend at best toward a mutual instrumentalism or self-interest. We have the tendency toward nominalism, according to which the many bear no inner unity in terms of a one, and the one bears no inner-inclusive openness toward the many in their many-ness. We have the tendency toward pelagianism, according to which one's relation to the other is conceived first in terms of power construed as somehow native to oneself alone, and not in terms of power that is anteriorly *given* to oneself and thus *originally participated in* by oneself. We have a body that lacks any immaterial or interior center within itself, and hence we have matter as inert stuff. We have a causality consisting primarily in external, "efficient" relations of force rather than in the communication of meaning via the interiority of form and finality, or purpose.[15] We have the separation of the true from the good, of fact from value. We have a technological approach to cosmology and a scientific knowledge of nature that views the world exhaustively as an *instrument:* nature is no longer a matter of "being born" *(nascor)* but of an object ready-to-hand for making, thus no longer good *qua ens* but only *quia factum*. We have extroverted patterns of life consisting in endless outwardly directed movement and activity. We have voluntarism and moralism, according to which freedom, or the will, operates without anterior mediation by intelligence.[16] We have rationalism and mechanism, whereby intelligibility is coerced out of an x whose identity has in principle been analytically closed.[17]

In the academy, we have the abstractions (from *abstrahere,* to pull out or drag away) characteristic of the modern disciplines, according to which what is abstracted is treated *methodologically* as though it were, or could be, *indifferent* toward what is left aside in the act of abstraction, or again as though the *limited aspect* of an entity "pulled out" in an abstraction was, or could be, indifferent to what lies "outside" or beyond what is pulled out, in the concrete world of "real" being.[18]

---

15. See D. C. Schindler, "Truth and the Christian Imagination: The Reformation of Causality and the Iconoclasm of the Spirit," in *Communio: International Catholic Review* 33, no. 4 (Winter 2006): 521-39.

16. To be sure, rightly understood, the intelligence's mediation of freedom itself presupposes, in a different order, freedom's own mediation of intelligence: cf. Aquinas, *ST* I, q. 82, a. 4.

17. Cf. in light of this paragraph Balthasar's suggestion that the deepest theme of modern thought lies in "the divorce between spirit and life, between the theoretical and practical reason, between Apollo and Dionysus, idea and existence, between [modernity's] conception of the spiritual world as valuable but impotent, and of the practical world as one of power but spiritual poverty. This dualism in philosophy has prevailed at least since Kant . . ." ("Theology and Sanctity," in *Explorations in Theology I: The Word Made Flesh*, pp. 193-94).

18. The methodological abstractions of modern disciplinary inquiry are of course both necessary and legitimate. How they are to be conceived, however, in terms of the Christian doctrine of creation, rightly understood, is a matter requiring qualification, when and

Recalling the language of equivocity and univocity used above, then, we see that, in accord with the modern Cartesian ontology of identity and distinction, every x is logically simply different from non-x, resulting in what appears to be, and in a significant sense is, a radical pluralism. And yet every x is different from non-x by virtue of a *single idea* of identity and distinction, and hence modernity's radical pluralism takes the form at once of a radical monism. There is, on the one hand, a radical fragmentation that presupposes a nominalist equivocity of being and meaning, even as, at the same time, this fragmentation is mediated by a univocal conception of being and meaning, of x and of its distinction from and relation to non-x.

It thus does not seem improper, echoing Nietzsche, to characterize modern patterns of thought in terms of a kind of nihilism, a superficial nihilism (from *super-facies,* staying on or along the surface), or indeed, as Nietzsche also says, in terms of "homelessness." We conceive both x and non-x in terms of an identity lacking the depth and interiority that alone can establish each as an order of inherent meaning and worth; and we consequently conceive any relation between the two in terms of a movement that can now only be dispersive, without end. It is just this endlessness, this identity and movement that are without an interior *center* and thus without ordered relation to, hence ability to rest in, any end, that promotes the *distraction from the depths* of things characteristic of modernity's peculiar nihilism. It is also what constitutes the peculiarly modern form of homelessness: the lack of a capacity really to indwell the familiar and the here and the now, investing it with life-giving passion.

What is crucial to notice here, in sum, is the way in which modernity's dominant Cartesian ontology of distinction affirms a mechanical identity of x and non-x, and consequently an original "negative" relation of mutual indifference between the two that then unfolds into "positive" relations only of arbitrariness and force. Modernity's characteristic pluralism thus of its inner nature hides, and just so far imposes or "dictates," a certain monism, resulting in a double nihilism whereby the identity of each lacks the interior depth and order that give meaning, even as each, when it relates or moves, can then only simply disperse. The modern nihilism of mechanical identity, in other words, opens of its inner dynamic into

---

insofar as the God of creation is understood as the God of trinitarian love: cf. note 14. See "Trinity, Creation, and the Order of Intelligence in the Modern Academy," *Communio: International Catholic Review* 28, no. 3 (Fall 2001): 406-28.

the postmodern nihilism of dispersal, though, as we can now see, the "post" in postmodernity signals what is in fact only the later arrival of what is structurally implied already in modernity's characteristic Cartesianism.

IV.

The patterns of modern thought as sketched here are, from the point of view of Balthasar, best understood in terms of an absence of an ontology of generosity. Indeed, my reading of these patterns is reasonable only on the presupposition of such an ontology. By an ontology of generosity I mean an ontology according to which what is naturally given (x) bears within it, precisely coincident with its own identity as such, an order of relation, or an ordered relation, toward and from others. This relation is a matter first not of forceful power but of the power proper to love, or, in the case of non-spiritual beings, of a power that participates in an analogical way in love.[19] The key to understanding properly the relation of x to non-x lies above all in the recognition that the relation is *given in and with the constitution* of each's identity *as such* and hence as a matter of the original-natural order of the one and the other.[20]

The point, then, is that the Christian understanding of creation entails this constitutive relationality of each entity, to the creator God who is

---

19. A power, in other words, that is rooted in metaphysical interiority. Cf., for example, Balthasar's *Theo-logic I: Truth of the World* (San Francisco: Ignatius Press, 2001), pp. 84ff., and Kenneth L. Schmitz, *The Gift: Creation* (Milwaukee: Marquette University Press, 1982); and Schmitz, "Immateriality Past and Present," in *The Texture of Being: Essays in First Philosophy*, ed. Paul O'Herron, in *Studies in Philosophy and the History of Philosophy* (Washington, DC: Catholic University of America Press, 2007), pp. 168-82.

20. It is crucial here to see that the character of being "in itself" that is necessary for one's identity must not be set in opposition to one's being simultaneously "for" or "from" another. Indeed, a thing is "*in itself*," and thus bears an interiority or "within," and indeed is also *for itself* and *from itself*, precisely *coincident with* and *by virtue of* its being constituted *by* another, a constitutive relation given its first and "transcendental" meaning in the act of being created by God. There is thus no identity or "in itselfness" without this constitutive relation *from* and *toward* another that creates the "within" of x presupposed in x's being "*in itself*" in the first place. Rightly understood, then, relationality does not attenuate but on the contrary enables and deepens identity. Cf. here the link discussed above between an identity construed originally mechanistically and the relative order of such an identity toward dispersal.

a God of love, and indeed to all other creatures in and through their common relation to God. The being of everything that is, is a *being-given* in and by love, above all by God's love but also by the love of all creatures by virtue of their creation in the image of, or as analogically conceived signs or symbols of, God's love.[21]

The ontology of generosity indicated here, once again, does not reject *tout court* any of the distinctions that modernity has deemed necessary and that indeed undergird and render possible its characteristic and genuine achievements. On the contrary, such an ontology recuperates all of these distinctions, precisely in the *relational-analogical way demanded by a universal community of being and meaning under God*.

Although, as I said earlier, thinkers like Dawson and Newman and Gilson, and professors like Moreland and Cobb, and behind them, Aquinas and "neo-Thomism" and indeed Greek thought generally, had led me toward the reading of modernity sketched above, it was Balthasar who reconfigured from the inside out, and immeasurably deepened, what is referred to here as an ontology of generosity. The terms of this ontology, of course, were reached only gradually and after many years of reading and reflecting upon his work. What Balthasar showed me, in his life as in his work, is the indissoluble unity or convertibility of being and love in relation to God, and thus what is meant by living the catholicity entailed in Catholicism down into the heart of every being, in a way that spans the cosmos in its entirety. This formulation, however, still expresses things in a shorthanded way, hence still too abstractly. Just how does Balthasar distinguish between and relate God and the world, such that being and love are convertible inside this relation? As noted earlier, fundamental for Balthasar is the idea that God and love indicate their own manner of making distinctions, in a way that affects the original and most basic logic of all distinctions and relations of whatever sort anywhere in the cosmos. How are we to understand this?

As mentioned above, Balthasar emphasized throughout his life the inner link between theology, or the order of reason and reality, and sanctity, a link that lies at the heart of his lifelong engagement with the form of consecrated life that remains in the world. The depths of this link between theology and holiness become evident when we see how it is holi-

---

21. See Adrian J. Walker, "Personal Singularity and the *Communio Personarum*: A Creative Development of Thomas Aquinas' Doctrine of *Esse Commune*," in *Communio: International Catholic Review* 31, no. 3 (Fall 2004): 457–80.

ness itself that brings to completion the claim that being and love are convertible, in relation to God. The meaning of being as love, in other words, can be realized fully and properly only in persons, i.e., in substances possessing the capacities of intelligence and freedom. Sanctity, if you will, is but the personal-subjective realization, the realization in and by a human subject, of the objective convertibility of being and love in relation to God. Once again, Balthasar's argument is that this convertibility obtains analogically all the way down through the entire order of created being. It is important, then, to see how the very content of this claim of convertibility — namely, that all of being participates in a genuinely analogical way in love — presupposes that every being is a *subject*, in the sense that every being bears some metaphysical immateriality or interiority, again analogically conceived.[22] However, it is only in beings possessing spirituality, in human beings, that there exists a subject in the full and proper sense. What we are terming a saint, then, is the human being who realizes in a profound and proper way the objective meaning of being as a subject ordered toward and called to participate in God-centered love, in the grateful love or worship of God and the love of all other creatures in relation to God.

Here, then, we see in all its radicality Balthasar's C(c)atholicity: all of created being and meaning is ordered in its depths toward participation in sanctity, in and through the human persons who alone among the beings of the cosmos realize sanctity in the proper sense.

But we must take this further. Sanctity realizes the proper creaturely response both to God's gift of the creature to itself that constitutes the act of creation, and also to God's gift of himself to the creature in Jesus Christ that constitutes the creature's re-creation, or justification. This double gift of God to the creature takes the form of a Covenant, a promise of unfailing fidelity to the creature. This Covenant of God with his creatures, with man and with all other creatures in relation to man,[23] comes to fulfillment in

---

22. A center or a "within" is required for something to be at all, and it is this center that establishes something as a subject. Which is to say, a pure object, or an exhaustively objective being, does not properly exist. Cf. here the works by Balthasar and Schmitz cited in note 19; cf. also note 20.

23. See Genesis 9:8-13: "God spoke to Noah and his sons, 'See, I establish my Covenant with you, and with your descendants after you; also with every living creature to be found with you, birds, cattle and every wild beast with you: everything that came out of the ark, everything that lives on earth. I establish my Covenant with you: no thing of flesh shall be swept away again by the waters of the flood. . . . Here is the sign of the Covenant I make

Jesus Christ and thus in the Church where Christ continues to abide sacramentally. For Balthasar, it is crucial to see that the Incarnation of the Son of God in Jesus Christ, and thereby the beginning of what becomes a sacramental-ecclesial community in Christ, elicits and presupposes a response on the part of the creature, a response given its primordial form in the *fiat* of the virgin-mother Mary; and indeed to see further that Christ's founding of his sacramental-ecclesial community is completed when Christ, from the Cross, unites Mary's love with that of Peter, in and through the love of John that has always abided.[24]

The point here, then, is twofold. First, God's Covenant indicates God's total gift of himself to creatures, a gift that affirms the inherent dignity and worth of the creature in its integrity as such, by virtue at once of God's act of creation and of God's willingness himself to suffer death and abandonment in his Incarnate Son on behalf of the creature. Thus we might say, in light of the Covenant, that God desires to appear to the world as the whole God, and desires at the same time that the world appear as the whole world within the appearance of the whole God. God in Jesus Christ desires to be all in all, such that each being can simultaneously be all *it* is, at once in itself and in God. In Jesus Christ and his Covenant, the center of God is revealed to be open to the heart of the world, even as the heart of the world is now seen to be opened to the center of God.[25]

---

between myself and you and every living creature for all generations . . . a sign of the Covenant between me and the earth."

24. Cf. in this connection the statement of Cardinal Ratzinger: "In his last words on earth, the Crucified One says to his mother: 'Woman, behold your son' and to the disciple: 'Behold your mother.' These words are the document on which the Church is founded, or, let us say, one of the fundamental statements in the document in which Jesus founded the Church and established his covenant with her. They make clear the meaning of 'Church' and the manner in which God established his covenant, the New Covenant, with us. He does this above all by laying claim to Mary's Yes in a new and more general and even greater context. Her first Yes was to the Son that God willed to bestow on her and to the will of God that required her total and mysterious acquiescence to his incomprehensible and great design. But now, in the hour of the Cross, . . . she must say her Yes anew and in an even greater dimension. It is now a Yes to a new and different son, who becomes, through her, the same Son. It is a Yes in this new Son to all the sons and daughters that will be hers throughout all history. It is a Yes to whatever he may ask her to do for them throughout all history. And vice versa: the Lord founded the Church by the very fact of giving his mother to the disciple" (Roman homilies, September 18, 1985, cited in *Co-Workers of the Truth* [San Francisco: Ignatius Press, 1992], p. 319).

25. Cf. in this connection the important work of Orthodox theologian Alexander Schmemann on sacramentality and the symbolic nature of the world, particularly in *For the*

Secondly, this total gift of God expressed in the Covenant, in Jesus Christ, and in his sacramental Church, elicits and presupposes a total gift of self on the part of creation, in and as a grateful response to God's total gift. This grateful response, which is first and above all that of Christ as the Son (Col. 1:15-18), the firstborn among creatures, is, from the side of the creature, embodied in Mary (the virgin-mother), and upon Christ's death sacramentalized in the Church in and through the mediation of John (the first son in the Son, so to speak). The point, then, is that God's love makes its entry into the cosmos in and through his Son, Jesus Christ, and, from the side of the creature, in and through Mary as his Mother and John as the first son in the Son. But what it is crucial for present purposes to see is that, though the feminine-motherly love of Mary and the masculine-filial love of John both give primordial form in Jesus Christ to the Petrine sacramental Church, they do so *while remaining in the world,* and thus *while giving form to the meaning of creatureliness as such.* Mary and John give primordial form to the *Church* not as (objective) office but as (subjective) state — as the lay state.[26] And, retaining their lay character, Mary and John simultaneously also give the *world* its most basic form in Jesus Christ.

The point, in a word, is that Mary and John provide for Balthasar the privileged or archetypal form of the sanctity to which the world *as world,* in and through human persons in Jesus Christ, is called from its original creation. And what is that form? A gift of self that is total — *of the whole self* and *forever* — *in and as obedient, grateful response* to God's total gift of self expressed in his Covenant that is sacramentalized in Christ's Church. As Balthasar says, total love can only be given once, and is thus ordered toward taking a vow, toward a state of life.[27] It is this total love as state, as embodied in the form of a vow, that defines the most proper meaning of the

---

Life of the World: Sacraments and Orthodoxy (Crestwood, NY: St. Vladimir's Seminary Press, 1997); *The Eucharist: Sacrament of the Kingdom* (Crestwood, NY: St. Vladimir's Seminary Press, 2003); and *The Journals of Father Alexander Schmemann, 1973-1983* (Crestwood, NY: St. Vladimir's Seminary Press, 2000). Cf. also Nicholas J. Healy, *The Eschatology of Hans Urs von Balthasar: Being as Communion* (New York: Oxford University Press, 2005), and "Liturgy and the Integrity of Cosmic Order: The Theology of Alexander Schmemann," pp. 288-309 in this volume.

26. Of course, John, in uniting Mary and Peter, shares in both lay state and office.

27. See Hans Urs von Balthasar, *The Glory of the Lord: A Theological Aesthetics,* vol. 5 (San Francisco: Ignatius Press, 1991), p. 654. In connection with the argument here regarding a state of life, cf. "Living and Thinking Reality in Its Integrity: Originary Experience, God, and the Task of Education," pp. 310-27 in this volume.

sanctity to which the whole of creation, in and through human persons in Jesus Christ, is called. It is from inside this sanctity, in other words, that the whole God in Jesus Christ becomes present in the world, coincident with the world's appearance in its own wholeness *as world*, such that God can now, in Jesus Christ, be all in the "allness" of all. For Balthasar, it is essential to see that Mary, precisely as mother, and John, precisely as son (and thus ultimately the reality of both in their virginal-familial-spousal relations) are the creaturely point of intersection between this mutual, albeit radically asymmetrical, appearance in Jesus Christ of God's love in the world and the world's love in obedient, grateful response to God's love.[28]

In sum, the whole world is ordered from and toward the sanctity of God himself in Jesus Christ that abides sacramentally in Peter (Church as office), in and through the form of that sanctity as personalized above all in Mary and John (Church as state of life).

Needless to say, this brief discussion of the sanctity, the realization of the unity of being and love in relation to God, to which the world as world is ordered from its creation carries an abundance of further presuppositions that bring into play all the major themes of Balthasar's theology. It will nevertheless suffice for our purposes now to provide a sketch of the ontology implied in the foregoing account, to indicate, that is, how the world in its given creaturely being as such is ordered from and toward a God-centered love that takes its proper "worldly" form in human persons, a form whose perfection is realized in sanctity.

V.

(1) First, since our question concerns the heart of the world, we must go to the world's first and last word about itself, so to speak: that it *is*. We must go to the world in its primitive revelation as being. Here Balthasar follows

---

28. It is important for Balthasar that we recognize the "circumincessive" relation between the vows pronounced in consecrated virginity on the one hand, and in marriage on the other. On this, see the work of David Crawford, e.g., his "Christian Community and the States of Life: A Reflection on the Anthropological Significance of Virginity and Marriage," *Communio: International Catholic Review* 29, no. 2 (Summer 2002): 337-65; *Marriage and the Sequela Christi* (Vatican City: Lateran University Press, 2004); "Love, Action, and Vows as 'Inner Form' of the Moral Life," *Communio: International Catholic Review* 32, no. 2 (Summer 2005): 295-312; "Of Spouses, the Real World, and the 'Where' of Christian Marriage," *Communio: International Catholic Review* 33, no. 1 (Spring 2006): 100-116.

Aquinas, and Aquinas's different contemporary interpreters such as Gilson and Ferdinand Ulrich, in affirming that being *(ens)*, which takes its name from the existential act of being *(esse)*, is the word that articulates first and most basically the meaning of the world. *Esse,* as Aquinas says, is the act of acts and thus the perfection of all acts. Nothing falls outside of *esse; esse* is what is innermost in a thing.

(2) In this context, however, Balthasar follows Ulrich in making central Aquinas's dictum that *esse* is *completum et simplex sed non subsistens: esse* is complete and simple, hence "perfect" in the sense indicated, but nevertheless is so, paradoxically, only as itself non-subsistent, not itself existent in the proper sense. *Esse creatum,* the very act through which God communicates being to the creature, depends for its proper existence on the very things that are called into being via that communication. *Esse,* so to speak, lends its wealth or perfection as act of being to the things to which it is communicated only by way of being emptied into those things, thus becoming poor. At the same time, the things to which *esse* is communicated, originally poor in their utter need for the act of being, themselves contribute a wealth of content to that act of being coincident with their enactment by the latter.[29]

The inner structure of being as created thus, for Balthasar, is disclosed as gift: being is "rich" or "perfect" *qua received from another.*

(3) Balthasar develops his own discussion of what is termed the "real distinction" between *esse* and *essentia,* or the ontological difference between Being and beings, in terms of a personal relationship, in the form of the mother-child relation. For Balthasar the mother's smile at her newborn child reveals being as gift, and the smile thereby sets in motion what will gradually become a conscious wonder in the child, a grateful response confirming being as gift. The child grasps himself as recipient of the gift of being permitted to be. And yet in time the child comes to see that his mother, like himself, is also the recipient of the gift of being permitted to be, indeed that all beings are in this same condition. The Being that shares

---

29. Once the matter is formulated this way, we can began to see a further implication: namely, that the concrete *ens,* whose unity is the *fruit* of a duality of principles *(esse* and *essentia),* and as such transcends that duality, just so far bears a kind of triplicity. And this in turn enables us, following Balthasar, to see already in the individual *ens* (existing substance) traces of God as a Trinity. Thus, for Balthasar, it is not only in the *relationality among beings (persons)* that these traces can be discovered (as in the tradition following Richard of St. Victor), but also in the *relationality within each being* (as in the tradition following Augustine). It is, however, beyond my purposes to explore this complex matter further here.

itself with all beings, that gives its act of being to all beings, and that is thus transcendent of beings, itself exists only in and as those beings, such that Being appears to reduce to beings, even as beings threaten to absorb Being into themselves. Either beings are some form of explication of Being, or Being is some form of projection by beings, or both. In either case, there is an oscillation within the structure of Being/beings in their mutual relation that threatens to drain the world as a whole of the giftedness that called forth gratitude and that seemed, originally and most deeply in the mother-child relation, to constitute the reality of the world as such, the reality of its giftedness coincident with the giftedness of its reality.

(4) Insofar as we would sustain all the way through and with consistency the originary experience of the child in relation to its mother, then, we are led reasonably, in and through the distinction between Being and beings in light of this originary experience, to affirm that Being *(Esse)* itself subsists, and at the same time to affirm that this Subsistent Being must somehow be generous, in the sense that it can both (in its transcendence) give beings their being while (in its simultaneous immanence) staying with those beings and caring for them, in a manner analogous to that of a mother or father in her or his parental love for the child. We are led reasonably to the conclusion that Subsistent Being must somehow be personal in the way expressed in such love.[30]

And yet it is just here that we have already begun to cross a threshold. We are led necessarily, that is, reasonably, to conclude that Subsistent Being must exist and must somehow be a personal, or parental, lover, but we cannot conceive properly or fully how this is so. In other words, we reach the point where the ontological difference must become in turn, *simultaneously,* the difference between God and the world, and thus the point at which the metaphysical act must become at once a theological act. But it is important to be clear here: reason, reflecting on the implications of what it finds in being itself as it appears in the world, is led in an intrinsic way to God; which is to say, the metaphysical act is led into what may be termed a natural theological act. It is important to stress this lest we slip into a fideism rejected by Balthasar. At the same time, however, precisely from inside its logical movement that has "naturally" reached toward the reality of God,[31] reason must await God's own self-revelation as (tri-personal) love.

---

30. For more on Balthasar's fourfold distinction, see *The Glory of the Lord,* vol. V, pp. 613-27.

31. "Naturally," that is, in the sense indicated by Balthasar *Theo-logic* I ("General In-

Which is to say, reason must remain open, in Marian fashion, to the theological-Christian act properly speaking.[32]

In sum, being is created for love, even as the fullness of this love for which being is created cannot finally be conceived or sustained on its own. On the contrary, the very structure of being entails a "waiting" for the Being (Subsistent *Esse*) that makes it be to reveal itself as a lover, one who can be provident for it and look after it and share life with it in the intimate fashion of a parent. The revelation of being as a gift calling forth wonder and gratitude, which takes place above all in the relation between mother and child, awaits the revelation of divine being itself, Subsistent *Esse,* as creator-giver of the gift of being in his Son, Jesus Christ.

This, then, is what it means for the metaphysical, or natural theological, act to break open to the theological, or Christian, act, which goes beyond even as it contains and presupposes the metaphysical act. Thus, as Balthasar sums up in *Herrlichkeit:*

> The fundamental metaphysical act is love within the Ontological Difference . . . ; the fundamental Christian act is love within the God-world distinction. . . . In each case love means here the total human act which comprehends the totality of mind and body, and in particular, percipient intelligence. As metaphysical intelligence, it perceives the relation of the existent and Being which defies formulation and, as Christian intelligence, it perceives God's free word of absolute love which utters itself as a medium within this relation. But we must guard here against both false distinctions and false equations. We are following the right path when we genuinely locate the metaphysical act within the Ontological Difference — even if it naturally points to God

---

troduction," especially pp. 11-13): while philosophy can identify certain fundamental natural structures of the world and knowledge — because grace and the supernatural "do not do away with, or even alter the essential core of" these structures — it is nonetheless impossible to know the precise extent to which, in the concrete order of things, elements of grace and the supernatural may be present. Hence "there is simply no way to reconstruct [nature] in its pure state *(natura pura)."* But see the further qualifications of Balthasar in his text here.

32. See John Paul II, *Fides et Ratio,* n. 108: "And just as in giving her assent to Gabriel's word, Mary lost nothing of her true humanity and freedom, so too when philosophy heeds the summons of the Gospel's truth its autonomy is in no way impaired. Indeed, it is then that philosophy sees all its enquiries rise to their highest expression. This was a truth which the holy monks of Christian antiquity understood well when they called Mary 'the table at which faith sits in thought.' In her they saw a lucid image of true philosophy and they were convinced of the need to *philosophari in Maria."*

as its depths — and understand the Christian act as a new response to the new word of God which, of course, contains the metaphysical act within itself and, beyond that, contributes also to its fulfillment.[33]

And again:

> Only this much can be said: in the love between human beings a mystery already operative at the origin is foreshadowed, because the loving persons (in whom the all-encompassing Being of reality prevails) never close themselves off from one another. On the contrary, they are open to the original mystery of Being in their (always conditioned) fruitfulness. The fruitfulness they share, rooted in nature (as when a child is conceived), indeed remains an important but still limited parable of this fruitfulness of love, which at the most archetypal level must have some inexpressible analogue within the divine identity.[34]

The radical comprehensiveness finally intended by Balthasar here is captured in the following summary formulations:

> The non-subsistence of the *actus essendi* is the creative medium which suffices for God to utter his kenotic word of the Cross and of glory and to send it as his Son into the world to experience death and resurrection.[35]

> The Incarnation and the Cross have their "place" where the *actus completus non subsistens* is at work in created reality, which is realized only in individual beings. The Son of God in no way replaces this act. But if "everything in heaven and on earth has its being in him," then he is the head of everything that has been created from that identity. And the free assumption not only of human nature but also of its alienation can ensue only "above" or "beneath" the situatedness of all natural beings.[36]

Thus from the very core of being as such there is an opening to love. Everything that is, and insofar as it is, participates in this logic of love, even as this logic is adequately and properly expressed only in and through

---

33. Balthasar, *The Glory of the Lord*, vol. V, p. 637.
34. Balthasar, *Epilogue* (San Francisco: Ignatius Press, 1991), p. 57.
35. Balthasar, *The Glory of the Lord*, vol. V, pp. 631-32.
36. Balthasar, *Epilogue*, p. 120.

personal-spiritual beings. Being as gift, to fully realize its meaning as such, must pass through — must be, as it were, brought home to itself through — the interior acts of giving and receiving, the obedient wonder- and gratitude-filled fruitfulness, proper to human lovers who have become saints.

In short, the point for Balthasar is that all human beings are meant to recapitulate personally the meaning of being as such, to perform the metaphysical act. Human persons are ordered in their constitutive reality as such to the gathering up of the being of the cosmos in its entirety and recapitulating it in love, in their total gift of self, lending the cosmos their own gift of self, as it were; and they must do this in openness to the Christian act that goes beyond this metaphysical act even as it contains and fulfills it. In other words, metaphysical love must finally be taken up within and comprehended by God's act of love in Jesus Christ, expressed in the total gift of his self in death and abandonment, a death and abandonment that recapitulates and fulfills in an utterly new and inconceivable way the original meaning of being as such in its dual unity of *esse-essentia!*[37] And this "upward" participatory love, which enables even as it is comprehended by God's "descending" love, receives its archetypal form in the Marian and Johannine love that remains in the world even as it mediates Christ's love as expressed sacramentally in the office of Peter.

The foregoing, then, reveals the burden of Balthasar's work: that the

37. Here, then, is the framework within which the Trilogy finds its order. Taking over the Thomistic understanding of being rooted in the "real distinction," Balthasar humanizes this distinction even as he lifts it in turn into a theological context, which is to say, places it finally within the horizon of the Trinitarian God's revelation of divine love in Jesus Christ. The relevant point is that the meaning of being is placed within the polarity presupposed in the encounter between a one and an other that reveals love in the proper (spiritual) sense. Thus being in such an encounter reveals itself most basically as a self-showing (beauty, glory), a self-giving (goodness, drama), and self-expressing (truth, logic) that occurs mutually, though always somehow asymmetrically, in every encounter, insofar as that encounter is faithful to its most proper meaning as love. But, as indicated above, this metaphysical act must itself be situated within the theological act, and this means that the encounter between beings must finally be placed within the encounter between the world and God, the Father of Jesus Christ, through the *fiat* of the Virgin-Mother, Mary. And thus the "transcendentals" of being become matters of *Herrlichkeit, Theodramatik,* and *Theologik,* that is, matters involving the appearance, giving, and speaking of creatures vis-à-vis the appearance, giving, and speaking of God's Word in Jesus Christ, in and through the responsive love that abides in Mary (and John). On the philosophical meaning of the transcendentals, cf. D. C. Schindler, *Hans Urs von Balthasar and the Dramatic Structure of Truth* (New York: Fordham University Press, 2004), pp. 350-421, and *passim*.

heart of the whole God of love in Jesus Christ appear at the heart of the whole world in the integrity of its worldly being and meaning; and that the heart of the whole world be opened to the heart of the whole God of love in Jesus Christ in the integrity of his divine being and meaning. God's reality as a total gift of self in Jesus Christ makes its entry into the world precisely coincident with, and indeed from inside or "beneath" and as the ground of, the world's recovery of its own inner meaning as ordered to a total gift of itself in and through the saints to God.

VI.

Balthasar's C(c)atholic ontology is thus fulfilled and recapitulated in a sanctity that takes every reality and every thought "captive" in Jesus Christ, *generously:* in a way that "assumes," while thus not "absorbing" but rather gathering up and perfecting, every being and meaning of the cosmos in its singular creaturely integrity as such. It is love inside the double distinction between *esse* and *essentia* (the ontological difference) and between God and the world (the Christian difference) that gives all cosmic identities, distinctions, and relations their most basic onto-logic, and thereby establishes the cosmos as a whole and in each of its parts as an analogically conceived generous community of being and meaning under God, and as a participatory sign of God's presence. It is the horizon set by love inside this double distinction, then, that enables us for the first time fully to understand what has been termed a Cartesian ontology of identity and distinction. This Cartesian ontology of identity, which is both rooted in and serves to bring about a forgetfulness of Being and of God, expresses even as it promotes the failure (however unintended) to live and think reality as a matter of love, or, *a fortiori,* to live and think sanctity as a matter of the perfection of being.

In conclusion, let me note briefly how Balthasar's position stands with respect to major alternative streams of Catholic thought, in response to modernity.

(1) Viewed in light of Balthasar as presented above, we should say that the dominant stream of modern Catholic theology and philosophy, even when harshly critical of modern patterns of life and thought, has nevertheless left intact the root assumptions of those patterns as reflected in a Cartesian ontology of identity. Modern Catholic thought has itself typically taken the identity of x to be originally-conceptually *closed to* non-x or to any implication of the presence of non-x in x. Which is to say, much of

modern Catholic thought has itself presupposed just the structural indifference between the two that, on Balthasar's understanding as outlined above, lies at the root of a modernity that mechanizes the order and intelligibility of things even as it then moralizes or voluntarizes (i.e., conceives as arbitrary and just so far not integral to the order and intelligibility of things) relation and love and religious piety. Catholic thought in the modern period, in a word, has had its own version of modernity's forgetfulness of Being, in relation to beings, and of God, in relation to the world: its own version thus of modernity's forgetfulness of love *in its ontological meaning* as signified and expressed in this double distinction.

The stream of Catholic thought referred to here is above all that of a certain modern scholasticism. Much is often made of the question of how Balthasar stands with respect to the thought of Thomas Aquinas. In fact, Aquinas is a pivotal figure for Balthasar as well as for modern scholasticism. The issue between Balthasar and scholasticism bears rather on what each takes to be the basic achievement of Aquinas. And this question turns finally on what each takes to be the Thomistic ontology of identity and distinction: how each conceives the double distinction between *esse* and *essentia* (the ontological difference) and between God and the world (the Christian Difference), and how each consequently understands the relation between being and love under God. Modern scholasticism's assumed, even if unintended, Cartesian ontology of identity manifests itself in its construal of these two distinctions in terms of what amounts to an original-structural indifference of *essentia* in relation to *esse* and the world in relation to God. That is, scholasticism overlooks both the significance of *esse* in its constitutive implications for being and the significance of God in his constitutive implications for the world, and thus misses the significance of love in its constitutive implications for the world — the world in the dual sense of its being created, hence its originally being-given, and of its being invited, simultaneous with its being created, to share in God's own love as revealed in Jesus Christ.[38]

---

38. Contemporary scholastic thinkers not infrequently accuse Balthasar of a theological reduction, a precipitous move from the order of nature and reason to that of faith and the supernatural. In point of fact, however, these critics typically make this accusation while also presupposing a metaphysics different from that of Balthasar, in the way already suggested in the text. That is, they read differently from Balthasar the distinction between *esse* and *essentia,* with all that this distinction implies for Balthasar in terms of the inner openness of being to God, and indeed in terms of the nature of being, in its given structure as such, as gift. Balthasar's argument, in other words, shows being to be open already in its nat-

The point, then, is that scholasticism lacks just the ontology of generosity ordered to sanctity whose absence is the bane of modernity, an ontology that Balthasar takes to be implied in the symphony of all great Catholic theologian-saints. Balthasar reads Aquinas, and indeed grants him his pivotal place, within this symphony. Key for Balthasar is Aquinas's articulation of the ontological difference, which eliminates Cartesian (mechanistic) identity at its source even as it restores identity in its genuinely catholic sense as warranted by the Christian doctrine of creation rightly understood.[39]

Modern scholasticism often insists that inscribing generosity, and thus relationality, within the original logic of being and meaning leads to relativism. Such a fear, however, from the point of view argued above in the name of Balthasar, overlooks the crucial fact that it is the *very relation to God* by which the creature is constituted in existence that gives the creature its substantial *identity* in the first place. Relationality and identity are constitutively, thus simultaneously, given. It follows that each presupposes even as it always already shapes the original and proper meaning of the other. The relationality of the individual creature to God (and the transcendental relationality thereby of the individual creature to all other creatures in God)[40] on the one hand, and the substantial identity of the individual creature, on the other hand, can never be simply juxtaposed or simply opposed to each other. Identity and relation, in a word, are *both* integral to the original-constitutive *order of being and intelligibility*. This is why the identity of things can never be most basically mechanistic, even as relationality can never consist most basically in arbitrary or forceful movement. And this is why, further, the proper intelligibility of things, which

---

ural philosophical meaning (in the one concrete order of history) to God-related love and generosity. The charge that Balthasar's understanding of the world in terms of God-centered love implies *eo ipso* a precipitous move to the order of faith and the supernatural thus begs what Balthasar himself takes to be *also* the crucial *philosophical* issue — namely, the relation between *esse* and *essentia*. Balthasar holds that this issue is necessarily invoked in any theological account of the world-God difference. The scholastic charge of a theological reduction on Balthasar's part, in a word, misses the crucial fact that the difference between scholasticism and Balthasar regarding the meaning of being in its relation to God-centered love is a matter at once of a properly philosophical *and* a properly theological argument. To be sustained in a reasonable and non-question-begging fashion, therefore, such a charge must defend itself also in philosophical terms, by providing its own account of the "real distinction" relative to Balthasar's account.

39. Cf. in this connection "The Given as Gift."
40. Cf. Walker, "Personal Singularity and the *Communio Personarum.*"

necessarily presupposes a conceptual identity just so far subject to power and control, is *simultaneously* a matter *also* of *mystery* — of the mystery entailed by an identity that is generously conceived.

Regarding the problem of relativism, then: the burden of the earlier criticism of modernity's Cartesian ontology is that the latter's originally assumed mechanistic, and just so far closed, identity of x is what first gave rise to, and indeed required, the idea that relations between x and non-x were arbitrary and dispersive and thus a matter of *relativism*, or better, for the reasons adduced earlier, of relativistic *nihilism*. In sum, it is Balthasar's originally generous identity that alone enables us reasonably to reject relativism, while on the contrary modern scholasticism's mechanistic identity generates, of its own inner logic and dialectically, the very relativism that it is scholasticism's intention to oppose.[41]

(2) Here, then, we can see the difficulty also with another stream of Catholic thought that has emerged in recent decades, as a kind of "postmodern" response to modernity, including modernity in the above scholastic form. Certain Catholic thinkers argue that love and God are, strictly speaking, beyond or other than being. Such a position, however, itself continues to presuppose modern patterns of thought, *precisely coincident with*, and in a way that thus anteriorly shapes, what is intended as a fundamental postmodern criticism of these patterns. Love, or God, needs to be placed "beyond" or "without" being only insofar as one has already, however tacitly and unintentionally, assumed that being in its original-proper meaning as such lacks generosity; insofar, that is, as one presupposes that the being of the world in its constitutive identity as such is not always already open to the *esse* that opens being to God and the love that images God — in a word, insofar as one continues, however contrary to one's intention, to presuppose the Cartesian ontology of identity whereby x is not properly *open* to non-x coincident with x's substantial self-identity *as x*. In short, the Catholic postmodern claim that love or God is "beyond" being is in fact but the later arrival of what is already logically implied in modernity's characteristic Cartesianism.

The difficulty with both modern Catholic scholasticism and its post-

---

41. The point, in other words, is that, while modern scholasticism has clearly insisted on the truth of Catholic dogma, precisely against modern, or modern liberal, forms of relativism, it has done so typically while failing to provide an adequate opening in the *structure of being* to relationality to God and God's love. Catholic dogma in such a framework, therefore, insofar as it speaks of God and God's love, can only appear to be, and be, an *arbitrary-adventitious imposition from without* on reality and reason in their naturally given logic as such.

modern Catholic alternative is that both, albeit from opposite directions, are simultaneously too modern and too anti-modern. They both remain caught in the dialectic that is the bane of the modern cultural situation: between an identity that is mechanistic, on the one hand, and relations that are (consequently) purely arbitrary and dispersive, on the other.

It is crucial, then, in light of these two Catholic responses to modernity, to see that Balthasar's own response, expressed in what has been termed his catholic ontology of generosity, is one that shares the assumptions neither of modernity nor of postmodernity, or better, that adopts the assumptions of both modernity and postmodernity but only as it transforms these. As we have repeatedly insisted, the identity of modernity and the relationality of modern postmodernity[42] both need to be recuperated, *precisely in terms of the community* of x and non-x that originally constitutes the order of reality as love and love as the order of reality, under God and in the image of God — in creation, hypostatically in Jesus Christ, and sacramentally in the Church.

But here in conclusion we need to emphasize what has been implied all along, that this recuperation, which is finally realized only in and through the lives of the saints, necessarily involves, in the one order of history that is weighted with sinfulness, a transformation at the heart of which stands the Cross. "Worldly" identities, all of which are disfigured by the sin of the first human persons, are restored in their originally given and intended meaning through the total-personal gift of self: first and above all through Christ's total gift of self, which is then truly symbolized in and through the saint's total gift of self, which lends itself to the cosmos, thereby gathering the cosmos itself up into the love of God revealed in Christ and in his saints.

The point, then, is that all identities of every age, in their real and in their cognitive being, are always to be recuperated and never simply rejected, but only from within the dynamic toward love which, in the one order of history, involves a crucifying conversion, following Christ into his suffering death and abandonment on the Cross. This following is realized in the saints, precisely as they extend themselves in an embrace of the cosmos in its entirety, in its unity and in each of its "parts," so that the cosmos as a whole may be drawn up into its needed conversion into love.

It is just here, then, and finally only here, that we can understand rightly what it means to affirm *in love* the identity peculiar to being in each

---

42. And thus, for example, the subjectivity and history that are characteristic achievements of the modern era.

of its epiphanies in every time and place of history, including modern Western history.

*   *   *

In sum, then, according to Balthasar what we need to see today — need to see in all cultures, but especially in our modern liberal-technological culture whose hallmark is to deny it — is that, in identifying *this* or *that*, or distinguishing between *this* and *that*, in life (reality) or in thought (concept), we necessarily invoke *an ontology of creation*. We invoke, at least implicitly and however unconsciously, some view of what constitutes the meaning of being, of a one in relation to a many, and hence *ultimately*, originally and finally, some response to the question of the nature and existence of God.[43] In the one concrete order of history, this necessarily implied view bears the further implication of some response to God as he has revealed himself in Jesus Christ and as he remains sacramentally present in the Church, whose primordial form is given in Mary and John, as state, and Peter, as office, of holiness. It is to this holiness that all "worldly" being, in and through the human persons whose meaning is archetypically embodied in Mary and John, is called.

The point is thus that every being in the cosmos, "real" or cognitive, realizes its perfection finally only from within the love whose katalogical-analogical meaning is revealed in the Christ-centered doctrine of creation and redemption. Sanctity alone, in realizing this love, liberates being into its deepest and most proper identity as such, as ordered toward the depths of God himself.

This, then, is the truly catholic and Catholic burden of Balthasar's work, which, it seems to me, articulates well the core meaning of the Second Vatican Council, in its renewed sense of the Church's Trinitarian God- and Christ-centered mission of love to the heart of the world.[44]

---

43. This in fact is one of the two main points of Pope Benedict XVI's lecture to the faculty of the University of Regensburg, September 12, 2006, which emphasizes that the West needs to see that reason of its inner logic is open to God even as the major religions of the world (e.g., Islam) need to see that God is innerly open to reason, that God himself is reasonable.

44. It thus seems difficult not to see the work of Balthasar as of a piece with that of the constellation of Catholic thinkers — including de Lubac, John Paul II, and Joseph Ratzinger/Benedict XVI — who have influenced and guided the Church in and since the Second Vatican Council, insisting that the Council's basic teaching is rightly understood in

terms of Christ's revelation of the mystery of the love of the Father (*Gaudium et Spes*, n. 22; see John Paul II, *Dives in Misericordia*, n. 1). Balthasar's work demonstrates that the renewal of the Church and the Church's relation to the world, as conceived at the Council and in the pontificates of John Paul II and Benedict XVI, is a matter of ontology and thus of reason and reality, and not merely of moral or spiritual intentionality. Cf. in this connection the Council's new, or renewed, understanding of Christ's revelation of divine trinitarian love as the key to understanding the reality of the Church (the idea of the Church as *communio*), and the developments since the Council regarding man, the body, and the world (the ideas of *communio personarum*, the "nuptial" attribute of the body, and man as a unity within distinctness of *eros* and *agape*), and regarding the laity and the call to live sanctity at the heart of the world (on the latter, cf. Balthasar's "The Council of the Holy Spirit," *Explorations in Theology*, vol. III: *Creator Spirit* [San Francisco: Ignatius Press, 1993], pp. 245-67).

The Given as Gift: Creation and Disciplinary Abstraction in Science

Introduction

> If the God of the Bible is creator of the universe, then it is not possible to understand fully or even appropriately the processes of nature without any reference to that God. If, on the contrary, nature can be appropriately understood without reference to the God of the Bible, then that God cannot be the creator of the universe, and consequently he could not be truly God. . . . To be sure, the reality of God is not incompatible with all forms of abstract knowledge concerning the regularities of natural processes, a knowledge that abstracts from the concreteness of physical reality and therefore may also abstract from the presence of God in his creation. But neither should such abstract knowledge of regularities claim full and exclusive competence regarding the explanation of nature and, if it does so, the reality of God is thereby denied by implication. The so-called methodological atheism of modern science is far from pure innocence. It is a highly ambiguous phenomenon. And yet its very possibility can be regarded as based on the unfailing faithfulness of the creator God to his creation, providing it with the inviolable regularities of natural processes that themselves become the basis of individual and more precarious and transitory natural systems.[1]

---

1. W. Pannenberg, "Theological Questions to Scientists," in A. R. Peacocke, ed., *The Sciences and Theology in the Twentieth Century* (Notre Dame: University of Notre Dame

This chapter was first presented in summary form at the international symposium "Science, Reason, and Truth," co-sponsored by the John Templeton Foundation and Euresis (Associazone per la promozione e la diffusione della cultura e del lavoro scientifico), Repubblica di San Marino, 17-19 August 2007.

This statement by Protestant theologian Wolfhart Pannenberg helps to set the context for the question posed in the present chapter. It goes without saying that abstraction — the consideration of a thing or an aspect of a thing apart from the totality of its meaning or context, for methodological or disciplinary purposes — is necessary and legitimate in scientific research. Indeed, such abstraction is made possible by the Christian understanding of creation itself. The creator God in his generosity grants to the creature its autonomy, a law *(nomos)* proper to its own nature *(autos,* "self"). At the same time, as Pannenberg suggests, the relation of the creature to the creator God is *sui generis,* by virtue of its utterly foundational character: rightly understood, creation in Christianity is *ex nihilo*.[2] If God is the source of my being and the being of all else, then relation to God is just so far *given with* and *constitutive of* being.[3] Indeed, as Aquinas says, "God is in all things, and innermostly."[4] This means that this relation to God cannot but accompany each being everywhere and at every moment and indeed from its deepest depths.

The reality of God as creator implies a distinction, further, between God and the world that shapes the nature of the distinctness among cosmic entities. Creation implies an openness in each thing to the Creator who makes them be in their beginning and all along the course of their existence.[5] This inherent openness of each thing to the Creator implies an openness of each thing to all others. Creation, in a word, implies a universe, a "turning" of all things toward a "one," a

---

Press, 1981/1986), pp. 3-16, at 4-5. The paper was originally presented at the Oxford International Symposium at Christ Church in September 1979. Reprinted in *Communio: International Catholic Review* 15, no. 3 (Fall 1988): 319-33.

2. Creation *ex nihilo* does not imply "creationism." An absolute origin of being is not incompatible with evolution, though which theory of the latter is most adequate need not occupy us here. Cf. Michael Hanby, "Creation Without Creationism: Toward a Theological Critique of Darwinism," *Communio: International Catholic Review* 30, no 4 (Winter 2003): 654-94; and Adrian Walker, "Schöpfung und Evolution. Jenseits des Konkordismus," *Internationale katholische Zeitschrift Communio* 35, no 1 (Spring 2006): 55-70.

3. Cf. the *Compendium of the Social Doctrine of the Church,* n. 109: "*The likeness with God shows that the essence and existence of man are constitutively related to God in the most profound manner. This is a relationship that exists in itself, it is therefore not something that comes afterwards and is not added from the outside.*"

4. Thomas Aquinas, *ST* I, q. 8, a. 1.

5. Cf. Aquinas on conservation in being: *ST* I, q. 8, a. 1: "Now God causes this effect [of being] in things not only when they first begin to be, but as long as they are preserved in being; as light is caused in the air by the sun as long as the air remains illuminated."

unity established by virtue of the common relation to God in which all things participate.[6]

Again, this constitutive relation of the creature to God, with its implications as sketched, does not eliminate the autonomy of each creature but indeed makes that autonomy possible even as it gives autonomy its original and proper meaning. The relation to God that *establishes the creature in its own being* is truly *in* the creature. It follows that each entity is independent in its being and acting even as this independent being and acting, which at every moment is *given* by God and *received* by the creature, just so far bears the constitutive feature of *openness from and toward God*, and indeed *from and toward the universal community of creatures* under God.

This Christian understanding of creation has two consequences relative to scientific abstraction. On the one hand, it renders possible and legitimates the study of an entity (x) in itself and just so far without explicit reference to its relation to God and other entities. At the same time, it requires that this abstraction, rightly conceived, take account of each entity's constitutive relation to God as origin and end, and indeed to the universe of creaturely entities implied by their common relation to God. Any rightly conceived abstraction, in other words, needs to take account of the qualitative "difference" that is always already operative *in* x by virtue of its constitutive relation to God and others (non-x).

The upshot is that abstractions in science are not and can never be indifferent to the reality of God or a universe under God. Each abstraction in science will imply, even if unconsciously, some conception of the unity or identity of the thing abstracted relative to God and to the universal community of beings. The God-world distinction as disclosed in the act of creation shapes the primitive nature of all distinctions, and hence all abstractions, in the cosmos. Indeed, every distinction and abstraction *most basically is* a sense of the God-world relation.

I propose to show this in terms of those scientific abstractions conceived as "merely disciplinary" in nature. It is commonly assumed that problems of reductionism in science (positivism, empiricism, mechanism, and the like) could be avoided if the practitioners of science simply ob-

---

6. On the interconnectedness of things, cf., for example, Marco Bersanelli, "An Echo of Ancient Questions from Contemporary Cosmology," in Charles L. Harper, ed., *Spiritual Information: 100 Perspectives on Science and Religion* (Philadelphia: Templeton Foundation Press, 2005), pp. 121-26.

served the limits specified by a science's particular mode of abstraction. Such problems would be avoided, so the argument runs, were it recognized that science does not claim to exhaust the intelligibility of an object in the integrity of its existing being: were physics or biology, for example, to remain just physics or biology and not venture onto the terrain of philosophy or theology. While recognizing the important sense in which this is, of course, true, I argue that such a claim, nevertheless, is governed by an idea of abstraction needing further differentiation, and just so far instantiates a *petitio principii.*

Abstractions and distinctions, which involve separating an entity or pulling it out or excluding it from the web of relations to other things that characterize its concrete existence at any moment,[7] necessarily evoke the notion of limit: of a boundary that sets the object off from its environs. This idea of limit, even if intended to be only disciplinary in nature, will inevitably carry some tacit conception of what lies beyond the entity's limit, some tacit conception, that is, of the relation of x to non-x, and just so far some conception also of both x and non-x. The idea of limit presupposed in any abstraction of an entity from its relations will imply, in a way that makes a difference already from within the limit that constitutes that object in its methodologically abstracted state, some tacit conception of the entity relative to the existence and nature of God, and a universe of beings under God: in a word, it will imply some ontology of creation.[8]

Insofar as this is so, claims to avoid reductive science by appealing to

7. *Abstrahere:* to pull from, drag away, take out, exclude; *distinguere:* to divide or separate.

8. The term "ontology" as used in the present chapter indicates a metaphysics that opens into a metaphysical ("natural") theology, in a sense indicated already by Aristotle. The term is understood just so far to bear definite implications with respect to what Christians understand to be revealed theology. As a "logic" of "being" (onto-logy), it is understood, further, to include in its most basic terms the logic of the whole person in his encounter with the totality of things. Finally, as my introductory remarks make clear, the ontology of creation affirmed in this chapter is understood to be a Christian ontology of creation, even as Christian faith itself is understood to enable and indeed to require, even as it reconfigures the meaning of, this ontology's *autonomy as an ontology.* Cf. in this connection the statements of Joseph Ratzinger in his "Faith, Philosophy and Theology" (*The Nature and Mission of Theology* [San Francisco: Ignatius Press, 1995], pp. 13-29): "Only when it takes up the cause of philosophy does [faith] remain true to itself" (p. 29). "A philosopher who really gets to the bottom of things can never rid himself of the goad of the question of God, which is the question regarding the origin and goal of being as such" (p. 22). The "*analogia entis* is simply a term for the ontological option of Catholic theology, for its synthesis of the philosophical idea of being and the biblical conception of God" (p. 19).

the idea of abstraction as methodologically limited require ontological qualification as a condition of their being soundly argued. Indeed, the assumption that the idea of limit can be originally empty of or neutral toward ontology already embeds a hidden ontology itself, one that is rightly termed mechanistic. Such an ontology implies a reductive view of God, of the universe, and indeed of the identity of the abstracted entity itself. The claim that an abstraction in science can be neutral toward an ontology of creation, in other words, effectively contradicts what is entailed in the constitutive relation of a given entity to God and to other creatures, in favor of a mechanistic sense of this relation — which thereby reveals such an abstraction to be reductive. The present chapter proposes to clarify how this is so.

As these introductory remarks make clear, my proposal presupposes a definite understanding of the Christian doctrine of creation, and thus a definite ontology as implied by this doctrine. I will have more to say about this understanding later. It is important to see at the outset, however, that although I take this ontology to be true, acceptance of this truth is not necessary to sustain the burden of the argument in the limited form advanced here. It suffices for my argument only that it succeed in showing that abstractions in science, even those made with purely disciplinary intentions, cannot avoid assumptions bearing on the meaning and truth of the Christian understanding of creation, *already from inside these abstractions in their limited disciplinary character.*

My proposal is developed in terms of the notion of the given as gift, which I take to lie at the heart of the ontology of the Creator-creature distinction affirmed in Christianity. The argument unfolds in five stages: first, an exposition of an argument that defends what is commonly considered a legitimate, methodologically limited abstraction in science, in a way that means to avoid reductive views of science (I); a description and evaluation of mechanism, and of modern and postmodern ways of conceiving scientific abstraction in light of mechanism (II and III); a description of what I take to be the implications of the Christian doctrine of creation's ontology of gift relative to the problem of mechanism, and of modern and postmodern views of scientific abstraction (IV); finally, a sketch of an idea of abstraction in science by a twentieth-century scientist and philosopher of science that I take to be consistent with this ontology of gift (V).

The overarching purpose of my reflections is to indicate, in terms of an ontology of gift, the significance for the form and content of human knowledge of the way the limit that constitutes disciplinary abstraction is understood: that is, whether a researcher's methodology embeds an *objective logic* of wonder or, to the contrary, and perhaps quite apart from his subjective intentions, a *logic* of mechanistically conceived technological power.

I.

Carlo Lancellotti, a mathematical physicist from the City University of New York, in a paper presented in November 2006, defends a non-reductive notion of science.[9] Science, he says, in its proper understanding is "an essentially contemplative activity," a "discernment of harmonious structures hidden in the workings of the cosmos" (2). Noting what are obviously many "ambiguous" factors in play, he nevertheless says that, based on his own experience as well as the testimony of many great scientists, "the ultimate motivation that has led to the triumphs of western science is essentially esthetic" (1). He cites Henri Poincaré:

> The scientist does not study nature because it is useful; he studies it because he delights in it, and he delights in it because it is beautiful. If nature were not beautiful, it would not be worth knowing, and if nature were not worth knowing, life would not be worth living. Of course I do not speak here of that beauty that strikes the senses, the beauty of quality and appearances, not that I undervalue such beauty, far from it, but it has nothing to do with science; I mean that deeper beauty coming from the harmonious order of the parts, and that a pure intelligence can grasp. (1)

Such an understanding of science, Lancellotti says further, "presupposes certain crucial metaphysical assumptions, many of which originated from the Judeo-Christian tradition, and chiefly from the biblical doctrine of creation" (2).

Lancellotti acknowledges that a "positivistic mentality . . . is still prevalent in many sectors of academia" (2). Many scientists nevertheless are able "to glimpse the inadequacy of a dogmatic positivism, simply because the guiding light of their work is not just some set of raw experimen-

---

9. "Science, Contemplation, and Ideology," given at the Baylor University conference "The World and Christian Imagination," Waco, Texas, November 9-11, 2006. All citations of Lancellotti in the text are from this paper.

tal data (the notorious 'facts'). Rather it is the discovery of unexpected and beautiful structures in the fabric of nature that seem to point to a deep, mysterious design which ultimately is always beyond the grasp of human intelligence" (3). Furthermore, he says, it is important to be aware that there has been a trend in physics over the last century toward "dematerialization." That is, in the eighteenth and nineteenth centuries, physicists were more likely to argue that "the role of mathematics in physics was just to describe the laws of motion of solid, 'positive' material bodies, where materiality was taken to be a primitive, self-standing notion" (3). In the twentieth century, however, this "naive notion of 'matter' has gradually dissolved into more and more 'immaterial' mathematical structures. When a physicist is trained to identify elementary particles with complicated and abstract mathematical objects, he/she will easily start wondering what is ultimately real, and will become open to the notion that there is an 'ideal' side to reality" (3).

The main points of Lancellotti's argument, in sum, are three: first, science is originally "born as the contemplation of harmonious mathematical/organizational structures that seem to be embedded in natural reality" (3). Secondly, "it is not coincidental that historically this endeavor started in cultures marked by Judeo-Christian ideas" (3). Indeed, Lancellotti says that "it is hard to imagine a conception of the universe more favorable to the birth of science than one in which the cosmos is brought out of nothingness by a loving *Logos,* who at the same time transcends the whole universe and is the immanent source of its being and rationality" (2). According to him, it could even be argued that "the birth of science was, in fact, largely the fruit of a Christian imagination of the cosmos" (2). Finally, Lancellotti argues that "even today true science in some ways rebels against its more reductionist interpretations" (3).

Relative to the issues raised in my introduction, then, Lancellotti acknowledges that scientism (which he defines as "the presumption that rationality coincides with empirical sciences") and reductionism (which he defines as "the ideology that every aspect of being can be 'analyzed down' to physical mechanisms"") are among the greatest threats we face today. His claim, however, is that these pathologies stem from certain *philosophical* attitudes that "are not *intrinsically* related to science, although they often accompany it in a parasitical fashion" (4). They are extra-scientific, and thus have nothing to do with science *per se.*

Professor Lancellotti bases his case for this conclusion on the notion of abstraction in science. Human reason, he says, is "capable of looking at reality according to different modes of abstraction" (4). "The word abstraction," he notes, "derives from the Latin root *abstrahere*, which literally means 'to pull from' or 'to take out'" (4). The scientist thus pulls or takes out certain aspects from objects "by applying to experience appropriate 'categorical selections.' For instance, physics abstracts from real existing beings one very specific aspect: spatial and temporal extension, and these only inasmuch as they can be measured by comparison with appropriate measuring instruments" (4). "Every object," he says, "comes to us with a 'form,' which makes it recognizable to intelligence and is the starting point for every further analysis. . . . The process of abstracting the manifold, harmonious structures that can be discovered in nature is completely contingent on the preliminary perception (or imagination) of a world of forms that offer themselves to our intelligence 'gratis,' *a priori* [relative to] our constructions" (5). The problem occurs only when the "abstraction is not recognized as such and claims to exhaust the intelligibility of the object" (5). It is this failure that is "the root cause of scientism . . . and reductionism. . . ." (5).

The burden of Lancellotti's argument is thus that the problems regarding dogmatic positivism and reductionism in science are not, properly speaking, scientific problems. Though science does rest on metaphysical assumptions, and although the ones often associated with modern science have been empiricist and mechanist in nature, he says, such assumptions are "not at all intrinsic to [science's] inner workings" (5). These assumptions "can and must be changed, but this change will not necessarily impact what scientists do *as scientists*" — though it may in some cases affect the direction of future research and will in any case affect what scientists do as "amateur philosophers, . . . social reformers, and high priests of secular humanism," and the like (6).

The decisive point for Lancellotti, then, is that "at the core of science lies a method 'dictated by the object,'" and that the problem regarding dogmatic positivism and reductionism has to do rather with what he calls "the moral dimension of the dynamics of knowledge" (6). What needs to happen, for example, is that "the human heart be 'wounded' again by the beauty of the cosmos" (6). Only this will enable the researcher to break through the walls of ideology and not allow his reason "to close upon itself but to open itself up to the infinite mystery of being. This is the rebirth of reason in its full breadth that [Pope Benedict XVI] called for in Regensburg: a return to the original position of openness and wonder in front of Being in all its dimensions" (6-7); and "it has been the Christian experience that this 'redemption' of reason can only happen as a fruit of the encounter with the beauty of Christ" (7).

I cite Lancellotti's article at length because it rightly identifies the elements needed regarding a non-reductive science, while raising the issue that I nonetheless wish to examine further, that of the rightful mode of abstraction in science. I agree with Professor Lancellotti's rejection of positivism and reductionism, that these are a function properly of philosophical judgments (tacit or otherwise) and are not intrinsic to the study of the natural world, but rather have been superimposed on it during a particular historical period. I agree that abstraction is legitimate and necessary for the proper practice of science. I agree that the method of the scientist is rightly to be dictated by the object and that, if the logic imposed by the object is followed, the scientist will not necessarily in his practice bear out what may be his originally "bad" philosophical presuppositions, which may not be explicit or reflective. I agree that the undertaking of science in principle may rightly be seen to derive from the biblical doctrine of creation. I agree that contemporary science needs a rebirth of reason in its full breadth, opening itself in wonder to being in all its dimensions and indeed in its infinite mystery.[10]

My question, nonetheless, bears on the nature of abstraction, and its relation to what Lancellotti calls "the moral dimension of the dynamics of knowledge." The heart of Lancellotti's argument lies in the claim that, as long as "abstraction is ... recognized as such" by the researcher, and thus is not taken by him or her "to exhaust the intelligibility of the object," the problems identified as empiricism or mechanism will be largely avoided.

What Lancellotti's argument is resisting, in other words, is a reading of the relation between philosophy and science that would make the practice of science too much a function of the scientist's philosophical assumptions. What he is affirming is that "bad" philosophical assumptions do not *determine* the scientist to reductive practice and that, indeed, in the end they may not even be very significant for that practice: if one follows faithfully a method dictated by the object, the moral-affective-aesthetic dimensions of the dynamics of knowledge will guide one to a non-reductive view of the thing.

---

10. It is important perhaps to note here, though the point will be mentioned again in my own ontological reflections later, that mystery as Lancellotti is rightly intending it here is a matter of an *excess of intelligibility*, that is, of what contains intelligibility precisely *in* its excess. The point, then, is that opening to the infinite mystery of things is reasonable, not a matter of what contradicts or simply eludes reason, i.e. of the irrational or the "mystical."

The problem on which I wish to focus begins to emerge, however, as soon as we recognize that every appeal to the limits of scientific abstraction, including Lancellotti's own, already, *eo ipso,* embeds a philosophy, an implicit ontology (and indeed theology) of creation;[11] and that Lancellotti's own appeal to limit, with its implied ontology, needs just so far to be further qualified, relative to the culturally dominant ways of conceiving this limit that would in fact undermine the intention of his argument.

Thus, according to what is perhaps the most widely held view in today's academic culture, whatever is to be added to x from beyond its limit as abstracted for disciplinary purposes can be safely added "later" (in a logical, not necessarily temporal sense), in a manner that presupposes a simply external relation between x as originally abstracted and what is left aside in that abstraction. The limit of an entity is just so far conceived in terms of its original indifference, hence closure, toward what lies beyond and thus transcends it. Such indifference thereby (implicitly) denies that what lies beyond or transcends this limit makes a pertinent difference to x already from inside its abstracted limit as x. The problem, I wish to argue,

---

11. The larger context for the argument I am introducing here presupposes a reading of Thomas Aquinas on three main points: (1) regarding the mutual internality of intellect and will in the unity of each human act (cf. *ST* I, q. 82, a. 4); (2) regarding what may be termed the "ontological weighting" of each human act, due to the fact that reference to being, as the first object of the intellect, is implied in every human-conscious act; (3) finally, regarding what is termed the "real distinction" between *esse* and *essentia* that fundamentally structures every created being, a distinction that implies an openness from within the core of every being to a Creator-Source and indeed to all other beings *(esse commune).* These three presuppositions undergird Aquinas's view (which echoes in its own way that of Augustine) that man knows and loves God implicitly in all that he knows and loves, in each of his conscious acts (cf. *De Veritate,* q. 22, a. 2, ad 1). On these points I am indebted in different ways especially to the work of Etienne Gilson, Hans Urs von Balthasar, and Ferdinand Ulrich. I also take the three points to be presupposed in and to undergird the argument of Luigi Giussani's *The Religious Sense* (Montreal: McGill-Queen's University Press, 1997), an important book for the problem of reductive conceptions of human consciousness in our time. The upshot of these points for my argument is that there is no act of freedom that does not always already presuppose an act of intelligence (and vice versa), even as this dual act of intelligence-freedom is most basically ontological, and finally also theological, in nature. The burden of my argument, of course, is not that every scientist needs to work out his implied ontology for himself, but only that it is important for him to be aware that ontological-theological assumptions are in any case always operative in, and helping to shape, his scientific abstractions. The argument of John Paul II's encyclical *Fides et Ratio* has very much in mind the philosophical claims that are often embedded in the practice, and hiddenly shape the conclusions, of the sciences, especially the social sciences.

is that this prevalent understanding of the limit involved in disciplinary abstraction presupposes a mechanistic ontology. Indeed, it *is itself* already a distinct expression of this ontology.

Lancellotti's argument appeals to the idea of limit as such, and thus leaves this dominant view of abstract limit philosophically unqualified, in a way that implies that an appeal to the idea of limit is or can be innocent of an ontology. He then emphasizes the moral-affective-aesthetic dispositions necessary to sustain the researcher in his respect for the limited nature of abstraction and in his wonder before the whole of being. But this way of proceeding does not take account of the sense in which the idea of abstract limit is already, in the current cultural situation, fraught with a mechanistic ontology that reinforces the very logic of the reductive science Lancellotti decries.[12]

---

12. All of this is not to deny what Lancellotti insists is the crucial importance of the moral-affective-aesthetic dimension of the dynamics of knowledge in avoiding reductive science. I take that as given. *It is to say, simply, that this dimension of the dynamics of knowledge is properly located within, and indeed is a response to, the ontological order of things.* Reductive science is a matter not only of an inadequate "subjective" disposition but *also-intrinsically* of a faulty notion of the ontological order of things, which must therefore be clarified as an integral part of recuperating properly those very dynamics. As implied by what is stated in the preceding note, this does not mean that one's always implied view of order will *determine* one's freedom, such that an anticipation of a reductively conceived ontological order will lead *necessarily* to reductive scientific practice. On the contrary, freedom and intelligence are each inside the other in the unity of the human act, and are therefore always *mutually* "causal," with each having its own distinct priority within this mutuality (cf. my "History, Objectivity, and Moral Conversion," *The Thomist* 38 [July 1973]: 569-88). It is for this reason, then, that the practitioner of science is able to be, and indeed in the case of the best scientists almost always is, better in his or her practice than his or her (mechanistic) theory logically allows. The point is simply that each act of freedom is mediated by some sense of ontological order, and this sense of order will always just so far, even if only unconsciously, *dispose and shape, without determining,* one's scientific practice, which remains simultaneously also a matter of freedom. As will become clear below, the history of mainstream science in modernity itself testifies abundantly to this fact.

Note, in light of the foregoing, the statements of Marco Bersanelli in his "Wonder and Knowledge: Scientific Investigation and the Breadth of Human Reason," presented at the international symposium "Science, Reason, and Truth" (Repubblica di San Marino, August 2007): "Every cognitive process involves the entirety of our person: reason and affection"; "In order to account for what we know about the universe through science, it is necessary to broaden our notion of what we normally mean by *reason*. Affective elements, not separable from our intellectual abilities, are essential for the onset and duration of any scientific enterprise." Again, Bersanelli says that the scientist at his best is moved by the great questions of existence: for example, "for an astronomer at work, the fundamental questions

Here, then, is the neuralgic issue evoked by Lancellotti's argument and urgently needing to be clarified today, at least from the point of view of a Christian ontology of creation: not simply whether wonder and beauty have an important place in the intentions of scientists, but whether on the contrary they are *integral to the logic of scientific abstraction and the order of the world properly understood*. It is just this view of wonder and beauty as pertinent to, indeed as primary within, the *objective* order — both the given causal order of things and the method of scientific knowledge — that the mechanistic ontology dominant in today's culture denies. We must take account of all that is implied in this denial if we are to enable a fuller and more adequate science *precisely as science*, which is to say, if we are to sustain the main burden of Lancellotti's own argument.

Thus, in a word: Lancellotti is right that recovery of the full breadth of reason in science entails renewal of the knower's openness to the beauty of the cosmos. My purpose is to secure the ontological-cognitional foundations of this assertion by examining, in light of the Christian doctrine of creation, the sense in which this renewal will have to involve *also simultaneously* a transformation of the *intelligence* enabling one to *see* this beauty as a matter truly of the *order of things*.

Indeed, without the further ontological qualification entailed in this transformation of intelligence, the prevalent mechanistic idea of scientific abstraction, which excludes from the *inner logic of science as science* the very features Lancellotti rightly insists are characteristic of science in its fullest realization, will be left intact. These features will continue to be viewed as they have commonly been viewed in modern academic culture, as essentially *extra-rational, extra-scientific, hence moralistic and merely aesthetic, additions* to science.[13]

---

on the origin, destiny and meaning of the universe are not an object of his research in the same way as are the telescope and instrumentation he is using or the quasars he is trying to observe; but those ultimate questions are continuously sustaining his deep motivations: they are not 'elsewhere' with respect to his scientific work, rather, they act as silent and powerful engines moving his desire to know and understand." Apropos of these statements of Bersanelli, whose paper was not yet available to me in the original writing of the present chapter, my purpose is to indicate the ontological foundations and significance of (1) a reason expanded to include wonder *precisely as integral to the proper functioning of reason as such*, as well as (2) a scientific method expanded to include openness to the great questions *precisely as integral to the proper functioning of that method in its scientific objectivity.*

13. Note that what I am proposing does not deny a necessary distinction between philosophy/theology and science. What it denies is only that this necessary distinction should be construed to mean that the abstractions proper to science, in form or content, *can be sep-*

II.

In general terms, then, the mechanistic idea of abstraction implies on the part of the researcher, whatever his *intention* to the contrary, a *method* that emphasizes the primacy of controlling power in its quest for the intelligibility of the object. Such control is predicated on the possibility of an exhaustive intelligibility of things, and of its inner logic seeks such an intelligibility. This dynamic for exhaustive intelligibility presupposes and indeed demands that the object be accounted for in terms of "parts" related externally, via forceful movements that are in principle deterministic and thus exactly measurable or calculable. This, on the mechanistic view — which gives way of its own logic to a technologistic view of nature and knowledge — is what makes up the order of things that is properly accessible to reason. Whatever is not ordered in this way is considered not to be a proper matter of reason and hence science (whether one conceives the discipline as engaging reality only within a certain limit or not), however important it may be for human life in other respects. Causal activities in a given entity that arise from within the entity itself — which is to say, genuinely interior causes (such as form and finality) that elude reduction to forces exerted from outside the entity — resist the determinism and just so far the kind of exhaustive intelligibility sought by mechanism, and hence are excluded from the purview of science.[14]

---

arated from, and thus *remain empty of and not always already shaped by,* some notion of being and God.

14. Cf. in this connection the works of late theoretical physicist David Bohm: *Causality and Chance in Modern Physics* (Philadelphia: University of Pennsylvania Press, 1971); *Wholeness and the Implicate Order* (London: Routledge, 1980); *Undivided Universe: Toward an Ontological Interpretation of Quantum Theory* (London: Routledge, 1993); and the exchange between Bohm and myself in *International Philosophical Quarterly* 22, no. 4 (December 1982): David Schindler, "David Bohm on Contemporary Physics and the Overcoming of Fragmentation," 315-28; David Bohm, "Response to Schindler's Critique of My *Wholeness and the Implicate Order*," 329-39. Fundamental to Bohm's argument is the claim that uncertainty in the behavior of things as affirmed in the dominant interpretation of quantum physics does not really overcome mechanism, but rather leaves it intact, albeit now as a matter of "statistical probability." Bohm's lifelong concern was in fact to show that the "uncertain" or non-mechanical aspects of things were manifestations of what was truly *order*, even as the idea of order needed thus to be expanded to include integration of explicit mechanical *and* implicit non-mechanical features. Without implying complete agreement between Bohm and Bersanelli regarding their respective conceptions of order (for example, with respect to quantum physics), the burden of Bohm's work as just stated is nevertheless entirely consistent with Bersanelli's statements in "Wonder and Knowledge": "Chance and order:

In historical terms, what is presupposed here in the mechanistic view of abstraction is a Cartesian understanding of distinction, coincident with a Baconian understanding of knowledge as an act primarily of power. Reason as exercised in science, on this understanding, is rightly seen to be primarily *technological*[15] in nature, in the sense that its logic is primarily intent, not on seeing or understanding the object as it appears, but on controlling its intelligibility as exhaustively as possible in order to produce things as efficiently as possible. What is not controllable in this fashion may be important in other respects, but is not pertinent to reason in its properly scientific exercise.

How does all this translate in terms of the problem of disciplinary abstraction in science? How the disciplinary limit of each science is to be conceived will depend, of course, on how the limit of the abstraction proper to that science is conceived. As I have already suggested, according to the dominant contemporary view, whatever is to be added to an object (x) from beyond the limit of x as abstracted for disciplinary purposes can be safely added later, in the manner indicated above. The limit of x is thus conceived in terms of an *original indifference, hence closure,* of x toward what (non-x) lies beyond, hence transcends, x. Such indifference thus implicitly denies that what lies beyond this limit makes a pertinent difference to x already *from inside its abstract limit as* x.

This notion of limit presupposes a Cartesian understanding of distinction. Distinction for Descartes is conceived in terms of the straight lines proper to geometry as he studied it. Straight lines enable clarity, by virtue of what is (as conceived by Descartes) a line's purely abstract

---

both collaborate to [yield] the aesthetic dimension of nature as we know it. Nature offers to us a feature that may be even more elegant and fruitful than the stability of the laws of nature on one side, and the novelty of unpredictable events on the other: the indissoluble unity of the two. Perhaps both chance and order need to be understood as manifestations of a deeper reality" (9). And again: "Nature blossoms in its beauty and diversity from a delicate interlacing of symmetry and symmetry-breaking, of laws and unpredictable events, of order and chance" (ibid.). Strictly speaking, Bohm's point, which, again, I take to be in agreement with the burden of Bersanelli's statements here, is that what is usually conceived as *chance* is in fact a matter of genuine *order,* albeit of a qualitatively different, and enlarged, sort — a "manifestation of a deeper reality."

15. The term "technology" as used here thus presupposes its modern form, which is to be clearly distinguished from (premodern) Christian or Greek *technē*. The point is important, because the burden of the argument I am proposing is to secure *a kind of technology,* albeit one informed by a sense of creaturely gift. What this means will be clarified as we proceed.

externality. A line so conceived establishes a limit that externalizes the relation between x and non-x, thus enabling an entity to be and to be known without any implication of reference beyond itself. Hence we have the mechanistic idea of limit as simple closure of x to non-x. Further, considering that matter is commonly defined primarily in terms of externality, we see that Descartes's mechanistic idea of limit is in fact a mechanistically materialized idea of limit.[16]

It is crucial to see here that this Cartesian understanding of limit as mechanistically conceived indifference, hence closure, of x to non-x operates decisively within what is at once the *method* of knowing and the *content* of knowledge as described above. A logical — not necessarily intentional — primacy of controlling power in quest of exhaustive, fully "clear and distinct" intelligibility on the one hand, and forcefully-causally related discrete bits of information or "stuff" on the other hand, are indissolubly linked: mechanistic method and mechanistic content are but two sides ("subjective"-cognitional and "objective"-causal) of the same mechanistic materialism.

Of course, this mechanistic and externalized idea of limit in one's scientific abstractions allows for a certain kind of openness in the method and content of one's knowledge. A researcher rarely takes his abstraction to exhaust the intelligibility of a given object *simply*. On the contrary, he typically recognizes that there is always more to find out about it. Indeed, that is just Lancellotti's point. But let us ponder what openness to this "more" means. On the Cartesian view just described, such "openness" signals little more than an anticipation that the intelligibility of x will require the ongoing addition of further x's, each of which, or indeed all of which as summed, remain exhaustively intelligible in principle. Fuller understanding of x comes only from the *external addition* of more x's, all of which bear *the same logic as x in its principled mechanistic character*. Such addition is thus but the ongoing extension of a limit still conceived simply as closure, a limit that thus still presumes a relation of indifference of x to non-x in x's originally constituted abstract limit as x.[17] Such "openness," in

---

16. In scholasticism, matter in its ordinary as distinct from "primary" sense is defined in terms of "parts outside of parts"; and in Hegel, matter is defined in terms of "what has no center within itself." But the crucial point is that, for both the Scholastics and Hegel, though in importantly different ways, matter as it actually exists always bears an interiority given it by form (Aristotle) or spirit (Hegel). It is in this light that we judge Descartes's matter to be at once purely abstract (i.e., not matter as it actually exists) and a "materialistic" reduction of the proper meaning of matter.

17. Cf. in this connection the statement of Adrian Walker: "What science can explain

a word, retaining the basic features of mechanism, is rightly termed reductive, not genuine openness at all.[18]

---

in its own domain, in fact, has to do with quantitatively measurable aspects of material substances. There is, however, a potential infinity of quantitatively measurable aspects in any given material substance. This fact accounts, at least in part, for the unlimited open-endedness of scientific discovery. In this sense, there is no limit to what science can discover within its own domain. Nevertheless, if one does not reflect on the difference between quantitative accident and substance, one is just so far tempted to forget or overlook that the unlimited open-endedness of scientific discovery is limited from the first moment, indeed, *a priori*, to one category of entity, namely, the quantitatively measurable. By the same token, one is tempted to forget or overlook in one way or another that *there exists any entity* but that." Hence, in this sense, *inter alia*, "Science itself is constitutively vulnerable to scientism."

Walker continues: "The distinction between methodological naturalism and ontological naturalism doesn't help deal with this problem. 'Methodological naturalism,' after all, can only really be just a shorthand for this: Science constitutes its domain of inquiry by setting up as its formal object (of which the following is admittedly only a partial description) 'whatever can be sufficiently explained *as if* materialistic naturalism *were* a true account of the being of the world'" ("Four Sets of Theses on Scientism," unpublished text prepared in connection with the December 2009 symposium "The Nature of Experience: Issues in Science, Culture, and Theology," held at the Pontifical John Paul II Institute for Studies in Marriage and the Family, The Catholic University of America).

18. Such openness may be termed a "bad" infinity consisting of endlessly summed, mechanistically conceived, intelligible objects.

See the *New York Times* editorial "The Cons of Creationism" (June 7, 2008) for an example of the false form of science's "openness" based on the dualistic-reductionistic notions of science and of the nature of things that the present chapter calls into question:

> The trouble is, a creationist system of science is not science at all. It is faith. All science is "naturalist" to the extent that it tries to understand the laws of nature and the character of the universe on their own terms, without reference to a divine creator. Every student who hopes to understand the scientific reality of life will sooner or later need to accept the elegant truth of evolution as it has itself evolved since it was first postulated by Darwin. If the creationist view prevails in Texas, students interested in learning how science really works and what scientists really understand about life will first have to overcome the handicap of their own education.
>
> Scientists are always probing the strengths and weakness of their hypotheses. That is the very nature of the enterprise. But evolution is no longer a hypothesis. It is a theory rigorously supported by abundant evidence. The weaknesses that creationists hope to teach as a way of refuting evolution are themselves antiquated, long since filed away as solved. The religious faith underlying creationism has a place, in church and social studies courses. Science belongs in science classrooms.

From the perspective of the argument advanced here, neither creationism nor evolutionism takes adequate account of the radical givenness of things that is the source, simultaneously, of their autonomy, intelligibility and mystery (each understood as directly

On the other hand, a researcher still assuming the dominant Cartesian categories may in fact be open to a non-x bearing a character different from that of x, a non-mechanistic character. It is essential here, however, that non-x be anticipated to make a difference to x *already from within* what is taken to be x's proper intelligibility and limit as x. Failing this, non-x will be seen to make an important addition to x, but at the expense of being judged not to be properly intelligible, and hence not properly an object of knowledge or a matter of reason, at all.[19] The result in this case, in other words, is a dualism that leaves mechanistic limit in place as the proper form of intelligibility and thus of rationality, even as it allows for something lying simply beyond this limit and hence beyond what is intelligible and rational in the strict sense. An openness that is dualistic in this manner remains reductive, in the sense that it still presupposes the equivalence of intelligibility and mechanistic limit even as it seeks to *add* something that is simply beyond both.

Note, then, that it is irrelevant whether the researcher here, in conceiving the limit characteristic of abstraction to be a matter of simple closure, understands this closure in a (would-be) purely disciplinary sense that anticipates an eventual releasing of that closure in another context. The crucial question, rather, bears on how one conceives "eventual releasing of closure." The crucial question, in other words, is whether, in his merely strategic abstraction of an entity, the researcher takes it to be open *here and now, from within its very limit as abstracted,* to a "more" *implying an order other than that of the entity itself,* and whether this "more" thus makes a "difference" to **the entity** already in its nature as abstracted, even if the abstraction is only for disciplinary purposes. Failing this, we are left with what will be merely a swinging back and forth between reductionism and

---

proportional to the others). The "openness" of science, as conceived in the editorial, is in fact a form of closure, inasmuch as "further evidence" is tacitly conceived in exhaustively mechanistic terms, and is otherwise not pertinent to scientific reason.

19. Note that the problem indicated here is not overcome simply by appealing to two different kinds of knowledge, since this would simply beg the question. Two different kinds of knowledge, *eo ipso,* share in something called knowledge, and if so, they bear some unity that just so far characterizes the inner form of *both* kinds of knowledge. This, then, is just the dilemma forced by mechanistic assumptions: if knowledge, then mechanistic; if not mechanistic, then not knowledge.

It should perhaps be pointed out again here that the burden of my own argument is not to deny but to affirm a plurality of ways of knowing (e.g., philosophical and scientific) while reconfiguring the conventional terms in which the relative unity *and* distinctness of these ways of knowing are conceived in the contemporary academy.

dualism in the relation between the abstractions characteristic of the various disciplines.[20]

The burden of my argument here, therefore, is that, to move successfully beyond a reductive sense of limited abstraction in science, and thus also beyond the dualism that presupposes this reduction, one must go to the roots of mechanism as such, as expressed in the primacy of methodical power and the quest for exhaustive (fully clear and distinct) intelligibility in terms of forceful-causal relations among discrete entities. One must go to the roots of knowledge as a mechanistically conceived technological act.

Before commenting on the vast influence of the mechanistic understanding of abstraction in modernity, it is important to consider briefly a current alternative way of conceiving the openness of x to what lies beyond its limit as x: what may be termed a "postmodern" reading of abstraction. We have noted how the intelligibility of x can be conceived as exhaustive by virtue of what may be an endless addition of further x's. The relevant point is to notice what is implied in the qualifier "endless." Endlessness entails a kind of *infinity,* in such a way as to redound back upon the intelligibility of the object from the beginning and thus in each of its instances. The result, on the postmodern reading, is an undercutting of the stability, hence intelligibility, of the thing in its identifiable limit as such. For the openness of x on this alternative is seen to signal an openness *here and now* and from within x to a quasi-infinity of additions, each of which would introduce a (possible) difference to it in its original intelligibility as such. The intelligibility of x would thus, in short, be *essentially elusive.*

This postmodern view clearly rejects mechanism insofar as the latter implies a primacy of controlling power and determinism and exact measurability and calculation, all of which are necessary for the exhaustive intelligibility of an object. Indeed, this second view draws attention to an openness to infinity, and thus infinite openness, inherent in every object.[21]

---

20. It is important to see, then, that reductionism and dualism, in their very opposition, remain mirror images of each other, because and insofar as both are governed by the same Cartesian logic of limit as simple external closure. Here, then, is the root of what is commonly the *confusion simultaneous with fragmentation* among the contemporary academic disciplines. In spite of radical differences in other respects, these disciplines share a common understanding of distinction, of what it means to "divide" one thing from another.

21. As Professor Nancy Cartwright suggested in the discussion at the international symposium "Science, Reason, and Truth" (Repubblica di San Marino, August 2007), postmodern thinkers like Michel Foucault, for example, share an openness to infinity with

Nevertheless, the relation of this alternative view to mechanism is paradoxical. For postmodernity, the infinite depth and breadth of a "more" that is implicit in an entity — the infinite relativity of x to non-x — implies a kind of infinity that is empty of intelligibility insofar as intelligibility bears mechanical features. The infinity of a "more" in this sense, which makes a difference to every instance of x, is thereby taken to be destructive of x in its (would-be stable) intelligibility as such. The object's putative intelligibility as such is in the end "nihilated," dissolving into a kind of infinite nothing, or unending difference.

From the perspective of the argument proposed in the present chapter, then, this postmodern view, despite its obvious fundamental challenge to mechanism, does not really question the link of the intelligibility of a thing with the mechanistic identity and exhaustive determinism and controllability of it, even as in a basic sense postmodernism of course rejects both mechanistic identity and exhaustive determinism and controllability. The crucial point, in other words, is that postmodernity, continuing to assume this link, understands an entity's inherent openness to infinity to signal not so much a density as an absence of intelligibility, construing the lack of completely controlled intelligibility as a simple absence of intelligibility in the strict sense. Mechanistic order is thus rejected in favor of what eludes intelligibility, even as mechanistic order is still presumed to be the necessary condition of intelligibility. In a word, the order of reason strictly interpreted retains its mechanistic character, even as this order is now a target of deconstruction. Postmodernity thus repeats in its own way a modern dualistic form of reductionism.[22]

As I will show later, neither modernity's mechanistic idea of intelligible limit nor postmodernity's infinite going-beyond of intelligible limit suffices to overcome the problem of the reduction of reason in science from the point of view of an adequate Christian ontology of creation. But before turning to this task, it is important to see the vast *intellectual-ontological revolution* that has been wrought in modernity by what we have described as a mechanistic idea of abstraction in science.

Christianity. I will clarify later the distinct sense of openness to infinity entailed in the Christian doctrine of creation.

22. See Kenneth L. Schmitz, "Post-Modern or Modern-Plus?" in *Communio: International Catholic Review* 17, no. 2 (Summer 1990): 152-66.

III.

To this end, we offer a description of the dominant stream of science in modernity, drawing on the work of twentieth-century Jewish philosopher of science, and especially of biology, Hans Jonas. At the heart of methodical abstraction as commonly conceived in modern science, argues Jonas, lies a "theoretical manipulability," a manipulability that he takes at once to presuppose and to anticipate a mechanistic or reductively technological view of order in the cosmos. But let us see how.[23]

Jonas suggests that the modern scientific revolution "was a change in theory, in world-view, in metaphysical outlook, in conception and method of knowledge." He states that the scientific revolution did not "at first — and for a long time — concern itself with the realm of practice," that indeed modern science "started mainly with the astronomer's reform of *cosmology*, and the cosmos, the stellar universe, does not lend itself to manipulation." And thus "technology, historically speaking, is the delayed effect of the scientific and metaphysical revolution with which the modern age begins" (47).

Jonas emphasizes, however, that this effect was scarcely "accidental":

> The very conception of reality that underlay and was fostered by the rise of modern science, i.e., the new concept of *nature*, contained manipulability at its theoretical core and, in the form of experiment, involved actual manipulation in the investigative process. Not that Galileo and others undertook their experiments with practical intent: their intent was to gain knowledge; but the *method* of knowledge itself, by the active intercourse with its object, anticipated utilization for practical ends.... Technology was thus implied as a *possibility* in the metaphysics, and trained as a *practice* in the procedures, of modern science. (48)

Thus "the present global technological situation of man has itself a metaphysical side to it besides the more obvious practical one. The meaning of

---

23. For present purposes, I will draw direct references from Jonas's "Seventeenth Century and After: The Meaning of the Scientific and Technological Revolution," Chapter 3 of *Philosophical Essays: From Ancient Creed to Technological Man* (Englewood Cliffs, NJ: Prentice Hall, 1974), pp. 45-80. But see also Jonas's books, *The Phenomenon of Life* (Evanston, IL: Northwestern University Press, 2001 [1966]; *The Imperative of Responsibility: In Search for an Ethics for the Technological Age* (Chicago: University of Chicago Press, 1984 [1966]).

the technological revolution is thus part of, indeed the completion of, the metaphysical meaning of the scientific revolution" (48).

Jonas characterizes as follows what he takes to be three important developments in the wake of Galileo's new conceptualization of motion. "The first is the geometrizing of nature and consequently the mathematization of physics" (62). Descartes had raised this to

> the dignity of a metaphysical principle when he split reality into the two mutually exclusive realms of the *res cogitans* and the *res extensa* — the world of mind and the world of matter: the latter is in its essence nothing but "extension"; therefore nothing but determinations of extension, i.e., geometry, are required for a scientific knowledge of the external world. (63)

> Secondly, the program of an analysis of motions necessitated a new mathematics, of which Descartes' analytical geometry was only the first step. (63)

> Thirdly, the conceptual analysis of motions permitted an actual dissociation of its component parts in suitably set-up *experiments*. It thus inspired an entirely new method of discovery and verification, the experimental method. It must be realized that the controlled experiment, in which an artificially simplified nature is set to work so as to display the action of single factors, is *toto caelo* different from the observation, however attentive, of "natural" nature in its unprocessed complexity, and also from any non-analytical trying out of its responses to our probing interventions. It essentially differs, in one word, from *experience* as such. What experiment aims at — the isolation of factors and their quantification — and is designed to secure by the selective arrangement of conditions, *presupposes* the theoretical analytic we have described; and it repays theory by its results. (63)[24]

---

24. Cf. in this connection the following statements by Walker: "Regardless of whether or not it rests on some prior ontology in any scientist's mind, experimentation itself enacts an ontology of its own — one that could fairly be described as technological. Regardless of whether or not scientists do science in order to enable the technological manipulation of nature *after* the science is done, experiment itself is already the technological manipulation of nature. It is also looking, of course, but the looking is, as it were, an aspect — and it is just one aspect — of experiment materially considered. Formally considered, however, experiment is technological manipulation of nature."

Turning to the task of evaluation, Jonas says that the innovation in modernity's theoretical revolution in dynamics was not originally about the principle of causality *per se*, but about the idea of change. However, "the altered conception of what constitutes a change, i.e., an *effect*, naturally reacted on the conception of what constitutes a *cause*" (65).

> Now, "change" had been redefined as acceleration of mass, and to this its primary form all (phenomenally) other kinds of change — such as qualitative change — must be reduced. Accordingly, "cause" is redefined as that which imparts (or resists) acceleration — i.e., as *force*, whose *sole effect* is acceleration (or its negative), and whose magnitude is precisely measured by the amount of acceleration it imparts to a given mass: and to this, its primary form, all (phenomenally) other kinds of "causes" must be reduced. (65)

Jonas notes what he calls the "extraordinary physical as well as metaphysical consequences" that follow from this conception of cause (66). "First of all, with the quantifiability of all changes in nature, the cause-effect relation has become a quantitative relation, namely that of strict *quantitative equivalence* of cause and effect. . . . Consequently, any physical state can be represented as a determinate configuration of masses and forces from which the next state follows necessarily and — more important — can be computed rigorously by a calculus of the represented magnitudes, if all of them are known" (66). Negatively put, this implies "the denial of the possibility of any nonphysical, e.g., spiritual, cause intervening in the physical course of things" (66). This "new metaphysics of science" clashed with "our most immediate and common experience (viz., that we are authors of our actions from purpose and

---

Further, then, Walker says that "technology is not first about devices; rather, the devices that we recognize as expressions of technology are indeed just that. Technology itself, however, is first the novel interpenetration of knowing and making which George Grant speaks of in his essay 'Thinking about Technology' [in *Technology and Justice* (Toronto: Anansi Press, 1986), pp. 11-34]."

Finally, "Experimental method doesn't merely abstract certain features of physical process from the whole in which they naturally occur. In the case of experimentation, abstraction is active re-configuration that just so far makes the re-configured reality accessible under a very definite profile: qua re-configurable. To the extent that experiment is an enacted ontology in this sense, it is the place where science (taken as an institution that comprehends, but is not reducible to, experiment) is constitutively vulnerable to scientism" ("Four Sets of Theses on Scientism").

design)," and relegated "this basic experience to the realm of mere appearance" (67).

Furthermore, in addition to eliminating any reasonable account of "the causal efficacy of *human* purpose," this new metaphysics of science sets aside

> *end-causes* of any kind — i.e., *teleology* as such which, in whatever attenuated analogy of striving and satisfaction it is conceived, must share with human purpose a transmaterial, quasi-mental aspect. That Nature is devoid of even the most unconscious bias toward goals, and of the formative power to serve it, that final and formal causes are struck from its inventory and only efficient causes left, follows simply from the principle of quantitative equivalence and invariance in cause-effect relations which is the distinguishing mark of the "determinism" of modern science. . . . [This determinism] means that always and only the immediate antecedent determines the next instant, that there are no long-term trends toward something, but only a transfer of the mass-energy sum from moment to moment, and the *vis a tergo* of this propagation — in short, no pull of the future, only the push of the past. (67-68)

Here, then, are the summary implications that Jonas sees for the fostering of a reductive technological attitude that has become prevalent in our time:

> What has neither will nor wisdom and is indifferent to itself solicits no respect. Awe before nature's mystery gives way to the disenchanted knowingness which grows with the success of the analysis of all things into their primitive conditions and factors. The powers that produce those things are powerless to impart a sanction to them: thus their knowledge imparts no regard for them. On the contrary, it removes whatever protection they may have enjoyed in a prescientific view. The implication this has for man's active commerce with the equalized manifold is obvious. If nature sanctions nothing, then it permits everything. Whatever man does to it, he does not violate an immanent integrity, to which it and all its works have lost title. In a nature that is its own perpetual accident, each thing can as well be other than it is without being any the less natural. Nature is not a norm (which to Aristotle it was) and a monstrosity is as natural as any "normal" growth. (70)

> Furthermore, if nature is mere object and in no sense subject, if it is devoid of "will," then man remains as the sole subject and the sole will. The world, after first having become the object of man's knowledge, becomes the object of his will, and his knowledge is put in the service of his will. And the will, of course, is a will for power over things. The heavens no longer declare the glory of God; but the materials of nature are ready for the use of man. (71)

In addition to these "spiritual" aspects of the new science that showed its intrinsic readiness for a reductive technological attitude, Jonas says that there were also more technical aspects that pointed in the same direction: for example, "the role of analysis and that of experiment" (71).

> The analysis of any complex phenomenon into its simplest geometrical, material, and dynamical factors is tantamount to finding out how even the most sophisticated natural entity comes about — is *brought about* — from the collocation of primitive components. But knowing how a thing is made of its primitive elements leads of itself to knowing how one can make it up oneself out of those elements. The passage from analytical knowledge to making, i.e., to providing the requisite components and manipulating them so as to secure the desired results — the passage, in short, from analysis to synthesis is open on principle whenever the former is completed in a given case. And so is the passage from experiment as a means of knowledge to applied science as a means of use. Practice in the service of theory, which is what experiments are, is readily converted into theory, in the service of practice, which by now most of "science" almost automatically becomes. (71)

Further, then,

> with the advent of molecular engineering man assumed a more sovereign role, involving a deeper meddling with the patterns of nature — indeed a redesigning of such patterns. We now are in an age where by imposed dispositions of molecules, substances can be made to specification — substances nature might produce but in fact does not produce. Man steps into nature's shoes, and from utilizing and exploiting he advances to creating. This is more than merely shaping things. Artificiality enters the heart of the matter. (77)[25]

---

25. Jonas of course does not object to artifice as such. On this, see the further comments below regarding nature rightly understood as itself inclusive of artifice.

"With its new, synthetic substances, [this technology] introduces things unknown before into daily use and thoroughly refashions the habits of consumption" (77).[26]

Needless to say, these statements can be qualified and elaborated much further. In their main lines, the patterns he describes are familiar to us. Although I find Jonas's portrayal of modernity to be brimming with profound insights, my purpose in offering it here is not to argue its truth but simply to indicate the significant sense in which the method of abstraction in science and a definite conception of order in the universe mutually imply one another.

Jonas makes clear how this is so in mainstream modern science and the culture shaped by that science. The primacy of what he terms "theoretical manipulability" in modern science implies a method whose logic is primarily that of controlling power with respect to the object of study, a power that tends toward completeness insofar as this method of science itself innerly anticipates effective utilization for practical or productive ends. But such a method, *eo ipso*, presupposes and leads to conceiving the order of the universe objectively as one that lends itself to this kind of control — leads to conceiving the universe, that is, in terms of mechanistic order. This order construes entities in terms of external identities initially closed to one another, the sum of whose (external-forceful) interactions can then, at least in principle, be exactly measured. "Theoretical manipulability," in a word, is a reductive way of conceiving the knower's relation to the world that itself already instantiates a definite, reductive notion of being, man, and God. Indeed, "theoretical manipulability" itself expresses what is but the cognitional version of an order consisting essentially of external-forceful relations, here between the subject-knower himself and the object known. My argument is that this reductiveness can therefore be overcome only by transforming "theoretical manipulability" at once as a mechanistic method of abstraction and in its presupposed and anticipated mechanistic ontology.

Note that what is most relevant here is not primarily a matter of the scientist's *intention*. As Jonas points out, for example with respect to Galileo, the issue is not whether a scientist approaches the object with the intention simply of seeing or understanding an object, which is granted in the case of Galileo. The pertinent issue concerns rather the presence or ab-

---

26. In connection with these citations from Jonas, cf. the remarks of Walker cited in note 24 above.

sence of genuine theory (contemplation, wonder) *in the very logic of the method* followed by the scientist in his quest for intelligibility.

What is relevant to recognize, then, is that the interlocking of mechanistic abstraction and mechanistic ontology is not undone simply by insisting on a disciplinary limit for mechanistic method, which in the end amounts to a form of question-begging. The question is whether the scientist, in his abstractions of x — whether these are assumed to be limited methodologically or not — takes x to be embedded in, and shaped from within by, a non-mechanistic order in which its mechanical properties are given both their stability and their proper intelligibility as such. The scientist whose primary cognitional logic is that of theoretical manipulability, and hence of mechanism — even if this is *intended* to be strictly limited methodologically — just so far denies this kind of primordial embeddedness. The inevitable result is some variant of modern monolithic or dualistic reductionism in what one takes to count as science and hence knowledge in the proper sense, or some variant of postmodernism, which simply repeats the modern problematic from the opposite direction.

Jonas refuses both of these alternatives. He critiques modern science and its reductively technological sense of abstraction with the aim of *integrating* scientific rationality into a broader and more ancient rationality, which remains rational and includes mechanical order even as it transforms and transcends the mechanistic notion of order. He affirms the necessity and legitimacy of technological progress, even as he sees the urgency of its integration into this broader rationality.[27] He insists that the task today is not merely to *add* something extra-rational and extra-scientific, which is to say, something purely willful-moral or affective or aesthetic, to a dominant cognitional-ontological order conceded to be legitimately mechanistic. On the contrary, he understands that such a response merely repeats the dualistic form of mechanistic reduction that lies at the source of modernity's problematic technologizing of ontology in the first place.

My simple point with respect to any appeal to the limited nature of disciplinary abstraction as a means of avoiding reductive science is that such an appeal needs to be qualified in light of these claims by Jonas regarding the nature and implications of abstraction as conceived in the

---

27. See in this connection Jonas's critique of Heidegger in *The Phenomenon of Life*, pp. 235-61, the burden of which, relative to my point here, is that "no philosophy of nature [that is, no causal understanding of things in a proper sense] can issue from Heidegger's thought" (253, note 16).

dominant stream of modern science, and indeed the dominant patterns of modern thought.

But this leads to the concluding stages of my own proposal: first, to show how a Christian ontology of creation takes up Jonas's task of integrating the now mechanistically conceived features of order in scientific rationality into a broader conception of order and scientific rationality; second, to offer an example from within science itself of this broader conception of order and rationality.

IV.

In an important lecture at the University of Regensburg in September 2006, Pope Benedict XVI addressed the theme of "Faith, Reason, and the University."[28] Western thinkers tended to fasten onto one main point of the lecture, that which concerned dialogue with Islam: that the Christian God has revealed himself as *logos* and thus as reason and word. This reason, as love, "is creative and capable of self-communication, precisely as reason," and God therefore acts with reason (σὺν λόγῳ), and not simply "willfully" or arbitrarily. Equally important, however, was Benedict's insistence from the other direction that reason rightly understood opens organically to God. Benedict pointed out that a restriction of science to the mathematical and the empirical elements of things, along with a restriction of demonstrable or certain truth to verification or falsification through experimentation, leads to a conception of method that excludes the question of God as *eo ipso* unscientific or pre-scientific.

Benedict intended his lecture to initiate a dialogue, in other words, not only in the direction of Islam but also and equally importantly in the direction of the West and its universities. On the one hand, he affirmed that it is the nature of God to be "reasonable," in the face of a terrorism often justified in the name of God and religion. At the same time he insisted that it is of the nature of reason rightly understood to open to the question of God, that the question of the "divine" *(das Göttliche)* should not be excluded from the universality of reason, and that the measure of what is to count as scientific should not be restricted to a certain conception of the mathematical and empirical. In a word, Benedict insisted that reason bears

28. Benedict XVI, "Faith, Reason, and the University: Memories and Reflections," Meeting with the Representatives of Science, University of Regensburg, 12 September 2006.

an intrinsic-logical movement toward God, and he did so expressly in the face of the problem of the Western university, which, he said, has in recent centuries harbored a reason or science that is deaf to God, relegating him to the realm of the merely "subjective."

Benedict concludes by saying that "modern scientific reason with its intrinsically Platonic element [by which he means matter's intrinsic rationality] bears within itself a question that points beyond itself. . . . Modern scientific reason quite simply has to accept the rational structure of matter and the correspondence between our spirit and the prevailing rational structures of nature as a given, on which its methodology has to be based."[29]

What does Benedict's proposed "expansion" of scientific reason imply for the question posed in this chapter?

(1) First of all, it presupposes a definite doctrine of creation. Creation is an act of love, which means that creatures come into being through an act of giving: to be a creature is to be a gift. Since creation, on the Christian understanding, is *ex nihilo*, the creature's being as such is constituted as gift.[30] Benedict's theology echoes that of his predecessor, John Paul II, who stated that it was opportune today to "turn anew to those fundamental words that Christ used, that is, the word 'created' and to the subject 'Creator,' introducing . . . *a new criterion of understanding and of interpretation that we will call 'hermeneutics of the gift.'* The dimension of gift is . . . at the very heart of the mystery of creation. . . ."[31]

---

29. Cf. also the Pope's statement: "the correspondence between [the] structures [of mathematics] and the real structures of the universe . . . implies . . . that the universe itself is structured in an intelligent manner, such that a profound correspondence exists between our subjective reason and the objective reason in nature. It then becomes inevitable to ask oneself if there might not be a single original intelligence that is the common font of both of them. Thus, precisely reflection on the development of science brings us toward the creator *Logos*. The tendency to give irrationality, chance and necessity the primacy is overturned. . . . Upon these bases it again becomes possible to enlarge the area of our rationality, to reopen it to the larger questions of the truth and the good, to link theology, philosophy and science between them in full respect for the methods proper to them and of their reciprocal autonomy, but also in the awareness of the intrinsic unity that holds them together" (Benedict XVI, Address to Participants in the Fourth National Ecclesial Convention, Verona, Italy, 19 October 2006).

30. See Kenneth L. Schmitz, *The Gift: Creation* (Milwaukee: Marquette University Press, 1982).

31. John Paul II, General Audience of January 2, 1980, in *Man and Woman He Created Them: A Theology of the Body*, trans. Michael Waldstein (Boston: Pauline Books and Media, 2006), p. 179.

What is entailed by the original nature of the creature as gift, relative to the problem of disciplinary abstraction in science? To prepare us to respond to this question, I begin with a brief description of some of the main features of creaturely entities in their nature as at once gifted and autonomous.

The crucial point, as already indicated in the introduction, is that the relation to God that *establishes the creature in its own being*, and indeed that implies a shared relation of each creature with all other creatures, is truly *in* the creature. What the creature most basically is, is a *being-given*. This being-given that is constitutive of the creature implies a receiving on the part of the creature that is just so far also constitutive. What is it that is being-given to, and being-received by, the creature?

The answer is, a participation in the self-diffusive generosity of God as good. As Aquinas says, *bonum est diffusivum sui:* it is the nature of the good to diffuse or give itself.[32] The basic truth about the creature, therefore, is its goodness. Or indeed, drawing on the classical language of the "transcendentals" employed by Aquinas, and developed further by twentieth-century theologian Hans Urs von Balthasar, we can say that God's act of creation is at root a creative *communication* to creatures of a participation in the truth of being as an order of goodness and beauty.[33] What the creature *receives* most fundamentally in the act of creation is thus a share in this communication, in the *giving* characteristic of God's creative act. In saying that these features of receiving and giving are constitutive of the creature, we mean to say that they are characteristic of both the *being (ens)* and the first and most basic *act (agere)* of the creature.[34] This receiving-giving, in other words, which is immediately also a giving-receiving, characterizes not only what the creature *does* but what the creature always already, at the most basic level, *is*.

Each creature, then, in the most primitive structure of his being and

---

32. Thomas Aquinas, *ST* I, q. 5, a. 4, obj. 2, referring to Dionysius, *The Divine Names*, iv. This does not mean that creation is necessary, but that what God does freely in creating necessarily expresses the generosity proper to his goodness.

33. Cf. the dictum common to many theologians in the patristic era of the Church: *"pulchrum est splendor veritatis"* (cited in Bersanelli, "Wonder and Knowledge").

34. Cf. Ferdinand Ulrich, *Homo Abyssus: Das Wagnis der Seinsfrage* (Einsiedeln: Johannes Verlag, 1998). See also Martin Bieler's article on Ulrich: "Causality and Freedom," in *Communio: International Catholic Review* 32, no. 3 (Fall 2005): 407-34; as well as his "The Analogia Entis as an Expression of Love According to Ferdinand Ulrich" (paper given at the conference "The Analogy of Being: Invention of the Anti-Christ or the Wisdom of God? A Symposium," Washington, DC, April 4-6, 2008).

acting, is a *recipient* of gift in relation to God and to others. This is not a matter of passivity, but rather a recognition of the fact that the creature's *acting* with respect to the other is at root *responsive* to the other. The creaturely act is first *contemplative* or *theoretical*.[35] What it does first (ontologically, not temporally) in relation to the other is receive the other, or more fully stated, receive itself in receiving the other. The creaturely act first "lets the other be" in its givenness as such. This letting be, as a response to being which, as created, is good and beautiful, is an act of wonder. Letting be and wonder, in other words, are but *the subjective-cognitional forms of participation in the objective nature of being as gift.* Which is to say, letting be and wonder are themselves, already in their theoretical character as such, distinct forms of participation in gift-giving.

Further, the creaturely act is characterized at once by *immanence* and *transcendence*. Immanence, in the sense that the relation to God and others that is constitutive of the creature presupposes the creature's capacity to receive the other *within itself*, and the creature is just so far marked by *interiority*. Transcendence, in the sense that the relation to God and others that is constitutively (hence continuously) *given to* and *received by* the creature presupposes the creature's openness to an other who is always already "beyond" the self. Immanence and transcendence in the creature cannot be dissociated: they are dual aspects of the same act. Each creature bears *within itself* as gift an *excess* signifying the presence of a transcendent other-giver. This excess we may term mystery, and, given that the creature's constitutive openness is to the whole of being, to all other creatures inside openness to God, this mystery lying at the heart of every creature opens to infinity. It is crucial to see that this openness to infinite mystery, as always already bound up with the original identity of the creature, is just so far integral to the intelligibility proper to the creature in its very identity as such; and indeed, further, to see that infinity is itself, in its character *as infinite*, inclusive of intelligibility.

Important also is the statement of Aquinas: "As the soul is wholly in every part of the body, so God is wholly in all things and in each one."[36] As the spiritual writer Dom Eugene Boylan elaborates: "The pattern of the whole is found in each of its parts, and in fact the parts are only incorporated into the whole by being made conformable to the whole. . . ."[37] What this

---

35. From the Greek *theorein*, to look at.

36. *ST* I, q. 8, a. 2, ad 3.

37. Dom M. Eugene Boylan, *This Tremendous Lover* (Notre Dame: Christian Classics, 1964) (cited in *Magnificat*, 6 May 2008).

means, in terms of the ontology of creation, is that the parts of things have their being as parts only in relation to the whole and thus as participatory in the pattern or image of the whole, and this in three analogically conceived senses: most basically in relation to God, but also in relation to the whole being of which they are a part and to the universal community of beings with whom each being shares a common relation to God.[38] Every "part" of being in the cosmos, in a word, is structurally a "part" of a greater whole, and thus always already constituted in community, analogically conceived.

There are many more features that could be adduced in describing the structure of creaturely being, of course, but this will suffice for purposes of our theme. Three qualifications will help to clarify the sense in which these features are constitutive and thus present in every creature all the time.

First of all, we normally associate acts of receiving and giving with human being, rather than with all of creaturely being, including sub- or non-human being. Though of course features such as giving and receiving and wonder and interiority are, among the beings of the creaturely cosmos, uniquely characteristic of human beings, the Christian doctrine of creation entails some genuinely analogical sense of generosity that reaches through the entire order of creation.[39] Every creature qua creature, for example, is receptive of relation to the Creator, and this receptiveness just so far presupposes an interior capacity enabling the presence of the other *within* each creature.[40] It is this rhythm of receiving-giving/giving-

---

38. The difficult question of how, precisely, the whole or wholeness indicated here is to be articulated is beyond the purview of the present reflection. Suffice it to say, in light of the classical-Thomistic philosophical tradition, that the idea of an analogical wholeness of things implied in the texts cited involves articulations, *inter alia*, of the notions of substance and form (soul) and *esse,* each in relation to the others and to God. In this connection, see Adrian Walker, "Personal Singularity and the *Communio Personarum:* A Creative Development of Thomas Aquinas's Doctrine of *Esse Commune,*" *Communio: International Catholic Review* 31, no. 3 (Fall 2004): 457-79. See also the discussion below regarding the rightful meaning of identity or limit in terms of the ontology of creation.

39. See the argument of Kenneth L. Schmitz regarding the need for a recovery of a metaphysical, and not merely anthropological, kind of interiority within created entities: *The Gift: Creation* (Milwaukee: Marquette University Press, 1982). See also Schmitz, "Immateriality Past and Present," in *The Texture of Being,* ed. Paul O'Herron (Washington, DC: Catholic University of America Press, 2007), pp. 168-82.

40. Such a position is implied by what is termed John Paul II's "theology of the body." Cf. also Bersanelli's comments in "Wonder and Knowledge": "Every new insight recalls the secret friendship of the universe with us, and satisfies for a moment our 'natural desire for

receiving that is affirmed in the insistence of John Paul II and Benedict XVI that the idea of gift, or love, analogically conceived, lies at the heart of creation and creaturely reason.

A second difficulty: the foregoing comments appeal expressly to the *Christian* doctrine of creation, and the features I have described might thus be set aside as convincing only to those who share the Christian faith. The burden of my argument, however, is that the Christian doctrine of creation itself, rightly conceived, carries an ontology, a distinct understanding of worldly being. The Christian doctrine of creation implies a metaphysics that opens of its inner dynamic into what Aristotle long ago identified as a (natural) theology. This claim, to be sure, demands elaboration, which nevertheless must await another forum. What I have been presupposing here is simply that the Christian doctrine of creation bears a distinct ontology which *eo ipso* carries the implication that the features of gift such as those noted above *are really present in things,* and that it is thus possible in principle for all reasonable beings, and not only Christians, to recognize these features. Indeed, the ontology carried in the doctrine of creation implies that all human beings will necessarily grasp these features, even if only confusedly. That doctrine also implies, of course, that the full depth and breadth of such features will be recognized only in faith. The further point, then, in light of Benedict XVI's Regensburg address, is that the accessible traces of gift, of their inner dynamic, bear sufficient implications of the presence of God that the *question* naturally arises regarding whether he truly exists and indeed what the nature of this God must be if the implied or "intuited" sense of being as gift is to be sustained. This *natural implication* of God's presence in the beings of the world suffices for the rational character of what has been proposed.[41]

Finally, it is also the Christian view of creation, rightly understood, that we do not live in a perfect or sinless world. Therefore it is not surprising that what is constitutively given as the nature of human being and cognition is historically weighted with a disorder that obscures being and cognition in their original meaning. Again, nothing that has been said above

---

connectedness with the universe' (L. Zagzebski), normally unconsciously lived. In letting itself be more understood, the physical world shows an attitude of openness to us, and we perceive ourselves as destined to a relationship with everything. It is as though for a fleeting instant the appearance of things allowed a glimpse of an ineffable familiar face at the roots of reality."

41. Cf. the view of Aquinas that every cognitive being knows and loves God implicitly in all that he knows and loves (*De Veritate,* q. 22, a. 2, ad 1).

implies that human beings are always fully aware of this primitively given nature of things. My claim is simply that what we have described does indicate the constitutive natural structure of things,[42] which, even if obscured or rejected or unwittingly ignored, still lies implicitly at the heart of every instance of being or acting, and hence always resonates in the depths of our experience, even if only confusedly and in the form of a restlessness for a generous way of being and acting.[43]

In sum, my proposal, in light of Benedict's Regensburg address, is that wonder lies embedded in the primitive structure of the human cognitional act, and that this act itself presupposes and already signifies a view of being as structurally *worthy or evocative of* wonder, hence as an order, the causal meaning of which consists most basically in giving and receiving goodness and beauty. Which is to say, conversely, that the primitive structure of being harbors a causal order of goodness and beauty which of its inner logic elicits receptive wonder as the most basic human cognitional act. The two are onto-logically inseparable: wonder and gift are the same reality viewed, respectively, subjectively and objectively. What human creatures do in a preeminent way, both subjectively-cognitionally and objectively-causally in their relations to God and to one another, is to communicate this order of being as goodness and beauty.[44]

---

42. It is helpful to recall in this connection the Catholic understanding regarding the enduring integrity of nature: sin penetrates nature in an utterly profound way (however much this was insufficiently emphasized in modern Catholic theology); but sin does not thereby destroy nature in its basic order as created.

43. On the unity coincident with distinctness of *eros* and *agape*, see Benedict XVI, *Deus Caritas Est.*

44. Cf. D. C. Schindler, "Truth and the Christian Imagination: The Reformation of Causality and the Iconoclasm of the Spirit," *Communio: International Catholic Review* 33, no. 4 (Winter 2006): 521-39, at 524-26, 528:

> The Greek word for cause (αἰτία) is a broad one, i.e., it doesn't initially have a univocal technical meaning. Used in a philosophical context, it indicates anything that accounts for a thing's being the way it is, that which is responsible for the how and why of a thing.... Plato affirms that causality always occurs according to a model, which is another way of saying that what comes to be is not simply a self-contained entity, but a revelation or manifestation of something else: to say that the causal agent always makes according to a model means that *agency is the communication of form*. Causation is not, in other words, simply the bringing about of a thing or the setting of something in motion, i.e., an essentially *formless* event or activity, which may or may not *subsequently* give rise to something with form and therefore something intelligible....
>
> To say that agency is the communication of form means that all of the things that come to be have the character of image — the Greek word is εἰκών, whence the En-

(2) We turn to the question regarding the autonomy proper to the creature and his agency. As pointed out earlier, this autonomy is necessarily presupposed in the regularities of the processes of nature and thereby

---

glish "icon" — or, in other words, that they reflect a meaning of which they are not themselves the source. It is crucial to see that there is no dualism here, as it were, between being and significance, as if things had a sort of opaque reality which subsequently indicated an intelligible content. To posit such a bifurcation would be to deny the meaning of cause as Plato clearly intends it, namely, as the communication of form in the bringing about of a thing. We could say that, for Plato, ontology *is* semiotics. Being an image is what makes a thing *real*. . . .

[T]he form that is communicated by agency is necessarily a reflection of goodness. And, finally, insofar as this form most basically determines what a thing is, and is itself an imitation of the first cause, the gift of the being of each thing is at the very same time the gift of the ultimate purpose of each: namely, to be what it is by imitating in a particular way the ultimate source of all that is, i.e., by pursuing goodness. In a word, what would eventually be differentiated by Aristotle into three causes, appears first in Plato in its unity: the *what* of things is inseparable from their goodness, their purpose, and indeed their "thereness." For this very reason, goodness represents the paradigm of causality — the goodness at the origin of the cosmos, as we saw, is the "best of all causes" — and thus all causes in the cosmos are, *as* causes, a reflection of goodness. Nothing is so causal, for Plato, as goodness and the beauty he takes to be essentially identical with it. . . .

To say that the presence of Beauty is the cause of beautiful things *qua* beautiful is simply to say that the sensible beauty we perceive in things is the intelligible form of beauty manifest in space and time; in other words, it is to say that sense experience is the expression of a *meaning*, that it has intelligible content, which, *as* intelligible, cannot simply be identified with the particularity of its manifestation. . . . [P]hysical objects, insofar as they are intelligible, are the expression of *meaning*, intelligible content, in a spatial and temporal mode. We can go further: there is, in fact, no content whatsoever in our sense experience that is not an expression of intelligible meaning. . . . There is nothing in what we would call the "physical" world that is not derived from form except its not being itself form, and this is simply a way of saying that the physical world is nothing but meaning made tangible.

The idea of causality as most basically a matter of the communication of meaning was held, albeit not in the same sense as in Schindler, by Bohm. It is important to see that such a claim is not, or not necessarily, an expression of "idealism." On the contrary, for a Christian the foundation of this claim can be found in the Gospel of John, whose Prologue states that in the beginning was the Word, the *Logos* of God, in and through whom everything was created. Insofar as all creaturely creativity (causality) images that of the Creator-God, this creaturely creativity communicates a "word": communicates a meaning and indeed what is always, in some significant sense, a natural participation in the wisdom of God.

Cf. also here, and more generally in relation to the argument advanced in this chapter, D. C. Schindler, *Hans Urs von Balthasar and the Dramatic Structure of Truth: A Philosophical Investigation* (New York: Fordham University Press, 2004).

renders both possible and legitimate the abstract study of nature. The heart of the response to this question is already implied in the foregoing comments. Creation is something given unconditionally *(ex nihilo)*. It is a gift that is really given over: what God gives to the creature is precisely the creature's *own being* as such. This of course means granting agency and power to the creature in (and for) itself. The crucial question concerns how this is to be rightly understood, given the above ontology of creation.

First of all, the movement from and toward God proper to creaturely being presupposes God's giving the creature to itself, and thus presupposes a creature that is just so far "in itself." The term for this is "nature," which may be characterized for our purposes as an *origin* that is *given*.[45] The creature is original, as it were, but only and always as given by another, hence as always recuperative of an *absolute origin that is from another*.[46]

The point here bears emphasizing: the creature's characteristic "in itselfness," on the one hand, and its reference to another (God and others), on the other hand, are directly and not inversely related, as conventional liberal patterns of thought dispose us to assume. On the contrary, the whole of the thing in itself is related from inside to others, even as this constitutive relation to others presupposes the whole of the thing in itself as the "what" that is in relation.[47]

Further, in giving creatures a nature, the Creator gives to each its own "substantial" identity. Each creature "possesses" a self-identity that is *different from* the identity of all others. This is what at root makes possible what may be called the "mechanical" properties of creatures, which structure each entity as just so far *outside* the others and able to act on them from outside. Such mechanical properties provide an essential condition for what is each entity's legitimate external-forceful activity in relation to other entities.

---

45. Cf. Aristotle's definition of nature as what is in itself the source of movement and rest, as always already given, in the sense that, in their deepest order, the things of this world are eternally there (see *Physics,* Book II). Of course, Aristotle's understanding of the character of nature's givenness relative to an ultimate Creator-giver differs profoundly from that affirmed in Christianity, even as both insist on the feature of givenness as essential to the idea of nature and its goodness.

46. Joseph Ratzinger/Benedict XVI repeatedly refers in this connection to what he terms the "filial" structure of creaturely being. Cf., for example, his *Jesus of Nazareth* (New York: Doubleday, 2007), which shows how Christ, as the *Son* of the Father, reveals all of creation to be filial in nature, to be from another.

47. It is *the whole being in itself* that is *related from within* to everything else, in relation to the Creator-God.

What it is in each creature that accounts for its *specific* and indeed simultaneously *individual* identity is a difficult question that need not be addressed fully in the present forum.[48] It will suffice simply to indicate how "identity" as implied by a Christian ontology of creation contrasts with that sketched earlier in the name of Descartes. For the latter, identity is a matter first of external, mechanistically conceived limit. The identity of x, in other words, is a matter of simple closure to non-x. What *distinguishes* the one *simply divides* it from the other.

The ontology of creation as outlined, on the contrary, *relativizes* closure, though not in a sense that attenuates at all the identity of the thing. The identity that constitutes the creature as substantially "in itself" is at once *given to* and *received by* it.[49] As noted above, this implies in the creature the double movement of immanence and transcendence, of receiving the other *within* oneself even as this receiving is itself already a *going out to* the other. The crucial point, then, is that the very act of being by which x is established "in itself" distinguishes and so far *divides* x from non-x and *simultaneously also opens* x to non-x. It is in this sense that I am proposing, in the name of an adequately conceived Christian ontology of creation, that the limit that sets x off from non-x is, always and everywhere, a matter of *relational closure*.[50]

---

48. Showing how "matter," form, and *esse* all perform in their own proper ways this function of determining, hence "closing," the identity of a thing, all the while opening it intrinsically to others, is a difficult task reaching beyond the purview of the present argument. Suffice it to say that each of these principles contributes to the "singularization" or "individualization" of a worldly being, even as each simultaneously "universalizes" the meaning of that being. Each individual, in other words, is a kind of concrete universal (though in Balthasar's sense, not Hegel's).

49. Thus each creaturely being has a triplex character: (a) a "substantial in-itselfness" that is at once (b) a receiving from the other and (c) a giving to the other *(esse in, esse ab, esse ad)*. The triplex character is crucial: a "third," which is to say the substantial identity or unity of an entity, is what gives it the stable, enduring center whereby it can serve as both origin and end for its movement *from* and *toward* an other. This stable, enduring center is at once the presupposition and the consequence (ontological, not temporal) of each entity's dual-dynamic relation to the other. Without this stable identity, what we are terming the gifted character of being would necessarily dissolve into a purely processive, formless relationality which, as such, would just so far lack the capacity for *its own* participation as gift in the generosity of creation. The generosity implied in the double movement of giving and receiving can be sustained only in terms of a "third" principle, a "substantial in-itselfness" in and through which giving and receiving are brought into original-final unity.

50. The phrase "relational closure," then, is meant to indicate the paradoxical way in which the in-itselfness proper to each being is a matter of real closure, but is so all the while

(3) My simple but basic argument, in light of this, is that legitimate abstract limit in science always and in each of its instances remains a matter of relational closure, because being itself is always and in each of its instances, in its "substantial" as well as its individual identity, a matter of relational closure. This does not entail denial of the mechanical aspects of abstraction in method and in content; on the contrary, it is relation itself that establishes and just so far always secures these mechanical aspects. However, that relation, given first by God, includes these mechanical aspects only as integrated within the logic of gift, in all the ways indicated above.

The crucial point is thus that these mechanical aspects realize their true character as matters of being and knowing only by virtue of being *integrated* into love, a love that remains from its depths God-centered. The logic of integration is just the point.[51] Simply to affirm the importance of adding wonder to a scientific reason tacitly understood to be a matter primarily of manipulative control — and just so far to affirm the importance also of adding (God-centered) goodness and beauty to a cosmological order understood to be a matter primarily of externally conceived efficient and material causes — leaves intact the fragmented, hence reductive, view of the mind and reality that an adequate ontology of creation calls into question.

Here, then, is the ontological reason why, in the words of Wolfhart Pannenberg, "it is not possible to understand fully or even appropriately the processes of nature without any reference to . . . God." The world's relation to God is the *analogatum princeps* for every inner-worldly distinction, even for those that are putatively purely methodological in nature. In a word, *simple addition* in construing the relation between any x and any non-x, in the method or content of knowledge, always implies an atheism

---

remaining open from its depths to the other. Substantial in-itselfness and openness to the other, in other words, are directly and not inversely related. This is so finally because *esse* in its singular actualization qua *each* being remains "common" to, and thus shared by, *all* beings. On this, cf. notes 40, 49, 50, and 51.

51. The term "integration" suggests a logic simply of continuity, while love and gift rightly understood just so far also demand the discontinuity entailed in relation to an *other*. That the latter is the case follows from what was stated above about the act that establishes x as x, an act that distinguishes and thus "divides" as it simultaneously relates x and non-x. The upshot is that the idea of "integration" needs to be further qualified in terms of the distance ("divides") as well as the nearness ("relates" or "unifies") that are both characteristic of an integration that is one of love or gift. But this qualification is a task for another occasion.

that is far from pure innocence: it obscures the nature of the universe, draining it of its constitutive creaturely character.

The suggestion that the birth of modern science is the fruit of a Christian imagination of the cosmos, at the heart of which lies the cosmos's being brought into being *ex nihilo* by a loving *Logos*, while not untrue, requires substantial qualification in light of these ontological considerations. The doctrine of creation gives rise to and sustains the methodical abstract study of the cosmos even as such study enables efficient making. But, in doing so, this doctrine, rightly understood, demands a transformation of modernity's notions of both making and knowing.[52] Rather

---

52. Cf. in this connection the comments of Adrian Walker:

Thomas, following Aristotle, says that finality is the "cause of causes." It is causality, then, in the primary sense, the *analogatum princeps* in which all other senses of causality participate — including efficiency. In fact, it is just this participation that distinguishes efficiency in the true sense, as communication of actuality, as generosity, from mechanical pushing and pulling. Or, to put it another way, *Gestalt* contains the principle thanks to which what we would think of as the mechanical aspects — pushing, pulling, etc. — derive their causal relevance and causal efficacy. For the "merely mechanical" as such does not exist; it is an ideal limit that is never actually reached because there is always a form determining, hence giving reality to, the mechanical causes. Mechanical causes are causes only to the extent that they are never merely mechanical, but always already participate in efficiency-as-generosity thanks to form. Yes, pushing and pulling will contribute, but not by reason of being pushing and pulling *simply*, but by reason of their specification with respect to a goal, that is, as *this particular* pushing and pulling. The sculptor cannot sculpt unless the chisel impacts the marble, but the impact would not be a cause unless it produced a specific kind of impact, whose specificity derives from the idea of the statue.

This presupposes, of course, that meaningfulness is actually a basic feature of nature, one more basic in a way than even efficient causality insofar as it has a material dimension and unfolds over time. Indeed, it is because this is the case that conventional experimental science already lives tacitly from the perception of something like *Gestalt*. This is true not only in biology, but also, analogously, in chemistry and physics. Now, if this is the case, why should biology, or any other physical science, not admit thematization of the *Gestalt* as part of science, indeed, as the more important part of science than the experimental part — more important because architectonic? Why should it not admit that *Gestalt* is the principle, middle, and end of experimental research?

True, the thematization of *Gestalt* would not be a particular experimental result or set of such results. Rather, it would be a way of returning all experimental results to the principle of their relevance and existence insofar as they are in any way causes. That is, it would be a way of re-reading their meaning in light of the whole. It would also work the other way around: It would include a re-reading of the meaning of the

than dividing to conquer, the *logos* implied in this doctrine seeks rather to distinguish or separate in order to relate more profoundly, in a sense that includes while transforming what is meant by "division" and "conquering." The Christian doctrine of creation thus insists that all methodical-scientific abstraction and all would-be efficient making be placed in the service of this distinguishing in order to relate ever more profoundly, finally to enable participation in the Christological love that bears all of being in its return to God.[53]

(4) The upshot of the foregoing comments is that there is no need to set aside love in the scientific-abstract study of the world, even for disciplinary reasons. There is no need to set love aside because love, rightly conceived in its creaturely nature, accommodates the mechanical properties of things, albeit as integrated in terms of (God-centered) love and gift.[54] What

---

whole in light of the details. In fact, it would be mistaken to think of what is being proposed here as just another fuzzy holism. . . . There is always as much to be learned from the bottom up as from the top down. In fact, the real unity of the whole is neither at the top nor at the bottom, with the universal or the particular, but in the interplay of both.

So the issue is: If meaning is basic in nature, even with respect to the mechanical aspects dealt with by conventional empirical science, then why should it not also be basic to the science of nature? Again, this may not be immediately "useful," but why should it be, if the main business of science is in fact to *understand* the way nature is, and this is in fact the way nature is? (From unpublished notes: "Thoughts on Evolution," pp. 2-3)

Cf. in this connection science as conceived by the following: Adolf Portmann, *Animal Forms and Patterns: A Study of the Appearance of Animals* (New York: Schocken Books, 1967); Leon Kass, *Toward a More Natural Science* (New York: The Free Press, 1985), and *The Hungry Soul* (Chicago: University of Chicago Press, 1999); and, for a different argument against mechanistic reduction: R. Lewontin, *The Triple Helix* (Cambridge, MA: Harvard University Press, 2000); *Biology as Ideology: The Doctrine of DNA* (New York: HarperCollins, 1991); R. C. Lewontin, Steven Rose, and Leon J. Kamin, *Not in Our Genes* (New York: Pantheon Books, 1984). See also the work of skin pathologist Wallace Clark.

53. It is important to emphasize (again) here that the unity sought in Christianity always presupposes and promotes *further differentiation:* each creature becomes *more itself* as it grows *more deeply into relation with* God and other creatures. This again is the way of a unity that images the Creator-God whose unity is always already differentiated into an infinite Tri-unity.

54. Gavin D'Costa, in his book *Theology in the Public Square* (London: Blackwell, 2005), engages *(inter alia)* the question of the unity of the disciplines in the writings of Pope John Paul II, focusing especially on the natural sciences. Reviewing the different ways in which the relation between theology and the natural sciences is commonly conceived today, D'Costa links John Paul II with what he terms a "harmonious direct implication model"

such a science would look like is a profoundly difficult and comprehensive question, which I will address in the present forum only by citing the example of a twentieth-century scientist and philosopher of science, Michael Polanyi, who advocates the practice of the sort of abstraction in science that seems to me consistent with the ontology we have set forth.

Before turning to this concluding task, however, it is important that we take note of one powerful objection to the need for the integration of ontology into science, in the sense advanced here: simply, that science with its dominant modern mechanistic idea of method and order has *worked*. But if it has worked, then this fact alone seems sufficient to demonstrate the "realism" of mechanism as a way of conceiving the order of things as intended by God.

One can scarcely exaggerate the profundity and complexity of the issues implied in this objection. Certainly the ontology sketched above anticipates that things conceived, analyzed, and experimented with carefully and intelligently will "work." The mechanical-forceful properties of things, after all, are really *in* the thing, are truly part of things in their identity and

---

(213), by which he means that theology bears direct implications for science, in a way that nonetheless accords science its legitimate autonomy. Although "harmonious" implies a consonance between theology and science, D'Costa says that priority must nevertheless be "given to theology because its 'data' are revealed" (211). Recognizing, as D'Costa does, the limitations of "models," the present argument is in agreement with his position, with one important qualifier, namely that what is termed a relation of "direct implication" between theology and science cuts both ways. The idea of creation as conceived in Christian theology demands some sort of reciprocal priority between theology and science, albeit a reciprocal priority conceived in asymmetrical terms.

Regarding the relation between theology and natural science, then, we must recognize first that this relation is one of mutual implication, such that the exercise of each in its proper method always bears internal implications for the other. Each, rightly understood, needs to remain open to and move toward genuine integration with the other, in a way that both presupposes and demands the legitimate autonomy of each. The relation between theology and natural science, in short, is neither extrinsic, after the manner of a kind of harmonizing "addition" of the results of their respective inquiries ("concordism"), nor is it properly deductive, such that the "theories" of one are construed simply-necessarily as inferences of the other. However, and this is the second point, the mutuality involved in this relation of harmonious or integrative implication between theology and science is not for all that symmetrical. Theology and science both make "normative" "truth-demands" on each other, *differently*: science, indeed science *as always mediated by a distinct ontology*, retains a "relative" priority, but within the *"absolute" priority of theology*. The relation between them, in a word, is genuinely mutual, while nonetheless asymmetrical. I do not think D'Costa would disagree with my qualifier here, as long as the "absolute" priority of theology is maintained in the way suggested. But this need not be argued here.

their behavior. For the present context, however, it will suffice to note only that any claim to justify modern science's abstraction of the mechanical-forceful aspects of things in terms primarily of technological power, on the grounds that this abstraction has "worked," remains just so far question-begging. Of course no one denies the vast successes of modern science, for example, in medicine and medical technology. The simple but crucially important implication of the foregoing argument, however, is that the appeal to the practical effectiveness of modern science, even in the face of its obviously vast successes, still begs the crucial issue.

Such an argument invariably has built into it the very fragmented patterns of thought needing to be challenged, if the idea of "it works" is to be assessed in terms of an integrated view of reality as created by and destined for God. The burden of the above ontology of creation is that we cannot know the true meaning of "it works" except in terms of what is implied originally and finally by things' integrity, relative to the ever-higher levels of being to which any given entity, or part of an entity, is related, all the way up to God. We cannot know the true meaning of things without recuperating memory of what they are in their givenness as gifts, in their concrete reality as created by God. What needs to be pondered, not in spite of but precisely coincident with and from inside those successes, is the extent to which our highly mechanistic and abstract culture, in the logic of its academy, its economy, its politics, indeed of its scientific technology that englobes all of these, has assisted in reducing the fundamental meaning of things, leaving man able to respond only in fragmented fashion to the universal ecology of being intended by God in his creation of the cosmos.[55]

---

55. Apropos of this, however, two comments: (1) In light of my argument regarding the order of gift as more basic than, while nevertheless including, mechanical order, I understand that any claim that artifice based effectively or exhaustively on the mechanical order "works" *eo ipso* expresses a fragmented sense of "works." In this case, "it works" can only signify what is at best an approximation, a matter of statistically frequent occurrence — that is, what is at best a fragmented part of the whole of what it means to "work" (cf. note 52 above). This may seem a less significant matter in the case of simple machines, since here mechanical properties do predominate. Even in the case of machines, however, a richer causality than mere efficient causality obtains, with consequences for the "working" of the machine — i.e., not even machines can be accounted for in exhaustively mechanical terms. Nonetheless, the significance of reductive-mechanistic modes of conceiving and treating entities becomes much more evident in the biological order.

(2) The ambiguity of "it works" can also be shown in a broader cultural sense. One might say, for example, that a cell phone or a computer "works." Each effectively and technically enables some form of communication between human beings and fosters some form of

Jonas has indicated some important aspects of what is meant here, perhaps most radically that, with the logic of modern mechanistic modes of abstraction, what has been set into place is a dynamic for the penetration of artificiality into the very core of the naturally given. Jonas's point is not that artifice is not integral to human culture, but that, in its prevalent mechanistic-technological form, artifice fails to integrate itself into what is permanently, anteriorly *given*, as gift. Indeed, it is important to see here that, from the point of view of an adequately conceived Christian ontology of creation, and also in a significant sense from the point of view already of Greek thought, *human artifice is itself part of nature*. This is the implication, for example, of Aristotle's treatise on the soul *(De Anima)*, which is conceived as part of the science of nature. Artifice and nature thus should not be opposed to each other, because in the most basic sense they cannot be so opposed. The point of my argument is simply that modern technologistic (Cartesian, Baconian) artifice fails to recuperate itself from within the *natural giftedness* that it shares with the rest of creation.

Modern artifice, in other words, insofar as it is shaped by mechanistic patterns of thought, bears a technological logic that would of its inner dynamic overtake things *in their origin, in their original-natural givenness as created by God*.[56]

The claim that the undeniably great successes of modern science, with

---

knowledge and experience. But whether this means that either *actually works in an adequate, fully integrated and thus non-question-begging sense* can be answered only by considering what is meant by human communication and knowledge and experience in their integrity. What is the logic of communication toward which the cell phone is ordered, or the logic of knowledge and experience toward which the computer is ordered? Toward what habits of human communication and consciousness do the cell phone and the computer *of their inner order as such* logically dispose us? To be sure, much more qualification is needed than can be offered in the present forum. My point is simply that the assertion that a product of mechanistically conceived artifice "works" can be truly assessed only in terms of the integrity of what the product is and is for, and ultimately in terms of the nature and destiny of the producers and users of the artifact in relation to other human beings, the cosmos, and God.

56. Thus nature is no longer good *qua* given *(bonum qua ens)* but only good *qua* subject to human *facere (bonum quia factum)*. Cf. Joseph Ratzinger, *Introduction to Christianity* (San Francisco: Ignatius Press, 2004), pp. 59-69. It is helpful to recall here the root meaning of nature *(natura, physis)* as something brought into being through "begetting" and "birth," hence as something whose *origin* is always already *given* (as good). Cf. in this connection the statement of twentieth-century philosopher Gabriel Marcel, who says that the "human being who denies his nature as a created being ends up by claiming for himself attributes which are a sort of caricature of those that belong to the Uncreated" (*Man Against Humanity* [London: Harvill Press, 1952], p. 184).

its dominant modes of mechanistic abstraction, suffice of themselves to mute the demand for transformation needs to be pondered in light of the question of these successes' reductive technological character. Such a claim needs to be pondered, that is, insofar as these successes would be measured in terms of fidelity to the ontology of creation carried in Christianity.

I conclude, then, simply by suggesting an alternative way of conceiving abstract limit in science, an alternative that I believe is consistent with the conception of limit entailed by the Christian ontology of creation outlined above. The cognitional theory is that of twentieth-century physical chemist and philosopher of science, Michael Polanyi.[57]

V.

In contrast to the dominant mechanistic theory, Polanyi's cognitional theory understands the abstract study of things in science to involve granting primacy to what is *implied* in an entity's relation to ever-greater and more comprehensive levels of reality.

The heart of his conception of knowledge lies in his notion of "indwelling," together with the dual features characteristic of knowledge as an act of indwelling. For the idea of indwelling, Polanyi draws on how we know our own body. "All extension of comprehension," he says, "involves an expansion of ourselves into a new dwelling place, of which we assimilate the framework by relying on it as we do our own body" (FR, 244). We recognize, for example, that "when we attend from a set of particulars to the whole which they form, we establish a logical relation between the particulars and the whole, similar to that which exists between our body and the things outside it. . . . We may describe this relation by saying that the act of comprehending a whole *is an interiorisation of its parts, which makes us dwell in them* in a way that is logically similar to the way we dwell in our

---

57. I will focus here on several important articles: "Faith and Reason" (=FR), *The Journal of Religion* 41, no. 4 (October 1961): 237-47; "Science and Religion" (=SR), *Philosophy Today* 7, no. 1 (Spring 1963): 4-14; "On the Modern Mind" (=MM), *Encounter* 24 (May 1965): 12-20; "The Structure of Consciousness" (=SC) in *The Anatomy of Knowledge*, ed. Marjorie Grene (London: Routledge and Kegan Paul, 1969), pp. 315-28. Key books by Polanyi include *Personal Knowledge: Towards a Post-Critical Philosophy* (=PK) (Chicago: University of Chicago Press, 1974); *The Tacit Dimension* (Gloucester, MA: Peter Smith, 1983); *Knowing and Being: Essays by Michael Polanyi*, ed. Marjorie Grene (Chicago: University of Chicago Press, 1969).

body" (SR, 7). This implies a duality in each of our acts of knowledge: in the act of knowing things, we attend *to* the things, but *from* within our body, or again from within the framework on which we tacitly rely *in* our focus on things.

In sum, Polanyi's cognitional theory holds that "our *explicit knowledge of a thing invariably relies on our tacit awareness of some other things*" (SR, 5). Polanyi says that the interplay of "detailing and integrating is the royal road for deepening our understanding of any comprehensive entity" (FR, 239-40). This points him toward what is a main burden of his theory, that there is an indissoluble link between the logic of reason and the structure of reality. Thus he states, following the assertion just cited:

> In saying this I have pronounced a key word. I have spoken of understanding. Understanding, comprehension — this is the cognitive faculty cast aside by a positivistic theory of knowledge, which refuses to recognize the existence of comprehensive entities as distinct from their particulars; and this is the faculty that I recognize as the central act of knowing. For comprehension can never be absent from any process of knowing and is indeed the ultimate sanction of any such act. (FR, 240)

Thus Polanyi insists that "an adequate theory of knowledge must involve a true conception of man and the universe and be itself supported by it. The absurdity of the world view which a false ideal of knowledge has spread in our time may bear this out" (SR, 8).

There are several further features implied in this notion of knowledge as indwelling with its duality of cognitional acts, its *polarity* within *unity* of each act of knowledge. To begin with, Polanyi says this notion addresses the problem raised by Plato in the *Meno*, regarding how our search for knowledge is always a knowing-unknowing, as it were. The knower relies on a kind of tacit or implicit knowledge *from* which he attends in coming to an explicit knowledge of something. In this sense, all knowledge presupposes a kind of memory.

Furthermore, Polanyi says that his conception of knowledge as indwelling overcomes a longstanding dualism between I-It and I-Thou kinds of knowledge. There is no dichotomy between the kind of knowledge involved in knowing a thing and that involved in knowing a person, indeed all the way to the person of God (FR, 245-47). In fact, all knowledge is like the knowledge of other persons. Indwelling is not a matter of mere feeling or sympathy (cf. Dilthey's *Einfühlung*), and thus not a matter appropriate only for the humanities: there is no dichotomy between the natural sciences and the human sciences *(Naturwissenschaften* and the *Geisteswissenschaften)*.

Polanyi says that each level of reality operates toward boundary conditions, in the sense that physics and chemistry, for example, are open to higher levels of reality that in fact "control" these lower levels (MM, 14-15). He says in this connection that "*what is most tangible has the least meaning and it is perverse then to identify the tangible with the real*" (MM, 15). "The world view of Galileo, [therefore], accepted since the Copernican Revolution, proves fundamentally misleading" (MM, 15). Focusing on "part" of something to the neglect of an abiding subsidiary awareness of the greater whole or more comprehensive levels of which it is a "part" turns that "part" into an extrinsic aspect of an object without functional meaning (i.e., without relation to the higher levels in relation to which it has its true or non-reductive meaning). Thus Polanyi says that biological entities presuppose the laws of physics and chemistry but are not determined by them. They are "comprehensive entities," not mathematically definable (SR, 8-9). Regarding Descartes, Polanyi says that the Cartesian dualism of mind and body is eliminated when one sees that mind and body do not "interact explicitly" (e.g., after the manner of two discrete entities), but rather relate "according to the logic of tacit knowing" (SC, 327).

Polanyi points out the implications of his theory for the problem of the relation of science and religion, countering the view of some theologians who would insist that science can contradict religious teachings only insofar as religion makes statements that bear on physical events, as these theologians think it should not (SR, 4). On the contrary, according to Polanyi knowledge leads organically to ever-higher and more comprehensive levels of reality. We always know more than we can tell, and the focal dimension of knowledge never exhausts the reality it is seeking to know. Each level opens toward boundary conditions that require moving on to ever-higher and more comprehensive levels of being (SC, 321). The structure of knowledge leads on to a panorama akin to Christian views of man's position in the universe (SR, 4-5). Indeed, Polanyi states that the true logic of knowing is disclosed finally in the faith-reason scheme of St. Paul. No act of knowledge is ever exhaustive, and the search for knowledge leads organically to the Pauline scheme (SR, 14):

> These subjects [of divinity and the possibility of knowing God] lie outside my argument. But my conception of knowing opens the way to

them. Knowing, as a dynamic force of comprehension, uncovers at each step a new hidden meaning. It reveals a universe of comprehensive entities which represent the meaning of their largely unspecifiable particulars. A universe constructed as an ascending hierarchy of meaning and excellence is very different from the picture of a chance collocation of atoms to which the examination of the universe by explicit modes of inference leads us. The vision of such a hierarchy inevitably sweeps on to envisage the meaning of the universe as a whole. Thus natural knowledge expands continuously into knowledge of the supernatural.

The very act of scientific discovery offers a paradigm of this transition. I have described it as a passionate pursuit of a hidden meaning, guided by intensely personal intimations of this yet unexposed reality. The intrinsic hazards of such efforts are of its essence; discovery is defined as an advancement of knowledge that cannot be achieved by any, however diligent, application of explicit modes of inference. Yet the discoverer must labor night and day. For though no labor can make a discovery, no discovery can be made without intense, absorbing, devoted labor. Here we have a paradigm of the Pauline scheme of faith, works, and grace. The discoverer works in the belief that his labors will prepare his mind for receiving a truth from sources over which he has no control. I regard the Pauline scheme therefore as the only adequate conception of knowledge. (FR, 246-47)

In this connection, Polanyi repeatedly points out that hope (FR, 243) and faith (PK, 208-52ff.) are part of the structure of knowing, and he points out the continuity between his theory of knowledge — which involves assimilating a framework of meaning and dwelling within it the way we dwell within our body — and religious conversion (FR, 244; cf. SR, 7-8). He suggests that the dynamic of knowing operates through attraction, and that intellectual beauty is a sign of man's contact with reality (PK, 145, 149). He speaks of the need to accept nature as the cosmic home of man, in which man is both a child of creation and a bearer of prospects beyond his own range of control (SR, 14). The idea of self-determination, he says, is meaningless (SR, 14), and this should make us willing to see that the task of knowledge in fact involves a calling (SR, 14). Here, then, in a word, "is the close neighborhood of science and religion to which a revised theory of knowledge leads us" (SR, 14).

Thus we have in Polanyi a way of abstracting with a distinctive way of understanding limit: limit is *relational* closure, relational in a sense that implies openness, precisely *from inside* what is abstracted and the manner of its abstraction, to being through all of its ever more comprehensive levels, up to God. Pertinent to my argument is how the manner of abstraction and the order that obtains in reality interlock in Polanyi's theory. Abstraction is a matter of relational closure because and insofar as things themselves are a matter of relational closure.

There are questions that might be put to Polanyi relative to the dominant mechanistic mode of abstraction and view of reality, in light of Jonas's discussion of modern science indicated above, and indeed in light also of the ontology of creation we have set forth.[58] It suffices for the purposes of the present argument, however, simply to point out in conclusion how Jonas's and Polanyi's respective arguments serve to confirm what we have meant to argue here, which is that the idea of limit implied in the disciplinary abstraction necessary for any scientific study of nature is never neutral with respect to what we have termed the nature of the given as gift, nor to the nature of the giver of the gift — in short, to the question of creation and the Creator-God.

Polanyi's insertion of an essentially tacit dimension into the heart of scientific abstraction involves rejection of the Cartesian idea of limit. Instead of simple external closure, limit becomes a matter of relational closure, a closure serving clearly to identify x in its difference from non-x all the while leaving each open from within to the other. Changing the nature of the limit proper to abstraction in science in this way may seem to some a trivial and easily negotiated matter. The burden of my argument, however, has been that carrying through this seemingly small change in science's method of abstraction will involve in its wake a reconfiguring of the idea of order in the universe — in its relation, finally, to the Creator-God.

---

58. The themes I would propose for further reflection are three: (1) the relative priority of the explicit and the tacit in his cognitional theory; (2) the need for an account of his argument in *distinctly ontological,* as well as cognitional, terms, especially relative to the mutual relation between the mind and the structure of the cosmos as implied in that argument; (3) further exploration of the significance of his argument in its bearing on what he terms the "exact sciences," as distinct from, say, biology, psychology, and sociology. I note this third question, for example, in light of the statement from *Personal Knowledge*: "I start by rejecting the ideal of scientific detachment. In the exact sciences, this false ideal is perhaps harmless, for it is in fact disregarded there by scientists. But we shall see that it exercises a destructive influence in biology, psychology and sociology, and falsifies our whole outlook far beyond the domain of science. I want to establish an alternative ideal of knowledge, quite generally." I should say that I do not necessarily pose these questions for critical purposes, but primarily for the sake of further clarification and possible development of Polanyi's argument.

The Anthropological Vision of *Caritas in Veritate* in Light of Economic and Cultural Life in the United States

"The truth of development consists in its completeness: if it does not involve the whole man and every man, it is not true development" (n. 18). This, says Pope Benedict in his recent encyclical, is "the central message of Paul VI's *Populorum Progressio*, valid for today and for all time" (n. 18).

> Integral human development on the natural plane, as a response to a vocation from God the Creator, demands self-fulfillment in a "transcendent humanism which gives [to man] his greatest possible perfection: this is the highest goal of personal development." The Christian vocation to this development therefore applies to both the natural plane and the supernatural plane. . . . (n. 18, citing *PP*)

According to Benedict, God-centered charity in truth is the key to this "integral human development." "Everything has its origin in God's love, everything is shaped by it, everything is directed towards it" (n. 1). Love is "the principle not only of micro-relationships (with friends, with family members or within small groups) but also of macro-relationships (social, economic and political ones)" (n. 1).

The call to love is thus not imposed on man from the outside, as an

---

Earlier versions of the present chapter were presented at the conference "Tradition and Liberation: *Charity in Truth* and the New Face of Social Progress," sponsored by the Center for World Catholicism and Intercultural Theology at DePaul University, Chicago, IL (April 20-23, 2010) and the Vatican II International Symposium of University Professors "*Caritas in Veritate*, Towards an Economy Supporting the Human Family: Person, Society, Institutions," organized by the Pontifical Council for Justice and Peace, Rome, Italy (June 24-27, 2010).

extrinsic addition to his being, nor is it something in which only some are meant to participate. On the contrary, "the interior impulse to love" is "the vocation planted by God in the heart and mind of every human person," even as this love is "purified and liberated by Jesus Christ," who reveals to us its fullness (n. 1). "In Christ, *charity in truth* becomes the Face of his Person" (n. 1). The Church's social teaching thus, in a word, is "*caritas in veritate in re sociali:* the proclamation of the truth of Christ's love in society" (n. 5).

This, in sum, is the root proposal of the encyclical. My purpose is to discuss the anthropological vision informing the Church's social teaching as summarized in this statement and articulated in the encyclical, in its meaning for economic and cultural life.

I.

To get at the heart of what I wish to propose, let me begin by indicating some questions raised by various commentators in America regarding the encyclical. I limit my discussion here to representative responses from "mainstream" Catholic academic and cultural leaders which, while favorable in many respects, also raise critical questions, and thereby bring into relief the most basic claims of the encyclical.

(1) One author suggests, for example, that "the intellectual style and philosophical-theological underpinnings seem noticeably different from that of the preceding tradition of the Church.... Benedict XVI's repeated appeal to metaphysics, as important as it is to his own theology and to his social message, seems to return to an earlier deductive model of teaching on social questions." This model, the author says, has been "abandoned by Vatican II's move to the symbolic rhetorical style of positive theology and reading the signs of the times in its social teaching." The author says further that the encyclical's approach risks making the terms of the encyclical "less accessible for many readers" because, as Benedict himself recognizes, "modern Western culture generally no longer articulates its fundamental convictions in metaphysical terms."[1]

(2) Not unrelated to these concerns, another author has suggested that, "where John Paul II or Paul VI cultivated an ecumenical voice when they wished to speak about global problems, Benedict cultivates a dog-

---

1. Drew Christiansen, "Metaphysics and Society: A Commentary on *Caritas in veritate*," *Theological Studies* 71 (March 2010): 3-28, at 7.

matic one." Consistent with his Regensburg address in 2006, Benedict invites dialogue, but then sets "the Catholic synthesis of faith and reason as a prerequisite for that dialogue." To be sure, says the author of this criticism, in "a de-secularizing age" such as our own, we should be free to draw on the wisdom of each of our traditions. Nevertheless, if such "teachings are to contribute to global 'unity and peace,' they will have to be taught in a way that seeks to transcend the boundaries of the traditions that produced them." The author says that Pius XI and John Paul II both understood this, and, although Benedict presents *CIV* as a continuation of their teaching, he does not follow their example. On the contrary, "Benedict's 'love' is narrowed by his 'truth.'"[2]

(3) Also pointing toward a discontinuity between *CIV* and earlier documents of the Church's social teaching, though in a different vein, a third author has said that Catholics must ask themselves whether there are now two social-doctrine traditions, one reaching from Leo XIII's *Rerum Novarum* to *Centesimus Annus*, the other from *Populorum Progressio* through *Sollicitudo Rei Socialis* to *Caritas in Veritate*. The author sees these two traditions stressing, respectively, freedom, virtue, human creativity, and the market economy, on the one hand, and such things as the benefits of "world political authority" and the redistribution of wealth over wealth-creation, on the other. He emphasizes in this context that *Centesimus Annus* had "jettisoned the idea of a Catholic 'third way' that was somehow 'between' or 'beyond' or 'above' capitalism and socialism — a favorite dream of Catholics ranging from G. K. Chesterton to John A. Ryan and Ivan Illich" — and implies that *CIV* weakens this claim. This critic also points toward what he thinks is the incomprehensibility of such views expressed in *Caritas* as that "defeating Third World poverty and underdevelopment requires a 'necessary openness, in a world context, to forms of economic activity marked by quotas of gratuitousness and communion.'"[3]

Likewise questioning in a similar spirit the comprehensibility, or "realism," of *CIV*, another author, writing in the journal *First Things*, asks whether the encyclical's call for "a true world political authority" may not involve Christians in "merely baking bricks for some yet more calamitous Babel." He suggests that we need to recall in this context St. Augustine's doctrine of the two cities, in which Augustine distinguishes clearly be-

---

2. David Nirenberg, "Love and Capitalism," *The New Republic*, September 23, 2009.
3. George Weigel, "*Caritas in Veritate* in Gold and Red," *National Review* online, July 7, 2009.

tween the Church and the world, and their respectively eternal and temporal forms of community.⁴

(4) There is the further suggestion that the encyclical "reflects only the most limited insight into the practical moral problems of people" in business. According to the author of this criticism, "Benedict reiterates recurring themes from Catholic social teaching on the rights of workers but offers no further counsel on how to resolve the difficult employment, sourcing, safety, and environmental challenges business executives face." In a word, the Pope chooses to address moral decisions only at the "systemic level."⁵

(5) Another author asks for a greater recognition by the encyclical of "the contested nature of the 'truly human' in a global society and a deeper epistemological humility in expressing 'the truth about man.'" She finds, for example, that the connections made in *CIV* between "human ecology" and "physical ecology" are unsatisfactory. The encyclical rightly critiques liberal rights and freedom, but in a way that is nevertheless too narrow, in its rejection *tout court* of same-sex marriage, contraception, and medically assisted reproduction. According to this scholar, the encyclical's appreciation of sexual difference and gendered roles gives insufficient attention to the social, economic, and political conditions that undermine genuine equality between men and women, and, more specifically, block recognition of the importance of empowering women "as the cornerstone of sustainable development."⁶

(6) Finally, discussing what she terms Benedict's "global reorientation," one theologian notes that

> Benedict's longstanding concern with the recovery of Christian religious faith in Europe [had led] him to accentuate the divinity of Christ, a Word Christology, and the availability to humans of transcendent communion with God. Yet Benedict's emergent investment in reform of global social structures requires a Christology in which

---

4. Douglas Farrow, "Charity and Unity," *First Things* (October 2009): 37-40, at 39. For a discussion of *CIV*'s theology of grace, and its concept of nature, see Philipp Gabriel Renczes, S.J., "Grace Reloaded: *Caritas in veritate*'s Theological Anthropology," *Theological Studies* 71 (June 2010): 273-90.

5. Kirk O. Hansen, "What's the Business Plan?" in "Papal Correspondence," in *America*, November 30, 2009.

6. Maura A. Ryan, "A New Shade of Green? Nature, Freedom, and Sexual Difference in *Caritas in veritate*," *Theological Studies* 71 (June 2010): 335-49, at 345-48.

the Incarnation, resurrection, and Pentecost offer the possibility of historical transformations modeled on Jesus' eschatological ministry of the kingdom or reign of God.

The author suggests in this connection that there has been a development in Benedict's *CIV* and other recent papal writings that contrasts, for example, with his first encyclical and his book *Jesus of Nazareth*. Implied in these developments is "a view of Christ and Christian faith as enabling charity and hope, not only as interior dispositions or gateways to eternity but also as active, practical virtues through which Christians join with others to work for global justice and structural change."[7]

These brief comments to be sure scarcely capture the nuances of the arguments in each case. Nor do my comments call attention to the authors' positive assessments of various aspects of the encyclical. I direct attention to their questions mainly to set a backdrop for the theme I wish to address, and limit myself in response to summary statements of principle in their regard. The questions all draw attention in different ways to what is perceived, not incorrectly, as the anthropological, metaphysical, or "dogmatic" nature and emphasis of *Caritas in Veritate*. My purpose is to demonstrate, against the background of the critical questions as outlined, that the methodological role played by anthropology is just the point. The burden of the encyclical, in other words, lies decisively in its anthropological orientation — and in this sense its development within continuity — of Catholic social teaching. What I therefore hope to show is that *CIV* conceives the Church's social teaching in a way that challenges the terms of that teaching as presupposed in the criticisms.

My presentation thus has two main parts: to consider the basic anthropological terms of Catholic social teaching; and to indicate how these terms reconfigure in subtle but crucial ways the dominant approaches to socioeconomic life in today's increasingly global liberal order.

II.

Let me then begin by saying that the "integral human development" introduced by Paul VI in *Populorum Progressio* and reaffirmed by Benedict in

---

7. Lisa Sowle Cahill, "*Caritas in veritate:* Benedict's Global Reorientation," *Theological Studies* 71 (June 2010): 291-319, at 291-92.

CIV is entirely consistent with what *Centesimus Annus*, published shortly after the political events of 1989, affirms as "the positive value of an authentic theology of integral human liberation."[8] *CIV* recalls the teaching of John Paul II in this latter encyclical, which states that a comprehensive new plan of development is called for not only in the formerly Communist countries of Eastern Europe but also in the West. Benedict emphasizes that this is "still a real duty that needs to be discharged" (n. 23). The Church, in other words, has a duty in relation to *both* the socialist economies that had prevailed in Eastern Europe *and* the liberal market economies of the West, even if this duty is not symmetrical in its respective implications for the one and the other.

On the one hand, then, the purpose of the Church is not to suggest a distinct economic system *as an economic system*. Catholic social teaching has no intention of providing technical solutions with respect to economics and development (n. 9). At the same time, by virtue of her sacramental embodiment of the truth of Christ as Creator and Redeemer, the Church does become an "expert in humanity,"[9] to use the words spoken at the United Nations by Paul VI, in the sense that she has "a mission of truth to accomplish, in every time and circumstance, for a society that is attuned to man, to his dignity, to his vocation" (n. 9).

The point is that the Church proposes principles that affect all human activities from within, including activities in politics and the public realm (n. 56) and in economics (n. 37). This implies that the Church does not begin by simply accepting the terms of freedom and rights and liberation as conceived in the dominant forms of either socialism or the liberal market, while then *adding* a Christian intention. The Church accepts what is true in the dominant forms of social-economic activity, but only as it dynamically reorders these in a way that reaches to their roots, in light of man's nature as destined for fulfillment in the love of Jesus Christ. In a word, the Christian difference, as it affects the economic and political order, is one not merely of *additional motivation* but of *inner transformation*.

---

8. *Centesimus Annus*, n. 26. This statement references the CDF's Instruction on Christian Freedom and Liberation, *Libertatis Conscientia* (March 26, 1986): AAS 81 (1987), pp. 554-821.

9. Pope Paul VI, *Discourse to the General Assembly of the United Nations Organization*, 4 October 1965, n. 3.

III.

But if the Church's social teaching is not a set of technical solutions or simply an alternative economic system, even as it informs, or indeed dynamically transforms, all such solutions and systems, then what is it?

What I take to be the answer of *CIV* is this: Catholic social teaching is a vision of reality — an understanding of being, man, and God — that unfolds an entire way of life, at the heart of which is a moral-social practice. Catholic social teaching, in a word, is a social practice only as at once a matter of truth. Four brief comments will clarify what this means.

(1) The foundation for this claim lies in the encyclical's affirmation of the unity of truth and love in the person of Jesus Christ as the revelation of the Trinitarian God. Jesus Christ is the *Word* or *logos* of God as the *deed* of God's love. Christ embodies in his person the original unity of truth (hence "theory" or "dogma") and love (hence deed: *pragma, praxis*), the original unity of truth and social practice.[10]

(2) This unity of truth and love is also disclosed in the structure of creaturely being as gift. Our being is a being-given meant itself to give. As St. Augustine says, citing the words of the apostle John: "We cannot love unless we are first loved."[11] "In this is love, that God has first loved us" (1 John 4:10).

(3) Love whom or what? We love God naturally above all things. As Augustine and Aquinas both say in their different ways, we naturally love God more than ourselves, because he is more interior to us than we are to ourselves.[12] And we cannot but naturally love all other creatures with whom we share a common relation to God: above all, other persons, but also non-personal entities that share proportionately-analogically in the creaturely meaning of being as gift, which makes them good in themselves, by virtue of their creation.

Our love, in other words, is in its roots *filial:* we are not the unorigin-

---

10. Ratzinger already developed this theme in a profound way in his early book, *Introduction to Christianity* (San Francisco: Ignatius Press, 1968), which shows that, according to Christian belief, at the origin of things lies the Creator who is characterized by the unity of reason and love, or freedom. Ratzinger comments on the Trinity in this light, and then shows how Christological dogma, and in turn each of the articles of the Creed, articulate the concrete meaning of love: articulate the *meaning* or *doctrine* of God in relation to the world, as *love* and thus already as *action* that is *social*.

11. St. Augustine, Sermon 34, 1-3.

12. Cf. Augustine, *Confessions* 3, 6; Aquinas, *ST* I, q. 8, a. 1 and *De Veritate*, q. 22, a. 2.

ated origins of love but participants in a love that is always first given to us by God. And this love is by nature radically *social:* it is at once God-centered and inclusive of the whole of creation, of all being and of each singular, unique being.

(4) This filial-social love that we participate in *by nature,* by virtue of creation, is destined for, and fulfilled in, our participation *by grace* in God's own love, as revealed in Jesus Christ through his sacramental Church.

It is helpful, in light of these four comments, to recall here the text that both John Paul II and Benedict XVI take to contain the central teaching of the Second Vatican Council: *Gaudium et Spes,* n. 22, which states that, in his revelation of the trinitarian love of God, Jesus Christ discloses the meaning of man and, by implication, of all physical creation, to itself.

In a word, truth is a *logos* of love, and love is the way of truth, as revealed by God in Jesus Christ and, naturally-analogically, in creation itself.

IV.

Thus we have the fundamental principles in terms of which *CIV* is able to respond to the criticisms noted briefly above.

(1) First, regarding the metaphysical character of the encyclical and its so-called "deductive model" of social teaching: the relevant point is to see that this criticism is mediated by its own notion of truth ("theory") and love ("social practice") and of the relation between them, though this notion remains implicit and thus unaccounted for. The criticism implicitly disjoins truth from love in a way that *CIV* does not. The author's different way of approaching the relation between the two is thus a function not of no metaphysics but of what is rather an alternative metaphysics, one containing an alternative understanding of what it means for God to be author of, and present in, his creation. It is true that Western culture today no longer articulates its vision of things in metaphysical terms, and that explicitly metaphysical language is not readily accessible to contemporary readers. However, metaphysics — some vision of reality inclusive of ideas about being, man, and God — does not cease to operate, and to guide one's social practice, simply because it is ignored or left tacitly implied. It is in this context that we see the importance of *CIV*: to recuperate the authentic meaning of social practice *as a vision of reality* whose most basic content is God-centered love; and in so doing to expose the inadequate alternative visions of reality that are implied in and give the basic form to the

conventional economic models of socialism and the liberal market, even where these alternative visions remain unconscious as *metaphysical,* and at least by implication also *theological, visions.*[13]

(2) Second, regarding dialogue and the recovery of an ecumenical voice: the key again is *CIV*'s unity of truth and love. Genuine dialogue need not, and should not, fracture this unity. In entering into dialogue, the weight should not be placed on bracketing the truth in its fullness — though of course not everything needs to be made explicit on every occasion — but rather on demonstrating ever more fully the nature of truth as the *logos of love,* and thus on giving integrated witness to truth *as* love. *CIV* presumes that the way of dialogue for Christians is given in Jesus himself, who testifies with his whole being, in a way that wholly respects and does not impose on others, even as he demonstrates that truth rightly understood tends toward witness, even unto the suffering of death. Benedict in other writings also offers the non-Christian Socrates as an example of one who testifies to the transcendent origin and reality of truth with his entire life — and martyr's death — all the while imposing nothing on others, but inviting them when he is questioned to look at what has convinced him and why.

CIV thus finds the common ground necessary for dialogue in man's concrete nature as restless to be loved and to love, all the way to the ultimate source and end of this love. The author who criticizes *CIV*'s lack of an ecumenical voice seeks instead a more abstract common ground, one that disposes the dialogue partners to leave implicit their own concrete search for meaning and to bracket what matters most to them, indeed to separate their verbally articulated claims from the wholeness of their reality as embodied in deed and social practice. From the perspective of *CIV,* dialogue rooted in such an abstract common ground can give only fragmented witness. And in fact such an abstract ground seems to be accepted as genuinely common, as universally accessible and meaningful, only by those who already hold to Western liberal assumptions. *CIV* thinks on the contrary that a truly common ground can be found for all persons only by starting from within the reality of each person in the concrete wholeness of his or her search for meaning in its ultimate source and end.

(3) Regarding the question of a "third way": what I have said above

---

13. Pope John Paul II's publication of the encyclical *Fides et Ratio,* with its emphasis on the recovery of metaphysics in the articulation of faith, is not at all unrelated to the concern indicated here.

already answers this in principle. Let me add only that those who criticize *CIV* for implying openness to a "third way" beyond socialism and the liberal market fail to grasp that what is at stake in Catholic social doctrine is precisely the nature of God's relation to the world, as expressed in Christ and his Church. These critics invariably assume that there realistically exist today only two economic alternatives, socialist-liberationist on the one hand and liberal-capitalist on the other; and that the task of the Church in this context is to add a distinct Christian-moral intentionality that would provide support for, but without truly *informing*, either alternative. But this implies a reductive understanding of the rightful "worldly" implications of the reality of God, Christ, and the Church for socioeconomic institutions and practice. The critics thus leave intact in their different ways, from the left and from the right, the fragmentary vision of man that may be termed *homo economicus,* a vision that wrongly abstracts the economic meaning of man from the ontological and theological roots of his being.

Regarding the question of the "realism" of such economic and political proposals: it is not the case that *CIV* does not appreciate the difficulties involved, or indeed does not recognize that the realization of what it proposes cannot be fully accomplished short of the eschaton. The point is that Christians, nevertheless, have a responsibility to work at all times and places, private and public, for the true end for which man was created. The nature of this end, which is participation in God's love, itself determines the appropriate means of its realization. These appropriate means demand patient and prudential rather than coercive action toward others in one's economic and political activity. Patient and prudential action, however, emphatically does not obviate the need for a witness in economic and political life that involves sacrifice and suffering.

(4) Regarding the objection that *CIV* neglects to provide counsel on how to resolve the practical moral problems in business: this objection fails to see that the Church rightly considers herself to be an "expert in humanity" in the sense indicated above, not an expert in the technical aspects of employment, sourcing, safety, environmental problems, and the like. This does not mean that the Church has no concrete interest in such problems. Rather, as *CIV* insists, the purpose of the Church, and the purpose of the teaching expressed in her social encyclicals, is to demonstrate that God-centered love affects all human activities and makes a significant difference to *every* technical solution, ordering each from within toward the common good and toward an integrated view of human dignity.

(5) Regarding gender and the sexual difference and the connections

between "human ecology" and "physical ecology": these matters of course raise profound questions regarding the nature of the human body. The argument of *CIV* in their regard presupposes, in accord with Pope John Paul II's teaching on the body, that the body is itself an order of love. This teaching runs counter to the physicalist views of the body prevalent in the West especially since the seventeenth century. The author who criticizes *CIV*'s position regarding gender and the link between human ecology and physical ecology, if her criticisms are to be adequate, must first recognize and provide an argument with respect to the differences between John Paul II's notion of the human body and the understanding of the body implied in her criticisms.

(6) Finally, regarding the claim that Benedict's theology has developed from an emphasis on the divinity of Christ and on charity as an interior disposition opening to eternity: in response it seems to me that we need only ponder more deeply here the implications of what Ratzinger said already in his 1960s commentary on *Gaudium et Spes* regarding the importance of the social nature of man. Though of course historical circumstances have drawn out the further implications of Ratzinger's views in this matter, he has never held a position that could rightly be interpreted to imply a dichotomy between so-called interior virtues and active virtues, relative to the question of global justice and structural change. What Ratzinger said in his *Gaudium et Spes* commentary, what he said as Prefect of the Congregation for the Doctrine of the Faith regarding liberation theology in the 1980s, and what he says in *CIV* all affirm the same principles, albeit articulated in ways that fit the different historical circumstances of each document.

But let me conclude this first part of my discussion simply by taking note of persons whose lives seem to me to render concrete the unity of truth and love or social practice articulated by Benedict in *CIV,* and thereby provide concretely embodied responses to many of the above criticisms of Benedict. I have in mind, for example, Peter Maurin and Dorothy Day in America and Madeleine Delbrêl in France, the latter a contemporary of Day who lived and worked among the Communists who were dominant in the economic and political institutions of Ivry, near Paris.[14] In their different ways, each of these persons recognized that God is a social good, that meaninglessness is the deepest form of poverty, and that "social work" takes place at the intersection of time and eternity. They un-

---

14. See Madeleine Delbrêl, *We, the Ordinary People of the Streets* (Grand Rapids: Eerdmans, 2000), with its fine introduction by Fr. Jacques Loew.

derstood that the question of the meaning and existence of God lies at the core of social practice, and that wealth consists most fundamentally in the quality of one's relationships to those with whom relation is given constitutively, in the act of creation: God, family, other persons, and all the creatures of nature.

These persons, in a word, all lived the truth articulated by Mother Teresa when she said that her "social work" involved at root being a "contemplative in the heart of the world."[15]

The persons named here are sometimes criticized for emphasizing too much a personal approach to social justice that fails really to transform or liberate institutions. But these persons show us what is in fact the true meaning of such liberation as presupposed in *CIV* (and *CA*): that personal transformation of meaning in love is the inner condition of, and gives the anterior form to, any institutional change that would be genuinely human and not simply a rearrangement of external structural machinery.[16]

V.

We turn to the second part of the argument. As indicated, the main presupposition undergirding the argument of *CIV* is the universality of the vocation to love. According to Pope Benedict, all of us know, even if only implicitly and thus not fully consciously, that we "are not self-generated" (n. 68). An implicit sense of the Creator abides in each of us, which Cardinal Ratzinger/Pope Benedict describes in other writings in terms of *anamnesis,* the memory of God that is "identical with the foundations of our being."[17] This memory of God can be ignored or denied, but it is never absent from any human consciousness. In a word, a dynamic tendency toward communion with God, and with other creatures who share relation to God, lies in the inmost depths of every human being and not only Christians, even as this tendency is fulfilled only in the grace of God's own love that is revealed in Jesus Christ.

The encyclical's call for a new trajectory of thinking informed by the principles of gratuitousness and relationality takes its starting point from

---

15. 1994 National Prayer Breakfast, Washington, DC.
16. Cf. the *Compendium of the Social Doctrine of the Church,* n. 42.
17. Cardinal Joseph Ratzinger, *Values in a Time of Upheaval,* trans. B. McNeil (New York/San Francisco: Crossroad/Ignatius Press, 2006), p. 92.

this universal *anamnesis* of love and God (cf. n. 53, 55). Let us now consider how this new way of thinking reorders some key aspects of the prevalent approaches to social-political justice.

(1) Regarding tendencies expressed in Western socioeconomic institutions, *Caritas in Veritate* rejects the reading of *Centesimus Annus* that would understand the three "subjects" of the social system — the state, the economy, and civil society — each to have a logic of its own, only extrinsically related to the others (cf. n. 38-40). As Cardinal Bertone stated in an address to the Italian Senate: "This conceptualization . . . has led to identifying the economy with the place where wealth or income is generated, and society with the place of solidarity for its fair distribution."[18] *CIV* rejects this dichotomy between "subjects" that would undermine the call to love as integrative of every human activity and of all development. To paraphrase Cardinal Bertone, we must supersede the dominant view that expects the Church's social teaching, involving as it does the centrality of the person and, in this light, solidarity, subsidiarity, and the common good, to be confined to societal-cultural activities, as it were, while "experts in efficiency" are charged with running the economy, and indeed the order of politics.

This rejection of the idea of three different logics proper to each "subject" of the social system presupposes reaffirmation of the idea of the common good. The common good, says Benedict, concerns the entire "complex of institutions that give structure to the life of society, juridically, civilly, politically, and culturally, making it the *polis*, or 'city' . . ." (n. 7). Commitment to the common good shapes "the *earthly city* in unity and peace, rendering it to some degree an anticipation and a prefiguration of the undivided *city of God*" (n. 7). The Pope insists that economics cannot resolve social problems simply through the application of *commercial logic*, but "needs to be *directed towards the pursuit of the common good*, for which the political community in particular must also take responsibility" (n. 36). "The *principle of gratuitousness* and the logic of gift as an expression of fraternity can and must *find their place within normal economic activity,*" as expressed in *commercial relationships* (n. 36).

Benedict's rejection of an extrinsic relation between the three "subjects" of society, tied to a consequent emphasis on the common good,

---

18. *Address of Cardinal Tarcisio Bertone, Secretary of State, During His Visit to the Senate of the Italian Republic*, 28 July 2009, http://www.vatican.va/roman_curia/secretariat_state/card-bertone/2009/document s/rc_seg-st_20090728_visita-senato_en.html, p. 3 of typescript.

bears two especially important implications. On the one hand, it entails rejection of the dualism between temporal and eternal that is a hallmark of liberal societies. Contrary to the view of John Locke, for example, and countless of our contemporaries, Benedict holds that public-economic activity is not a matter exclusively of the temporal order, as though the eternal order, or the heavenly city, arrives only *after* life on earth, or in any case remains in this life something purely "private."[19]

CIV thus also makes clear that the Church affirms the notion of the *common good*, rather than that of *public order*, as the proper purpose of political and economic activity. The encyclical, in other words, implies rejection of the "juridical" idea of political and economic institutions, according to which such institutions do not project any view of human nature or destiny, but are on the contrary limited simply to the securing of the procedural mechanisms necessary for the fair and equal exercise of freedom by citizens. This juridical understanding of institutions has been a prevalent reading not only of John Paul II's *Centesimus Annus*, but also, for example, the Council's *Dignitatis Humanae*. As noted above, however, this reading is subject to the criticism that *CIV* makes regarding those who interpret *CA* to affirm an extrinsic relation between the end of civil society and the end of the market and the state.[20]

In light of the foregoing comments, we should see that *CIV* carries a significant challenge with respect to the dominant logic of economic and political institutions as conceived in liberal societies. *CIV* challenges the assumption that these institutions are simply procedural mechanisms whose purpose is to create space for the exercise of freedom, and not to offer any pedagogy regarding the meaning, order, and end of man. Such an understanding is inconsistent not only with this encyclical but also with

---

19. Thus Locke's view, from the perspective of *CIV*, is already the beginning, not of "legitimate secularity," but of secularism. The point here is important in connection with Benedict's call for a new reflection on the concept of "laïcité." See, for example, his statement in the opening address of his apostolic visit to France: "I am firmly convinced that a new reflection on the meaning and importance of 'laïcité' is now necessary" (12 September 2008).

20. The juridical idea of political or constitutional order is advanced with respect to both *Dignitatis Humanae* and the American constitution by American theologian John Courtney Murray, S.J. Indeed, Murray affirms an identity in the two documents with respect to their understanding of the right to religious freedom as a primarily "juridical" right. For a defense of Murray, which contrasts Murray's view with that of John Paul II, see Herminio Rico, S.J., *John Paul II and the Legacy of Dignitatis Humanae* (Washington, DC: Georgetown University Press, 2002). For a critical study of Murray's juridical idea, see my "Civil Community Inside the Liberal State: Truth, Freedom, and Human Dignity," pp. 65-132 in this volume.

the *Catechism of the Catholic Church,* which states that "every institution is inspired, at least implicitly, by a vision of man and his destiny, from which it derives the point of reference for its judgment, its hierarchy of values, its line of conduct" (n. 2244).

In sum, we can say that a central task of an "authentic theology of integral human liberation" and "integral human development" with respect to the West lies in a dynamic transformation of the core meaning of the West's liberal economic and political institutions in light of a common good infused with the idea of truth as an order of love.

(2) The idea of humanity as a single family, together with the encyclical's emphasis on the social role of marriage and family, plays an important role in providing a foundation for, and in giving original form to, the principles of gratuitousness and relation, and indeed the logic of freedom and rights, that is implied by the notion of the common good as outlined above.

Strikingly, Benedict says that *"the development of peoples depends, above all, on a recognition that the human race is a single family . . ."* (n. 53); and that "the Christian revelation of the unity of the human race presupposes a *metaphysical interpretation of the 'humanum' in which relationality is an essential element"* (n. 55). The idea that all human beings make up a single family derives from the common origin of each in the Creator. "The unity of the human race is called into being by the Word of God-Who-is-love" (n. 34).

This idea of a single unified family deriving from a common relation to the Creator invites further reflections drawn from the theological anthropology of Joseph Ratzinger/Pope Benedict and Pope John Paul II, notably regarding the idea of filiality, in the former, and regarding the "original solitude" of man, in the latter. *CIV* emphasizes that love is first received by us, not generated by us. Already in his commentary on the anthropology of *Gaudium et Spes,* Ratzinger stresses the capacity for worship as the primary content of man's imaging of God. This is so because human beings are most basically sons and daughters in the Son: they are images of God in and through Jesus Christ who is God precisely as the *Logos* who is from-and-for the Father (cf. Col. 1:15-18); or, as Ratzinger puts it succinctly elsewhere, "the center of the Person of Jesus is prayer."[21] Likewise, John Paul II affirms the primacy of man in his "original solitude," by which he

---

21. Cardinal Joseph Ratzinger, *Behold the Pierced One,* trans. G. Harrison (San Francisco: Ignatius Press, 1986), p. 25.

means that man's relationality begins most radically in his "aloneness" before God. The point is not that man is originally without relation, but that man's relationality, his original being-with, is a being-with God before (ontologically, not temporally) it is a being-with other human beings. Man's being-with God, as creaturely, is first a *being-from*, in the manner of a child who participates in being only as the fruit of the radical generosity of the One Who Is.

Here, in what we may call the filial relation associated with the family, we find the root meaning of the encyclical's central category of relation as *gift*. Indeed, once we see the radicality of this relation, which originates in God as the Creator, we see that it must include not only all human beings (though especially and most properly these), but *all* creatures, including also all natural, physical-biological entities. Benedict states in this connection that "*nature expresses a design of love and truth. It is prior to us . . . and speaks to us of the Creator* (cf. Rom 1:20) *and his love for humanity. It is destined to be 'recapitulated' in Christ at the end of time* (cf. Eph 1:9-10; Col 1:19-20). *Thus it too is a 'vocation'. Nature is given to us . . . as a gift of the Creator who has given it an inbuilt order, enabling man to draw from it the principles needed in order 'to till and keep it'*"(Gen. 2:15) (n. 48). We could thus say that, in its own analogical way, and with the help of man, nature participates in the prayer constitutive of the creature in its inmost filial movement toward the Creator.

A further implication regarding filiality: we teach our children to say "please" and "thank you." But, rightly understood, this is not a matter merely of manners. On the contrary, it is a matter of teaching them who they are in their deepest reality: gifts from God who are thus meant to be grateful, to act in gratuitous wonder, in *response to* what is first *given*, as *gift*. Here is the origin of that recognition of being as true and good and indeed beautiful — *qua given* and not simply *quia factum* or as a function of human making — which must lie at the basis of any healthy human society. Here is the root of the encyclical's call for new lifestyles centered around the quest for truth, beauty, goodness, and communion with others (cf. n. 51).

Of course, children are sons and daughters of God only through a human father and mother, and the child is born as itself apt for either fatherhood or motherhood. The fruitfulness of the union of the father and the mother is a continuing sign and expression of the creative generosity of God. Ratzinger in his commentary on *Gaudium et Spes* refers to this spousal communion between a man and a woman as the immediate consequence *(Folge)* of the content *(Inhalt)* of the person's imaging of God that lies first in the person's "unitary" being as child of God.[22] John Paul II refers to this constitutive aptness for spousal union-fruitfulness as the "original unity" of man and woman. This aptness for spousal union, established first in man's and woman's common filial relation to God, is constitutive of the human being.[23] Each human being is a member of the single family of creatures under God, in and through membership in a particular familial genealogy of his own. This is the ground for the encyclical's calling on the state to promote "the centrality and the integrity of the family founded on marriage between a man and a woman, the primary cell of society, and to assume responsibility for its economic and fiscal needs, while respecting its essentially relational character" (n. 44).

The implications of this constitutive relationality affirmed in *CIV* are radical: *no relations taken up by human beings in the course of their lives are purely contractual*, or simply the fruit of an originally indifferent act of choice, as in liberal "contractualism."[24] Man is never, at root, "lonely," which is to say, in the language of *CIV*, never poor in the sense of "isolated" (n. 53). On the contrary, his being is always a being-with.

Hence, *regarding human freedom:* freedom is an *act* of choice only as already embedded in an *order* of naturally given relations to God, family, others, and nature (cf. n. 68). And *regarding human rights:* just as the juridical idea of rights presupposes a contractualist idea of freedom, so does a truthful order-bearing idea of rights presuppose a relational idea of the self. Just as the contractualist idea entails a priority of rights over duties, so does the relational idea entail a priority of duties over rights,[25] though of course rights remain unconditional coincident with this anterior responsibility (cf. n. 43). Rights, in a word, are properly invested in every person, but no person is a solitary agent who can be abstracted from relations. On the contrary, the creaturely person as he or she concretely exists by nature

---

22. Joseph Ratzinger, "Introduction and Chapter I: The Dignity of the Human Person," in *Commentary on the Documents of Vatican II*, vol. 5, ed. Herbert Vorgrimler (New York: Herder & Herder, 1969), Article 12 ("*Erster Hauptteil: Kommentar zum I*," in *Lexikon für Theologie und Kirche* 14: *Der Zweite Vatikanische Konzil*, vol. 3, ed. Vorgrimler et al. [Fribourg: Herder & Herder, 1968], Artikel 12).

23. Cf. the *Compendium of the Social Doctrine of the Church*, n. 37, 110, and 147.

24. In the liberal societies of the West, the tendency is to conceive human relations most basically in contractual terms. And, when such relations appear rather to be natural or "constitutive," as for example in the case of the family, the tendency is then to reduce such "constitutive" relations to matters merely of physicalist biology.

25. Duties are not to be understood here as opposed or extrinsic to charity and the logic of gift: see *CIV*, n. 6, 34, and 38.

is innerly ordained to God, is conceived by a father and a mother and born into a family, is sexually differentiated, and is intrinsically related to the whole of humanity and all cosmological entities.[26] An adequate idea of rights must take into account this order of relations that is constitutive of each person. The prevalent liberal idea of rights and freedom in America, on the contrary, presupposes a Cartesian human subject that bears no constitutive relations to other beings or to his or her own body.

(3) Thirdly, *Caritas in Veritate* says that Paul VI's encyclical, *Humanae Vitae*, is "highly important for delineating the *fully human meaning of the development the Church proposes*" (n. 15). This encyclical makes clear "the *strong links between life ethics and social ethics*, thus ushering in a new area of magisterial teaching that has gradually been articulated in a series of documents, most recently John Paul II's encyclical *Evangelium Vitae*" (n. 15).

The Pope notes in this connection *HV*'s emphasis on the unitive and procreative meaning of sexuality, thereby locating "at the foundation of society the married couple [who] are open to life" (n. 15). He suggests that the tendency to make human conception and gestation artificial contributes to the loss of "the concept of human ecology and, along with it, that of environmental ecology" (n. 51). The point here, though not explicitly developed in *CIV*, is that *HV*, in its affirmation of the unity of the personal and the procreative meaning of sexuality, implies a "new" understanding of the body as a bearer of the objective order of love, in a way consistent with and instructive for *CIV*'s view that the nature of the physical-biological cosmos as a whole "expresses a design of love" (n. 48).

Regarding the relation between life ethics and social ethics, the Pope notes in this connection the inconsistency of societies which, affirming the dignity of the person and justice and peace, tolerate the violation of human life when it is at its weakest and most marginalized (n. 15). He thus insists that "*openness to life is at the center of true development*" (n. 28), and that we

---

26. I am presupposing a concept of nature with respect to the features affirmed here as characteristic of the human person, and this concept of nature requires an argument beyond what can be undertaken in the present forum. To be sure, strong objections are posed today regarding the universality of one or another of these features. My statement presupposes that exceptions to these features, when and insofar as they obtain, are signs of objective disorder and do not suffice to call into question the natural order rightly understood, or to overturn its natural dynamisms. Nor, it should go without saying, does the presence of "objective disorder" in a person attenuate his or her human dignity. But, again, all of this needs to be argued more extensively elsewhere.

need to broaden our concept of poverty and underdevelopment to take account of this question of openness to life. It is precisely in its increasing mastery over the origin of human life, manifest, for example, in *in vitro* fertilization, the harvesting of human embryos for research, and the possibility of manufacturing clones and human hybrids, that we see "the clearest expression" of a supremacy of technology in contemporary society (n. 75).

(4) *CIV* takes up the complicated question of technology in its last chapter. Benedict of course acknowledges that technology "enables us to exercise dominion over matter" and "improve our conditions of life," and in this way goes to "the heart of the vocation of human labor" (n. 69). The relevant point, however, is that "technology is never merely technology" (n. 69).[27] It always invokes some sense of the order of man's naturally given relations to God and others. Technology thus, rightly conceived, must be integrated into the call to holiness, indeed into the covenant with God, implied in this order of relations (cf. n. 69): integrated into the idea of creation as something first *given to* man, as *gift*, "not something self-generated" (n. 68) or *produced by* man.

Here again we see the importance of the family. It is inside the family that we first learn a "technology" that respects the dignity of the truly weak and vulnerable — the just-conceived and the terminally ill, for example — for their own sake. It is inside the family, indeed the family as ordered to worship, that we first learn the habits of patient interiority necessary for genuine relationships: for the relations that enable us to see the truth, goodness, and beauty of others as given (and also to maintain awareness of "the human soul's ontological depths, as probed by the saints"; n. 76). It is inside the family that we can thus learn the limits of the dominant social media of communication made available by technology, which promote surface movements of consciousness involving mostly the gathering of bits of information, and foster inattention to man in his depths and his transcendence as created by God. It is in the family that we first become open to the meaning of communication in its ultimate and deepest reality as a *dia-logos* of love that is fully revealed by God in the life, and thus also the suffering, of Jesus Christ (cf. n. 4).

---

27. That is, technology is never "premoral," to use the language employed by *Veritatis Splendor*, n. 48, in its rejection of the idea that the body as body is neutral with respect to human-moral meaning.

The Anthropological Vision of Caritas in Veritate | 449

*   *   *

In light of the foregoing, we can see, in sum, why *Caritas in Veritate* insists that the social question today "*has become a radically anthropological question*" (n. 75); why "*the question of development is closely bound up with our understanding of the human soul*" (n. 75); and why "only a humanism open to the Absolute can guide us in the promotion and building of forms of social and civic life — structures, institutions, culture and *ethos*..." (n. 78).

Index

Abortion, 71, 110n.47, 203-4. *See also* Liberalism: and violence

Abstraction: as mechanistic, 392-93, 395-401; as "merely" disciplinary, 363, 385-87, 392-93, 399; proper sense of, 384-85, 419-22, 425-29; in science, 385-87, 389-400, 408, 429; of self from others, 185-88; of world from God, 288, 294-96, 297, 331-35, 338, 358

Academy, the, 12, 22, 326, 342, 363, 400n.20. *See also* Abstraction; Distinction; Education

Americanism, 97n.36, 267-70. *See also* Liberalism: and Catholicism

Anamnesis, 5-6, 21, 42n.16, 90, 118, 243, 273-74, 311, 318, 441

Aquinas, Thomas, 344, 377-78, 392n.11

Asymmetrical reciprocity: and being as gift, 298-99, 301; of body and soul, 244n.4; and distinction, 255-56; of self and other, 180-81, 197, 299-300, 305

Autonomy of creation (*iusta autonomia*), 126, 148-49, 305-9, 359, 360n.14, 384-85, 416-18

Balthasar, Hans Urs von, 282, 303, 336-38, 349, 358-60, 360-61, 366-81

Beauty, 173, 301, 347-49, 388, 394, 415n.44

Being as gift, 1, 4-8, 15, 35, 39-41, 88-96, 154-56, 172-74, 228-35, 246-52, 259-60, 262-70, 299-300, 313-18, 365-67, 371-80, 384-85, 410-18, 436-37, 445

Benedict XVI/Joseph Ratzinger: on the academy, 22; on America, 19-25, 56; on *anamnesis*, 5-6, 21, 42n.16, 90, 118, 243, 273-74; on conscience, 21, 42n.16, 59-60, 89-90, 243; on creative minorities, 56-60, 63-64; on distinction between church and state, 23, 56-58; on evangelization, 42n.16, 57-58, 148-49; on filiality, 248-50, 258, 317, 444-45; on interreligious dialogue, 26-27; on liberalism, 22-23, 273-74; on marriage and family, 55, 134, 139; on natural law, 21, 244; on pluralism, 55, 61; on reason, 11n.18, 20, 22, 29-33, 58-59, 326, 409-10; on relativism, 32-33, 60-64, 106; on religious freedom, 60-62; on science, 409-10; on social justice, 144-50; on suffering, 22, 24-25, 147, 438; on technology, 29-30, 46n.21, 448; on the West, 54-64, 273n.44. *See also Caritas in Veritate; Deus Caritas Est*

Bernanos, Georges, 324-25

Berry, Wendell, 331-32

Body, the: and freedom, 219-20, 223-35; and gift of self, 228-33, 252-54, 261-66,

269; as "pre-moral," 223-25, 252-53; reductive understanding of, 38, 136, 223-25, 309; as (pre-)sacramental sign, 224-28, 252-53, 264-65, 269, 292-93, 344; soul as form of, 199n.38, 224, 227, 229-30, 244-46, 344; theology of, 225-29, 242n.1, 251-54, 261-67, 316-18
Bohm, David, 355-56, 357n.11, 395n.14

Capax Dei, man as, 36, 52, 90, 251-52, 254n.22, 317
Capitalism. *See* Economy, the
Caritas in Veritate, 127-28, 161n.12, 248n.10, 430-49
Centesimus Annus, 70, 127-28, 161n.12, 201n.44, 342, 442
Church, the: absence of in America, 48-49; charitable activity of, 134-35, 142-53; and clericalism, 307-8; and *communio* ecclesiology, 121-24, 140-42, 146-47, 308n.22, 368n.24, 369; and evangelization, 49-50; and the laity, 121-24, 148-49; as positivist or voluntarist sect, 112-19, 198-200; as sacramental reality, 114, 117-19, 121-24; social teaching of, 144-53, 302, 430-49; and the state, 56-57, 67-71, 77, 111-24, 145-47, 198-200, 270-74. *See also* Liberalism: and Catholicism
Cobb, John, 354-55
Common good vs. public order, 63n.4, 77-80, 83, 86-87, 145, 442-44
Community, 164, 168-75, 200-203, 208-10, 229-31, 264, 361, 444
Compendium of the Social Doctrine of the Catholic Church (CSDC), 35-36, 89-90, 246, 247n.9, 253, 314n.7
Conscience, 21, 42n.16, 59-60, 89-90, 243
Contemplation, 27-29, 50-51, 141-42, 278-81, 323-24. *See also* Interiority; Wonder
Creation as gift. *See* Being as gift
Culture: of death, 37-39, 188-94; of life, 190; and nature, 232-33, 235-38; transformation of, 24-25, 32-33, 130-32, 163-65, 236-38, 270, 280-81, 286n.33, 349

Dawson, Christopher, 351
Descartes, René, 99n.39, 114n.52, 178, 199n.38, 255-56, 344, 361-62, 396-97, 403
Deus Caritas Est, 21, 53, 133-53, 157
Dialogue: between believers and unbelievers, 57-59, 61, 270-73; ecumenical and interreligious, 26-33, 431-32, 438; in the liberal state, 13, 71-73, 105-8, 270-74, 438
Dignitatis Humanae, 60-62, 77n.11, 82-83, 88n.21, 124-26
Distinction: Catholic understanding of, 361, 365-66, 376, 380-81, 385-87, 419-21; between church and state, 12-13, 23, 56-57, 77, 111-24, 145-47, 198-200, 270-74; modern (Cartesian) understanding of, 344, 357-58, 360-65; between state and society, 12-13, 66, 70-73, 98, 101-4, 127-28, 199n.38, 442. *See also* Abstraction
Dominum et Vivificantem, 8n.12, 190n.30, 230, 237, 339-40
Drama, 34-36, 40-43, 301
Dualism. *See* Abstraction; Distinction

Economy, the: alternative form, 162-65; and the Church, 302, 432-33, 435, 439; Distributism, 164; globalization, 210-16; and instrumentalism, 156-62, 177-80, 193; and love, 175-85; and materialism, 206-7; as (allegedly) neutral institution, 160-61, 175, 207-8, 342; and profit, 177-81; and self-interest, 156-61, 180-83; and wealth, 155-56, 174-75, 183-85, 206-10. *See also* Liberalism: as formalist-instrumentalist
Education, 22, 323-26, 351
Enlightenment, 22, 99, 258-59
Esse. *See* Ontological difference, the
Eucharist, 140-41, 289, 320
Evangelium Vitae, 37-39, 41-42, 51n.31, 88-89, 188-90

Evangelization, 42n.16, 49-50, 122-23, 148-49, 270, 349. *See also* Culture: transformation of

Experience: and experiment, 403; as originary, 310-18, 325-27

Faith and reason, 14-15, 19-22, 58-59, 92-93, 130, 145-46, 148-49, 167-68, 372-73, 414, 427-28

Family. *See* Marriage and family

Femininity and feminism, 294-95, 299, 302-9

Fiat ("letting be"), 41, 52, 123, 174, 262, 294, 297, 316, 320n.15, 321n.17. *See also* Filiality; Receptivity

Fides et Ratio, 15, 373n.32

Filiality, 45, 94-95, 225n.8, 248-52, 254n.22, 258-59, 260n.30, 262-64, 269-70, 296n.8, 316-18, 444-45

Forgetfulness of God, 5, 19, 29, 37-39, 48-50, 52, 189, 377. *See also* Abstraction: of world from God

Freedom: and the body, 219-20, 223-35; as formal or indifferent exercise of choice, 43-46, 61-64, 87-88, 94, 104, 131, 185-88, 234; and intelligence, 151-53, 175-78, 223-25, 295, 306-7, 333-48, 393n.12, 394, 407-8, 415, 419; and love, 5-6, 13, 36, 40, 75, 131, 233-35; as receptive response, 36, 40-42, 44, 86, 88-89, 92, 164, 196, 221-22, 233-35, 262, 265, 306, 446; religious, 60-64, 82-83, 198-200; and truth, 5-6, 13, 60-64, 65-66, 70-71, 75, 82-83, 86-88, 123, 124-26

Free market. *See* Economy, the

Fruitfulness, 252n.18, 269, 298-99, 300n.11, 301, 374, 447

Gaudium et Spes, 25, 167n.2, 126, 262-64

Gender. *See* Sexual difference

Gift: being as, 1, 4-8, 35, 39-41, 88-96, 154-56, 172-74, 228-35, 246-52, 259-60, 262-70, 299-300, 313-18, 365-67, 371-80, 384-85, 410-18, 436-37, 445; and the body, 228-34, 252-54, 261-66, 269; economy of, 175-85; freedom as, 233-35; life as, 37-38; nature as, 229-33, 445; and receptivity, 7, 15, 35, 39-41, 171-74, 185-88, 256-58, 262-67, 297-98, 306, 315, 413-14; of self, 226-27, 234, 261-65, 318-22, 369-70, 375

Gilson, Etienne, 352-54

God: abstraction of world from, 288, 294-96, 297, 331-35, 338, 358; and *anamnesis*, 5-6, 21, 42n.16, 90, 118, 243, 273-74, 311, 318, 441; forgetfulness of, 5, 19, 29, 37-39, 48-50, 52, 189, 377. *See also* Jesus Christ; Trinity

Grace and nature, 2-3, 7-8, 126, 151-53, 220-21, 290-91, 368-70, 372-76, 377n.38, 381

Grant, George, 277-87, 345-47

Home and homelessness, 168-75, 364

Humanae Vitae, 447

Imago Dei, 45, 208, 225-28, 242-43, 246, 247n.9, 251-54, 263-64, 317

Instrumentalism: in the economy, 156-58, 160-62, 177-81, 194-216; legitimate forms of, 9, 96n.34, 158, 202, 231-33, 348; and liberalism, 73-81, 93-99, 102-4, 105-8, 116-17, 185-94, 343; of nature, 278, 281, 334, 405-6

Intelligent (objective) order and (subjective) intention, 151-53, 175-78, 223-25, 295, 306-7, 333-48, 393n.12, 394, 407-8, 415, 419

Interiority, 34-36, 94-95, 107n.44, 108-9, 162, 323-24, 412. *See also* Contemplation; Wonder

Jesus Christ, 41, 126, 139-40, 185, 221, 291-92, 296n.8, 316, 320, 367-68, 374-76

John Paul II/Karol Wojtyla: on community, 209-10; on creativity, 207-9; on culture, 232-33; on culture of death, 188-90; on freedom and truth, 36, 125-27; on liberalism, 70; on structures of sin, 189-90, 200-201, 236-37, 339-40; on theology of the body, 225-

29, 252-54, 261-67, 316-18; on women, 303. *See also Centesimus Annus; Dominum et Vivificantem; Evangelium Vitae; Fides et Ratio; Sollicitudo Rei Socialis; Veritatis Splendor*
Johnson, Elizabeth, 302-9
Jonas, Hans, 402-9
Justice: and charity, 142-49, 161n.12, 283, 434, 440-41; as fairness, 66-67, 73, 79-80, 105-6, 109. *See also* Common good vs. public order

Laity, the, 121-24, 148-49, 320n.16, 369
Lancellotti, Carlo, 388-94
Liberalism: achievements of, 23-24, 43-50, 73, 100-101, 194, 217, 283-84, 360; Anglo-American vs. Continental, 23n.9, 82-83, 126; and Catholicism, 49-50, 67-71, 77, 81-83, 97n.36, 121-28, 204-6, 267-74, 432-33, 435; definition of, 65, 71-73; and distinction between church and state, 12-13, 23, 56-57, 77, 111-24, 145-47, 198-200, 270-74; and distinction between state and society, 12-13, 66, 70-73, 98, 101-4, 127-28, 199n.38, 442; as formalist-instrumentalist, 71-74, 80-88, 101-4, 185-88, 343; and freedom, 43-46, 61-64, 87-88, 94, 104, 131, 185-88; and metaphysics, 12, 69-76, 98-99, 101-4, 128-32, 270-74, 437-38; (alleged) neutrality of, 12, 61-64, 73-76, 80-81, 101-4, 120, 129, 204-6, 212-13, 239-41, 342, 443-44; and pluralism, 61, 66, 101-4, 210-16, 284n.31, 364; and public order vs. common good, 63n.4, 77-80, 83, 86-87, 145, 442-44; and rights, 43-46, 63n.4, 82-88, 108-11, 195-98; and technology, 46-48, 161-62, 213-16; and truth, 12-13, 30-31, 66-67, 76-81, 101-8, 125, 128-32, 271-72; and violence, 37-39, 73-75, 103-4, 106-8, 109-11, 128-29, 132, 216-17
Liturgy. *See* Worship
Locke, John, 114-16
Love: and the body, 225-29, 251-54, 261-67; charity, 134-35, 142-53; *eros* and *agape*, 21, 133-40, 148-49; and freedom, 5-6, 13, 36, 40, 75, 131, 233-35; as order (*logos* of), 1, 4-8, 126-27, 151-53, 175-85, 326, 347-48, 436-37, 438; as order, objections to, 1-14; of self and others, 2-3, 21, 94-96, 131-32, 133-40, 148-49, 156-57, 181. *See also* Being as gift
Lubac, Henri de, 331n.4

MacIntyre, Alasdair, 285-87
Madison, James, 77n.11
Marcel, Gabriel, 15, 286n.33
Marriage and family, 52, 55, 170, 202-3, 250n.14, 252-54, 264, 319n.13, 445-48. *See also* Nuptiality
Mary, 41, 142, 174, 181, 222, 293-94, 296-99, 301-6, 368n.24
Maximus the Confessor, 259-60
Mechanism, 224, 343-44, 378-80, 387, 393-94, 395-401, 407-8, 422-25
Memory of God. *See Anamnesis*
Mission. *See* Evangelization
Moralism. *See* Intelligent (objective) order and (subjective) intention
Morality: body as "pre-moral," 223-25, 252-53, 292n.6; conscience, 21, 42n.16, 59-60, 89-90, 243; and faith, 141, 220-23; intention, 151-53, 175-78, 189-90, 223-25, 265; natural law, 21, 148, 244; and public order, 56-60, 61-63, 76-80, 115-17, 160, 175, 203-4, 270-74
Morse, Jennifer, 190-94
Murray, John Courtney: anthropology of, 83-87, 94, 97-99; on "articles of peace," 65-66, 81-82, 99, 342; on distinction between state and society, 66, 98, 127-28; on (religious) freedom, 82-87, 124-26, 198-200; on rights, 83-84

Natural law, 21, 148, 244
Nature: and grace, 2-3, 7-8, 126, 151-53, 220-21, 290-91, 368-70, 372-76, 377n.38, 381; physical nature, as indifferent mechanism, 224, 278, 281, 334,

343-44, 348, 378-80, 387, 393-401, 405-8, 422-25; physical nature, (sacramental) order of, 224-33, 252-53, 289-93, 344, 348, 356, 445
Neuhaus, Richard, 194-200, 201n.44, 203-6
Newman, John Henry, 351
Nietzsche, Friedrich, 57, 135
Nominalism, 129, 258, 266-67
Novak, Michael, 200-201, 206-10
Nuptiality, 225-28, 234, 252-54, 255, 264, 269, 292-94, 296n.8, 316-17

Obedience, 44-45, 173, 252n.17, 256-58, 293-94, 296n.8, 301, 303
Ontological difference, the, 1, 4-7, 91n.26, 231n.25, 249-50, 259, 266, 314-15, 353, 355, 371-75. *See also* Being as gift
Order (objectivity) and intention. *See* Intelligent (objective) order and (subjective) intention

Pelagianism, 129, 187, 266-67, 306, 363
Person, the: as autonomous individual, 37, 83-86, 91-92, 108-9, 118, 126, 171-74, 185-86, 194-96, 270, 297, 305-9; creativity of, 94-96, 185-86, 206-9, 213-16; as dependent, 38, 88-89, 171-74, 190-92; dignity of, 54-55, 83-85, 191, 195, 297; as embodied, 38, 244-46, 252-53, 425; as mediator of creation, 4-5, 259-60, 367, 374-75, 380; and self-determination, 91-92, 94-96, 185-88, 294, 297-300, 305-6. *See also Imago Dei*; Substance and relation
Philosophy: and liberalism, 12, 69-76, 98-99, 101-4, 128-32, 270-74, 437-38; and science, 389-92, 394n.13; and theology, 336-38, 353, 372-73, 386n.8
Plato, 25, 46n.21, 415n.44
Pluralism, 55, 61, 66, 101-4, 210-16, 284n.31, 364
Polanyi, Michael, 425-29
Postmodernity, 97n.35, 341n.19, 379-80, 400-401

Public order vs. common good, 63n.4, 77-80, 83, 86-87, 145, 442-44
Public vs. private, 3, 10-13, 71-73, 115-17, 119, 160-61, 358, 443. *See also* Liberalism: and distinction between state and society
Puritanism, 48-49, 99, 112n.49, 215, 331-33

Ratzinger, Joseph. *See* Benedict XVI
Rawls, John, 66-67
Realism, 3, 8-10, 24-25, 130-32, 158-59, 181-85, 283-87, 439
Reason: expanded notion of, 326, 393n.12, 394, 408, 409-10, 425-29; and faith, 14-15, 19-22, 58-59, 92-93, 130, 145-46, 148-49, 167-68, 372-73, 414, 427-28; in liberal state (public reason), 71-73, 105-8, 119-20, 129-30, 271-72, 358
Receptivity, 7n.10, 15, 35, 171-74, 185-86, 256-58, 262-67, 293-94, 312, 315, 411-12. *See also* Responsivity
Relation as constitutive. *See* Substance and relation
Relativism, 32-33, 60-64, 75, 105-8, 378-79
Religiosity in America, 19-20, 38-39, 56, 112n.49, 120, 328-49
Religious freedom, 60-64, 81-88, 124-26, 198-200
Responsivity, 39-41, 90-91, 95, 109, 172-74, 293-94, 315, 320n.15, 411-12. *See also* Receptivity
Rhonheimer, Martin, 67-71, 111, 122n.62
Rico, Hermínio, 125-26
Rights: and the Church, 44, 49; as immunities, 43-46, 82-88, 108-11; and relation to the other, 86-87, 109, 131, 196-98, 446-47

Sacrament: body as, 224-28, 252-53, 264-65, 269, 292-93, 344; world as, 289-93, 294-96, 348, 445
Schindler, David C., 319n.13, 415n.44
Schmemann, Alexander, 117, 288-94

Science: and abstraction, 385-87, 389-400, 408, 429; and beauty, 388, 394; and creation, 383-85, 419-21; as mechanistic, 387, 393-94, 395-400, 407-8, 422-25; and philosophy, 389-92, 394n.13; and reductive scientism, 389-90, 391, 397-98, 404-8; and technology, 402-9, 424-25; and theology, 421n.54, 427-28

Secularism and secularity, 67-71, 93, 117-20, 122, 126, 271-74, 288-96, 328-49, 443n.19. *See also* Autonomy of creation *(iusta autonomia)*

Self-interest, 2-3, 11, 95-96, 136-38, 156-58, 180-83, 187, 300. *See also* Love: of self and other

Sexual difference, 203, 251-59, 269, 293-94, 302-4, 306-9, 433, 440

Sin: and the integrity of nature, 8-10, 414-15; and liberalism, 131-32, 158-59, 182-83; original, 45, 260n.30, 294; structures of, 24, 146-47, 189-90, 192, 200-201, 236-38, 339-41

Smith, Adam, 156-59, 177-81

Socrates, 21, 25, 438

Sollicitudo Rei Socialis, 236, 340

Stackhouse, Max, 210-16

State of life, 40-41, 51-52, 164, 250n.14, 315-26, 369-70

Stratton, Lawrence, 210-16

Substance and relation: and abstraction, 185-88, 392, 396-400, 428-29; and being as gift, 2, 5-7, 39-43, 88-93, 154-55, 169-74, 246-52, 313, 365-66, 378-79, 412-13; and the environment, 202; and experience, 311-13; and the family, 202-3; and freedom, 40-42, 43-45, 84-88, 94-96, 262-67; and interiority, 35-36; and liberalism, 43-46, 84-88, 94-99, 156-58, 174-75, 185-88, 267-70, 362-63; and rights, 44, 85-87, 195-98; and self-identity (autonomy), 91-92, 94-96, 171-72, 180-81, 186-87, 195, 247-48, 256-58, 297, 299-302, 305, 314n.7, 361-64, 384-85, 416-18; and sexual difference, 251-52, 269

Suffering, 22, 24-25, 132, 147, 173-74
Symbol. *See* Sacrament

Technology, 46-48, 106n.43, 161-62, 213-16, 325, 423n.55, 448; as ontology, 277-87, 345-46, 396; and science, 402-9, 424-25

Testem Benevolentiae, 267-70

Theology of the body, 225-29, 242n.1, 251-54, 261-67, 316-18

Time and eternity, 28-29, 114-19, 164-65, 321-25, 443

Tocqueville, Alexis de, 99n.39, 106n.43

Totalitarianism: and liberalism, 108-11; of relativistic democracy, 63; of the strong over the weak, 37-38, 45-46, 75, 109-11, 188-89

Transcendental properties of being: and being as gift, 7, 9-10, 91n.25, 259, 375n.37, 411, 445; and liberalism, 79-80, 158, 179-80; as revealed in the family, 52, 448; as "useless," 28, 30

Trinity, the, 248n.10, 252n.16, 263

Ulrich, Ferdinand, 91n.25, 371
Utilitarianism. *See* Instrumentalism

Vatican Council II, 124-28, 381n.44. *See also Dignitatis Humanae*
Veritatis Splendor, 219-25
Virginity, 51-52, 250-51n.14, 269-70, 320n.16
Vow. *See* State of life

Waldstein, Michael, 7n.9, 261-67
Walker, Adrian, 244n.4, 397n.17, 403n.24, 420n.52
Weber, Max, 48-49, 99n.37
Weil, Simone, 280, 347
Wojtyła, Karol. *See* John Paul II
Wonder, 27-29, 31, 51n.31, 107n.44, 173, 301, 393n.12, 394, 412, 415. *See also* Contemplation; Interiority
Worship, 50, 117-18, 140-41, 259-60, 288-92

www.ingramcontent.com/pod-product-compliance
Lightning Source LLC
Chambersburg PA
CBHW021350290426
44108CB00010B/178